ORGANIZATION THEORY

A PUBLIC AND NONPROFIT

PERSPECTIVE

THIRD EDITION

HAROLD F. GORTNER
George Mason University

KENNETH L. NICHOLS
University of Maine

CAROLYN BALL
University of Maine

WADSWORTH
CENGAGE Learning

Australia • Brazil • Japan • Korea • Mexico • Singapore • Spain • United Kingdom • United States

WADSWORTH
CENGAGE Learning™

Organization Theory: A Public and Nonprofit Perspective, Third Edition

Harold F. Gortner,
Kenneth L. Nichols and
Carolyn Ball

Acquisitions Editor: David Tatom

Assistant Editor: Rebecca Green

Technology Project Manager:
Inna Fedoseyeva

Marketing Manager: Janise Fry

Marketing Assistant:
Teresa Jessen

Senior Content Project Manager,
Editorial Production:
Paul Wells

Creative Director: Rob Hugel

Art Director: Maria Epes

Print Buyer: Nora Massuda

Permissions Editor: Joohee Lee

Production Service: International
Typesetting and Composition

Copy Editor: Meg McDonald

Cover Designer: Jeanette Barber

Compositor: International
Typesetting and Composition

For product information and
technology assistance, contact us at **Cengage Learning Customer & Sales Support, 1-800-354-9706**

For permission to use material from this text or product, submit all requests online at **www.cengage.com/permissions**
Further permissions questions can be e-mailed to
permissionrequest@cengage.com

Library of Congress Control Number: 2006906712

ISBN-13: 978-0-495-00680-0

ISBN-10: 0-495-00680-7

Wadsworth Cengage Learning
20 Davis Drive
Belmont, CA 94002-3098
USA

Cengage Learning is a leading provider of customized learning solutions with office locations around the globe, including Singapore, the United Kingdom, Australia, Mexico, Brazil, and Japan. Locate your local office at **www.cengage.com/global**

Cengage Learning products are represented in Canada by Nelson Education, Ltd.

To learn more about Wadsworth, visit
www.cengage.com/wadsworth

Purchase any of our products at your local college store or at our preferred online store **www.cengagebrain.com**

Printed in the United States of America
3 4 5 6 7   18 17 16 15 14

Preface

Two premises directed the revision of this book. First, effective management of public organizations differs in key respects from the management of private organizations. Second, nonprofit organizations play an increasingly important role in our society, and they are recognized as an important part of the public sector in society. Both of these premises are important to understanding what we attempt to accomplish in our discussion of organization theory as it applies to the public sector (government and nonprofit). Both types of organizations are administered in a demanding political, legal, and economic environment.

For both government and nonprofit organizations, the political system plays a major part in their everyday actions. Government agencies are charged with administering often ambiguous laws in a setting filled with well-organized opponents scrutinizing every action, zealous supporters, reluctant clients, and strict but often conflicting guidelines for procedures. Legal constraints for equality and consistency of action dominate the design of programs and procedures. The political system drives public organizations. Agencies in currently popular policy areas are supported and well financed *regardless of past efficiency or effectiveness.* Likewise, the same agencies, faced with a public mood of cutback and reduction in government, find their programs diminished *regardless of past efficiency or effectiveness.*

Nonprofit agencies operate in a world where they must make clear to a fickle public the causes and goals that are their raison d'être. In a society where new issues and crises are constantly occurring, nonprofit administrators must be especially sensitive to public swings in issue interest and attention. Maintaining the public trust is critical to survival, so issues of ethics, efficiency, and effectiveness are central to both decision making and action. And as nonprofit organizations play an ever bigger role in developing and implementing public policy, collaboration while maintaining independence is a constant calculation.

Managers in the public sector must work to develop organizational systems that respond to demands that change once the systems are in place; they must understand that the reasons for such change do not necessarily follow operational rationality. The market does not function for public agencies the way it does for private profit-seeking organizations. In consequence of the distinctiveness of the public mission and setting, public sector management differs from private management and requires a distinctive approach to the literature of organization theory and management behavior. Organization theory for public agencies must consider issues that do not appear in traditional, generic organization theory or in management behavior texts.

This is not a new organization theory, but rather a selection from and interpretation of the existing literature. The basic literature in the organization theory field is discussed from an applied management perspective. A special set of questions is asked about that literature and how each of the basic topics of organization theory can best be applied to the problems of public sector administration. To do so, we must examine the requirements of, say, control systems in public organizations, and then discuss what the existing literature tells us about this organizational function.

In addition to material traditionally included in organization theory texts, considerable research in areas such as political science and economics must be acknowledged and examined by students of public sector organizations. One cannot discuss leadership in public organizations, for example, without including material about chief executives that is not usually covered by most organization theory authors (much to their loss). Nor is it possible to understand leadership at the executive level in public organizations if one is ignorant of the fact that leaders rotate, and fluctuate in their abilities and desires, relatively rapidly in most public organizations (especially at the state and national levels of government). In general, public sector administrators must have a special sensitivity to the political, social, and economic implications of their environment.

In this edition of the text we have removed the cases and most of the readings. We encourage teachers to use our website at Wadsworth, Cengage Learning (www.cengage.com) and to make use of "The Electronic Hallway" (also listed on our website) at the University of Washington, which houses a large and varied inventory of excellent cases. Likewise we have noted in the "For Further Reading" sections of our chapters the readings in the Shafritz, Ott, and Jang text *Classics of Organizational Theory,* 6th edition (published by Thomson) that are closely related to the material in our text. We believe it is important to introduce students to the original writings of important scholars and practitioners in the field.

This book is geared toward students at the upper division of undergraduate school and those in the graduate programs of public and nonprofit administration across the country; therefore the material is presented both pragmatically and theoretically. Only upon reaching the doctoral level is one likely to study organization theory primarily with the intent of focusing on the theory itself. Students at the bachelor's and master's levels are ultimately interested in the application of theory in the real world of the public sector organization.

For these reasons we feel that this text offers something special to the field of public administration around the United States, and perhaps in other Western countries as well. As individuals study (and work in) public sector organizations, it is important to remember that in a liberal democratic society, the organization's ultimate function is to be a means by which society can make its democratic institutions meet the needs of its citizens.

In revising and updating this volume, Harold Gortner has been joined by Carolyn Ball and Kenneth Nichols, professors at the University of Maine–Orono. The combination of continuity and new perspectives has been a valuable element in reenvisioning the material. Obviously much of the prior volume is valid and dynamic—that remains, though we have added and reorganized material to better fit the new and broader vision of the constituency of this text. We have especially tried to retain the ease of reading and understanding that was a strong point of the earlier editions. We have avoided jargon, obfuscation, and unnecessary complication in explaining the organizations in which we spend so much of our lives.

A virtual organization of people contributed to the development and completion of this revision. We especially appreciate the reviewers of the second edition—Gleb Nikitenko, University of San Francisco; Robert W. Smith, Clemson University; and William M. Leavitt, Old Dominion University—for their useful suggestions. As would be expected, we did not heed all of their advice, so any errors in judgment or presentation are solely ours. The editors and production staff at Cengage Learning have been untiring in keeping us on track and transforming our raw material into a burnished prose. Students in the graduate programs of our universities have consistently forced us to think differently about organization theory as it applies to their public sector experiences and needs. They have felt free to comment on the book and suggest ideas that have improved the current edition. Colleagues on our faculties have also given us thoughtful and helpful input regarding the presentation of many theoretical constructs. Carolyn Ball wishes to thank graduate alumni Miranda Johnson and Shakeel Mahmood, who assisted in conducting research and making corrections, and undergraduate Michelle Hayes, who helped with editing and corrections. Carolyn thanks her husband Merl Williams for making it possible for her to work nonstop at times. Ken Nichols offers appreciation to his wife Barbara, whose energy and intellect he taps incessantly; to the spouses of his two collaborators, who became most valued coconspirators; and to Brack Brown, Aaron Milligan, and Ed Colley, from whose minds spring vital organizational images. Hal Gortner especially wants to thank his wife Sylvia, who has once again contributed in innumerable ways—most importantly by always being there when needed.

No book can be the final word on the field of organization theory and its application to public organizations. This is because both good theory and good public organizations accrete and evolve to meet the needs of those who use them. For us and, we suspect, for our readers as well, exploring the field is both rewarding and fascinating.

Hal Gortner, Ken Nichols, and Carolyn Ball
December 2006

Contents

Chapter 3 The Pivotal Controversies   55

Chapter 4 Structure   105

Chapter 5 Communication   154

Chapter 6 Accountability to Transparency   194

Chapter 7 Decision Making   242

Chapter 10 Change and Stability   374

Chapter 1

Varieties of Organization Research and Theory

INTRODUCTION

The subject of this text is organization theory for public organizations. We survey many of the most prominent explanations and theories of organizations as political, social, and economic phenomena; however, we interpret *political* in a broader way than most theorists. First, both government and nonprofit organizations are considered *public*. We clarify and justify this special definition of *public organization* in this and the next chapter, and then we include both types of organizations in our discussions of the unique characteristics of public organizations throughout the rest of the book. Second, all public organizations, both government and nonprofit, have an internal political nature—recognized by most organization theorists—and an external political environment that is not considered by generic theory. By adding the political environment, and its impact on inter- and intra-organization functions, we hope to help both government and nonprofit administrators devise their own effective and successful strategies for organization management, informed by these theories.

We do not intend to offer a new theory of organization that is unique to the public sector; rather, our purpose is to integrate and highlight the existing research and theory around an understanding of public sector organizations and the problems of public sector management. This effort is undertaken with the hope that we can get beyond the usual bias toward the problems and environments of the private sector and the idea that whatever is good for business is good for government and related public service organizations.

Thus the emphasis here is on the implications of the public nature of agencies along several dimensions. How do the demands of constituencies and clients, rather than markets, suppliers, and customers, affect what we know about designing organization structures, communication networks, and systems of control? How do the legal requirements and the mission of public organizations affect power, authority, and leadership? What are the sources of organizational ethos, commitment, and motivation in public agencies? What are the pressures on intelligence and decision-making systems in public sector agencies as opposed to for-profit firms?

In this chapter we address some of the basic definitions, assumptions, and questions posed by organization theory as it is applied to nonprofit and government agencies. We look at the contributions of various disciplines to the body of research and theory in the field, and we introduce the wide variety of theories and explanatory perspectives that have emerged in the field. We hope to help the reader to see organizations at many levels and perspectives simultaneously and to use the organization theories presented here as a set of conceptual tools for analyzing problems in government and nonprofit organizations and finding solutions to them.

WHAT IS AN ORGANIZATION?

In one sense this is an easy and obvious question; we generally agree on what counts as an organization. A government agency, a professional association, and a private firm are organizations. Pillsbury, the Girl Scouts, and the Office of Management and Budget are organizations; but the people in line to buy stamps at the post office, the crowd at a soccer game, and this week's panel of reporters on a Sunday morning interview program are not. Both size and the ongoing interrelatedness of the people in the group contribute to the state we call *organization*.[1]

The most common formal definition of *organization* is a collection of people engaged in specialized and interdependent activity to accomplish a goal or mission. Typically organization theorists further define their interest as large, complex organizations that are specialized and highly interdependent collectivities. Size often allows specialization. Specialization of function or division of labor permits efficiency; it also creates interdependency and a demand for mechanisms that can coordinate these different but interdependent tasks. The activities in which members are engaged are typically not personalized or personally determined, but rather are codified in job descriptions or roles, thus ensuring that the organization will survive even if personnel change.

This definition, while acceptable, is a bit misleading. For example, the vast majority of organizations are not large and complex, and the technology of some small organizations may be so simple that little specialization of work is necessary or possible. Perhaps an even more serious limitation is that not all the members of organizations (public, nonprofit, or private) are there to accomplish some formal, perhaps intangible, or abstract goal. They may simply want to earn a living, or in some cases they enjoy interaction with other people while doing something that is socially acceptable. (Considering the dark side of human nature, it is possible that some people wish to interact with others while doing something socially unacceptable; however, that is the subject of other fields of study and will not figure in our discussion.) Thus questions of control, motivation, and supervisory style immediately become important.

Other limitations in the definition concern the desirability of nonpersonalized work roles, the lack of real freedom and democratic values, and what some see as an inappropriate focus on behavior rather than the culture of the organization and the intentions of the organization's members. Karl Weick provides an interesting insight into the *activity of organizing* as opposed to whatever constitutes the *organizational institution.*

> Organizing is like a grammar in the sense that it is a systematic account of some rules and conventions by which sets of interlocked behaviors are assembled to form social processes that are intelligible to actors. (1979, 3)

But the grammar really becomes important once we begin to write the story. Once organizing has occurred, and routine and structure come into being, does it matter? There is a general consensus that structure does influence function and that both are critical to success in achieving goals. There is certainly much railing about "the bureaucracy" in the political world, and in their campaigns many politicians "run against the bureaucracy." Increasingly nonprofit organizations are judged, at least in part, according to "percentage of revenue expended in administrative costs"—which is one way of saying that structure, function, and therefore efficiency and effectiveness are important. There is much debate about what missions should be entrusted to nonprofit or government organizations, with the debate often focusing on the

---

[1]Howard Rheingold (2003) argues that many groups often deemed as "mobs," or seemingly disconnected groups of individuals, are beginning to achieve the ability to act almost spontaneously and without traditional organization because of the ubiquitous and instant communication achieved through modern technology (cell phones, pagers, text messaging, and handheld computers). This will be an important development to watch over the next few decades, and it may change organization theory in interesting and critical ways.

flexibility—or lack thereof—allowed by carrying out tasks within or outside the government. Other people make their living trying to move organizations from the "bureaucratic age" into the "postbureaucratic age of the moment"—be that the information age organization, the participative–democratic organization, or the learning organization.

At the same time there is an underlying feeling among many that organization is not that important. James Q. Wilson comments that "only two groups of people deny that organization matters: economists and everybody else" (1989, 23). Economists, he argues, see organizations and the people in them as individuals maximizing their utility under a set of market or political constraints—just another social phenomenon explained by marginal cost economics. We address this particular view occasionally as we discuss public choice theory (the ultimate economic explanation of organizational activity) and its impact on public organizations.

Other people, says Wilson, argue that the organization is unimportant; it's the people in it who matter. He responds by saying there are two errors in the "only people matter" view. The first is that people are influenced by their membership in, and positions in, an organization just as they are affected by biological, social, and educational factors. Wilson quotes Herbert Simon, who says a person

> does not live for months or years in a particular position in an organization, exposed to some streams of communication, shielded from others, without the most profound effects upon what he knows, believes, attends to, hopes, wishes, emphasizes, fears, and proposes. (1976, xvi)

Some people would summarize this idea by stating that "people are influenced by the organizational culture"; but the influence is more than ideas, values, and perceptions because it includes the inculcation of understanding through action (both repetitive, rational, and irrational). The second error in the "organization doesn't matter" argument is pointed out by simply noting that what people accomplish depends on their having the authority and resources with which to act (Wilson 1989, 24). Why cannot people accomplish the things they do *in* organizations *outside* of organizations? Position, authority, and resources available only in organizations matter.

If organization matters, then it is important to understand how organizations come into being, develop structure, maintain resources and procedures, and accomplish goals. Much of the debate about "bureaucracy" and its impact on society, politics, and individuals occurs in ignorance: Many individuals shouting the shrillest imprecations do so without in-depth knowledge of the phenomenon against which they rail. Their debate would be greatly enlightened by an increase in knowledge about what they see as the enemy. We hope this book presents the knowledge needed to enlighten the debate; we cannot, however, ensure that these critics will partake of the knowledge.

At the same time, serious discussions are occurring around issues related to the core meaning of the term *organization* and numerous concerns about how organization can be best utilized as a tool of society. In these cases, as Gareth Morgan notes, our debate is based on our understanding of the phenomenon we study, and our understanding of "organization is always shaped by underlying images and ideas" (1986, 343). These images and ideas are broadened and deepened by coming to understand what has been learned about organizations through research over the last century. Of course the concepts, theories, and models have raised new issues. These issues are raised by organization theorists and public administration theorists in their critiques of conventional approaches to organization theory. We look briefly at some of these critiques in this chapter and throughout the text.

Public Organizations

It is necessary to distinguish public organizations, with which this book is concerned, from the whole universe of organizations. For the sake of simplicity let us break formal organizations into three categories: government, nonprofit, and private. Let us briefly discuss private organizations (which we also call *firms*) first and then look at the other two types of organizations. Private organizations, or firms, are established by entrepreneurs (individually or in concert) to make a profit and, except when breaking the law, are accountable only to owners and stockholders. Other factors further define or describe the firm; but this one sentence cuts to the core and presents the major difference.

We include both government agencies and nonprofit organizations under the rubric of "public organizations." It is true that government and nonprofit organizations have major differences, but their similarities are sufficient to justify combining them while we discuss organization theory and its application. Government organizations are created as agents of some unit of government, whether a local school district or the executive office of the president. *They are created by law to administer the law.* Public oversight and accountability are prominent and necessary features of government organizations. Nonprofit organizations come into existence to fulfill public needs that are not or cannot be carried out by business *or* government. Lester Salamon argues that there is a continuum from private to nonprofit to government organizations and that the latter two are "partners in public service" (1995). In fact, in discussing the role of voluntary (that is, nonprofit) organizations, he argues that they are more likely than government organizations to be the initiators of collective goods provision (2003):

> For government to act, substantial segments of the public must be aroused, public officials must be informed, laws must be written, majorities must be assembled, and programs must be put into operation. By contrast, to generate a voluntary sector response, a handful of individuals acting on their own or with outside support can suffice. It is reasonable to expect, therefore, that the private, nonprofit sector will typically provide the first line of response to perceived "market failures," and that government will be called on only as the voluntary response proves insufficient. (1995, 44)

Thus both government and nonprofit organizations usually exist to fulfill visions of the public interest and public service, and neither type of organization exists for the end, or ultimate, goal of making a profit (the primary reason for private organizations). Although nonprofit organizations operate without constant public oversight and accountability, they must depend on public trust as they carry out their missions because their support comes from voluntary fees or donations and grants from philanthropic organizations or the government, and in both cases the continuation of support depends on the donors' goodwill.

As nonprofit organizations, often referred to as "the third sector," have grown in importance within society, it has become increasingly important to decide where they fall on the public–private spectrum. Obviously it is our belief that third-sector organizations fall much closer to the public than the private end of that spectrum. If the claim that these organizations operate in a quasi-public fashion is correct, the material in this book should be especially applicable to them. The next two chapters discuss both the characteristics of public agencies in contrast to other types of organizations and the implications of a focus on such organizations.

Bureaucracy

The term *bureaucracy* is used both to identify a particular type of organization structure and to deride or criticize it (Downs 1967). The definition of bureaucracy offered by Max Weber (1947), the German sociologist who wrote from the turn of the century to the 1920s, is the most authoritative and still serves as the point of departure for contemporary organization theory. Based on historical and contemporary study of several great social and economic institutions, including the Prussian military, the Roman Catholic church, and the Chinese civil service, Weber identified a number of characteristics of organization structure and personnel policy that set the bureaucratic institution apart from all other, less neutral, stable, and expert means of administering the law and coordinating the intricate activities of vast numbers of people in a predictable and efficient manner.

The characteristics of bureaucracy that Weber noted included the specialization of function; the hiring and promotion of officials based solely on expertise; the exercise of authority through a centralized, hierarchical chain of command; and the development of an intricate system of rules to cover all possible actions and to minimize discretion. These and other characteristics of bureaucracies are described and analyzed in detail in Chapter 3 as an example of one prototype of public agencies.

Alternatively, Downs's formulation of the idea of bureaucracy highlights its economic foundations (1967). He distinguishes between government and nonprofit entities and firms based on public sector organizations' lack of a market. Without a market to set the value of the organization's work, managers rationally focus on obtaining a larger share of inputs, funds for expansion, or greater authority. The basic purpose and motivation of the public sector organization becomes not efficiency in the usual sense but greater recognition and support from funders. All government agencies, many nonprofit organizations, and some special offices in the private sector are therefore "bureaus." The implications of the lack of a market are felt in many areas of these bureaus' existence: growth, motivation, communications, control systems, leadership styles, and especially decision making. In the matters of organization size and structural characteristics, Downs agrees with Weber.

Still other formulations of bureaucracy are offered by a number of contemporary theorists. Hummel (1994), who also begins with Weber's formulation, focuses on what Weber saw as the considerable dangers of bureaucracy for the personality of its officials and for society at large. Though Weber chronicled the rise of the bureaucratic form and was able to see its advantages for the control of far-flung enterprises, he was also extremely critical of the way bureaucracy destroys spontaneity—which, as one raised in the Romantic literary tradition, he equated with human freedom. The bureaucratic personality must always be oriented to the efficiency of any proposed course of action; thus he or she loses the capacity to act in a spontaneous and fully human manner. Even worse, the trend Weber saw (and we continue to observe) is that more and more institutions—public, private, and even familial—have become bureaucratic, which makes us increasingly captive of the bureaucratic mentality and less able to see or to act on our plight.

Hummel notes that ultimately

> Bureaucracy gives birth to a new species of inhuman beings. Peoples' social relations are being converted into control relations. Their norms and beliefs concerning human ends are torn from them and replaced with skills affirming the ascendancy of technical means, whether of administration or production. Psychologically, the new personality type is that of

the rationalistic expert, incapable of emotion and devoid of will. Language, once the means of bringing people into communication, becomes the secretive tool of one-way commands. Politics, especially democratic politics, fades away as the method of publicly determining society-wide goals based on human needs: It is replaced by administration. (1994, 3)

Other definitions of *bureaucracy,* also highly critical and negative, derive from a variety of theoretical foundations. Some view bureaus as complex linguistic games, as cultural constructions rather than the objective realities we assume we perceive, as "psychic prisons," or as instruments of class domination (Burrell and Morgan 1979; Denhart 1981, 1993). We look further at these characterizations in this and subsequent chapters.

The question of whether public organizations must have the negative characteristics associated with a bureaucracy lies at the heart of most contemporary organization research, and we hope to examine this question in this text. Government agencies are often referred to as "bureaucracies," but this appellation is used more in a derogatory way than as a descriptive term.[2]

Nonprofits usually avoid the charge of being bureaucratic; however, the model actually describes almost all organizations better as they grow in size. The larger an organization, the more likely it is to have bureaucratic characteristics. The effort to devise a better form of organization, one that balances the many and sometimes contradictory beliefs about what would be a better form, is a major occupation of the organization research field. What are the alternatives to bureaucracy? What are the advantages and limitations of alternative organization forms, in general and in particular, for public administration? What can the radical critics of bureaucracy teach us about the obligations of public agencies?

WHAT IS ORGANIZATION THEORY?

Organization theory is *not* a single theory. Rather, it is a loosely knit community of many approaches to organization analysis. Its themes, questions, methods, and explanatory modes are extremely diverse. Dwight Waldo noted in a review of work in the field in 1978, "Organization theory is characterized by vogues, heterogeneity, claims, and counterclaims" (597), and even greater differentiation in theory and practice have developed since then. Organization theory certainly cannot be described as an orderly progression of ideas or a unified body of knowledge in which each development builds carefully on and extends the one before it. Rather, developments in theory and prescription for practice show disagreement about the purposes and uses of a theory of organization, the issues it should address (supervisory style, organization culture, efficiency, and effectiveness), and the concepts and variables that should enter into such a theory.

The interdisciplinary (really multidisciplinary) character of the field is both the cause and effect of the diversity of questions, methods, and theories and of the considerable energy in the field. Most social sciences contribute to organization theory. Theorists and practitioners   these fields for answers to critical (and everyday) problems; and the fields, in turn,

his *The Case for Bureaucracy: A Public Administration Polemic* (2004), distinguishes
    s an organization type and "the bureaucracy" as a pejorative term for government depart-
    distinction is important to remember throughout this text.

introduce new concepts and models that create new perspectives and questions. Psychology (and its more applied branch, industrial psychology) has contributed behavioral studies on such topics as leadership, motivation, group interaction, and conflict. Sociological research has produced insightful research, including case studies, about the unintended consequences of official organization rules and the effects of informal social relations. Sociologists have also studied organization structure, interorganization coordination, and organization–client relations and their impact on both groups—to name only a few topics. Economic analyses of organizations have focused on the many theories of decision making, among other subjects, and more recently have introduced into the study of organizations the general *public choice theory* with its emphasis on the self-interest of organizational actors. Anthropologists and communications analysts have studied the linguistic and cultural dimensions of organizational life. Systems analysts have provided applied mathematical, process, and value-added models for planning and program management. Public administrators and political scientists have concerned themselves with policy analysis (and implementation) and have investigated the ways in which the political, professional, and technical characteristics of government (and more recently nonprofit) organizations influence the making and execution of government policy. These disciplines study the relationships between public organizations and their political environments. Box 1–1 gives examples of typical questions posed by each of the disciplines that contribute to the field of organization theory.

This variety of disciplines clearly contributes to the richness and complexity of theory in the field, as well as to the conflicts over theories and the absence of conceptual agreement on fundamental assumptions about the nature of organizations or the uses and purposes of organization theory. The tension around organization theory is further exacerbated by the expectations of those studying it. For some scholars and practitioners, the theories are expected to provide clear and direct guidelines for the selection of particular management styles or practices; for others the purpose of theory is to explain phenomena; and for still others its purpose is to activate resistance to the role organizations can play in political oppression.

There are, of course, overlaps, continuities, and some disagreements as the various disciplines are considered within the larger field of organization theory. Real interdisciplinary exchange results from the extensive borrowing of concepts, findings, and questions. Often, however, this borrowing is characterized by extensive reinterpretation and shifts in meaning and emphasis so that the result sometimes resembles piracy more than interdisciplinary cooperation in theory development. This state of affairs is fairly common in the social sciences generally (Kaplan 1964), but it sometimes seems to reach new heights in organization theory because of its multidisciplinary nature. These debates can be confusing, but they serve a healthy and interesting purpose—they offer a rich bazaar for ideas about organization.

Organization theory has also been open to the currents of political thought. For example, various organization theorists since the 1960s and 1970s have advocated more democratic decision-making procedures and greater participation by citizens and officials. Theoretical movements in the social sciences have also had an impact on the field. The behavioral revolution, the popularity of general systems theory, and the current reemergence and acceptance of interpretive research on the intentions, meanings, and symbols of organizations rather than on behavior alone are some examples. Theory in the field has sometimes gone to extremes in its search for a conceptual wedge that can open the secrets of successful organizations. All of these currents have been combined in new "action theories" that attempt to create organizations with more sensitivity to internal and external changes, increased capability of learn·

BOX 1-1　Questions about Organizations Posed by Various Social Sciences

Anthropology: the social science concerned with the origins of humankind and its physical, social, and cultural development.

> **Questions:** What are the cultural values and norms of the organization, and how are they manifested in stories, rituals, and symbols? How are organizational values and norms related to those of the larger culture? How do they affect implementation of policies and strategies of the organization?

Sociology: the science of society, social institutions, and social relations; specifically, the systematic study of the development, structure, interaction, and collective behavior of organized groups of people.

> **Questions:** What is the relationship between the formal organization and the informal social life of the organization? How are organizational activities coordinated and controlled? What are the key social institutions, roles, and values in the organization? How are they related to external institutions and values? How do organizations interact? How are they linked? What are the relationships between the organization, its clients, and other interested parties in society?

Psychology: the social science that examines personality, cognition, emotional life, and behavior.

> **Questions:** How are we motivated? What attitudes or personality types lead to behavior that is valued in organizations? How do perception and learning influence organizational behavior such as work motivation and productivity? What are the processes of effective communication?

Social psychology: the social science concerned with attitudes, cognitions, and behavior in social settings and the interactions of people.

> **Questions:** What is leadership, and what are the most effective forms of leadership behavior? How are attitudes formed in organizations, and how do they influence work behavior? How do cohesive groups form, how do members interact, and what are the implications for organizational functioning?

Economics: the social science concerned with the analysis of markets and the systems by which goods and services are produced, distributed, and consumed.

> **Questions:** What are the differences in market relations and economic motivations between public and private organizations? What economic conditions are necessary for the formation of a public agency? How is decision making linked to the economic characteristics of organizations?

Political science: the social science concerned with the institutions and processes of government, public policy, and politics.

> **Questions:** What is the role of government bureaus? What is the role of nonprofit organizations, and when should they play a primary role in guaranteeing the public good? What are the political responsibilities of government organizations (and nonprofit agencies)? How are power and influence exercised within government bureaus (nonprofit organizations) and in their relations with other actors, government bodies, and constituencies?

and changing to meet constant challenges to existence, and, especially, greater chances for individual growth and fulfillment in conjunction with organization success (Senge 1990; Heckscher and Donnellon 1994). And of course all of these theoretical and applied theories and models have been occurring in an extremely turbulent technological environment that has rewritten many of the accepted ideas about structures and roles in organizations.

Given these factors (and the list is not complete but indicative of the quantity and complexity of factors influencing the daily lives of organizations and the people who work in them), it is understandable that organization theory is a disorderly and fascinating field. To produce a useful overview of it is a difficult—almost presumptuous—task. But we feel that it is important to try because we believe that the field makes an important and useful contribution to the study of government and nonprofit management.

VARIETIES OF ORGANIZATION THEORY

The varieties of organization theory can perhaps best be understood by differentiating them at three levels. First, they differ in subject matter (what is studied). Second, there are differences in their explanatory forms (how it is studied)—that is, whether systems analysis, political economy, or some other approach is the basis for the explanation offered in the theory. Finally, theories can be differentiated in terms of their purposes (why they are studied). We look briefly at each of these distinctions.

Essentially the perspective taken here on the application of these theories might be called a multi-theory approach in which the question is not which theory to accept and which to discard, but how to establish a basis from which managers, *informed* by theory, can pick and choose useful concepts and devise strategies for action. Concerning the application of the theories, we see them as a set of conceptual tools for diagnosing and acting on organization problems. Within limits, the larger the number of theories and the more varied the conceptual tools at our disposal, the greater the likelihood that we will find an approach that suits the conditions we face. Thus having a variety of theories at our disposal makes us more capable managers because we have the ability to see and conceptualize problems in alternative ways and to evaluate these alternatives. So let us begin to consider the variety of theories.

Differences in Subject

Organization theorists study various phenomena and use different levels of analysis. Some research focuses on the individual, whereas other studies are concerned with groups or the organization as a whole. Studies at the organization level include work on structures and hierarchies and on processes such as communication or decision making. In this way, four main subject areas in organization research and theory can be identified:

1. Theories of individual and group behavior.
2. Theories of organization structure.
3. Theories of organization processes (such as communications and decision making).
4. Global or overall theories of organization.

These topics do not, however, constitute unrelated or mutually exclusive categories. In fact, the *mutual use* of these theories in examining organization understanding and action is synergistic. For example, theories of structure focus on the formal chain of authority, but intelligence gathering and information processing also rely on some of these structures while using other nonformal aspects. Thus the topics are related in ways we discuss in detail later in this chapter.

At the level of *individual* behavior is, for example, research on motivation where inborn needs, attitudes, and perceptions are studied in relation to productivity or other desirable organization outputs. However, groups, and the interaction of individuals within them, are important parts of understanding phenomena such as motivation. The investigation of *groups and intergroup relations* encompasses such subjects as the dynamics and effectiveness of workgroups or decision-making groups, conflict management, and leadership. At the overall or *global* level of analysis are found research and speculative theory about such issues as what the reigning values of the organization should be; what its relations with outside clients or constituents should be; or what its means of motivation, coordination, or leadership are. A total picture is provided—usually at the speculative level—that energizes our efforts in theory and research at the other two levels. Over the last four decades some examples of attempts at global theory include the constant appeals for "team building" (Larson and LaFasto 1989), creating "learning organizations" (Senge 1990), using total quality management (TQM) as originally developed by Deming (Walton 1990), the "excellent" organization of Peters and Waterman (1982), the "Z" organization that reflects aspects of Japanese management (Ouchi 1981), and Orion White's "dialectical" organization (1969). As can be seen from this list, there is a constant effort to develop global, or universal, theories about and for organizations. At the same time such effort at theory building is equally and constantly frustrated by changes in environment, technology, society, and numerous other factors. In spite of the frustration in trying to generate such theories, the simple effort to do so is important because it forces everyone interested to stay up to date with (often subtly) changing forces that students and practitioners must face every day. To a lesser extent, the same frustrations exist for all those studying organizations and trying to manage them. Herein lies one of the most frustrating and yet exciting aspects of studying organization theory.

Research on organization structure and processes constitutes yet another distinction in the field's subject matter. *Structural* research is concerned with the organization's hierarchical pattern, centralization and decentralization, the shape of the organization chart and its lines of authority, the formation of organization subdivisions, and the coordination of those subdivisions. An important question in this area is how organizations adapt their structures to changes in the environment or technology. Organization *processes* include the basic activities of the organization. Such topics as decision making, control, communication, budgeting, evaluation, and program implementation are all key processes in making and implementing policy and in management.

The subjects mentioned here are the basic topics discussed in this text. Differences in the types and purposes of theories, which are described next, are discussed within this subject framework as we proceed.

Differences in Type

The type of theory or the form of explanation offered is another distinction that can be made among organization theories. Some of the most common theories include systems theory, theories of political economy, public choice theory, theories of group politics and influence, theories of personality and attitude formation, theories of psychological humanism, theories of culture interpretation, and theories of social change. We illustrate just a few of these to show the diversity of explanations used in the field. Usually any one organizational subject is explained by several different types of theories, which makes for a great diversity of explanations and richness in perspective on any single subject. Thus each subject that is discussed in this book is typically covered from several theoretical perspectives.

Systems theories are used to explain many aspects of an organization. The technology for resource transformation, from inputs to outputs, and the influences of various environmental conditions are often described as particular patterns of activity called *systems*. Systems theories point out how activities in the system are interrelated, sometimes in mathematical terms. Here events are explained as the product of natural, often unintended, patterns of interactivity. Organizational communication and control theories make frequent use of systems theory.

The political economy approach explains events in terms of the relations between political and economic systems (Wamsley and Zald 1976) and the nonmarket setting (Downs 1967) of bureaus, showing how these factors influence the choices of organizational actors. Incremental decision making, for example, is seen as the rational response when the costs of new information and reprogramming the rules and personnel are high relative to the value of a new, severely different policy for the organization (Allison 1971).

A third type of theory attempts to explain how social and cultural factors influence the internal operation of organizations and how those organizations interact with clients, interest groups, political policy makers, and other external forces in the larger society. Internal theories include everything from the "bureaucratic model" of Max Weber (1947), to theories about "socialization" into groups, to ideas about "learning organizations" (Senge 1990), "participative management" (Kearney and Hays 1994), and "team management" (Larson and LaFasto 1989). Likewise, theories about the spread of values and mores within and between groups and cultures also help explicate the challenges faced by organizations as they try to remain relevant and effective in the larger social environment (Rheingold 2003).

Finally, it is important to note one further current theory. "Postmodern theory" challenges all of the other theories just presented by asking "What is real?" According to Adrian Carr (1997), postmodernists

> convey the idea or a sense of being **after** what has been previously referred to as an era of modernity. . . . Modernity . . . is typified as an age of reason, rationality, enlightenment, and progress. Many postmodernists situate postmodernity not just as being **after** modernity but against, anti, or the antithesis of such an age. (4–5)

Based on this "truth," postmodernists argue that all knowledge formation and authentication is relative, and "reason is, itself, transitory and an illusionary construction of text" (5). Truth can develop only from discourse between individuals with their various constructs of existence based on experience and personal understanding. Although total acceptance of this theory strikes us as destructive of science and rationality—and therefore of the ability to arrive at useful theories and models of organizations' structure and function—remaining sensitive to the multiple perspectives related to personal and social experience is critical to success in both understanding and prescribing for organizations.

Differences in Purpose

Even though the accepted and used theories are diverse in explanatory content and topical focus, they share basic assumptions about the nature of organizations and the purpose of organization theory. In general, the mainstream theories are empirical—that is, they are based on quantitative or qualitative observations, and they assume that there is a more or less objective reality that can become knowable through observation.

The theories also share the assumption that the purpose of organization research and theory is to uncover that reality and to use the knowledge of how to predict and sometimes control that reality to improve the functioning of organizations from the standpoint of the organization's "owners," including administrative professionals, the public or clients, and the variety of government and nonprofit policy makers. Because these assumptions fit naturally with the assumptions and purposes of practicing administrators, the mainstream orientation to organization theory has generally been useful for practitioners.

Other responses to questions about the nature of organizational knowledge and the purposes of organization theory have been emerging (especially in public administration) in the past few decades. Although these theories, for the most part, lack the "scientific objectivity" of the theories just mentioned and therefore are centers of debate about their applicability to public organizations, they show some noteworthy developments that are outside the mainstream theories, assumptions, and methods, as Burrell and Morgan (1979) note. Hummel's critique of the standard bureaucratic model of organization, based at least in part on phenomenology, illustrates one alternative model. According to this theory, what one thinks and perceives—the precepts and concepts of the mind—actually determines what is reality to the individual. And the assumptions inherent in the bureaucratic model organize the minds of most people because of the time spent in, and the impact on life of, bureaucratic organizations. According to Hummel,

> Unless a model can be found in bureaucratic policies of programs for a real individual trying to become a client, that individual can never come to exist for the bureaucracy as a client. Reality itself is defined according to ideal models. In bureaucratic speech, the client experiences this power to declare him or her existent, or a nullity, in terms of a number of demands by bureaucrats: Speak our language or get no help; answer our questions (according to some secret code unknown to you) or we will think you don't exist. (1994, 217)

In other words, phenomenology says bureaucratic organizations are mechanistic and depersonalizing; everyone in them and affected by them is forced into a category, a class, and treated with generic procedures and remedies to achieve universal goals. The painful and conflicting pressures that conscientious officials experience, caused by the bureaucratic system, often have the effect of creating either loss of freedom or disobedience. Naisbitt (1982) refers to this phenomenon as the divided need for "high tech" and "high touch" in society. As more technology, bureaucracy, and "order" take over life there is a corresponding need for connectedness and meaningful interaction with others as human beings. Some groups and individuals have tried to escape bureaucracy by reverting to premodern existence and seeking charismatic guidance. The desire of many people to leave large corporations and either work in or set up smaller businesses, the emergence of literalist religious movements, and attempts by groups to force societies to revert to social and political customs from prior ages may be signs of this revolt.

For phenomenological critics like Robert Denhardt (1981, 2003), a way to begin reforming organization culture is to adopt what Hummel calls an "intentionalist" position (a form of phenomenology), which focuses on the intentions and the beliefs of workers as well as on the perceptions and language that link one human being to another. We would then no longer treat workers or clients as objects to be motivated or manipulated. Instead we would focus on our status as coworkers, use the discretion available to us as managers to increase interaction, and thereby enhance the power, capacity, and creativity of officials to perform their mission. Theories that build, at least in part, on these assumptions include many of the current participative and team-building models that appear throughout this book.

Michael Harmon (1981), like Hummel, emphasizes the subjectivity of organization and social life and suggests that attention be paid to the ways in which all officials try to make sense of their worlds by positing theories and engaging in linguistic and other symbol-sharing activities. As an outgrowth of this view, Harmon argues that cooperation and freedom of interaction will be more justice producing than the methods of social domination and control that are more commonly found in organizations and in society at large. Burrell and Morgan (1979) sketch a conceptual framework for describing and comparing these theories, and Denhardt (1981) reviews and critiques these and other organization theories as they apply to public administration. Janet and Robert Denhardt (2003) go further and argue that the interorganization milieu in which public policies are currently determined and implemented makes it impossible for hierarchical authority and control systems to function either efficiently or effectively; thus new organization patterns (both structural and procedural) must be discovered. Senge (1990) depends on many of these assumptions as he argues for the building of an organization that searches for a more specific reality than that which is normally accepted and then learns from its experiences, thus turning into an organization that constantly builds on its experiences in ways that improve the overall functioning and success of the entity.

Another theory, related to economics, that has gained attention over the last two decades is public choice theory and its application to bureaucratic actors (Tullock 1987). These theorists believe that people in public bureaucracies almost inevitably move away from dutiful behavior in carrying out the law or the goals established by their external masters—often the legislature or the chief executive. Instead, quoting Garvey,

> Drawing their premises primarily from the economic theory of the market, (public choice) theorists emphasize individual self-interest, not group goals. The appeal to an internalized sense of public trust may work partially or temporarily, but human egoism will eventually challenge the pattern of strict accountability that the machine model of bureaucracy implies. Bureaucratic actors have interests of their own to advance. Inevitably, these interests will come into conflict, at least to some degree, with the goals of the organization. The temptation of a conflicted employee to sacrifice the group goal for the personal one is likely to be irresistible. Thus, . . . if subordinates have any latitude for discretion, they will sooner or later abuse it. (1993, 29)

Public choice theory, if accepted, has strong explanatory and prescriptive power. It especially prescribes strong systems of control for decisions and actions of employees in any public bureau. This theory also speaks to the size of government: Proponents of this theory believe government should be minimal and the bureaucracy small.

Although we discuss the insights and criticisms of these newer theoretical orientations throughout this text, we do not advocate one or another of them. Neither do we advocate any of the more conventional organization theories. Rather, we present a variety of theories organized around a fairly comprehensive set of topics in the field to permit and encourage readers to develop a way of using the insights from as many theories as possible.

OUR THEORETICAL PERSPECTIVE

As noted earlier, the approach we are taking here is multitheoretical. From an application perspective, we see the theories outlined here and discussed throughout the text as conceptual tools for diagnosing problems and assessing the potential of different solutions. The larger the number and variety of conceptual tools that we have to work with, the more facets of the organization problem we can see, and the better and more intelligent our choice of action can be.

For example, in most organization theory classes, students confronting their first discussion of a management case will typically see all problems as personality conflicts and will try to find ways to get rid of the offending actor. After a few weeks of reading, however, they begin to see that the same case has other dimensions, such as problems in the form of the communication network, in the supervisory style of a manager, or even arising from factors external to the organization. Reading organization theory helps us to see organizations as multidimensional entities and allows us to identify alternative lines of analysis and action.

A variety of theories and research findings contributes to both understanding and action in organizations. Different theories are useful in different circumstances and for different kinds of managers. While we are not suggesting that managers should simply make up a personal theory without recourse to the analysis and research in the field, we are suggesting that public managers can and do judge which dimensions of a problem are most critical, which aspect of the organization is in the most trouble, and what his or her own particular talents and predilections are. Based on these factors, the offerings of the field of organization theory should be studied and selectively used.

Some work has already been done on identifying the circumstances under which a particular theory or research finding is most appropriate. What is called a *contingency theory* or *metatheory* (a theory about how or when to use other theories) has been developed in several subject areas of organization theory and is presented in later chapters. These contingency theories prescribe different courses of action, depending on the circumstances in the organization. For example, one contingency theory of supervisory behavior leads to a recommendation of different styles of behavior, based on the psychological maturity and skill levels of the work group; another suggests that different decision-making models fit distinct situations. We present a number of these theories wherein such factors as the environment of the agency, its program technology, its political support, and others influence our evaluation and selection of the available courses of action.

CHAPTER TOPICS FOR THIS TEXT

The chapters in this text are, for the most part, organized around subjects or themes central to organization theory. Two further introductory chapters follow this one, however. Chapter 2 discusses the differences between public and private organizations and how those differences affect the development of public organization theory. Chapter 3 discusses pivotal areas of interest to organizations that work in the public sector (both government agencies and non-profit organizations) and how major global theories of organization address or fail to address these issues. Our purpose in these introductory chapters is to identify some of the issues with which we are particularly concerned, given our focus on public organizations.

Chapter 4 addresses theories of organization structure. It overviews traditional theories and presents a detailed review of contemporary research and theorizing on the design of organizations. This review takes into account the public organization's needs for program support, its program technologies, and its environment.

Chapters 5, 6, and 7 discuss the organization's intelligence system; communication, control, and decision making are the subjects covered. We consider the various types of formal and informal communication networks, their pathologies, and some partial remedies. The control system, of course, depends on the communication structure for the gathering and processing of information, which means that problems in one part of the system affect the other parts. Various forms of control using quantitative, behavioral, and social psychological approaches to the subject are discussed. Finally, the various descriptive and prescriptive theories of decision making or policymaking are described, and the prospects for a contingency theory of decision making are discussed.

Individual behavior is the focus of Chapters 8 and 9. Theories of motivation, largely borrowed from research on for-profit firms, are discussed in Chapter 8, and the alterations that would make them applicable to nonprofit and government agencies are considered. Leadership, managerial, and supervisory behaviors are discussed in Chapter 9. The traditional and behavioral approaches are examined in terms of their appropriateness for different hierarchical levels and managerial settings. Techniques of planned organization change based on technological developments, behavioral research, and the human relations values mentioned earlier conclude the book in Chapter 10.

FOR FURTHER READING

At the end of each chapter there are suggestions for further reading in that subject area. Here let us note some of the numerous journals that are the source of the latest information on research about, and application of, organization theory. The most recent behavioral research is often presented in the *Administrative Science Quarterly*. Among the several journals in public administration that should be scanned for information about both research and current practice in government agencies are the main journal of the field, *Public Administration Review*, and the *Journal of Public Administration Research and Theory*. Current nonprofit research can be examined in journals such as *The Nonprofit Quarterly* and the *Journal of Volunteer Administration*. General management journals, such as the *Harvard Business Review* and the *California Management Review*, although usually focusing on the private sector, present much valuable information on research in complex organizations. Another set of journals, represented by *Organizational Dynamics*, deals with the application of behavioral theory to current businesses or organizations. Each of the major disciplines involved in particular aspects of organizational research (psychology, sociology, economics, and so on) has journals that make contributions to the field of organization theory. And finally there are journals dealing with each of the major subject areas covered in the latter chapters of this volume (communication, decision theory, leadership, and the like). This review of journals is cursory, meant only to point the researcher in the right direction. A little effort will return great rewards in learning about the latest research about organizations and its real-world application.

Another universe of potentially valuable information is the Internet. Government organizations have home pages with substantial amounts of information available to the public. Likewise businesses, universities, and many professional organizations with an interest in organization theory are sharing information about current research and activity through the Internet. Incredible amounts of research data and findings can also be found on the Internet—plus lively discussions of issues related to the subject matter presented throughout this book. The increasing availability of online journals must also be noted. Some professional journals are changing to online formats, and some universities are creating consortia to make data and research available online. Also numerous issue-related websites are springing up. A major challenge faced by anyone using the issue-related material, however, is being able to separate the serious and useful information from the conjecture and misinformation that can just as easily be found on the Internet. Given that caveat, undoubtedly this area of potential information will continue to grow, and the Internet is an important source for up-to-date information.

REVIEW QUESTIONS

1. Before continuing through this book, think about the goals you wish to achieve from reading this material. What do you want to know about organizations after this experience?
2. Remember that this book presents an introduction to the field, and it is possible to delve much deeper into every topic. How much more do you need to know about specific topics to accomplish the goals you have established for yourself?
3. As you read the following chapters, consider to what extent the materials presented are *particular* to government organizations, *particular* to nonprofit organizations, or apply to both.

REFERENCES

Allison, Graham T. 1971. *Essence of decision: Explaining the Cuban missile crisis.* Boston: Little, Brown.
Burrell, Gibson, and Gareth Morgan. 1979. *Sociological paradigms and organisational analysis.* London: Heinemann.
Carr, Adrian. 2003. Putative problematic agency in a postmodern world: Is it implicit in the text—Can it be explicit in organization analysis? In *Postmodernism, "reality" & public administration: A discourse,* 3–18. Ed. Hugh T. Miller and Charles J. Fox. Burke, VA: Chatelaine Press.
Denhardt, Janet V., and Robert B. Denhardt. 2003. *The new public service: Serving, not steering.* Armonk, NY: M. E. Sharpe.
Denhardt, Robert B. 1981. *In the shadow of organization.* Lawrence, KS: Regents Press of Kansas.
_____. 1993. *Theories of public organization.* 2nd ed. Belmont, CA: Wadsworth.
Downs, Anthony. 1967. *Inside bureaucracy.* Boston: Little, Brown. (Reissued Prospect Heights, IL: Waveland Press, 1994.)
Garvey, Gerald. 1993. *Facing the bureaucracy: Living and dying in a public agency.* San Francisco: Jossey-Bass.
Goodsell, Charles T. 2004. *The Case for Bureaucracy: A Public Administration Polemic.* 4th ed. Washington, DC: Congressional Quarterly Press.
Harmon, Michael. 1981. *Action theory for public administration.* New York: Longman.

Heckscher, Charles, and Anne Donnellon. 1994. *The post-bureaucratic organization: New perspectives on organizational change*. Thousand Oaks, CA: Sage Publications.

Hummel, Ralph P. 1994. *The bureaucratic experience*. 4th ed. New York: St. Martin's Press.

Kaplan, Abraham. 1964. *The conduct of inquiry*. San Francisco: Chandler.

Kearney, Richard C., and Steven Hays. 1994. Labor management relations and participative decision making: Toward a new paradigm. *Public Administration Review* 54: 44–51.

Larson, Carl, and Frank LaFasto. 1989. *Teamwork*. Newbury Park, CA: Sage Publications.

Morgan, Gareth. 1986. *Images of organization*. Beverly Hills, CA: Sage Publications.

Naisbitt, John. 1982. *Megatrends: Ten new directions transforming our lives*. New York: Warner Books.

Ouchi, William. 1981. *Theory Z: How American business can meet the Japanese challenge*. Reading, MA: Addison-Wesley Publishing.

Peters, Thomas P., and Robert H. Waterman. 1982. *In search of excellence*. New York: Warner Books.

Rheingold, Howard. 2003. *Smart mobs: The next social revolution*. Cambridge, MA: Perseus Publishing.

Salamon, Lester M. 1995. *Partners in public service: Government–nonprofit relations in the modern welfare state*. Baltimore: Johns Hopkins Press.

———. 2003. Voluntary failure theory correctly viewed. In *The study of the nonprofit enterprise: Theories and approaches*, 183–86. Ed. Helmut Anheier and Avner BenNer. New York: Kluwer Academic/Plenum Publishers.

Senge, Peter M. 1990. *The fifth discipline: The art and practice of the learning organization*. New York: Currency/Doubleday.

Simon, Herbert A. 1976. *Administrative behavior*. 3rd ed. New York: Free Press.

Tullock, Gordon. 1987. *The politics of bureaucracy*. Lanham, MD: University Press of America.

Waldo, Dwight. 1978. Organization theory: Revisiting the elephant. *Public Administration Review*: 589–97.

Walton, Mary. 1990. *Deming management at work*. New York: G. P. Putnam's Sons.

Wamsley Gary, and Mayer Zald. 1976. *The political economy of public organizations*. Bloomington, IN: Indiana University Press.

Weber, Max. 1947. *Theory of social and economic organization*. Trans. A. Henderson and T. Parsons. Glencoe, IL: The Free Press.

Weick, Karl. 1979. *The social psychology of organizing*. 2nd ed. Reading, MA: Addison-Wesley Publishing.

White, Orion. 1969. The dialectical organization: An alternative to bureaucracy. *Public Administration Review* 29: 32–42.

Wilson, James Q. 1989. *Bureaucracy: What government agencies do and why they do it*. New York: Basic Books.

Chapter 2

Blurring Sectors: Public and Private

Organizations are one of the building blocks of the world we humans create for ourselves. Modern civilization would not exist without organizations—modest and enormous, simple and complex, public and private, and every combination in between. In fact, organizations are a *social* technology. We painstakingly design organizations or haphazardly muddle them into being; then we use them to help shape our personal lives, our work lives, and the societies we live in. Organizations are woven into the fabric of our social, economic, political, and spiritual lives. Our accomplishments through them inspire admiration and loyalty even as we feel fear and anger in the face of their power, inflexibility, and attention to petty detail (Blau and Meyer 1987).

This book centers on *public* organization theory and *public* management. Its principal assumption is that public and private management differ in many respects because public organizations (government and nonprofit organizational entities) are significantly and fundamentally unlike private organizations (for-profit business organizational entities) in crucial ways (Brody 2003). This chapter examines the public–private spectrum of contemporary organizations in the context of organization theory, highlighting the distinctiveness of each family of organizations—government, nonprofit, and privately owned—as well as the commonalities they share. The chapter also explores aspects of their shared public environment, ethics, technology, globalization, and privatization, along with other trends and issues.

GENERIC THEORY AND PUBLIC ORGANIZATIONS

Chapter 1 defines an *organization* as "a collection of people engaged in specialized, interdependent activity to accomplish a goal or mission." A thumbnail definition of a *public organization* is an organization whose primary goal or mission is providing goods or services that benefit members of the public rather than the stockholders and owners of the organization. (See Box 2–1 for key synonyms.) As Chapter 1 explains, nonprofit groups and government entities meet this definition, whereas for-profit firms do not. The real world gets much more complicated, of course, but we'll get into those matters shortly.

All formal organizations share many traits, enabling us to consider a generic or general theory of organization. *Management*, too, is inherently "a generic process with universal implications and with application in any institutional setting—whether a private firm or a public agency" (Murray 1975, 364; also see Anheier 2000). Concern about achieving organizational goals is the common thread in defining management; and as Hersey and Blanchard state in *Management of Organization Behavior,*

> This definition . . . makes no mention of business or industrial organizations. Management, as defined, applies to organizations whether they are business, educational institutions, hospitals, political or military organizations, or even families. (1996, 5)

Many forms of human behavior and interaction retain their similarities under different organizational conditions and settings, but does this make a universalistic approach to organization theory valid? The answer is a qualified yes when considered on the general level. Does the generic approach provide a sufficiently useful basis for informing the action and choices of the public manager? No, often it does not. Generic theory is a fine starting point for every manager; but for managers of for-profit, nonprofit, and government organizations

BOX 2–1 What's in an Organization-Oriented Term?

This book uses a number of terms that have both distinct and interchangeable meanings. Of them, the most broad-based term is *organization*. As a noun, an *organization* is a collection of people engaged in specialized, interdependent activity to accomplish a goal or mission. Departments, agencies, and bureaus are types of organizations, but each is a term that can also have a special meaning.

Department A *department* is a major subunit of a larger organization, such as an accounting department, English department, or department of public works. At the U.S. federal level the term refers to the most basic organizational unit within the executive branch, a cabinet-level office such as the Department of the Interior, headed by the secretary of the interior.

Agency Generically an *agency* is an administrative division of government. It can also mean a nonprofit organization, such as an adoption assistance agency, or of a private firm, such as an insurance agency. At the U.S. federal level the term formally refers to an independent regulatory agency, such as the Federal Communications Commission. Less formally, it can reflect a major subunit of a cabinet-level department, such as the Agency for International Development, which is associated with the Department of State, and the General Services Administration, a bureau within the Department of Commerce.

Bureau A *bureau* is a division of a government department or an independent administrative unit. At the U.S. federal level it refers to a major subunit of a department, such as the Federal Bureau of Investigation, part of the Department of Justice. As a concept, a bureau is also a cost center within a larger organization, as opposed to a profit center (Downs 1967).

Bureaucracy *Bureaucracy* has several meanings relevant to organization theory. It is an organization concept that German sociologist Max Weber analyzed in 1922 as an "ideal type" (Weber 1947). It refers to the institutions of public administration in general and of government in particular. It can be a pejorative term suggesting rule-bound, overly complex organizations. Typically the word *bureaucracy* unadorned by an article (such as *the* or *a*) refers to the organization concept, whereas *the* bureaucracy refers to government, to American government as a whole, and particularly to the unelected portion of government (Goodsell 2004).

alike, it is only a starting point. Each management setting offers unique challenges and opportunities, and all are subject to local environmental characteristics and to inevitable changes over time:

> Although the elements of organizations have remained relatively constant, their purposes, structures, ways of doing things, and methods for coordinating activities have always varied widely. The variations largely (but not exclusively) reflect an organization's adaptation to its environment, because organizations are "open systems" that are influenced by and have an impact on the world around them. (Shafritz, Ott, and Jang. 2005, 2)

Public organizations—both nonprofit and government—differ from private organizations in ways that warrant their being treated separately, even though the preponderance of books about organization theory, leadership, and management concentrate on the corporation and other for-profit organizational forms. But, after all, the private organization is itself a special case rather than a generic institution. In fact, when examined closely, many distinctions between clearly private and clearly public become surprisingly ambiguous even though the core distinction remains.

Organization Theory in a Blurred Environment

Organizations increasingly display a blending or overlapping of privateness and publicness. Dwight Waldo, the late dean of American public administration scholars, observes that "the separation of public and private has been one of the defining features of the modern world." But he cautions that this is changing: "In the United States—and I believe more widely— there is a movement *away* from a sharp distinction between *public* and private, and toward a blurring and mingling of the two" (1980, 164).

At all levels of government, privatization (through contracting out work as well as by divestment of government organizations and functions) continues to blur the lines between public and private functions. Likewise, grants and mandates (often unfunded or underfunded) blur distinctions among national, subnational, and transnational activities. Moreover, holistic management systems such as total quality management and other techniques commonly associated with business (market segmentation, customer–client emphasis, operations research, benefit–cost analysis, productivity measurement) soften operational differences between the public and private spheres (National Performance Review 1993).

Blurring among sectors is likely to become more pronounced over the coming decades—a forecast that has at least three implications for today's and tomorrow's managers. First, the blurring phenomenon underscores the need for good generic organizational theory. Second, it likewise underscores the need for a practical understanding of when generic theory gives way to sector-specific insights. And third, those insights must themselves be sensitive to the complex geography of this public–private continuum. After all, few concepts exist in a pure state in the real world.

And that's a challenge. To be truly generic, theory must also be comprehensive, embracing the entire range of its subject matter. This makes the need to explore the nature and implications of publicness in organizations especially compelling (Brody 2003). Recognizing when differences matter makes organization theory more relevant and useful for managers in all organizations: the solidly private, the earnestly nonprofit, the manifestly governmental, and the growing ranks of organizations with hybrid features.

The Public–Private Continuum

Visualize a continuum line that at one end represents entirely private, profit-based organizations—from *Fortune* 500 companies down to mom-and-pop street-corner businesses. At the other end of the continuum line, picture governmental organizations—from massive bureaucracies such as the Department of Defense to the part-time, volunteer-staffed offices of a small town or village. Somewhere along the middle of that continuum line, envision nonprofit organizations—from massive humanitarian agencies such as the International Red Cross to barely formalized neighborhood cleanup groups. With these three checkpoints you've begun to populate a continuum (or spectrum) of contemporary organizations.

Figure 2–1 is an illustration of that continuum. The left side of the continuum line identifies the type of organization that falls at a particular point along the continuum. On the right side are examples of organizations—some large, some small—that fall on the continuum at that point.

FIGURE 2–1 Public–Private Continuum

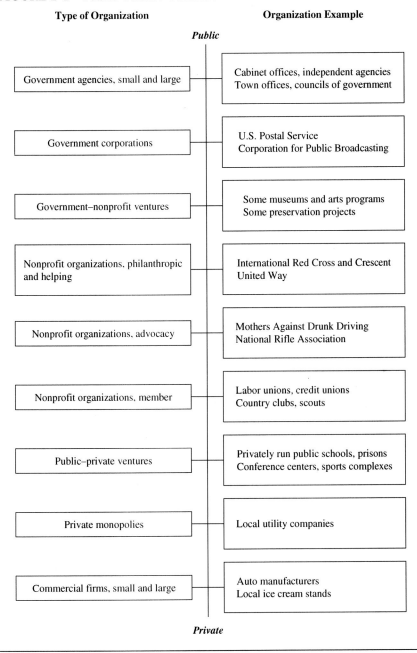

Type of Organization / Organization Example

Public

| Government agencies, small and large | Cabinet offices, independent agencies / Town offices, councils of government |

| Government corporations | U.S. Postal Service / Corporation for Public Broadcasting |

| Government–nonprofit ventures | Some museums and arts programs / Some preservation projects |

| Nonprofit organizations, philanthropic and helping | International Red Cross and Crescent / United Way |

| Nonprofit organizations, advocacy | Mothers Against Drunk Driving / National Rifle Association |

| Nonprofit organizations, member | Labor unions, credit unions / Country clubs, scouts |

| Public–private ventures | Privately run public schools, prisons / Conference centers, sports complexes |

| Private monopolies | Local utility companies |

| Commercial firms, small and large | Auto manufacturers / Local ice cream stands |

Private

Though incomplete and necessarily arbitrary, Figure 2–1 establishes a basis for discussing distinctions and similarities of organization that populate various parts of this public–private continuum.

PUBLIC ORGANIZATIONS: HOW ARE THEY DIFFERENT? HOW AREN'T THEY?

Unlike wholly private organizations, public organizations are not in the business of making money (a financial profit) for their owners and shareholders. Consequently, *purpose* distinguishes private organizations from nonprofit and government organizations. Moreover, unlike government organizations, private and nonprofit organizations are at liberty to decide *what mission* they wish to pursue. Consequently, self-determination distinguishes nongovernmental organizations from others along the continuum.

Differences between public and private organizations have been approached in a variety of ways. Typologies have been constructed on the basis of ownership and funding (Wamsley and Zald 1976), classified based on who benefits from the organization (Blau and Scott 2003), and subcategorized through other typologies (Lohman 1992; Anheier 2000). Public and private organizations have been arranged on a continuum according to the extent of outside interference they face in policy decision making (Gortner 1986). According to Anthony Downs, the distinguishing characteristic of a bureau is that it does not face an external market (1967); hence bureaus can be cost centers within for-profit organizations and nonprofit service organizations as well as government agencies. These approaches are useful and enlightening; but for the most part they cover only specialized or partial aspects and do not provide a broad overview of public–private differences.

Three public administration researchers achieved more comprehensive results when they looked at the literature about differences between public and private organizations (Rainey, Backoff, and Levine 1976). They summarize their review as a list of propositions about public organizations (with more emphasis on the government component than the nonprofit component) compared to private organizations. Table 2–1 draws upon their findings and the research of others to compare government, nonprofit, and private organizations on a number of characteristics.

As Table 2–1 illustrates, public organizations are fundamentally unlike private organizations in their legal, economic, and political nature and roles. Public organizations exist for different purposes than for-profit organizations; they are controlled or funded differently; their determinants for success are not simply profit; and they affect and must be accountable to constituencies who often have no choice about being constituents. The next section of this chapter explores these differences at their broadest and most general levels, as well as consequences that flow from them.

Legal Differences: The Constitution, the Law, and Public Management

The Constitution and the law are major forces in determining the context and content of public organization activities. This is especially true for government organizations because the law itself sets out the purposes of government organizations and often their structures.

TABLE 2–1 Comparison Matrix of Government, Nonprofit, and For-Profit Organizations

	Type of Organization		
	Public Sector		Private Sector
Comparison Characteristic	*Government*	*Nonprofit*	*For-Profit*
Societal role	Administer the law.	Help address unmet needs.	Serve as economic engine.
Fundamental purpose	Benefit all within the political jurisdiction by serving a specific function.	Benefit designated recipients, typically by providing specific services.	Benefit owners by selling goods and services.
Who determines purpose	Officials outside the organization.	Officials inside the organization or members.	Owners of the organization.
Principal funding	Legislated appropriations from taxes.	Fundraising and/or member dues.	Sale of goods and services.
Basic accountability	To the public through legislative oversight.	To donors and board of directors.	To owners, including stockholders.
Trust expectation	Extreme.	High.	Moderate.
Level of operational transparency	Moderately high to high.	Moderate to moderately high.	Moderately low for publicly held firms; very low for privately held firms.

Statutory requirements and constraints—in the form of laws, ordinances, and regulations—create a vital legal framework for managers of all types of organizations.

Empowerment (Agency/Organization/Legal Empowerment)

Government organizations differ from nonprofit and for-profit organizations in a profound way: *The mission of government organizations is to administer the law.* Their function is authoritative in the deepest and most formal sense. Their role is as active and pervasive as the reach of law and governmental purpose. They are an intimate, integral part of constitutional and legal systems of our society—a society based on the "rule of law." Discussions about whether public and private organizations differ significantly overlook this role, concentrating instead on the greater legal constraints placed on public organizations in our system. We address these constraints in later discussions. The major point here, however, is that *empowerment* is a distinguishing, even paramount, characteristic of government entities.

The characteristic of empowerment in nonprofit organizations differs completely from for-profit and government organizations. We grant special powers to nonprofit organizations, enabling them to serve people in unusual ways, to raise funds in ways not necessarily available to other types of organizations, and, in the case of tax-exempt nonprofit organizations, to forgo paying certain taxes as a means of helping sustain the work of the organization. In return,

BOX 2–2 Of Games and Gains. . .
Eileen Siedman

Each game—politics, business, governance—affects the lives of each of us as citizens in a capitalist democracy. Without attempting to weigh the relative strengths and weaknesses of the three or to equate them, it seems evident that their objectives are distinctly different—and so are their rules. It follows, then, that players who don't learn the rules, or assume there are no differences in the rules, are asking for trouble. For example, successful businesspeople who enter government service for the first time, learn (sometimes the hard way)

1. That government organizations are not just another form of business corporation.
2. That the Constitution and its diffusion of power are the underpinning of government behavior.
3. That elected officials and political appointees are temporary policy makers who have been given an opportunity to establish and promote their points of view through new or modified laws and regulations.
4. That efficient use and control of public resources includes accountability for their use in conformance with the law.
5. That there is a double standard of ethical behavior that is far more stringent for public servants than it is for anyone in business or private life.

They also learn that politics is the difference between public administration and business administration. . .

(M)anaging a government organization is infinitely more challenging and complex than managing a business because public office is a public trust and government employees are

1. Responsible for enforcing and implementing the laws as mandated.
2. Openly accountable to everyone—elected officials, appointed officials, news media, and the multiple publics (only one of which is the business sector).
3. Collecting and spending public money.
4. Using, preserving, and protecting public resources and property.
5. Responding to frequent shifts in policy as laws change and elected officials come and go.
6. Protecting the health, safety, welfare, and national security of all the people.
7. Carrying out their duties and responsibilities in conformance with their oaths of office, professional standards, official codes of conduct, and restrictions on their personal and political activities.

The governance game, then, includes transitory amateurs at the very top, supported by career executives, technicians, and other professional staff who do the work and provide the continuity, institutional memory, and stability that are public administration. Do we need reminding that the first person on the moon was a federal bureaucrat—a GS-15?

Because careerists maintain the government's stability, they are experts in accommodating to periodic changes in administration philosophy and policy. When organizations and programs work well and apparently effortlessly, their products are taken for granted—what has been called the art of hiding the art. It is only when dysfunction occurs that citizens notice or care about systems or management problems.

SOURCE: Reproduced from *The Bureaucrat*, Summer 1984, Vol. 13, No. 3, with permission from The Bureaucrat, Inc.

tax-exempt nonprofit organizations are bound by legal constraints against many forms of political advocacy—a constraint they share with government agencies and, to a lesser extent, with the individuals working for those agencies (Harvard Law Review 2001).

For-profit entities, in contrast with government and nonprofit organizations, derive much of their empowerment by being comparatively the most unfettered of the three types of organizations: As a category, they have the fewest legal constraints on what they engage in and how they operate. Certainly for-profit organizations are subject to a variety of laws and regulations (environment, safety, reasonable access for persons with disabilities, employment taxes, and many others). With few exceptions, however, such constraints apply equally to government and nonprofit organizations. This is discussed further in Chapter 4.

But the premier empowerment distinction among for-profits, nonprofits, and government organizations is the government's power to implement and administer the law. As with other constitutional democracies, ours includes both a governmental system and a source of authority. Actions undertaken within the constitutional framework carry the formally sanctioned weight of the governmental system's legitimated force. This means that in our system, as in other representative democracies, those who exercise this formidable form of empowerment do so as governmental actors for publicly sanctioned purposes. Of course, private advantages may be furthered; however, governmental action requires and carries the force of formal sanction.

Compliance with private rules and regulations is voluntary. Compliance with the public sphere is mandatory to the extent that government organizations embody the power and authority of the state. In fact, it is this power that Blau and Meyer (1987) argue we resent more than any supposed inefficiency on the part of the public organizations. Therefore, legal empowerment raises other questions, especially questions of accountability and control.

Accountability

In a representative democracy, the scope of a public institution is broad. "Its obligations extend not just to a particular group of shareholders or sponsors," George Berkley points out, "but to the public at large." A government organization, moreover, "is supposed to do what the public wants in ways the public or its elected representatives have decreed" (Berkley and Rouse 2004, 11).

The writers of the Constitution were vitally concerned about ensuring that government structures and processes focus on serving the public interest rather than the private interests of elected and appointed officials and their compatriots. The framers viewed human nature as essentially flawed: Self-interest was the primary motivator. Theirs was not the modern view of self-interest as the mark of rational calculation; rather, self-interest was synonymous with invidious selfishness. The framers attributed the tendency to selfishness and greed to public official and common citizen alike, but it was in the governmental sphere that they saw its implications as most alarming.

Their solution was to divide and diffuse authority among the various levels and institutions of government, and even to divide and diffuse power *within* an institution (as they did in the bicameral legislature). As a further safeguard, power was to be shared as well as separated (such as by presidential veto of legislation, Senate confirmation of executive appointees, and judicial review of statutes and of executive action). As Peter Woll points out,

> The Constitution, on the other hand, does not completely separate the powers of the three branches of government, but rather blends them so that each branch will be able to check the other branches by interfering with their functions. (1977, 18–19)

The authors of our Constitution sought mechanisms for accountability in the exercise of governmental authority by the president, the Congress, and the judiciary, but not for the scant bureaucracy contemplated at that time. This fact of history in no way diminishes the significance of the many consequences of a system of fragmented authority for today's public bureaucracy—a bureaucracy that is large and vigorous beyond the imagination of our Constitution writers.

To whom and by what means are government organizations and managers accountable? The fragmented system of authority created by the separation and blending of powers creates lines of authority that are both multiple and overlapping. In contrast to those for private firms and the majority of nonprofit organizations, which are primarily internal and relatively clear, lines of authority for government are external as well as internal to the organization and are exceedingly unclear.

The Constitution states, "The executive power shall be vested in a President of the United States of America" (Article II, Section 1), but it leaves the power undefined. The president may and does initiate proposals to Congress, but it is through legislative action that government organizations and programs become law and their legal empowerment is established. The legislature authorizes the size of and funding for the personnel force of federal agencies. Congress appropriates money, though often at the request of the president and subject, of course, to executive veto. Top bureaucratic leaders are appointed by the executive but confirmed by the legislature.

Both Congress and the president oversee administrative actions. The judicial branch, in accordance with its own powers and procedures, also practices oversight. Courts may judge whether a statute or executive order under which an agency acts is legally valid. Chief executives, legislatures, or courts may all ask whether an agency is acting within the limits or intent of a statute or rule, or whether its administrative procedures are fair. All of these institutions and actors charged with external control of government organizations have some power, but no single institution or actor has sufficient authority for control; thus these actors often disagree and end up in conflict with one another.

Government organizations are drawn into the processes by which chief executives attempt to influence legislators and by which both branches of government seek to create public evidence of their responsiveness or the rightness of their position. Even the president cannot dictate major policy; the president's power has been aptly described as the "power to persuade" (Neustadt 1960). Lacking blanket formal power, the president must achieve cooperation and action by collaborating with others whose interests coincide with the chief executive. If collaboration fails, agreement is achieved in more overtly political ways—through persuasion, negotiation, bargaining, compromise, confrontation, and even threat. Similarly, Congress must obtain political support to supplement its formal power. In this dance of power bureaucracies may be tools useful to everyone else.

These or similar patterns of fragmented authority, simultaneously external and internal, divided and overlapping, are found in state and local government as well. In fact, governmental authority at the state and local levels may be even more fragmented than at the national level. The chief executive's power over governmental organizations is diminished by the practice in some states and localities of electing rather than appointing heads of government organizations. The prevalence of independent boards and commissions whose members have long and overlapping terms also dissipates the power of chief executives (governors, mayors, city managers) and legislators alike. And the problem of holding government organizations accountable is further compounded where they have a degree of fiscal autonomy through such means as charging fees for services or being recipients of earmarked funds. In countless ways, then, the accountability of government organizations is complicated by often intentional fragmentation of authority and responsibility. (Also see Chapter 6.)

Accountability works differently for public organizations in the nonprofit arena, though with occasional parallels. A notable difference is that the need for and degree of accountability in the nonprofit arena, although great, is less than for government organizations. Two factors diminish this need. First, unlike government organizations, nonprofit organizations do not enforce the law; second, their spheres of influence are limited when compared to those of government organizations. Nonprofit organizations are accountable to their donors (as government organizations are to taxpayers), to those their organizations serve (because many government agencies serve defined target groups), and to a board of directors (akin, in government, to legislative oversight). Tax-exempt nonprofit organizations have an additional level of accountability: To qualify for exemption from paying federal income tax, a nonprofit organization must demonstrate its standing as a charitable institution—that is, one whose purpose is to provide benefit to others (CFR 26 § 501(c)(3)) rather than pursue financial profit or political gain. Tax exemptions can be complicated. Nonprofits such as the Sierra Club and the League of Women Voters organize as 501(c)(4) entities and must confer benefits on the community as a whole and not a particular group. Contributions to 501(c)(4) organizations are not tax-deductible to the donor, but contributions to 501(c)(3) organizations are. Both 501(c)(3) and (4) organizations are tax-exempt.

To look briefly at the groups public organizations serve, Brookings Institution scholar Albert Hyde (1991–92) notes that government organizations have three types of constituents: *customers*, with whom dealings are casual, occasional, and elective on the part of the customer; *clients*, who have stronger, longer-term, usually contractual relationships; and *captives*, who have no choice but to deal with the public organization, such as a law enforcement or regulatory agency. This can be true for nonprofits as well, depending on their missions. Though accountable to each of these groups, organizations are most strongly accountable to captive constituents precisely because those constituents do not have the option of choosing whether they interact with that organization (consider the Internal Revenue Service, a local code enforcement office, or a monopoly-based utility service). By extension, nonprofits are more likely to have captive constituents where they contract to provide a government service. Organizational accountability is discussed further in Chapter 6.

For-profit, private sector organizations similarly are accountable to their customers, owners, and shareholders, as well as (for many for-profit organizations) boards of directors. For-profit and public organizations all must comply with the law, such as collecting and remitting payroll taxes for their employees and meeting safety standards for employees and their constituents. And that brings us to a nested aspect of "rule of law."

Administration Subordinate to Law

Accountability and control of government authority apply to all branches and officials in a democratic system. However, the bureaucracy, being mostly unelected, raises particular problems. How is the power of government organizations restrained and controlled? The answer relates in part to the philosophy toward the role of law in determining administrative discretion.

Managers of private, for-profit organizations and of nonprofit organizations can generally take any action, establish any policy, or use any means of operation not specifically prohibited (a common law approach). Government managers are bound by these prohibitions as well. However, in contrast to for-profit and nonprofit managers, managers of government organizations are not at liberty to operate in the absence of specific grants of authority (a Roman law approach). Nongovernmental organizations can act *unless* proscribed or forbidden; government organizations may act *only* if authority is granted.

The most general and important way in which law controls administration is that goals for public organizations are both established and circumscribed by the law. But the role of law also extends to other crucial aspects of public management, such as the prescription of means and the provision and control of resources.

Lack of managerial control over budget and personnel resources often complicates, even thwarts, policy implementation. For example, passage of the national Freedom of Information Act (FOIA) resulted in a sudden, high-volume increase of citizen requests to federal agencies for information disclosure. But Congress appropriated no additional agency funding or staffing increases to carry out the policy (in other words, this was an *unfunded mandate* within the federal structure), and existing procedures made personnel reassignments slow and difficult. In particular, the Federal Bureau of Investigation (FBI), which had engaged in widespread domestic surveillance during the turbulent 1960s and early 1970s, was deluged with requests. Thus backlogs built quickly and long delays were commonplace. The public naturally directed its ire at the FBI and its administrators. Allegations of obstructive agency attitudes notwithstanding, it is difficult to see how the bureau's managers, saddled as they were with budget and personnel constraints, could have implemented the new law efficiently and effectively.

State and local administrators face similar obstacles in implementation. In addition to the other limitations on taxes, budgets, and personnel created by state constitutions, state and local governments are told what they must do by higher levels of government. Unfunded mandates—programs created by law but with no concomitant financial support—often limit alternatives for state and local officials. For example, states accepting federal education funding must comply with federally established education policies that require public school access for students with emotional and physical disabilities and that set specific standards and testing requirements for all students. But most school administrators find they must contend with an inadequate increase in budget, teachers, or the special support personnel such policies require for effective implementation.

Entitlement programs such as unemployment compensation and Temporary Assistance for Needy Families (TANF) are in greater or less demand based on broad social and economic forces. However, the personnel levels of state and local agencies administering these programs do not naturally adjust to correspond to these fluctuations in demand. Thus caseworkers, who are typically overloaded under normal economic conditions, are swamped when the economy worsens. This affects related nonprofits in the same manner because state and local government agencies often contract with nonprofit organizations for these services.

The legal framework of public organizations, then, dictates that the public manager must accomplish the objectives set by others with resources that are often determined by still others; and the manager must do so within a general organizational framework established by law and interpreted by political appointees. The objectives set by external forces may be unclear or unrealistic, and resources and structures may be inadequate or inappropriate (Smith and Lipsky 2001). The result may be goals that cannot be met and inefficient, inflexible, or ineffective action. Consequently, managers must often attempt to accomplish changes through the political process.

In contrast, private executives have the flexibility to adopt various courses of action with little external kibitzing. Procedures may be changed and the organization redesigned; projects may be reduced, canceled, expedited, or enlarged. New markets may be entered. Resources may be shifted from one purpose to another, workers laid off or additional workers hired directly or through contracts with other organizations, which are thereby bound by essentially the same constraints as the governmental organization (which is to say that contracts can impose substantial control from outside the organization). So although legal requirements and prohibitions are sometimes placed on almost all organizations (such as nondiscrimination and sexual harassment policies), the role of law for most private organizations is contextual and relatively peripheral.

Economic Differences: Nature of the Public Organization's Role and the Market

What is the nature of the economic role of the public sector—both nonprofit and government institutions? The usual answer is articulated in terms of prescriptive, free market theory. This is an illuminating perspective as far as it goes, but it overlooks the place political values and processes occupy in our system in determining the nature of governmental roles—including those that are ostensibly economic.

Free Market Theory and the Role of Public Organizations

According to market theory, private sector organizations seek economic enhancement. Their objective is to increase financial profitability through voluntary exchange and transactions, with government playing only a supplementary or at most a complementary role. Government action is considered appropriate only when private resource allocation fails or operates very inefficiently.

Markets may fail as allocation mechanisms in a variety of ways. For example, some goods are public in that the benefits are held in common. Exclusion is not feasible. If the cost is high, the free or private market is especially unlikely to provide such goods. For instance, streetlights increase safety for an entire area regardless of who pays and who does not; however, their cost is prohibitive for a single individual or organization. In such instances, action carried out by government organizations is conceded to be an acceptable, or even indispensable, mechanism for providing public goods and is considered more efficient in ensuring that costs as well as benefits are shared—through compulsion and coercion if necessary.

Sometimes actions or exchanges between individuals or organizations result in costs to people not involved in a given transaction. Noise abatement, antipollution, and building height restriction laws are examples of governmental intervention in such circumstances.

Relevant markets may not emerge or exist under the usual workings of the private market system. As Stokey and Zeckhauser point out,

> In some areas the meagerness of private markets has been especially significant for public policy. One of these is insurance against income loss; government unemployment insurance and welfare programs may be thought of as efforts to remedy this market deficiency. Another is insurance against living too long after becoming disabled or retiring and thereby using up one's savings; the Social Security system serves as a response to such needs. (1978, 300–301)

Even in free market theory, government and nonprofit organizations are not linked to markets in the same way as private sector organizations. By giving public organizations responsibility for tasks for which the market is inappropriate or for unprofitable services such as care of the poor, market theory implicitly recognizes differences in the economic roles of private and public sector organizations. It does not go far enough, however, because the functions of the public sector are far broader than performing the passive or supplemental economic role left to it by market theory. More significantly, market theory fails to recognize that the economic role of public organizations essentially is not economic in nature.

Rather than accepting classical market theory's artificial watertight categories of inviolate private and public spheres, we must recognize that "[p]ublic and private are not categories of nature; they are categories of history, culture, and law" (Waldo 1980, 164; see also Hall 1987). In other words, as Figure 2–1 illustrates, the line between public and private offers many shades of private and public, and even those shadings shift and change in response to historical and political forces. The goals of public organizations are products of the legal and political process and embody values legitimated through these systems. Because the role of government is determined through cultural and political forces as well as economic considerations, organizations falling within the public sphere are charged with promoting and protecting both cultural and economic values.

Without question, the free market and economic competition are values with widespread acceptance in our culture; therefore, policies that reflect the values and ideas of the free enterprise system receive a great deal of government attention. In fact, our government's economic activities conform, to a large extent, to the role market theory prescribes. Nevertheless, the important consideration here, especially where government organizations are concerned, is that economic policies are adopted not so much because of their desirability as economic theory, but due to political acceptability, demand, and expediency. Indeed, economic policy is adopted primarily as a means to achieve politically sanctioned ends. The long-standing Cuban trade restrictions, the freezing of rogue nations' assets, and a requirement that when states receive grant money the distribution formula must include "tax effort" are examples of the use of economic policy as means to political ends.

Public organizations certainly have functions that do not directly involve the economic system and that entail basically noneconomic objectives. Enforcing affirmative action laws, protecting endangered species, and administering elections are examples of such functions. Some may argue that even these policies have economic implications, which is true. But the key point is that the objectives of public sector organizations are varied; social and political, not economic, considerations are paramount.

Both market theory and organization theory have focused on the private sector organization to such an extent that the implications of political rather than economic values and goals for organizational behavior have been overlooked or dismissed. More puzzling is the fact that although market theory recognizes different markets and functions for government organizations and, to some extent, nonprofit organizations, it does not examine the significance of these differences.

Economic versus Political Markets

Public and private sector organizations exhibit marked differences in the nature of their markets and in their relationships to these markets. In an economic output market, each producer engages in voluntary transactions with buyers who exchange money for the producer's output.

Anthony Downs points out the effects of output markets and discusses how the lack of such markets affects nonmarket-oriented organizations.

First, output markets provide a built-in tool for evaluating the work (output) of the organization. If the producer "can sell his outputs for more than his inputs cost . . . then he knows his product is valuable to its buyers" (Downs 1967, 29). If the market price does not cover the costs of producing the product, then the organization knows the output is not valuable enough.

Second, output markets are a means of allocating resources among organizations. A third function of the market is that of producing a standard for evaluating the individual performance of members of the organization; for example, when one salesperson sells more than another, she or he is more valuable to the firm. And as Downs explains, even individuals performing different functions can be objectively compared through cost accounting and related techniques.

Because most government and nonprofit organizations have no economic output markets, they cannot evaluate the costs of producing their output or its value on this external basis. Their income does not directly relate to their services. As a result, an organization's ability to obtain income in a market cannot serve as an objective guide to the appropriateness of its level of current expenditures. Nor can it aid in determining how to use the resources it controls, or in appraising the performance of individual bureaucrats. In short, the major yardsticks for-profit organizations use for decision making are unavailable or less salient to those who run bureaucratic organizations (Downs 1967). The attempt to put profit-based criteria into a service context can, in fact, lead to disastrous results, as Jerry Knight reports in classic terms (Box 2–3). Anheier (2000) refers to this as the "copycat principle," borrowing management practices from another sector (usually from business) whether or not they fit (Mintzberg 1996). As Charles Goodsell summarizes, after examining studies of government and business productivity for similar functions,

> Many direct measures of performance cast quite a favorable light on bureaucracy. . . . With respect to its overall productivity over a quarter of a century, the federal government has posted impressive and steady gains, averaging 1.1 percent growth per year, not greatly different from that of the private sector. Productivity increases—particularly in finance, accounting, and social services—have no doubt saved taxpayers many dollars. (2004, 38)

Public sector productivity can, of course, be ascertained. It cannot be evaluated in exactly the way private sector organizations are, with their markets and objectively measurable standard of financial profitability. Public organizations do not lend themselves to such a single universal standard. We must measure both efficiency and effectiveness—along with process, output, and outcome measures—examining the functions and the goals of the particular organization, and leading to many separate, specialized measures of productivity. For example, a job-training program may record intake figures, attrition, number of applicants trained, number of trainees placed in jobs, training-to-placement ratios, and cost of training per placement to measure its productivity. The Federal Aviation Administration (FAA) uses measures such as number of successful landings, number of airplane inspections, number of "near misses," and passenger miles-to-accident ratios.

However, financial measures are certainly relevant for all public organizations as one set of performance measures. For some public organizations, they are dominant measures. Nonprofit fundraising organizations such as the United Way, for example, pay close attention to the total funds raised in a given fiscal year, how these totals compare to target amounts and years past, contribution patterns of donor segments, and responses to the organization's

BOX 2–3 Run It Like a Business, No Matter How Much More It Costs

One of the most pernicious myths of Washington business is that the government—and virtually everything else—would be vastly improved if the people in charge would just "run it like a business."

Candidates have captured every office from dogcatcher to president of the United States by promising that the moral equivalent of the profit motive would become the guiding principal of their administration.

Worse yet, they've kept their promises, giving us such a stunning success as the U.S. Postal Service. Freed from the perils of politics and patronage and now "run like a business," the mail service costs more and delivers less.

Despite such self-evident shortcomings, the urge to "run it like a business" continues to flourish, infecting Washington with ill-thought initiatives like the plan to sell the Weather Bureau.

Neither rain, nor sleet, nor gloom of night would seem to be ingredients of a profitable enterprise. But no doubt a weather bureau run like a business could market the exigencies of nature with as much success as the postal service defies them. Like the mail, the weather forecast might not arrive when expected, but that would be a small price to pay for the ideological satisfaction of knowing the weather bureau is run like a business.

The run-it-like-a-business bug is even spreading into the private sector, where it is demonstrating the ability to transform perfectly adequate nonprofit institutions into bungled "businesses."

Ironically, the U.S. Chamber of Commerce was the first private, nonprofit organization to get burned by its businesslike approach; but now other Washington institutions have fallen victim, including National Public Radio.

. . . The U.S. Chamber has run up multimillion-dollar deficits. . . . Instead of using its magazine, *Nation's Business,* as a service to communicate with its members, the Chamber decided to run *Nation's Business* like a business. While the magazine vigorously expresses the Chamber's views, it has apparently been less successful as a business. In recent months the

campaign strategies. Government organizations—from state universities to city zoos to parks charging entrance fees—often depend on special revenue streams, even when a portion of their funding comes through legislated appropriations. Government organizations whose missions involve revenue collection—such as for taxes and government loan programs—use financial data to monitor program performance. Local tax assessment offices, state tax agencies, and the Internal Revenue Service, for example, measure crucial aspects of their performance in terms of revenue collections, yield-to-cost ratios of their compliance enforcement programs, and a productivity measure often calculated as "cost to collect $100"—a ratio somewhat comparable to return on investment (ROI) analysis in for-profit organizations. The IRS, which operates on an annual appropriation of around $10 billion, calculates that it spends under 50 cents for each $100 it brings into the U.S. Treasury. In business terms this would be an ROI of 200 percent, which is $200 of tax revenue for every dollar invested in internal revenue operations.

Chamber has had to explain why the magazine's circulation fell several hundred thousand subscribers short of what advertisers were charged for.

There is, perhaps, a certain justice in the Chamber of Commerce being seduced by its own rhetoric. It would be hard to find an organization that has preached the virtues of "running it like a business" more often than the U.S. Chamber.

But National Public Radio is no captive of corporate ideology. The likes of the Chamber of Commerce have been known to suggest that NPR is virtually socialized radio, the commercial-free antithesis of free enterprise.

So what did NPR do when government subsidies and corporate contributions ran short? You guessed it—they decided to go into business, forming profit-making partnerships that were supposed to finance nonprofit broadcasting. But now, just like the Chamber of Commerce, NPR is laying off people and canceling projects because its business ventures are proving to be something less than hoped for.

That's the first lesson that ought to be taught to people who believe government and non-profit associations should be run like a business: Businesses can and do fail with predictable regularity.

Even well-run businesses fail; but more often, failure is the result of management mistakes.

More than just management style is involved. The reality is that weather forecasting, mail delivery, business advocacy, and public broadcasting are not businesses. Their first and foremost goal is to deliver services, not to make a buck.

One of the marvels of the free market economy is that when services can be provided at a profit, somebody does it. The Mafia in several cities collects garbage cheaper and better than government employees; the National Geographic Society uses profitable publications to finance its educational activities; Federal Express and United Parcel Service make money competing with the mail.

But UPS doesn't want to deliver all the mail—just the profitable part—and there are services that even the Mafia couldn't make money on. The inescapable conclusion is that the goals of service and profit are often incompatible.

SOURCE: From "Run It Like Business, No Matter How Much More It Costs" by Jerry Knight from *The Washington Post*, March 21, 1983. Copyright © 1983 The Washington Post. Reprinted with permission.

Because different measures must be used to evaluate public organizations with different functions, the most reasonable approach to comparing organizations is to use those with similar functions and goals. Thus organizations of a given type should usually be compared with others of the same type, as Paul Taylor did in his commentary on the 100th anniversary of the civil service (Box 2–4).

In the political arena, of course, criticisms of government organizations do not go away. "The bureaucracy" is unresisting as a general target for many reasons, some of which are genuine and some of which are convenient for demagogy. This failure to please critics is partly an "outrider" problem—that is, some unit of an organization is likely not to meet the standards of the overall organization, its oversight bodies, or consumers of its products or services. (An example at the beginning of this century is faulty intelligence integration and analysis in the years around the terrorist attack on the Pentagon and World Trade Center and leading into the invasion of Iraq.) For news media and the news-consuming public, such stories

BOX 2–4 Civil Service Turns 100, Burdened by Stereotypes

Since Federal Express has raised the question of postal efficiency, let us ponder it. It makes an especially good topic. Productivity measures are a lot cleaner at the Postal Service than they are at, say, the State Department.

The fact is the U.S. Postal Service delivers more mail, more efficiently, for less money than any other nation on earth, and it is getting better.

It moves 110 billion pieces of mail per year, or some 161,879 pieces per employee, a productivity per worker rate that is 44 percent above that of the closest competitor, Japan.

The cost of mailing a first-class letter in the United States is 12th lowest of the 14 industrialized nations surveyed last summer, with only Belgium, at an equivalent of 19.9 cents, below the Postal Service's 20 cents. Germany charges the equivalent of 33 cents.

Rates here have been rising at a slower pace than inflation since 1974, and in 1979 for the first time in four decades, the Postal Service operated in the black. It did again last year, and it is now operating on a fee basis. There are no subsidies any more from Uncle Sam.

Speed of delivery is on the rise, too. In 1982 the Postal Service met its next-day-delivery standard for first-class mail traveling within a metropolitan area 95.5 percent of the time. In the two-day category, performance was 88 percent, and in the three-day delivery, 90 percent.

Productivity measurements are difficult to apply to most of the federal government, which produces policy, information, and services, not widgets. But coarse standards have been devised for roughly two-thirds of the federal work force. And they show that since 1967, the average annual increase in productivity has been 1.4 percent among federal workers. This is a growth percentage that would make most sectors of the private economy envious, though comparisons are difficult because the standards of measurement vary.

SOURCE: From "Civil Service Turns 100, Burdened by Stereotypes" by Paul Taylor from *The Washington Post*, January 16, 1983. Copyright © 1983 The Washington Post. Reprinted with permission.

are understandably more newsworthy than routinely successful nonprofit and government program operations. Failure to please is also a consequence of naturally rising expectations, which are the tendency of customers to expect more after a specific level of service is achieved and maintained. Thus the displeasure with the U.S. Postal Service (a public corporation, not a government bureau) continues unabated decades after Paul Taylor's article, with calls from time to time for postal privatization. Such debates are an integral and healthy—though occasionally uncomfortable—part of being in the public's purview.

Because public organizations do not have exclusively economic outputs, their markets and consumers are targeted individuals and groups (property owners, families eligible for public housing, children who join groups such as the Y and the Scouts), organized interest groups, and political elites. These are in addition to the overall population because citizen–constituents, both today's and tomorrow's, are a standard by which government must consider what is "in the public interest." Organizations engage in exchange relationships with these essential actors to achieve legitimacy and domain (Thompson 1967), as well as political support for resource allocations. Political exchange dominates market and environmental transactions, and the evaluation or response to an organization's outputs is political.

Further, public sector and private sector outputs do not lend themselves to the same classifications. A useful way of classifying public organizations' policies or outputs places public organizations in three categories: distributive, regulatory, and redistributive (Lowi 1964). Each output category comes with its characteristic pattern "of consensus–conflict, group alignment, and breadth and intensity of group involvement" (Wamsley and Zald 1976, 35; Lowi 1964; Sharkansky 1965). Distributive arenas usually enjoy consensus in an environment supportive of the organization's output. Not surprisingly, conflict marks regulatory policy arenas—either between government organizations and the groups they regulate or among interest groups watching the regulatory process. This, at least, is a common pattern during the early life of a regulatory organization. Older regulatory agencies are prone to developing accepted parameters of behavior and decisions with the regulated industries, and those relationships can lead to charges of co-optation. Conflict in redistributive arenas often touches on divisions among social classes and consequently tends to be broader than in the other policy arenas.

Nonprofit organizations are more conveniently classified by whom they serve than by the nature of their outputs: Some nonprofits primarily serve their memberships while other nonprofits serve other clientele. Member-oriented nonprofit organizations include labor unions, trade associations, professional societies, religious institutions, social clubs, and homeowners' associations, among others. Member-focus organizations tend to be funded by the members themselves, though other revenue streams are also common. Client-oriented nonprofit organizations usually receive little or no economic support from those they serve because these nonprofits often focus on providing services to individuals and groups in need, including assisting with government-sponsored distributive outputs. Nonmember-oriented nonprofits include philanthropic and social services organizations (such as foundations and emergency aid organizations). Some member and nonmember organizations focus on individuals and families (unions, churches), whereas others serve governments and other organizations (governors' associations, trade associations). Moreover, some nonprofit organizations have built-in or allied organizational components that are explicitly for-profit and typically provide an additional revenue stream for the overall organization. Economist Burton Weisbrod finds "no support for the view that nonprofits act essentially like private firms." At the same time he sees enough differences among types of nonprofit organizations "to be cautious about generalizing about nonprofits as a whole. Institutional form does seem to matter, but some nonprofits are more 'nonprofit' than others" (1988, 159).

Whatever the classification, a public organization's internal characteristics can vary according to type of policy output. Lowi, for example, finds that the rules and procedures of public organizations in redistributive arenas tend to be specific and detailed (1964). This is an organization's way of adapting to external political conflict, close observation by interested parties, and the widespread effects of government action.

To summarize, unlike the primarily economic nature of the private sector organization, the public sector organization's purposes and roles are more complex and are fundamentally political. And political factors, both within and external to public organizations, have an important influence on organizational structure and process in the same way that economic factors influence corporate organization and operation.

Political Differences: Internal and Environmental Politics of Public Organizations

Probably the two best known and most frequently cited definitions of politics are Lasswell's statement, in 1958, that politics is the study of "who gets what, when, how"' (1990) and Easton's phrase that politics is the process of society's "authoritative allocation of values" (1979). Public organizations, especially in their role of influencing and interpreting legislative choice, are integral to the authoritative process of determining who gets what, when, and how.

The processes by which policies come about and the interests they promote or maintain (whether broad public interest or those of organized groups, elected or appointed officials, or even public organizations and their members) are political in nature. The political process is, of course, not limited to the confines of government institutions and nonprofit advocacy organizations. It is the process by which various individuals, groups, and institutions seek to influence public policy and government action or inaction. The boundaries of the political system are elastic and changeable; they encompass all interactions and activities that affect or seek to affect government action or inaction.

Among public organizations, nonprofits have major roles in the political process in that nonprofits serve as both *shapers* and *implementers* of policy. Consider the range of nonprofit advocacy organizations—from the political parties themselves (Democratic National Committee, Republican National Committee) to local environmental groups or from liberal and conservative policy think tanks (Brookings Institution, American Enterprise Institute) to policy groups that eschew political labels (League of Women Voters). Each of these nonprofit organizations has, as a major mission objective, influencing political, social, and economic policy in the United States. Nonprofit organizations such as labor unions (American Federation of Labor and Congress of Industrial Organizations or AFL-CIO) and professional societies (American Medical Association or AMA), whose principal missions are not policy shaping, devote time and resources to policy advocacy of potential benefit to their memberships. Even nonprofit entities whose mission in no part includes policy advocacy find themselves in that role from time to time—for example, homeowners' associations from adjacent neighborhoods banding together to influence the proposed location of a new road, school, shopping area, or landfill.

Also consider the vast range of nonprofit organizations we rely on to implement policies and make them work. On an international level, transnational nongovernmental organizations (NGOs) are often first on the scene when responding to disaster situations. The International Red Cross and Crescent and Doctors without Borders are two such organizations. Governments from around the globe help supply, fund, and coordinate operations with them in responding to floods, famines, and even the aftermath of war. Domestically we use nonprofit (and for-profit) social service agencies and hospitals to carry out health care policy goals. We also entrust much environmental and historic preservation work to local historical societies and land trust groups.

In what ways do the political contexts and purposes of public sector organizations differ from private sector organizations, especially with nonprofit organizations themselves serving in multiple roles (Gronbjerg and Salamon 2001)? At first glance the answer seems blurred and ambiguous. Certainly for-profit organizations participate actively in the political process, and governmental policies sometimes address even the internal activities of both private and public organizations. For example, private personnel practices, insofar as their effect or intent is discriminatory, are the object of equal employment opportunity requirements.

For-profit and nonprofit organizations are also involved in the governmental–political system in a variety of other ways, such as environmental regulation, health and safety, and licensing requirements. Through activities such as participation in government job training and employment programs, performance of government contract work, or the use of businesses as collectors of state or local sales taxes, for-profit and nonprofit organizations become instruments of public policy. But even when directly involved in government work, such organizations may choose to contract with the government or to function in other areas of economic activity; they choose with whom they do business.

Government organizations are themselves pervasively enmeshed in the political process. *Every* public organization is an object of the political process; *any* aspect of its goals, structure, and operation may be subject to that process. Government organizations exist to implement and enforce public policy, inextricably engaging them as participants in the policy and political process. The differences between the political context and nature of public compared to private organizations dictate that, at times, different skills are needed in managing and leading public organizations and differently weighted values (from a shared menu of societal values) may drive internal decision making and consequent action. Further contributing to the distinctive nature of public organizations are the servant nature of their relationships with clientele and interest groups, their more inclusive—and often ungainly—approaches to goal setting, their higher goal ambiguity and diversity, and the role of the organizations' managers in each of these areas.

External Groups and Public Organizations

The nature of American public sector organizations is political in great measure because of their prewired accessibility to (and through) external influences—elected officials, political interest groups, and the like. Private sector organizations are typically more closed. Their access points (boards of directors, marketing and customer service departments, stockholders' meetings) are fewer and more controlled. This is especially true for privately held businesses, particularly firms whose shares of ownership are not publicly traded through stock market transactions.

Life in the "sunshine" world of public management means that legislators, chief executives, clientele, journalists, and hosts of others may legitimately scrutinize the actions of public managers and other public employees. (The term *sunshine* here refers to the practice throughout most non–law enforcement government entities of operating through public meetings, public budgets, and public records.) Based on his executive experience in both the public and private spheres, Fredric Malek writes,

> The corporate executive is accustomed to the usually informed and generally sympathetic scrutiny of his colleagues, his stockholders, and occasionally the public through annual reports and news releases. The government executive, however, lives in a fishbowl; depending on the level and nature of his job, he must expect to be exposed at any moment to the glare of publicity and notoriety. (1972, 64)

Nonprofit executives inhabit a world between the two, though more akin to their government counterparts. Nor is public scrutiny restricted only to what public organizations do or how they do it. The spotlight of publicity lays bare ideas for future activity, however tentative and unformulated. Premature disclosure of programs or ideas is a public manager's occupational hazard. A given agency often has a contingent of journalists who specifically follow it and who, because of their familiarity with the organization and their internal personal contacts, are often able to reveal matters that are merely under consideration. Such publicity can have a strong, troublesome effect; painstakingly laid plans may be disrupted. Equally distressing (though occasionally handy) is the airing of proposals or suggestions at an exploratory stage in which future commitments, if any, are still vague and distant.

> The glare of publicity and the concomitant power of public opinion make it important to gain public support and acceptance of a department's or agency's goals and essential to gain public understanding before proceeding with any major initiative or change of policy. This notion is unfamiliar to the average business executive. (Malek 1972, 64)

In varying degrees, nonprofit and government organizations seek or receive broad public support; but such support comes with the problem of having both the intensity and direction of public opinion shift with events that may have little to do with the life and goals of the organization. Compared to general public opinion, attentive clientele and related special interest groups provide more stable support. Unlike the general public, their interests are tangible and direct, and typically both clientele and regulated groups have vested interests in a public organization's actions (Rourke 1984; Wamsley and Zald 1976). Of course, as public managers work with positive interest groups, which is essential, our political system encourages opposites—and groups fighting an organization, policy, or program can be as troublesome as positive groups are helpful (Schattschneider 1975; Fisher, Kopelman, and Schneider 1994). This phenomenon is common on the government side of the public sector, but nonprofit organizations delivering controversial types of service (drug treatment programs, women's health clinics) find themselves in this situation too.

Ties between government organizations and interest groups are reinforced in many ways. Public service action or inaction affects the material interests and welfare of clientele and other related groups. The public organization provides a channel for political representation within the governmental structure. For their part, groups support requests to legislators and chief executives for empowerment and for resources; they oppose legislative and executive action that threatens the organization's status, authority, and resources. Moreover, considerable movement among employees of government organizations and their for-profit and nonprofit constituencies occurs in both directions.

The phenomenon is sometimes derisively referred to as the "revolving door," but it has both healthy and unhealthy aspects. Personnel movement between organizations occurs in part because frequent, long-term interaction breeds personal ties; in part because interests and expertise are frequently similar even when policy positions are not; and in part because, for many managers and other professionals, the cachet of serving in multiple sectors adds value to a person's résumé. Hence similar professional training and experience further foster mutual identification between public administrators and related interest groups.

This bond is not limited to public organizations and private interest groups; it also exists between government organizations and between nonprofit organizations. In intergovernmental programs, organizations at lower levels (state or local) have a clientele relationship to organizations at higher levels (national or state). Here, too, shared professional specialization and values lead to a joining of forces and political strength between subject matter specialists at one level of government and their counterparts at other levels.

Laws may grant interest groups access to the policy process and even membership in public organizations. Statutes mandating membership in or certification by professional groups as conditions for appointment as administrators are common at the state level for boards, commissions, and other entities.

Citizen participation and interest group involvement are fostered through legal orders requiring government entities to hold hearings, consult with, or secure the consent of these groups before they can enforce their regulatory power or adopt or change procedures. This situation in itself leaves public managers with considerable ambiguity about their own power in the decision processes, as well as uncertainty about what criteria are appropriate for the policy decisions they must make.

The general imperative to avoid "political" decisions is juxtaposed with the inconsistent expectation that government organizations and some types of nonprofit organizations be politically responsive to "the public," which in practice usually means a special and attentive public or set of organized interests. In the face of conflicting expectations of neutrality and responsiveness to adversarial groups, government organizations must, as part of their decision process, include achieving consensus or forming coalitions among diverse forces. As a result, the processes of organizational decision making in government are certain to be slower and more disjointed than the more direct decision process favored in private sector organizations. Thus public managers typically need greater skills in conflict resolution and consensus building.

Goal Making and Politics

Although for-profit organizations depend on the environment for resources, consumption of their product or service, personnel, and so on, their means for obtaining these are primarily economic, not political, and decisions about their actions or exchanges are made internally, not externally. On the other hand, goals, available resources, and even basic procedures are determined for government organizations through legislation, executive orders, court decisions, and input from clients and interest groups. Goal setting for nonprofit organizations generally falls between these two poles. For member-based nonprofits, the members themselves play a significant role in determining the organization's goals; for other nonprofits, the board of directors and management typically work together to map out basic goals and the strategies for accomplishing those goals.

Because decision making in government organizations is often limited to interpretation of goals set externally and politically, politics is inescapable in public management. Externally governed decision making deeply affects other crucial organizational factors—such as power relations among individuals in the organization, the role of the manager, the development of operating routines, and relationships with external groups.

Public goals that direct the organization's efforts are typically a product of coalitional support and thus reflect a mixture of means and ends, often based on an uneasy compromise among conflicting claims for public benefits or recognition (Lindblom 1959). Although, within the public sector, this applies most strongly to government organizations, nonprofit organizations also deal with coalition support and so must be sensitive to accommodating the underlying interests of their supporter groups. Throughout the goal-setting process, public managers simultaneously pursue both means and ends through the political arts of persuasion, bargaining, and compromise—valuable management tools that help defuse paralyzing stalemates among the struggling forces (Braybrooke and Lindblom 1970; Gawthrop 1971).

The various means–ends conflicts that arise and the shifting coalitions of interest groups and politicians associated with them are kaleidoscopic. Public organizations and their managers enter these conflicts either because of the needs and demands of other participants or because of organizational or personal values. The organization's expertise and clientele support provide public managers with opportunities to initiate or shape (to a degree) policies set outside the organization. In a patently political vein, public managers sometimes leak information or indirectly mobilize interest group support; however, doing so is properly rare and raises ethical questions about responsibility and public trust. (See Chapter 7 for a discussion of principled reasoning.) Public organizations far more commonly play crucial roles in shaping policy through reports, studies, recommendations, and other forms of information collection, analysis, and dissemination.

In fact, public organizations' input to the policy process is irreplaceable when considering how to craft policy that is practical and administrable. The simultaneous and political nature of ends–means determination raises numerous problems for the public manager. For example, one result may be a poor match between ends (goals) and means (procedures to achieve goals), in which case the organization's effectiveness is seriously hampered when it must work with—or around—inadequate and inappropriate means.

Just as goals for government organizations are set externally, so too is judgment about public sector actions. Again, this is true (but less intensely so) for nonprofit organizations. Although public managers play a limited though important role in evaluating the effectiveness and efficiency of the organizations they manage, public organizations are still extremely dependent on and vulnerable to the external environment. A police administrator, for example, might adopt a policy of blanketing high-crime areas with foot patrols. Crime may drop, but the overpowering presence of many uniformed police may be viewed as creating an oppressive and even racist climate, especially if mostly white police officers are used in a minority neighborhood. Community protests may ensue. The bottom line is that the public manager must answer in some fashion to the external standards of political acceptability.

The Problem of Goal Ambiguity

Goal ambiguity is more of a challenge for government organizations than for nonprofits because government organizations have little control over their fundamental goals. Statutes creating government organizations or establishing programs usually set forth their goals in general and ambiguous terms. For example, the federal government's first independent regulatory agency, the former Interstate Commerce Commission (1887–1995), was charged with regulating railroads in a "just" and "reasonable" fashion, as well as "in the public interest." For more than a century the ICC did its imperfect best to meet that set of goals. Agencies at all levels of government receive equally undefined charges. In general, broadness and ambiguity in goals and purposes give public managers responsibilities and opportunities for exercising power. As Rourke notes,

> Control over the implementation of policy becomes especially important as a source of bureaucratic power when it includes the authority to exercise discretion in achieving policy goals. As used here, the term "discretion" refers to the ability of an administrator to choose among alternatives—to decide in effect how the policies of the government should be implemented in specific cases. (1984, 32)

Administrative discretion is extensive in the everyday, routine decisions of public organizations. For example, the community health officer enforcing both state and local sanitary standards decides whether to give an informal reprimand, issue a warning notice, make a formal violation charge, or even invoke an order to close a restaurant. Police officers similarly decide whether to warn, charge, or arrest an individual. Of course they are expected to do so within legal limits and in accordance with the norms of the organization in whose name they carry out their duties. For public administrators, then, the exercise of authoritative political power is an everyday fact of life.

Public goals are general and ambiguous not only because legislators and others lack sufficient time and expertise to spell out every specific implication and application of legislation, but also because ambiguity and generality are useful in blurring the lines of conflict over both means and ends. This blurring promotes sufficient coalitional cohesion and support to get legislation passed, but the political struggle does not end; only its locus shifts. The Office of Coastal Zone Management, for example, was created with a charge both to protect the coastal environment and to foster orderly development in coastal areas because Congress had been unable to decide between these goals, to define them more specifically, or to set priorities between them. Such indecisiveness and lack of clarity help explain why and how conflict among contending interests is transferred from a legislative to an administrative setting.

Vague and general goals also mean that government organizations must make decisions about interpretation, activities, and means. Public administrators are expected for the most part to base their decisions on "professional" grounds, which include objectivity and equity among a range of professional values (Gortner 1991). This prescription stems from the belief that using professional criteria removes political factors from administrative decisions. In theory, policy is to be made externally by politicians, and those inside the organization are to be passive except for implementing externally prescribed goals. In real bureaucratic life, however, so passive a role is not possible given the generality and ambiguity of goals. This gives rise to the rationale that if public managers use professional criteria, they will be prevented from making political decisions. But professional values are not apolitical. They may be nonpartisan, but they are political in the broader sense of benefiting some groups and not others and of advancing some values but not others. Ultimately, whether they are based on professional and technical criteria or on more obviously political considerations, the decisions of public administrators have basically political effects. The policy debate over whether the U.S. Bureau of the Census should provide a decennial census based on the science of statistical sampling in historically underreported locations such as inner cities or whether it should retain comprehensive enumeration of individuals is an example of a tug-of-war between interest groups that is framed in terms of technical issues but weighed largely in terms of policy outcomes.

The emphasis on professional or technical values affects the internal organization in a variety of ways, particularly in the areas of internal conflict and power. Conflict between political appointees and professional careerists is one dimension (Rourke 1984; Heclo 1977). Superior–subordinate conflict is rendered more complex. Conflict occurs among contending and different professionals at the same levels and among those at different levels. Likewise, in the fragmented world of public organizations—both government and nonprofit—conflict between professionals in different organizations or sectors is also a fact of life.

In the process of interpreting and implementing vague legislation, public managers may increase political support for their organizations and programs, but they also risk political attack and loss of support. Client groups usually support aggressive action that promotes the organization and its programs but demand a broad interpretation of their eligibility to receive services. However, influential legislators or the chief executive may not have embraced a program, even though it gained sufficient power to pass; or they may prefer a limited, even symbolic, program. A regulated clientele may resist and oppose an assertive agency, whereas other groups and their elected officials may demand greater regulatory fervor. This was certainly the case for the Office of Coastal Zone Management discussed earlier. The organization's legal charges and goals placed it between conflicting pressures from coastal developers and environmentalists and their respective elected supporters. Local planning agencies constantly face pressure from these two conflicting community interests. For public managers, action may satisfy some interests but upset others, and inaction undoubtedly has equally disparate results.

On the nonprofit side, service-oriented nonprofit organizations may face a less intense set of impacts related to goal ambiguity because they have more control over their mission definition and goals. (See Chapter 7 for a discussion of organizational missions and strategic planning.) For these organizations, political considerations are most likely to come when the mission involves socially controversial issues (such as drug rehabilitation or abortion) but constituencies among their stakeholders are not comfortable with the organization's presumed or expressed goals or, alternatively, with their methods of pursuing those goals (consider a county health service funding a nonprofit agency's drug treatment program in a suburban neighborhood). Advocacy-oriented nonprofit organizations are often a source of policy polarity and criticism regarding other public sector and private sector organizations. Even so, they themselves encounter goal ambiguity and its fallout effects when they are disunified within the organization or supporter groups about the mission goals. The Sierra Club, for example, has a lengthy record of strong environmental conservation positions; in recent years anti-immigration groups have tried to win enough seats on the Sierra Club's board of directors to drastically change the goals of the organization. In short, organizations within the public sector share differences in the degree of their sensitivity to the political environment, but no public organization is immune.

HOW ARE ORGANIZATIONS ALONG THE PUBLIC–PRIVATE CONTINUUM THE SAME?

Thus far we've addressed differences between public sector and private sector organizations and differences among public organizations. These are key to understanding organization theory from a public and nonprofit perspective. Also important are characteristics and situations that contemporary organizations have in common, at least by and large.

Scale

One of these universal attributes is scale: the size of the organization itself. The common element is that the range in size is enormous in every sector. How do we measure scale? Probably the most common yardstick is workforce (staffing) size, which can range from a part-time volunteer to hundreds of thousands of full-time employees. Another common measure of scale is annual operating budget, which can be entirely pro bono or can top hundreds of billions of dollars (as in the Department of Defense). Geographic dispersion, number of worksites, value of assets managed, and number of people or constituents directly affected can also be useful when we determine an organization's scale.

Shared Public Environment

Public or private, all contemporary organizations operate in the same basic environment or context. True, this context has modulations, varying from place to place in a number of ways. But by and large, all organizations must react to the same stimuli—whether social and demographic, economic and environmental, technological, or legal and political.

Demographic trends, for example, affect organizations in consistent ways. The baby boomer bulge (people born in the years following World War II) that provided North Americans with an abundant workforce and consumer base is now aging toward retirement. This creates not only a change in the available workforce but also a continuing shift in the needs and wants of the people organizations are designed to serve. Globalization, too, is not sector-specific: For-profit, nonprofit, and government organizations alike are influenced by threats and opportunities that come with ever more routine interactions with others all over the globe. Likewise, the pace of technology innovation and dissemination leaves both private and public organizations scrambling to take advantage of previously unattainable possibilities and absorbing the impact of accommodating those technologies in the workplace.

Over the last several decades the public's confidence in government and other social institutions has declined—a trend not unique to the United States (GlobalScan 2005). The public sector first saw the brunt of this phenomenon. Its roots are often linked to the Watergate scandal that forced President Richard Nixon from office and to disillusionment with the Vietnam War, followed by the practice of a series of presidential candidates—and scores of contenders for other public offices—of employing campaign strategies that included "running against the bureaucracy." The anti-institution phenomenon reached into the private sector as well, marked by declining allegiance to American-built automobiles and other products in the face of overseas competition, savings and loan scandals, investment and tax shelter abuses, and the exposure of high-level corporate corruption that destroyed the jobs and investments of millions of people. The nonprofit world, too, saw its public standing decline—a loss of confidence derived in part from the growing disaffection with the institutions we all depend on and in part from widely publicized instances of misuse of donor funds (such as the United Way's chief executive diverting donated funds for personal use, as well as the Red Cross's reallocating donations in the wake of the September 11, 2001, terror attacks on the Pentagon and the World Trade Center and having to destroy, unused, part of the related surge in donated blood) (Light 2005).

The September 11 tragedy, itself, had its impact on the environment in which organizations operate. The event altered the character of the environment to one of less complacency and more caution, one slightly less tolerant of variance with societal norms and somewhat more tolerant of limiting personal rights—for organizations as well as for individuals. The event disrupted portions of the economy: It hit some parts of the for-profit sector especially hard over the next several years, and it created spartan times for some nonprofit organizations while showering others with new attention and a temporary rush of contributions. Coming when it did—only six years after an act of domestic terrorism, the 1995 bombing of the Murrah Federal Building in downtown Oklahoma City—the 9–11 tragedy had a unique impact on government organizations and the women and men in public service. The public's growing skepticism about the essential purpose of government and the value of public workers began to reverse (Goodsell 2004): Government was seen more as necessary, not just a nuisance. Abraham Lincoln held that the purpose of government is to do what the people need but will not or cannot provide for themselves. In this instance "the people" turned to governmental institutions to address the scary problem of terrorist mayhem on American soil; but, by extension, other levels and aspects of government were treated more seriously.

Has the long-term trend of reduced confidence in organizations and institutions bottomed out? Changed direction? Aside from rare, high-impact events, such perceptions typically change only slowly over time. For now, public perceptions of administrative government, elected leaders, nonprofit institutions, the press, and big business remain gloomy.

Ethics

If many of these trends and events have an underlying theme, it is one of erosion of trust in contemporary organizations. The struggle to deal with this disillusionment involves ethics as its most important tool. *Ethics*, at its heart, is "doing the right thing" based on broadly accepted standards of behavior that, in turn, are based on important societal values. Not all values are oriented toward ethics (such as aesthetic values), but many are. Among these ethical values are honesty and integrity, compassion and loyalty, fairness and respect for others, personal responsibility and civic participation, and doing one's best. Ultimately society expects organizations as well as individuals to exhibit these and other ethical values—irrespective of whether they are public or private sector entities, and even though parties may differ over which values are relatively more and less important.

The bottom line is that ethical principles transcend professional and organizational boundaries because society holds those values in common and weights them in approximately the same way. *Weighting* means that when values come into conflict for a particular situation (such as honesty versus compassion), the more strongly held or weighted value likely takes precedence.

Then what about "business ethics," "legal ethics," "medical ethics," and fill-in-the blank ethics? At times such terms are used as rationalizations for ethically troubling decisions. Mostly, however, these labels come into play when an issue's description is laced with jargon specific to a particular discipline or when complexities of an ethics situation are largely discipline-specific. For example, "public service ethics," to the extent there is such a thing, involves giving especially high weight to ethical standards that come into play for people in public organizations. One such standard is maintaining public trust: When trust in public institutions erodes, the utility and effectiveness of those institutions diminish. Another standard for people in public service is avoiding impropriety and the appearance of impropriety—even in areas of personal behavior unrelated to job performance (Josephson 2005). Those behaviors color perceptions of the organization's character, contributing to cynicism about public institutions and their effectiveness.

In facing situations with ethical implications, some managers consciously or unconsciously use a decision process called *principled reasoning* (see Chapter 7) to help figure out the "right thing"; some rely on an inner compass; and some simply muddle through. Some managers fail to recognize (and often fail to deal with) many ethics issues when they arise. In organizations both public and private, managers come to their jobs from every background and with vastly different formal education and training portfolios. Of those with formal management training, ethics is emphasized more strongly in typical public management curricula (masters of public administration degrees) than in typical business management curricula (masters of business administration degrees) (Denhardt 1987). Research indicates that formal ethics training increases sensitivity to ethics issues (Jurkiewicz and Nichols 2002), and ethics-related indictments and disclosures have raised fresh calls for strengthening ethics training in all sectors, but particularly in the private sector.

As discussed earlier, organizations and those who lead them must confront political and ethical questions about ends and means. The classic question is whether the ends justify the means. A contemporary version of the question is "How do we minimize harm while maximizing benefit?" And a variant of that question is "Who benefits, who is harmed, and to what degree?" Programmatic and policy considerations in any organization can spawn these questions—or ought to. That said, these questions typically weigh most heavily for public sector organizations because they work for the benefit of us all. The standard answer schoolchildren learn is that worthy ends do not justify harmful means. But old-world administrative writers—of whom Niccolò Machiavelli is arguably the most often cited—advocate quite the opposite: Ends are paramount, so employ draconian means as needed.

One means-oriented debate regarding public organizations addresses the extent to which public organizations need to be consistent and neutral in the application of law and extent to which they need to be sensitive and flexible in dealing with individual cases (Thompson 1967; Dvorin and Simmons 1972). Both positions reflect ethical principles, but the principles conflict; so the position an organization chooses depends on the relative weight its managers and other stakeholders assign to those values. The ethical dilemma becomes one of "right versus right"—and those dilemmas are difficult to resolve.

Postmodernism

Public organizations do not enjoy coming across as "bureaucratic" in the definition of the term that connotes being unresponsive, rule-bound, officious, and antiquated (Goodsell 2004). As ways of updating themselves, organizations may adopt new names, logos, mottos, and websites. This is not new and not a U.S. phenomenon. Under President Dwight Eisenhower in the 1950s, the Bureau of Internal Revenue became the Internal Revenue Service. Under President Richard Nixon, in 1971 the Post Office—one of the original Cabinet-level departments—became a government corporation called the U.S. Postal Service. Under President Jimmy Carter the Civil Service Commission changed into the Office of Personnel Management. Under President Ronald Reagan the agency-level Veterans Administration was elevated to Cabinet rank and became Veterans Affairs. Federal agencies in Canada have adopted names such as Statistics Canada and Environment Canada. The U.S. Forest Service (a bureau within the Department of Agriculture) adopted, retired, and reactivated a mascot the world knows as Smokey the Bear. The Library of Congress, which is part of the legislative branch, operates "Thomas" (named for Thomas Jefferson, who donated his personal library to establish the original Library of Congress), an extensive website that tracks congressional activity.

Organizations—and people who study organizations—want to be contemporary, effective, and even fashionable. In other words, they want to be modern and sometimes postmodern. *Postmodernism* is, in part, a reaction to the traditional approach to organization theory, which often emphasizes rationality, formality, rule-reliance, and hierarchy. (See the "Models of Organization" section of Chapter 3.) Postmodernism dismisses, or at least bends, these precepts:

> Postmodernity transforms established ways of thinking, although no single set of postmodernist views exists; rather, postmodernists have different views, and many of them would deny the label. No positive program, no neat system of concepts, and no promise of future benefits are proposed. The title itself is not sacrosanct; next year, postmodernity might be called something else. (Farmer 1995, 5)

Postmodernists consciously try to step outside a topic as they consider it, and then engage in arms-length critique. Though managers often lack the time and intellectual predilection to step away from a situation and ponder it, several postmodern premises make sense.

One theme is a concern that society and the organizations within it have become technology-driven and are rapidly evolving into a technocracy, which seems almost a contraction of "techno-bureaucracy." To the extent that machines in general and information technologies in particular offer new ways to structure and operate organizations, this observation is true— not necessarily bad, but certainly true. To the extent that administrators increasingly tend to treat data as decisions rather than as one basis for making decisions, the observation is true and likely bad. However, to the extent that we can make our technology smart enough to handle many routine decisions (and to know when circumstances are not routine), the observation is true and mostly good.

Postmodern scholars sometimes refer to "constructivism," which pertains to being skeptical about a rational, objectivist reality. They hold that we construct "our own social realities" and make them our "global models of justice or order" (Bergquist 1993). We often do. An example of this took place in a hall in Philadelphia during the 1780s, when a group of men hammered out what became the U.S. Constitution and in the process created our governmental structure—a public meta-organization that has proven quite durable. In fact, most people realize that both social and organizational institutions change from time to time and place to place. Consequently, organization theory tends to be pragmatic and, for the most part, tacitly bounded by "approximately now" and "approximately here" rather than concerned with being timeless and ubiquitous.

In keeping with the premise of constructivism, postmodernists assert that language itself shapes much of our reality. This is very true, though the shaping process is a two-way street. Managers in most contemporary organizations consciously use gender-neutral terms and strive for politically correct communications. We try to "talk with" someone rather than "talk to" someone. We prefer active, concise, and efficient styles of communication that reflect and reinforce our preference for active, effective, and efficient organizations. But we also resculpt our language to keep up with our changing knowledge, environment, and values (quark, tsunami, e-mail, sustainable development, sunshine laws, open-door policies).

Postmodernists hold that society is at once both more global and more differentiated. Yes, society is more global than it has ever been. As for being more segmented, people more readily recognize that "not everyone in the world lives just like me"—which is an acknowledgment of a phenomenon rather than the creation of one. On the other hand, we select ourselves into groups that would not before have been practical to coalesce. This phenomenon of increased awareness of and access to other parts of the world is often referred to as our *global village*, a term Wyndham Lewis (1949) coined after World War II and Marshall McLuhan (1962) subsequently popularized. However, a village metaphor is less apt than the image of a city. Unlike a village, a city is a large place that encompasses distinct neighborhoods: During the day we interact with people from many places; we then go home to our own neighborhoods at day's end.

Fads, trends, fragmentation, and inconsistency are major elements in the postmodern outlook. One theme is that organizations and systems introduce chaos rather than manage it—a Kafkaesque viewpoint that most of us recognize on bleak days. Traditional public administration and organization theory have long incorporated the vein of "muddling through" as a means of looking at the long-term effects of short-term or superficial decisions and actions (Lindblom 1959).

In short, in the context of organization theory, postmodernism tends to be incomplete, self-absorbed, and somewhat jargonistic. But these negatives are offset by important positive characteristics. Postmodernism encourages organization theory, public administration, and other social science and artistic disciplines to rethink fundamental assumptions and concepts, to be creative and open to change, and to keep in mind the larger perspective and the longer view.

The Organizational Jumble

Postmodern thinkers note the contrast between organization theory, which is laid out as logically as possible and is frequently discussed in ideal terms (without the barnacles of reality), and the more disjointed context of what, in practice, organizations look like and how they work. In the public realm as well as the private sector, reality involves variety and messiness.

The public sphere and the private sphere both have behemoth organizational structures (such as an automobile manufacturer or the United Nations) alongside structures whose reach belies their modest size (such as a major stock exchange or the World Trade Organization). Both have tight, vertically integrated organizations and rambling, conglomerate organizational constellations. And in keeping with observations at the beginning of this chapter about blurred sectors, public and private sector activities link in formal as well as informal ways.

Table 2–2 describes examples of linkages among for-profit, nonprofit, and government organizational activities. In the automobile industry, a "foreign" car has become a fuzzy concept. (Who owns the company? Where were the parts, or at least most of the major parts, manufactured? Where was the vehicle assembled? How nearly identical is the design to another make, foreign or domestic?) In a similar fashion, people who deal with organizations are not necessarily aware of whether they are dealing with a private firm, a nonprofit organization,

TABLE 2–2 The Jumble: Front Office/Back Office

Front Office	*Back Office*
National Aeronautics and Space Administration (NASA)	Private science and engineering contractors
Agency for International Development (USAID)	Private U.S. contractors
National Science Foundation (NSF)	Private and state educational institutions
State department of transportation	Private contractors paid from federal and state funds
State health care program for the poor	Federal Medicaid Program and funding
State bureau of mental health services	Nonprofit and for-profit mental health care providers
Fundraising campaign for nonprofit organization	For-profit marketing firm
Privately funded housing and student loans	Government loan guarantee programs
Weather forecasts from commercial broadcasters	National Oceanic and Atmospheric Administration (NOAA)
Global positioning system (GPS) devices	Satellites funded for U.S. Geological Service (USGS) and military agencies

or a government agency. The front office (the label we see and place we might visit) may well be in one sector while the back office (where the work itself gets done) may be in another.

Some types of work take place in both public and private settings. Hospitals and schools are examples of this because some are for-profit entities, some are nonprofit, and some are government-run. The movement to privatize various functions also contributes to jumbling. The list of such functions ranges from garbage collection to tax collection, from health care and retirement funding systems to building maintenance and management. Although these are ultimately political and economic decisions, they add complexity to the public–private dynamic in an ever-evolving constellation of for-profit, nonprofit, and government organizations.

CONCLUSION: PUBLIC AND PRIVATE ORGANIZATIONS LOOK SIMILAR BUT DIFFER FUNDAMENTALLY

In summary, public organizations differ from for-profit organizations in substantial and fundamental ways. In the nonprofit sphere, some organizations are policy advocates while others primarily help implement policy. Because of the political roles and ambitions of other major governmental actors and institutions, they and their managers are plunged into politics. Public sector organizations, principally because of their expertise and their access to the client groups they serve, are important political resources and allies to legislators and chief executives. Our government system creates an opportunity structure not only in which organizations in the government sphere are drawn into politics by others, but also in which officials pursue and exercise political influence.

The climate and role of public organizations are unlike those of the for-profit entities in varying degrees and in crucial ways. Clearly the extent of external control, especially coupled with conflict among the overseers, fosters a climate of uncertainty, hostility, and risk. Moreover, circumstances dictate an essentially political role for public organizations, whether they are passive, defensive reactors, or active influence pursuers. In considering where organizations fit in a public–private continuum, nonprofit organizations inhabit the midsection of the spectrum, sharing attributes of both governmental and for-profit organizations; fundamentally, however, nonprofits are fully public because they exist to achieve a mission or goal other than financial gain for those who own and control them.

Generic organization theory, concentrating as it commonly does on the private firm, emphasizes a relatively closed system view. Competition, efficiency, self-interest, and unilateral decisions are dominant parts of that view, whereas instability, power, and conflict receive less emphasis. Organization theory addressing the realities of public organizations looks more to the interaction between them and their environments, questioning more closely how their environments affect them.

FOR FURTHER READING

For an excellent summary of the literature about the differences between bureaus and private organizations, see Hal G. Rainey, Robert W. Backoff, and Charles H. Levine, "Comparing Public and Private Organizations," *Public Administration Review* 36 (March/April 1976): 233–44. The major economic and market differences between private and public organizations are presented by Anthony Downs in *Inside Bureaucracy* (Boston: Little, Brown, 1967; reissued Prospect Heights, Illinois: Waveland Press, 1994). For theories about the roles and distinguishing characteristics of nonprofits, see Avner Ben-Ner and Benedetto Gui, "The Theory of Nonprofit Organizations Revisited," in *The Study of Nonprofit Enterprise Theories and Approaches,* ed. Helmut Anheier and Avner Ben-Ner (New York: Kluwer Academic/Plenum Publishers, 2003). James Q. Wilson, in his book *Bureaucracy: What Government Agencies Do and Why They Do It* (New York: Basic Books, 1989), discusses the implications of the political nature of bureaus and the inseparability of politics and public organizations. Among Lester Salamon's many substantive writings about nonprofit organizations and about the changing face of public organizations as a whole, his 2002 edited volume, *The Tools of Government: A Guide to the New Governance* (New York: Oxford University Press, 2002), is especially comprehensive. A serious and insightful investigation of the necessity of combining traditional managerial values with essential political functions and the complexity of administering public organizations is presented by Dwight Waldo in *The Enterprise of Public Administration* (Novato, California: Chandler & Sharp Publishers, 1980). Finally, an excellent response to the antibureaucratic rhetoric common in current politics and scholarship is Charles T. Goodsell's *The Case for Bureaucracy: A Public Administration Polemic*, 4th ed. (Washington: Congressional Quarterly Press, 2004).

The sixth edition of *Classics of Organization Theory*, edited by Jay M. Shafritz, J. Steven Ott, and Yong Suk Jang, presents excellent articles examining aspects of organizations in general and public organizations in particular. Among the articles pertinent to this chapter are "Organizations in Action" (1967) by James D. Thompson; "External Control of Organizations: a Resource Dependence Perspective" (1978) by Jeffrey Pfeffer and Gerald R. Salancik; "Institutionalized Organizations: Formal Structure as Myth and Ceremony" (1977) by John W. Meyer and Brian Rowan; "Democracy and the Iron Law of Oligarchy" (1915/1962) by Robert Michaels; "Theory of the Firm: Managerial Behavior, Agency Costs, and Ownership Structure" (1976) by Michael C. Jensen and William H. Meckling; "Bureaucracy" (1922) by Max Weber; and "Foundations of the Theory of Organization" (1948) by Philip Selznick.

REVIEW QUESTIONS

1. Public organizations differ from private organizations in critical ways. What seem to you to be the most significant differences? In what fundamental ways are all organizations similar?
2. Among public organizations, nonprofit and government organizations share many characteristics even though key differences distinguish them. What major differences do you see?
3. Given the political influences basic to public organization, how does structural change generally take place for government organizations? For nonprofit organizations? When public organization leaders want to shape that structural change, how does what they must do differ from their counterparts' actions in for-profit organizations?
4. How do the clients or customers of public organizations differ from those of private organizations?
5. What role does ethics play in public organizations?

REFERENCES

Allison, Graham. 1992. Public and private management: Are they fundamentally alike in all unimportant respects? In *Classics of public administration.* 3rd ed. Ed. Jay Shafritz and Albert C. Hyde. Pacific Grove, CA: Brooks/Cole Publishing.

Anheier, Helmut K. 2000. Managing nonprofit organizations: Toward a new approach. Civil Society Working Paper, January 1.

Ben-Ner, Avner, and Benedetto Gui. 2003. The theory of nonprofit organizations revisited. In *The study of nonprofit enterprise theories and approaches.* Ed. Helmut Anheier and Avner Ben-Ner. New York: Kluwer Academic/Plenum Publishers.

Bergquist, William. 1993. *The postmodern organization: Mastering the art of irreversible change.* San Francisco: Jossey-Bass.

Berkley, George E., and John Rouse. 2004. *The craft of public administration.* 9th ed. New York: McGraw-Hill.

Blau, Peter M., and Marshall W. Meyer. 1987. *Bureaucracy in modern society.* 3rd ed. New York: McGraw-Hill.

Blau, Peter M., and W. Richard Scott. 2003. *Formal organizations: A comparative approach.* Stanford, CA: Stanford University Press.

Braybrooke, David, and Charles E. Lindblom. 1970. *A strategy of decision: Policy evaluation as a social process.* New York: Simon & Schuster.

Brody, Evelyn. 2003. Are nonprofit organizations different? In *The study of nonprofit enterprise theories and approaches.* Ed. Helmut Anheier and Avner Ben-Ner. New York: Kluwer Academic/Plenum Publishers.

Denhardt, Robert B. 1987. The contemporary critique of management education: Lessons for business and public administration. *Public Administration Quarterly* 11 (v. 2, Summer): 123–33.

Downs, Anthony. 1967. *Inside bureaucracy.* Boston: Little, Brown. (Reissued Prospect Heights, IL: Waveland Press, 1994.)

Dvorin, Eugene P., and Robert H. Simmons. 1972. *From amoral to humane bureaucracy.* San Francisco: Canfield.

Easton, David. 1979. *A framework for political analysis.* Chicago: University of Chicago Press.

Farmer, David John. 1995. *The language of public administration: Bureaucracy, modernity, and post-modernity.* Tuscaloosa: University of Alabama Press.

Fisher, Roger, Elizabeth Kopelman, and Andrea Kupfer Schneider. 1994. *Beyond Machiavelli: Tools for coping with conflict.* New York: Penguin.

Gawthrop, Louis C. 1971. *Administrative politics and social change.* New York: St. Martin's Press.

GlobalScan, Inc. 2005. Trust in governments, corporations, and global institutions continues to decline. Survey report. Geneva: World Economic Forum; available from www.weforum.org/trustsurvey.

Goodsell, Charles T. 2004. *The case for bureaucracy: A public administration polemic.* 4th ed. Washington, DC: Congressional Quarterly Press.

Gortner, Harold F. 1986. *Administration in the public sector.* 2nd ed. New York: Krieger.

———. 1991. *Ethics for public managers.* New York: Greenwood.

Gronbjerg, Kirsten, and Lester Salamon. 2002. Devolution, marketization, and the changing shape of government–nonprofit relations. In *The state of nonprofit America,* 447–71. Ed. Lester Salamon. Washington, DC: Brookings Institution Press.

Hall, Peter. 1987. A historical overview of the private nonprofit sector. In *The non-profit sector: A research handbook.* Ed. W.W. Powell. New Haven: Yale University Press.

Harvard Law Review. 2001. Developments in law. In *Understanding nonprofit organizations,* 61–79. Ed. J. Steven Ott. Boulder, CO: Westview Press.

Heclo, Hugh. 1977. *A government of strangers: Executive politics in Washington.* Washington, DC: Brookings Institution.

Hersey, Paul, Ken Blanchard, and Dewey Johnson. 1996. *Management of organizational behavior: Utilizing human resources.* 7th ed. Englewood Cliffs, NJ: Prentice-Hall.

Hyde, Albert. 1991–92. Customers, clients, and captives. *The Bureaucrat* 20 (Winter): 49–53.

Josephson, Michael S. 2005. *Preserving the public trust: The five principles of public service ethics.* Bloomington, IN: Unlimited Publishing.

Jurkiewicz, Carole L., and Kenneth Nichols. 2002. Ethics education in the MPA curriculum: What difference does it make? *Journal of Public Administration Education* 8 (April): 103–14.

Knight, Jerry. 1983. Run it like a business, no matter how much more it costs. *Washington Post* (March 21): B1.

Lasswell, Harold D. 1990. *Politics: Who gets what, when, how.* Magnolia, MA: Peter Smith Publisher.

Lewis, Wyndham. 1949. *America and cosmic man.* Garden City, NY: Doubleday.

Light, Paul C. 2005. Rebuilding public confidence in charitable organizations. *Public Service Brief #1* (October).

Lindblom, Charles. 1959. The science of muddling through. *Public Administration Review* 19 (Spring): 79–88.

Lohman, Roger. 1992. The commons: A multidisciplinary approach to nonprofit organizations, voluntary action, and philanthropy. *Nonprofit and Voluntary Sector Quarterly* 21: 309–24.

Lowi, Theodore. 1964. American business, public policy, case studies and political theory. *World Politics* 16 (July): 677–715.

Malek, Frederick V. 1972. Mr. Executive goes to Washington. *Harvard Business Review* (September/October): 63–68.

McCurdy, Howard E. 1977. *Public administration: A synthesis.* Menlo Park, CA: Cummings Publishing.

McLuhan, Marshall. 1962. *The Gutenberg Galaxy: The making of typographic man.* Toronto: University of Toronto Press.

Miller, Hugh T., and Charles J. Fox, eds. 1997. *Postmodernism, "reality" and public administration: A discourse.* Burke, VA: Chatelaine Press.

Mintzberg, Henry. 1996. Managing government: Governing management. *Harvard Business Review* (May/June): 75–83.

Murray, Michael A. 1975. Comparing public and private management: An exploratory essay. *Public Administration Review* (July/August): 364–71.

National Performance Review (U.S.) 1993. *Creating a government that works better & costs less: Report of the national performance review* (Vice President Al Gore). New York: Plume/Penguin.

Neustadt, Richard E. 1960. *Presidential power: The power to persuade.* New York: John Wiley & Sons.

Rainey, Hal G., Robert W. Backoff, and Charles H. Levine. 1976. Comparing public and private organizations. *Public Administration Review* 36 (March/April): 233–44.

Rourke, Francis E. 1984. *Bureaucracy, politics, and public policy.* 3rd ed. Boston: Little, Brown.

Salamon, Lester, ed., and Odus V. Elliott. 2002. *The tools of government: A guide to the new governance.* New York: Oxford University Press.

Schattschneider, E. E. 1975. *The semi-sovereign people: A realist's view of democracy in America.* Fort Worth: Harcourt College Publishers.

Seidman, Eileen. 1984. Of games and gains. . . . *The Bureaucrat* 13 (Summer): 4–8.

Shafritz, Jay M., J. Steven Ott, and Yong Suk Jang. 2005. *Classics of organization theory.* 6th ed. Belmont, CA: Wadsworth.

Sharkansky, Ira. 1965. Four agencies and an appropriation committee: A comparative study of budget strategies. *Midwest Journal of Political Science* 9 (August): 254–81.

Smith, Steven, and Michael Lipsky. 2001. "Dilemmas of management in nonprofit organizations." In *Understanding nonprofit organizations,* 256–67. Ed. J. Steven Ott. Boulder, CO: Westview Press.

Stokey, Edith, and Richard Zeckhauser. 1978. *A primer for policy analysis.* New York: W. W. Norton.

Taylor, Paul. 1983. Civil service turns 100, burdened by stereotypes. *Washington Post* (January 16): A1.

Thompson, James. 1967. *Organizations in action*. New York: McGraw-Hill.

Waldo, Dwight. 1980. *The enterprise of public administration: A summary view*. Novato, CA: Chandler & Sharp Publishers.

Wamsley, Gary L., and Mayer N. Zald. 1976. *The political economy of public organizations*. Bloomington, IN: Indiana University Press.

Weber, Max. 1947. *Theory of social and economic organization*. Trans. A. Henderson and T. Parsons. Glencoe, IL: The Free Press.

Weisbrod, Burton A. 1988. *The nonprofit economy*. Cambridge, MA: Harvard University Press.

Wilson, James Q. 1989. *Bureaucracy: What government agencies do and why they do it*. New York: Basic Books.

Woll, Peter. 1977. *American bureaucracy*. 2nd ed. New York: W. W. Norton.

Chapter 3

The Pivotal Controversies

As was pointed out in the first chapter, organization theory is a disorderly and fascinating field (Waldo 1978). Each theory starts with a unique set of assumptions, asks a different set of basic questions, and, not surprisingly, arrives at different—sometimes diametrically opposed—answers. Nevertheless, certain themes are constantly addressed as the frantic debate among public organization theorists goes on. These controversies about, or perspectives on, organization in the public sector can be categorized under the following four general headings:

1. *Law and/or legal authority:* Questions pertaining to the interpretation and implementation of the law are of central importance to public and nonprofit organizations. Public agencies are established by law to administer the law. How these organizations fulfill their mandated functions and how society is affected by the result are issues of constant debate. Nonprofit organizations are established by individuals or groups to deliver services and accomplish goals that have important social and political implications for part or all of society. Nonprofit organizations exist in an environment where it is critical to maintain public trust, and the most basic requirement for such organizations is to clearly show compliance with all laws regulating their fiduciary and governance practices.

2. *Rationality and efficiency:* Public and nonprofit organizations use material resources furnished by the public. These resources may be mandatory (taxes, fees, and the like) for governmental agencies or voluntary (donations, grants, fees, and so forth) for nonprofit organizations. Whatever the source, how efficiently and rationally the resources are used is of utmost importance to everyone because of the necessity of maintaining the public's trust.

3. *Psychological and social relations:* Civil servants and nonprofit workers are human beings (even though some politicians might have us believe otherwise). Human beings choose where they work on the basis of numerous factors, and many if not most individuals working in the public and nonprofit arenas have special reasons for choosing to be there rather than laboring in some other sector of the economy. Therefore, managers must understand the psychological and sociological aspects of their organization if they are to accomplish good human resource management and achieve organizational goals. This is especially true if there is any commitment on the part of management to allowing members of the organization to maintain individual professionalism[1] while maintaining high motivation and involvement among employees. This is a special problem because those workers cannot be rewarded in ways that are typical in the private sector.

4. *Politics and/or power relations:* All organizations have a political aspect. However, in addition to the ubiquitous internal politics in organizations, all action in the

---

[1]Because *professionalism* is often a factor in individual beliefs and actions and is a recurring idea in our discussion, let us define what is meant by the term. Central to this concept is a set of beliefs that include

1. Belief in the need for *expertise* in the body of abstract knowledge applicable to the profession.
2. Belief that professionals should have *autonomy* in work activities and decision making.
3. *Identification* with the profession and fellow professionals.
4. *Commitment to a life's work* in the profession as a calling.
5. A feeling of ethical *obligation to render service* to clients without self-interest and with emotional neutrality.
6. A belief in *self-regulation* and collegial maintenance of standards—that is, that fellow professionals are best qualified to judge and police each other (Filley, House, and Kerr 1976).

public sphere takes place in a politically charged environment. Therefore, the decisions and actions of the principal actors in these organizations must be considered within this dual political context.

The second and third controversies noted here (rationality/efficiency and psychological/social relations) are especially universal and must be considered in any discussion of organization theory, although they must be interpreted in the context of the particular sector under consideration. However, because public service organizations exist for reasons (and have obligations) quite dissimilar to those in the private sector, the first and last of these pivotal perspectives (law and political/power relations) assume a special significance that does not exist for organizations in the private sector. The reason for this emphasis on the law and the political environment should be relatively clear thanks to the last chapter, but it may be worthwhile to comment briefly on the importance of these two areas.

Chapter 2's discussion centered on the way public service organizations are involved in the formulation and interpretation of the law, but a further impact of the law must be noted: The law places serious limitations on the way public organizational structures and functions can be instituted and carried out. While focusing on mission, striving for optimal efficiency, and attempting to achieve the best possible social and psychological arrangements in the agency, the public manager must always be cognizant of "what the law will let one do." A story, perhaps apocryphal but passed on to the authors as true, can best explain the difficulty faced in this area.

In a Midwestern state it was discovered that one particular employment office was extremely successful, over an extended period, in placing unemployed individuals in permanent jobs; in other words, not only were more than the usual number of people placed in available openings, but those people were remaining on the job longer than was usual compared with other offices in the state. When a state auditor made his biennial visit to the office to examine the files and validate the records, he found that the records were indeed correct. He also found that the director of the office was using a unique motivational system that apparently accounted for the tremendous record: She was rewarding the office employees with an extra day off after they had successfully placed X number of clients (determined by placement in a position where the client remained on the job for a predetermined time period that was longer than the statewide mean). In spite of the program's success, the auditor had to inform the director that she could not use such a reward system because it violated state law. One year later the record of that particular employment office was slightly lower than the state average for both placements and length of time remaining in the new job. Everyone believed that the unique reward system was the causal factor in the success of the office, and that removal of the system led to the immediate return to mediocrity. But all they could do was shake their heads, shrug their shoulders, and say, "It was a great idea, but it was against the law."

Government organizations must use existing theories in ways that meet the letter of the law. Solid proof that an experimental system works is not adequate justification for action, although such proof might be used to try to persuade the legislature to change the law. Therefore, public organization theory must include a consideration of the law as it relates to bureaus, its reason for existence, and the limitations that it places on freedom of action. Doing so creates a more complete and rational picture of the real world of public organizations.

Nonprofit sector organizations may have greater flexibility to try experimental systems and procedures, but probably not to the extent available to private organizations. Success in meeting established goals may be foremost in the minds of donors and interested participants and observers. But short-term success may be undermined by longer-term loss of credibility and trust if nonadherence to laws and regulations is found. Therefore the nonprofit administrator walks a constant fine line between achievement and adherence to accepted procedures.

When dealing with the fourth controversy just noted (politics/power), students of public and nonprofit sector agencies need to be aware of the assumptions and thinking behind the questions asked about organizations. These questions and their answers are political in nature; they often express, implicitly or explicitly, criticism of the political system and the predominant culture and agendas for change. Therefore they rest on a particular set of assumptions about authority, conflict, power, and the proper criteria for choice within organizations. Any organizational theory, when studied and applied to public service agencies, should be examined for such assumptions, especially before we attempt to apply it in the hope of improving management or changing the operations of any established group.

Similarly, as we examine public organization theory, it is important to consider the politically charged environment as a prominent factor. How does the theory take into account the existing political system, which in turn helps to explain why bureaus currently function as they do? Equally important, understanding the political environment helps us understand why interested parties have a particular perception of any public sector organization. And these factors must be considered whenever an attempt is made to apply organization theory to a specific establishment. How do actors (interest groups, community leaders, donors, clients) in the environment interpret what is attempted? And how do they react to that effort given their political or social philosophy, position within the political or social system, and the perceptions that both factors give them of the world? How will the reactions of these actors affect the implementation of any change? Different types of political and managerial rationality exist based on different sets of basic values and on whether substantive or instrumental rationality is being considered. (Rationality will be discussed later in this chapter.) These different rationality systems are used simultaneously in defining the goals of public service organizations and in assessing their rationality and efficiency.

Thus the inclusion of the four controversies[2] in this particular combination makes public organization theory different from that related to business, especially the heavy emphasis that must be placed on the first and last principles. If, when studying organization theory, such an emphasis is not included, there is no way to recognize the special problems faced by public service organizations or the special interpretations that must be understood when the traditional theories are applied to these unique sectors of our society. The addition of these issues creates additional problems for private organizations when they are carrying out public policy or public service functions.

In the next section, after presenting models of organization that will help us focus the discussion throughout this chapter, we examine the four pivotal themes of public organization theory. Finally we take a special look at the influence of political history on the understanding of what falls within the context of public service and what the impact of that understanding is on public organization theory and on public management practice.

---

[2]Some would suggest that a fifth controversy should be addressed here: What is the proper distribution of service delivery, or when should private, nonprofit, or government organizations be used to carry out the functions of society? That important question is addressed by authors such as Savas (2000) and Salamon (1995), and the origin of an organization is important to its ongoing operation; however, the genesis of organizations is determined by political and social factors existing at the time of their appearance and is outside the focus of this book.

MODELS OF ORGANIZATION

Let us briefly present the classic view of complex organization developed by Max Weber—usually referred to as the *bureaucratic model*—and then examine three approaches to a new view of organizations—or a *postbureaucratic model*. Throughout the chapter, as we discuss the four controversies, we will refer to these views in an effort to understand the larger field of organization theory and how perspectives differ in importance within the nonprofit and private sectors. Both views of organization are important in all three sectors of society; but the idea of bureaucracy is primarily, and perhaps wrongly, attached to public sector organizations, whereas the three models in the other view have played a larger role in the private sector. Although government organizations get tagged with the "bureaucratic" moniker, private sector organizations are often just as bureaucratic—perhaps even more so because of the lack of democratic input from employees in favor of hierarchical decision making. Refer back to the discussion of the differences between public and private organizations in Chapter 2.

The first and traditional model of bureaucracy presented by Max Weber is widely accepted as the basis on which discussion of organization structure and function normally begins (see Chapter 4). Many people, usually pejoratively, see the bureaucratic model as the norm for public organization. By *norm* we mean that Weber's model describes the way public organizations look; it says nothing about how they should be structured or how they should operate. In fact, Weber decried some of the inherent problems created by such a structure; nonetheless, he described it in an objective and scholarly manner. Weber's use of the term *ideal type* means "the organization that most perfectly meets the criteria of bureaucracy" and *not* the best organization.

The second view is actually a set of three models (total quality management, the information organization, and organization development) about how to organize the successful modern organization in a highly competitive and rapidly changing environment. After discussing the bureaucratic model we will briefly present these three models and then discuss their commonalities.

Probably the most influential model of organization ever presented is Max Weber's description of the internal characteristics of the ideal type bureaucracy. According to Weber, within the bureaucracy

> The whole administrative staff under the supreme authority consists, in the purest type, of individual officials (employees or "office holders" but *not* elected politicians or political appointees) who are appointed and function according to the following criteria:
>
> 1. They are personally free and subject to authority only with respect to their impersonal official obligations.
>
> 2. They are organized in a clearly defined hierarchy of offices.
>
> 3. Each office has a clearly defined sphere of competence in the legal sense.
>
> 4. The office is filled by a free contractual relationship. Thus, in principle, there is free selection.
>
> 5. Candidates are selected on the basis of technical qualifications. In the most rational case, this is tested by examination or guaranteed by diplomas certifying technical training, or both. They are appointed, not elected.
>
> 6. They are remunerated by fixed salaries in money, for the most part with a right to pensions. Only under certain circumstances does the employing authority . . . have a right to terminate the appointment, but the official is always free to resign. The salary scale is primarily graded according to rank in the hierarchy; but in addition to this criterion, the

responsibility of the position and the requirements of the incumbent's social status may
be taken into account.

7. The office is treated as the sole, or at least the primary, occupation of the incumbent.

8. It constitutes a career. There is a system of promotion according to seniority or to
achievement, or both. Promotion is dependent on the judgment of superiors.

9. The official works entirely separated from ownership of the means of administration and
without appropriation of his position.

10. He is subject to strict and systematic discipline and control in the conduct of the offices.
(1947, 333–34)

Weber's model is descriptive; this means that the model describes major aspects of the
structure that appear, to a greater or lesser extent, in almost all organizations. In cases where
the characteristics do not describe what is present in any organization, entities are generally
categorized by the extent to which their structures vary from the bureaucratic standard. Built
into this model is a series of assumptions about the functions of an organization within the
larger society, the goals of the organization and where they are established, and the individuals within the organization and how they think and act. For these reasons the model may be
described as universal or as an attempt to present facts and relationships that must be understood anytime we talk about complex organizations, which has certainly been the case. At the
same time the bureaucratic model has been especially applied to governmental organizations,
in part at least to the necessity of maintaining control and accountability within governmental
services where privacy, constitutional rights, and the use of citizens' money (taxes) play a central role in decisions and actions.

During the 1980s a series of major changes that had been occurring in the larger
social/cultural/technological environment culminated in a new emphasis on the way productive organizations were perceived and evaluated, and that change has continued under a
number of rubrics over the last few decades. Perhaps the most widely recognized of these
new ways to view organizations is through the concept of participative management, which
includes the many models for team building and team management. The package of ideas
that perhaps best summarized the movement toward participation by all parts, or members,
of the organizations is total quality management (TQM), which represented the first comprehensive attempt to respond to a changing, increasingly international economic and productive system that required rethinking how American business operated. Whereas Weber's
model is descriptive, TQM is prescriptive: It presents an action plan for making organizations more efficient and effective. As American businesses felt the threat of foreign competition and the pressure for both efficiency and quality, the teachings of the quality theorists,
especially W. Edwards Deming (2000), were accepted by an increasing number of organizations and management theorists. It is unnecessary to give much historical background to this
movement; however, TQM was "borrowed back" by Americans, after having been rejected
earlier and then being successfully implemented by Japanese businesses.

Deming (2000) presents 14 principles for successful total quality management (see
Box 3–1). From these TQM principles, originally developed for manufacturing companies,
comes a universal organizational and managerial model that Deming argues is the structure
necessary for success in the competitive environment of capitalist free enterprise. This
model, like Weber's, operates from a set of assumptions about the functions of organizations
within the larger society, the goals of the organization and where they are established, and
the individuals within the organization and how they think and act.

BOX 3–1 Deming's 14 Points for Management

1. Create constancy of purpose toward improvement of product and service, with the aim to become competitive and to stay in business, and to provide jobs.

2. Adopt the new philosophy. We are in a new economic age. Western management must awaken to the challenge, must learn their responsibilities, and take on leadership for change.

3. Cease dependence on inspection to achieve quality. Eliminate the need for inspection on a mass basis by building quality into the product in the first place.

4. End the practice of awarding business on the basis of price tag. Instead minimize total cost. Move toward a single supplier for any one item on a long-term relationship of loyalty and trust.

5. Improve constantly and forever the system of production and service, to improve quality and productivity, and thus constantly decrease costs.

6. Institute training on the job.

7. Institute leadership. The aim of supervision should be to help people and machines and gadgets to do a better job. Supervision of management is in need of overhaul, as well as supervision of production workers.

8. Drive out fear so that everyone may work effectively for the company.

9. Break down barriers between departments. People in research, design, sales, and production must work as a team to foresee problems of production and in use that may be encountered with the product or service.

10. Eliminate slogans, exhortations, and targets for the workforce asking for zero defects and new levels of productivity. Such exhortations only create adversarial relationships because the bulk of the causes of low quality and low productivity belong to the system and thus lie beyond the power of the workforce.

11. a. Eliminate work standards (quotas) on the factory floor. Substitute leadership.

    b. Eliminate management by objective. Eliminate management by numbers and numerical goals. Substitute leadership.

12. a. Remove barriers that rob the hourly worker of his right to pride of workmanship. The responsibility of supervisors must be changed from sheer number to quality.

    b. Remove barriers that rob people in management and in engineering of their right to pride of workmanship. This means, *inter alia,* abolishment of the annual or merit rating and of management by objective.

13. Institute a vigorous program of education and self-improvement.

14. Put everybody in the company to work to accomplish the transformation. The transformation is everybody's job.

Manufacturing systems and government/nonprofit systems are quite dissimilar and exist for radically different reasons; therefore changes must be made in the rules of TQM as they apply to public organizations. A translation of the principles to meet the needs of public agencies has been developed by James E. Swiss (1992), who argues that the TQM model for a successful government organization includes seven primary tenets:

1. The customer is the ultimate determiner of quality. If the product does not meet the desires of the customers, it is bad quality, no matter how "perfectly" made.

2. Quality should be built into the product early in the production process (upstream) rather than being added on at the end (downstream). Proper early, upstream design saves later redesigning or reworking and makes customers happier. TQM opposes mass inspections—quality is everyone's task, not someone's at the end of the process.

3. Preventing variability is the key to producing high quality. Quality slips when variation occurs. Therefore process control charts that track deviation from the optimum are analyzed to prevent deviation in product or service.

4. Quality results from people working within systems, not individual efforts. The system usually creates quality slips, not the individual. With committed people working together, it is a mistake to focus on individuals. The system should create intrinsic motivators that lead all workers to perform well.

5. Quality requires continuous improvement of inputs and processes. This continuous improvement should be in processes and inputs—not in outputs (defined as profits).

6. Quality improvement requires strong worker participation. The workers must do it right the first time, so managers and workers must work together "without fear."

7. Quality requires total organizational commitment. Managers must create an organizational culture where everyone focuses on consistently producing quality products and improving them constantly (Swiss 1992, 357–58).

TQM in its original form is no longer seen as the panacea that it once was; however, numerous approaches to organizational improvement have sprung from that first model. Individual or combined elements of that model may be emphasized or reconstructed in new forms (for example, the participative management movement) to address the problems and opportunities faced by current public or private organizations.

During TQM's greatest popularity two correlative paradigms, or ways of looking at organizations, were being developed by other scholars and practitioners. These were parallel perspectives on what were the essential elements affecting organizations in our environment. The first is descriptive and the second prescriptive. The first of these parallel new paradigms might be called the "information organization model." It was introduced by Harlan Cleveland in 1985, when he noted that information (organized and refined data that equal knowledge) had become the crucial resource in society and in government; therefore the inherent characteristics of information, and the development of an "information society," required everyone to think in new ways about organizations. Cleveland points out that at least six characteristics of information must be taken into consideration:

1. Information is expandable. "(T)he capacity of humanity to integrate its collective experience through relevant individual thinking is certainly expandable—not without limits, . . . but within limits we cannot now measure or imagine."

2. Information is not resource hungry. "Compared to the processes of the steel-and-automobile economy, the production and distribution of information are remarkably sparing in their requirements for energy and other physical and biological resources."

3. Information is substitutable. Information can and increasingly does replace capital, labor, and physical materials.

4. Information is transportable—at close to the speed of light. As a result, remoteness is now more choice than geography.

5. Information is diffusive. It tends to leak—and the more it leaks the more we have. This means that "monopolizing information is very nearly a contradiction in terms; that can be done only in more and more specialized fields, for shorter and shorter periods of time."

6. Information is shareable. "(I)f I give you a flower or sell you my automobile, you have it and I don't. But if I sell you an idea or give you a fact, we both have it. An information-rich environment is thus a sharing environment. That needn't mean an environment without standards, rules, conventions, and ethical codes. It does mean the standards, rules, conventions, and codes are going to be different from those created to manage the zero-sum bargains of market trading and traditional international relations" (Cleveland 1985, pp. 186–87).

Thus Cleveland argues that the inherent characteristics of physical resources (natural and fabricated) made possible the development of hierarchies of power based on control (of products, manufacturing technologies, energy, markets, and so on); hierarchies of influence based on secrecy; hierarchies of class based on ownership; hierarchies of privilege based on early access to valuable resources; and hierarchies of politics based on geography. However, these bases for rank and power distribution are crumbling because the old means of control are declining; secrets are harder and harder to keep; and ownership, early arrival, and geography are of dwindling significance. Therefore knowledge and wisdom, which have become the virtual legal tender of our time, are available to a much larger portion of society; and the hierarchical system, which hoarded tender to maintain authority, tends to break down. This means that people will in the future come together in productive arrangements to make quite different products that will, accordingly, lead to different organizational structures and procedures. What happens will depend on the continuing evolution of technology and the mission of each particular organization.

The second, parallel approach to organization that appeared at about the same time as TQM was "organization development," which is discussed in Chapter 10. As will become apparent in that discussion, organization development was a broad-based and multifaceted attempt to prescribe and implement a process of planned change for the purpose of organizational improvement—as opposed to a focus solely on performance (Waclawski and Church 2002). Organization development (OD) has been built around a set of models or systematized theories rooted in the social and behavioral sciences. OD advocates felt confident in proposing such change because of the tremendous increase in the amounts of information about organizations and the people in them and the OD experts' increasing confidence in the application of the scientific method in human research. This model developed two parallel activities. First, methods for the study and analysis of personal and organizational behavior were developed based on similar practices in several social sciences; and second, the actions taken to change individuals and organizations were based both on the findings of the analysis and on normative and humanistic values generally accepted by practitioners and scholars of the combined fields. The field of OD became popular in the 1970s and has continued to grow in its diversity of use in all types of organizations.

The importance of the OD and information society organization paradigms is to show there was a broad movement in the latter half of the twentieth century to redefine the perspectives and values that shaped our perception of management over time. The two extreme models, the bureaucratic and the total quality perspectives, are both important and cannot be ignored. An acceptance of these models, as well as the strengths and weaknesses of each, has led to several movements to restructure public organizations over the last few decades. Several state and local governments, and many nonprofit organizations, have been and are involved in trying to take advantage of the new perspectives to improve both the efficiency and effectiveness of government services. Many organizations, in fact, have as their missions the assistance of public sector entities in carrying out these changes in organizational structures, processes, and cultures. Elements of TQM and the other approaches mentioned here appear in a variety of critiques of government organizations and operations, including but certainly not limited to Osborne and Gaebler's *Reinventing Government* (1992) and the report of the National Performance Review, *Creating a Government That Works Better & Costs Less* (1993). An examination of the *9/11 Commission Report* (National Commission on Terrorist Attacks upon the United States 2004) shows constant references to weaknesses in specific programs caused by the inability of agencies to master the concepts of what we might call the new management. And in the nonprofit sector constant efforts are under way to apply these new concepts—with varying degrees of success (Durst and Newell 2001).

Each of the models just mentioned addresses some, and deemphasizes other, of the four perspectives that we suggested are central to the study of public organizations. It is the thesis of this discussion that placing too much emphasis on any one of these perspectives is unproductive, whereas combining them creates a useful picture. After each perspective is examined separately, we will try to bring them together in a meaningful synthesis.

THE CONTROVERSY AROUND THE FOUR PERSPECTIVES

Law and Legal Authority

We take it for granted that government organizations operate on a legal basis or according to the law. We also recognize that the purpose of any government agency is to execute the law. However, we may fail on occasion to recognize that the effort to execute the law according to structures and processes established by law may cause great difficulty for these agencies. An obvious example of this difficulty is seen in law enforcement's attempt to control organized crime, or the federal government's attempt to carry on our struggle against terrorism, where the strict limits placed on surveillance and collection of evidence and the broad interpretation of individual rights create problems for police operatives and the many other organizations at all levels of government that are supposed to work together on these critical problems. While all of the agencies involved in antiterrorism activities are derided for not doing a better job, there is also a fear that government might intrude into the lives of innocent individuals throughout society. Prime examples are the debate over the national government's use of telephone logs—through the National Security Agency—and the monitoring of international transactions of money, both hot issues during the summer of 2006. Security organizations are closely watched by civil and human rights groups and by most interested citizens to see that the necessary activities are carried out under procedural proscriptions strongly ascribed to by most citizens. Antiterrorist and law enforcement agencies must find a way to protect society while staying within the procedural limits placed on them by that same society.

In a similar vein, it is not uncommon for legislative adversaries, once aware that they cannot block passage of a new program, to attempt to place it in an already existing organization that is inimical or at best coldly neutral to that program. Another ploy regularly used by enemies of programs is to create, in the enabling act, procedures or structures that will hobble or make inefficient the delivery of the service or good in the hope they may reopen the debate about the issue at a later date with "proof" that the decision to create the program was a mistake because of the problems that have been shown to exist in administering it.

That the government and its agencies should operate according to law is a widespread belief. Even in totalitarian states, the government and its agencies at least pay lip service to this idea and function under a constitution and laws that, while failing to guarantee some of the most important human rights, attempt to create the semblance of legality for the imposed order. In our society the few public organizations that we suspect may not always operate according to law (the Central Intelligence Agency, for example) cause considerable discomfort to interested observers because such activity, while perhaps necessary, is considered amoral. Even though it is endured, attempts are made to limit the amounts and types of covert activity, and various checks are created to oversee the organizations. As a result, leaders of such organizations sometimes complain of being hamstrung in their operations and of being unable to respond to, or counter, similar organizations elsewhere in the world or in organized crime.

The concept of the law as the basis of authority is relatively new in organization life. Authority, according to Max Weber (1947), used to be based on charisma and tradition. Although examples of increasing dependence on legal authority can be invoked from earlier times (the Athenian democracy, the Magna Carta, and canon law), the concept became fully developed and widely accepted only during the last few hundred years. Today, however, we take for granted Abraham Lincoln's statement that we have a government of laws, not of men. The administrative or implementation and service arm of government is based on laws. Laws establish the policy direction, or the goals, of departments and programs, thereby spelling out what is expected in the way of output or results. Likewise, laws define proper organizational structure, due process in rule making and implementation, reporting procedures, and conflict of interest. In other words, the law clarifies both structural and procedural questions. It even establishes the system by which personnel are selected, rewarded, or punished within an organization.[3]

Public bureaucracy and dependence on the law grew together, as is noted by Herbert Spiro:

> Modern law and modern bureaucracy were created to fill the same needs. On the Continent, especially, the birth and growth of each cannot be conceived of without the other. Administrative law was designed to make responsible conduct possible for the ruler's new instruments, the bureaucrats, by giving them reasonable expectations of the probable consequences of their acts. . . . In the days of the youth of modern bureaucracy, the bureaucrat's accountability normally

---

[3]Although the laws specify all the elements of organization mentioned here, it must be understood that the elements may not, indeed cannot, be specified completely, concisely, and clearly in many if not most cases.

stood in fair proportion to his causal responsibility. He knew the extent of his accountability, i.e., it was explicit. What he should or should not do, and how he should go about his tasks, were laid down for him with greater exactness perhaps than for anyone else who acts politically. The statutes creating or regularizing his position told him from the outset what would happen to him if he committed "nonfeasance, malfeasance, or overfeasance." (1969, 86–87)

The centrality of law and the concomitant responsibility for the execution of the law required the development of the modern public bureau. This is especially true if it is assumed that government organizations should *react to and fulfill* citizen desires and demands rather than *create* social objectives because the bureaucracy is geared toward objectivity, independence from personal pressure, and control over discretionary actions by bureaucrats. Looking back at Max Weber's model of bureaucracy, or at his description of the internal characteristics of bureaucratic organizations, we can see how these characteristics help guarantee that public agencies will automatically obey the law.

Weber argues that organizations of this type exist in both the private and public sectors—and this is certainly true; however, public organizations, especially those in government, probably match this model more closely than private ones. In the first place, government agencies, having been established by the legislature to achieve certain objectives through specified processes—all spelled out by the law—are creatures of the law.

A second aspect of the relationship between the law and public organizations becomes overwhelmingly apparent as we look at Weber's model and the ways in which it guarantees that the law will be the basis for bureau action. By examining Weber's criteria, spelled out in the model presented earlier in this chapter, we can clarify the way in which the bureaucratic system guarantees an inordinate focus by public employees on the law. Central to this point is the fact that each office has a clearly defined sphere of competence (criterion 3). And where is that sphere defined? In the law—if not in the enabling act, then in the rules, regulations, and other materials that are based on and interpret the inert law as it is put into action. Note also that bureaucratic officials are subject to authority only when it applies to their offices (criterion 1); these offices are at least their primary occupations (criterion 7); and the officials are entirely separated from ownership (criterion 9). These factors limit the possibility of conflict of interest; thus employees of bureaus are under no other pressure except to know and obey the law. Furthermore, the fact that positions in the bureaucracy are filled by free contractual relationships (criterion 4) after being selected on the basis of technical qualifications (criterion 5) and are then paid fixed salaries in money (criterion 6) guarantees their loyalty, expertise, and objectivity. The officials are not forced to participate; they are presumed to be knowledgeable in the field; and their rewards are fixed. Therefore, no person has an undue power over, or claim on, their services. They are not distracted by personal claims from the objective administration of the law. Finally, the hierarchical structure of offices (criterion 2) and the natural desire to advance in a career (criterion 8) mean that all officials are held accountable for their actions. Strict accountability breeds close adherence to the law, and deductive rules and rigorous control are the major objects of design and management.

Within government organizations, adherence to the law is central to all activities. Accountability and control, especially as spelled out in the law, are ensured by the structure of organizations. Structure, as portrayed in the organizational chart, is the formal aspect of organizational life. If the chief executive, or an external body such as the legislature, wishes to have an impact on the operation of an agency, the primary line of attack is through either budgetary cuts (contained in the budget act passed by the legislature), which can severely affect the ability of the agency to carry out its charge, or changes in the law that force reorganization. Likewise, the easiest and most direct way for top officials to make an imprint on their agencies is through reorganization. The result is instantaneous and visual, whereas attempts to influence the informal portion of a bureau take an indeterminate amount of time and often cannot be concretely measured. Nor are these officials often able to get the enabling law changed to accomplish the shift in agency direction that they would like. In addition, appointed officials, bringing with them a portfolio of experience from their prior positions (often from the private sector), are convinced that by restructuring the bureau they can increase the efficiency and effectiveness of the public agency. Such changes and "improvements" always appear, ultimately, in formal rules and regulations or some similar lawlike format.

Interest in the effect of organizational structure on the success of public organizations as executors of law actually existed before the time of Max Weber, but no one had formalized the theory. Apparently the structure of the governmental bureaucracy was not an issue of importance to the framers of the Constitution (Wilson 1887); little mention is made of such factors in records of the day, including the record of debates at the Constitutional Convention or the explanatory and laudatory *Federalist Papers* (Rossiter 1961). However, although the founders may not have recognized it, the civil service reformers who became active in the second half of the nineteenth century did. They argued that to improve the efficiency and effectiveness of government, a structural change was needed in public organizations and that such change had to occur through the establishment of law (the Civil Service Act, the Hatch Act, and similar reform legislation). Interest in the public sector can then be traced through a series of reorganization commissions (the Brownlow Commission, the first and second Hoover Commissions, the National Productivity Commission/Gore Report), each of which led to new laws and, in some cases, to the reduction of laws and regulations.

What attention do the developers of current private management theorists pay to the law as they present their models for the successful business organization? Almost none! It is assumed that any business will operate within the general parameters established by society and spelled out in regulatory law (apparently an increasingly risky assumption), and that is all that matters. No further comment on the law is required. Occasionally, when a flurry of illegal activity stirs press coverage, there are calls for more laws to control the activities of business; however, that clamor usually dies away quickly after some initial, and often rudimentary, changes are made in the law. This cycle of events is neither surprising nor malevolent: Our society holds as one of its values that entrepreneurs should be allowed maximum flexibility in carrying out their business so long as those activities are not obviously iniquitous.

Students and managers of nonprofit organizations find themselves in the familiar middle ground between public and private entities. The law is not as central to a nonprofit as it is to a public agency; however, it is important to maintain the organization's activities carefully within the limits circumscribed by laws specifically related to nonprofit operations. The goal of the nonprofit organization is not entrepreneurial or to make a profit. The nonprofit organization seeks to fulfill a mission related to achieving specific public goods. At least two factors are constantly in the purview of those involved in the governance of nonprofit organizations. First, boards, executives, and managers must constantly remember that they

> do not own the public benefit corporation, nor do they have any right to its assets. Their rights pertain to governance and access to information about the organization. The corporation's assets are held in charitable trust for the benefit of the public. (Silk 2005, 72)

Therefore nonprofit leaders cannot operate from an entrepreneurial value set (see Chapter 2). They must operate from a perspective of "maintaining the public trust," and one of the foundations of maintaining that trust is making sure that one is not only operating within the law but that one is also *perceived by others* as doing so.

A second reason for focusing on the law is the fact that nonprofit organizations are given special status—including tax-exempt status on revenues—when they operate within the limitations placed on them by federal statute. Along with the special status comes the requirement that specific rules related to the utilization of funds are followed (such as not passing along profits to equity owners of the nonprofit organization). The special status given to nonprofits is one of the most important symbols of the special roles they play and the high esteem they have in society. Any damage to that perception of dependability cuts at the heart of survival in this highly competitive sector of society, where many voices ask for support both in resources and goodwill.

Efficiency and Rationality

The principles of efficiency and rationality are grouped together here because many social theorists, especially during the first third of the twentieth century, used the terms almost interchangeably. Whether they realized the synonymy of the two concepts is unclear; but their recognition or lack thereof is not important to the major thrust of our argument. In the interest of clarity we will first discuss the two principles separately. Then we shall point out how they overlap.

Efficiency

In its simplest sense, efficiency equals maximization of productivity, or the greatest possible output for the least input. The founders of this school of administrative study came from both industry and public administration, with their ideas being adopted in both sectors. Let us look at the two approaches to this principle and then note the common assumptions from which the founders operated.

The first school, occurring primarily in the manufacturing area of the economy and dubbed *scientific management*, came directly from the research of Frederick Taylor on work methods. Taylor was interested in increasing productivity because he firmly believed that everybody benefited from the result:

> It is perfectly clear that the greatest permanent prosperity for the workman, coupled with the greatest prosperity for the employer, can be brought about only when the work of the establishment is done with the smallest combined expenditure of human effort, plus nature's resources, plus the cost for the use of capital in the shape of machines, buildings, etc. (1998, 11)

Productivity was achieved by applying Taylor's interpretation of the scientific method to the human–machine system in industry. Because little had been done up to that time by way of systematically examining how workers and machines interacted as a single task or process (series of tasks) was carried out, Taylor zeroed in on this most obvious factor.

Industry had moved from the production of goods by tradespeople who made complete items to production by specialization, where items were produced by a combination of machines and workers, each of whom performed part of a complex process that yielded finished items more rapidly and in a more standardized form. The specialization occurred somewhat randomly, however, and no careful scientific analysis of how jobs were done, or how tasks interconnected, had been carried out. Machines were responsible for much of the improvement in productivity; they would continue to account for much of the improvement because there appeared at that time to be an almost infinite potential for technical development. However, little effort went into examining how the weak link in the system—the human—could be made to operate more efficiently, either in conjunction with the machines operated or in jobs that tended to require people to work without the aid of technology (because either machines were not appropriate to the job or they were not yet developed).

Taylor's approach to the study of work soon became known as scientific management. He best defines the central concepts of the scientific management approach at the end of his treatise when he says that

> It is no single element, but rather [a] combination, that constitutes scientific management, which may be summarized as:
>   Science, not rule of thumb.
>   Harmony, not discord.
>   Cooperation, not individualism.
>   Maximum output, in place of restricted output.
>   The development of each man to his greatest efficiency and prosperity. (1998, 141)

By using his version of the scientific method, Taylor was convinced that it was possible to discover the single best way to structure any job or process. With the discovery of this best way, the principle of efficiency was realized.

A second group of individuals, in both the public and private sectors and operating in the early 1900s, was attempting to apply scientific principles to administration, which Luther Gulick defined as "the phenomena of getting things done through cooperative human endeavor" (2003). Whereas politics is concerned with the process of getting elected to office and setting objectives for the country, Gulick argued that "administration has to do with getting things done; with the accomplishment of defined objectives" (2003, 191). If administration is removed from the value-laden field of politics, then a science of administration becomes possible:

> In the science of administration, whether public or private, the basic "good" is efficiency. The fundamental objective of the science of administration is the accomplishment of the work in hand with the least expenditure of manpower and materials. Efficiency is axiom number one in the value scale of administration. (2003, 192)

The way to achieve that efficiency is by "scientifically" examining the structure of organizations, and this is what is done throughout Gulick's and Urwick's *Papers on the Science of Administration* (2003). Questions such as what is the proper span of control for a supervisor, what should be the basis for assigning supervisors over workers, and what principles should control the division, or structure, of large organizations are analyzed throughout the book in one of the first attempts to find the "one best way" to structure organizations to guarantee efficiency in both administration and production of goods or services.

The followers of Taylor, Gulick, and the other expounders of the principle of efficiency are legion (including the proponents of all the newest management theories). Industrial engineering, which has as its goal improvement in efficiency and productivity, traces its beginning in the United States directly to Frederick Taylor (1911). Although the techniques that are used have become more sophisticated, industrial engineers still accept the basic premises Taylor postulated at the beginning of the last century. Likewise, many current students of work flow and office design are convinced that there is one best way to establish the physical layout of a workplace so that all tasks can be completed with optimal efficiency. On a larger scale, information scientists are striving to achieve the greatest possible efficiency in the flow, impact, and use of information; this requires an acceptance of the idea that there is, if not one best way, at least an optimal way to structure both organizations and information systems. The principle of efficiency lives on.

Rationality

The principle of rationality was accepted as an undisputed law by all of the writers just mentioned. When Weber defines the phenomenon that he calls *bureaucracy,* he is simply describing the organizational construct that has been established to guarantee rationality in a highly interdependent world. Taylor, Gulick, Urwick, and the other proponents of scientific management and scientific administration (created during the early part of the 1900s) prescribe rational procedures and structures. Both groups, whether descriptive or prescriptive, accept the idea that what organizations seek and need is rationality. Rationality (the quality or state of having or being based on reason) is central to all organizations in our modern, technological, interdependent world. This idea is alluring in the public sector due to the government's influence on all of society. In the private sector it is believed that rationality and efficiency will maximize profits. And in the nonprofit sector, rationality is supposed to maximize the ability to fulfill the mission of a particular organization.

The fact that rationality is alluring, of course, does not necessarily mean it is easy to achieve. These theorists are overly simplistic in their definition and perception of essential elements. This simplicity is best understood by examining the term *rationality* and by recognizing the narrowness of their definition as opposed to the complexity that exists when the concept is given a full explication.

First, there are two levels of rationality: instrumental and substantive (Weber 1947). Substantive rationality is concerned with the *ends* that an organization attempts to achieve— what are the right, appropriate, or best goals to be sought? Instrumental rationality is concerned not with ends but with *means*, or how an organization attempts to achieve a given end or set of ends. The two levels are both essential, but the types of logic and analytic tools involved differ dramatically. Second, Paul Diesing (1962) defines five types of rationality that currently exist in our society: technical, economic, social, legal, and political. He discusses the social conditions in which these five types of rationality exist—conditions that, as Diesing points out, they partially help to create. Careful consideration leads to even more rational systems based on other premises (axioms) commonly accepted by major active sectors of society. For example, major religious groups in our society have their own rationalities that determine both the substantive and the instrumental decisions of their organizations.

Weber recognizes the need for rationality as one of the central causes for the development of bureaucracy. Bureaucracy is a necessary result of the development of modern technology, with its incredible level of interdependence among all parts of society. Technological interdependence creates a requirement for stable, strict, intensive, and calculable interactions, and "it (bureaucracy) is superior to any other form (of organization) in precision, in stability, in the stringency of its discipline, and in its reliability" (Weber 1947, 339). Like them or not, bureaucracies are rational; and because that principle is central to our lives, the bureaucratic structure and values will continue to exist until a form of organization is discovered that improves on the delivery of this particular characteristic. Even within the information technology organizations springing up today, with all of their storied flexibility in structure and processes, there is still an ultimate need for rationality and for some person or office to have the final say in order to keep all the creative and independent workers headed in some semblance of a single direction. All of this discussion, however, focuses on instrumental rationality—getting things done efficiently—rather than focusing on what should be done, which is determined by the superior powers (politicians or governing boards) outside the bureaucracy. This is especially true in the government, where the legislature, chief executive cadre, the courts, and other powerful players determine what should be done and work to express that ideal state through mandate. Government bureaus then carry out the procedural steps, to the extent of flexibility allowed within the law, to achieve the assigned goals.

On the other hand, students of scientific management and administration prescribe rationality rather than describe it. It is significant that Gulick (2003) referred to efficiency as "axiom number one in the value scale of administration." The use of the term *axiom* was not accidental. Axioms (self-evident truths that require no proof) are a part of science. These theorists believed that by building a full set of axioms, or propositions of obvious truth, administration could become a part of science just as geometry became a part of mathematics. The axioms sought by the scientific administration group were related to the structures of organizations as those structures related to the functions of administration—or as Gulick referred to them, the functions of the chief executive—because all administrators simply fulfilled roles and exercised the powers delegated to them by the chief executive, either directly or indirectly. Through the use of axioms and rationality, many important problems could be solved by finding the one best way to organize; and the one best way was considered the most efficient way (a value judgment). A similar type of logic applied to the followers of Taylor.

The model presented by those advocating TQM also accepts much of the scientific management philosophy of Taylor. "TQM practitioners are expected to focus their attention on work processes rather than on outcome measures and to use scientific methods to improve those processes continuously" (Hackman and Wageman 1995, 325). Scientific methods—such as benchmarking and the establishment of best practices—are used to monitor performance and to identify points of high leverage for performance improvement. Thus although there is continuous improvement in performance, there is a best process at any moment, arrived at rationally by teams of workers and managers through use of the scientific tools at their disposal, and it is to be followed by workers.

The goals behind this rational approach to work procedures ultimately have a specific meaning for business organizations—a very special definition of rationality and efficiency—a bottom-line definition that says rationality and efficiency are measured by how successful the organization is in achieving the goals of profit, size, and growth. Despite a strong argument against short-term measurement of these goals, they still exist over the long term; consequently the success of any organizational change—through TQM, restructuring the organization to take advantage of information technology advancements, or behavioral and attitudinal improvements—is measured by the strength of the corporation within the total market.

Substantive rationality plays a role in the internal decision-making process in the private sector—corporations care about what they make, and in many cases, what effect that product has on society. However, their decisions about what ought to be are biased by the basic assumptions about the goals of businesses. If the product or service makes a profit and is not illegal, then it is okay to carry on that activity, to maximize productivity, and to reap the available profit. Such ends are usually not appropriate for the public manager. There may be vociferous debate about the impacts of alcohol and tobacco products on society, but perfectly legitimate businesses will continue to make those products until they are specifically banned from doing so.

Both government and nonprofit agencies generally cannot be involved in such debatable activities unless there is believed to be a need for an activity in spite of its questionableness; and then the goals of the operations are specifically stated and procedures are stringently regulated.

It is interesting to note that to achieve the bottom-line success that is assumed to be the goal of all organizations, a countertrend to the "one best way" has developed over time. This system, labeled by Peters and Waterman (2004) as a "loose-tight" relationship, which includes a substantive (what we are trying to accomplish) rather than just an instrumental (how we do our tasks) approach, asserts that if everyone in an organization understands and shares the same goals, then managers need not prescribe in detail how to achieve those goals. People will work together to find appropriate ways to accomplish their common cause. (Actually this idea was also presented early in the twentieth century by Luther Gulick [2003] as he discussed the concept of "leading an organization through an idea.")

Advocates of organizational change accept structures and procedures that would be highly questionable in the public sector. For example, they argue that it is rational to break the employees of the corporation into small, independent teams, under management direction, to examine the work being done and to make changes once agreement is achieved on optimal procedures. This step, of course, accepts the basic tenet that the organization should cater to its customers. Both of these eminently rational suggestions for corporations may raise howls of protest if implemented by many of their public counterparts (Swiss 1992). It can also be suggested to private managers that they remain in the business the company knows best and that the administrative structure be kept lean and simple (Peters and Waterman 2004). Such a focus on quality often leads to success and growth for a private company. However, public sector managers often do not have the luxury of deciding such matters; therefore, such advice may be useless to them. The public served, and the services to be rendered, are often decided before the public manager begins to get involved in the decision-making process. Rago (1994) also points out that public agencies often pay a price for success:

> Many companies in the industrial sector undertake new management systems to improve their bottom lines by increasing market share or by improving quality. Increased market share means new customers and new revenues. Conceivably increased revenue enables companies to hire employees and purchase equipment as necessary to ensure that supply keeps up with demand. In many government service organizations, the order of business is opposite that of industry. That is, the more customers the organization has, the less money is available to provide the service.
>
> As the government service organization gains efficiency in the delivery of services as a result of organizational or procedural improvement, it expands its customer base by providing services to citizens who needed services but who were too far down on the waiting list to obtain them. Typically this expansion occurs without a correlated expansion in revenue. (63–64)

Government administrators may focus on process and improve it dramatically,[4] but that does not guarantee more resources or more satisfaction from clients. Still procedural efficiency

---

[4]Any organizational change model assumes top management support, but political officials operate under a different concept of rationality than do business officials (see the later section in this chapter about "Politics and Power"). TQM-based organizational change models focus, ultimately, on economic factors—in the long term businesses strive to increase profits or gain a larger segment of the market. Public officials focus on the short term—the next election. They must get reelected, or the politician who appointed them must. There are few incentives for public officials to focus on management. For example, Joseph Sensenbrenner, the mayor of Madison, Wisconsin, who was committed to TQM in the 1980s, enumerates the tremendous gains made in efficiency within the city. It gained him accolades from across the nation. "But this recognition was not enough to win me a fourth term. Other political factors were more compelling" (1991, 75).

and rationality are the goals of TQM-related management theories and practices, and these two terms continue to dominate public organization debate even when in new rhetorical clothing.

Likewise, nonprofit organizations operate in an environment where improvement of both substantive and procedural rationality is important; however, the governance of these groups is carried out by boards of directors that have as members individuals from outside. These individuals set the goals and determine policy related to procedures; they usually have perspectives of the organization that are colored by these multiple loyalties, and they are pressured by outside forces such as government rules or the demands of donors or grantors. Any decisions about models to be used in managing such an entity must usually be reached through consensus; therefore, clear adherence to any system is less likely to occur. Fluidity or flexibility in applying models or perspectives is often the requirement for leaders in such organizations; and sensitivity to the internal and external environments of policy makers, managers, employees, and volunteers is an essential talent. Ironically these circumstances may also characterize small municipalities where local council members share many of the characteristics, and much the same role, as a nonprofit's board of directors (especially in a council–manager form of government).

Rationality–Efficiency

By closely examining the multiple approaches to organization theory, and by probing for the more basic assumptions on which the approaches are built, we see that although different terms are used, they are used in almost identical ways. Early theorists—Weber, Taylor, Gulick, and so forth—consider only the instrumental level of rationality and define rationality and efficiency identically. According to these theorists, "The efficient achievement of a single goal is technical rationality (Taylor), the maximum achievement of a plurality of goals is economic rationality (Gulick, Weber), and no other types of rationality are admitted" (Diesing 1962, 1). Substantive rationality is irrelevant; goals are established outside the organization or outside the part of the organization being considered. Technical rationality, as developed by Taylor, was specifically geared toward increased output for the same amount of input; that equals efficiency. Gulick, Urwick, and the others who were scientifically examining administration were interested in efficient organization or structures that maximized the managerial functions; good management guaranteed efficiency in operation and maximum return for tax dollars spent. Weber argues throughout his writing that technical efficiency, a term he uses interchangeably with rationality, is the major benefit to be gained from bureaucracy and the reason that bureaucracy developed in the first place. Modern organizational theories in all three sectors discussed here search for efficiency in procedures and use scientific methods to achieve the one current best way of production. The issues of rationality, efficiency, or both, if they are in fact the same, are central to many debates that rage between advocates of different approaches to the study of public and nonprofit operations (Auteri 2003). Attempts to achieve rationality and efficiency must not be downplayed. However, focusing on such concepts inspires us to ask only some of the vital questions, and our horizons must expand, even when we are considering the place of reason or rationality in organizations. Both levels of rationality, and at least the five types of reason mentioned by Diesing, are required to understand or operate in a public service organization.

Psychology and Social Relations

Interest in the social relations of organizations developed in part as a reaction to the formal approaches emphasized by the early students of management and organization and in part as the logical evolution of interest or curiosity by those who desired to examine all aspects of organizational life. The reaction to the formal emphasis, and the ensuing recognition of the fact that informal relations within an organization are equal in importance to the structures and processes established by law or in writing, occurred for at least three reasons. Some manager/scholars such as Chester Barnard (1968) began to point out that both a formal and an informal life existed side by side, if not intertwined, in the structure and functions of any human association, and that both aspects of organizational life had to be considered. At the same time some programs attempting to reach the goals of increased productivity and rationality did not achieve the expected results (such as the Hawthorne experiments—Roethlisberger and Dickson 1970). At least part of the reason for the failure of such efforts was the fact that after a certain point in the development of productivity programs and increasing rationality in structures, the individuals operating in the organizations began to resist further change. To comprehend the attitudes and reactions of employees, it became important to focus on both the individuals and groups in the organizations and how they interacted outside the formal structures and procedures. Finally, with the developing interest and skill in testing and evaluating individuals, and to a certain extent groups, which was hastened and increased by World War II, it became obvious that the informal side of organization theory added a great deal to our knowledge about the total field.

The interest in the informal aspects of organization led to two major categories of theories: (1) those dealing predominantly with individuals, and (2) those concerned with groups. The first can be considered the psychological approach and the second the sociological approach. Each obviously deals with an important aspect of the organization, and each has theories that try to explain and predict what has happened or will happen in organizations as different elements change. After examining both types of theories, we will go one step further and note how by combining the two, a third level of theory appears that adds even more to our understanding.

Focus on Individual Behavior (The Psychological Approach)

The focus on individual behavior is in many ways a continuation of the interests noted by Frederick Taylor as he emphasized the study of individual jobs and how the "man–machine system" could be made to function more efficiently. However, the new focus on the individual recognized an aspect of human nature that Taylor tended to overlook, even though students of psychology were emphasizing it. While Taylor was expounding on the principles of scientific management (which, in part, accepted as its basis the rationality and economic motivation of humans), Walter Dill Scott, a psychology professor at Northwestern University, was arguing that people were not fundamentally reasoning creatures. Scott (1914) argued that the power of suggestion influenced human decisions and that it was therefore essential to study individuals so as to understand their personal makeup, which might, in turn, influence their habits.

The importance of examining the individual's skills and aptitudes (issues also important to Taylor) is recognized by everyone; but equally important is the study of individual traits and attitudes, with the second gaining major impetus from the surprises at Hawthorne. Central to the examination of individual skills and aptitudes is the area of testing and measurement.

Personnel selection, for instance, has been one of the principal areas of interest to industrial and organizational psychologists since the field's earliest days. The goal of those involved in testing and measurement is to choose, from a larger group, the best individual or group of individuals to fill positions within an organization. These decisions are frequently based on tests that purport to measure people's ability to perform specified mental or physical tasks and to measure attitudes and personality traits or attributes that are believed to predict future success on the job. With the evolution of demands for equal employment opportunity, this field in the study of individual behavior has come under increased scrutiny and attack.[5] In this area psychologists cannot lose for winning even though they cannot win for losing: The more tests—usually prepared with the help of psychologists—are challenged, the greater the demand for psychologists skilled in test validation to examine the testing procedures.

Central to understanding individuals' skills and aptitudes and using that knowledge in an organizational setting is a series of questions: What is the impact of the human resource system, with its rules and incentives, on recruiting top-notch individuals, motivating them to do good work and, above all, keeping them? What skills are needed by an individual to communicate, make decisions, and deal with formal and informal pressures on the job? How does an individual interact with new technologies being introduced into the workplace? Organization structure, job design, and even the physical layout of offices have an impact on how individuals interact and carry out their tasks. All of these factors must be considered as managers define "appropriate preparation" for applicants seeking a job—and for those already in the organization, what kinds of knowledge, skills, preparation, and training are required for promotion to higher positions or for the new jobs being created by technological change. In the Hawthorne experiments, carried out at a plant in the suburbs of Chicago, Roethlisberger and his researchers set out to examine the impact of the immediate physical surroundings on worker productivity. But they ultimately concluded that one of the most important factors influencing individual behavior was the morale or motivation of the subject workers. In other words, the most important factor influencing the workers was not the physical environment, but the attitudes that resulted from the workers seeing themselves as important to the ongoing experiment. Even though the Hawthorne research is methodologically suspect in retrospect (Carey 1967; Roethlisberger 1941), it started a line of inquiry that continues today. In the ensuing decades a variety of theories about motivation and about the impact of motivation on productivity have been developed. Indeed a great deal of work continues in this area and is the theme of Chapter 8 in this text. The relationships between job satisfaction, material rewards, productivity, the physical and psychological environment of work, and numerous other factors associated with individual attitudes have been found to be correlated with the success of organizations in varying ways and degrees. In addition, the unique aspects of public and nonprofit organization environments create peculiar challenges for those interested in these sectors of society.

The focus on the individual extends to the examination of the functions and processes of organizations. The functions of management are described in numerous ways; but however described, it is essential to understand how an individual thinks, acts, and reacts to the various stimuli that constantly bombard him or her. When public officials—whether the secretary of

---

[5]In the public sector an examination of the testing and selection process for either police or fire department employees serves as a fine example of the development of, the complexity of, and the challenge to the idea of tests and measurement as the chief tool for decisions about hiring.

state, the city auditor, or the chief clinician in a hospital—have to make decisions, they normally go through a series of steps, and a variety of individual factors determines how they see the problem, who or what influences their thought processes, and what alternatives they believe are possible, which ones are acceptable, and which one is ultimately chosen. These and other issues are examined by psychologists, economists, decision scientists, and others. Indeed Herbert Simon, whose intellectual roots are in public administration, has been awarded the Nobel Prize in economics because of his work in decision theory, which, in part and in a very sophisticated way, addresses the issues just noted. The role of the individual in other management activities, such as objective setting, planning, communication, and coordination, also plays an important part in the theory of the individual in the organization.

Finally, the study of leadership focuses much attention on the individual; considerable effort is expended, through systems such as the widely used Myers–Briggs test, to understand the personality characteristics or traits of leaders and potential leaders. Likewise Stephen Covey writes about "the seven habits of highly effective people" (1989). Do individuals who become leaders have certain traits in common? Are certain traits always necessary in particular types of situations? These and similar questions have emerged as a persistent theme within the psychological approach to leadership, especially as people's career paths in all sectors make them likely to move from organization to organization and from sector to sector throughout their working lives. These issues are addressed further in Chapter 9 of this text.

Focus on Group Behavior (The Sociological Approach)

The common thread in every preceding case is the researchers' interest in the individual. A parallel interest exists in the role of the group and how it affects and is affected by the organization. The informal organization, which comprises groups that form outside or despite the formal structure, plays a significant part in determining the perceptions and attitudes of group members, as well as in establishing the values and norms of behavior. One of the early discussants of the importance of the informal aspects of organization was Chester Barnard (1968), who argued that informal organization preceded the formal in existence. Barnard also pointed out that each type of organization needed the other if both were to continue existing for a significant time because each fulfilled functions that could not be accomplished by the other.

Of course the recognition of the importance of informal groups meant that a new fact of organization life had to be examined if we were to be fully cognizant of all the forces that influence organizations. The most inclusive term for this study is *group dynamics,* which is defined by Cartwright and Zander as "a field of inquiry dedicated to achieving knowledge about the nature of groups, the laws of their development, and their interrelations with individuals, other groups, and larger institutions" (1968, 4). From this research came numerous explanations of and theories about group behavior.

Of special interest is the recognition of the importance of informal groups in establishing values, norms, roles, and status. *Values,* the ideas that are considered to have intrinsic worth or desirability and that are the basic standards and principles that guide action, are greatly influenced by groups (Gortner 1994). Individuals do not create their values in a vacuum; instead values are developed in a group context. Thus the result is inevitably different than it would have been if an individual interacted with groups holding contradictory persuasions. *Norms,* the social rules or authoritative standards or patterns against which attitudes and behavior can be measured, are directly related to group interactions. Without groups, norms could not be developed. *Roles,* the behavior that is expected from an individual by the others in the group, are assigned to the person or position by the other group members. Although a formal role may be spelled out by the official organization chart, job description, and official pronouncements, there is just as assuredly an informal role established by the group or groups with which the individual interacts, and the two roles may or may not coincide. Likewise, groups develop roles that they play in the larger institutional setting and that develop both formally and informally. Finally, the whole idea of *status,* one's position or rank in relation to others, is again possible as a concept only in a group setting.

These and other similar concepts help to describe the workings of the informal side of an organization, which is essential because it has become apparent that formal structures and processes are always matched by informal systems. When, for example, a formal organization chart establishes a hierarchy that spells out from whom an employee is to seek help and who is to evaluate that employee's work (usually an immediate supervisor), a second system develops that allows an employee to go to selected peers for help and advice—usually people with recognized expertise (Blau 1955). Individuals often consider peer evaluations of work performance just as or more important than the opinions of the boss. This type of informal structure is apparent in almost every organizational setting and is a key element in such matters as job satisfaction and morale, as well as efficiency and productivity. Such factors are important for public and nonprofit managers for several reasons. Both environments contend with limitations on the availability of material rewards such as pay raises or bonuses. Public managers often face seemingly torturous limitations placed on them by formal rules and regulations. Nonprofit managers often work in organizations lacking clear rules and regulations concerning worker evaluation; in addition, the importance of volunteers in many nonprofit workforces creates a need for a substantially different set of procedures to generate motivation and goodwill in workers. In both the government and nonprofit sectors managers need to find ways to foster team spirit and reinforce appropriate behavior among employees by using the informal system that exists in every group.

The recognition of this group side of organizational life led to the development of the *human relations school,* which emphasizes the importance of employee morale in productivity. The keynote theme of the school is that successful organizations generally have employees who are happy with and challenged by the organization's environment. One applied approach to the field, first broadly recognized in the 1970s and continuing in many forms, is organization development (OD), in which behavioral scientists use the findings about organizational culture in an attempt to make changes so that bureaus will be better (more satisfying) places to work (and in the public and nonprofit worlds more effective in serving the public). Behind the theories of OD lies a complex set of values that can be summarized here by noting the three essential components mentioned by Waclawski and Church:

> First, . . . OD is fundamentally a data-driven process. . . collected through a process known as *action research.* Second, the OD model represents a *total systems approach* (which targets) organization-wide issues, problems, and challenges. Finally, values represent a third key component to the field. OD is (or should be) a *normative and humanistic values-based approach* to organizational improvement. (2002, 9)

In OD we see the combination of the scientific method with the values of the human relations school. But what is meant by the "normative and humanistic values-based approach"?

Robert Simmons, an advocate of the concept of a "humane organization," perhaps best defines the idea when he says

> The first essential step in provisioning humane organization is to confront the full meaning of groups, organizations, and bureaucracies in the context and fabric of our political, social, and personal lives. . . . The attainment of humane bureaucratic organizations is crucial for the full achievement of human dignity in industrial urban society. The social "payoff" is creative and producing human beings fulfilling their own capabilities, contributing to stable social institutions, and challenging the unknown horizons of human existence and understanding. (1981, 241)

Closely related to the idea of organization culture and its impact is the understanding of leadership in the group context. Success in changing the attitudes and habits of individuals and groups usually depends on the commitment of the leaders: If they support change it has a chance; if they do not support change it probably will not occur. The relationships between groups and their leaders have become an increasingly important aspect of organization theory (see Chapter 9). Social exchange theory, for example, bases leadership effectiveness in a group not on formal position but on the benefits the leader can generate for the group in return for his or her acceptance in the position (Jacobs 1971). In other words, leadership is a role or position granted by the group in exchange for services rendered. This and other similar theories point out the difference between management and leadership, the first being based on position in the organizational hierarchy and the second on power relationships in a social situation (French and Raven 1958).

Group behavior is also a major focus when we examine the processes of organizations. Much effort has gone into noting how decisions are influenced by groups. Irving Janis (1972), for example, has looked at what he refers to as the dangers of groupthink; other students of decision making, attempting to find productive ways to use groups, have promoted the use of group decision-making techniques such as synectics, brainstorming, and Delphi. Likewise, all of the management processes (POSDCORB) discussed by Gulick (2003) or other writers about public management have a group aspect to them. Among the current major prescriptions for improving group processes in organizations are the attempts at creating learning organizations that use groups to constantly evaluate ongoing processes searching for improvements (Senge 1994) and the movement to create teams and teamwork that use many of the informal aspects of group dynamics within the formal organization context (Smith 2004).

Combining the Individual and the Group

Our understanding of organizations increases immensely if we examine the individual or the group and how each interacts with the organization. Perhaps even greater progress has been made by combining the various theories into a more comprehensive network. When we look at theories about individuals in organizations, then add the element of individuals in informal groupings that also are operating within the formal organization, and finally recognize that the formal organizations themselves operate in larger environments where each organization may be thought of as an individual within the larger system, the complexity (and subtlety) of organization theory is brought home rather forcefully. The result of such an interconnected view of individuals and organizations creates an incredibly rich tapestry that allows great detail to be developed at multiple levels. It also lets us see the interrelationships between numerous factors that, considered singly, cannot be explained appropriately or adequately.

In looking back at the models presented at the beginning of the chapter, we find that Weber seems to separate consideration of the individual and the group (although he does look at both). This separation occurs because of the strictly formal view he takes of bureaucracy. Social relations—at least the formal ones—within the bureau are spelled out by the criteria of each job and the structure of the organization, whereas the informal side of the organization is ignored.

On the other hand, advocates of the new management models created in the latter part of the twentieth century recognize both the formal and informal relationships in organizations. They encourage a formal structure that serves as the instigator and modulator of group processes—both formal and informal—that flourish as work teams focus on production processes. Management's job is to guarantee that the total organization, formal and informal, is focused on the major value of the firm (which is to guarantee satisfied customers or to deliver services in a way that serves the public good). By recognizing that productivity occurs through people, this model emphasizes the importance of motivating employees. Those working for organizational change, and improvement in efficiency and effectiveness, recognize that a broad, multifaceted view of the psychological and social principles operating in any organization is necessary. The problem becomes one of figuring out what parts of their ideas can be applied, and how, in the public and nonprofit sectors.

A good example of this more inclusive approach to organization theory was developed in the systems theories of Kenneth Boulding (1956), an economist, and Talcott Parsons (1956), a sociologist. Parsons, for example, argues that

> Like any social system, an organization is conceived as having a describable structure. This can be described and analyzed from two points of view, both of which are essential to completeness. The first is the "cultural/institutional" point of view, which uses the values of the system and their institutionalization in different functional contexts as its point of departure; the second is the "group" or "role" point of view, which takes suborganizations and the roles of individuals participating in the functioning of the organization as its point of departure. (1956, 67)

Other scholars, notably March and Simon (1993), Katz and Kahn (1982), and Thompson (2003), also use the systems approach in their consideration of complex organizations. And this approach continues to be central to many current debates about how to improve organizations.

Currently the areas of organization development and team management are based on attempts to apply all of the theories in a way that will open communication channels, increase trust, and create a more democratic environment in organizations while improving overall productivity. Although there is a fierce debate about the feasibility and propriety of these objectives and about the methods used to achieve them, the debate includes all aspects of organization theory. In a similar manner, the quality/participative management movement includes a broad interpretation of organization theory—which sometimes disagrees with commonly held ideas about motivation and reward, for example—and attempts to maximize quality in performance through the combination of human understanding and scientific methods; therefore, these theories about organizational change and improvement encourage a scope of integration that is beneficial to those wishing to improve their understanding of how public sector agencies work, regardless of what happens to the ideas generating the debate.

Politics and Power

In spite of the differences noted in the discussion of the prior three perspectives, it is in the area of politics and power that the greatest disparity between organizations exists. All organizations have internal political systems and exist in a larger political environment; however, there is a distinct increase in the importance of politics in the short- and long-term success of units as we move from business to nonprofit to public entities. In this area most of the generic or universal models have failed; they simply do not address the issue of politics, and they interpret power as an internal phenomenon usually related to the area of leadership. Weber, when describing bureaucracy, spends little time in discussing power; and to the extent that he does discuss it, internal power relations are defined by the law (or rules and regulations) and its formal interpretation in the hierarchy and in individual spheres of competence. Ultimate power and the relationship of each organization with the others in society are determined either totally outside the organization or are considered by only those few in formal positions at the top of the hierarchy, where such matters fall within their sphere of competence.[6]

The adherents of the more modern models of participative and learning organizations presented in this chapter either ignore the subject of power and politics within organizations or make assumptions about the willingness of those in higher positions to share that power. However, power relationships within the corporation remain basically the top-down system traditional to American industry. Unless the leaders, formal and informal, buy into the organizational change being attempted, it will almost certainly not work. Thus "quality is ultimately a management responsibility . . . attempts to improve quality must begin at the top" (Hackman and Wageman 1995, 315). The success or failure of the performance enhancement programs depends on the holistic implementation of the principles noted earlier. People advocating organizational change through organization development or the use of team management focus on the interpersonal relations of groups, offices, and programs; this interpersonal phenomenon is often referred to as "office politics." Nevertheless power still rests ultimately with top officials, and it is conceded that those at the top of the hierarchy must support the concepts and models being presented or the attempts at change and improvement will not succeed. How to achieve this support by organizational leaders is ignored or seldom directly faced as part of the overall program of change. It is assumed that such must take place, but there is no way to bring this about other than hope that the leaders want the change. The external (especially political) environment is seldom considered as a major factor in the potential success or failure of groups to seek and achieve change.

When we look at nonprofit entities, they once again appear to fall between private and public organizations in regard to the importance of politics. Nonprofit agencies are not restricted in their internal operations by regulations similar to those imposed in the public sector; however, they obviously do not have the freedom of action that exists for businesses because of resource limitations (among which resources government contracts often make up a major part) and the involvement of donors and special interest groups in establishing the goals and procedures of nonprofits. In fact, the changing political environment may be more immediately critical to leaders in a nonprofit group because in an environment where the

---

[6]Private organizations also must pay attention to the political setting. An example that shows the difficulty that may be caused when two sociopolitical systems are involved is the case of international corporations bribing government officials in foreign countries to gain contracts. Such behavior is common in some countries, but the practice—even though taking place in another country and in an environment that accepts the behavior—causes an uproar in the United States and has been declared illegal. Businesspeople therefore must be politically sensitive and astute in their actions. Industries that are regulated by government or that depend on government for much of their business are naturally much more cognizant of the principles of politics and power; however, these are generally seen as external factors, only peripherally affecting internal operations. Review the discussion of the political environment of public, especially government, organizations in Chapter 2.

READING 3–1   On the Primary Role and Essential Importance of Associations in America

Alexis de Tocqueville, early in America's life as a nation, pointed out the importance of what we now call "the third sector" or nonprofit organizations.

In no country in the world has the principle of association been more successfully used or applied to a greater multitude of objects than in America. Besides the permanent associations which are established by law under the names of township, cities, and counties, a vast number of others are formed and maintained by the agency of private individuals.

The citizen of the United States is taught from infancy to rely upon his own exertions in order to resist the evils and the difficulties of life; he looks upon the social authority with an eye of mistrust and anxiety, and he claims its assistance only when he is unable to do without it. . . . (However) there is no end which the human will despair of attaining through the combined power of individuals united into a society. . . .[*]

The political associations that exist in the United States are only a single feature in the midst of the immense assemblage of associations in that country. Americans of all ages, all conditions, and all dispositions constantly form associations. They have not only commercial and manufacturing companies, in which all take part, but associations of a thousand other kinds, religious, moral, serious, futile, general or restricted, enormous or diminutive. The Americans make association to give entertainments, to found seminaries, to build inns, to construct churches, to diffuse books, to send missionaries to the antipodes; in this manner they found hospitals, prisons, and schools. If it is proposed to inculcate some truth or to foster some feeling by the encouragement of a great example, they form a society. Wherever at the head of some new undertaking you see the government in France, or a man of rank in England, in the United States you will be sure to find an association. . . .

Thus the most democratic country on the face of the earth is that in which men have, in our time, carried to the highest perfection the art of pursuing in common the object of their common desire and have applied this new science to the greatest number of purposes.[†]

SOURCE: Alexis de Tocqueville, *Democracy in America* (New York: Vintage Books, 1990).

[*]Vol. I., pp. 191–92.

[†]Vol. II., pp. 106–7.

public regularly shifts its attention (and giving and volunteering) from one hot social problem or issue to another, the ability to respond appropriately to the whims of public interest may be critical to success (Marwell 2004). This requires a high level of political savvy.

Public employees operating at lower hierarchical levels, especially those buried in the heart of their organizations, may not recognize or care much about the political environment because the way they work may be somewhat similar to the way employees work in the private sector. However, when we examine positions at higher levels, or when the behavior of the public organization as an entity is the focus of attention, the political environment becomes an essential element in the equation—which obviously includes a lot of other factors in addition to politics. In this case it is necessary to note the development of theories related to political values and power, which in turn have an impact on resource distribution, coalition building, and political goal setting and decision making. A grasp of these theories is essential to an understanding of the political factors that profoundly influence public organization.

The oldest of the continuous studies of politics—political philosophy—has much to say that is relevant to students of organizations. Herbert Kaufman (1993) points out that organization theory and political theory have produced findings and inferences that are "closely parallel in many important respects." (See Reading 3–3 at the end of this chapter.) The values espoused by the political system also have a dramatic impact on how government administrative structures actually operate. Basic premises about the state and the citizen vary significantly depending on whether organizations with identical structures are located in an authoritarian–communist state, an authoritarian–fascist state, a democratic–socialist state, or a democratic–capitalist state because their objectives will operate quite differently.

Actually we must consider political philosophy when examining either government or nonprofit agencies, although it may be more critical when dealing with the government. Using the U.S. government as an example, we must look carefully at its culture, which includes such factors as (1) the history of government, or how it developed; (2) the role of government as perceived by members of society; (3) the structures and processes considered proper to government; and (4) the values, mores, and habits of the primary actors, especially the elected and appointed officials and the bureaucrats working beneath those officials. All of these factors help to define reality for public officials, employees, and the organizations they represent.

READING 3–2   Government: A Necessary Evil

Presented here are some interesting thoughts from Garry Wills on the prevailing political culture of the United States. Whether you agree or not, he cuts to the heart of the "political culture" debate.

Henry David Thoreau put in extreme form what many Americans want to believe about their government:

> I heartily accept the motto, "That government is best which governs least"; and I should like to see it acted up to more rapidly and systematically. Carried out, it finally amounts to this, which also I believe, "That government is best which governs not at all."*

Government is accepted as, at best, a necessary evil, one we must put up with while resenting the necessity. We want as little of it as possible, since anything beyond that necessary minimum instantly cancels one or other liberty. There is more to this attitude, in our culture, than the normal and universal resistance to authority. Americans believe that they have a government which is itself against government, that our Constitution is so distrustful of itself as to hamper itself. The great Supreme Court Justice Louis Brandeis pronounced, in 1926, that "the doctrine of the separation of powers was adopted by the Convention of 1787, not to promote efficiency but to preclude the exercise of arbitrary power" (*Meyers v. United States*). So common is the assumption that the Constitution is deliberately inefficient that Chief Justice Earl Warren could echo Brandeis in 1965, saying that the Constitution was "obviously not

---

*Henry David Thoreau, "Civil Disobedience," in *Walden and Civil Disobedience*, ed. Owen Thomas (New York: Norton, 1966).

instituted with the idea that it would promote governmental efficiency" (*United States v. Brown*). . . . Our very liberty depends so heavily on distrust of government that the government itself, we are constantly told, was constructed to instill that distrust. . . . Our government does this by checking and balancing itself, each of its three major parts being so equal that deadlock occurs unless all three are brought in guarded and grudging agreement.

I (believe) that the historical and constitutional evidence constantly used in these debates is largely bogus. But that just raises another question. Whence comes this determination to distort the history of our legal system? The distortion began very early, when the arguments of Antifederalists *against* the Constitution were said, only a decade or so after that document's ratification, to be embodied *in* the Constitution. People could stay loyal to the Constitution only if they felt it was structurally disloyal to itself. . . .

(T)o the arguments about the shape of our government and our history are added, always, certain attitudes that tend to come in a cluster, each reinforcing the other. After studying the ways our fear of government has found expression, I was struck by the persistence, through these different forms of opposition, of values that not only recurred but recurred in relatively stable proximity to each other. At times these values uphold liberal positions, at time conservative ones. They can show up on the left or on the right; but wherever they show up, they bring along all or most of their fellows. They can be found in a hippy commune or a modern militia camp. These are all good American values, and it is no wonder that people want to uphold them, especially if they believe (as they often do) that government would weaken or obliterate them. That sincere belief is behind much of the need to oppose any increase in government.

Here are the values we shall find recurring wherever government is opposed: a belief that government, as a necessary evil, should be kept at a minimum; and that legitimate social activity should be provincial, amateur, authentic, spontaneous, candid, homogeneous, traditional, popular, organic, rights-oriented, religious, voluntary, participatory, and rotational.

Values contrasting with those are not polar opposites, but distant points on the continuum of approaches to government—namely, a belief that government is sometimes a positive good, and that it should be cosmopolitan, expert, authoritative, efficient, confidential, articulated in its parts, progressive, elite, mechanical, duties-oriented, secular, regulatory, and delegative, with a division of labor. Ideally, I suppose, government should combine all these values in a tempered way, since the one set does not necessarily preclude the other. But as a matter of empirical fact I find that group after group in our history does treat the first cluster of values as endangered by the second, under siege from them. And a recognition of this fact helps explain things that look merely perverse or irrational unless one sees what values are at work and what are their interconnections.

SOURCE: Garry Wills, *A Necessary Evil: A History of American Distrust of Government* (New York: Simon and Schuster, 1999), 15–18.

The same or quite similar factors are equally important to a nonprofit executive or boundary-spanning employee because the political/governmental culture determines how one approaches the government when looking for collaborative arrangements and how one presents his or her organization to the interested publics who might support the proposed program or collaboration. Even relatively small differences in political culture may create important variations in the way government and nonprofit actors perceive the world, the way they operate in it, and with whom they are willing to cooperate.

For example, political culture has played a major role over the years in attempts to resolve the problem of acid rain in the northeastern United States and eastern Canada. While Canadian officials urge the United States to take firmer action against the industrial air pollution that is responsible for a major portion of the problem, members of the U.S. Congress bitterly complain that Canada should strengthen its own laws. One of the major causes of this controversy is the different ways in which government agencies are expected to behave as they enforce laws. In the United States government agencies are expected to enforce rules to the letter of the law, but only to the letter of the law.[7]

Actions are often opposed in the courts by private corporations that, for whatever reason, wish to drag their feet concerning compliance. On the other hand, Canadian officials argue that their government agencies tend to operate in such cases through persuasion and unofficial agreements, and that therefore the overall level of compliance with air pollution abatement goals is superior in Canada. Needless to say, members of the U.S. Congress doubt this. Much of the difficulty here is not related to the blindness of political expediency; it is simply hard for U.S. legislators to believe that attitudes toward the legitimacy of government regulation vary that much, and, therefore, that organizations can operate that differently on opposite sides of an arbitrary line on a map. To understand the relevant public agencies, their objectives, and their processes, it is necessary to understand the political cultures in which they operate.

Political culture may lead to results that are the opposite of the objectives stated in the law. Weisband and Franck (1975) note that top officials in the United States are guaranteed by the Constitution the right to resign and use whatever nonclassified information is available to them to fight policies proposed by the president if they are convinced those policies are wrong. On the other hand, in Great Britain cabinet officials operate without a formal guarantee of protection if they release information that is damaging to the government. However, in almost every case, politically appointed officials in the United States resign quietly, without taking up the battle against the policy that caused them to resign. Notwithstanding legislation to protect whistleblowers, in the few cases where these officials have protested publicly, they have often been viciously attacked and their public careers ruined, if not their private careers as well. In Great Britain, on several occasions where officials not only resigned but also released information damaging to the government's cause, the officials were not punished for the infraction, and in fact they often found themselves at a later date holding equal or higher posts in the cabinet (Weisband and Franck 1975, 95–98). By looking only at the law or the formal rules and by not understanding the structural and cultural context in which the law and the relevant public organization operate, an observer would be totally bewildered.

The culture of a political system is inextricably bound up with the existing governmental structure. A mayor–council or a council–manager form of government exists in a city not by chance but because of the size of a community, the heterogeneity of its population, and the political values of the citizens in the community. (Smaller and medium-sized communities that are socioeconomically homogeneous tend to have city manager–council governments,

---

[7]There is much disagreement about what the letter of the law is. The constant debate over equal employment opportunity shows the drastic differences that can exist between politicians, civil servants, and the interested public in interpreting a law.

whereas larger and more socioeconomically heterogeneous communities tend to have mayor–council systems.) To a great extent the structure of local government is a formalized statement of the citizens' values as they relate to such vital issues as political empowerment, decision making, communication, conflict resolution, and control. The structure in turn influences the procedures around and in the bureaus established to carry out city policy. Therefore theories about how the political system works, who has access where, and what is considered proper within the political sphere are vital to understanding how public structure develops, how it is maintained, and what are the proper ways for those outside government to try to influence it or work with it. These factors become extremely important to nonprofit entities wanting to be an active part of the politics of the community. Understanding whom and where to approach, what is acceptable as a strategy, and when to interject one's organization into the process is critical to successful interaction with the relevant governments and their agencies.

Pluralist and Elitist Theories of Government

There are two major theories of democratic politics: the pluralist and the elitist. Despite disagreement as to which offers the best description of the political process, both theories are useful in examining how bureaus attempt to operate as actors in the political system.

The pluralist[8] or group theory of politics presents a systematic statement of the role of interests and interest groups in the U.S. governmental system. In a definition commonly accepted by all pluralists, David Truman says, "An interest group is a shared-attitude group that makes certain claims upon other groups in the society. If and when it makes its claims through any of the institutions of government, it becomes a political interest group" (1993, 37). These groups—many of which organize as nonprofit entities—create a mosaic of actors who influence governmental policies and processes, with a balance developing as the power and influence of the groups become known. But that balance is never static:

> The moving pattern of a complex society such as the one in which we live is one of changes and disturbances in the habitual subpatterns of interaction, followed by a return to the previous state of equilibrium or, if the disturbances are intense or prolonged, by the emergence of new groups whose specialized function it is to facilitate the establishment of a new balance. (Truman 1993, 44)

Sometimes public agencies are the recipients of group action; at other times they become actors attempting to influence the policies or processes of other parts of the government—other bureaus, branches of government, or levels of government. In fact, the departments in the national government have been established around a set of related interests, and it is easy to identify the roles played by the Departments of Labor, Veterans Affairs, Housing and Urban Development, Agriculture, Energy, and Transportation in the policy making free-for-all. To the extent that pluralist theory describes reality in our political process, it helps to explain how public organizations decide whom to listen to, what to hear, and how to use information. It also explains many of the tactics used by informal groups, nonprofit entities, and government agencies as they try to influence other agencies or other parts of the government.

---

[8]The pluralist school of politics traces its beginnings to Arthur Bentley (1994). Other major contributors include David Truman (1993), Robert Dahl (2005), and Dahl and Charles Lindblom (1992), especially Chapters 10 and 11.

The elitist theory of politics[9] contends that the prominent actors in the political arena are a few powerful individuals or groups, often outside formal positions in government, who control the rules of the political game as well as the resulting politics and activities of government. Briefly summarized, the elitist theory argues that

1. Society is divided into the few who have power and the many who do not. Only a small number of persons allocate values for society; the masses do not decide public policy.

2. The few who govern are not typical of the masses who are governed. Elites are drawn disproportionately from the upper socioeconomic strata of society.

3. The movement of nonelites to elite positions must be slow and continuous to maintain stability and avoid revolution. Only nonelites who have accepted the basic elite consensus enter governing circles.

4. Elites share a consensus about the basic values of the social system and the preservation of the system. They disagree only on a narrow range of issues.

5. Public policy reflects not the demands of the masses but the prevailing values of the elites. Changes in public policy will be incremental rather than revolutionary.

6. Elites may act out of narrow self-serving motives and risk undermining mass support; or they may initiate reforms, curb abuse, and undertake public-serving programs to preserve the system and their place in it.

7. Active elites are subject to relatively little direct influence from the apathetic masses. Elites influence masses more than masses influence elites (Dye and Ziegler 2003, 5).

To the extent that elites control politics and government as just described, theories about individuals, groups, and formal organizations in the public sector must reflect the realities of the situation. Both government and nonprofit organizations will fall into a hierarchical arrangement based on such factors as which units serve members of the elite (as opposed to agencies serving nonelite groups such as welfare recipients), receive the elite attention and accolades, or in some other way gain the support or fulfill the programmatic desires of those who control the political environment. The tactics used, even the goals perceived as feasible and appropriate, will match the perception if there is agreement that power rests in gaining the ear and influencing the decisions of an elite rather than in coalition and majority building.

Technocratic Theory

A technocratic theory has also been espoused recently that argues that experts, through their professions and their positions of authority in both public and private organizations, actually make most of the important political decisions (Fischer 1990). This theory could be considered a specific derivation of the elite theory just presented. "Technocrats" use their expertise and positions of power to dominate in the policy formulation and implementation process. This occurs for two reasons: (1) The increasing complexity and interdependence of society (technologically and economically, nationally and internationally) create a need for expertise and attention to both broad and specific impacts that are beyond the time—and perhaps intellectual—capacity of much of society; and (2) at the same time, technocrats are aware of

---

[9]The elitist theory of politics is as old as history, but the first presentation of it as a model of local government in the United States can be traced to Floyd Hunter (1953).

their monopoly on information and use this very powerful tool to make their positions secure. Technocrats find it relatively easy to interact, whether in public or private positions, and to arrange public policy to suit their technological needs.

This approach to politics, which postulates an elite theory based on technological training rather than socioeconomic position in society, is further defended by its supporters, who point at the decreasing levels of participation by the general citizenry in the political process. The steadily declining portion of citizens who vote or take part in any electoral activities is offered as proof of this growing lack of citizen interest. According to one group of theorists, the citizenry has lost interest because it recognizes that it is being manipulated by the technocrats; according to theorists viewing the phenomenon from the other side, citizens cannot comprehend the complex issues that they are inappropriately asked to settle through a single vote in an election. In either case political decisions are ultimately made by the military–industrial complex, by the Madison Avenue marketing and advertising group, or by an international conspiracy made up of bankers and industrialists.

There is often a tendency to dismiss the technocratic theory completely because of the pejorative and sensationalistic nature of those at the fringes of this theoretical group. But such a response fails to recognize the elements of truth in the theory. It is easy to miss, or at least fail to give enough credence to, the important questions that are raised by this group of theorists as we attempt to understand how organizations operate everywhere, especially in the public sector. For example, do public employees place their loyalty in their organizations or in their professional associations? Do policy makers and agency administrators make their decisions based on organizational or professional perspectives and information? Are people with technical training and experience able and willing to look beyond their specialties and recognize the social and political consequences of their decisions and actions? It is impossible to comprehend the impact of government and nonprofit agencies and of the many specialists within those entities without understanding the power of technology in society and hence of the technocrats in public organizations.

Public Choice Theory

A more recent development in the field is known as *public choice theory*. This political theory attempts to use economics as the basis for explaining and predicting decisions and actions of individuals and groups operating in the political world. Public choice theory combines decision theory, motivation theory, and economics to improve the "scientism" in the study of politics (and public organizations), which means that both explanations and predictions can be improved. According to this theory, founded by James Buchanan and Gordon Tullock (2004), public organizations—and individuals within those organizations—should be considered rational decision makers who carefully weigh the costs and benefits of all actions where they have a choice. Both organizations and individuals will make choices in their own interest. (See Box 3–2). According to Harmon and Mayer, in "public choice theory, the rational bases for voluntary cooperation are deducible from, to put it baldly, people's selfish nature" (1986, 246). For public choice theorists individual interests are given a priori legitimacy, and the individualistic postulate "goes beyond the scientific concerns of prediction and explanation because it influences their theory of values, as well" (246). They reject a "collective good" and argue that important values

> are not found in moral codes and philosophies, but are instead synonymous with the private wants or interests of individuals. Insofar as collective values can even be considered, they are

---

BOX 3-2 Public Choice Theory's Assumptions about Individuals in a Democracy

---

Individuals:

- Are motivated mainly by considerations of self-interest
- Are rational in the sense that they are able to rank alternative choices known to them
- Have varying amounts of information regarding the probable consequences of pursuing those alternatives
- Prefer an orderly context within which to engage in those pursuits
- Will choose strategies that will maximize their interests

SOURCE: Vincent Ostrom, *The Intellectual Crisis in American Public Administration, rev. ed.* University, Ala: University of Alabama Press, 1974: 551.

---

derived from the coincidence of people's shared interests. These are empirically identifiable, rather than postulated in advance on the basis of metaphysical speculation. Thus "private gain" should be the goal of institutions and legal constraints. (Harmon and Mayer 1986, 247)

There is much debate about the applicability of public choice theory,[10] and the success of this marriage may be in doubt; still it is an interesting effort that portends future theoretical efforts. To the extent that public choice theory successfully describes how bureaus operate— at least in their choice of policy—a valuable addition will be made to our understanding of how public organizations interact within the political system (see Chapter 7).

The Impact of the Political Setting on Public Organization Theory

Some readers may not be convinced that the political setting is important to a discussion of organization theory—even after the argument for this idea in Chapter 2. It may be impossible to convince those who do not wish to agree, but a brief history of the interaction between the political arena and public organization theory may help to make the point. What is important

---

[10]Gerald Garvey represents a major segment of those attacking public choice theory when he makes a special plea to reject it in *Facing the Bureaucracy* (1993). He believes that self-interest is a dangerous tool to use when attempting to guarantee *the public interest* in a society. He argues that our culture, including its democratic underpinnings, developed as a product of *human experience in society*, a group, a larger collectivity than that portrayed in the egoistic model of public choice; therefore individuals can be inspired to identify with larger values related to that society and culture.

No one doubts that worker self-interest may be harnessed to move a public agency, like a private firm, toward efficiency. But more than efficiency is involved in public service. . . . (I)n any large technically based bureaucracy, organizational distance and increasing information costs limit a supervisor's ability to monitor subordinates. To try to remedy this deficiency with a self-regarding rewards-and-punishments calculus would be to reaffirm precisely the wrong values among our public servants. For this reason, I would (give) a nod . . . of approval for the progressives' ideal—an internalized standard, an *ethic of public service*. (218)

to note in the following review is that every time a new historical development occurred, a concomitant new perspective of public organization was introduced. No attempt to prove a cause-and-effect relationship is made here. The authors simply wish to note that the two factors—political developments and public organization theory—were and are interconnected.

At the beginning of the formal study of organizations, for example, the two major theories (those of Weber and Taylor) melded perfectly with the major thrust of the reformers.[11] Reformers were trying to remove the "business of government," as Woodrow Wilson referred to it, from the political arena, at least to the extent that decisions and actions could be made independent of politicians. Second, a major claim of reformers was that by separating politics and administration, efficiency and neutrality could be dramatically improved. The theories of Wilson and Taylor gave rational and powerfully persuasive support to the reform movement, which in turn gave impetus to the development of the civil service system, the anchor point of the reform movement. If we examine the merit personnel system from beginning to end, it is obvious that it almost perfectly matches the bureaucratic system as described by Weber—even if the reformers were not aware of Weber's writings. The structure also allowed specialization and development of expertise as defined by Taylor. In spite of temporary setbacks, such as the refusal of civilian naval employees, during World War I, to allow stopwatches in the armories, the technological complexity of society led to an increasing acceptance of specialization and its focus on efficiency.

With the arrival of President Roosevelt's New Deal, two major political facts of life (the Great Depression and World War II) influenced the development of organizations and the way scholars thought about them in government. For the first time government was expected to be responsible for the state of the economy and to help people who were out of work or had other serious economic needs. The increased charge led to two phenomena, the first of which was the general growth of government and new agencies. Government could not take on all of the new functions that became part of its sphere without growing immensely; therefore the magnitude of governmental organizations became increasingly important. This growth brought an influx of new people into public service, many of whom were well-educated and highly specialized individuals who would be leaders of public organizations for the next two generations. Second, many people coming into government had been trained in political science, economics, history, and other disciplines by scholars who wholeheartedly accepted the politics–administration dichotomy as presented by Woodrow Wilson, Frank Goodnow, and numerous others writing between 1880 and 1930.

The storm of World War II, which broke over the United States with the Japanese attack on Pearl Harbor, also attracted many highly talented and well-trained individuals to federal government positions. After the war many of these people either continued their careers in government or began a routine of moving regularly between government and academic or private sector positions. Not only did government benefit from the infusion of intellectuals, but scholarly understanding of public administration was expanded dramatically because many of these intellectually inclined individuals, upon returning to the more objective and

---

[11]Although Weber's writings were not translated from German to English until the 1940s, it is probable that the intellectual leaders of the reform movement were familiar with his writings and those of his intellectual predecessors. Wilson, for example, notes the impact of German sociologists on the Progressives of his day. It is not possible at this point to debate the questions of intellectual causality and to attempt to decide whether the reform movement was a result of the developments in the social sciences or if the two developed coterminously but independently.

neutral environment of the university, took advantage of the opportunity to thoughtfully consider their experiences as practitioners.

At the same time nonprofit organizations became a larger and more important part of society's attempt to solve many of the social and economic problems of modern life, often working in tandem with government but in many cases taking on particular social issues without any governmental prodding. Both groups, government and nonprofit, developed a quite different view of the public organization. Nonprofit organizations saw involving themselves in politics as a natural part of their task. If political issues were relevant to programs they ran, nonprofit administrators assumed they should be part of the ongoing debate. At the same time a new view emerged of government organizations that included the agencies and their top managers as active participants, by necessity as well as desire, in the overall public policy process. The idea that politics and administration were separate and autonomous functions was put aside, and a more viable theory that recognized the overlap of the two fields became the standard doctrine of public administration. The concepts of efficiency and effectiveness and the belief that public organizations were just like private ones were rethought and enriched by the addition of political theory, both in philosophical terms and in terms of political system mechanics and the roles of public organizations and administrators in that process.

Over time the demands of the Cold War, space exploration, global economics, and technological development in general required a larger and more sophisticated government bureaucracy to carry out the government's work. Even the social programs needed greatly expanded capabilities in information science to keep pace with increased demands for record keeping and for any planning or decision making based on models of facts, trends, and potential outcomes. Thus when examining public organizations, the information and decision sciences firmly established themselves as a major component of a required knowledge base. At the same time nonprofit organizations continued to take on more tasks within society and to grow larger and more sophisticated in their planning, fundraising, and administering of public and social programs. Their presumed independence from government, however, helped them to maintain public trust.

In government, as the bureaucracy grew in size and scope, and the growth replicated the impact of government on everyone's life, the inevitable occurred: People became distrustful of the organizations for which they had clamored. To carry out the functions that the citizens demanded of government, it grew; and as it grew there was increasing fearfulness of big government. Of course the same phenomenon was occurring throughout society.[12] While governmental organizations were becoming more numerous and larger, people saw largeness in the government as a threat to their everyday lives because government played such a central and visible role, especially at the national level.

The complaints about government and its workers are legion, but perhaps three themes can illustrate the attitudes of the citizenry. The first "antigovernment/antibureaucracy" theme is that the public bureaucracy lacks "humaneness." Ralph Hummel describes this attitude with the proper rhetorical inflection when he recites the following litany:

> The bureaucrat has to be a truncated remnant of a human being. Bureaucrats are allowed to feel emotion, but only those emotions specified in the work orders. They are allowed to be

---

[12]Nonprofit organizations are also subject to this phenomenon. As they grow or lose their local roots by serving larger areas, they tend to have to combat a fear of size (and growing impersonality) and to prove they are staying on mission. The three criticisms of larger government can also be translated into language that corresponds to complaints about some larger nonprofit organizations.

responsible for their actions and in fact will be held responsible, but only if the action performed falls within their jurisdiction. The bureaucrat is not officially responsible and will not be held responsible for the action or nonaction of another bureaucrat in a different and independent part of the bureaucracy. The bureaucrat has a will, but it is an officially limited will: It cannot transcend his or her role. It is a will whose origins lie, not in personal conscience, but in machinery set in motion by a superior, the work rules, or the understanding of one's jurisdiction. (1994, 5–6)

Although not everyone expresses feelings about government functionaries quite as negatively and passionately as does Hummel, we can all remember times when "the bureaucracy" (a term often used to denigrate governmental organizations) treated us as if we were dehumanized objects. We also tend to forget the overwhelming number of things the bureaucracy accomplishes and remember only occasions when something goes wrong.

Because of this universal phenomenon of selective memory, the government and its agents were painted with the highly negative image of being inhumane to both its members and clients. To change this situation, several new administrative remedies were proposed. Among these were:

1. Representative bureaucracy, which argued that public employment patterns should mirror, or represent, the composition of the general population because public employees could then better serve all of the people.

2. Affirmative action, which argued that to achieve a representative bureaucracy it was necessary to go beyond strict neutrality, to actively recruit minorities and then discriminate in their favor during the selection and promotion process to make up for systemic and societal discrimination that had worked against them in the past.

3. The new public administration, which advocated active participation by public administrators in the policy process, with a special emphasis on their being surrogate representatives for members of the population not currently represented in the political system.

4. Community participation in public agency decision making and implementation of policies, which insisted that the public could be served well only if they had input into the interpretation and implementation of public policy because only those being served could know what they wanted and needed.

5. Organization development, which was internal to the public bureaucracy and attempted to apply behavioral science to bureaus in a way that would increase openness, trust, and sensitivity so that public agencies would be more humane and democratic in dealing with their employees.

Even though there are relatively vociferous advocates for each of these particular approaches to organizational reform, there are also people who see these steps as overreaching by government to the detriment of the greater society. The debate about such approaches to public administration continues, and none of them has been totally adopted into the mainstream of public organization theory. On the other hand, each has had some important influence in the public sector in that many of the basic premises have been accepted, and some efforts have been made in individual organizations or in the larger public administrative system to accomplish at least some of the goals of the groups. This again is typical of the political arena; as Woodrow Wilson noted more than a century ago, "Wherever regard for public opinion is a first principle of government, practical reform must be slow and all reform must be full of compromise" (1887, 9).

The second antigovernment/antibureacracy theme argues that the structures and processes of government administration have gotten completely out of control. According to these complainants, departments have become the equivalent of independent agencies. Civil servants, who are appointed by the merit system (which operates well in guarding entree to a position but has serious shortcomings in attempting to maintain high working standards), do their work with little guidance from elected officials. The merit system is a complex set of formal rules that has the effect of forcing job performance evaluations of both marginal and superior employees into a vast body of "satisfactory" workers with significant financial protection. Because the employees have special knowledge and expertise about their programs and processes, and because there are so many programs that it is impossible for the general public to watch over them, agencies tend to become their own power bases. The public perceives the agencies as independent and powerful when instead it is frequently private special interest groups that have power, with the public agencies that serve these interests as the visible proof.

Many attempts have been made to increase control over the public bureaucracy and its pluralistic set of interests; some are primarily political (usually on the part of Congress and competing interests), whereas others attempt to use the new systems of information science (usually appointed top officials and technically oriented interest groups or clients). An attempt at increasing control by appointed officials over merit civil servants, which was hoped to improve morale and motivation, was carried out by the Carter administration when it sponsored the Civil Service Reform Act and the establishment of the Senior Executive Service. Another major effort at controlling bureaucracy while improving efficiency and effectiveness was carried out in the Clinton administration's National Performance Review (1993). The second Bush administration has emphasized two approaches to the problem. The first effort is a continuation and intensification of privatization—moving many of the activities carried out by the public bureaucracy into the area of contract services (thus making many public servants contract administrators instead of program managers). This movement has again led to a larger role for nonprofit organizations in carrying out governmental policies. The other Bush administration approach has been to move toward decentralization of personnel functions by giving departments more say over their human resource systems. The framers of these efforts to "reform" the bureaucracy were affected both by current political philosophy and by modern organizational theories—theories about motivation, competition (economic and social), and employee empowerment, for example. It may also be arguable that some important discoveries of organization theory were downplayed in these cases, again by design or default. That is the way of the political world. Nevertheless, it is impossible to believe that the academics and practitioners who designed these efforts were not influenced by their intellectual backgrounds.

The third antigovernment/antibureaucracy theme is that government and its agencies are too large. When all levels of government are considered together, they comprise by far the largest single portion of our economy. By 1980 the rebellion against the size of government was a factor in the election of Ronald Reagan, which brought into the national government people with attitudes that were already having an impact at the state and local level. In 1994 the Republicans gained power in Congress, at least in part, on a platform of reducing the size of government. As a result of this groundswell of public opinion, government faced new questions at all levels. Should we cut back on services, employees, and revenues? Such an effort was carried out for a while, but government expenditures have gone up again over the last few years even though the Republicans came to power on a "smaller government" platform. Whatever the level of expenditure, when services are essential, should they be offered by the government and its employees, or can people be better served by the government's contracting out those functions to nonprofit and private organizations? Although nonprofit organizations have always been active in the delivery of such services, the role of such organizations has expanded quickly over the last few decades. In addition to the level, or amount, of public services delivered by nonprofit organizations, another question has been voiced. What nonprofit groups should be included in fulfilling these public functions? In social services, for example, should "faith-based agencies" be allowed to contract with the government? These are major questions in the political debate swirling around public services. To answer these new questions and still maintain public expectations, employee morale (in all types of involved agencies), and overall program effectiveness, it is necessary to call on every bit of knowledge that has been developed and then to discover innovative ways of applying it.

PUBLIC ORGANIZATION THEORY TODAY

All of the forces just discussed have led to an intense interest in organization theory as it applies to both nonprofit and government organizations—and this discussion is a greatly simplified review of the environment in which both scholars and managers have to work. It is no wonder that so many theories have appeared, given the multitude of perspectives from which to examine organizations. In most cases we have a situation similar to that of the group of blind men who examined an elephant. Any single theory about public organizations may appear to be wrong, even ludicrously wrong, at least in part because the theory focuses too closely on one particular aspect of the organization at the expense of the others. But by examining the full range of theories, we can move toward the creation of a set of perspectives useful to practitioners and students of public management. Most readers of this book are primarily looking for a basis of knowledge that will help them accomplish the daily task of managing public sector organizations. To accomplish this task, all four perspectives presented in this chapter must be considered, and it is the fourth dimension— the political environment of public management—that is usually missing in the study of organization theory. While important, the legal dimension is not so much a central consideration in the private sector. Likewise, while focusing on rationality and efficiency, it is important to recognize that managerial, political, and economic definitions of these terms are dramatically varied by sector or interest. An understanding of these differences and how to either bring them together or accept the impossibility of doing so, and discovering ways to survive in the resulting conflictual environment, is essential to managing public organizations.

In a similar vein, it is not enough for managers in the public and nonprofit sectors to know all about the psychological and sociological theories related to complex organizations. When any attempt is made at application of these theories (and that is the prevalent goal), it is essential to understand the legal, political, and social environments in which that attempt is being made. Public managers, for example, cannot use all of the methods of motivation that are open to managers in the private sector. Nonprofit managers must in many cases comprehend the special challenges that come from trying to accomplish subtle and complex goals with volunteers while seeking financial resources and political support from individuals who have a keen and sometimes single-minded interest in specific causes. Likewise theories about organization, when applied in the public and nonprofit sectors, must be adjusted to meet the demands of the general political culture and the specific political or social actors who are relevant to the bureau in question. Organization theory must address all four perspectives in the controversy if it is to develop a comprehensive picture of public and nonprofit service organizations and how they work.

FOR FURTHER READING

Obvious first reading for any serious student of organization theory is Max Weber, *The Theory of Social and Economic Organization*, translated and edited by A. M. Henderson and Talcott Parsons (New York: Oxford University Press, 1947)—especially Section III, "The Types of Authority and Imperative Control," and within it pages 329–41, which discuss "Legal Authority with a Bureaucratic Administrative Staff." Alongside Weber, in order to understand the political world of the public administrator, one should read James Q. Wilson, *Bureaucracy: What Government Agencies Do and Why They Do It* (New York: Basic Books, 2000). As a presentation of modern popular thoughts about management that differ greatly from Weber, see David Osborne and Ted Gaebler, *Reinventing Government, How the Entrepreneurial Spirit Is Transforming the Public Sector* (Reading, MA: Addison-Wesley, 1992); and Peter M. Senge, *The Fifth Discipline: The Art and Practice of the Learning Organization* (New York: Doubleday/Currency, 1994). For a presentation of the classic view of public administration and the rules governing it, see Luther H. Gulick and Lyndall Urwick, eds., *Papers on the Science of Administration* (London: Routledge, 2003, but originally published in 1937 by the Institute of Public Administration in New York). For an explication of the impact of law on government workers in several societies, see John A. Rohr, *Civil Servants and Their Constitutions* (Lawrence: University of Kansas Press, 2002). The classic presentation of the psychological and sociological aspects of generic organization theory is found in Daniel Katz and Robert L. Kahn, *The Social Psychology of Organizations*, 2nd ed. (New York: John Wiley & Sons, 1978). Numerous "how to" books related to team leadership are constantly appearing in the popular management press. A good recent example is Geoff Smith, *Leading the Professionals: How to Inspire & Motivate Professional Service Teams* (London: Kogan Page, 2004). To see a controversial but thoughtful and interesting discussion of the political culture of the United States and the way it colors debate and action in the political arena see Garry Wills, *A Necessary Evil: A History of American Distrust of Government* (New York: Simon & Schuster, 1999).

For complementary excerpts from the classics, see most editions of Jay Shafritz and J. Steven Ott's (and coauthors) *Classics of Organizational Theory* (Belmont, CA: Thomson Wadsworth); Xenophon, "Socrates Discovers Generic Management"; Max Weber, "Bureaucracy"; Frederick Taylor, "The Principles of Scientific Management"; Robert Merton, "Bureaucratic Structure and Personality"; Jeffrey Pfeffer, "Understanding the Role of Power in Decision Making", William Ouchi, "The Z Organization"; and Daniel Katz and Robert Kahn, "Organizations and the System Concept."

REVIEW QUESTIONS

1. What are the major theses of each of the four pivotal approaches to organization theory? What impact does the fourth (politics and power) have on each of the other three?
2. Given the differences described in the prior chapter, how would the interpretation of these four theoretical foci vary in their application to government, nonprofit, and private organizations?

REFERENCES

Auteri, Monica. 2003. The entrepreneurial establishment of a nonprofit organization. *Public Organization Review* 3: 171–89.
Barnard, Chester. 1968. *The functions of the executive*. Cambridge, MA: Harvard University Press.
Bentley, Arthur F. 1994. *The process of government: A study of social pressures*. New Brunswick, NJ: Transaction Publishers.
Blau, Peter M. 1955. *The dynamics of bureaucracy*. Chicago: University of Chicago Press.
Boulding, Kenneth E. 1956. General systems theory—The skeleton of science. *Management Science* 2: 197–208.
Buchanan, James M., and Gordon Tullock. 2004. *The calculus of consent*. Indianapolis: Liberty Fund.
Carey, Alex. 1967. The Hawthorne studies: A radical criticism. *American Sociological Review* 32: 3–16.
Cartwright, Dorwin, and Alvin F. Zander. 1968. *Group dynamics: Research and theory*. New York: Harper & Row.
Cleveland, Harlan. 1985. The twilight of hierarchy: Speculations on the global information society. *Public Administration Review* 45: 185–95.
Covey, Stephen R. 1989. *Seven habits of highly effective people: Restoring the character ethic*. New York: Simon and Schuster.
Dahl, Robert. 2005. *Who governs? Democracy and power in an American city*. 2nd ed. New Haven: Yale University Press.
Dahl, Robert, and Charles E. Lindblom. 1992. *Politics, economics. and welfare: Planning and politico–economic systems resolved into basic social processes*. New Brunswick, NJ: Transaction Publishers.
Deming, W. Edwards. 2000. *Out of the crisis*. Cambridge, MA: MIT Press.
Diesing, Paul. 1962. *Reason in society: Five types of decisions and their social conditions*. Urbana: University of Illinois Press.
Durst, Samantha L., and Charldean Newell. 2001. The who, why, and how of reinvention in nonprofit organizations. *Nonprofit Management & Leadership* 2: 443–57.
Dye, Thomas R., and Harmon Ziegler. 2003. *The irony of democracy: An uncommon introduction to American politics*. 12th ed. Belmont, CA: Wadsworth/Thompson Learning.
Filley, Alan C., Robert J. House, and Steven Kerr. 1976. *Managerial process and organizational behavior*. Glenview, IL: Scott, Foresman.
Fischer, Frank, ed. 1990. *Technocracy and the politics of expertise*. Newbury Park, CA: Sage Publications.
French, John R. P., and Bertram Raven. 1958. The bases of social power. In *Studies in social power*, 150–67. Ed. Dorwin Cartwright. Ann Arbor, MI: Institute for Social Research.
Garvey, Gerald. 1993. *Facing the bureaucracy: Living and dying in a public agency*. San Francisco: Jossey-Bass.
Gortner, Harold F. 1994. Values and ethics. In *Handbook of administrative ethics*, 373–90. Ed. Terry L. Cooper. New York: Marcel Dekker.

Gulick, Luther H., and Lyndall Urwick, eds. 2003. *Papers on the science of administration*. London: Routledge.

Hackman, J. Richard, and Ruth Wageman. 1995. Total quality management: Empirical, conceptual, and practical issues. *Administrative Science Quarterly* 40: 309–42.

Harmon, Michael M., and Richard T. Mayer. 1986. *Organization theory for public administration*. Boston: Little, Brown and Co.

Hummel, Ralph. 1994. *The bureaucratic experience*. 4th ed. New York: St. Martin's Press.

Hunter, Floyd. 1953. *Community power structure: A study of decision makers*. Chapel Hill: University of North Carolina Press.

Jacobs, T. O. 1971. *Leadership and exchange in formal organizations*. Alexandria, VA: Human Resources Research Organization.

Janis, Irving L. 1972. *Victims of groupthink*. Boston: Houghton Mifflin.

Katz, Daniel, and Robert L. Kahn. 1982. *The social psychology of organizations*. 3rd ed. New York: John Wiley & Sons.

Kaufman, Herbert. 1993. *The forest ranger*. Washington, DC: Resources for the Future.

March, James, and Herbert A. Simon. 1993. *Organizations*. 2nd ed. Cambridge, MA: Blackwell.

Marwell, Nicole P. 2004. Privatizing the welfare state: Nonprofit community-based organizations as political actors. *American Sociological Review* 69 (2): 265–91.

Mosher, Frederick C., and Richard J. Stillman, eds. 1982. *The professions in government*. New Brunswick, NJ: Transaction Publishers.

National Commission on Terrorist Attacks upon the United States. 2004. *9/11 Commission Report*. New York: Barnes and Noble Books.

National Performance Review (U.S.). 1993. *Creating a government that works better & costs less: Report of the national performance review*. Vice President Al Gore. New York: Times Books.

Osborne, David, and Ted Gaebler. 1992. *Reinventing government: How the entrepreneurial spirit is transforming the public sector*. Reading, MA: Addison-Wesley.

Ostrom, Vincent. 1989. *The intellectual crisis in American public administration*. 2nd ed. Tuscaloosa: University of Alabama Press.

Parsons, Talcott. 1956. Suggestions for a sociological approach to the theory of organizations. *Administrative Science Quarterly* 1: 63–85.

Peters, Thomas J., and Robert H. Waterman, Jr. 2004. *In search of excellence: Lessons from America's best-run companies*. New York: HarperBusiness Essentials.

Rago, William V. 1994. Adapting total quality management (TQM) to government: Another point of view. *Public Administration Review* 54: 61–64.

Roethlisberger, Fritz J. 1941. *Management and morale*. Cambridge, MA: Harvard University Press.

Roethlisberger, Fritz J., and W. Dickson. 1970. *Management and the worker*. Cambridge, MA: Harvard University Press.

Rohr, John A. 2002. *Civil servants and their constitutions*. Lawrence: University of Kansas Press.

Rossiter, Clinton, ed. 1961. *The federalist papers: Alexander Hamilton, James Madison, John Jay*. New York: New American Library.

Salamon, Lester M. 1995. *Partners is public service: Government–nonprofit relations in the modern welfare state*. Baltimore: Johns Hopkins University Press.

Savas, Emanuel S. 2000. *Privatization and public–private partnerships*. New York: Chatham House.

Scott, Walter Dill. 1914. How suggestion works on the prospect's brain. *Advertising & Selling* (May): 11, 59.

Senge, Peter M. 1994. *The fifth discipline: The art and practice of the learning organization*. New York: Doubleday/Currency.

Sensenbrenner, Joseph. 1991. Quality comes to city hall. *Harvard Business Review* 69: 64–75.

Silk, Thomas. 2005. The legal framework of the nonprofit sector in the United States. In *The Jossey-Bass Handbook of Nonprofit Leadership and Management*, 63–80. Ed. Robert D. Herman. San Francisco: Jossey-Bass.

Simmons, Robert H. 1981. *Achieving humane organization.* Malibu, CA: Daniel Spencer Publishers.

Smith, Geoff. 2004. *Leading the professionals: How to inspire & motivate professional service teams.* London: Kogan Page.

Spiro, Herbert. 1969. *Responsibility in government: Theory and practice.* New York: Van Nostrand Reinhold.

Swiss, James E. 1992. Adapting total quality management (TQM) to government. *Public Administration Review* 52: 356–62.

Taylor, Frederick W. 1911. *Principles of management.* New York: Harper & Row.

_____. 1998. *Principles of scientific management.* Mineola, NY: Dover Publications.

Thompson, James. 2003. *Organizations in action.* New Brunswick, NJ: Transaction Publishers.

Truman, David. 1993. *The governmental process: Political interests and public opinion.* 2nd ed. Berkeley: Institute of Governmental Studies, University of California.

Waclawski, Janine, and Allan H. Church, eds. 2002. *Organization development: A data-driven approach to organizational change.* San Francisco: Jossey-Bass.

Waldo, Dwight. 1978. Organization theory: Revisiting the elephant. *Public Administration Review* 38: 89–97.

Weber, Max. 1947. *The theory of social and economic organization.* Trans. and ed. A. M. Henderson and Talcott Parsons. New York: Oxford University Press.

Weisband, Edward, and Thomas M. Franck. 1975. *Resignation in protest.* New York: Grossman Publishers/Viking Press.

Wills, Garry. 1999. *A necessary evil: A history of American distrust of government.* New York: Simon & Schuster.

Wilson, James Q. 2000. *Bureaucracy: What government agencies do and why they do it.* New York: Basic Books.

Wilson, Woodrow. 1887. The study of administration. *Political Science Quarterly* 2 (June): 197–222. In *Classics of public administration.* Ed. Jay M. Shafritz and Albert C. Hyde. Oak Park, IL: Moore Publishing, 1978.

READING 3–3   Organization Theory and Political Theory

If two men of similar talents, identical training, shared values, and common interests were to study the same phenomena it would not be at all remarkable if they approached the phenomena in the same way, described them in the same terms, employed the same logic in analyzing them, drew the same conclusions from them, and formulated the same theories about their causes.

If, however, two men of similar talents but of rather divergent training, professing differing objectives, and displaying varied (perhaps even conflicting) concerns were to pursue studies of phenomena each believed to be quite distinct from the other's field of inquiry, it would be most astounding if their findings and inferences should turn out to be closely parallel in many important respects, particularly if there were little evidence of communication between them.

That is why the parallels between political theory, probably the oldest of the social sciences, and organization theory, perhaps the newest such discipline, are so totally unexpected. If there is any conscious agreement between the two fields, it is on their separateness from each other: Political theorists and organization theorists alike seem to take for granted the impossibility of encompassing within a single theoretical framework propositions about states—that is, the relation of governments to subjects, and the relations of governments to each other—and propositions about other forms of human association. In the literature on organization theory, one rarely finds references even to contemporary political theorists and almost never to those who wrote in the past. By the same token, political theorists rarely seem to find anything relevant to their interests in the work of students of organization. Measured by the acknowledged exchange of information between the disciplines, the gulf between them is wide and seldom bridged.

Perhaps such a gulf is inescapable. Political theorists draw heavily upon history, philosophy, and personal experience for their ideas and evidence; organization theorists rely heavily upon sociology, social psychology, economics, and, when possible, on controlled experimentation. Political theorists are frankly normative; organization theorists generally believe their work is value-free. Political theorists deal willingly with the intangible aspects of human associations, for it is difficult to measure the outputs of governments and governmental agencies; organization theorists are more at home with organizations producing tangible products and measuring their performance ultimately in terms of profit. The fields do seem to have quite different traditions, methods, goals, and subject matters.

But all this merely makes the similarities in the problems they investigate and in their findings more surprising and intriguing.

I

For example, both organization theorists and political theorists encountered the same enigma: In order that the human systems may come into being and continue, men often have to do, at the behest of others, tasks that are unpleasant or even hazardous (such as working on assembly lines or going to war), and must refrain from doing what they would greatly enjoy (such as helping themselves to the property of others or saying whatever they please wherever and whenever the spirit moves them). What accounts for obedience and docility entailing such self-sacrifice, self-restraint, self-denial, without which neither states nor other associations could long survive?

Political philosophers and organization theorists have offered essentially the same range of explanations: the rationality of men and the conditioning of men's minds.[*]

Because men are rational, they can calculate what they would lose if everyone were to follow his own impulses and preferences without restraint. They can also see that collective action will be taken against individuals who disobey. Out of fear of the consequences, they

---

[*]A third explanation, offered initially by political philosophers of classical antiquity, was that some men are by nature followers and others are by nature rulers. The followers obey because it is their nature to do so, just as leaders command because that is their nature. This argument has few defenders among contemporary political theorists, and it is seldom articulated by organization theorists. But one may wonder whether the batteries of personality and aptitude and intelligence tests used for selecting executives do not rest ultimately on the assumption that there are "natural" leaders who should be identified, separated from the "naturally" subservient mass, and elevated to their "natural" managerial roles.

submit. They can calculate, too, the advantages they may gain from organized life and activity. They can see that the gains usually outweigh the costs. Out of hope for the benefits, then, as well as out of fear, rational men yield to the will of others.[†]

At the same time, according to many political and organization theorists, men obey because obedience to certain commands from certain sources is a conditioned reflex. Even in infancy, every individual is introduced to the exercise of authority; maturation is in many ways a process of learning when to obey, whom to command, and under what circumstances to do either. That is, from his social environment generally, and also by virtue of the deliberate drill and indoctrination to which he is subject, every man is prepared for his social roles. He comes to yield to others because he learns it is right and proper to do so, and he may even come to cherish his submission. The will to obey is implanted in him; depending on the discipline one draws upon for appropriate language, he is educated, indoctrinated, trained, socialized, acculturated, programmed, or brainwashed.

Interestingly enough, political theorists have from the very beginning made more strenuous efforts to incorporate the nonrational (i.e., the conditioned) elements of men's behavior into their hypotheses than have the organization theorists. For men are born into political systems, and the possibilities of withdrawal are much more limited. It is not clear that joining or remaining in a political system is really a matter of rational choice at all, except in isolated instances. Organization theorists, on the other hand, deal more extensively with associations that men presumably choose to enter and may leave at any time. To explain membership and all it entails, students of organization lean toward a rather literal application of social contract theory and utilitarianism; many 18th- and 19th-century political philosophers, who employed these concepts as metaphors to aid in understanding the rational component of behavior, would find little in most modern organization theory with which to quarrel. And some organization theorists would doubtless be surprised to discover how many political philosophers in ancient and medieval times were aware there were social norms and group loyalties that a ruler dared not violate without risking extensive disobedience.

At any rate, more or less independently of each other, drawing in different ways on different bodies of experience, political theorists and organization theorists have dealt in very similar fashion with the obedience of man to man.

II

They have also dealt similarly with organizational structures for the achievement of coordination. For purposes of this discussion, coordination means ordering the direction, volume, and timing of flows of activities, goods, and services so that the functioning of one element in a system at least does not prevent or negate or hamper the functioning of other elements,

---

[†]This reasoning underlies most social contract philosophies of the origins of civil and political society. The emphasis was placed in some cases on escape from the risks and uncertainties of anarchy (as in Hobbes and Locke), in others on ascension to a higher, richer, distinctively human and civilized life (as in Rousseau, whose logic, in turn, parallels that of classical political theory). The hypothesized reasoning in men's decisions to form or join groups in which they must then submit to others is not far removed from the analysis by J. G. March and H. A. Simon (1957, Chapter 4) of individual calculations regarding "the decision to participate" in organizations. See also Simon's assertion that a distinctive feature of organization theory is its treatment of joining an organization as an "all-or-none choice of participation or nonparticipation" (1957, 74; Chapters 10 and 11).

and at best facilitates and assists the functioning of other elements. Coordination is not always a goal of system designers; the separation of powers, for example, encourages some contradictions and deadlocks in order to protect other values. But it is often among the principal values, and practically never is a matter of total indifference. And when political theorists and organization theorists discuss methods of promoting coordination, they end up in much the same positions.

Fundamentally, coordination is accomplished by two processes: central direction, which means that the activities of the elements of a system respond chiefly to cues and signals from some common source, and reciprocal relations, which means that the elements respond to cues and signals from each other. Every system employs some blend of the two processes. Moreover, the systems are not mutually exclusive; an increase in reliance on one does not necessarily produce a decrease in the other. On the contrary, effective central direction often permits a higher degree of reciprocal cueing, as in a well-trained platoon, and vice versa. Whatever the blend of modes of coordination and whatever the general level of coordination in any system, these may be explained in terms of the relative weight assigned to each of the two underlying processes.

Political theorists who believe men are inclined to take advantage of one another tend to stress central direction as the best means of coordinating them. Without an overriding central figure, according to them, any system breaks down in disorder, confusion, and internal warfare. Hobbes, of course, presented this argument in its purest, most logical form. On the other side, philosophers who assume the interests and tendencies of men are harmonious emphasize the possibility and desirability of coordination through reciprocity, and regard central direction as an exploitative or disturbing factor in what would otherwise be a highly coordinated system distributing maximum satisfaction to all its members. The anarchists, both Marxist and non-Marxist, pushed this reasoning to its logical extreme. It matters little for this discussion whether the extremists on both sides meant their doctrines to be taken literally or as analogies for the sake of clarity and vigor of statement. They bracketed the range of possibilities. In the history of political thought, not only the extremes, but virtually all conceivable intermediate positions, have at some time or other been advanced or defended.

During most of the short history of organization theory, few theorists seriously questioned the premise that central direction (expressed structurally as a hierarchy of authority because of the need of leaders to delegate formal powers and because of the assumed inability of men to supervise directly more than a small number of colleagues) is the primary method of achieving coordination; indeed, hierarchy and organization were sometimes treated as almost synonymous. Yet very early some questioning voices were heard, particularly after experimental studies in the sociology of industry drew attention to the responsiveness of workers to cues and signals emanating from sources other than (and sometimes hostile to) the designated managers of the firms examined. Mary Parker Follett, a political scientist of Pluralist persuasion, became well known to students of organization for her advocacy of "power with rather than power over" and for her criticism of "the illusion of final responsibility." Later on, Argyris and Thompson and others would search explicitly for a pattern of organization that is nonhierarchical. . . . It would be grossly inaccurate to equate these organizational analysts with the anarchists, but there can be no question that organization theory has begun to display an awareness of a range of positions on the central–reciprocal scale that political philosophers have explored extensively for centuries.

I do not intend to imply that political philosophy is somehow superior to organization theory, or that organization theory is a mere branch of the history of political thought. My object in pointing out similarities between their treatments of coordination is simply to demonstrate that these seemingly unrelated disciplines confront common problems in common ways.

III

Another such problem is the reconciliation of individual or other narrow objectives with the objectives of the collectivity. Political theorists discuss it in terms of special interests as against the general or public interest. Organization theorists speak of personal or subgroup goals vis-à-vis organizational goals. But the issues are the same.

In both fields, the dominant opinion seems to be that every collectivity is in some sense goal-seeking, or purposive. That is, there is some general interest or organizational goal shared or at least acknowledged by nearly all the participants in the system, and although the overarching purpose is accomplished by the labor of individuals, it is distinct from the goals or interests of individuals; rather, it is viewed as an attribute of the system as a whole. There is little agreement on the specifics of the general interest, and even a given commentator may switch from one to another interpretation as conditions change. (Implicitly, however, one goal can be discerned in every interpretation: the survival of the system.) Yet, although students of states and of organizations may never arrive at a consensus on exactly what the shared interests of human associations are, many of them tend to take it for granted that one exists for every human association.‡

A substantial number of political theorists, on the other hand, have taken the view that virtually every definition of the public interest is but a reflection of the personal interests of the definer, and consequently, the only realistic way to understand the performance of a system is to construe its output (or its policies) as nothing more than the resultant of the interplay of many special interests. The representatives of each interest may invoke the symbol of the public interest as an honorific, perhaps even with sincere conviction that the actions they espouse are better for the system and all the members of the system, but what is actually

---

‡Plato and Aristotle, for example, saw as the purpose of the city–state the promotion of the highest moral development of its citizens. For Hobbes, the end of government was the preservation of order. For Locke, it was the protection of "natural rights," such as the right to private property. For the Utilitarians, it was to produce the greatest good for the greatest number. For the early liberal economists, it was to furnish just enough service and regulation to permit the reciprocal processes of the marketplace to operate effectively. In all these instances, selected haphazardly from the broad array of goals postulated in political thought, the existence of a common purpose and interest is axiomatic.

The same is true of most contemporary organization theory, although the specification of common interests is rarely articulated as explicitly as in political philosophy. Rather it is assumed that every human association has some goals shared by all its members, and can be understood only in terms of those common purposes; for example, in H. A Simon, D. W. Smithburg, and V. A. Thompson, purpose and cooperative action are described as the "two basic processes of what has come to be called administration. . . . Administration can be defined as the activities of groups cooperating to accomplish common goals" (1950, 3). Similarly, P. M. Blau and W. R. Scott declare that what organizations "all have in common is that a number of men have become organized into a social unit—an organization—that has been established for the explicit purpose of achieving certain goals" (1962, 1). And C. Argyris hypothesizes "that organizations are intricate human strategies designed to achieve certain objectives," and that the objectives of any organization include "achieving its goals (intended consequences)" (1960, 10–11).

decided and done is the product of negotiations and understandings among specialized groups and individuals.

Among organization theorists, the counterpart to this point of view is seldom advanced even tacitly, let alone explicitly; it is distinctly a minority position. Barnard, however, comes close to it. Although he discusses organizational purposes at length, and attributes great importance to them, they are not central to his analysis. He defines formal organizations without referring to goals, and he describes them largely in terms of individual motivations and objectives coordinated with each other through an "economy of incentives." The "absolute test" of efficiency is survival of the organization. An organization is thus portrayed as a kind of marketplace in which each man pursues his own goals by offering a contribution in return for those inducements (selected from the range of inducements provided, consciously or unwittingly, by the system) that appeal to him. The enterprise is an arena in which each participant offers his wares and services in exchange for what he can get. From the elaborate network of agreements, accommodations, and behaviors come products, wages, salaries, profits, prices, dividends, interest, taxes, working conditions, and all the other outputs of a complex system. Managers, workers, suppliers, customers, stockholders, creditors, competitors, government regulators, consultants, academics, and others may all see different transcendent purposes in the undertaking, so that its ends are in a sense the sum of all the special purposes. To this extent, this view resembles in many respects the view of the state espoused by the political theorists mentioned above. What is sometimes referred to as a collective purpose is merely the resultant of a constantly shifting adjustment among individual and subgroup purposes.

Over the relationship of private interests to the general interest, organization theorists and political theorists have divided into similar camps. Again, the resemblances between the fields are impressive.

IV

The foregoing illustrations do not exhaust the parallels between organization theory and political theory. But they are probably sufficient to establish the point of departure for this discussion—namely, that striking similarities have developed in two disciplines that seem to be quite different in their interests and methods.

Why should this occur? Why should two fields of study with such discrepant premises and perspectives converge?

Perhaps it is because the discrepancies are, after all, merely the distinctions between different species of the same genus. When all is said and done, they both treat phenomena that encompass vast areas, if not all, of human life. We are all members of at least several organizations, and organizations give characteristic content and general form to our lives. Moreover, states, governments, the branches and agencies of governments, political parties, and interest groups are organizations like other organizations even though they have their unique attributes. What aspect of civilized existence then lies outside the scope of organization theory?

At the same time, every organization is sometimes construed as a political system, with all the problems of leadership, policy formation, succession, strategy, rivalry, resistance, revolution, and influence that this implies. If organizations are an all-embracing subject of inquiry, politics is an equally comprehensive theme. To be sure, organization theorists tend to avoid political institutions in searching for data, and political philosophers tend to concentrate on those institutions immediately associated with public governments. But they may end with strong similarities because they are both addressed to phenomena permeating the whole of human affairs. Fields that take so much for their province must have far more overlap than is immediately obvious.

Furthermore, they both start from normative bases. Political theorists were historically engaged in a quest for the ideal political system; organization theorists began by seeking "the one best way"—the most efficient way—to organize production and distribution. There are probably some in both disciplines who still believe such ideal arrangements, superior to all alternatives under any conditions and at any time, are attainable; most contemporary theorists, I believe, now adopt a relativist position, holding that the definition of the ideal changes as circumstances change, and perhaps even that a wide variety of organizational and political patterns may satisfy equally well these requirements of any particular definition. At any rate, men in both fields set out to discover the "laws" or "principles" governing social behavior so as to formulate proposals for improvement consonant with the constraints imposed by reality. Sometimes they try to sharpen their thinking by reasoning from admittedly oversimplified hypotheses, such as man in a state of nature or completely rational man. Eventually, however, they complicate their models by adding variables that render the hypotheses better approximations of the real world. (Such variables are more often discovered by nonnormative research of an historical or experimental kind than by intuition.) Conceivably, the fields may come to resemble each other because they have parallel normative underpinnings.

But the explanation of the resemblances may not lie in the character of the disciplines at all; perhaps it is to be found rather in the nature of the world the disciplines purport to describe. The convergence could result from the existence of such pronounced and persistent regularities in large-scale human associations that no matter which such associations one examines and what approach one adopts, the sum of the findings of each set of observers will inevitably be much the same as those of any other set. When all the blind men compare their notes, they do end up with a description of an elephant, and the description by each team of blind men will not differ materially from the description produced by any other team, because, after all, it *is* an elephant they are studying. The consensus of two relatively insulated fields, when the whole range of their content is reviewed, lends corroboration to the impression that our ideas about organizations and politics have a substantial degree of validity. . . .

SOURCE: Herbert Kaufman, American Political Science Review 58 (March 1964):5–14. Copyright 1964 by The American Political Science Association. Reprinted with permission from the publisher and the author. Only selected footnotes have been included, and citations have been changed to the format used in this text. If interested, the reader should look at Kaufman's numerous citations supporting his argument in the original essay.

REFERENCES

Argyris, Chris. 1960. *Understanding organizational behavior*. Chicago, IL: Dorsey Press.
Blau, Peter M., and William R. Scott. 1962. *Formal organizations*. San Francisco: Chandler & Sharp Publishers.
March, James G., and Herbert A. Simon. 1957. *Organizations*. New York: John Wiley & Sons.
Simon, Herbert A. 1957. *Models of man*. New York: John Wiley & Sons.
Simon, Herbert A., Donald W. Smithburg, and Victor A. Thompson. 1950. *Public Administration*. New York: Alfred A. Knopf.

Editor's Note

In this essay Herbert Kaufman argues for a position shared by the authors (although we do not necessarily agree with all of the points that he makes). The argument seems to be especially true when one is looking at public organizations, which must operate in a political environment. When reading any such essay, however, it is important to understand the perspective from which the author proceeds when writing; therefore, it is important to consider the following questions:

1. What basic assumptions and political values are accepted by Herbert Kaufman as he argues for the overlap of political and organizational themes?
2. Come back to this essay after reading Chapters 8 and 9 of this book. How do Kaufman's assumptions about people in organizations differ from those of behaviorists such as Fiedler, Hersey and Blanchard, Porter and Lawler, or Vroom, whose theories and models are presented in those chapters?

Chapter 4

Structure

We trained hard but it seemed that every time we were beginning to form up into teams we would be reorganized. I was to learn later in life that we tend to meet any new situation by reorganizing, and a wonderful method it can be for creating the illusion of progress while producing confusion, inefficiency, and demoralization.
Gaius Petronius the Arbiter (~AD 27–66)

The quote is attributed to Petronius the Arbiter, who died in AD 66; yet it could be the comment of most employees in large organizations. Reorganization often is seen as largely cosmetic and negative—sometimes improving organizational operations, but perhaps more often serving political or ideological ends or portraying policy makers and leaders as innovative administrators curing intractable problems. So though useful on occasion—that is, when the existing structure impedes rather than assists the organization in achieving its mission— reorganization is no magic pill.

In simplest terms *reorganization* means realigning subunits within an organization or rearranging boxes on an organization chart such as the chart in the cartoon illustrating this chapter. The fact that we have practiced reorganization for at least two thousand years—long, long before inventing the "org chart"—says two fundamental things. First, *the structure of an organization is important*; second, *the structure is ours to shape*. The purpose of this chapter is to examine traditional and contemporary models of organizational structure with a view that, to a large degree, we can prescribe appropriate organizational forms to suit different organizational needs.

As a verb, *organize* pertains to process. As a noun, *organization* pertains to form. Reorganization focuses on an organization's form or structure. More recently a whole series of related words has been used to describe improvements in organizations. *Reorganizing* is just one of these words; *centralizing, decentralizing, regionalizing, consolidating, downsizing, privatizing, reengineering, redesigning,* and *reinventing* are also part of this lexicon (Carr, Littman, Condon 1995), as are *contracting out, merging, collaborating,* and *partnering.*

THE VALUE OF MODELS

Many scholars have identified reasons behind reorganizations such as breaking up dysfunctional patterns of organizational behavior, emphasizing a new or modified mission, following management fads, meeting political needs, and rewarding excellent performers by providing increased promotional opportunities in management (Cohen 1988, 57). Lester Salamon (1981) and Guy Peters (1994) are among those who theorize about why reorganizations occur. Peters notes that most theories lack the ability to predict the outcome of reorganization. The theories are based on four types of explanatory models. *Economic models* posit that actors will act rationally to maximize the size of their organizations. *Political science/public administration models* suggest that reform and reorganization are related to some external change in the environment such as a shift in public opinion, an innovation, a new technology, or an economic change. Related *institutional models* assume that at least some aspect of the change comes from within the organization; the culture helps create the need for change, and then the change influences further adaptation (see Chapter 10 for an expanded discussion).

The final model, *population ecology*, is one of the most interesting, drawing on analogies from science. Organizations are viewed as organisms having birth, life, and death cycles. They interact with other organisms to establish their niches. Over time the collective group of organizations, rather than individual organizations, will adapt to a changing environment. Some individual organizations will win and others will lose. The applicability of this approach is obvious to anyone who has noticed that older organizations seem to have more rules and policies and larger units (Mintzberg 1979, 227, 233) compared to younger organizations. This model becomes more tenuous if we apply the idea of death to the life cycle of organizations because few public organizations actually "die." More often they are merged or absorbed. Critics argue that mergers (and voluntary closures of organizations that have accomplished fixed goal missions) do not comfortably fit the population ecology model because mergers and voluntary closures are not equivalent to the death of most organisms.

Peters (1994, 166) finds that all these models, rather than predicting the type of change, focus on what may happen once reorganization is complete. The models' value, even given their limitations, is that (1) ecological and political models examine interrelationships between organizations and their environments and (2) institutional and economic models examine roles and relationships of organizations and individual stakeholders.

Although Peters leaves us wishing for better explanatory modeling, Salamon (1981) avoids the issue of predictive power, instead approaching organizational structure (and the tool we call reorganization) from an analysis of purpose. Any reorganization is purposive, with those who support and influence a particular reorganization having an end state in mind (Peters 1994). Salamon postulates that based on goals, reorganizations can be subsumed into no more than three categories—improving efficiency, improving program and policy effectiveness, and serving tactical or political ends:

1. *Efficiency,* the most common goal for reorganization, rests on the idea that economies of scale are lost because of duplication of effort and the potential for working at cross-purposes. This creates unnecessary costs for citizens in time and money. This goal is probably most difficult to achieve because ultimately administrative cost savings are limited, efficiency can be elusive to measure well, and redundant systems are essential for vital functions (Landau 1973). Of course there are one-time savings when individuals are laid off or offices closed. Increasing centralization often means a trade-off must occur between responsiveness and efficiency. Ultimately Salamon believes that substantially increasing efficiency may actually require legislation to change policies. Changes in, say, health care or child welfare costs are more likely to occur when and if fundamental programs or policy changes occur—not simply through reorganization.

2. Improving *program/policy effectiveness,* often by gathering programs together to implement policy, focuses on the output side—in particular, on outcome. Programs relevant to a particular issue are combined. As Salamon notes, the Hoover Commission (1949) on reorganization pointed out the importance of placing programs together for policy effectiveness. Grouping programs can increase mechanical coordination and reduce interest group pressure on isolated programs. By the same token, organizationally separating some programs or aspects thereof may improve overall program effectiveness. Examples might be serving mainstream and special needs constituents through separate organizational mechanisms or placing enforcement and assistance aspects of a program in separate organizational subunits to prevent one activity overshadowing the other. A problem is that effectiveness may be in the eye of the beholder. Grouping related programs does not give officials authority to

change purposes, so the underlying problem may remain. Reorganization is not and cannot be an "alternative to policy [change]" (Salamon 1981, 493).

3. *Tactical or political ends* is Salamon's third category, which he characterizes as a residual category. Reorganizations might occur to downgrade or eliminate a person or program or as a symbolic initiative to convey understanding of problems. Laurence J. Peter and Raymond Hull (1969) label the results of such reorganizations as "lateral arabesques" when they result in moving a key employee to another part of the organization and "free-floating apexes" when the managerial employee is left in place but the organizational unit is moved or disbanded. Reorganizations might also occur to gain access, representation, or visibility for a particular interest. In the latter case, a new organization might break off from a larger one. Guy Peters (1994) identifies these cases as those in which government is seen as ungovernable or overloaded. It also includes reorganizations that yield layoffs and contracting out of government functions.

These purposes are similar for nonprofit organizations, though the theory relating to nonprofits is less fully developed (Young, Bania, and Bailey 1996) than in regard to government organizations.

Mergers—the combining of two or more organizations—can be considered a major form of reorganization. Among nonprofit organizations, mergers can be as controversial to boards, staffs, and client constituencies as are mergers and major reorganizations in government. Nonprofit mergers take place for similar reasons: to improve efficiency and effectiveness but also to increase resources and reduce competition among nonprofits (Oster 1992; 1996). Mergers that threaten original missions can be among the most difficult. Women's colleges and traditionally black colleges have had difficulty merging with their opposites. Although the Young Men's Christian Association (YMCA) and Young Women's Christian Association (YWCA) have many similar programs, they have different missions and rarely merge. Effectiveness depends on the stakeholders.

A merger or reorganization in government is subject to the same controversies, but doubled. It is controversial because of the need to meet constituency, special interest group, and employee concerns, but even more so because of the political process normally used to enact substantial reorganizations. Consider the difficulty of merging small community schools. So political are closure and reorganization of defense bases that congresses and presidents turn to commissions to make the hard decisions.

The recently created U.S. Department of Homeland Security (DHS) illustrates some of the reasoning behind reorganizations. Its official purposes are to prevent terrorist attacks within the United States, reduce U.S. vulnerability to terrorism, minimize damage of an attack, and assist in recovery from terrorist attacks. The freshly formed department carries out this mission by (among other things) centralizing terrorist information gathered from other agencies. This reorganization involved the merger of 22 agencies or agency divisions to improve effectiveness in fighting terrorism. In addition, it gave the administration more flexibility in hiring of personnel (outside the civil service), the most controversial and political aspect of the merger. Finally, it served a political purpose by responding to 9/11 in a dramatic way. Interestingly, policy effectiveness, rather than efficiency, was the primary goal. Even so, the new agency did not gain police powers. Rather police powers remain with the Federal Bureau of Investigation (FBI), Central Intelligence Agency (CIA), and other information-collecting and law-enforcing agencies. These agencies report information to this central collecting agency.

READING 4–1   Merger/Reorganization in County Government

In the second stage of a government reorganization promised to go on for four years, Montgomery County Executive Douglas M. Duncan proposed yesterday creating a single public works and transportation department from two existing departments and part of a third.

If approved by the County Council, the change will eliminate 22 jobs and save $1 million a year, according to Duncan. "This consolidation will allow us to provide essential services at an affordable cost, which is what local government is all about," Duncan said at a news conference.

Half of the lost jobs would be managers and the rest clerical workers. The plan cuts the number of divisions from 11 to 7.

Council member Isaiah Leggett (D-At Large) said he expected the council to approve the move.

"I'm optimistic that we can realize some saving," said Leggett, chairman of the council's Transportation and Environment Committee. "I'm not sure they'll be as great as projected."

But the head of the affected union complained that Duncan had not given adequate notice of the change.

"He continues to give us false assurances that he will not make final decisions without consulting the unions," said Gino Renne, president of the Montgomery County Government Employees Organization, the United Food and Commercial Workers local that represents about half of the 7,000 county employees.

"The morale of this work force is at an all-time low," Renne said. "There is not confidence in [Duncan's] leadership as an employer."

The new department would be headed by Graham Norton and replace the Department of Transportation, which Norton currently heads, and the Facilities and Services Department. The directorship of Facilities and Services is vacant.

The trash collection and recycling functions of the Department of Environmental Protection, which were transferred to the transportation unit in the budget year that began July 1, also would come under the new department.

In March, Duncan announced the consolidation of four departments into a new Health and Human Services Department, saving $4.4 million while eliminating 163 jobs.

The council approved that consolidation, but only after restoring programs for the homeless and working poor that trimmed about $1 million from the projected saving. Leggett suggested the council might do the same with the public works department.

Under county personnel rules, any employee whose position is eliminated becomes eligible for a comparable or lesser vacancy elsewhere in the government. Renne said that no union member has been laid off so far as a result of the Health and Human Services consolidation.

SOURCE: Karl Vick, "Duncan Urges Merger of 2 Montgomery Departments; Public Works, Transportation Functions Would Be Combined in 2nd Stage of County Restructuring," *Washington Post* (July 27, 1995): C6.

READING 4–2   The Creation of the Department of Homeland Security

The new [D]epartment [of Homeland Security] will merge at least 170,000 federal employees from 22 agencies who perform a vast array of missions, from agricultural research to port security to disaster assistance. Under H.R. 5005, the Homeland Security Department would include the Transportation Security Administration (TSA), Customs Service, Immigration and Naturalization Service, Secret Service, Coast Guard, and Federal Emergency Management Agency. The agencies will be reorganized into four directorates within the department: Information Analysis and Infrastructure Protection, Science and Technology, Border and Transportation Security, and Emergency Preparedness and Response.

The information analysis unit would absorb all of the functions of the FBI's National Infrastructure Protection Center, the Defense Department's National Communications System, the Commerce Department's Critical Infrastructure Assurance Office, the Energy Department's National Infrastructure Simulation and Analysis Center, and the General Services Administration's Federal Computer Incident Response Center.

The Border and Transportation Security Directorate would have jurisdiction over the Coast Guard, TSA, Customs, Border Patrol, Federal Protective Service, and Federal Law Enforcement Training Center. It would also include a new Bureau of Citizenship and Immigration Services to handle visa applications and absorb up to 3,200 agriculture inspectors and other employees of the Animal and Plant Health Inspection Service from the Agriculture Department. The Treasury Department would keep the portion of Customs that deals with trade and revenue collection.

In a departure from the Bush proposal, the Justice Department's Office of Domestic Preparedness and FEMA's Office of National Preparedness will move to the Border and Transportation Directorate. The White House would have put these offices in the Emergency Preparedness Division of the Homeland Security Department.

Agriculture's Plum Island Animal Disease Center, the Energy Department's Lawrence Livermore National Laboratory, and Defense's National Bioweapons Defense Analysis Center would all move to the Science and Technology Directorate, which would focus on developing chemical, biological, radiological, and nuclear countermeasures. This division would also create several research labs to develop homeland security technologies.

The National Oceanic and Atmospheric Administration would lose its Integrated Hazard Information System to the Emergency Preparedness Division of the new department. The Federal Emergency Management Agency; the FBI's National Domestic Preparedness Office; and the Health and Human Services Department's National Disaster Medical System, Metropolitan Medical Response System, and Office of Emergency Preparedness would also transfer to this division, along with the Justice Department's Domestic Emergency Support Teams. The Secret Service would be an autonomous agency within the department, falling under none of the four directorates.

The new department will include an undersecretary for management; chiefs of information, human capital, finance and civil rights; and an inspector general.

SOURCE: Tanya Ballard, "Homeland Security Organized along Administration's Proposal," Daily Briefing, November 20, 2002. Accessed June 2005. Retrieved from *Government Executive* at www.govexec.com.

Note: To see the most current organization chart, see www.dhs.gov. One additional directorate, the Office of Preparedness, and a superexecutive office, the National Office of National Intelligence—to coordinate the budgets of DHS, Defense, and other intelligence-gathering agencies—were created in 2005.

Mergers and reorganizations are dynamic aspects of organizations and their basic structure. The concept of structure involves aspects worth looking at in detail. The next section addresses types of structure, from bureaucracy to its alternatives, as theoretical constructs.

STRUCTURE AS A THEORETICAL CONSTRUCT

Why study the structure of organizations? As Brandl (1989) states, "organization matters." Different organizational (structural) forms affect the efficiency, effectiveness, responsiveness, and accountability of the organization.

Organizational structure has many meanings, including "the way in which the parts of the organization are arranged" (Hall 1991, 48), a formal set of rules governing behavior (Scott, W. R. 1987; Simon 1947), or the officially prescribed distribution of authority and task responsibility among offices and officials. An organization chart shows these relationships graphically. An "org chart" may also show the names of employees holding higher-level positions, their specific responsibilities, and the coordination prescribed in the structure (see Box 4–1). Mintzberg (1979, 24–34) defines an organization in terms of five basic parts:

1. The operating core—the staff who perform the basic work of the organization to provide a product or service.

2. The strategic apex—the executives responsible for the overall organization.

BOX 4–1   Organization Charts: Rigor Mortis

They have uses: for the annual salary review; for educating (individuals) on how the organization works and who does what.

But draw them in pencil. Never formalize, print, and circulate them. Good organizations are living bodies that grow new muscles to meet challenges. A chart demoralizes people. Nobody thinks of himself as *below* other people. And in a good (organization) he isn't. Yet on paper there it is. If you have to circulate something, use a loose-leaf table of organizations (like a magazine masthead) instead of a diagram with the people in little boxes. Use alphabetical order by name and by function wherever possible.

In the best organizations, people see themselves working in a circle as if around one table. One of the positions is designated chief executive officer because somebody has to make all those tactical decisions that enable an organization to keep working. In this circular organization, leadership passes from one person to another depending on the particular task being attacked—without any hang-ups.

This is as it should be. In the hierarchical organization it is difficult to imagine leadership anywhere but at the top of the various pyramids. And it's hard to visualize the leader of a small pyramid becoming temporarily the leader of a group of larger pyramid leaders that includes the chief executive officer.

The traditional organization chart has one dead giveaway. Any dotted line indicates a troublemaker and/or a serious troubled relationship. It also generally means that an unsatisfactory compromise . . . has been worked out and the direct solution has been avoided.

SOURCE: Abridged from Robert Townsend, *Further Up the Organization* (New York: Alfred A. Knopf, 1984), 159–60.

3. The middle line—the managers who join the operating core to the strategic apex.

4. The technostructure—those who serve the core and affect the work of others, often by standardizing functions.

5. Support staff—those outside the core work flow who provide service for the organization.

Perrow (1972 generally; and 1984, Chapters 1 and 5) defines *organization structure* as a complex, open system that includes the organization's form, environment, technology, informal and formal communication, and its culture.[1] He further defines most organizations as bureaucracies. For Perrow, the words *structure* and *bureaucracy* are largely synonymous for large organizations (1972, 50) in that both typically involve hierarchy and share other characteristics. This chapter examines these ideas of structure, including the concept of an open system, but defers the main discussion of communication and culture to Chapters 5 and 8.

The officially sanctioned government organization is recognized through legislative enactment; for nonprofits, formal recognition comes through the incorporation process. The authority of officials and board members to decide, act, and delegate responsibility is prescribed in the legislative enactment (or executive order) or incorporation documents. Such enactments may also specify the mission, the structure of the major subdivisions, procedural requirements, and even the size of the agency. For example, the document creating the Office of the National Intelligence Director states that the office can transfer no more than 100 employees from other intelligence agencies. Some statutes are intentionally vague about these points to avoid the political implications of a choice. For example, the Department of Homeland Security statute delegates organization details to the organization itself. The act (2002) specifically lists the agencies to be merged and reorganized, but it requires the new department to submit a reorganization plan to Congress.

Organizational structure became a hot topic in the 1980s when Thomas Peters and Robert Waterman published the now classic *In Search of Excellence* (1982). Excellent companies, they note, strive for excellent customer service and not simply profits. Peters and Waterman identify a series of structural characteristics including lean top management, using small task forces, and "chunking" or subdividing major tasks to get things done, along with cultural characteristics such as a bias for action (124). The excellent companies in their case studies purposely ignore economies of scale to gain greater innovation and higher morale through smaller groups.

Ten years later interest in government structures took off with David Osborne and Ted Gaebler's *Reinventing Government* (1992). They too focus on the value of the customer and on being mission driven. They favor decentralization to centralization and contracting out to providing services directly. Both *In Search of Excellence* and *Reinventing Government* view organizational structure as affecting the ability of the organization to successfully adapt to external demands. Both books are based on case studies, and both have been criticized for advocating contradictory ideas (Williams 2000). Be that as it may, they provided insights that unleashed broad interest in business and then government organization. No equivalent book examines nonprofit organizational structure, but nonprofits have been "bitten" by the reorganizing, reinventing movement. This has led to nonprofits becoming more mission driven, competitive, and engaged in measuring performance (Durst and Newell 2001).

---

[1]In *Normal Accidents* (1984) Perrow continues his theories of organizations to encompass groups of organizations as complex systems. See the next section for details.

THEORIES OF ORGANIZATIONAL STRUCTURE

Of course studying organizational structure began well before the 1980s. Structural function-alism, a sociological school of thought, theorizes that the factors of structure and function intertwine. The structure of an organization affects what can be done and what will occur (Parsons 1969, 1970, 1964; Perrow 1972), whereas the actual functions of an organization determine the structure.

As with its sociological counterpart, the administrative science school of public admin-istration (Fayol 1949; Barnard 1938/1968; Gulick 1937; Wilson 1887/1978) looks at the structure of organizations—not so much for guiding what can be done as for scientifically and rationally developing the best organizations. The approach assumes that finding a set of universal principles about structure is key to successful management; a well-structured organization would be more efficient and nearly manage itself. The search for universal prin-ciples that apply to all, or almost all, organizations occupies many analysts, managers, and researchers. For a partial list of principles, see Box 4–2.

BOX 4–2 Some Principles of Administrative Science

Unity of command: An official should receive commands from and be responsible to only one supervisor to avoid confusion, unfair expectations, divided loyalties, and uncoordinated action.

> **Comments:** Henri Fayol, one of the earliest and most prominent of the administrative sci-entists, maintained, "For myself, I do not think that a shop can be run in flagrant violation of [unity of command]" (Fayol 1949, 69). As we will see, however, many contemporary organization designs, such as the matrix organization, do not follow this principle.

Line staff: An unbroken chain of command should be carried by line officers from top to bottom in the organization. Technical support and advisory staff should be attached to the offices with decision-making authority and command responsibility without disrupting the line of command.

> **Comments:** The distinction between line and staff is based on the difference between decision-making authority and advisory or support work; but this distinction is not always easy to main-tain in practice, especially in bureaus where technical analysis is at the core of the mission.

Span of control: The optimal number of subordinates that can be successfully commanded by a supervisor.

> **Comments:** Working on the problem as a question of the mathematical combinations of possible relationships among superiors and subordinates, administrative scientists arrived at the conclusion that five or six was the optimal span (Urwick 1943). But little agreement on the ideal span ever emerged. Each branch of the military, for example, had its own scheme.

The functional and scalar principles: The search for the optimal basis for determining the appropriate type and degree of specialization in subordinate offices, and the optimal point at which to add another level in the hierarchy.

> **Comments:** Firm conclusions about the optimal point for either type of expansion are, not surprisingly, rare (Scott, Mitchell, and Birnbaum 1981, 36–37).

Affecting both the work of sociologists and public administration theorists is the work of Max Weber, one of the foremost thinkers guiding the understanding of organizational structure.[2] Max Weber's definition of the *ideal-type bureau* (discussed in the previous chapter) sets the stage for the analysis of structures. The ideal type is not found in reality but is a concept by which to judge organizations and their structures for their efficiency above other values. The ideal type serves us (and Weber) as part of an overall worldview, an observational tool, to summarize what is essential—the unique character of an organization.

To define the ideal type, Weber (1947) examined government, the military, and the church. Weber identified three bases of authority for leaders of organizations: rational–legal (based on election or merit), charismatic (based on personality), and traditional (based on caste, bloodline, or other societal determinants). (Chapter 9 more fully discusses leadership in public organizations.) The ideal-type organization is based on laws and official competency (today we would use the term *employee* rather than *official*) as opposed to decision making based on favoritism. Three key structural elements of ideal-type bureaucracy are the principles of hierarchy with one leader, specialization or division of labor, and delimited authority of professional employees.

The idea of *hierarchy* is that authority of offices and employees is rank ordered on a descending scale of subordinate relations. Officials at the top of the ordering have greatest authority, perfectly matched in the ideal bureau to their knowledge, expertise, and specialization in office operations. Almost everyone would agree that few real agencies, and certainly not the ones they work for, reflect this ideal completely (see Figure 4–1).

In two seminal works, "Proverbs of Administration" (1946) and *Administrative Behavior* (1947), Herbert A. Simon calls into question the rationality of administrative science principles. Simon observes that although these principles are designed to guide the development of administration (that is, efficient bureaucracy), they frequently contradict one another. Simon consequently refers to them as "proverbs" rather than principles. He points to a lack of evidence on how to centralize administration, create specializations, divide work, or determine the span of control of supervisors. His critiques raise questions such as these: Is bureaucracy truly efficient? How centralized is centralized? What exactly is the appropriate level of specialization? How should a workforce be divided? Moreover, what is the value of hiring, promoting, and firing members of an organization's workforce based on experience and seniority?

Proverbs and principles, hierarchy, and ideal-type bureaucracies have begun our look at the elements of organizational structure. The following sections examine specialization, span of control, centralization, departmentalization, line and staff, and the formalization of organizations.

Specialization

In the ideal-type bureaucracy, a professionally designed, technically rational order to positions and tasks exists; and this order produces the stability, consistency, and efficiency hailed as the hallmarks of traditional organizational structure. Employees specialize in a body of knowledge to provide the services of the organization. *Specialization,* both vertical and horizontal in the organization, creates a need for *differentiation.* The greater the number of specializations, the greater is the necessary differentiation among groups of employees. Specialization and the

---

[2]Max Weber lived from 1864 to 1920. His works were published posthumously in German in 1922 but not translated into English until 1947. Prior to 1947, Weber's ideas were introduced to sociologists by Talcott Parsons. Thus Weber's influence beyond German-speaking countries has taken place largely since the mid-twentieth century. Weber is usually pronounced "Vaber" with a long a.

FIGURE 4–1   Is Your Organization a Bureaucracy?

Most people believe that government is more bureaucratic than the private sector. No study has been conducted regarding nonprofits. In bold are the ratings of government (*G*) and private sector (*P*) survey respondents.

Rate your own organization on a scale of 0 to 10 with 0 being the lowest, 5 being average, and 10 being highest rating.

Category	0	1	2	3	4	5	6	7	8	9	10	
Hierarchy				*P*		*G*						
Few Layers												Many Layers
Task Specialization						*P*	*G*					
Little												Great Deal
Record Keeping							*P*	*G*				
Few												Great Many
Formal Credentials								*P*	*G*			
Little Concern												Great Concern
Standardized Treatment									*G*	*P*		
Much Discretion												Highly Standardized

SOURCE: Bozeman, Barry. *Bureaucracy and Red Tape*, 1st Edition Copyright © 2000, p. 19. Reprinted by permission of Pearson Education, Inc., Upper Saddle River, NJ.

resulting differentiation of positions enable employees to become highly proficient in relatively narrow professional tasks and generally allow employees to become more productive. Simply put, organizing complex work increases the speed of production.

Yet specialization, and the stability it brings, is a mixed blessing for organizations. We want and need this degree of predictability in a law enforcement institution, but we regret the rigidity that is the seemingly inevitable side effect. Although specialization brings expertise, it can lead to an unwillingness or inability to see alternative solutions or appreciate divergent points of view about what a program or policy should mean or how it could be implemented. There is no better place to examine the conflict than in health care. We value health care specialists for their expertise yet criticize them for not being able to cross specialty lines when a diagnosis is inaccurate: Is it the X-ray, the ultrasound, the CAT scan, or the MRI that will yield the right diagnosis? Each of these tests is conducted by different technician specialists and often read by different medical specialists. This organizational specialization, too, may have an unintended consequence that pulls organizations away from democratic principles when the narrowness of specialized knowledge obscures them.

Integration and Span of Control

Greater differentiation in specialties not only requires a greater integration of functions within an organization but also creates a need to determine each manager's *span of control—* that is, the number of subordinate managers or workers who report directly to that manager. How many supervisors are needed to manage the required number of specialists? Simon (1946) notes there is no scientific way to determine this. The more differentiated the organization is, the smaller the span of control by supervisors and managers—and therefore the more complex the organization's structure and, very likely, the greater the number of hierarchical layers. Ultimately greater differentiation increases costs and likely reduces efficiency, so balance becomes important. Reducing or increasing the degree of specialization has policy implications as well as technical consequences. Hospitals are a classic example of the highly differentiated organization, with supervisors and managers for each specialty (laboratory, X-ray, physical therapy, nursing, and so on). The newly created Department of Homeland Security (DHS) subdivides into four directorates, which further divide into additional specializations.

Span of control is typically narrower at supervisory and managerial levels and at working levels where diverse specialties report to a given supervisor. (By contrast, one supervisor can often handle many direct subordinates who are doing essentially the same work, such as at a service call center.) Narrow spans of control create a greater need for methods of *integration* such as hierarchical command and communication systems, processes of task coordination, program rules and regulations, plans, and schedules. When handled properly (as Chapter 5 discusses with regard to communication), staff meetings, committees, procedures for circulating memos about policy changes, informal consultations, and even departmental grapevines all contribute to organizational integration.

Balancing differentiation and integration is a key to designing effective organizational structures, yet there is no clear means to proceed. Optimal span of control broadens and narrows to meet different goals of the organization (Theobald and Nicholson-Crotty 2005). Administrative costs, technical requirements, and professional assumptions all help shape appropriate choices for balancing differentiation and integration even though, as Salamon (1981) suggests, the outcome of greater efficiency is not guaranteed. As we will see, alternative structural forms exhibit different solutions to the balancing of differentiation and integration.

Centralization

The terms *centralization* and *decentralization* refer to the degree to which decision-making authority is confined to the top echelons of an organization or dispersed to lower-echelon employees. Centralization and decentralization come in degrees, with every arrangement having both advantages and drawbacks. Fundamentally, centralization promotes consistency and stability, whereas decentralization promotes flexibility and responsiveness. Centralization can be used to achieve greater control; to monitor operations; to clarify policy making and assure consistent application of policy; to create communication channels; and, in the end, to improve efficiency and effectiveness. All of these uses can be critical to the survival and effectiveness of the organization. For example, demands for greater centralization often accompany political claims that an agency is exceeding or misinterpreting its mission (the Central Intelligence Agency and the Pentagon's Defense Advanced Research Projects Agency), failing to achieve its mission (the Federal Emergency Management Agency), abusing its powers (the Defense Intelligence Agency and law enforcement in general), or has been captured by special interests or by a special viewpoint (the U.S. Department of Agriculture) (Wilson, J., 1989, Chapter 5). This debate also is present in the different organizational arrangements of churches from the centralized Roman Catholic church to decentralized Baptist churches.

The term *centralization* is often used to describe situations in which certain management functions are unified in a headquarters office and other functions in regional or local offices (see Reading 4–3). This occurs when a support function is centralized, such as

READING 4–3   Centralization or Decentralization: What Is Right?

Supper at Shirley Barger's house has been downsized to bologna sandwiches. Barger is one of nearly 20,000 jobless Hoosiers whose unemployment claims are backlogged at the Indiana Department of Workforce Development. After a centralization of the unemployment insurance offices in May that cut the claims processing staff from 120 to 41, paperwork has piled up.

Barger's claim has been waiting more than five months for a ruling on whether she's even eligible for unemployment. Other jobless residents are waiting as long as 10 weeks for a check that, according to federal guidelines, should have arrived in three.

The centralization has affected not only the jobless awaiting checks—it has cost some state workers their careers. And it has left employers vulnerable to higher unemployment insurance rates in the future if the state continues to miss its deadlines.

Commissioner Ron Stiver [of the Department of Workforce Development] . . . takes responsibility for the centralization of the agency, which last year handled $723.8 million in claims for 263,548 jobless residents. He said he's concerned about jobless Hoosiers, but he also believes the agency he inherited in January is in dire need of repair.

Streamlining

When Stiver took over nine months ago, the agency was $2.5 million in debt, he said. He immediately went to work to cut costs—leaving vacant positions empty, laying off a handful of information technology workers, and canceling the pagers and cell phones of employees.

But, he said, he needed a way to shave more off the deficit. After considering a long list of alternatives, Stiver opted for the centralization. It required that all claims deputies throughout the state move to Indianapolis or lose their jobs. Just 41 of 120 deputies came on board.

. . . Stiver argues, "It was the best of a rough batch of alternatives." He expects the centralization to save his agency $1.7 million annually and bring its debt to zero by the end of the fiscal year. The second best option for relieving the deficit would have removed unemployment insurance from the agency's 27 satellite WorkOne offices, meaning jobless residents wouldn't have local sites at which to file claims and get questions answered, he said.

Many Democratic lawmakers aren't buying the reasoning.

"Centralizing the eligibility process set us back by many, many steps," said State Senator Vi Simpson, D-Ellettsville. "We're saving federal dollars on the backs of people who can't get unemployment dollars." The agency is hiring full-time claims deputies, bringing the final tally to 76. In the meantime, Stiver has rallied the help of current employees who have a background in claims processing to work overtime on the backlog. "We're going to get it under control by the end of December," Stiver said. "We're going to improve the timeliness of this agency and meet deadlines."

Longtime Problem

Department records show that for the past seven years, the agency has missed the deadline requirement for claims processing. The U.S. Department of Labor requires that eligibility claims be processed within 21 days. In fall 2004 the agency was processing just 74.8 percent of claims within that time period. About 14,000 claims sat in a backlog.

U.S. Department of Labor records show that Indiana's unemployment insurance was far from running smoothly before Daniels and his team took office. The appeals process showed a "glaring deficiency," according to a letter sent by the U.S. Labor Department. In that letter the Labor Department criticized the agency's record, saying the timeliness of Indiana's hearing decisions was the lowest in the nation, averaging less than 1 percent within 30 days and 3 percent in 45 days. The Department of Labor requires 60 percent of hearing decisions within 30 days and 80 percent of hearing decisions within 45 days.

Higher Insurance

The centralization isn't affecting just jobless residents; it soon could touch employers, he said. According to federal law, if a state doesn't comply with guidelines set for processing unemployment insurance, the government may impose higher insurance rates on employers.

Stiver continues to stress that this issue will be a nonissue by the first of the year. "We will have the backlog completed by the end of December."

Former claims deputies question whether Stiver's goal is a reasonable one to set. As construction companies shut down for the winter and factories start layoffs, the fourth quarter is traditionally the busiest time for claims.

SOURCE: Abridged from Dana Knight, "Jobless and Waiting: Changes Delay Claim Processing; State Says Reform Is Overdue," *Indianapolis Star,* March 3, 2005. Accessed October 2005. Retrieved from www.indystar.com. Reprinted with permission.

---

personnel services or information technology. In some cases the centralized function may serve (or "cross service") a number of organizations, usually for a fee; for example, the payroll system at the U.S. Department of Agriculture has for many years handled payroll operations for a number of federal departments (Halachmi and Nichols 1997).

The type of alliance is another aspect of centralization. Nonprofit organizations, in particular, range from separate independent organizations (community food pantries, research institutes such as the American Enterprise Institute), to independents with weak umbrella coordination, often known as alliances (United Ways, Chambers of Commerce, some Protestant churches), to franchise federations (Ys, Scouts, unions), to unitary organizations in which much of the decision making is centralized (Catholic church, Friends of the Earth, Save the Children) (Standley 2001; Young 2001; Young, Bania, and Bailey 1996). Local governments within a geographic area commonly form a council of government (COG) to coordinate interjurisdictional issues; similarly, states form regional alliances, usually around important common issues (airborne pollution, regional economic development). Alliances among federal organizations occur less frequently and tend to emerge from shared responsibilities, such as the Chief Financial Officers (CFO) Council, or from proximity, such as cooperative administrative services units (CASUs) that operate in many federal buildings throughout the country. Authority and funding typically remain with the individual organizations for government coalitions, but this varies for nonprofit alliances (see Table 4–1).

When nonprofit organizations cross national boundaries, they often operate as alliances with a shared logo but multiple central offices organized by country. Save the Children, for example, acts as a unitary organization in each of the 22 countries in which it has headquarters:

TABLE 4–1   Structure of Nonprofits

	Level of Accountability (in Percentages)		
	Decentralized*	*Shared Authority*	*Centralized*
Regulation by *National Organization*			
National has authority to suspend affiliates.	24	41	54
Limit activities.	05	32	62
Regulate client service activities.	13	27	54
Financial practices.	13	50	85
Governance policies.	20	50	62
Establish fundraising area.	09	23	38
Permitted to raise funds whenever it wishes.	53	52	92
Audit finances.	00	02	08
Influence of Locals *over National*			
Participate in national board elections.	80	80	54
May withhold dues from national.	62	30	08

N=122

*Decentralized: National organization represents the interests of diverse collection of autonomous affiliates and provides services. *Shared authority*: National organization provides leadership and direction to autonomous affiliates or authority for programs is shared. *Centralized*: Centrally directed organization in which affiliates have limited discretion.

SOURCE: Table modified from Dennis Young, Neil Bania, and Darlyne Bailey, "Structure and Accountability: A Study of National Nonprofit Associations," *Nonprofit Management & Leadership* 6 (1996): 355, 357–58.

Each national organization sets its own goals but shares a common international logo and mission (Lindenberg and Dobel 1999). The International Save the Children Alliance acts as an umbrella organization for common policy or programs but exerts no control over each Save the Children. The national organizations ally as needed among themselves, such as after the December 2004 Indian Ocean tsunami that killed almost a quarter of a million people. Transnational governmental bodies (such as the North Atlantic Treaty Organization, better known as NATO) typically operate in a more coordinated fashion. However, even in organizations such as the United Nations and the World Trade Organization, much funding and legitimacy ultimately rest with a handful of key players.

With multiple sites or levels of organization also comes the pull each site or level feels toward unit autonomy and the conflicting need for organizational affiliation. Sometimes organizational culture, discussed in Chapter 8, leads people to identify more closely with the overall organization and sometimes with the unit within that organization. If this discussion were about citizens rather than about workers and members of public organizations, the comparison might be framed in terms of political allegiance: "I'm an American" versus "I'm a New Yorker." Allegiance, however, is a characteristic of the organization's culture rather than its formal structure; hence it does not necessarily align with the degree of centralization or decentralization within an organization.

At the same time, if centralized organizational structures tend to be more efficient than decentralized organizations (because of internal consistency and economies of scale), decentralized structures tend to foster organizations that are more responsive to clientele needs and changing environments. Decentralized structures, by definition, permit greater autonomy within the organization's divisions and make broad participation in more decisions possible. Decentralization can also increase the visibility of local offices or organizations and emphasize their importance in a civil society, whether it is the Department of Agriculture (USDA), a local school, or the Girl Scout Council. Being closer to the people allows greater flexibility in dealing with problems and external demands. Faster decisions are also associated with decentralization (Kaufman 1960).

Decentralization has negative as well as positive attributes. One danger is straying from an organization's central mission in response to local pressure. As Simon (1946) suggests, decentralization may make it difficult to determine program accountability or to establish consistent policies throughout the organization when many employees are active decision makers. Blau (1966) finds that decentralized decisions in organizations primarily composed of professionals may result in a high ratio of managers and more layers in the hierarchy; in such situations accountability becomes dispersed and decentralization becomes costly.

In coalitions and alliances characterizing certain large nonprofit organizations, the theoretical problem, as Standley (2001) observes, is "to what degree is the national organization accountable to the locals and vice versa?" Among nonprofits, public realization in the 1990s about highly paid executives in the YMCA and United Way and, in the 2000s, the chair of the Wall Street Stock Exchange (a nonprofit) created a sense of scandal, as did extensive reporting about child molestation by clergy in the Catholic church. When dysfunctional practices surface regarding extended public organizations (whether these examples or any others), assigning responsibility for their causes and remedies can be frustrating and elusive. Large, decentralized government organizations exhibit similar accountability challenges—as with Abu Ghraib prisoner humiliation while in U.S. military custody in post-Saddam Iraq. Ultimately, however, the innate hierarchical structure of government places ultimate ethical (if not legal) accountability with the organization's top-level officials. Irrespective of centralization or decentralization in a hierarchical organization, final responsibility rests with the individual or group having final authority.

Departmentalization

Simon (1946) points out that public organizations are structured around purpose, process, clientele, or place (geography). The structural arrangement is commonly for efficiency; yet efficiency can escape us because it is unclear that one method of departmentalization is better than another. Specialized tasks in work flow typically result in grouping employees with related specialties into departments, offices, and other subdivisions. The idea behind departments based on *purpose*—that is, a program-based structure—is that all of the organization's resources, professional specialties, command and communication structure, and management procedures then focus on administering policy and program goals. Departments based

FIGURE 4–2   Processes and Stovepipes

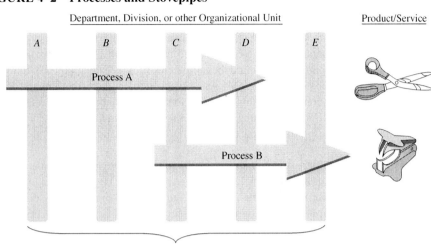

Stovepipe—Specialized activity contributing to a process.

on similarity of purpose (more commonly called *programs* in public organizations) are probably the most familiar; many federal executive departments are structured in this way. Environmental protection agencies at federal and state levels and nonprofit health agencies (such as those for addictions, illnesses, and obesity) share the fact that they are often organized around programs and a set of policies.

A drawback is that departmentalization tends to create "stovepipes" or "silos" of specialized knowledge at the expense of comprehensive understanding of or responsibility for the programmatic processes and services to which they contribute. As Figure 4–2 depicts, specialty functions operate vertically within a bureaucratic hierarchy's traditional lines of authority (inquiry or intake processing, information and publications, record storage and retrieval, legal advice, case handling and resolution, accuracy monitoring). Processes operate horizontally, embedded in *projects* (which have an anticipated completion state) and *programs* (which are ongoing); these create outputs in the form of services (trash collection, vehicle licensing, public education, law enforcement), products (public works), or both (land trusts, which acquire and maintain land holdings for public use). Typical environmental protection agencies, for example, are structured as a set of silo-like departments, one dealing with air, another water, and another land. This kind of departmentalization leads to the need for more and more formal organizational communication (integration methods) to ensure that all departments obtain the same information at the same time. Informal communication across departments between employees can overcome some of the silo problems, but not all.

In some situations a department or division is a self-contained administrative unit devoted to one program, with all management functions (administration, policies, budgeting) and support services (personnel, information systems, procurement) established on a small scale. Often specialists in the most prestigious field associated with the type of program become executives in the agency (Mosher 1982). This can protect established program goals, increase visibility, and create a strong advocate in a leadership position. Thus firefighters traditionally manage fire departments and superintendent–educators manage schools, although in both cases the departments are formally part of local governments. Often, in fact, the head of the department must, by statutory requirement, be a member of the profession.

Drawbacks to self-contained units are not hard to imagine. This situation creates duplication of effort among departments and may be inefficient from the standpoint of economies of scale. Some organizations—including YMCAs—take a middle road by merging most management functions across communities but retaining local boards and executives. The political costs of eliminating self-contained units are often enormous. As in the case of schools, such a self-contained structure is ingrained, part of our cultural history, and consequently difficult to change.

The last two bases of departmentalization, by *clientele* and by *geography,* are common organizational schemes in both nonprofits and in government. These two arrangements define subdivisions within organizations. Examples of agencies organized by client type include corrections departments and nonprofit contractual agencies providing support services to those with special needs. Recreational organizations often subdivide by their major clientele groups, such as the elderly, adults, youth, and preschoolers.

Most federal and state agencies have geography-based subdivisions, frequently called regions or districts. Geography-based subdivisions normally provide direct ("frontline") services to the public—from Social Security offices to post offices to state agricultural services. Cooperative extension offices are a classic case. The purpose is to be closer to the actual customer or citizen. Geographically based nonprofits include public television outlets, Red Cross offices, and chambers of commerce. Nonprofit economic development corporations and "friends" organizations of national and state parks are specifically established around a geographical concern. The U.S. Agency for International Development (AID) and the United Nations (UN) organize by country and region.

For all its benefits, organizing by geography raises an additional dilemma for many nonprofits and for government organizations such as those involved in higher education. How much competition should be allowed in one geographic area? In the private sector, competition may be viewed as absolutely necessary for the market to work. In the government and nonprofit sector, competition is viewed as a problem. Public higher education systems often attempt to regulate the types of majors offered on each campus (with minimal success). For organizations engaged in decentralized alliances or confederations, mechanisms may not exist to regulate competition. For example, the Washington, D.C., region enjoys three public television outlets and at least four public radio stations overlapping one another.

The upside of this competition is that it can increase responsiveness to customer concerns. The downside is its effect on the mission of organizations. First, mission-driven nonprofits experience pressure from corporate donors to modify their practices or goals in ways that may be inconsistent with their missions but meet the donors' desires. Competition has the potential to shift the mission emphasis to the bottom line when working with donors. Universities feel this pressure when they establish special contracts with service companies to be the sole provider of soft drinks and other products. Second, competition can sometimes cause confusion in the public's eye. This occurs when government agencies such as sanitation departments compete with private sector garbage haulers. The public may not understand differences in the purposes of an organization or how each is organized (see Reading 4–4). Third, competition can sometimes reduce coordination of services if organizations are

READING 4–4   No Switch in Bills for Some Communities

Residents of communities with their own municipal light departments don't have to worry about how restructuring will affect their bills. Municipal utilities—unlike privately owned utilities such as NStar or Massachusetts Electric—are not included in the Massachusetts energy restructuring law.

There currently are 40 nonprofit municipal utilities serving 800,000 people in Massachusetts according to David Tuohey, spokesman for Massachusetts Municipal Wholesale Electric, the state's municipal utility collaborative.

North Shore and Merrimack Valley communities that own their own electric utilities include Peabody, Danvers, Ipswich, Rowley, Middleton, Merrimac, Groveland, Georgetown, Marblehead, and Wakefield.

Last week the state-controlled rate for customers at privately owned utilities was eliminated. For average households that consume 500 kilowatt-hours of electricity a month, the change will mean a $3.59 increase to the average $63.42 monthly bill. But municipal electric customers will see none of that.

Danvers Electric Utilities Director Coleen O'Brien-Pitts said Danvers 11,600 customers pay an average of $59.67 per month for 500 kilowatt-hours of electricity. A municipal board of directors will continue to set that rate.

The state's 40 municipal utilities generally have been able to offer lower rates than private utilities because many still own their power generation plants, Tuohey said. Municipal utilities generally produce one-third of the electricity they consume and buy another third in the form of long-term contracts from suppliers and the balance on the large daily electricity markets.

Under deregulation, private utilities are limited in the length of supply contracts they can sign and must service most of their electricity demands on the open market, which is sensitive to swings in the price of natural gas or other fuels used to generate electricity.

SOURCE: Abridged from Andy Murray, "No Switch in Bills for Some Communities," *The Salem News* (Salem, MA), March 7, 2005, C7.

competing for the same clienteles and donors (see Chapter 6's discussion of responsiveness). Finally, for government, another concern occurs when consolidations or closures are planned, usually for efficiency reasons. Efficiency turns out to be not enough of a reason for a consolidation or closure; the public may demand the continuation of, for example, a post office, military base, civil rights office, or school for reasons of employment, responsiveness, and community civic enhancement.

In reality, agencies often use a variety of organizational arrangements and associated departmentalization (Simon 1946). Large police departments show the realities of the different arrangements in action. As city agencies, large police departments are self-contained with their own planning, budgeting, and personnel departments. The titles and organization charts show a traditional hierarchical bureaucracy: a police chief at the highest level, with descending responsibilities at each level to the entry level of the officers. However, large police departments often stray from the traditional bureaucratic model, thereby losing a unity of command and clear hierarchy. Typically there are specializations (traffic control, drug enforcement, and investigation) with separate responsibilities and reporting requirements. These operate as part of a bureaucracy insofar as a clear hierarchy remains. By adding geographic precincts, the hierarchy may become less clear, depending on whether each division has specialists reporting to it and to the central office. At the same time community policing officers—who combine responsibilities that cross specializations—work with officers across the city, police from other jurisdictions, employees from other city departments, and citizens to identify and resolve problems. Rather than decision making being strictly hierarchical, it is participative using problem-solving techniques.

Line and Staff

In a classic ideal bureaucracy, a clear chain of command exists from the lowest-level position to the final authority in a clear unbroken line. *Line* managers have formal authority to make decisions, whereas *staff* managers have advisory or service functions. Line administration has functional authority in a given area in contrast to hierarchical authority. So the director of human resources, the chief of facilities maintenance, and the director of management information systems have functional authority over direct staff and can advise line executives about matters within their expertise. This distinction has importance in many organizations, but it may serve as barrier in some cases if followed to the letter. For example, if the head of security or a website development supervisor, both line functions, cannot make unilateral decisions about threats, then he or she may put the whole organization at risk. Further, line managers may not have the expertise to make key decisions and may rely on staff. The use of technology is increasingly part of the core process (e-government) rather than a staff support function.

The use of teams composed of those with functional and line authority further blurs the difference and makes the line of authority up the chain of command indistinct. In a *flat organization,* one in which teams are created that have cross-functional purposes and teams members are cross-trained (Ostroff 1999), the need for hierarchical authority is decreased. Teams are built around the operating core processes to deliver the ultimate objectives of the organization. Flat organizations reduce reliance on specialization and differentiation because specialists are part of the team. The teams implements and manages the service and outcomes. Managers are needed as liaisons between teams rather than as conveyors of decisions and recommendations up and down the hierarchy.

Formalization

Formalization is the extent to which written or legal rules, procedures, instructions, and policies govern organizations (Hage and Aiken 1969). It is what today makes *bureaucracy* a dirty word, yet more of us work for bureaucracies closer to the ideal than when Weber wrote. In fact, even the word *bureaucracy* as defining a department or agency is disappearing from our lexicon. The federal Bureau of Budget was long ago renamed the Office of Management and Budget, and the Bureau of Internal Revenue became the Internal Revenue Service. In Canada even the word *department* is disappearing in favor of agency names such as Health Canada and Environment Canada. We criticize bureaucracy for its "sins"—(arbitrary) rules, paperwork, and hierarchical decision making. Yet these are formal organizational characteristics that lead insufficiently attentive organizations toward rigidity, lack of accountability, and dehumanizing treatment of subordinates and customers (see generally Perrow 1972 and Salamon 1999 for nonprofits). The very rules that make organizations efficient are implicated in making them inefficient.

But one of the overriding criticisms of today's governmental bureaucracy relates to its employee protections through civil and merit service rules.[3] Civil service rules create a formal system of hiring, promotion, and wage determination; these rules are designed to keep the personnel process free of political favoritism and treat employees equitably. Civil service rules affecting hiring have been modified or eliminated in the states of Georgia, Texas, and Florida and in federal agencies such as the Department of Homeland Security and the National Aeronautics and Space Administration (NASA). With their emphasis on fairness, these formal systems are viewed as excluding the best and brightest potential employees, decreasing efficiency, stifling innovation, and protecting unsatisfactory employees from termination. The criticisms ignore the fact that not all government employees are part of civil service systems; falling outside the civil service process are employees in many local and county governments, certain departments in state government (often civil rights agencies; planning departments; medical examiners' offices; and judicial, legislative, and executive employees), state universities, and governmental authorities such as water districts. Whatever the merits of these arguments, formal civil service rules closely fit Weber's concept of the ideal-type bureaucracy discussed in Chapter 3.

Given these criticisms of formal bureaucracy, Perrow asks, are better alternatives available? He is referring to bureaucracies not just in government but in the private sector as well. He poses this viewpoint:

> [S]ins generally attributed to bureaucracy are either not sins at all or are consequences of the failure to bureaucratize sufficiently. . . . [T]he extensive preoccupation with reforming, "humanizing" and decentralizing bureaucracies, while salutary, has served to obscure . . . the impact upon society [that is] incalculably more important than the impact upon the members of a particular organization. (1972, 6)

By this Perrow means that what we are criticizing are examples of maladministration.

So one way of thinking about alternatives is simply to apply the principles more carefully. One alternative is for the public organization to retain focus on the ends it strives to achieve (usually a public good articulated in the organization's mission) and not, instead, lower its focus to the means (programmatic tools, procedures, organizational structures) crafted to help achieve those ends. (See the means–end discussion in Chapter 2.) A second alternative is to include some flexibility. Never making exceptions is a pathology (Bozeman 2000). Exceptions to rules can be made, and most organizations have a specific process for doing so. Some organizations refer to sanctioned exceptions as "authorized deviations" or "variances from practice." A third alternative is designing robust structures, policies, and procedures. "Good rules are those that are rarely noticed," even as conditions change (Newell and Simon 1972, 31). They fit many different situations. Public sector hiring practices offer an example. New processes of direct hiring of employees by departments do not violate Weber's ideal; the means change, but not the ends. The ideal requires hiring competent professionals who conduct their job by

---

[3]Personnel theorists but not organizational theorists often attack the civil service and its pay systems (Risher and Fay 1997). See Zeller (2005) for discussion of federal civil service reform.

written rules. Certainly no one would argue for hiring unqualified staff; neither would anyone argue for never changing rules.

If theory is strong, we should see practice follow theory. Practice, however, is often a combination of principles (Simon 1946). Every real-world configuration involves trade-offs and conflicting principles at work. The ideal bureaucracy of Weber can be updated and configured in many ways. Simon's contribution to our understanding of bureaucracy is that administrative science is a set of hypotheses. Each approach should be considered a hypothesis rather than a principle of universal or scientific administration. Administrative science assumes all other things to be equal when, in fact, political, economic, technical, and professional factors intrude to complicate the formal arrangements of organizations.

ALTERNATIVE STRUCTURES

The search for guidelines to modify bureaucracy or create alternative organizational structures is ongoing (Huber et al. 1995). Cleveland (1985) presumes that one reason for "an erosion of hierarchies" (including bureaucracies) is because of the increase in availability of information. No longer does one level of the hierarchy routinely gain privilege based on early or primary access to information or ownership of information. The increased use of committees and teams has also led to modifications in bureaucracies. Practitioner and writer Alfred Sloan, chair of General Motors, introduced one early modification. Under Sloan (1964) General Motors began running on a model of "centralized control of decentralized functions." Key control activities such as strategic planning, board management, budgeting, and finance were centralized, while the automotive subdivisions were given considerable discretion in design, marketing, and competing with each other. Chandler (1962) described GM's success in the 1920s as structure following strategy in response to increasing size and changing technology. This is similar to Peters and Waterman's (1982) idea of loose–tight properties in excellent companies. Management controls the emphasis on the major values of the organization—such as customer service or cost savings—but leaves substantial autonomy in other matters to the employees. These explanations anticipate concepts discussed later in the chapter: the effects of technology, environment, and type of organization on choice of structure.

Alternative forms of organization structure are visible throughout the public sector and are defined in the theoretical literature. These alternatives often modify the hierarchical principle The next sections discuss project management organizations, ideal-type matrix organizations, participative management organizations, adhocracies, collegial structures, "structureless" organizations, and virtual organizations. Many of these structures are more team-oriented than those found in a classic bureaucratic hierarchy. For teams to be part of a changed structure they must be more than a temporary gathering of employees to make a recommendation; in such organizations organizationally cross-cutting teams must be considered legitimate with acknowledged status and acceptance in the organization. (See Chapter 10 for additional discussion of teams.)

Project Management and Matrix Organizations

Project management is a limited-objective oversight and execution process for achieving a specific objective—such as developing or implementing a new program or project—within given constraints in time, resources, and quality expectations. It involves organizational arrangements using teams. Project teams have full responsibility for the work flow of a project from the beginning to completion. Team members are selected for the project team because of their specializations and skills. Members report to the team leader but maintain ties with their home functional departments, creating a dual reporting system violating the traditional hierarchical principle of unity of command. The team leader may have real authority or simply be an expediter of the project management process. But what makes project management different from the bureaucratic model is that it provides for team decision making in ways not possible in the classic hierarchy.

Baber (1983) uses the literature about project management to offer an ideal-type matrix structure (see also Kingdon 1973). The ideal-type matrix structure in Figure 4–3 embodies several characteristics:

- Two or more intersecting lines of authority.
- Achievement of goals by task-oriented groups.
- Team membership drawn from functional departments.
- Temporary membership in teams.
- Continuation of functional departments to provide personnel functions, professional development, and the like.

Individual teams are temporary because they disband when a project is completed, but the team approach is permanent because of its routinized use within matrix organizations or organizational units. Because team members come from different functional departments, they need teamwork skills. The matrix form's strength—the diversity of skills and specializations—may also be a weakness because of innate professional differences in culture and perspective, possible ambiguity of roles, and the potential for conflict about authority. Just as the ideal bureaucracy does not exist, neither does the ideal matrix organization. Whereas the ideal bureaucracy emphasizes efficiency, the ideal matrix emphasizes adaptability and effectiveness.

For many programs and projects, a team approach can be more successful and effective than an individual working alone or than passing work from one stovepipe to another. But for teams and matrix organizations to operate well, administration support is critical (Baber 1983, 42). The matrix form of organization can be costly with its heavy reliance on the availability of team members and management personnel to meet the needs of the team. In this case every professional works under two superiors. Traditional accountability is also weakened because of the need for greater time spent on coordination. Functional department heads, the project team leaders, and even the professionals themselves may have to negotiate who will work on what parts of each project and when they will and will not be involved.

Peters and Waterman, stressing the excessive costs, heavy paperwork, and control requirements of the model, noted that almost none of their "excellent" companies used a matrix structure (1982, 307). Despite the criticisms and actual costs, matrix-type structures are used. The extra expense and personnel needs of this form of organization are most often justified by three factors. Teamwork and the matrix structure and process work best when:

1. Costs, within limits, are not as high a priority as program goals.
2. The same people need to be involved throughout the process.
3. Work can be divided into clear, discrete segments or projects.

FIGURE 4–3   Ideal-Type Matrix Structure

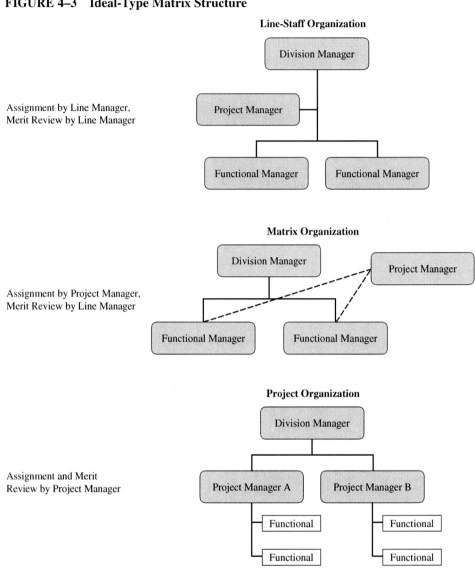

Line-Staff Organization

Division Manager

Assignment by Line Manager,
Merit Review by Line Manager

Project Manager

Functional Manager   Functional Manager

Matrix Organization

Division Manager   Project Manager

Assignment by Project Manager,
Merit Review by Line Manager

Functional Manager   Functional Manager

Project Organization

Division Manager

Assignment and Merit
Review by Project Manager

Project Manager A   Project Manager B

Functional   Functional

Functional   Functional

SOURCE: Adapted from Walter Baber, *Organizing the Future: Matrix Models for the Postindustrial Polity* (Tuscaloosa, AL: University of Alabama Press, 1983), 39.

Management consulting and accounting firms in the private sector find the matrix structure well suited to their needs. Among public organizations, NASA uses this model, as do some parts of the U.S. General Services Administration, many transportation agencies responsible for highway construction and renovation projects, and a range of nongovernmental organizations (NGOs) involved in humanitarian relief.

Ad Hoc Structures

Another team-based structure is the adhocracy (Mintzberg 1979, 431–65). Bennis and Slater first discussed adhocracy teams in 1964. Toffler, in his best-selling *Future Shock*, forecast that society is "moving from bureaucracy to [a]d-hocracy" (1970, 118), whereas Cleveland (1985) wrote of the "twilight of hierarchy." On the organizational level, Waterman (1992) embraced what he called adhocracies, which are even more flexible than project teams or matrix organizations. Waterman briefly defines *adhocracies* as any organizational form that challenges the bureaucracy to embrace the new and "to make change happen" (16). Here the focus is on innovation and change rather than efficiency or effectiveness. It is structurally the most fluid model, but the use of teams is a permanent component of an adhocracy versus simply appointing a team or occasionally using one. What remains of bureaucracy is to assign, support, and organize ad hoc team efforts to solve targeted problems (Waterman 1992; Mintzberg 1979, 433). What differentiates this structure from other organizational structures is that unity of command is not clear. Who provides information upward and downward depends on the problem. Decision making is decentralized to managers and teams alike to maximize innovation. According to Waterman's vision of an adhocracy, team leaders are not experts in a specific field but have good process skills. Mintzberg adds that team leaders (managers) are the ones who coordinate work among teams. It appears that this type of structure is useful in organizations with large professional staffs, particularly in creative organizations such as advertising and consulting firms.

Participative Organizations

Participative organizations turn the principle of hierarchy on its head and add another modification: democratic principles. The more senior manager or supervisor does not have complete authority. In participative management organizations, employees are given authority and have the knowledge to solve problems. Not unlike project teams or the ideal matrix organization, participative management organizations structure work in teams. In the most well-known form of participative management, total quality management (TQM), employees are trained in teamwork, problem solving, and statistical skills. Team members cross functional lines and are empowered to solve problems and implement solutions (Deming 2000, Walton 1990). Usually these teams are created as problems arise, but there also may be permanent teams responsible for a particular process. The latter case is most often found in organizations where line workers work in teams and solve assembly line problems as they occur. Though the term *total quality management* is used less and less, the ideas remain. TQM recognizes that

> organizations are systems of highly interdependent parts, and the central problems they face invariably cross traditional functional lines. [Therefore,] Deming and Juran are insistent that cross-functional problems must be addressed collectively by representatives of all relevant functions. (Hackman and Wageman 1995, 311)

Many organizations recognize and address functional interdependencies through teamwork principles, democratic problem-solving processes, and employee cross-training. For example, community policing is characterized by the use of teams of citizens, officers, businesses, and nonprofit representatives working together in a problem-solving process aimed at putting into effect solutions to crime.

Whereas matrixlike structures focus on effectiveness and adhocracies on innovation, organizations adopting classic quality management techniques focus on process improvement and customer/citizen satisfaction. Nothing in traditional bureaucratic organizations identifies customer service as part of a professional's responsibility. Rather, one of the principles is to treat individuals impersonally and equally without favoritism. But in many (perhaps most) cases this is the best way to satisfy the customer/citizen in the long term, especially considering that public sector managers must often look beyond the individual case to the public good. This is in contrast to private sector managers, who do not (Thompson 1967). Thus organizations adopting quality management principles must balance legal and ethical requirements of fairness and equity with the quality management emphasis on meeting individual needs.

Collegial structures are a form of participative structure found, as the name implies, in colleges and universities but also in scientific and research organizations and small nonprofits. This kind of structure emphasizes deliberative democratic decision making, with decisions often made through formal votes. Even when there are differences in positions in the hierarchy, each person's opinion is considered equally valuable. The drawback, of course, is that the organization is process driven, and the decision-making process can be time-consuming and even a delaying tactic. Perrow's critique of collegial structures is harsh. He asserts that university collegial structures are bureaucracies in disguise (1972, 32–35).

Could it be possible that even a collegial structure is too formal? A *structureless* organization is one in which the organization embodies no unity of command or formal leadership (Freeman 1975). Structureless organizations are found in some feminist and female-oriented organizations such as domestic violence prevention and assistance organizations. Such organizations reject the idea of formal and hierarchical authority and prefer to make decisions by consensus. They value horizontal equity over a hierarchical system. Decisions are made by consensus (or sometimes by vote). For example, the staff of the Spruce Run Domestic Violence Collaborative (one of the oldest domestic violence prevention agencies) emphasizes equality and equity by training all staff to conduct basic services such as handling hotline calls. Full-time staff take turns acting as shift managers and handling activities in the office. Staff members also work in groups such as in direct service, administration, or training. Full-time employees receive the same pay, with pay increases occurring for employees after 1 year, 2 years, and 10 years. The organization emphasizes democracy through weekly staff meetings where all staff, to some degree, participate in administrative duties, financial decision making, and employee evaluations. Decisions of both the staff and board are made through consensus.

Spruce Run comes close to being a structureless or collective organization. As Freeman (1970) observes, structurelessness probably occurs in name only. Equality of staff disguises cliques and may serve as a disguise for unelected leaders called upon to represent the organization. Some organizations start out with an egalitarian structure; but when organizations grow and become more formal, some structure inevitably must develop, as with Spruce Run. Research does indeed indicate that the size of the organization affects such behavioral outcomes as attendance, absenteeism, and termination rates (Indik 1965). So too it may affect the type of organizational structure (Pugh, Hickson, and Hinings 1969).

Virtual Organizations

Communication and information technologies have converged to vastly enrich how individuals and organizations interface with one another and how we collect, maintain, and share information. Videoconferences take place in the boardroom and on the kitchen counter, depending on the equipment at hand; wireless Internet access keeps workers in touch wherever they are and offers the potential for access to any electronically stored data or knowledge; moreover, the cost of *not* adopting these new technologies has substantially surpassed the cost of making them a routine aspect of how an organization operates. Consequently, technology and the role of knowledge workers have driven—and enabled—organizations to evolve to another form: the virtual organization (Drucker 1990). The *virtual organization* (often called a *network organization*) describes a multilocation organization or a network of many organizations brought together through information and communication technology.

Bekkers defines a virtual organization as an "informational space that facilitates the sharing of information, knowledge . . . [and] communication in order to support collective action" (2003, 91). It is a set of coordinating mechanisms. Because of the virtual structure, these organizations are purported to be more responsive and innovative (Chesborough and Teece 1996) while meeting the technological demands of complex systems.[4]

Virtual and networked organizations cluster into types (Bekkers 2003; Chesborough and Teece 1996)—federated, concentric, platform, portal, and internally networked:

- In a *federated* organization, each organization is responsible for its own information systems, but they share information to improve efficiency and service. A new organization to coordinate information may be created, or one member of the federation may serve as the coordinator. Federated organizations take place in government in larger municipalities and at the state level. At the national level the Department of Homeland Security has been assigned this responsibility for information pertaining to intelligence gathering and national security.

- In a *concentric virtual organization*, one organization usually sits at the center. Two or more organizations may couple their databases to the center organization. Employing each of the databases are users within and outside the organizations. In a simple example, a state agency may contract with a nonprofit to provide a service. The state agency monitors and audits the data of the nonprofit organization. The nonprofit enters data into its own network linked to the state agency network. In another example, law enforcement personnel in offices and vehicles statewide directly access motor vehicle license data from the state's department of motor vehicles. A still more complex situation may include a state agency that audits and reviews direct service contract work from nonprofit and for-profit organizations. One private firm might handle the agency's information technology support, another firm might handle its mailings, and several nonprofit organizations might provide services.

- In the *virtual platform* organization, organizations with a shared interest use a common space for information and knowledge. This creates a virtual meeting place closed to the public. More than 40 states share a virtual platform as a means to monitor complaints and abuse (such as "slamming" or changing a customer's long-distance service provider without the customer's permission) by energy and communication companies across state lines.

- A *portal organization* is based on a gateway to a variety of users. Each state's website serves as a portal. The portal gives employees and the public access to state-provided information and services, links to departments, online access to legislative resources, and

---

[4]Chesborough and Teece (1996) refer to product innovation rather than service innovation.

links to municipalities and other outside sources. It also contains gateways (intranets) restricted to specific employees and official functions.

- An *internal networked organization* is one in which employees may physically be anywhere but can communicate and be linked with their own organizations. They may work anywhere, rarely operating from the central office.

No clear-cut answer exists for when to use such organization models or how to combine elements of multiple models. The virtual organization, whatever its configuration, has the drawbacks of requiring a sophisticated information technology infrastructure, adequate training for all users, good systems security, extensive coordination, and flexibility to adopt appropriate technology advances. (See Chapter 10 about organizational change and stability.) Many state governments grapple with where to place responsibility for their information and communication technology needs, which must be broadly drawn for practical use and finely tailored for each agency's unique needs. Should a state establish a centralized information management function that serves all state government? Should each agency have its in-house information technology (IT) function? Should the IT function be contracted to private sector providers? Although no best configuration has emerged, some states are experimenting with a mixed approach that distinguishes among common services, less broadly shared services, and specialized IT services. Viewed top-down, a mixed approach might:

1. Place common functions such as Internet, e-mail, security, procurement, and technology policy responsibilities with a state-level office.
2. With the support of the state-level office, foster collaboration among specific government components having shared needs such as law enforcement, the courts, and the prison system.
3. Establish agency-level information technology functions that operate independently but within the statewide framework and policies.
4. Contract out development functions, maintenance functions, and some security functions.

Closed Systems

What these conceptual approaches to organizational structure have in common is they center inwardly on the organization itself without regard to the external environment. Organizations are treated as closed systems. This is not a wrong approach; however, a closed system approach does not explain how or why organizations modify and adapt their structures. To have a realistic understanding of the motivations and results of reorganization, we must comprehend organizing and reorganizing as both a methodical and a political strategy (Salamon 1981). The type of organization structure chosen serves political ends, employee needs, and technical concerns. Structures differ in their capacities to coordinate task activities, in their degree and form of specialization, in their capacity to permit organizations to respond adequately to changing environments and program technologies, and in their emphasis on employee involvement. Some structures emphasize efficiency, others customer service and responsiveness, others fairness and consistency, and others program effectiveness.

ORGANIZATIONS AS ADAPTIVE OPEN SYSTEMS

Organizations are often analyzed for their ability to adapt to and change with the demands of the environment. An open systems perspective recognizes the effect of the environment on the organization and the fact that the organization structure itself may change in responding to the effects of the environment. The environment includes social, political, economic, informational, and physical factors as illustrated in Box 4–3. An *open systems* perspective describes and explains the behavior of any dynamic, cyclical, recurring patterned process or event through inputs, throughput (that is, processing), output, and feedback (Katz and Kahn 1966, see also Thompson 1967):

1. *Inputs* can be raw materials, financial resources, human resources, information resources, and technology resources, as well as the political and economic environment, the societal and community environment, and the trigger element, which could be an inquiry, constituent request, or customer order.

2. *Throughput* is the transformation of the inputs. Employees and technologies within the system itself transform the input into output through processes that are embedded subprocesses, tasks, and layers of subtasks.

3. *Output* has to do with the effect the system has on other systems. Direct services and products are first-order outputs of most organizations. For public organizations, second-order outputs can be as important or more important; these carry labels such as results, impacts, and outcomes.

4. *Feedback* is information used to keep the organization in a steady state. Feedback can be negative (such as delays in serving clients or constituents) or positive (such as achieving project milestones on time and on budget).

From a systems perspective, some organizations (or portions of them) are relatively resilient to changes in their inputs; they have a relatively stable flow of resources and carry out routine tasks such as sending out checks or providing permits. Others respond to constantly changing needs such as are implied by the name of Vermont's information management office, the Department of Information and Innovation. It is also possible that there are organizations where two cultures that demand different structures and procedures have to coexist. Classic functions such as those involved in distributing unemployment insurance, a fundamentally legal and continuous process, demand objectivity, equity, and routine; whereas keeping up with the development of the technological support services demands creativity, intellectual participation by employees, and regular change. Perrow states that for organizations with many routine actions, Weberian bureaucracy probably constitutes the socially optimal form of organizational structure (1967, 204). Even organizations in less stable situations tend to make programs and activities as routine as possible—especially those at the heart of the organizational process or mission (Thompson 1967). Several organizational analysts describe the rigidity of organizations as the result of efforts to prevent deviant cases and situations from disrupting established routines (Allison 1971; March and Simon 1993). The sunk costs in trained personnel, procedures, and other resources for current programs make administrators reluctant to alter routines (Downs 1967).

Perrow (1967, 1984) and other theorists recognize that organizations have much that is also nonroutine, even complex, and that requires many exceptions to rules. The greater the

BOX 4-3 An Open Systems Perspective: Dimensions of the Environment

What aspects of the organization's environment have a bearing on its structure? Not all dimensions will apply equally to every organization. The first column lists the broad dimensions of the environment that affect any organization, and the headings list the descriptions of that environment.

Description of the Environment

Environment	Stable/ Turbulent	Hostile/ Benign	Homogeneous/ Heterogeneous	Scarce/Adequate/ More Than Enough
Societal/ community values				
Political				
Economic				
Informational/ technological				
Physical/natural resources				
Other organizations				

Stable/turbulent: Is the environment relatively stable in terms of values, resources, and the like, or is it rapidly shifting and turbulent in terms of technology, other organizations, and so on?

Hostile/benign: Is the economic and political environment welcoming to the organization's mission or hostile to it?

Homogeneous/heterogeneous: How similar are the other organizations in the environment for relevant matters? Are they like-minded or very different? For example, different organizations such as school, town government, and companies may serve different purposes, but they share a similar culture in terms of ideology and wealth.

Scarce/adequate/more than enough: How available are resources such as political support and appropriate technology?

specialization, both vertically and horizontally, the more complex the organization. These researchers move beyond specific characteristics to look at the whole organization and its environment as an open system. To determine the type of organization, Perrow examines whether employees perform routine or nonroutine tasks in meeting the goals or mission of the organization. He is also interested in the interaction of tasks and whether tasks are completed in a linear fashion or are more complex and nonlinear. *Complex systems* are systems with numerous interactions—some hidden, some unplanned, and many nonlinear. (See Chapter 10 for a discussion of complexity and chaos theory.) Complex systems describe many large organizations; public sector examples include city governments, universities, nonprofit research institutes, and public utilities, as well as federal and state regulatory agencies, NASA, and the military.

Because of their complexity, these organizations are subject to normal (inevitable) accidents (Perrow 1984; 4, 7, 62–65). *Normal accidents* are caused by two or more component failures interacting in a nonlinear fashion; that is, multiple actions are taking place at once. (See the excerpt from *Normal Accidents* in Reading 4–5.) In complex systems components of organizations are *tightly coupled*, thereby having little buffering or slack available to alter behavior or actions quickly (90); yet these large systems "require organizational structures that have internal contradictions" (5). Because of risks, procedures are detailed and centralized, but the employees who must carry out the decisions are decentralized, working in different departments or places. For example, utility companies are coupled through grids, but they also have methods to decouple. Redundancies and other safeguards are built in so that a problem at one utility company should not bring down others. Despite redundancies and safeguards, in July 2003 a power failure occurred in Ohio, triggering power blackouts eastward to New York City and northward to Toronto. Perrow would argue that because systems are so complex, we cannot fully understand them, and thus some accidents are inevitable.

READING 4–5 Normal Accidents: A Day in the Life

You stay home from work or school because you have an important job interview downtown this morning that you have finally negotiated. Your friend or spouse has already left when you make breakfast, but unfortunately he or she has left the glass coffeepot on the stove with the light on. The coffee has boiled dry and the glass pot has cracked. Coffee is an addiction for you, so you rummage about in the closet until you find an old drip coffeemaker. Then you wait for the water to boil, watching the clock, and after a quick cup dash out the door. When you get to your car you find that in your haste you have left your car keys (and the apartment keys) in the apartment. That's okay because there is a spare apartment key hidden in the hallway for just such emergencies. (This is a safety device, a *redundancy*, incidentally.) But then you remember that you gave a friend the key the other night because he had some books to pick up, and, planning ahead, you knew you would not be home when he came. (That finishes that *redundant pathway*, as engineers call it.)

Well, it is getting late, but there is always the neighbor's car. The neighbor is a nice old gent who drives his car about once a month and keeps it in good condition. You knock on the door, your tale ready. But he tells you that it just so happened that the generator went out last week and the man is coming this afternoon to pick it up and fix it. Another "backup" system has failed you, this time through no connection with your behavior at all (*uncoupled* or independent events, in this case, because the key and the generator are rarely connected). Well, there is always the bus. But not always. The nice old gent has been listening to the radio and tells you the threatened lockout of the drivers by the bus company has indeed occurred. The drivers refuse to drive what they claim are unsafe buses, and incidentally want more money as well. (A safety system has foiled you, of all things.) You call a cab from your neighbor's apartment, but none can be had because of the bus strike. (These two events, the bus strike and the lack of cabs, are tightly connected, dependent events, or *tightly coupled* events, as we shall call them, because one triggers the other.)

You call the interviewer's secretary and say, "It's just too crazy to try to explain, but all sorts of things happened this morning and I can't make the interview with Mrs. Thompson.

Can we reschedule it?" And you say to yourself, next week I am going to line up two cars and a cab and make the morning coffee myself. The secretary answers "Sure," but says to himself, "This person is obviously unreliable; now this after pushing for weeks for an interview with Thompson." He makes a note to that effect on the record and searches for the most inconvenient time imaginable for next week, one that Mrs. Thompson might have to cancel.

Now I would like you to answer a brief questionnaire about this event. Which was the primary cause of this "accident" or foul-up?

1. Human error (such as leaving the heat on under the coffee or forgetting the keys in the rush)? Yes/No/Unsure

2. Mechanical failure (the generator in the neighbor's car)? Yes/No/Unsure

3. The environment (bus strike and taxi overload)? Yes/No/Unsure

4. Design of the system (in which you can lock yourself out of the apartment rather than having to use a door key to set the lock; a lack of emergency capacity in the taxi fleet)? Yes/No/Unsure

5. Procedures used (such as warming up coffee in a glass pot; allowing only normal time to get out this morning)? Yes/No/Unsure

If you answered "unsure" or "no" to all of these questions, I am with you. If you answered "yes" to the first, human error, you are taking a stand on multiple-failure accidents that resembles that of the President's Commission to Investigate the Accident at Three Mile Island.* The commission blamed everyone, but primarily the operators. The builders of the equipment, Babcock and Wilcox, blamed *only* the operators. If you answered "yes" to the second choice, mechanical error, you can join the Metropolitan Edison officials who run the Three Mile Island plant. They said the accident was caused by the faulty valve and then sued the vendor, Babcock and Wilcox. If you answered "yes" to the fourth, design of the system, you can join the experts of the Essex Corporation, who did a study for the Nuclear Regulatory Commission of the control room.

The best answer is not "all of the above" or any one of the choices, but rather "none of the above." (Of course I did not give you this as an option.) The cause of the accident is to be found in the complexity of the system. That is, each of the failures—design, equipment, operators, procedures, and environment—was trivial by itself. Such failures are expected to occur because nothing is perfect, and we normally take little notice of them. The bus strike would not affect you if you had your car key or the neighbor's car. The neighbor's generator failure would be of little consequence if taxis were available. If it were not an important appointment, the absence of cars, buses, and taxis would not matter. On any other morning the broken coffeepot would have been an annoyance (an *incident,* we will call it) but would not have added to your anxiety and caused you to dash out without your keys.

Though the failures were trivial in themselves, and each one had a backup system, or a redundant path to tread if the main one were blocked, the failures became serious when they interacted. It is the *interaction* of the multiple failures that explains the accident. We expect bus strikes occasionally, we expect to forget our keys with that kind of apartment lock (why else hide a redundant key?), we occasionally lend the extra key to someone rather than disclose its

---

*The Three Mile Island nuclear accident occurred in 1978 near Harrisburg, Pennsylvania. President Carter appointed a commission to investigate the causes of the accident.

hiding place. What we don't expect is for all of these events to come together at once. That is why we told the secretary that it was a crazy morning, too complex to explain, and invoked Murphy's law to ourselves (if anything can go wrong, it will).

That accident had its cause in the interactive nature of the world for us that morning and in its tight coupling—not in the discrete failures, which are to be expected and which are guarded against with backup systems. Most of the time we don't notice the inherent coupling in our world because most of the time there are no failures, or the failures that occur do not interact. But all of a sudden, things that we did not realize could be linked (buses and generators, coffee and a lent key) became linked. The system is suddenly more tightly coupled than we had realized. When we have interactive systems that are also tightly coupled, it is "normal" for them to have this kind of an accident, even though it is infrequent. It is normal not in the sense of being frequent or being expected—indeed, neither is true, which is why we were so baffled by what went wrong. It is normal in the sense that it is an inherent property of the system to occasionally experience this interaction. Three Mile Island was such a normal or system accident, and so were countless others. . . We have such accidents because we have built an industrial society that has some parts, like industrial plants or military adventures, that have highly interactive and tightly coupled units. Unfortunately some of these have high potential for catastrophic accidents.

. . . Accidents can be the result of *multiple failures.* Our example illustrated failures in five components: in design, equipment, procedures, operators, and environment. To apply this concept to accidents in general, we will need to add a sixth area—supplies and materials. . . . The example showed how different parts of the system can be quite dependent on one another, as when the bus strike created a shortage of taxis. This dependence is known as *tight coupling.* On the other hand, events in a system can occur independently, as we noted with the failure of the generator and forgetting the keys. These are *loosely coupled* events because although at this time they were both involved in the same production sequence, one was not caused by the other.

One final point that our example cannot illustrate: It isn't the best case of a normal accident or system accident . . . because the interdependence of the events was comprehensible for the person or "operator." She or he could not do much about the events singly or in their interdependence, but she or he could understand the interactions. In complex industrial, space, and military systems, the normal accident generally (not always) means that the interactions are not only unexpected, but are *incomprehensible* for some critical period. In part this is because in these human–machine systems the interactions literally cannot be seen. In part it is because, even if they are seen, they are not believed. . . .

SOURCE: From Charles Perrow, *Normal Accidents.* Copyright © 1999 Princeton University Press. Reprinted with permission of Princeton University Press.

This open systems perspective regarding structures leads to questions about how to design organizations that adapt to changing environmental demands and that support increasingly complex programs and procedures. How can we make specific complex organizations safer? Technology, programs, and people are the independent variables that affect the type of structure needed. The next section considers inputs and the role of technology as a throughput.

Inputs from the Environment

Because the environment changes constantly, studying organizations involves studying their environments. A principal environmental factor for public organizations is the decisions of elected officials. Public sector organizations are responsible to elected officials, but they also seek to influence them directly or indirectly in an effort to control the organizations' autonomy. Government and nonprofit organizations use their program expertise, control of information, constituency ties, and technological capabilities to influence policy. Using technological changes such as e-mail and electronic networks, nonprofits have been able to mount huge advocacy campaigns for particular causes, especially environmental causes (Dov and Dennis 2003; Dighe 2002). Their efforts help formulate, critique, and oppose or support legislative budget and policy initiatives the organizations define as good (Berman and West 1995; see also Chapter 9's section "Executives as Implementers of Policy"). Hospitals are particularly vigilant about the status of health care legislation. This is not formal lobbying, which government agencies and nonprofit organizations are barred from doing; but the effect can be similar. At all times public sector organizations must be cognizant of the political landscape and the game playing necessary to influence politics (for nonprofits see Marwell 2004; Gronbjerg and Salamon 2002; Bernstein 2001; for government see Rourke 1984; Jones 1984).

Another aspect of the political landscape is the well-being and concerns of clients or citizens. The organization's mission and policies may drive public organizations to advocate for groups with little political power, such as the homeless and the mentally ill (Berman and West 1995). Within this political environment are clients, customers, and interest groups who support or oppose the organization's actions.

Broader public opinion is part of this external environment as well. Changes in national views of federalism have shifted many program responsibilities from the federal level to states, localities, contractual arrangements with nonprofit and for-profit service providers, and occasional abandonment of public responsibilities (such as trash pickup in some communities). At the same time the emergence of widespread public awareness about dangers such as obesity, drunk drivers, and terrorism has caused a rise in demands for the services of both government and nonprofit programs and public regulatory agencies (Barzelay 1992; Goldsmith 2000). In the post-9/11 era, natural and human-caused threats are emerging as major environmental factors that affect the decision making in organizations as diverse as the Salvation Army and transportation departments.

Using an open systems perspective we can see how changes in the political landscape, public opinion, the economy (now the global economy), and even technological advancements have an impact on the throughput—the budgets, the staff, the technology used, information management systems, the volunteers—of an organization. This can lead to changes in structure and mission and ultimately affect the final output of the organization.

Emery and Trist (1965) help summarize organizational environments according to four levels of complexity, depending on the number and predictability of other actors in the system. (See also Chapter 10's "Levels of Turbulence" section.) The simplest level is placid and relatively free of other cooperating or competing organizations. In this environment organizations can plan and act independently, without concern for the reactions of other organizations. In the second level organizations and problems cluster, although the environment is still relatively placid. An organization must develop a strategy and perhaps a distinctive competence. Organizations in this second type of environment tend to become hierarchical. The third level is one in which similar organizations in the environment take each other into account as they develop a strategy. They may be working to move in the same direction. The most complex level is an environment so unstable and densely populated with other actors and organizations that the consequences of independent action by any one organization are no longer predictable, and strategic action must be replaced by joint action and merger. Thompson (1967) similarly argues that the most important environmental dimensions for the structure of organizations are the stability and homogeneity of the organizations' task environment. *Stability* and *homogeneity* refer to the uniformity of the demands and resources from the environment over time and the similarity among the groups with which the organization deals. In other words, in a stable, homogeneous environment, an organization can keep and maintain a set way of doing business year after year. This is, of course, unlikely for most government and nonprofit agencies.

The Throughput: The Role of Technology

Perrow's focus is on the implications of the work processes; the technology of an organization has implications for the structure of the organization, other organizations, and the ability of humans to understand what is happening. Robey (1986) summarizes this and other work and finds that work processes, defined as technology (whether computers, assembly line, report writing, or clerical work), affect the type of organizational structure. The more routine, say mailing unemployment checks, the more bureaucratic and hierarchical. The flip side is that when jobs become more complex, such as working on the street with at-risk youth, it is less clear how to design an organization structure. The work process becomes a source of uncertainty (Robey 1986). Within the organization itself, the greater the differences between departments—say, the dietary department and a nursing unit at a hospital—the more difficult it becomes to cooperate and manage the organization. For Robey this means that organizational structure and job design must be considered together (163).

An alternative view is just the opposite: An organization's structure affects the work processes, which in turn affect the technology chosen (Robey 1986, 150). The argument here is that a bureaucratic form itself influences the perception and choice of the most appropriate work process for the organization, and this in turn influences the design of any new programs. Tasks that might not be properly subject to division of labor and serial production, for example, are set up in this manner anyway if this is the norm in other parts of the organization. According to this view, only a few public organizations will break out of serial routines and hierarchical models. Thus, for example, despite the creation of the new Homeland Security agency, bureaucratic routines are likely to remain much the same as before 22 agencies and divisions were brought together.

Implicitly theorists have assumed that only when the technology is appropriate and the structure supports it will the agency be successful and effective. Acknowledging technology as an important factor in the design of organizations in no way implies that choosing a structure is therefore a wholly technical, scientific task. On the other hand, if organizational design is to fulfill the promise of creating smoother and more efficient work flow by matching structure and technology, we need to consider questions about the appropriateness of the technology itself.

RESPONSES TO ENVIRONMENTAL CHANGE

Organizations respond to changes in their environment in several ways at once. Programs can be resized, relocated, and reorganized in efforts to be responsive. Organizations may choose to handle changes in the environment by reemphasizing their values and trying to maintain the status quo. These values may or may not fit with the emerging environment. Expansion or contraction can occur with board or political approval. For example, energy and environmental programs were added to many agencies in the 1970s just as health programs (obesity, drugs, alcohol) have become part of the mission of human services agencies, both public and nonprofit, in the 2000s. As the following discussion describes, collaboration, boundary spanning, and organizational learning are among the means organizations use to understand and better relate to their environments.

Partnerships and Collaboration

Complexity increases the potential value of collaboration. The theoretical concern is not identifying complexity (even though that is often critical), but how coordination and collaboration can and do occur (Salamon 2002). Awareness of real interdependencies can lead to voluntary cooperative adjustments among agencies and can result in more stable, effective interorganizational systems (Litwak and Hylton 1962; Benson 1975; Lindblom 1965; Walter and Petr 2000). This is not to say that turf wars do not occur (Wilson, J., 1989, 195), but we concentrate here on cooperation.

Walter and Petr (2000) reviewed the literature and characterized the degree of collaboration of human services agencies on a continuum spanning cooperation, coordination, collaboration, co-optation, and integration. This is a continuum of increasingly shared decision-making processes and structures, culminating in full service integration. *Cooperation* is an informal exchange between agencies "with more or less frequent communication." *Coordination* involves formal relations between agencies with staff meeting to share plans and joint activities; but each agency maintains its own goals and structures so that agencies are not accountable to each other. A familiar type of coordination is the arrangement across local jurisdictions for emergency services units (such as fire, rescue, and police) to come to one another's aid.

Collaboration is a partnership forming a durable relationship with mutual benefits, interdependence, and formal commitment to work together for a specific purpose or purposes. The level of pooling of resources affects the organizational structures. Collaboration can be at the service level, administrative level, or both. Walter and Petr include the following domains of interagency collaboration:

- Stakeholder involvement.
- Common goals or tasks.
- Shared responsibilities.
- Shared rewards.
- Shared authority or decision making.
- Shared evaluations.
- Shared structures.
- Shared visions and values.

Empowering clients, staff, and community is crucial for successful collaboration. New structures—such as interagency councils or steering bodies, joint mission statements, and membership of staff as well as managers, consumer representatives, and citizens at large—may also need to be developed.

Co-optation takes place when an organization "captures" other organizations or parties (which may not share the organization's priorities and objectives) by bringing them into the decision-making process—ultimately as allies rather than foes (Selznick 1957, 13). The process has the effect of shifting the other parties' loyalty and socializing them into the co-opting organization's culture and value system. This can occur under many circumstances, such as when regional environmental protection and economic development policy goals appear to conflict. Successful co-optation may evolve into one of the other points along the cooperation–integration continuum.

The last level is *integration*. The merger of numerous agencies into the Homeland Security Department in 2002 was designed to increase coordination and cooperation. Because this was a forced merger, the steps toward integration did not take place, and the agency is having growing pains. Only two years after its creation Congress saw the need for another new agency—the Office of National Intelligence—which both complicates and complements the Homeland Security Department's mission. The Office of National Intelligence is a "superexecutive" office created to coordinate agencies, align missions, and prioritize terrorism-related budgets that include those of Homeland Security, the Department of Defense, and others. As is typical of organizations involved in integration, Homeland Security exhibits its share of confusion, low morale, and persistent resistance within organizational levels and units.

For all of the benefits of cooperation, partnering, and other alliance approaches, they also have substantial drawbacks, and theory does not seem to guide when these forms should be used. Creating partnerships tends to be time-consuming, with no systematic, rational way to create them (Ostrower 2005; Lindenberg and Dobel 1999). "A Puzzlement," a song from Rodgers and Hammerstein's Broadway musical *The King and I*, summarizes the quandary:

> Shall I join with other nations in alliance?
> If allies are weak, am I not best alone?
> If allies are strong with power to protect me,
> Might they not protect me out of all I own?
> Is it a danger to be trusting one another,
> One will seldom want to do what other wishes;
> But unless someday somebody trusts somebody
> There'll be nothing left on earth excepting fishes!
> . . . Is a puzzlement. (Rodgers and Hammerstein 1951)
>
> SOURCE: Williamson Music, NY NY.

Boundary-Spanning Units

Rather than creating some form of partnership or cooperation, Thompson theorizes, organizations adapt to their environments by creating internal boundary-spanning units. *Boundary-spanning* units (see "Boundary Spanners" in Chapter 5) buffer the organization from outside interference and interact with other organizations and people (that is, the environment) on a regular, ongoing basis. Thompson proposes, "Under norms of rationality, organizations facing heterogeneous task environments seek to identify homogeneous segments and establish structural units to deal with each" (1967, 70). That is, organizations slice their environment and themselves in matching or complementing ways, making it easier to address diverse segments and perspectives.

Illustrating this proposition are the plethora of public information/public relations offices, marketing offices, legislative liaison offices, hotlines, interagency task forces, ombudsmen, contract offices, mediation offices, and other similar offices. The greater the number and diversity of groups in an organization's environment—other governmental bodies/nonprofits, interest groups, media outlets, business groups, and so on—the more specialized boundary-spanning units the rational organization is drawn to create. A further implication is that the greater the proliferation of these specialized boundary-spanning units, the more elaborate the integration mechanisms must be to coordinate activities with each other and with the technological core of the organization.

Thompson's proposition helps explain why we should expect organizations in tumultuous environments to have more complexity of specialization and more integration mechanisms than organizations in more placid environments. Although little systematic research on this point has been done, Thompson's proposition squares with considerable experience. As the public becomes more involved through formal processes (such as public meetings and other citizen participation requirements) and through informal processes (such as volunteering), political oversight and interest group demands may increase. Organizations are likely to respond to this elevated attention from the environment by creating structures to deal with additional duties. The more such demands apply, as is frequently true, the more organizational complexity becomes compounded.

Even though boundary spanning is a response to a complex environment, it too can become routine. Another Thompson proposition is that the greater the predictability of environmental activities, the more routinely the organization can handle them. Thompson notes, "The organization component facing a stable task environment will rely on rules to achieve its adaptation to that environment" (1967, 71). The routine application of rules, of course, costs less in time and other resources than direct feedback, negotiation, or an elaborate planning process.

On the other hand, unstable or unpredictable demands, complaints, and opportunities cannot be effectively handled by rules. Boundary-spanning units and executives negotiate between the organization and outside groups to resolve concerns. Uncertainty and the possibility of departure from standard operating procedures by a boundary-spanning unit can have a ripple effect on the rest of the organization, propagating greater uncertainty and possible departures from rules in the core work. If, for example, a regulatory or benefit agency makes an exception to some requirement in a particular case, other internal procedures will have to be altered to allow the case to proceed through the system.

These are frequent roles and impacts of an organization's boundary-spanning elements. Applying Thompson's propositions broadly, that is why the more heterogeneous, dense, and unpredictable the environment, the greater the number and complexity of boundary-spanning units, the more elaborate the means of integrating them into the core work, and the more complex the core work.

Learning Organizations

Still another response to environmental change is the learning organization. *Learning organizations* or *self-designing organizations* are organizations in which learning how to adapt occurs continually (Senge 1990). The principal thesis is that the organizational structure, associated work and technologies, and key operational systems should evolve, be unique, and expect to be impermanent in response to emerging knowledge and the environment. This systems perspective assumes that organizations, or the people in them, have a shared vision and are committed to improving processes and services or products in ways that ensure the success of the organization.

Senge describes five component disciplines that must converge for organizations to develop a culture that will tap the expertise and commitment of every member at every level. When that is accomplished, organizations "can truly 'learn,'. . . can continually enhance their capacity to realize their highest aspirations" (1990, 6). Senge identifies five disciplines critical to success as a learning organization:

1. *Systems thinking*—the ability to contemplate the whole of a phenomenon instead of simply any individual part of the pattern.

2. *Personal mastery*—the discipline of continually clarifying and deepening one's personal vision, of focusing one's energies, of developing patience, and of seeing reality objectively.

3. *Mental models*—the process by which individuals learn how to surface and challenge other individuals' mental models (deeply ingrained assumptions, generalizations, pictures, or images) that influence how one understands the work and therefore takes action.

4. *Building shared vision*—the skill of unearthing a shared "picture of the future" that binds people together around a common identity and sense of destiny, thereby fostering genuine commitment and engagement rather than compliance.

5. *Team learning*—the skill of sharing "dialogue," the capacity of members of a team to suspend assumptions and enter into a genuine "thinking together," and learning how to recognize the patterns of interaction in teams that undermine learning (1990, 6–10).

The existence of these five characteristics, or disciplines as Senge calls them, means that many traditional structures and patterns of behavior are radically changed. Senge defines *structure* as a process of decision making more than a structural form. Structure is the interrelationship of people, resources, and process, not just the offices shown in an organization chart (27, 44). According to Senge, the structure of the organization influences the behavior of people (42–47). Learning organizations and employees try to enhance their capacity and realize their highest aspirations (1990, 6).

For Senge, recognizing constraints in the system is important. If we view what we do in organizations as processes, we can then identify the constraints to success. This is also known as the *theory of constraints* (Goldratt 1990). Goldratt points out that for an organization to be effective, it must first be sure of its goal and then remedy the bottlenecks or the weakest links. Above all, resources should be used to eliminate such constraints; only then can the organization be truly effective. Each process and component within the organization has the potential to constrain (or contribute to) the organization's effectiveness; consequently remedying a bottleneck is likely to make the entire system more effective.

Senge's ideas build on earlier organizational research. Korten's (1980) study of rural development programs identifies three key attributes of learning organizations. First, "the learning organization embraces error" (1980, 498). Rather than denying that a program is failing or insisting that some other set of actors is responsible for the failure, the learning organization looks for problems, corrects those it can, and seeks change from other quarters when necessary to remedy other problems. For example, pilot projects and field experiments would be the first step in program development.

Second, the learning organization takes advantage of existing local knowledge and the technology of those who have been coping with problems the program seeks to remedy. Examining existing technologies, even those that have been inadequate, allows program developers to understand the priorities and constraints of the target group.

Finally, the learning organization links knowledge to action so that the implementing organizations are "built up from the teams that created the original program" (Korten 1980, 499). Peters and Waterman (1982) also see this as a way to ensure that the initial dedication and enthusiasm of project founders and "champions" are used and rewarded. Organization structures in successful programs are composed of teams of clients, researchers, and administrators, which allow "rapid, creative adaptation" necessary to build new knowledge into the developing programs.

Prior to Senge's work, Hedberg, Nystrom, and Starbuck (1976) identified the self-designing organization as an organization constantly searching for new approaches to solve problems. They identify complacency as a key reason organizations fail to continue to search. To remedy this, they suggest six organizational behaviors:

1. Act on minimal consensus rather than waiting for unanimity.

2. Strive for only minimal contentment among personnel, which sharpens their desire for change and their search for alternatives.

3. Work toward only minimal affluence because even though a "small buffer of flexible resources is an asset" (59), too much affluence breeds complacency and contempt for new opportunities.

4. Place only minimal faith in plans or goals. Even though they are needed to direct immediate action, they should be discarded easily.

5. Attempt to be only minimally consistent. Total consistency impedes the pluralistic bargaining process that produces incremental changes, thereby forcing a delayed and destructive revolution to achieve any change.

6. Aim only for minimal rationality in procedures. Even though basic managerial processes must be established, highly coherent and fully rationalized structures convey a false sense of control and prematurely define new problems and opportunities rather than encouraging their exploration. Some structural and procedural ambiguities will keep the organization in a state of readiness for change.

Whereas the views of Senge (1990), Korten (1980), and (we infer) Hedberg and his colleagues (1976) are that learning organizations are not hierarchical, Landau (1973) perceives a self-correcting organization as fitting the Weberian bureaucratic model. In essence, to be self-correcting, organizations must be more rational, more empirical, and much more open to continuous reexamination. Too often in organizations, Landau claims, "rationalization replaces verification" (1973, 540). The ways to bring about self-correction are periodic program audits, operations research, and cost analysis in the context of searching for error rather than trying to rationalize it. Interestingly, Korten rejects these self-examination techniques, arguing for case study interpretation over quantitative statistical analysis. His reasoning may be that quantitative analysis is more readily used to disguise failure and shut citizens out of the examination process.

Argyris and Schön's analysis of organizational learning (1978), while not specifically about organizational structure, focuses on the process of learning. *Single-loop learning* occurs when an organization recognizes and corrects mistakes it makes because of its processes and nonstrategic goals, then adjusts the processes and goals accordingly. *Double-loop learning* occurs when an organization also examines and adjusts its underlying values and strategic goals—a challenge more formidable than single-loop learning. In general, the idea behind the self-designing learning organization is to maintain a state of dynamic tension. The self-designing organization differs in its strategies to create and maintain the dynamic state. Self-designing organizations make satisfaction with the status quo difficult by permitting some degree of dissatisfaction and by adopting decision-making rules that make changes easier to achieve.

The prescription for the learning organization varies. Tom Peters (1992, 1987) professes a prescriptive, frenzied view of what organizations should be. He advocates a crazy, constantly changing organization that supports human imagination, independence, temporary employment, and networking. He imagines that employees will have no permanent offices. Rather, they might carry their materials from one space to the next, from one project to the next. Burns and Stalker (1994) similarly prescribe an organic, adaptive structure to address the criticism that bureaucracy fails to meet the demands of unstable conditions and is thus unable to adapt to changes. Tasks and work flow are flexible and subject to continual redefinition on the basis of new information. Formal authority roles and specializations are loosened to create a milieu for flexibility, creativity, and the growth of knowledge. Employees are loyal to their work and their professional communities, but not necessarily to a single organization. Movement from one organization to another is common, but so too is a strong organizational commitment while at one organization.

As with all structural models, learning organizations have practical challenges. Such organizations may be more difficult to put into practice in government and nonprofit organizations than in business (Senge 1990, 15). The political/board environment, which is interested in efficiency and accountability, constrains a learning environment. In government, developing and sustaining such organizations is problematic when the women and men filling top leadership positions may turn over rapidly and may see the public employee as the enemy. The value of intensive education and training for leadership and management may not pass muster in budgets. Theory in this area presumes a constant need for change when that may or may not be true. Also, by its very notion, learning organizations are less than clear on structures. Senge does not describe what the structure should look like; rather, he states that it is one in which there is an openness of communication, personal responsibility for actions, decentralized authority (as much as possible), decision making with a mind to the well-being of the whole organization, and forgiveness when mistakes occur (1990, 300). This description is similar to a participative organization without the major emphasis on teamwork.

Whatever the debate and difficulty, theory about learning organizations underscores that structure and flexibility or even innovation are not antithetical.

Complexity in Open Systems

Research on the relationship between environmental change and structure is mixed but appears to point to a consistent trend: Organizational success is enhanced when the complexity of structures and processes matches the complexity of the environment. This broad finding argues for open system organizations, which are designed to be in tune with the environment rather than to ignore it. Lawrence and Lorsch (1986) considered this relationship in a study of private sector firms; their findings have interesting implications for all organizations. They found that in more successful firms, the complexity of a firm's internal structure matched the rate of market change. Firms in the most unstable environments showed the greatest structural complexity, with a relatively large number and diversity of subdivisions. Further, subdivisions that interacted most with external groups (such as research and sales) were less hierarchically structured than routine production divisions. These facts suggest that the structural differences in these firms were not global matters of style; instead they were choices designed to meet environmental uncertainties.

Integration mechanisms also differed among the industries, with more complex task coordination methods used in plastics firms than in other industry segments. Special liaison units were created, for example, to improve interdepartmental coordination between research and production because their divergent goals and work processes sparked frequent conflicts. The relationship between environmental change and structure was stronger for successful than for unsuccessful firms.

Hage and Aiken (1969) conducted research that also supports the relationship between environment and structural adaptability. They list seven structural characteristics of adaptive or dynamic organizations of adaptive organizations:

1. Organizational complexity, defined as the number of professional occupational specialties in the organization, is positively associated with the ability of the organization to respond to external change because professionals are often oriented to developments in their fields and bring them to the organization.

2. Centralized authority in the upper echelons slows the rate of change because decision criteria are static and lower-ranking personnel, who often see the need for change, are excluded from decision making.

3. Formalization (the degree to which tasks are highly codified into rules and standard operating procedures) slows the rate of program change. When large portions of program and management activities are rule-governed, change is delayed and perceptions of the possibility of substantial change are limited. Extreme formalization also slows the process of implementing change because new rules must be developed and coordinated with existing rules.

4. Stratification (differentiation by rank and pay) decreases the rate of change. Stratification creates insecurities and fears of loss of status. It also discourages negative reports about organizational performance and open discussion of problems with superiors.

5. Emphasis on a high volume of production lowers the rate of change because change, almost of necessity, disrupts production.

6. Greater emphasis on efficiency delays change because new program ideas are usually oriented first to improvements in quality, not efficiency. Thus program changes will be adopted only when they have developed to the point of high operating efficiency.

7. Higher levels of job satisfaction are also associated with greater rates of change because satisfaction increases commitment to organizational success and enables the organization to overcome the strains involved in change.

What is missing from this research is a comparative analysis of the state of the environment and the subsequent success or failure of the organizations studied. Nevertheless, Hage and Aiken's work is important in that it offers explanations for the relationship between structural characteristics and the capacity to change.

ALTERNATIVE PARADIGMS?

Are there alternative paradigms? Perhaps it sounds impossible to have a learning organization or a constantly changing organization in which people come and go; but consider an alternative. Eggert (1990, 36–39) offers an entirely different organizational structure and argues that we limit ourselves by thinking within the bureaucratic paradigm. She suggests a contemplative paradigm, unrelated to the rational, efficient organization. In this organizational structure, the administrators are contemplative. Coworkers have inherent value without regard to what they produce or do. Human dignity, pain, and compassion are recognized. Managers do not need to be in control. "Impatience, tenseness, and anxiety are replaced with a relaxed, open awareness" (37). Listening to others is an important skill, as is being silent to think about what will happen next. Identification with the poor and the suffering "is an integral aspect of working in the public interest" (39). There is time to tell stories and share visions at meetings rather than just have dull, controlled meetings. Creativity is a gift that we cannot manufacture, but not all creativity should be valued. There are choices to make.

Does such a model work for public organizations? Does it exist among the tens of thousands of government and nonprofit organizations that operate today? Probably not; the closest model is the structureless organization, one used from time to time in small, help-oriented nonprofit agencies. But theory begets experimentation, and Eggert's model could be worth a try. Other good news is that (1) experimentation also happens when no theory paves the way—people just have an idea to try out and the moxie to glean support from others; and (2) serendipity happens—fortunate discoveries that people are not looking for. The critical point is that we can determine how our public organizations are structured; they are not frozen in place.

Today industrial psychologists and other researchers are adding another component to the study of organizational structure: the physical environment of the office. They seek understanding of the relationships between the physical layout of the office and employee performance, between space and human productivity. The U.S. General Services Administration is on the cutting edge of this research. Anyone who has suffered from aching wrists, back, or neck knows the importance of a well-arranged desk and computer. Anyone who has wondered why office space is often allocated by position—the higher the position, the nicer the office and the better the view—is familiar with the issue. Fixed wall space is increasingly uncommon for practical reasons and for organizational restructuring. The goal of this new approach to structure—the relationship of physical space to employee behavior—is the same as that of any other approach: to improve effectiveness, efficiency, and innovation.

CONCLUSION

This chapter has surveyed a variety of possible organizational structures from Weberian bureaucracy to learning organizations. Characteristics of the structure of organizations affect the ability to change and adapt (Huber, Sutcliffe, Miller, and Glick 1995). Structures vary in their emphasis on effectiveness, efficiency, innovativeness, responsiveness, transparency, and democratic decision making. Some seem to be more appropriate for small organizations, whereas others work best in large organizations. Often this has to do with complexity.

Many organizations and systems are complex both in everyday terms and in Perrow's definition. Considering environmental conditions focuses attention on the need for not only internal reorganization but also the coordination of multiple organizations. The symbolic functions of organization structures and reorganization can be as critical as their coordinative functions.

Traditional assumptions about reorganization have been that it changes the agency's internal processes and thus is a suitable remedy to improve efficiency and effectiveness of policy, program, budgets, and management issues. Organization theory posits that this may not be adequate; what is also necessary is a legal and policy change. What the structural organization literature does suggest is that different types of organizational structures serve different purposes: efficiency, effectiveness, democracy, innovation. We are not much nearer to a canned method for determining and optimizing structure than when Weber proposed the ideal bureaucracy, nor should we expect to be given the different emphases of structures. Rather, we recognize today that restructuring, creating new organizations, and merging organizations involve a whole series of conditions that include the political environment, the type of programs, the type of services, and the dynamics of both the external and internal environment. Structures can support or impede the efficient coordination of work—the work of the public sector.

FOR FURTHER READING

A great introduction to understanding the theories of organizational structure is Henry Mintzberg's *The Structuring of Organizations* (Englewood Cliffs, NJ: Prentice Hall, 1979). Frank Ostroff fleshes out the idea of a flat organization in a discussion of the reorganization of OSHA in *The Horizontal Organization* (New York: Oxford University Press, 1999). A review of the research on technology as a basis for structure is offered by Donald Gerwin's "The Relationship between Structure and Technology" in Paul Nystrom and William Starbuck, eds., *Handbook of Organization Design: Volume 2—Remodeling Organizations and Their Environments* (New York: Oxford University Press, 1981). Charles Perrow's book, *Normal Accidents* (Princeton: Princeton University Press, 1984), with a new afterword added in 1999, provides a classic discussion of the technological problems with large organizations using an open systems model. The impact of political agendas on design efforts is described by Lawrence Lynn in *The State and Human Services* (Cambridge, MA: MIT Press, 1980). Finally, Karen Hult and Charles Walcott, in *Governing Public Organizations: Politics, Structure, and Institutional Design* (Pacific Grove: Brooks/Cole, 1990), discuss decision models as they relate to organizational structure and different forms of contract.

For interesting examinations on the political effects of contractual relationships between nonprofits and government, see Susan Bernstein, "The Game of Contracted Services" in J. Steven Ott, ed., *Understanding Nonprofit Organizations* (Boulder, CO: Westview Press, 2001); and Kirsten Gronbjerg and Lester Salamon's "Devolution, Marketization, and the Changing Shape of Government–Nonprofit Relations" in Lester Salamon, ed., *The State of Nonprofit America* (Washington, DC: Brookings Institution Press, 2002), pp. 447–71. For information about the relationships between nonprofits and government, see the Fall 2004 (Volume 11) issue of *The Nonprofit Quarterly*.

For complementary excerpts from classics readings, see most editions of Jay Shafritz and J. Steven Ott's (and coauthors) *Classics of Organizational Theory* (Belmont, CA: Thomson Wadsworth): Herbert Simon, "The Proverbs of Administration"; Max Weber, "Bureaucracy"; Blau and Scott, "The Concept of the Formal Organization"; Burns and Stalker, "Mechanistic and Organic Systems"; Katz and Kahn, "Organizations and the System Concept"; and James Thompson, "Organizations in Action."

For complementary nonprofit case studies to go with this chapter, see Robert Goliembiewski and Jerry Stevenson's *Cases and Applications in Non-Profit Management* (Belmont, CA: Thomson Wadsworth, 1998): Case 26, "Changing Missions for Nonprofits," and Case 27, "Organizational Development in the Ashfield Youth Corps."

REFERENCES

Allison, Graham. 1971. *Essence of decision: Explaining the Cuban missile crisis.* Boston: Little, Brown.

Argyris, Chris, and Donald Schön. 1978. *Organizational learning: A theory of action perspective.* Reading, MA: Addison Wesley.

Baber, Walter F. 1983. *Organizing the future: Matrix models for the postindustrial polity.* Tuscaloosa, AL: University of Alabama Press.

Barnard, Chester Irving. 1938/1968. *The functions of the executive.* Cambridge: Harvard University Press.

Barzelay, Michael. 1992. *Breaking through bureaucracy: A new vision for managing in government.* Berkeley: University of California Press.

Bekkers, Victor. 2003. "E-government and the emergence of virtual organizations in the public sector." *Information Polity* 8: 89–101.

Bennis, Warren, and Philip Slater. 1964. *The temporary society.* New York: Harper and Row.

Benson, Kenneth. 1975. The interorganizational network as a political economy. *Administrative Science Quarterly* 20: 229–49.

Berman, Evan M., and Jonathan P. West. 1995. Public–private leadership and the role of nonprofit organizations in local government: The case of social services. *Policy Studies Review* 14: 235–47.

Bernstein, Susan. 2001. The game of contracted services. In *Understanding nonprofit organizations,* 267–75. Ed. J. Steven Ott. Boulder, CO: Westview Press.

Blau, Peter M., Wolf V. Heydebrand, and Robert E. Stauffer. 1966. "The Structure of Small Bureaucracies." *American Sociological Review* 31: 179–191.

Brandl, John, and Randall Bovbjerg. 1989. How organizations count: Incentives and inspiration. *Journal of Policy Analysis and Management* 8: 489–94.

Burns, Tom, and Gerald Stalker. 1994. *The management of innovation*. Rev. ed. Oxford: Oxford University Press.

Carr, David, Ian D. Littman, and John K. Condon. 1995. A lexicon of valid, pseudo-, and non-approaches to restructuring government. In *Improvement driven government: Public service for the 21st century*, 358–60. Arlington, VA: Coopers & Lybrand LLP.

Chandler, Alfred. 1962. *Strategy and structure: Chapters in the history of the industrial enterprise*. Cambridge: MIT Press.

Chesborough, Henry, and David Teece. 1996. When is virtual virtuous? Organizing for innovation. *Harvard Business Review* 74: 65–73.

Cleveland, Harlan. 1985. The twilight of hierarchy: Speculations on the global information society. *Public Administration Review* 45: 185–95.

Cohen, Steven. 1988. *The effective public manager.* San Francisco: Jossey-Bass.

Deming, W. Edwards. 2000. *Out of Crisis*. Cambridge, MA: MIT Press.

Dighe, Atul. 2002. Demographic and technological imperatives. In *The state of nonprofit America*. Ed. L. M. Salamon. Washington, DC: Brookings Institution Press.

Dov, Te'eni, and Dennis R. Young. 2003. The changing role of nonprofits in the network economy. *Nonprofit & Voluntary Sector Quarterly* 32: 397–415.

Downs, Anthony. 1967. *Inside bureaucracy*. Boston: Little, Brown. (Reissued Prospect Heights, IL: Waveland Press, 1994.)

Drucker, Peter. 1990. *Managing the non-profit organization: Practices and principles*. New York: HarperCollins.

Durst, Samantha L., and Charldean Newell. 2001. "The Who, Why, and How of Reinvention in Nonprofit Organizations." *Nonprofit Management & Leadership* 11: 443–457.

Eggert, Nancy. 1990. "Contemplation and administration: An alternative paradigm." in *How public organizations work*, 31–41. Ed.C. Bella Vita. New York: Praeger.

Emery, F. E., and E. L. Trist. 1965. The causal texture of organizational environments. *Human Relations* 18: 21–32.

Fayol, Henri. 1949. *General and industrial management*. Trans. Constance Storrs. London: Pitman.

Freeman, Jo. 1975. Political organization in the feminist movement. *Acta Sociologica* 18: 222–44.

———. 1970. Tyranny of structurelessness. [Accessed January 3, 2005.] Retrieved from Jo Freeman at http://jofreeman.com/joreen/tyranny.htm.

Gerwin, Donald. 1981. "The Relationship between Structure and Technology" in Paul Nystrom and William Starbuck, eds., *Handbook of Organization Design: Volume 2—Remodeling Organizations and Their Environments*. New York: Oxford University Press.

Goldratt, Eliyahu. 1990. *Theory of constraints*. Great Barrington, MA: North River Press.

Goldsmith, Stephen. 2000. Making government cheaper and better. *USA Today Magazine*, January 11–12.

Gronbjerg, Kirsten, and Lester Salamon. 2002. Devolution, marketization, and the changing shape of government–nonprofit relations. In *The state of nonprofit America*, 447–71. Ed. Lester Salamon. Washington, DC: Brookings Institution Press.

Gulick, Luther. 1937. "Notes on the theory of administration." In *Papers on the science of administration*. Ed. L. Gulick and L. Urwick. New York: Institute of Public Administration.

Hackman, J. Richard, and Ruth Wageman. 1995. Total quality management: Empirical, conceptual, and practical issues. *Administrative Science Quarterly* 40: 309–42.

Hage, Jerald, and Michael Aiken. 1969. Routine technology, social structure and organizational goals. *Administrative Science Quarterly* 14: 366–76.

Halachmi, Arie, and Kenneth L. Nichols, eds. 1997. *Enterprise government: Franchising and cross-servicing for administrative support*. Burke, VA: Chatelaine Press.

Hall, Richard. 1991. *Organizations structure, process and outcomes*. Englewood Cliffs, NJ: Prentice Hall.

Hedberg, Bo, Paul Nystrom, and William Starbuck. 1976. Camping on seesaws: Prescriptions for a self-designing organization. *Administrative Science Quarterly* 21: 41–65.

Homeland Security Act of 2002. HR 5005-8, P.L. 108-458 amended by Intelligence Reform & Terrorism Prevention Act of 2004.

Hoover, Herbert. 1949. A concluding report to Congress by the Commission on Organization of the Executive Branch of the Government (known as the 1st Hoover Commission), May.

Huber, George, Kathleen Sutcliffe, Chet Miller, and William Glick. 1995. Understanding and predicting organizational change. In *Organizational change and redesign*. Ed. G. Huber and W. Glick. New York: Oxford University Press.

Hult, Karen, and Charles Walcott. 1990. *Governing Public Organizations: Politics, Structure, and Institutional Design*. Pacific Grove: Brooks/Cole.

Indik, Bernard. 1965. Organization size and member participation. *Human Relations* 18: 339–49.

Jones, Charles O. 1984. *An introduction to the study of public policy*. Monterey, CA: Brooks/Cole Pub. Co.

Katz, Daniel, and Robert Kahn. 1966. *The social psychology of organizations*. New York: John Wiley & Sons, Inc.

Kaufman, Herbert. 1960. *The forest ranger: a study in administrative behavior*. Baltimore: Johns Hopkins Press.

Kingdon, Donald. 1973. *Matrix organization: Managing information technology*. London: Tavistock Publications.

Korten, David. 1980. Community organization and rural development. *Public Administration Review* 40: 480–511.

Landau, Martin. 1973. On the concept of a self-correcting organization. *Public Administration Review* 33: 533–42.

Lawrence Lynn. 1980. *The state and human services*. Cambridge, MA: MIT Press.

Lawrence, Paul R., and Jay W. Lorsch. 1986. *Organization and environment: Managing differentiation and integration*. Rev. ed. Boston: Harvard Business School Press.

Lindblom, Charles. 1965. *The intelligence of democracy*. New York: Free Press.

Lindenberg, Marc, and J. Patrick Dobel. 1999. The challenges of globalization for northern international relief and development NGOs. *Nonprofit and Voluntary Sector Quarterly* 28: 4–24.

Litwak, E., and L. Hylton. 1962. Interorganizational analysis: A hypothesis on coordinating agencies. *Administrative Science Quarterly* 6: 397–420.

March, James G., and Herbert A. Simon. 1993. *Organizations*. 2nd ed. New York: John Wiley & Sons.

Marwell, Nicole. 2004. Privatizing the welfare state: Nonprofit community-based organizations as poetical actors. *American Sociological Review* 69: 265–91.

Mintzberg, Henry. 1979. *The structuring of organizations*. Englewood Cliffs, NJ: Prentice Hall.

Mosher, Frederick C. 1982. *Democracy and the public service*. 2nd ed. New York: Oxford University Press.

National Performance Review (U.S.). 1993. *Creating a government that works better & costs less: The report of the national performance review*. Vice President Al Gore. New York: Plume/Penguin.

Newell, Allen, and Herbert Simon. 1972. *Human problem solving*. Englewood Cliffs, NJ: Prentice-Hall.

Osborne, David, and Ted Gaebler. 1992. *Reinventing government: How the entrepreneurial spirit is transforming the public sector*. Reading, MA: Addison-Wesley.

Oster, Stephen. 1992. Nonprofit organizations in a franchise age. *Nonprofit Management & Leadership* 2: 223–38.

———. 1996. Nonprofit organizations and their local affiliates: A study in organization form. *Journal of Economic Behavior & Organization*: 101–17.

Ostroff, Frank. 1999. *Horizontal organization*. New York: Oxford University Press.

Ostrower, Francie. 2005. The reality underneath the buzz of partnerships: The potentials and pitfalls of partnering. *Stanford Social Innovation Review*, Spring. [Accessed June 2005.] Available from Stanford University at www.ssireview.com.

Ott, J. Steven, ed. 2001. *Understanding nonprofit organizations*. Boulder, CO: Westview Press.

Parsons, Talcott. 1964. *The social system.* New York: Free Press.

_____. 1969. *Politics and social structure.* New York: Free Press.

_____. 1970. *Social structure and personality.* London: Free Press; Collier-Macmillan.

Perrow, Charles. 1967. A framework for the comparative analysis of organization. *American Sociological Review* 32: 194–208.

_____. 1972. *Complex organizations: A critical essay.* Glenview, IL: Scott, Foresman and Company.

_____. 1984. *Normal accidents.* New York: Basic Books.

Peter, Laurence J., and Raymond Hull. 1969. *The Peter principle.* New York: W. Morrow.

Peters, Guy B. 1994. Government reorganization: A theoretical analysis. In *Handbook of Bureaucracy.* Ed. A. Farazmand. New York: M. Dekker.

Peters, Thomas J. 1987. *Thriving on chaos: Handbook for a management revolution.* 1st ed. New York: Knopf.

_____. 1992. *Liberation management: Necessary disorganization for the nanosecond nineties.* New York: A. A. Knopf.

Peters, Thomas, and Robert Waterman. 1982. *In search of excellence.* New York: Warner.

Pugh, D. S., D. J. Hickson, and C. R. Hinings. 1969. "An Empirical Taxonomy of Structures of Work Organizations." *Administrative Science Quarterly* 14: 115–126.

Risher, Howard W., and Charles Fay. 1997. *New strategies for public pay: rethinking government compensation programs.* San Francisco, CA: Jossey-Bass.

Robey, Daniel. 1986. *Designing organizations.* 2nd ed. Homewood, IL: Irwin.

Rodgers, Richard, and Oscar Hammerstein. 1951. A Puzzlement. New York: Williamson Music.

Rourke, Francis E. 1984. *Bureaucracy, Politics, and Public Policy.* 3rd ed. Boston: Little Brown.

Salamon, Lester. 1981. The goals of reorganization. *Administration and Society*, 12: 471–500.

_____. 1999. *America's nonprofit sector: a primer.* New York: Foundation Center.

_____. 2002. Of market failure, voluntary failure, and third-party government: Toward a theory of government–nonprofit relations in the modern welfare state. In *The state of nonprofit America.* Ed. L. M. Salamon. Washington, DC: Brookings Institution Press.

Salamon, Lester, ed. 2002. *The State of Nonprofit America.* Washington, DC: Brookings Institution Press.

Scott, W. Richard. 1987. *Organizations: Rational, natural, and open systems.* 2nd ed. Englewood Cliffs, NJ: Prentice-Hall.

Scott, William, Terence Mitchell, and Philip Birnbaum. 1981. *Organization theory: A structural and behavioral analysis.* 4th ed. Homewood, IL: Richard D. Irwin.

Selznick, Phillip. 1957. Leadership in Administration: A Sociological Interpretation. Berkeley, CA: University of California Press, 1984. (Originally published by Harper & Row, 1957.)

Senge, Peter M. 1990. *The fifth discipline: The art and practice of the learning organization.* New York: Doubleday/Currency.

Simon, Herbert. 1946. Proverbs of administration. In *Classics of public administration*, 112–24. 6th ed. Ed. J. M. Shafritz and A. C. Hyde. Oak Park, IL: Moore Publishing, 2005.

_____. 1947. *Administrative behavior.* New York: Macmillan. (4th edition Republished in 1997 by Free Press.)

Sloan, Alfred P. Jr. 1964. *My years with General Motors.* Garden City, NY: Doubleday Publishing. (Reprinted in 1990 by Doubleday/Currency Publishing.)

Standley, Anne. 2001. Reinventing a large nonprofit: Lessons from four voluntary health associations. *Nonprofit Management and Leadership* 11: 305–20.

Theobald, Nick A., and Sean Nicholson-Crotty. 2005. The many faces of span of control: Organizational structure across multiple goals. *Administration & Society* 36: 648–61.

Thompson, James D. 1967. *Organizations in action: Social science bases of administrative theory.* New York: McGraw-Hill. (Republished in 2003 by Transaction Publishers.)

Toffler, Alvin. 1970. *Future shock.* New York: Random House.

Townsend, Robert. 1984. *Further Up the Organization.* New York: Alfred A. Knopf.

U.S. Dept of Homeland Security. 2002. *Reorganization plan.* November 25.

Urwick, Lydall. 1943. *The elements of administration.* New York: Harper.

Walter, U. M., and C. G. Petr. 2000. A template for family-centered interagency collaboration. *Families in Society* 81: 494–503.

Walton, Mary. 1990. *Deming management at work.* New York: G. P. Putnam's Sons.

Waterman, Robert. 1992. *Adhocracy.* New York: Norton.

Weber, Max. 1947/1992. *Theory of social and economic organization.* Trans. A. Henderson and T. Parsons. Glencoe, IL: The Free Press,.

Williams, Daniel. 2000. Reinventing the proverbs of government. *Public Administration Review* 60: 522–35.

Wilson, James Q. 1989. *Bureaucracy: What government agencies do and why they do it.* New York: Basic Books.

Wilson, Woodrow. 1887/1978. The study of administration. In *Classics of public administration.* Ed. J. M. Shafritz and A. C. Hyde. Oak Park, IL: Moore Publishing Co, 2005. (Original publication, *Political Science Quarterly.*)

Young, Dennis R. 2001. Organizational identity in nonprofit organizations: Strategic and structural implications." *Nonprofit Management & Leadership* 12: 139–57.

Young, Dennis, Neil Bania, and Darlyne Bailey. 1996. Structure and accountability: A study of nonprofit associations. *Nonprofit Management & Leadership* 6: 347–65.

Zeller, Shawn. 2005. OPM official touts governmentwide civil service reform. Daily briefing, April 13. Accessed June 2005. Available from *Government Executive,* www.goveexec.com.

Chapter 5

Communication

By Ed Colley

Communication and organization are inseparable. As early as 1938, Chester Barnard argued that "in any exhaustive theory of organization, communication would occupy a central place, because structure, extensiveness, and scope of organizations are almost entirely determined by communication technique" (1979, 8). Three decades later Katz and Kahn stated no less emphatically that communication is the essence of a social system or an organization (1978). The centrality of communication in organizational, and interorganizational, success was once again emphasized at the beginning of the twenty-first century when the 9/11 Commission stated that a major need related to intelligence about terrorism is to make sure that the numerous groups involved in trying to protect American citizens and interests communicate their knowledge about threats to one another fully, quickly, and accurately (National Commission on Terrorist Attacks Upon the United States, 2004, 416–19).

The technological revolution that has occurred over the last few decades has had a tremendous impact on just about all aspects of organizational life, but it perhaps has been felt the most in the area of communication. Larger organizations, nonprofit or governmental, have chief information officers who are charged with integrating technology and work processes so that people can at least optimize the utilization of communication systems and the information that has become overwhelmingly abundant. At the same time these information specialists have to be constantly on guard against efforts to break into the information resources and to use that information improperly. Thus the ability to communicate instantaneously and to share huge amounts of information has become an increasing blessing and, at the same time, an increasing burden.

Smaller organizations have no less need for information that is essential to understanding their world, staying aware of opportunities for (and threats to) their organization, and using the communication process to maintain employee and volunteer commitment to the group and the mission. Often the challenge for smaller groups is to take advantage of communication systems that are essentially designed for economies of scale and speed—thus focusing on the nonhuman aspects of communication—that are necessary to compete in the entrepreneurial environment of society while maintaining the combination of individual commitment and internal team spirit required for success.

Of equal importance is the effect of communication (from one-on-one conversations to the vast international networks now involved in collecting and using information) on organizational structures, processes, and cultures. There is a steady movement away from the classical Tayloristic model of organizations, which emphasized specialization, standardization, and formalization—the classic concepts of the assembly line. Certainly communication, organization structure, and process are powerful influences on one another, and the habits these three factors ultimately create in everyone's ongoing work relationships result in the development of an "organizational culture" that permeates all participants' behaviors and perceptions. The predictability and stability that come from operating within such an organizational culture make it possible to decide what to focus on, how to think about it, and what to do in one's daily routine, thereby allowing everyone to make decisions and accomplish their responsibilities in spite of the chaos of the larger environment surrounding them and their organization.

Communication, in turn, allows the organizational structures and processes to function. Organizational structure is differentiated in a variety of ways—hierarchical levels, departments, teams, task specialization, and so on—and must be integrated to achieve the organization's goals. Information about goals, rules, and functions of the organization's human and

BOX 5–1   Definition of Culture

Culture in organizations refers to the collective programming of members' minds (especially in the area of values and beliefs) that distinguishes the individuals in one group or category of people from another. People interacting in an organization create their culture through their interactions with one another; culture is produced not for them but by them.

> Like any social group, the complex web of messages sent and received by members in an organization is interpreted by these members, and the interpretation results in patterns and expectations. The interplay of messages and meanings creates a culture, or a set of artifacts, values, and assumptions, by which people choose their subsequent behaviors and messages, and against which the behaviors and messages are interpreted. Hence, culture is both a process and a product. (Keyton 2005, 18)

> In discussing organizational culture and communication it is important to remember that culture is a process and a product—as just noted; but culture is also confining (limiting what we see and how we interpret it) and facilitating (helping us to make sense of what might otherwise appear to be a chaotic environment).

other resources and its environment must be exchanged. Different activities and tasks must be coordinated. As noted in the previous chapter, the greater the organizational differentiation and complexity, the greater the need for integration. And an organization's communication system is a key mechanism for achieving integration and coordination—in other words for being successful.

The communication process also has a major impact on morale and commitment among those working in the organization who are there for more than a paycheck. Successful communication processes ensure commonality of purpose (a common bond) and an understanding of one's role in the organization; good communication helps create positive morale among participants because they have a reason for achievement.

The role of the communication system in public and nonprofit organizations has one additional level of complexity: It is a political process as well. In the government, expertise and control of information are major sources of bureaucratic political influence (Rourke 1984). Or in the simplest terms, information and its control equal power! In many cases much of that information exists in or comes from nonprofit actors working in tandem with government. And of course individuals who have information also use it as part of the internal organizational political process.

Communication may be instrumental, psychological, or incidental. Instrumental communication is purposeful or goal-directed: The sender intends to have an effect (related to knowledge, attitude, and behavior) on the receiver. Psychological communication arises and is emitted from the emotional state of the sender (such as enthusiasm, fear, or uncertainty). Incidental communication imparts information without the sender being aware of having done so. The first type of communication is formal and related to the mission, structure, and processes of the organization. The second and third types of exchanging information are informal: The communication may or may not be related to aspects of organizational mission and procedures, and there are only limited ways to control the content and impact of the information released into the system.

The focus here is on instrumental communication but with the understanding that emotional and unintended meanings may be present also. Because the purpose of communicating may be to exercise influence rather than simply to transmit information, we are concerned here with distortion in ways that depart from its usual treatment in organization texts.

Discussions of communication often assume that its only purpose is the accurate transmission and reception of information between senders and receivers. Accuracy in communication promotes greater organizational efficiency and productivity. Distortion, which is generally assumed to be unintentional, is dysfunctional, then, because it reduces the accuracy and completeness of the communication. But distortion may in fact be intentional, as in the distinction between *mis*information or error and *dis*information, in which a message includes a true factor to make a story credible and then adds deliberate distortion or untruth. Whether or not distortion is intentional, its significance in public and nonprofit organizations lies either in its political intent or in its programmatic consequences.

After introducing an interactive model of the communication process, we turn to the focus of this chapter: organizational communication. Formal and informal communications

---

READING 5–1 Ride a Pale Horse

The meeting was ended.

Not yet, thought Karen. "I have been doing some thinking. On disinformation. I could write two articles at least on that subject—if I had some solid facts as a basis."

"Disinformation?" That had caught his attention. He dropped the pen back on the desk.

"It's important—something we all ought to be aware of. Most of us don't really know the difference between misinformation and disinformation."

"But you know now—since Prague?" He was amused but interested. "Give me an example of that difference, Karen. No fancy language: just a simple explanation that any ignorant layman—like myself—can understand."

He is challenging me, she told herself. All right, let's show him this isn't just a Prague-inspired notion. "The scene is Paris. An attempt to shoot Mitterrand as he was entering his car. The actual facts are that he wasn't hit, his driver was wounded, and the two assailants escaped."

"An early press report of the incident said that Mitterand was wounded and his chauffeur was killed; two, possibly three terrorists had done the shooting. That report is a case of misinformation."

"Another press report starts appearing. It says that an attack on Mitterrand took place; he wasn't hit but his driver was wounded. The two assailants have been identified as gunmen used in previous killings by a West German intelligence agency. A reliable source states that the assassination of Mitterand was to have been followed by a right-wing coup, establishing in power a French general favored by fascist elements in Germany." Karen paused. "And that report is pure disinformation."

She knew what she was talking about. Schleeman nodded his approval. "It includes a fact or two to make a story credible, then adds the distortions."

SOURCE: From *Ride a Pale Horse*, Copyright © 1984 by Helen MacInnes. Reprinted by permission of Harcourt Brace Jovanovich, Inc.

and network research are discussed, followed by an examination of directions of communications and communication roles in organizations. Finally, some types of distortion and interference are explored, along with several techniques for coping with distortion.

INTERPERSONAL COMMUNICATION: AN INTERACTIVE MODEL

Human communication is an ongoing, interactive process that includes, according to Aristotle, the speaker, the speech, and the audience. Over thousands of years the phenomenon has remained the same. Each element in the process influences the others. In particular, an understanding that the receiver must perceive and accept any messages is critical in the interpersonal dimension of organizational communication.

When speaking of *process* we mean that it is essential to view events and relationships as dynamic, continuous, and ever-changing. Everett Rogers and Rekha Agarwala-Rogers describe this ongoing process as an intertwined activity:

> Communications is a **process** . . . (or) a continuous sequence of actions through time. It is not meaningful to talk about a beginning or an end of communication, because . . . (it) flows like a stream through time. Someone has suggested that all processes should . . . begin and end with the word "and." (1976, 17)

The classical model of the interpersonal communication process includes the basic elements of source–encoder, message, channel, and receiver–decoder plus feedback (see Figure 5–1). Because the model is exclusively concerned with human communication, the source and receiver are individuals or groups of individuals.

The strength of this model lies in its recognition of interpersonal communication as an interactive process. The concept of process as interactive is one of considerable subtlety and complexity, however, and cannot be fully depicted in a diagram. The concept of feedback must be attached to every element in Figure 5–1; the success in using each aspect of the model, in turn, has an impact on the next communicative sequence of the sender—and perhaps the

FIGURE 5–1   Classic Interactive Communication Model

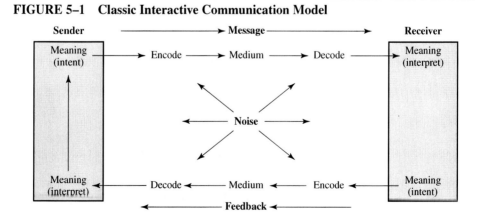

SOURCE: From *Organizational Behavior,* 5th Edition by Richard M. Steers and J. Stewart Black. Copyright © 1994 by HarperCollins Publishers. Reprinted by permission of Addison-Wesley Educational Publishers, Inc.

receiver if she or he recognizes that there is a problem. Successful or failed communication will lead to repeated or changed behavior by the participants in the effort. Likewise, the impact of noise on the communication process is confounded by the fact that noise comes from all directions (in the organization and in the larger environment) and from innumerable sources. Even then the diagram falls short of conveying the complexity of an interactive, ongoing process. Perhaps this is one of those rare times when a thousand words are better than a picture.

The *sender* has a purpose or reason for engaging in communication. An individual encodes a message that is intended to produce some desired result. In person-to-person communication, encoding is usually accomplished through speaking and writing. It is important to understand that one person (the sender) does not transfer meanings to another (the receiver); the receiver creates meanings in his or her own mind. If the sender and receiver use the same word but perceive different meanings, understanding may be illusory.

Communication behavior is affected by the sender's attitudes toward self, the subject matter, and the receiver. The expectations that sources have for themselves and others, the positions they hold, and the roles they play in the organization help determine the nature of the communication. The assumed knowledge about the subject matter on the part of the receiver also affects the language and style of communication. For example, a professional will communicate with other professionals quite differently than with clients. Thus a variety of social and cultural influences are a final factor in determining the communication process.

The *message* is the actual physical product of the source–encoder. The message may be spoken or written; if the communication is between visible actors, posture, body movement, or facial expression may also deliver an important message.

The *medium* is the means by which the message is physically transmitted from sender to receiver. To be effective, channels of communication must take into account not only the encoding skills of the sender but also the sensory and decoding skills of the receiver. Can or will the receiver be more attentive to a formal written memo, an e-mail message, a personal chat, or a phone call? Should only one channel be used? Or should the message be reinforced by the use of multiple channels? A common practice, for example, is the use of "power point" projections alongside an oral presentation. This book includes pictorial material, such as tables and figures, in addition to the standard text. And many books now include DVDs and CDs with data and practical exercises for those interested in learning procedures in detail.

The *receiver–decoder* is, according to many contemporary theorists, the most important link in the communication process. Much that has been said about senders applies to receivers as well. Like the sender, the receiver's communication behavior is affected by communication skills, attitudes, knowledge level, and social and cultural background.

In still another sense, the receiver is central to the communication process; this has to do with differences between meaning and message. Messages are transmitted, but words and other symbols have no meanings in themselves. Meanings are assigned by both the source and the receiver, and those meanings may not be the same. In particular, the roles of receiver perception, comprehension, and acceptance of messages must be recognized if organizational communication is to be more fully understood and more effectively used.

The interdependence of sender and receiver is critical to understanding communication as a process. Up to a point it is useful to talk about senders and receivers separately, but doing so can create one of the difficulties of thinking about communication as process: Calling one individual a sender and another a receiver implies a single finite act that stops at a given point; often communication is a process with no beginning (sender) or end (receiver). In interactive communication, a sender at one moment may be a receiver at another; the same rapid change of role is true for a receiver.

Feedback, the final element in the model, is the receiver's response to the source's message. It gives the source information about the degree to which an intended effect was achieved. Feedback, certainly in interpersonal communication, is a reciprocal process. The action of the source affects the receiver's reaction; the receiver's reaction affects the subsequent reactions of the source. Each can use the reactions of the other in a continuous, ongoing fashion. But feedback is more than a simple action–reaction concept; it is part of a dynamic and mutual interdependence.

People bring their own expectations to interpersonal encounters, and they also anticipate the expectations and responses of those with whom they communicate (Thayer 1986). These expectations have an ongoing effect on the communication process between sender and receiver. Successful communication between individuals requires that the two people put themselves into each other's shoes, perceive the world as the other person perceives it, and predict how the other will respond.

Finally, this process occurs in an environment where there is *noise*—unanticipated factors that cause a lack of clarity on the part of the source, garble the message during transmission, or distract the receiver. Noise may come from other actors in the area, technology, simultaneous social and political occurrences, or innumerable other factors. The danger of noise interrupting or distorting communication is constant; thus feedback becomes exceedingly important because it is the primary way to find out if the communication occurred as desired.

In the current environment of public and nonprofit organizations, there is one more aspect of communication that requires special attention. *Distortion,* the capacity of humans to anticipate the expectations and reactions of others and thereby attempt to deliberately shape the meanings that others will draw from messages, has important implications in the gaining of influence or avoidance of control. Modern organizational leaders must be aware of the problem of distortion both in and outside the organization and constantly look for ways to limit and control its impact on mission success. A special discussion of this phenomenon occurs later in this chapter.

COMMUNICATION IN ORGANIZATIONS

Organizations have both formal and informal communication systems, and both coexist and are relatively inseparable. Therefore our discussion of the two systems will be divided for definition and description and then merged to note how they work together, work against, or reinforce one another depending on how well their strengths and weaknesses are recognized and managed by leaders and group members.

An organization's formal structure (defined in Chapter 4) is the officially prescribed distribution of authority and task responsibility among its offices and officials. Formal communication networks coincide with the organization's formal authority structure. The formal communication system consists of interactions (official policy directives, orders, and reports) among the organization's members and its subdivisions that are prescribed by the formal structure (Downs 1994). When clear statements of agency policy and process are needed to guarantee that everyone is "on the same page," or when clear records of accountability and responsibility are needed, formal channels of communication are critical to success and survival.

On the other hand, formal channels can never meet all the communication needs of the organization and its members; therefore informal channels emerge when there is a need for organization members or officials to communicate and no formal channel exists—or when the use of a formal channel poses risks to personal or policy interests.

Informal communication is interaction that is not prescribed by the organization's formal authority structure or official procedures (although, over time, certain patterns can gain implicit official approval). Informal communication is ubiquitous and highly significant in organizations, sometimes overlapping with and sometimes existing outside the formal structure. Not only wide-ranging and flexible, informal communication patterns are also more dynamic and unpredictable than formal ones. This is not to imply that informal communication is random or without form, or that all individuals in the organization are linked to others in the same way. Informal communication may be either task related—such as sounding out unofficial ideas or information—or it may be personal or social. Informal communication—the grapevine—has often been thought of as primarily a face-to-face transaction. But with the blossoming of information technology, the importance of other types of informal communication must be carefully considered. The results of informal communication may be positive (creating trust and social support, allowing nonthreatening learning and feedback, filling in gaps in knowledge and information, and helping create high satisfaction and motivation) or dysfunctional (facilitating the growth of loyalties and norms that are at odds with formal goals and rules).

Interestingly, research indicates that informal communication channels are more effective for implementing change when risk and complexity are characteristics of that change. Informal channels provide those adopting innovations with social support. Informal communication is also more likely to meet the specific needs and questions of the adoption unit because of the immediacy of feedback and the situational specificity of the communication (Fidler and Johnson 1984).

From the perspective of bureau members and officials, unofficial communications have great advantages; they "can be withdrawn, altered, adjusted, magnified, or canceled without any official record being made" (Downs 1994, 113). In this way new ideas are encouraged and tested. "Trial balloons" can be generated regarding policies or implementation procedures to test member and public reactions for support and opposition. Depending on that reaction it is still possible to change positions without having to explain the inconsistencies of formal statements. Internally both bosses and subordinates can carry out the same procedure without having to take an official stand, and often with the added advantage of being able to "deny authorship" to most interested observers.

Just as informal communication can be a boon, it can also create a variety of problems. This becomes especially true when dealing with individuals outside the organization. Organization leaders must constantly be aware of the ubiquitous "unnamed source" who can create havoc with the best, most quietly laid plans and decisions. Therefore formal leaders often attempt to restrict informal communication about sensitive topics, especially with journalists or officials outside the bureau. In these areas specific officials may be designated as agency spokespeople.

Formal and Informal Networks

Network analysis provides a fruitful approach to the study of the human communication process in the organization. The unit of analysis in network research is the recurrent communication interactions that are evidence of communication networks. In other words, network analysis studies the structure of the organization's communication, not the structure of the organization. Such study is especially helpful in revealing the structure of informal communication networks. Unlike formal communication channels, which are explicitly set out and known, informal systems are more elusive and ephemeral.

Each of us knows from our own experience that every individual in a large organization cannot interact continually or even frequently with every other member. Within the formal organization, some individuals and groups become linked through more or less regularized channels of interpersonal communication. Communication scholars term such a set of individuals, interconnected by a patterned communications flow, a *network*. The size of networks is intermediate—somewhere between the individual and the organization. In other words, a network includes some, but rarely all, individuals or groups in an organization. In any sizable organization many networks may exist and can be linked to other networks.[1] From these patterned though often informal networks, an organization's communication structure emerges.

In their investigations of work and informal group communications, researchers have used two approaches: small-group laboratory experiments and network analysis. Their principal concerns have been the patterns of communication flow and how these patterns affect individual and group functioning.

Small-Group Experiments

Starting in the 1950s and 1960s, communication researchers conducted laboratory experiments with small-group networks. The structure of a network—that is, the pattern of communication flow—was predetermined and controlled by the researcher. In this way communication structure served as an independent variable, along with several others such as group size and task complexity. In the controlled laboratory setting these variables could be manipulated to determine their effect on dependent variables such as task performance, member satisfaction, and leadership. The principal types of communication networks studied were chains, circles, and wheels. All-channel and "Y" networks were also investigated. Each type is characterized by a different communication flow.

In experiments with small communication structures or networks, group members are placed in separate cubicles and allowed to communicate via written messages. Different types of networks are imposed on each group. In each type of network an individual can communicate only with those to whom he or she is connected; these communication patterns are indicated by the solid lines in Figure 5–2. Information given to each member of a group has to be shared for an assigned task to be completed, and the solution to the task has to be conveyed back to all members.

This research revealed several interesting relationships between communication structure and task performance. For simple routine tasks, a centralized network (wheel) is more effective (Bavelas 1950; Leavitt 1951). For more complex problem solving that requires pooling information, a decentralized network is superior. Decentralized networks may also be preferred if accuracy is important because it was found that centralized groups, although faster, had a higher error rate.

Position in the network was found to be related to leadership and satisfaction. Bavelas, for example, devised an index of relative centrality: The more people with whom an individual could interact, the more central she or he would be. In Figure 5–2 the most central person is

---

[1]Some of these networks may reach into other organizations or serve boundary-spanning functions.

FIGURE 5–2   Small-Group Experiment Networks

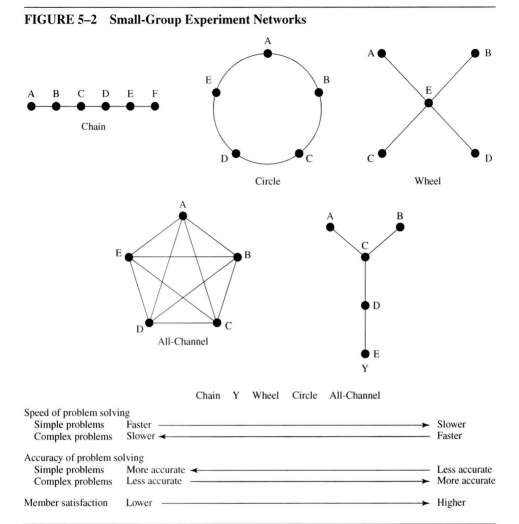

SOURCE: Adapted from R. Daft and R. Steers. *Organization: A Micro/Macro Approach* (Glenview, IL.: Scott, Foresman, 1986), 534. Copyright © 1986 Scott, Foresman and Company.

individual E in the wheel; next is individual C in the "Y." The circle and all-channel networks do not differentiate among member centrality. The more central an individual is in the communication structure (1) the more information they are likely to have compared to other members and (2) the more they are regarded as leaders by other members of the group (Bavelas 1950; Leavitt 1951).

Centrality and satisfaction are linked (Bavelas 1950). In highly centralized networks like the wheel, the most central (therefore independent) person is also the most satisfied person (Shaw 1954). In networks that are decentralized and allow the most independence or freedom to interact, satisfaction is more equally experienced by all members of the group. The negative effects of centrality were also explored. For example, saturation, or information overload, can occur. Overload lowers performance in group tasks.

The small-group experiments yielded considerable information about communication flows and their effects, but their application to organizations is limited by the methodology used. The experiments brought together individuals who were strangers, and there was no expectation that their relationships would continue. Tasks were artificial. Perhaps the greatest flaw was that of setting or context: Interaction occurred in a vacuum of sorts, devoid of the larger structure or system in which organizational communication—formal and informal—usually occurs.

Organization Network Analysis

When research on networks moved into real-life organizations, studying communication networks required changes in research procedures. The general approach used for identifying the communication structure within an ongoing system—whether group or organization—is network analysis. By means such as questionnaires, interviews, and observation, researchers gather sociometric data about interpersonal communication relationships (basically who interacts with whom and how frequently). In this way networks and communication flows can be identified and relationships between formal and informal structures can be determined. Moreover, network analysis has assisted researchers both in recognizing specialized communication roles performed by individuals and in assessing certain systemwide variables.

Most individuals have personal (informal) networks of other individuals with whom they interact frequently—at least about certain types of concerns. An informal network may be radial or interlocking in structure. In a *radial network* a person interacts directly with others, but these people do not interact with one another. In an *interlocking network* the people with whom a person interacts also interact with one another (see Figure 5–3). It is useful to regard these terms (radial and interlocking) as descriptive of a quality rather than as designating categories. To some degree, informal networks are more likely to be both radial and interlocking; that is, some individuals in a personal network may interact with one another while others may not. On balance, however, personal networks tend to be more interlocking than radial (Granovetter 1973; Rogers 1973).

FIGURE 5–3   Personal Networks: Radial and Interlocking Types

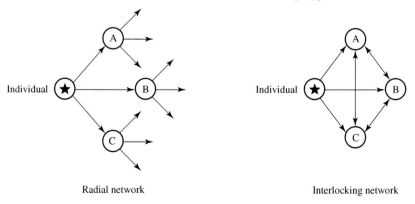

Radial network   Interlocking network

Communication occurs quickly and easily within interlocking networks, but the closed nature of such a network reduces its informational strength. Although the ties among individuals may be weaker in radial networks, communication researchers have noted what they term the "strength of weak ties" (Granovetter 1973). That is, communication is unlikely if there are no ties or links among individuals, but weak sociometric ties (which are more characteristic of radial networks) promote the exchange of more information that is new to members of a network. For example, Figure 5–3 portrays a network that is almost completely interlocking. Its members communicate only with each other, except for one individual who communicates with people outside the group. (This individual is often a boundary-spanning actor because the outside contacts may be from other parts of, or even outside of, the organization.) That individual, then, has weaker ties to the interlocking network than its other members, yet he or she can be an important conduit for new information. Through such links, information passes from one network to another.

DIRECTIONS OF ORGANIZATION COMMUNICATION

Organizational structure influences both the direction and substance of communication. The authority hierarchy provides a vertical axis for the flow of communication. *Vertical* communication occurs between superiors and subordinates; it may flow downward (from superior to subordinate) or upward (from subordinate to superior). Vertical communication is often formal in that its substance is in some sense official. In general, the greater the degree of formalization or status and power differences, the higher the proportion of vertical communication, and the more likely the direction will be downward.

Horizontal communication links related tasks, work units, and divisions of the organization. Some horizontal communication is formal but to a lesser extent than that within vertical channels. Two structural factors, task specialization and the diversity of organizational structure, stimulate internal horizontal communication. Organizational diversity is interpreted as complexity and sheer number of occupations and professions, and not as the microdivision of labor implied by task specialization (Thompson 1961). Task specialization increases the need for coordination and integration. Similarly, the proportion of horizontal task communication is greater as the occupations in an organization increase in number and become more professional (Hage, Aiken, and Marrett 1971).

Most organization theory concentrates on communication *within* the organization. But the study of communication related to public and nonprofit establishments requires a special focus on external communication (or communication between organizations). Public organizations especially operate in an environment of great visibility and accessibility due to their political roots. They must understand and use external communication skills as an everyday element of their existence. Nonprofits operate increasingly in an environment of collaboration with other nonprofits, public agencies, and even private sector firms, so communication with these outside actors and forces is of paramount importance. Obviously such interorganizational communication occurs in the private sector also; however, it is not nearly as central to success as in the two public sectors of our society. Therefore external communication must also be considered. Moreover, whereas the study of internal communication dictates an emphasis on interpersonal behavior patterns, external communication includes a macro perspective (that is, organization-to-organization patterns) as well.

Downward Communication

Downward communication provides a mechanism for the policy command process in organizations. Government organizations are usually carrying out a specific mandate (protection of the community or nation, collection of taxes, protection of the environment) or implementing services for segments of society (health and education services, transportation planning and construction, managing parks). Nonprofit agencies also implement services, but in many cases they have a second duty to serve as protagonists for their members in societal or political conflicts. Downward communication generally furnishes information about why and how tasks should be done, and it also helps to create the ideological framework within which workers go about their activities. Thus downward communication includes at least

1. Information of an ideological nature to foster a sense of mission—inculcation of ends and goals.

2. Information about organizational procedures and practices—explanation of organizational means to ends.

3. Specific task directives—job definition.

4. Information designed to produce understanding of the task and its relation to other organizational tasks—job context.

5. Feedback to the subordinate about his or her performance—job evaluation (Katz and Kahn 1978).

Job instructions are communicated to subordinates in a variety of ways—oral directions, written directives, manuals, and training sessions—and often with great specificity. Information about organization procedures may pertain to job tasks (and how they fit into organizational functions) or to the rights and obligations (salary, promotion, security procedures) of members of the organization. Too often communication about tasks and procedures is given priority while ideological information and feedback about job performance, including the impact of the workers' activities on the larger system, are neglected. Why do these patterns occur, and how are the organization and its membership affected?

Strong emphasis on job instruction and organizational procedures is understandable in light of the requirement for managerial and supervisory individuals to direct and control those below them in the hierarchy. But overemphasis on directives can foster the kind of authoritarian atmosphere that leads to problems in control. If the organizational climate is repressive, subordinates may "go by the book" and meet minimum requirements when allowing them to exercise greater individual discretion would do more for task performance and the achievement of organizational goals. Or rather than becoming passive, subordinates may react with resentment and respond to organizational rigidity by subverting organizational control. Either way, an insidious spiral may be set in motion—new directives and efforts at control followed by more subversion or passivity followed by more new directives, and so on.

The emphasis on direction and control in government agencies is further strengthened by the political environment in which they operate. Government bureaus are open to external accountability. At the same time there has been an apparent polarization of many parts of society in relation to important policies and programs. Whatever is done by public administrators is likely to generate heated opposition from one or more groups interested in the policy or program. Yet there is a commonly held idea that civil servants should be politically neutral. In spite of the policy ferment, it is demanded of public servants that they treat professionally, impartially, and equally the citizens who are served or regulated. Such competing forces or demands inevitably create pressure for rigid standardization and limited discretion, and only constant vigilance keeps leaders from focusing on this issue.

Given the pressures just mentioned, we should not be surprised that managers usually give less attention to communication about job rationale. Yet an understanding of the importance of a job can increase motivation and commitment; similarly, individual decision making may be improved. Helping workers understand how their jobs are related to organizational goals can promote better overall coordination. On the other hand, coordination may not be as well served if the organizational goals are understood but not the interactive processes. Katz and Kahn note that workers who think they understand why they are doing something may attempt to do it in other than the specified fashion, and the organization's leaders may not want the variability of behavior this introduces into the system (1978). Nonprofit organizations must be especially sensitive to these last two points about downward communication. Nonprofit agencies have no formal authority such as the law to turn to for an authoritative, final statement defining the organization's mission. The nonprofit workforce often combines professionals, nonprofessionals, and volunteers in a polyglot of knowledge and commitment that requires both underscoring the nonprofit's mission and creating a common approach to organizational procedures. There must be some common voice and similarity of process when interacting with one another, clients, and the larger public.

Despite its motivational and control significance, feedback to subordinates about their individual performance is another type of downward communication that is often overlooked and poorly handled. Some reasons for neglecting such feedback stem from general cultural values. American ambivalence toward authority, emphasis on self-determination and individual freedom, and generally egalitarian principles may inhibit superiors—especially when negative evaluations are involved. The psychological tendency to avoid conflict and discomfort also explains to some degree the unpopularity of supervisory evaluation for superior and subordinate alike.

Superior–subordinate communication has as one of its purposes the promotion of organizational goals. Both nonprofit and governmental agency leaders can impart a sense of mission and commitment to followers. After all, these organizations make major contributions to social welfare (Katz and Kahn 1978). On the other hand, civil servants often fear that strong and overt identification with ideological positions and goals will endanger their career progress and job security.

Unlike the internally set goals of firms and most nonprofits, external and often shifting political processes help determine bureau goals. For example, one administration may actively pursue a policy of vigorous expansion of environmental policies related to air and water pollution by appointing activist advocates to top agency posts, creating new laws and regulations, and using class action suits to emphasize its philosophy. A change of goals and ideological emphasis may occur when the next administration appoints opponents to (or weaker advocates for) the environment, removes or reduces the number of environmental regulations, and curtails the government's adversarial role by changing from a class action to an individual, case-by-case approach. When one administration is succeeded by another, an official who has advocated and is identified with an ideology and goals that are no longer in favor is open to attack by new forces and actors inside and outside the bureau. This occurs at one time or another to leaders at all governmental levels.

Upward Communication

Upward communication functions as a reporting and control system for the organization. It is also an adjunct to decision making to the extent that higher officials use or need information from lower ones in making decisions and setting policy. Upward communication is necessary to organizational functioning, but it faces numerous difficulties. Some are structural, but others stem from the desire of subordinates to influence policy and to protect themselves from the actions or control of their superiors.

The hierarchical structure of organizations in particular discourages open and free upward disclosure of information. Because of authority relationships and reward systems, subordinates (especially those with strong aspirations for upward mobility and promotion) are likely to distort or omit information that will reflect adversely on themselves, that may lead to decisions they do not favor, or that their bosses do not want to hear (Wilensky 1967, 42–48; Sinetar 1988). Likewise, supervisors may distort or stop messages that they do not want to forward for any reason. A tragic instance of this type occurred moments before the attack on Pearl Harbor:

> At 7:00 a.m. the army shut down its five mobile radar units, as it did every morning at that time. When an army private turned on one radar set for practice, he saw a huge flight of planes. He telephoned his lieutenant, who told him to forget it. The Japanese "surprise" attack began at 7:55. (McCurdy 1977, 209–10)

One of the major debates after the beginning of the Iraq War in 2003 was about the amount and quality of information given to the Bush administration about the presence of "weapons of mass destruction" and the level of troop strength that would be needed to accomplish the mission of toppling Saddam Hussein and establishing a democratic government in Iraq. Was there enough information? Was it all considered seriously, or was some material emphasized while other information was downplayed? Was all of the information forwarded through the organizations and up to the policy makers? Finally, was all the relevant information released, or was some held back because it did not fit the desired end? This debate on a national level is reenacted regularly in all organizations and at all levels of society.

In an effort to improve upward communication (in fact, communication in all directions) an emphasis was recently placed on increasing personal authenticity and openness and the disclosure of feelings and thought in communication. Techniques such as transactional analysis (James and Jongeward 1991) and Johari windows (Luft 1984), along with group exercises that increased self-worth, empathy, and openness, were stressed in the 1960s. In addition to fostering personal growth and satisfaction, it was assumed that the skills learned in these exercises would foster openness in communication within organizations. However, the belief that such training would open communication, remove hierarchical barriers, reduce conflict, increase worker morale and motivation, and therefore increase productivity was only partially realized.

Despite its appeal and the advantages it offers, the personal authenticity approach proved to be of limited utility in communication situations governed by power and influence considerations. In fact, this approach can lead to the manipulation of individuals who practice it by those who do not—and those who do not, whether inside or outside the bureau, are likely to be legion in number in the public arena. Inside the organization, even if there is an honest attempt to develop open communication, organizational hierarchy, specialization, and diversity create impediments that require strenuous efforts to overcome.

Therefore emphasis has now shifted to an attempt to create a "learning organization," where the total membership communicates openly with understanding. As described by Luthans, Hodgetts, and Lee,

> Every complex organization has a variety of subcultures—departments, divisions, levels of management, and the like. Each has its own special interests, mental model of how the (organization) works, and, quite possibly, its own language (jargon). Dialogue,[2] as the discipline is now emerging, is a technique for helping individuals recognize and put aside these basic differences. Consequently, higher levels of collaboration are possible. (1994, 13; see also Schein 1993 and Isaacs 1993)

The emphasis in much of this activity is aimed at reducing the impact of hierarchical status and power on organizational communication. Especially in public sector organizations this is quite difficult. The "power game" is played by subordinates as well as superiors, and the constant presence of outside forces wishing to influence organizational decisions and processes makes the possibility of achieving a learning state even more difficult for government organizations. For nonprofit agencies the environment may be somewhat more amenable to such activities so long as the leadership of the organization desires to use this strategy. Other factors such as size, structure, and clearness of mission also have a significant impact on the methods employed, success, and outcomes in upward communication activity.

As in downward communication, the size of the communication loop affects information transmitted upward. In general, the higher the organizational level, the more constricted the upward feedback tends to be. Some constriction or filtering is needed to prevent information overload; but a by-product, isolation of the organization's leaders, can be harmful.

Messages that must pass through many individuals or through numerous hierarchical levels tend to be distorted at each level in the hierarchy. The effects of distortion on information are aggregated as messages pass from one level to the next. The longer the communication loop and the more levels it involves, the greater the likelihood that significant distortion will occur. Conversely, communication loops may be too small. Typically the upward communication loop terminates with the immediate supervisor, who may choose to transmit some part of the message upward but usually in a condensed and modified form (Katz and Kahn 1978). All of these limitations on upward communication, of course, add to the importance of informal communication, about which we will talk later in this chapter.

Horizontal Communication

A substantial amount of communication flows laterally in organizations. These lateral flows connect individuals within the same work unit, span diverse but interrelated divisions and levels, or even link different organizations. Horizontal communication serves important

---

[2]*Dialogue* is quite different from the common discussion that goes on in organizations because in discussion the goal of the participant is "to win" or to get one's views accepted by the group. According to Senge (1994) the discipline of team learning starts with dialogue, in which "people become observers of their own thinking" (242) and "individuals gain insights that simply could not be achieved individually" (241). Bohm (1996) created the concept, which has three basic conditions:

1. All participants must "suspend" their assumptions, literally to hold them "as if suspended before us."

2. All participants must regard one another as colleagues.

3. There must be a "facilitator" who "holds the context" of dialogue (Senge 1994, 243). This means that the facilitator understands and practices the process of dialogue so faithfully that she or he can "influence the flow of development simply through participating."

purposes for the organization: task coordination, problem solving, information sharing, and conflict resolution. Some of this interaction is formal—intra- or interagency committees, task forces, coordinating boards, and so forth—but much, if not most, is informal. Most horizontal communication connects peers rather than superiors and subordinates; but even when officials of different ranks are involved, variations in status are likely to be played down (Downs 1994; Blau and Scott 2003, 116–39).

Horizontal flows, which are thought to be more frequent than vertical flows, are subject to less pressure for information distortion. For various reasons, organization members are more comfortable in using lateral channels and have less cause to restrict, withhold, or distort messages. Research shows that the more threatening a message, the more likely it is to be ignored or distorted. Unlike the authoritative (downward) or control-related information about performance (upward), horizontal messages are often concerned with coordination and are therefore less threatening. Also, lateral communication is more likely to be interactive than unilateral, informal rather than formal, and face-to-face/oral rather than written (although the Internet and e-mail have greatly increased the importance of almost instantaneous written communication). As a result, feedback occurs rapidly and often, and distortion is reduced. Because peers have a common frame of reference, their meanings are shared and similar. Openness and personal authenticity are easier and less risky to sustain in horizontal communication.

Communication between peers provides emotional and social support as well as task coordination. Socioemotional support is needed by individuals whether in organized or unorganized groups. It is often through the informal communication system that individuals learn about organizational culture, get feedback about their acceptance within their working sphere, and figure out whom to approach with problems or questions that they do not want to take to superiors or have surface within the formal communication network.

The question is whether the organization benefits from peer communication of this type. The answer is probably or a qualified yes. Katz and Kahn caution, for example, that if there are no problems of task coordination left to a group of peers, the content of their communication can take forms that are irrelevant or destructive to organizational functioning (1978). In authoritarian organizations leaders see the sharing of information as a check on their power; therefore information (or the lack thereof) is used to control members at lower levels, and controls and restrictions are placed on the horizontal flow of information. If members cannot communicate with one another, they will be unable to engage in any coordinated efforts not sanctioned by the leadership. In such cases horizontal communication may become destructive in a number of ways.

Of course new management systems, especially those based on learning or team management concepts, view horizontal communication as a central method of learning about problems and possibilities facing the organization and involving everyone in the common goal of improving quality. The new management systems teach that successful leaders learn to use informal and horizontal communication to achieve positive management or leadership styles (see Chapter 9). Horizontal communication is just as important, in these approaches to management, as either upward or downward communication.

The fact remains that horizontal interaction is inevitable. Organizations need task coordination, and the functions performed by horizontal communication will be increasingly important as organizational tasks become more complex and professionalism rises because individual members will continue to seek the stimulation, support, and identity with peers that come with lateral and informal interaction. In addition, the tasks performed by public and nonprofit organizations increasingly require horizontal communication and interorganizational cooperation both because of the complexity of the tasks and because of the political environment's increased demand for collaboration, contracting out, and privatization.

Communication with the Rest of the World

Government and nonprofit agencies are extremely permeable; information easily passes through in both directions. Individuals at all levels, responding to a variety of situations and for innumerable reasons, communicate with those outside their agencies. Their external and largely informal communication has wide-reaching implications for the public sector organization. Networks of private and public establishments, interest groups, politicians, and clients develop around policy fields and programs. Interesting combinations of rivalry and cooperation occur among these *current competitors who may be future collaborators*, or vice versa, and communication becomes a special art. When dealing with people outside the organization, constant questions in the minds of thoughtful communicators are these: "How much information do I give to whom?" and "How should I interpret the information that I am getting from those in this (probably temporary) coalition or collaborative group?" Employees at all levels play an important role in this dance of external communication. For example, civil servants who wish to maintain support for superiors or for specific programs can make positive information available to outside sources. On the other hand, government employees who disagree with the substantive policies of their superiors may appeal to, and supply information to, powerful actors outside the agency. In nonprofit organizations it is essential to build constituencies and work with other groups, but individuals generally also have a sense of loyalty to their own organization; therefore they must communicate with care while also helping to develop a level of trust between organizations that allows effective cooperation.

In some instances the accountability and responsiveness of an agency are improved by such external communication; in other cases damage may be done to programs and policies. In either case organizational structures and processes—the vertical authority system, managers' control over subordinates, and the organization's decision processes—may be disrupted. For the organization, the greatest significance of boundary-spanning activity depends on whether it results in favorable and ethical exploitation or containment of environmental factors.

One way in which an organization can make its environment more predictable and favorable is by coordinating information and actions with the relevant actors, both internal and external, who operate in that environment. Coordination is easier talked about than accomplished, however, because the channels of power and communication among fragmented policy makers, target clientele, and multiple entities are complex. Two major approaches are used to both control and improve interorganizational communication and coordination. The first approach focuses on the attempt *within the organization* to control, and to benefit from, information flow across its boundaries. Agencies often recognize, through the provision of special status, individuals who are major players in the interorganizational communication game. Status often involves special position descriptions, emphasis of the boundary-spanning activities in the individual's overall evaluation, and where possible, other perquisites such as special pay. It is hoped that such recognition will help to maintain the individual's loyalty to his or her home agency.

The second way in which organizations deal with cross-boundary communication is to neutralize and formalize the process whenever possible. Therefore special meetings of appropriate individuals (those with special interest in the issues to be coordinated) are regularly scheduled at neutral or mutually acceptable sites. In addition there are regular, often annual, conferences of groups interested in common policy problems or service programs. In this way valuable information can be shared in a neutral setting.

Within the public arena these complex channels among policy makers, agencies, and clientele are considered benign—as argued in most pluralist political theory. The shared interests and the increased efficiency and effectiveness that come from collaboration are, in fact, critical where government and nonprofit organizations must collaborate. In other situations, especially when dealing with issues and services of large size and nationwide importance, students of politics and administration have referred to the results with mixed feelings. Hugh Heclo (1977) speaks of "iron triangles" of administrators, politicians, and interest groups that have the capacity to be misused for power or profit. Likewise President Eisenhower warned about the development of a "military–industrial complex," a phrase he coined to describe the coalition that included the relevant politicians and bureaucrats in addition to business and defense organizations. These terms have not gone away. And much is made currently of the problems generated by regulatory agencies (for example, the Federal Drug Administration) that are so intertwined, through appointments of industry and interest group scientists and executives to commissions and top staff positions, that many people question whether industries (or interest groups) have gained control of policy making and policing in the regulated areas, thereby diminishing the objectiveness and reliability of the regulators' findings, rulings, and ability to act as watchdogs for the public.

As is implied by the designation of "iron triangles" and "the military–industrial complex," shared communication and interaction lead to the development of power channels among multiple bureaucracies. Agencies compete for the scarce resources that policy makers and funders allocate, especially in a period of economic downturn or budget cutbacks. They regularly compete for programs and target clientele. At the same time the need to cooperate with other organizations in achieving mission goals or providing more comprehensive or better clientele services also arises.

The communication channels linking organizations to one another take several basic forms (Figure 5–4). If the primary need in interorganizational communication is coordination

FIGURE 5–4   Models of Interorganizational Communication Channels

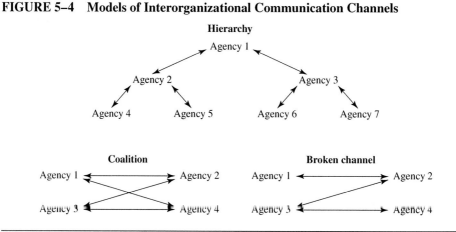

SOURCE: From *Bureaucracy, Policy and the Public* by Steven Thomas Seitz, p. 93. Copyright © 1978. Reprinted with permission from the author.

and commonality of action, then the hierarchy model is likely to be present. In this case there is a formal chain of command, and messages sent from the top agency often take the form of commands. Messages coming from the lower bureaus would contain information and reports desired by the top agency.

The hierarchy model implies that the top bureau would have authority over lower bureaus. Thus although the system may guarantee efficiency and effectiveness, at least a couple of negative factors are related to this model. First, political resistance to this arrangement will come from many, if not most, bureaus and their separate clienteles. The fact that an organization has achieved a dominant position in such a coordinative effort is a clear sign to the others that they may be diminishing in power and losing their status or independence. The agencies that are lower on the communication hierarchy will often feel threatened and take a defensive posture in the interorganizational relationship. That feeling of threat to the status quo is not always illogical. As the reorganization in antiterrorism and homeland security agencies has transpired, there has been more than one example of initial changes in communication structures being a portent of later institutional reorganization. For example, after the delivery of the report of the 9/11 Commission, the president created a director of national intelligence and made him the center of the communication system involving all intelligence and antiterrorist organizations. This immediately affected the director of the Central Intelligence Agency because the new intelligence tsar delivered the daily intelligence briefing to the president. Other departments were also nervous, and a few months later President Bush announced a shakeup of these services that included giving the intelligence tsar meaningful control over major segments of the Federal Bureau of Investigation (Eggen and Pincus 2005). Control of information is power, and all agencies—large and small, national or local—recognize the importance of interorganizational communication structures.

The second factor that may lead to resistance to a hierarchical communication structure is the existence of multiple jurisdictions in our government system *and* the involvement of public, private, and nonprofit organizations in carrying out many if not most public policies. If agencies are averse to being placed under the control of other agencies, clearly jurisdictional aversion is equally strong. For example, in the 1982 crash of an Air Florida jet into the Potomac River in Washington, D.C., emergency units from numerous local jurisdictions were needed. Rescue operations were plagued by lack of effective interagency communication and coordination. The hierarchy model offers a structural approach to such a problem, but reservations had to be accommodated from interjurisdictional as well as interagency viewpoints. Only after months of task force meetings, studies, and much formal and informal conferring among agency and political leaders could a plan be adopted to improve communication and the direction of future emergency and catastrophe operations. More streamlined and effective interagency communication channels were instituted, but the resulting design was considerably less pyramidal than a pure hierarchy. This outcome is common, given the resistance from agencies, clientele, and officials in different jurisdictions and levels of government, and can be expected when organizational design must take into account political actors and factors. The challenge of gaining voluntary cooperation and coordination is further increased when organizations from all three sectors of society (public, nonprofit, and private) are brought into the mixture (Walter and Petr 2000).

In the coalition network a complex set of channels links organizations. This model has the advantage of ordinarily achieving greater buy-in by all involved, but it has a cost in the time that is usually needed to reach the consensus that is the basis for decisions and actions in the coalition.

Direct channels exist among some organizations in the broken-channel model, but no agency is linked directly to all the others, and none has power over all the others by virtue of a formal chain of command. In coalition and broken-channel models, coordination occurs but is less centralized and systematic.

Coordination in the coalition and broken-channel models rests on how participants use power to achieve mutual adjustment. There are three approaches to mutual adjustment and power relationships among these types of sets (Seitz 1978, 95–101). First, agencies might agree to accept the current balance of power and to respect each other's turf. This approach is usually the modus operandi when the organizations are legally created entities such as local governments or special districts.

Second, bureaus may agree to actively coordinate their activities and facilitate each others' activity. This approach is often used when systematic coordination is required for specific functions, such as in the disaster response just mentioned.

The third approach is active competition among bureaus. The relationship between competing agencies and cooperation is somewhat surprising. "Under conditions of competition in the organization set, each agency must seek information about its competitors and must seek to match any improvements made by one agency with similar improvements of its own" (Seitz 1978, 96). Competition is now one of the central tenets among current "reinvention of government" (Osborne and Gaebler 1992) and "privatization" proponents (Savas 2000); one of the arguments is that it increases communication (both internal and external) about goals, processes, tasks, and effectiveness. At the same time, because of the increased communication and the need for efficiency, competition in public goods (as in capitalist markets) increases standardization of goods, services, and knowledge.

INDIVIDUALS IN THE COMMUNICATION PROCESS

Organizational communication, as we have seen, can be differentiated in numerous ways. The channels and the content may be formal or informal; the direction of communication may be upward, downward, horizontal, or external; a variety of networks may develop among individuals and groups; and some individual communication roles may be established within the organization's communication system.

It is of immense importance for everyone, from organization theorist to public manager to citizen, to understand that government agencies are not some mass of sameness. This fact is true, and perhaps more obvious, for nonprofit organizations. In organizational communication as in other areas of life, individual differences count. Researchers have identified specialized communication roles and functions that certain individuals may fulfill. Four of these individual roles deserve particular attention: gatekeeper, liaison and bridge, opinion leader, and boundary spanner or cosmopolite (Rogers and Agarwala-Rogers 1976, 132–40). (See Figure 5–5.) All of these roles are recognized in, and designed into, the formal side of organizations; however, it is often of even greater importance to recognize when these roles are often played informally (or without any official sanction).

Managers, clients, individuals from other organizations, and citizens can deal more effectively with agencies when they can identify individuals in terms of communication roles, recognize the behaviors associated with different roles, and understand the effects of those behaviors on organizational functioning. Some roles are "political" in the societal/governmental sense of

FIGURE 5–5   Individual Communication Roles in Organizations

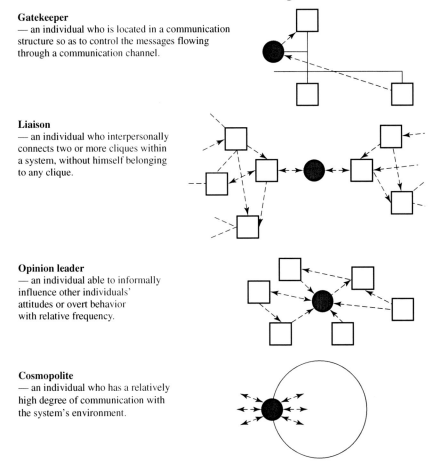

Gatekeeper
— an individual who is located in a communication structure so as to control the messages flowing through a communication channel.

Liaison
— an individual who interpersonally connects two or more cliques within a system, without himself belonging to any clique.

Opinion leader
— an individual able to informally influence other individuals' attitudes or overt behavior with relative frequency.

Cosmopolite
— an individual who has a relatively high degree of communication with the system's environment.

the term; some are related to group and "organization politics"; some "just develop" and may or may not have anything to do with the ongoing power plays that occur in all organizational life. Yet all have program and public management consequences.

Gatekeepers

Gatekeepers control the flow of communication through a given channel or network— formal or informal. Any individual in a position through which messages must pass plays the role of gatekeeper to some extent. For example, any individual in a chain network is a gatekeeper.

Because they act as a filter for message flows, gatekeepers perform an important function in reducing information overload, especially in upward communication. For example, voluminous proposals are reduced to two- or three-page memoranda for approval by the chief executive. Whether this is accomplished without harmful distortion and omission depends on the criteria used by gatekeepers in regulating information flows.

The selection criteria used by gatekeepers are critical to organizational intelligence and responsiveness. Information can be advanced or withheld by gatekeepers, but their power becomes most noticeable when they cause problems. In fact, inspectors general and ombudsmen in government organizations can be seen as structural responses to the vulnerability of communication within the usual hierarchy to distortion, omission, or suppression of information.

Not all gatekeeping is negative. Most of us have had reason to appreciate the helpfulness and responsiveness of gatekeepers, public and private. Gatekeepers can help individuals avoid the time and effort of following formal channels, and this is especially important when speed of communication is required. Knowing who the gatekeepers are and attempting to develop good relations with them are important parts of learning to operate successfully in many organizations.

Liaisons

Liaisons (also called "bridges" or "linking pins") are individuals who connect communication subsystems or networks in the organization. These roles can be formal or informal and can link networks both vertically and horizontally. A liaison does not belong to either of the subsystems he or she connects, whereas a bridge is a member of one of the connected subsystems. The coordinating function of liaisons and bridges is crucial to effective functioning of the organization. For simplicity, only the term *liaison* will be used in our discussion.

Liaisons may expedite the flow of information between groups and subsystems or serve as a bottleneck. Serious organizational consequences result from the loss or removal of liaisons; they have been called the cement that holds the organization's structural parts together. One of the major recommendations that usually comes from any study of failures to coordinate activities recommends greater use of liaisons to speed communication and to make plans in advance of expected needs for cooperation.

The structure and stability of organizational networks and individual roles are important from both theoretical and applied perspectives. Even though a small percentage of members usually play such a role, it is a matter of strategic importance that an organization considers—in terms of its tasks—its need for liaisons and where that need is located. In some instances liaison roles may need to be created formally if they do not exist informally. Even where a liaison role is informally filled, it may be advisable to make the position formal if that is necessary to coordinate important organizational activities.

Mobility of personnel may render performance of the liaison role unreliable. The information and influence liaisons have make their existence important to organizational functioning, but constant turnover can lead to difficulty in maintaining a reliable contact with others. This means, for example, that leaders of public organizations, where political appointees may remain in office for relatively short times, must constantly calculate the costs and advantages of using a career bureaucrat or a political appointee in the bureau's liaison positions.

Opinion Leaders

Opinion leaders are people who have "the ability to informally influence other individuals' attitudes or behavior in a desired way with relative frequency" (Rogers and Agarwala-Rogers 1976, 138). An opinion leader may hold a formal position in a work group, but most research findings conclude that opinion leaders are generally part of the informal structure of their organization and that they can be expected to be distributed throughout all status and hierarchical levels (Redding 1972; Carroll and Tosi 1977). Opinion leaders' influence is not based on formal authority; rather, it stems from their greater expertise and experience and their credibility with members of their group. (See the discussion of the bases of social power in Chapter 9.)

Opinion leadership helps create the norms of the group and may enhance coordination and control through organizational culture. Members are more motivated to achieve the organization's goals if the informal group norms correspond to the organization's formal goals. When this is not the case, however, and opinion leadership is based on conflicting norms, these individuals pose difficult problems for the organization's formal leaders.

Opinion leadership based on substantive knowledge facilitates informal decision making in the group. The wider knowledge and information of leaders on certain topics or issues is passed on to their followers. Radial networks appear more suited to knowledge-based opinion leadership, whereas the opinion leader in a tightly cohesive group may be part of the group's interlocking network (see Figure 5–3). Acceptance of their leadership may be limited to a specific topic or may embrace a wide range of concerns. The importance of opinion leadership in organizations is probably enhanced by the growing importance and numbers of professionals in public and nonprofit agencies.

Boundary Spanners

Boundary spanners, also called cosmopolitans or cosmopolites, are individuals whose interactions include numerous contacts in the external environment (Rogers and Agarwala-Rogers 1976). Many formally appointed liaisons are boundary spanners, but other individuals throughout any organization also play this role. In the sense that they control or filter the flow of communication and information coming into or going out of the organization, boundary spanners are like gatekeepers. Organizational openness—the degree of information exchange between an organization and its environment—is provided to a considerable degree by boundary-spanning communications. Not surprisingly, the personal networks of boundary spanners are open or radial rather than closed and interlocking (see Figure 5–3). "Adjustment to constraints and contingencies not controlled by the organization is the crucial problem for boundary-spanning components" (Thompson 2003, 81). They significantly affect the organization's ability either to adapt to or to exploit and control its environment.

Boundary-spanning jobs vary in the types of action and rewards they entail depending on the stability of the environment. The potential is greater for power and upward mobility in heterogeneous and somewhat unstable environments. Boundary-spanning jobs in such environments require the exercise of discretion to meet changing and unpredictable contingencies. This, in turn, gives the individual in a boundary-spanning job opportunities to learn through experience and provides for visibility inside and outside the organization; jobs that are routinized do not offer comparable opportunities for favorable visibility. The worker with standardized tasks is likely to be noticed only if she or he goofs, and will generally have poorer or slower chances to learn the contents and requirements of other better jobs in the organization (Thompson 2003, 107–11).

Boundary-spanning communication is part of the job of top officials and those with formal external liaison roles such as public information officers or liaisons with Congress or other important organizations. Individuals at the top of the organization obtain different kinds of information than that gathered by lower-level members. Higher administrators and political appointees may gather intelligence—that is, information of strategic importance. Such information is usually about changes in the larger system—the economic outlook, social movements, alliances with like-minded organizations or political groups, legislative climate with respect to bureau or nonprofit organization programs and policy areas, or potential policy initiatives by interest groups or elected officials. These environmental changes, although seemingly remote from the organization, are likely to affect it in the future.

Lower members of the hierarchy who directly deliver public services and serve the agency clientele may also occupy boundary-spanning positions. Boundary spanners—like police dispatchers, license clerks, and recreation specialists—also function as external gatekeepers and can affect the access and treatment of clientele. Lower-level employees handle much of the agency's incoming contacts or correspondence, as well as its material and equipment. Their information is likely to be related to the effectiveness of operational activities, changes in clientele demands and needs, the increase or decline in acceptance of agency activities, and the adequacy and quality of materials or services received by the organization.

The more cosmopolitan boundary spanners, whose identity with their specialized fields (education, law, accounting, or the like) competes with their organizational identification and loyalty, can present challenges to organization control. These individuals often maintain contacts with fellow specialists and membership and affiliation with professional organizations and groups, and they keep up to date with developments in their fields. To the extent that such a boundary-crossing identity is respected, these individuals may be opinion leaders in their work situations (Mosher 1982; Rourke 1984). On the positive side, their expertise is valuable in stimulating program development, innovation, and adaptability and in maintaining organizational ethics. Conversely, their policy objectives or preferences for program design may reflect professional values and standards that are not consistent with those of top agency officials or the relevant public. In addition, studies have concluded that informal ties between boundary spanners can constrain an administrator's choice of strategies for establishing linkages with other actors in interorganizational networks (Boje and Whetter 1981, 391). Finally, the greater mobility of this type of boundary spanner can add to organizational turnover and instability.

In summary, individual communication roles perform numerous functions for the organization—coordination, filtering, socialization, innovation. In many ways they make communication more accurate and effective. They also can be sources of distortion and interference. In any event, like other variables in public and nonprofit organizations, their ultimate significance lies in their impact on agency power, policy, and effectiveness.

DISTORTION AND INTERFERENCE IN BUREAU COMMUNICATION

Accurate exchange of information is necessary to efficiently and effectively achieve the goals of an organization. Distortion in communication is dysfunctional to this end. However, in any organization communication often has goals other than just transmitting information. Its purpose is to influence. Distortion here, rather than being dysfunctional, may be an influence tool.

Ambivalence is strong about attempts by unelected officials to influence policy—even without distortion. One concept of public accountability in our system holds that officials who make policy should be accountable to the public they represent. Elections provide one such mechanism. Bureaucrats, according to this reasoning, are not elected and therefore not accountable to the public, so they should not have policy roles, however inadvisable or impossible this may be in practice. Intentional distortion of information by a bureaucratic official causes even greater accountability concerns.

BOX 5–2 Types of Distortion and Interference in Communication

---

Systemic Problems

- *Information overload:* Too much information, often unorganized and received serendipitously, makes it difficult or impossible to find relevant or important information. In such a situation important information may be lost or misinterpreted because of a lack of context.

- *Information lost or distorted by noise:* Static and other distractions cause information to be distorted or portions of communication to be lost.

- *Manipulating and withholding information:* Communications may be shaped, selectively released, or sent through specific channels that will present the best possible face to the information.

Sender/Receiver Problems

- *Projection:* It is assumed that the person or people being communicated with have the same perception of the problem, and the same mindset, as the sender.

- *Distorted perception:* Perception of what is communicated is selective based on the cues received and one's attention, mental set, and location in social space.

- *Erroneous translation:* Closely related to distorted perception, communication is misinterpreted because the same words have different meanings to the sender and the receiver. Included in this category are:

  - *Abstraction errors:* Misinterpretation of abstractions or generalizations by emphasizing some details and omitting others.

  - *Differentiation errors: Indiscrimination* neglects difference and overemphasizes similarities, whereas *polarization* treats "contraries" (situations or factors involving graded variations and middle ground) as if they are "contradictories" (strictly either–or affairs).

Interpersonal Problems

- *Lack of congruence:* At the interpersonal level, nonverbal cues and behavior are inconsistent with spoken communication. Likewise, communication received through multiple channels and information from multiple channels is inconsistent.

- *Distrusted source:* Information received from sources thought to be biased is evaluated with greater weight given to unintended than to intended communication because receivers' defenses are not aroused by communication that they don't believe was intended for them.

- *Jargon:* Jargon is composed of specialized vocabularies, the meaning of which is known only by a select group or by insiders within a profession, career, or social group. It develops as a shorthand within an expertise, as a way of rationing information made available to others, or as a way of making information seem *mysterious, pretentious, or euphemistic,* thereby giving an aura of scientific impartiality or detachment to judgments.

Not all the types of distortion discussed in this section and elsewhere in this chapter are intentional: Sometimes distortion is intentional, sometimes it is unintentional, and sometimes it is both. But all distortions have the potential to affect policy implementation and control. Let us look at the problems (a decidedly limited set of the total) leading to distortion and interference under three general headings.

Systemic Problems

One of the factors creating miscommunication, or failure to communicate at all, is *information overload* created by the pervasive nature of communication in what is now referred to as the information society. Discarding or ignoring the vast majority of communication that has no relevance to ongoing organizational activities while finding the messages and data that are useful (often critical) to staying informed is a difficult task. Most information available to—indeed thrust upon—an individual or an organization is simply *noise* and must be ignored to avoid information overload. Being able to select from the chaos of communication the information that is important to the operation and fulfillment of mission is a critical skill.

It is equally important to be able to recognize if *important communication is being manipulated or withheld.* Are some aspects of the environment, or of the organizational operations, missing? Even if transmitted with the best of intentions, communication can easily be lost or distorted in the chaotic information environment. Nor is it being paranoid to assume that some information may be withheld or manipulated by individuals or organizations that have something to gain or lose (power, influence over policies, jurisdiction over programs, resources, maintenance of coalitions).

The first strategy for controlling detrimental information is to simply withhold it if possible. Given the multiple sources of information and the persistence of those seeking to tap them, withholding information seems to be increasingly difficult. In both the private and public sectors much information seems to get released no matter what effort is put into burying it. Drugs that have detrimental effects on users, reports that do not support policy decisions by the president, misuse of funds by an executive in a nonprofit organization all seem to become headlines in newspapers in spite of efforts to keep the information quiet. Likewise, rumor mills often make information, good or bad, common knowledge long before officials planned to release it.

A common strategy for controlling information is to selectively release it in an effort to present it in the best light and to either maximize its positive impact or minimize its fallout. One practice, although one hopes it is not too common, is to request studies from those who will give the desired conclusion. Given the complexity of most public policy issues and the diverse perspectives existing in society and among interest groups or think tanks, there will be numerous findings based on the same sets of statistics or data. Thus two carefully detailed studies may present facts in an authoritative fashion yet result in diametrically opposed findings. Facts may even be intentionally distorted if necessary—although this strategy is dangerous in a world of multiple information sources. Selective presentation of facts also includes the tactic of *not* reporting all the information if some of it reflects poorly on the wisdom of the agency's preferred policy or procedure. Environmental and health policy disputes often are classic examples of this type of debate. The constant discussion of Social Security reform is perhaps the classic example of this form of information interpretation. This kind of attempt at controlling information occurs at all levels of society and involves public and nonprofit organizations.

Not only does such distortion of information happen at the interorganizational level; it also occurs regularly within agencies. Members of a government bureau or a nonprofit organization often have longevity in office, expertise, familiarity with issue communication networks, and control of information as power bases that make higher-level officeholders dependent on them for information and advice. This allows employees in critical positions inside the organization to shape the flow of information in favor of the policies and decisions they prefer. They do this by use of selective information and structuring or choosing appropriate channels through which to release information so that it will present the best possible face on the issue when received by policy makers in the agency. Information conveyed in routine reports from lower-level members usually does not reach top officials in its original form; the information is synopsized or rewritten for digestion by superiors—often at their request because of information overload and limitations on time.[3]

Thus all three types of distortion discussed here must be understood by both decision makers and program managers in organizations. Public servants and higher organization officials have long been acquainted with the obscuring technique of supplying too much information and thus creating information overload. However, everyone should be aware that screened and condensed information may be biased or intentionally limited if such action appears beneficial (for whatever reason) to those preparing it. Finally, it must be understood that techniques for structuring channels to control information flow include circumventing formal channels, informally exposing target officials to those who hold the correct views, and keeping sources away who might report preferably suppressed facts.

Sender/Receiver Problems

At the opposite end of the spectrum from system problems in the distortion of communication is the fact that information usually flows between individuals. Even in the day of e-mail and instantaneous mass communication, much important business of organizational life occurs in one-on-one encounters (face-to-face or through electronic technology). To guarantee that sender and receiver are communicating clearly, a number of factors must be taken into account. Let us mention several of these factors here; the reader should extend that list based on his or her experience.

Probably the most common problem in communication between individuals is that of *projection* by the sender. Individuals in an organization or profession often are surrounded by a mindset created by an organizational or professional culture—that is, by shared experiences, language, values, and worldview. Police officers, lawyers, judges, corrections officers, and parole and probation officers all work in the same general justice system; but their mindsets are quite different. Especially when communicating with people outside the organization, the sender often sends a message using the "agency mindset" assuming it is shared by those with whom he or she is communicating. That assumption may be naive. This kind of projection leads to serious misunderstandings because the same words, indeed the same phrases, may be interpreted entirely differently by the two parties in the communication. It is essential to

---

[3]On most policy issues the president, when making a final decision, is given a position paper that is at most two or three pages long and has listed at its end the two or three alternatives being seriously considered. The president, after discussion with closely involved officials, checks the chosen alternative and signs the document. This occurs after all of the time and effort spent on studying the issue.

understand how outsiders think when communicating with clients, constituents, and even other organizations that may be working in the same general subject or program area. This problem also arises when someone moves between work sectors (such as from a private to a public or nonprofit setting).

Even within organizations members operate from different mindsets. Many factors may lead to *distorted perception*. Motivations, personality, and past learning determine both what we perceive and what we fail to perceive. Individual differences add richness to both our internal and social worlds, but they also introduce complexities and obstacles into interpersonal communication. Thus perception can often be the mirror image of projection. Receivers of communication are influenced by their perceptions of the senders.

Our mental set determines our perceptual readiness, "the tendency to perceive what one expects or wants to receive" (Haney 1992, 63). And perception is selective. Thus different individuals interpret the same message or behavior in different ways.[4] For example, the expertise and dedication of professionals to their special field may focus their attention on the achievement of objectives with little thought about cost (Rourke 1984). They tend to regard administrative rules and procedure as stifling the effectiveness of policy implementation. Administrators, on the other hand, are more concerned with the efficient use of resources and with the need to compromise and moderate policy objectives in light of competing political forces in and out of the agency. The same tension is regularly reported between line and staff employees in most organizations.

Communication research also confirms that individuals normally perceive and recall those messages that reinforce prior images (Sebald 1962, 149). This phenomenon conditions what we attend to and what meaning we attach to it (March and Simon 1993). First impressions, as we all know, are hard to shake. So strong is the impulse to self-perpetuate our mental set that "the tendency to distort messages in the direction of identity with previous inputs is probably the most pervasive of the systematic biases" (Campbell 1958, 346).

Researchers have described how we go about sustaining our existing perceptions and mental set: "When confronted with a fact inconsistent with a stereotype already held by a person, the perceiver is able to distort the data in such a way as to eliminate the inconsistency. Thus, by perceiving inaccurately, he defends himself from having to change his stereotypes" (Zalkind and Costello 1962, 227). In a similar vein, Salvatore Maddi's research indicates that longer exposure to threatening as opposed to nonthreatening stimuli is required even to recognize or register awareness of them (1996).

In no other respect is the tendency to selective perception so strong as when self-image is involved. S. I. Hayakawa asserts that "the fundamental motive of human behavior is not self-preservation, but preservation of symbolic self" (1961). Individuals feel threatened by any sudden and uncontrolled change to their self-image even if the change is favorable (Haney 1992).

Selective perception may lend stability to our internal state, but it frequently introduces distortion into our perceptions and communication. This type of *erroneous translation* (misinterpretation of terms or using two different terms for the same thing) leads to serious organizational

---

[4]In this regard it is important to remember that communication may occur through behavior or other nonverbal symbols as well as through the use of language. When given what is seen as an important assignment, new employees may interpret a lack of feedback from their superiors as a negative sign, whereas more experienced individuals in the organization may welcome that same behavior as a positive sign. (See Chapter 9's discussion of leadership.)

and individual misunderstandings. Organizational control and responsiveness to change may be complicated by perceptual distortion and resistance to change—depending on the nature of the stimuli or message. And this distortion, or misunderstanding of information, is doubtless an ingredient in both internal and external organizational conflict.

Other factors that lead to erroneous translation include *abstraction and differentiation errors*. By necessity much information is generalized and then must be interpreted to meet the specific condition or plan of action. If someone says that "the budget is balanced" that sounds good to an outsider; but an organizational veteran knows the devil is in the details. That generalization must be broken down in numerous ways (size, distribution, source of revenue, fixed costs or mandated expenditures, and so on) before the phrase takes on meaning.

Several types of differentiation errors contribute to miscommunication. *Indiscrimination* is neglecting differences while overemphasizing similarities. Linguists note that English-speaking people are particularly inclined to perceive and speak in terms of similarities and to generalize instead of differentiate. Our language has numerous general nouns and verbs; other languages have proportionately fewer of these terms but numerous specific ones. For example, the Eskimo language has many words for specific types of snow but no general word. The Navajo language distinguishes specific stages and manners of going but has no general word for this verb (Haney 1992).

Polarization is a form of differentiation failure that occurs when contraries (situations involving graded variations, middle ground) are treated as if they were contradictories (strictly either–or or winner-loser affairs) (Haney 1992). To say that people are either over six feet tall or not is a genuine contradictory. But saying that people are either short or tall is polarization because people of medium height are, of course, neither short nor tall. *Frozen evaluations* also cause differentiation errors: When we do not take the possibility of change into account, both thinking and communication suffer.

Any policy, of necessity, must be general. Especially in the public and nonprofit world, policy must satisfy a variety of similar individual circumstances. Yet its design should allow implementation to adequately reflect differences and varieties of people and situations. Individuals carrying out public policy must therefore be especially sensitive to balancing the overall goals of legislation (or governing board mission statements and principles) with the individual circumstances of those for or about whom the rule is written.

Interpersonal Problems

Interpersonal problems are closely related to sender/receiver problems in communication but involve a much larger portion of the organization. The final three categories reach beyond any individual communication (and the sender or receiver involved) and involve numerous people throughout the organization. It is also important to note that these three factors usually operate at the informal level; there is no formal recognition of their existence. Instead they might be considered part of the culture of the organization, which is discussed further in Chapter 8.

The first problem is a *lack of congruence* in messages. Organizations often verbalize an ideal type of behavior and process but practice another. This occurs both internally and in relations with other agencies. For example, if the body language or behavior of individuals does not match the words that people are hearing, the discrepancy may lead to ambiguity (and higher tension for the receivers). Managers in an organization may claim to have an open-door policy. Members of the organization may be told to come in at any time to talk about what is really on their minds. But if the workers meet with resistance from the outer office or experience excessive delays, the open-door message becomes incongruent. If the managers fret, glower, or read during exchanges with employees or react defensively or unsympathetically when problems are brought up, the overall message becomes ambivalent. For most workers the managers' verbal message is "the door is always open," but their behavioral message is "don't bother me, I'm busy with more important things" or "I don't want to know about problems; you take care of them."

Likewise, if one organization makes overtures to work cooperatively with a second but continues to carry out competitive practices in its public dealings, the second agency will find it hard to interpret or believe the communication received. In both cases the incongruence between verbal and nonverbal communication leads to difficulty in message interpretation, loss of trust, and an internal culture with destructive levels of frustration and cynicism or an inability to develop constructive cooperative relationships with important external constituents.

All other elements in the communication being equal, higher source credibility leads to greater acceptance of communication (Zimbardo and Ebbesen 1977). However, *distrust of a source* is a common result of incongruence. If for any reason information comes from a distrusted source, receivers of the communication judge the messages accordingly; and the distrust can lead to distortions of the message. For example, John McCone, director of the Central Intelligence Agency during the Kennedy administration, reported his suspicions that the Soviets were preparing to put offensive missiles into Cuba; it was the message the president least wanted to hear. Moreover, according to Graham Allison, "Kennedy heard this as what it was: the suspicion of a professional anti-Communist" (1999, 190). The president did not share the stance and outlook of such types. Later, however, other information verified the presence of offensive weapons, thus changing the course of administration action in dealing with this greater danger. The tendency to evaluate the sender, which we all share, is basically rational—as long as we are aware of how our own biases can distort our judgment. The inability to recognize biases—ours or those of others in the organization—creates serious problems.

Communication researchers report an interesting paradox concerning the effect of distrusted sources. If the sender is thought to have biased attitudes, greater weight is given to unintended than to intended communication because receivers' defenses are not aroused by communication that they don't believe was intended for them (Allyn and Festinger 1961; Jones and Davis 1965). Thus, for example, people will pay more attention to nonverbal communication from a distrusted source, or they will give greater weight to information that appears to be intended for others (rather than the person receiving the communication). Perhaps the importance given to information received through the organization's informal grapevine or leaked to the outside is related to this phenomenon. Rumor may engender less defensiveness and skepticism because it is seen as unintended or unguarded.

Finally, we need to note an increasingly ubiquitous phenomenon related to the increasing specialization in all aspects of society and in organizational life—the use of *jargon* by groups and individuals in society. Specialization, in the past, referred to separate task components in organizations. But the term has gained greater credence as both organizations and the substantive issues they address have become more complex and sophisticated. Some time ago knowledge (especially scientific knowledge) expanded beyond the capacity of the minds of single individuals and became fragmented into separate disciplines and bodies of knowledge. Thus specialized vocabularies have developed within discrete technical and professional areas. Inevitably in such situations communication gaps arise between those who have the specialized knowledge and vocabularies and those who do not. In many cases, however, the

BOX 5-3 Expertise, Influence, and Governance

Western societies in general, and the United States in particular, tend to accept the fact that technical matters should be left to professionals and experts; thus specialists within government bureaucracy and in special interest groups often have great influence on policy. There are, of course, constraints on the experts' influence in shaping public sector policy (in government or in nonprofit organizations). Two factors are especially important in calculating the level of power held by experts: (1) Is the issue perceived as technical or value related? (2) Are policy makers (legislators in government or governing board members in nonprofit organizations) able to match the expertise of outsiders by developing their own staff experts? Let us look at each of these factors.

Because of both pressure groups and their own personal values, legislators and governing board members are likely to perceive certain issues as value laden (religious or moral) rather than technical. Several of the most heated debates facing politicians, and administrators attempting to carry out public services in communities, are what are currently called "values-oriented issues." Communication between policy makers and experts, the influence of specialists, the distribution of influence, and policy outcomes are altered accordingly. Public health specialists, like some other experts, are frequently in control of presenting the alternatives from which policy makers choose. Yet in areas such as abortion, stem cell research, and the definition of when someone is legally dead, the influence of these specialists is limited. For example, elected officials at national, state, and local levels have initiated and enacted various abortion-related policies quite independently of public health or medical experts. Stem cell research is another issue in which the primary stimulus for decisions is related not to the science involved but to the various definitions of "life" and interpretations by religious groups of when life begins and whether the sanctity of an embryo is similar to that of a fully developed fetus. For those who define an issue in terms of their personal religious or moral views, technical or expert perspectives are not relevant.

Because policy makers (Congress is the prime example) feel dependent on experts who are often out of their control, the policy makers try to counter the expertise of outside sources. The Congressional Budget Office was created because Congress did not trust the figures from either the Office of Management and Budget or the outside interest groups who were lobbying about specific programs and financial policies; however, individual members of Congress refute or refuse the figures of the CBO when its numbers do not match their policy desires and they can present more favorable figures—usually prepared by their staff economic experts (often with the help of interest groups with whom the legislators are sympathetic). Likewise, issues like environmental regulation are often left to the experts in the Environmental Protection Agency; however, countering expertise has been developed by interest groups on all sides of the issues, and the EPA is now challenged, and often overruled, much more regularly on its decisions. In other cases, such as the closing of military bases, decisions are turned over to "experts" by Congress primarily because the politicians realize the issues are so volatile that (1) they do not want to have to handle them, and (2) the decisions must be handled by a group that can claim expertise and objectivity in its deliberations.

The relationship between officials and experts is best described as one of mutual dependence. Thus there is a special need for trust between politician and adviser. Successful professional and expert advisers are scrupulous about the veracity of their information; they also understand that politicians often will use the information they find most satisfactory from their personal political perspective. Top-level organizational leaders, as generalists, may do the same thing.

level of specialization in vocabularies and the requisite inability of outsiders or clients to understand the exchanges of insiders has reached levels not required for clarity and specificity in communication. When this occurs the result is referred to as the use of *jargon*.

As just noted, the fragmentation of knowledge creates a situation in which those who need, but do not have, a particular kind of expertise are dependent on those who do. This phenomenon gives rise to the tendency to defer to experts in technical matters and to follow the advice of experts in policy making. The vocabulary and jargon used by individuals with specialized knowledge identifies them as experts—and thereby enhances their power. Jargon erects communication barriers, but it also reinforces the tendency to follow the advice of experts in policy making.

In addition to fragmentation and specialization of knowledge, other factors foster the use of jargon. On one hand, workers in public and nonprofit organizations are expected to be responsive to their publics. This could reasonably include communicating in ways familiar and understandable to their clientele. On the other hand, the norms of impartiality and equal treatment create pressures that sometimes have unintended effects on communication. Language becomes depersonalized. Individuals in a bureaucratic setting tend to use passive expression or style; standardized terminology is coined that does not correspond to ordinary usage. One of the most frequent complaints of outsiders about government agency communication is the use of jargon—or worse, of "bureaucratese" or gobbledygook.

Bureaucratese, or jargon, can be used by service deliverers to give themselves an advantage in their interaction with clients or outsiders if any kind of power game is taking place. By using their specialized language, people who are supposed to be serving others can turn the tables on those with whom they are interacting. The inability of clients or outsiders to understand what is being communicated can create a sense of insecurity and bafflement that puts them at an instant disadvantage in any situation.

Some public and nonprofit agencies "ration services by manipulating the nature and quantity of information made available" (Lipsky 1980, 91). Street-level bureaucracies—those whose workers directly dispense benefits or sanctions—usually have inadequate resources. Confusing jargon, especially in conjunction with elaborate and obscure procedures, forms a barrier to many clients; thus the bureau may limit client access and demand—through noncommunication based on jargon—as a way of coping with its resource problem.

READING 5–2   Inflated Style, Euphemism, and Evasion:
A Special Use of Jargon

George Orwell points out in his classic essay on politics and language in the British public service that language is "an instrument which we shape to our own purposes" (1956, 355). Frequently those purposes are political, especially in public bureaus. Pretentious diction "is used to dress up simple statements to give an air of scientific impartiality to biased judgments" (Orwell 1956, 358). Speakers also use inflated style to keep their political intentions and alternatives unclear. Orwell notes that

> The inflated style is itself a kind of euphemism. A mass of Latin words falls upon the facts like soft snow, blurring the outlines and covering up all the details. The great enemy of clear

language is insincerity. When there is a gap between one's real and one's declared aims, one turns as it were instinctively to long words and exhausted idioms, like a cuttlefish squirting out ink. (363)

Even more alarming to Orwell was the use of meaningless words or euphemisms. These are used to make the unpalatable palatable. Sometimes political communication is the attempt to defend the indefensible, or things that can be defended "but only by arguments that are too brutal for most people to face" (Orwell 1956, 363). Instead we turn to "euphemism, question-begging and sheer cloudy-vagueness":

> Defenseless villages are bombarded from the air, the inhabitants driven out into the countryside, the cattle machine-gunned, the huts set on fire with incendiary bullets: This is called *pacification*. Millions of peasants are robbed of their farms and sent trudging along roads with no more than they can carry: This is called *transfer of population* or *rectification of frontiers*. People are imprisoned for years without trial, or shot in the back of the neck, or sent to die of scurvy in Arctic lumber camps: This is called *elimination of unreliable elements* (363).

SOURCE: George Orwell, "Politics and the English Language." In *The Orwell reader*, ed. Richard Rovere (New York: Harcourt Brace Jovanovich, 1956), 355–66.

COPING WITH DISTORTION

Various sources of distortion in communication—perceptual, social, structural, and political—have been raised. No single answer exists to the problem of distortion; it must be kept in mind that remedies can introduce new problems along with solutions. Nevertheless public and nonprofit administrators, and officials outside these agencies, can adopt strategies to reduce distortion, whether or not the distortion is intentional.

It is possible to shape the flow of information received from both inside and outside any particular agency or official position. At least five types of strategies are available to leaders, political officials, members of the organization, and others for obtaining better information and constraining the power of actors trying to use the communication process for personal or political gain. They are (1) creating alternative sources, (2) encouraging divergent views, (3) eliminating intermediaries, (4) using distortion-proof messages, and (5) counterbiasing.

Administrators and leaders can check distortion and achieve better verification of the information they receive by *creating alternative sources*. A fuller and more accurate picture emerges from a wider range and amount of information. Several independent groups can be set up within an organization to work on the same policy question (Downs 1994; Janis 1972). This technique introduces an element of competition combined with each group's lack of information about the reports and actions of the other groups and individuals. In government administration it is common to use the fact that there are regularly overlapping areas of responsibility in different bureaus. Coordination requires communication, often in a face-to-face format, so leaders can develop a sense of what is going on both inside and outside their agencies. Leaders of nonprofit organizations also use such alternative sources for "reality checks" on the information they receive.

Informal ties and friendships within one's agency create alternative sources to gather and verify information. In part this is learning to use the grapevine productively. Sources outside the bureau are useful also; these include the press, clientele, social acquaintances, reports of other agencies, and even gossip.

Certain leader behaviors and communication styles *encourage divergent views.* Leaders can surround themselves with individuals of differing views and still not achieve divergence in views and openness in communication of those perspectives. Much of the learning organization theory is built around the development of openness and sharing of knowledge, information, and perspective. Senge (1994), for instance, notes that there must be more than just "participative openness," which allows the freedom to speak one's mind. To learn from our environment and our experiences we must also practice "reflective openness," which leads to looking inward.

> Reflective openness starts with the willingness to challenge our own thinking, to recognize that any certainty we ever have is, at best, a hypothesis about the world. No matter how compelling it may be, no matter how fond we are of "our idea," it is always subject to test and improvement. Reflective openness lives in the attitude, "I may be wrong and the other person may be right." It involves not just examining our own ideas, but mutually examining others' thinking. (277–78)

The kind of reflective openness needed for encouraging and utilizing divergent views requires the skills of

- Reflection (slowing down our own thinking processes so we can become more aware of how we form our mental models).

- Inquiry (knowing how we operate in face-to-face interactions with others, especially in dealing with complex and conflictual issues).

- Dialogue (the examination of assumptions and willingness to play with new ideas).

- Dealing with defensive routines (breaking through perspectives and routines that form a protective shell around our deepest assumptions and defend us from pain or embarrassment).

For such a system—encouraging divergent views—to function successfully, a strong sense of trust must exist as part of the organization's culture, and this is exceedingly hard to create in organizations that are embedded in the overall political system. Constant turnover of political appointees at the top of the organization, and the seemingly unavoidable tension between those appointees and merit system employees, limit the development of trust. Thus it is difficult to create communication systems that do *not* soft-pedal disagreements or suppress bad news. Difficulty, however, does not let managers off the hook—divergent views are still necessary for successful operation in the public interest.

Opportunities for distortion and omission increase with the number of organizational levels communication must pass through. A structural approach to this problem is to *eliminate intermediaries,* or to flatten the hierarchy by having fewer levels. This approach is popular now, but for reasons primarily of economy. That does not, however, keep administrators from taking advantage of this opportunity to improve communication channels at the same time. A more informal technique for overcoming these structural sources of distortion is by-passing—that is, for officials to contact individuals considerably above or below themselves in a hierarchy.

When accuracy of reporting is critical, one way to make sure that information gets forwarded in its original format, and with its complete content, is to use *distortion-proof messages*—forms of communication that cannot be distorted because they are forwarded without screening or condensation. Standard forms, messages that go to multiple levels at the same time, and statistical reports are a couple of these communication devices. The National Aeronautics and Space Administration, after the explosion of the *Challenger* shuttle, found that critical safety information had not been passed forward to higher-level officials, so it changed its reporting system to require that conflicts be reported to the next higher level in all cases. This meant that distortion could not occur, nor could the information simply be withheld.

If administrators have experience in the organizations they lead, or if they have professional insight about the goals and processes, they can often *counterbias information*. They can estimate the distortion that occurs during communication and then make an appropriate adjustment in their interpretation of the information. For example, a line administrator who knows the tendency of the bureau's staff lawyers to include all remotely possible legal pitfalls as well as the more likely ones, can conduct his or her operation with more latitude than if she or he were to regard all the legal warnings as equally imminent or likely. By reading between the lines we can correct bias in information. However, other sources of correction are critical because it is always dangerous to depend too much on personal experience.

CONCLUSION

Communication is essential in all organizations. It is a process through which organizations inform and clarify goals for members. Internally, communication provides a medium for organizational coordination and control and, more informally, for social support among members. External communication is especially vital to organizations working in the public sector to (1) maintain political or community responsiveness and accountability, (2) foster coordination with other agencies and levels of government, and (3) promote external support. In this chapter we discussed accountability and power as well as communication. The two are closely related for public sector agencies because communication is a primary medium for exercising power. Communication is essential to creating a sense of mission and loyalty among employees and interested outsiders; however, it can also be used destructively. Organizations and their members can raise smoke screens to evade accountability. Information can be withheld or its timing and content manipulated to protect the agency's operating routines and policies from external scrutiny. By shaping the flow of information, bureaus and their members attempt to maintain or increase their power and resources, avoid the control of others, and reduce undesirable environmental turbulence. Policy outcomes and power relationships inside and outside the organization are affected.

Before organization and communication theory can fully encompass public organizations— and their important differences—much future research and integration of public–private perspectives will be needed. For now we point to some issues of special interest for communication and public sector organizations. In particular, the political nature of public sector organizations and their communications should be acknowledged and understood; we also need to understand the importance of organization–environment relationships and external communication in the public sector.

FOR FURTHER READING

A useful reference to earlier communication theorists, and an attempt to present a model of interpersonal communication as a dynamic process, is David K. Berlo's *The Process of Communication: An Introduction to Theory and Practice* (New York: Holt, Rinehart & Winston, 1960). A lucid and concise presentation of communication research in an organizational context appears in Everett Rogers and Rekha Agarwala-Rogers's *Communication in Organizations* (New York: Free Press, 1976). Anthony Downs, in *Inside Bureaucracy* (Boston: Little, Brown, 1967; reissued Prospect Heights, IL: Waveland Press, 1994), discusses the interaction between the communication process and bureaucratic structure and processes. He also looks at communication as one element in other functions such as decision making, motivation, and coordination and control. A particularly significant contribution to communication theory is made by Steven Seitz in *Bureaucracy, Policy, and the Public* (St. Louis: C. V. Mosby, 1978) because he includes external communication as an important element in the total managerial process. Seitz explores the influence of (especially external) communication patterns on policymaking and implementation. For an emphasis on sources of unintentional distortion in interpersonal communication, see William V. Haney, *Communication and Interpersonal Relations: Text and Cases*, 6th ed. (Homewood, IL: Richard D. Irwin, 1992). On the other hand, George Orwell's "Politics and the English Language," in Richard Rovere, ed., *The Orwell Reader* (New York, Harcourt Brace Jovanovich, 1956), and Morton Halperin's "Shaping the Flow of Information" in Halperin (with the assistance of Priscilla Clapp and Arnold Kanter), *Bureaucratic Politics and Foreign Policy* (Washington, DC: The Brookings Institution, 1974), both look at *intentional distortion* and its political significance.

For complementary excerpts from classics readings, see most editions of Jay Shafritz and J. Steven Ott's (and coauthors) *Classics of Organizational Theory* (Belmont, CA: Thomson Wadsworth): Mary Parker Follett, "The Giving of Orders"; and Scott Cook and Dvora Yanow, "Culture and Organizational Learning."

For a complementary nonprofit case study to go with this chapter, see Robert Goliembiewski and Jerry Stevenson's *Cases and Applications in Non-Profit Management* (Belmont, CA: Thomson Wadsworth, 1998): Case 16, "Conflicts on the Human Services Team."

REVIEW QUESTIONS

1. Note the differences between formal and informal communication. Considering the noise that occurs within and around communications, how can the formal and informal channels of communication help to correct any distortion or information loss?
2. How does communication differ when moving upward, downward, or laterally in the organization? What impact will the structure of the organization have on how communication flows in each direction?
3. Given the political environment of public sector organizations, how important is communication to the leaders (or managers or workers) of the organization? What political factors must be taken into account when the leader talks to those outside the organization

or those inside the organization? Will the message and the medium be different in those two situations?

4. Looking at the roles individuals play in the communication network, how many roles can a single individual play? How (and why) might peoples' behavior, and their power in the organization, change as they shift roles?

REFERENCES

Allison, Graham T., and Philip Zelikow. 1999. *Essence of decision: Explaining the Cuban missile crisis*. New York: Longman.

Allyn, J., and L. Festinger. 1961. The effectiveness of unanticipated persuasive communications. *Journal of Abnormal Social Psychology* 62: 35–40.

Barnard, Chester. 1979. *The functions of the executive*. Cambridge, MA: Harvard University Press.

Bavelas, Alex. 1950. Communication patterns in task-oriented groups. *Acoustical Society of America Journal* 22: 727–30.

Berlo, David K. 1960. *The process of communication: An introduction to theory and practice*. New York: Holt, Rinehart & Winston.

Berne, Eric. 2004. *Games people play: The psychology of human relationships*. New York: Ballantine Books.

Blau, Peter M., and W. Richard Scott. 2003. *Formal organizations: A comparative approach*. Stanford, CA: Stanford Business Books.

Bohm, David. 1996. *The special theory of relativity*. London: Routledge.

Boje, David M., and David A. Whetter. 1981. Effects of organizational strategies and contextual constraints on centrality and attributions of influence in interorganizational networks. *Administrative Science Quarterly* 26, no. 3: 378–95.

Campbell, D. T. 1958. Systematic error on the part of human links in communication systems. *Information and Control* 1: 334–69.

Carroll, Stephen J., and Henry L. Tosi. 1977. *Organizational behavior*. Chicago: St. Clair Press.

Downs, Anthony. 1994. *Inside bureaucracy*. Prospect Heights, IL: Waveland Press.

Eggen, Dan, and Walter Pincus. 2005. Spy chief gets more authority over FBI. *Washington Post*, June 30: A1, A7.

Eisenhower, Dwight D. 1965. *Waging peace, 1956–1961: The White House years*. Garden City, NY: Doubleday.

Fidler, Lori A., and J. David Johnson. 1984. Communication and innovation implementation. *Academy of Management Review* 9: 704–11.

Granovetter, Mark S. 1973. The strength of weak ties. *American Journal of Sociology* 78:1360–80.

Hage, Jerald, Michael Aiken, and Cora Bagley Marrett. 1971. Organization structure and communications. *American Sociological Review* 36: 860–71.

Halperin, Morton H. 1974. Shaping the flow of information. In *Bureaucratic politics and foreign policy,* 158–72. With the assistance of Priscilla Clapp and Arnold Kanter. Washington, DC: The Brookings Institution. Reprinted in Francis E. Rourke, ed., *Bureaucratic power in national politics*, 102–15. 3rd ed. Boston: Little, Brown, 1978.

Haney, William V. 1992. *Communication and interpersonal relations: Text and cases*. 6th ed. Homewood, IL: Richard D. Irwin.

Hayakawa, S. I. 1961. Conditions of success in communication. From an address presented to the Twelfth Annual Round Table of the Institute of Languages and Linguistics, Edmund Walsh School of Foreign Service, Georgetown University, Washington, DC, April 22. Cited in William V. Haney. 1979. *Communication and interpersonal relations: Text and cases*, 234–35. 4th ed. Homewood, IL: Richard D. Irwin.

Heclo, Hugh. 1977. *A government of strangers: Executive politics in Washington.* Washington, DC: The Brookings Institution.

Isaacs, William N. 1993. Taking flight: Dialogue, collective thinking, and organizational learning. *Organizational Dynamics* 22 (Autumn): 24–39.

James, Muriel, and Dorothy Jongeward. 1991. *Born to win.* Reading, MA: Addison-Wesley.

Janis, Irving L. 1972. *Victims of groupthink.* Boston: Houghton Mifflin.

Jones, Edward E., and Keith E. Davis. 1965. From acts to dispositions: The attribution process in person perception. In *Advances in experimental social psychology,* vol. 2, 219–66. Ed. Leonard Berkowitz. New York: Academic Press.

Katz, Daniel, and Robert L. Kahn. 1978. *The social psychology of organizations.* 2nd ed. New York: John Wiley & Sons.

Keyton, Joann. 2005. *Communication and organizational culture.* Thousand Oaks, CA: Sage Publications.

Leavitt, Harold J. 1951. Some effects of certain communication patterns on group performance. *Journal of Abnormal and Social Psychology* 46: 38–50.

Lipsky, Michael. 1980. *Street-level bureaucracy: Dilemmas of the individual in public services.* New York: Russell Sage Foundation.

Luft, Joseph. 1984. *Group processes: An introduction to group dynamics.* 3rd ed. Palo Alto, CA: Mayfield Publishing.

Luthans, Fred, Richard M. Hodgetts, and Sag M. Lee. 1994. New paradigm organizations: From total quality to learning to world class. *Organizational Dynamics* 22 (Winter): 5–19.

Maddi, Salvatore. 1996. *Personality theories: A comparative analysis.* 6th ed. Pacific Grove, CA: Brooks/Cole.

March, James B., and Herbert A. Simon. 1993. *Organizations.* 2nd ed. Cambridge, MA: Blackwell.

McCurdy, Howard E. 1977. *Public administration: A synthesis.* Menlo Park, CA: Cummings.

Mosher, Frederick. 1982. *Democracy and the public service.* 2nd ed. New York: Oxford University Press.

National Commission on Terrorist Attacks upon the United States. 2004. *9/11 Commission report: Final report of the National Commission on Terrorist Attacks upon the United States.* New York: Barnes & Noble Books.

Orwell, George. 1956. Politics and the English language. In *The Orwell reader,* 355–66. Ed. Richard Rovere. New York: Harcourt Brace Jovanovich.

Osborne, David, and Ted Gaebler. 1992. *Reinventing government: How the entrepreneurial spirit is transforming the public sector.* Reading, MA: Addison-Wesley.

Redding, William C. 1972. *Communication within the organization.* New York: Industrial Communication Council.

Rogers, Everett M. 1973. *Communication strategies for family planning.* New York: Free Press.

Rogers, Everett M., and Rekha Agarwala-Rogers. 1976. *Communication in organizations.* New York: Free Press.

Rourke, Francis E. 1984. *Bureaucracy, politics, and public policy.* 3rd ed. Boston: Little, Brown.

Savas, Emanuel S. 2000. *Privatization and public–private partnerships.* New York: Chatham House.

Schein, Edgar H. 1993. On dialogue, culture, and organizational learning. *Organizational Dynamics* 22 (Autumn): 40–51.

Sebald, Hans. 1962. Limitations of communication: Mechanisms of image maintenance in form of selective perception, selective memory, and selective distortion. *Journal of Communication* 12: 142–49.

Seitz, Steven Thomas. 1978. *Bureaucracy, policy, and the public.* St. Louis: C. V. Mosby.

Senge, Peter M. 1994. *The fifth discipline: The art and practice of the learning organization.* New York: Doubleday/Currency.

Shaw, M. E. 1954. Some effects of unequal distribution of information upon group performance in various communication nets. *Journal of Abnormal and Social Psychology* 49: 547–53.

Sinetar, M. 1988. Building trust into corporate relationships. *Organizational Dynamics* (Winter): 73–79.

Steers, Richard M., and J. Stewart Black. 1994. *Organizational behavior.* 5th ed. New York: HarperCollins.

Thayer, Lee O. 1986. *Communication and communication systems: In organization, management, and interpersonal relations.* Lanham, MD: University Press of America.

Thompson, James D. 2003. *Organizations in action: Social science bases of administrative theory.* New Brunswick, NJ: Transaction Publishers.

Thompson, Victor A. 1961. *Modern organization.* New York: Alfred A. Knopf.

Walter, U. M., and C. G. Petr. 2000. A template for family-centered interagency collaboration. *Families in Society: The Journal of Contemporary Social Services* 81: 494–503.

Wilensky, Harold L. 1967. *Organizational intelligence: Knowledge and policy in government and industry.* New York: Basic Books.

Zalkind, S. S., and T. W. Costello. 1962. Perception: Some recent research and implications for administration. *Administrative Science Quarterly* 7 (September): 218–33.

Zimbardo, P., and E. B. Ebbesen. 1977. *Influencing attitudes and changing behavior.* 2nd ed. Reading, MA: Addison-Wesley.

Chapter 6

Accountability
to Transparency

Law of ever-expanding control: "The quantity and detail of reporting required by monitoring bureaus tends to rise steadily over time, regardless of the amount or nature of the activity being monitored."

(Downs 1967, 150)

All organizations are under tremendous pressure to be efficient. But public organizations, whether government or nonprofit, are also under stress and scrutiny to be accountable, responsive, and effective. This chapter is about how public organizations are accountable—to themselves and to us, the public—and trends in accountability as an evolving principle in the public sector. Briefly, legal or *democratic accountability* refers to adhering to orders and laws and being able to substantiate that adherence to whomever the person or organization is accountable. As Downs states, this need for control and hence accountability seems to expand, becoming increasingly important for our understanding of organizations. *Responsiveness* means meeting the individual needs of customers and citizens. Accountability and responsiveness are organizational values interwoven into organization culture and are not merely externally mandated controls. Balancing these values are the individuals who must act responsibly. *Responsibility* emphasizes a personal commitment to duty; that is, individuals accept the personal obligation of determining right from wrong in the context of the rule, order, or law and act accordingly. Only when these values are engaged and in harmony can the organization be effective (see Figure 6–1).

Transparency brings these values together. For our purposes, *transparency* is visible decision making that is open to public input, allows the public maximal choice, and is conducted in cooperation with organizations working together for common public purposes. We will use this meaning, but we need to acknowledge that the word has another definition. A process is transparent if it occurs without the user having to be aware of or concerned with the underlying complexities of the action that is taking place. For instance, few taxpayers are aware of the accounting, communication, and verification requirements behind having their income tax refunds deposited directly into their personal checking accounts: The process is conveniently transparent or invisible.

FIGURE 6–1   From Accountability to Transparency

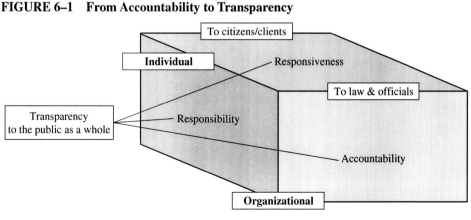

As we might expect, the principles or values of accountability, responsiveness, and responsibility can sometimes be challenging to reconcile, so trade-offs occur. Those who place more emphasis on the idea of accountability will place following the letter of the law and following the hierarchical chain of command above such factors as individual freedom of action within the organization. For them it is crucial to ensure that the organization remains within its sphere of competence and its mission. In such situations elected representatives and boards of nonprofit organizations make the discretionary decisions. Where policy is at issue, elected officials and board members—rather than employees—must be the ones who are responsive. At the day-to-day level of decision making, however, it is the organization's employees who must decide whether to make exceptions to rules. Should the employee be responsive to the individual situation or to the rule or law? In some situations the goals of accountability and individual freedom within the organization conflict; although individual satisfaction and career development are valid goals, accountability must take precedence.

Those who place more emphasis on individual responsibility to one's own moral code or to one's clientele are not necessarily arguing against accountability; they simply believe that it is achieved in another way. They argue that the long-term goal of maintaining democracy and the mission of the organization is best served when professionals (1) are sensitive to the needs and desires of those they serve and (2) have discretion and adequate freedom to influence policy and procedures. In other words, accountability pertains predominantly to those being served rather than to a formal oversight body.

These values are at the root of the public's questions about the effectiveness of public sector organizations. Classic rational economic theory suggests that nonprofit and government organizations are less concerned than private sector organizations about efficiency; public organizations put resources into providing services (such as providing rural mail delivery, public utilities, and health care to the poor) that otherwise might not be available because of high costs (Weisbrod 1975; Kingma 2003). Public sector organizations are motivated by an explicit social mission (Bacchiega and Borzaga 2003; Hansmann 2003). As such, they tend to be responsive to constituent needs. The reverse may also be true. The impersonal but fair rules of public sector organizations may make them less responsive. This is of particular concern to those who study nonprofit organizations and see a change in the behavior of nonprofits as their responsibilities are inextricably blurred with government in the provision of services (Salamon 1999 a and b; Brown and Troutt 2004).[1]

More generally, some phrases suggest the challenge and difficulty public organizations have in dealing with the sometimes competing values of accountability, responsiveness, and responsibility:

- The term *captured* describes agencies that make their decisions and policies with and for the benefit of a particular interest group rather than the public as a whole.

- The term *street-level bureaucrats* (Lipsky 1980) recognizes that police officers and other service professionals who work directly with the public make numerous official decisions,

---

[1]The highpoint of government-nonprofit coordination was in the 70s declining in the more conservative years of the 80s. More recently, there has been an expansion as states and the federal government have devolved responsibilities to nonprofits.

in a sense setting policy case by case; moreover, the term can sometimes mean that important organization decisions are out of the leaders' hands, and those employees closest to the public are not fully accountable to their superiors.

- *Red tape* suggests that an organization requires an excessive amount of paperwork or a complex process to obtain service, and its employees are not responsive to citizen needs because they follow the letter (without considering the spirit) of the law even in situations when doing so does not make sense (Bozeman 2000) and because they focus on processes rather than results—sometimes referred to as *ends–means displacement.*

- *Unfunded mandate* implies that an organization has little control over or responsibility for a set of rules and policies it oversees; a higher level of government has created requirements that are costly and perhaps burdensome but has not provided funding to mitigate those costs.

These phrases relate to the theory of political control (Frederickson 2003; Robey 1994). What and how much control should another organization or official have? A more positive point of view is expressed through the use of such terms as *best practices, performance evaluation, evidence-based medicine,* and *analysis.* All these connote organizations engaged in self-examination, ongoing improvement, and being accountable to others. "Sunshine" laws and the popular press term *transparency* indicate that organizational processes and proceedings are open to the public, creating accountability.

Accountability, responsiveness, and responsibility emphasize control at different and equally important levels. As we discuss in the next section, the basis for understanding accountability is the theory of political control. Accountability occurs when organizations report to a higher political authority or political body. We expand the discussion to include accountability to an accrediting organization, a parent agency, or a regulatory body. Most public organizations and agencies are accountable to elected officials, legislative bodies, and the courts at times, and, in the end, to the public. Nonprofits and some government organizations, such as government authorities (such as some utilities, civil rights commissions, transit and port authorities), are accountable to boards and the public and only indirectly accountable to elected officials.[2] Accountability is also discussed in terms of the internal reporting mechanisms used to create that accountability. Accountability involves an obligation to report. The discussion of accountability is followed by a discussion of responsiveness. Responsiveness emphasizes citizen or customer control rather than political or democratic control. Ultimately public organizations are accountable to the public. That involves direct responsiveness to the public rather than indirectly through a political official. A third section discusses how responsibility emphasizes individual self-control. We follow that discussion with an entirely different theory of control and accountability: cybernetic control. According to this theory organizations are self-organizing and self-sustaining, and they naturally seek to create an equilibrium of stability. Accountability becomes automatic. The chapter concludes by considering transparency as an important emerging value for effective organizational accountability.

---

[2]Public authorities are established to be independent of elected officials. Elected officials appoint board members but normally have no power to fire them.

ACCOUNTABILITY

How should we ensure that our organizations are accountable? The theory of *political control* or political accountability is based on the idea that policies and decisions of a public organization are best controlled through a chain of command or hierarchical control from political officials to the appointed executive and on to frontline employees (Frederickson 2003; Robey 1994; Kearns 1996). All employees are accountable to elected officials for fair, equitable treatment of citizens, clients, and customers; efficient and effective programs; and conformance with the law. Accountability and trust of both nonprofit organizations and government are critical to a democratic society. Government agencies, part of the democratic framework, are responsible for preserving the Constitution, exercising certain executive, legislative, and judicial powers, and even at times checking the power of elected officials (Terry 2003, 23; Rohr 1986). As citizens we delegate broad and often critical responsibilities through our elected representatives to government agencies, giving those agencies discretion and authority. To the extent that nonprofit organizations offer government services through contractual arrangements, they too assume this responsibility.

Political accountability does, however, become more difficult when government organizations contract with nonprofits for service. Nonprofits assume greater political accountability; but at the same time, this use of "indirect government" (Kettl 2002) dilutes direct hierarchical control to the extent that government agencies become conduits to the actual service providers instead of providing program services themselves. In these situations political officials must rely on other methods of accountability.

No similarly pervasive theory of accountability applies to nonprofits (Kearns 1996), but Brown and Troutt (2004) suggest an adaptation specific for nonprofit–government contractual relationships. Normally political accountability of nonprofits involves reporting and budgeting requirements, a process-driven approach. Using principal–agent theory, Brown and Troutt suggest a key component is that the agent's (the nonprofit organization's) actual responsibility and "felt" responsibility must converge. This can occur if the principal (government) invites its agent to be fully involved in creating the process, the principal and agent feel interdependent, performance measures and funding are appropriately tailored and tied to responsibilities, and principal and agent continually discuss the shared mission and mutual understanding of community needs or other objectives. This creates a new alliance of government and nonprofits (similar to those discussed in Chapter 4). Further, Brown and Troutt propose that this paradigm also pertains to relationships between government and nonprofits that are not strictly contractual relationships but relationships in which both parties work to solve a community problem.

The theories of regulation also provide a mechanism of accountability. For the greater public good, government organizations regulate or provide oversight of certain public, nonprofit, and private actions. Because individuals cannot make certain determinations about the value, quality, or amount of a service, a public mechanism must be created to do this work. Some goods, such as air and water, cannot be divided among individuals, so the public needs a mechanism to regulate their fair use. Regulatory agencies create these rules and regulations for others, and they in turn are subject to review by legislatures. The Occupational Safety and Health Administration (OSHA), for example, regulates worker safety in all sectors; federal and state environmental protection agencies monitor chemical storage and pollution-contributing workplace by-products; federal agencies and many state agencies must account to inspector general (IG) offices, the General Accountability Office (GAO) and its state-level counterparts, and guidance agencies such as the Office of Management and Budget (OMB). Academic and professional institutions solicit oversight from essential accrediting organizations, and many public and private organizations operate under the umbrella of higher-level and parent organizations. Organizations engaged in contracts and grants from other organizations are accountable to those organizations. The extent to which these bodies closely monitor and enforce their standards is a matter of politics, public agenda setting, and policy. When other controls fail, public organizations may be subject to control by the courts. Courts have assumed temporary responsibility for correction and mental health institutions, housing authorities, and schools when political and administrative officials have repeatedly failed to meet their responsibilities for funding and operating critical agencies and their services.

Perhaps a stronger means of accountability is one that is indirect and episodic. Public organizations are accountable through news media and watchdog organizations, as well. External critics, supporters, and interest groups may press for reports, investigations, and standards they believe are needed. Politicians, too, in office or preparing for an election, may impose or advocate tougher requirements on a city, university, state agency, or federal agency, which can in turn lead to changes in internal systems.

Means of accountability have led to new departments and agencies. Consider departmental labels found in large organizations: Quality Assurance, Quality Control, Evaluation, and Auditing. More specific examples include the Juvenile Justice Evaluation Center (nonprofit), Testing and Accountability Office (Department of Education, California), the Government Accountability Office (federal), the Stanford University Hospital Quality Improvement and Patient Safety Office (nonprofit), the Office of Public Evaluation and Accountability (Maine),

---

BOX 6–1 Federal, State Mandates Erode Local Flexibility

A county hospital in Maryland is required by state law to keep its hot water temperature at no less than 100 degrees. That same hospital is mandated by federal law to keep that very same water no more than 110 degrees. The hospital was forced to purchase highly sophisticated water heaters—$20,000 more expensive than ordinary ones—to keep water temperature maintained at 110 degrees.

San Bernadino County California was forced to move a stone wall 50 yards at $50,000 cost to local government because of a federal requirement dealing with historical preservation.

"It's called mandate madness," Roy Orr, a Dallas County Commissioner and the new president of the National Association of Counties (NACO) told President Carter, Congress, and federal agency heads September 17.

"Mandates erode local decision-making power and shrink already limited tax revenues," Orr said. "And if this mandate madness continues, local county officials will lose the control necessary to deal with complicated local issues." Compliance with state and federal mandates eats up as much as 80 percent of some county budgets.

SOURCE: Effie Cottman, *Public Administration Times* 3, no. 19 (October 1, 1980), American Society for Public Administration staff.

and the Inspector General's office (federal). Ombudspeople and internal civil rights offices also increase accountability. Federal laws have passed with prominent accountability features, such as the Health Insurance Flexibility & Accountability Act (HIFA), No Child Left Behind Act, and the Government Performance Results Act (GPRA). Accrediting organizations have arisen to ensure accountability of professions and organizations: the Joint Commission for the Accreditation of Health Care Organizations (JCAHO) for hospitals and other health care organizations, the American Camping Association for camps, the Association of State Highway and Transportation Officials (ASHTO) for transportation agencies, and the Commission on Accreditation for Law Enforcement Agencies (CALEA) for police agencies.

In the following sections we discuss the types of accountability, internal and external, in more detail. The distinction between internal and external accountability is useful. External accountability includes accountability to political oversight bodies, boards, councils, accrediting institutions, and parent bodies or higher levels of government. Internal accountability involves internal mechanisms that are used by management to create accountability. These range from performance measurement of the overall organization to performance measurement, commonly known as performance appraisal or evaluation of the individual employee, and other mechanisms such as employee involvement programs, employee monitoring, and socialization of employees to the organization's mission.

Types of Accountability

The discussion thus far has focused on *external accountability:* the extent to which an organization reports and is controlled by a political body, board, or commissioners. According to political control and democratic theory, elected public officials who oversee agencies are accountable to the public for the work of government organizations and agencies. Organizations are increasingly accountable to other bodies such as accrediting, contractual, and regulatory organizations.

Internal accountability mechanisms or control mechanisms range from subtle to explicit and range widely in their use from organization to organization. Control mechanisms become internalized into the process of an organization, ensuring compliance with the goals and mission of the organization. Organizational literature provides several typologies for distinguishing among internal accountabilities. Etzioni's (1965) theory of bureaucratic organizations identifies several sources of control: physical, material, and symbolic bases in which coercion, self-interest, or identification with certain values of the organization motivates compliance. Robey (1994) contrasts control through measured work outputs with behavior or activity levels that are only indirectly or indeterminately linked to organizational outputs. As a substitute, Robey considers compliance techniques based on identification with the organization that Etzioni describes. Weber's (1947) method is simpler: He considered professional training to be the backbone of a disciplined, professional, accountable bureaucracy. Total quality management (Walton 1986) and other systems of employee involvement take full advantage of employees' being accountable for their own work, often in teams, using performance data, statistics on problems or failures of products or services, and scientific examination of variations from the norm.

Included among the range of contemporary approaches to accountability are these:

1. Political accountability and board accountability.
2. Accrediting and contractual requirements, including reporting requirements to national organizations or higher levels of government.

3. Performance measurement—quantitative measures of outputs and outcomes based on standards.

4. Employee involvement in accountability systems, created by active participation of the employees themselves monitoring and taking corrective action.

5. Monitoring of employees.

6. Organizational commitment and socialization: employee identification with the organization and its mission.

Most large public organizations and their professional staff are involved in many of these methods of accountability. Political accountability, though not the same as board accountability, requires organizational reporting to a higher authority. Socialization of employees is ongoing in any organization. Data warehousing has made it possible to collect more and more information over time that can be used on a simple personal computer (PC) or laptop; this has led to the adoption of quantitative measures for accountability in both the government and nonprofit sectors. Large organizations may have designated organizational units responsible for program evaluation or quality assurance.

Let us consider each method. For each method ask yourself this: To whom is the organization accountable, how, and for what reasons (Brody 2002)

EXTERNAL ACCOUNTABILITY

External accountability—being responsible to parties outside the organization—involves political accountability for government organizations, board accountability for nonprofit organizations, and accrediting and contractual considerations for many public organizations.

Political Accountability and Board Accountability

Weber (1947) wrote that while the ideal-type bureau may be accountable to democratic as well as socialist regimes, externally generated laws form the basis of rational bureau activity. The theory of political control is concerned with the accountability of government organizations through politicians and policy makers (such as a town council, a state legislature, or Congress). It concerns the workings of democracy, "how to run a Constitution" as Rohr (1986) puts it, and the legal responsibilities of the organization (discussed in Chapter 2). In the United States and most Western democracies, executive branch agencies at every level of government are subject to numerous legal and political checks based on the principle of separation of powers. The duties of these organizations are delimited in their authorizing legislation and appropriations, and agency heads are held responsible to political officials, elected or appointed. Thus the organization is subject to control by outside authorities, whereas internal control is maintained through a chain of command leading to a politically accountable executive. Exceptions, such as commissioners of independent regulatory authorities who cannot be fired by the chief elected executive, compromise the accountability principle only to achieve another imperative—impartial judgment.

Requirements for political and legal accountability leave their mark on the control systems of agencies. To ensure that organizations perform in a consistent, equitable, and stable manner mandated by legislation, regulations, and court decisions, control systems may closely monitor program procedures. For example, the control systems in an employment office are strict in ensuring nondiscrimination toward any client and the process of referring clients to jobs; even so, client results (the number of jobs filled or number of clients placed) are more relaxed than one would expect in a service agency. Without such controls, legal and ethical requirements for consistency of action in public organizations could not be met; along with them, of course, the irksomeness and density of red tape increase.

Many theoretical problems arise when government organizations are held accountable through political mechanisms. First, citizens must care about the issues, and they must vote for political officials based on these issues. In turn citizens expect the officials to base their votes on their previously stated positions. The political mechanism used to convey the public's wishes, of course, is the enactment of law; but it is also the oversight that a legislative body provides (from a town council to Congress) to agencies or departments, through review of reports, by holding hearings and public meetings. If we carry this logic further, then government agencies must be attuned to these same issues.

This portrayal of the democratic cycle of accountability is drawn largely from public policy making literature (Page and Shapiro 1983). (This simple causal model is one of citizen opinion regarding issues—and the choice of whom they elect to office—affecting the votes of representatives according to classic representative democracy.) As we extend the democratic cycle model to the oversight of organizations, the accountability link becomes more tenuous. First, a relatively small portion of the population votes in any given election, and those who do are more apt to vote on the candidate's image or general stand on issues rather than on specifics. Second, this model requires "perfect information." The media must convey both the public's and the candidates' opinions. Individual and public interest, however, vary across issues, thus weakening the accountability link. It is also true that representatives may in fact shape public opinion, thus switching the causal relationship. Asynchronous election cycles in our federal system make it more difficult for citizens to obtain information through the proxy of political party identification, compounding the problem of obtaining perfect information.

The third problem relates more to our concern: the democratic cycle's impact on organizations. Not all public concerns require enactment of a new law or a change in law. Countering the weakness of the link between the public and their representatives' ability to hold organizations accountable are the direct links between the public and organizations. Public hearings and sunshine laws have made it much more possible for citizens to obtain information. Yet not all issues require a public hearing. In this democratic cycle of accountability, what citizens ask of their elected officials is to improve the responsiveness (discussed in the next section) of the organization or agency to an individual's specific concern rather than to an overriding issue. Citizens want to find out why the organization has not responded or has not responded in the way citizens feel is appropriate. These day-to-day concerns of citizens range from snowplowing to the receipt of Social Security checks.

A fourth problem of the model is that the actions and activities of some government organizations do not fit. As citizens we do not often think of the Government Accountability Office, the federal auditing and investigation agency; nor do we think much about departments that rent and maintain buildings for the various levels of government or the employees of the state legislature. There is little oversight of the judiciary (except through appointment or elections of judges), yet many public employees work for the courts providing an important service in our democratic system. Agencies with which we have direct contact, sometimes daily, are often at arm's length, and they are not directly accountable to a legislative body.

These include the U.S. Post Office, turnpike and transit authorities, and water and power authorities. Again, accountability becomes a question of responsiveness.

Although we have treated nonprofits and government agencies largely alike, some differences in accountability exist between government and nonprofits. Nonprofits are legally accountable to state attorneys general, who ensure that boards carry out their fiduciary responsibilities. State regulators also regulate fundraising activities. To a much lesser extent nonprofits are responsible to the Internal Revenue Service through the annual filing of the financial report Form 990 (Return of Organization Exempt from Income Tax). For example, tax laws limit the type of political advocacy that nonprofits may undertake. The "publicness" of a nonprofit (according to law), however, makes it similar to government entities. Nonprofits are accountable to the public as a whole for meeting their nonprofit mission. Board members have the following duties:

- Care generally includes the discharge of duties in good faith with due diligence, care, and the skill a person of prudence would exercise under similar circumstances.

- Loyalty that includes an allegiance to the organization, a level of confidentiality, a responsibility not to use the position for personal gain, and an obligation to act in the best interest of the organization at all times.

- Obedience that includes establishing the mission of the organization and remaining loyal to it, following the articles of incorporation and by-laws, and ensuring the organization's compliance with law.

How much accountability nonprofit organizations should have to the public and to their boards is debatable (and the wording of the legal responsibilities varies from state to state). First, the accountability and information link with the public is relatively weak. The public is generally unaware of meaningful data such as IRS 990 forms that nonprofits file.[3] Second, the responsibilities of a volunteer board are wider in scope than those of for-profit paid boards. Unlike boards of commercial corporations, nonprofit boards are expected to both exercise full government oversight and serve as fundraisers and image enhancers of their organizations. Even so, board members are often chosen for their fundraising ability or support of the nonprofit mission (Klausner and Small 2005; O'Regan 2005) rather than for their focus on fiduciary and management responsibilities. Research (Holland 2002) shows that supervision by boards is relatively minimal. Accountability can also be reduced by the choice of board members. Nonprofit board members with private sector backgrounds may be more apt to view decision making as a confidential rather than a transparent process (Herzlinger 1996). In addition, board member conflicts of interest are rarely addressed.

Countering the weakness of link between the public and the board's responsibility is the general oversight the media provide and state oversight provides in one area: accountability of organizations for the use of funds gathered through fundraising. State laws require nonprofits to explain how much of their donations actually are used for their organization and how much goes for the cost of fundraising.

---

[3]Form 990 ("Return of Organization Exempt from Income Tax") provides information about revenue from public support, contributions, membership, program services, expenses, achievements, primary purpose, clients served, and employee compensation. Tax-exempt nonprofit organizations file IRS Forms 990 and other paperwork with the office of the secretary of state in which they are based. Form 990 information about many nonprofits is available through www.guidestar.org.

Accrediting and Contractual Requirements

Organizations contract with one another for services (security, payroll, building maintenance), are subject to regulatory oversight (worker safety, environmental protection), and report to external accrediting bodies (certification boards). These arrangements often create methods and requirements for reporting errors in an organization's procedures and quality control processes and accomplishments. This "red tape" involves costs to the organization that end up being costs to taxpayers, other funders, and often the organization's clients or constituents. In fact, most accountability mechanisms come with a price tag in both time and money. But the red tape has genuine value: It helps ensure clear written records (Bozeman 2000, 8; Kaufman 1967), fairness, tolerance, diversity, and participation in the political process—and thus accountability.

In very real ways, regulatory and accrediting organizations depend on the organizations they monitor. This complicates and attenuates their influence, limiting their impact as agents of accountability. Several theories describe the consequences of this situation. *Capture theory* hypothesizes that the regulatory agency depends on regulated agencies for political support, and private decision makers conspire to use the agency as a tool of their own self-serving intentions (Garvey 1993, 25–34; Brandl 1989). A more moderate thesis, the *political economy* thesis, states that to survive, regulatory agencies must find a balance of support and opposition among clients and organized interest groups (Noll 1971). The Environmental Protection Agency, for example, cannot police every environmental hazard; therefore it cultivates the cooperation of firms and simultaneously needs the support of environmental lobbies to offset the fundamental opposition of the regulated firms. Similarly, accrediting agencies have no role without the consent and support of those they accredit. Accrediting agencies rarely implement new rules without the consent of a majority.[4] This common pattern of negotiated regulations and accreditation rules shows the ambiguous position of regulatory and accrediting agencies as vehicles for greater accountability (Katzman 1980). In a sense this interdependency brings added accountability to the oversight organizations themselves.

INTERNAL ACCOUNTABILITY

The requirement for political and legal accountability—external accountability—leaves its mark on internal control systems. Internal accountability is the *process* by which an organization takes stock of itself, reports that information to external authorities, addresses any deficiencies it finds, and implements any changes required by external authorities. Internal accountability involves performance measurement, employee involvement, and employee monitoring, supervision, and evaluation.

Performance Measurement

"About the time we can make the ends meet, somebody moves the ends."

Herbert Hoover, President of the United States, 1928–1932

Beyond reporting to political or board officials and accrediting organizations, perhaps the most embedded method of ensuring accountability and control of organizations is

---

[4]Conversely, professional links with external groups may lead to pitting one part of the agency against another so that aggressive regulators may encourage or even assist in suits against the agency to achieve compliance with regulations by recalcitrant staff.

performance measurement and evaluation. This type of accountability is the transition from external accountability (reporting to another organization or political body) to one of internal accountability (measuring for management's own internal use).

Evaluation and performance measurement have progressed in use from an analysis of efficiency and effectiveness of programs, completed by external contractors or scholars seeking to influence policy makers, to techniques used by today's organizations to measure not only efficiency and effectiveness but also productivity, quality, and customer service.

Daniels and Wirth (1983) characterize the early stages of evaluation as beginning between 1910 and World War II, when the goal was to determine efficiency and improve productivity of employees. Frederick Taylor testified before Congress in 1911 (compiled in *Principles of Scientific Management,* 1947) about his work on scientific management—to find the most efficient methods of production. Taylor searched for means to overcome management practices that caused workers to restrict their output. He promoted systematic analysis to reduce inefficient methods of work, known as the "one best way." Later the Brownlow Committee on Administrative Management (1937) recommended that White House staffing be modernized to create efficiency. Analysis and efficiency were the keys to modern management. Thus Chester Barnard, a member of the Brownlow Committee, recommended that quantitative measurement and statistical analysis be part of executive training (Scott 1992; Wolf 1974).[5]

As the techniques of evaluation progressed, their sophistication, in turn, led to more complicated demands for both efficiency and effectiveness. The studies collectively known as the Hawthorne experiments were conducted to assess the impact of changes in the environment on employee productivity. Their lasting effect was the recognition that the interaction of people and managers may have at least as much or more to do with improvements in productivity as do equipment and the general work environment.

Only since the Great Society programs of the Johnson Administration (1960s) has evaluation moved significantly toward examining (and seeking to influence) the effectiveness of policy and programs. Did government programs make a difference—did they improve the quality of life of citizens? As emerging programs were implemented, the press at local levels reported corruption and mismanagement. Analysts and scholars began to critique the programs of the Great Society. Evaluations were primarily add-ons and not fully incorporated into any ongoing process of accountability. They tended to look at the effect of a program as a whole and not at individual successes or failures. A critical study of black urban poverty, conducted in 1965 by Daniel Patrick Moynihan while he worked for the Department of Labor, was followed by another critical work, *The Other America,* by Michael Harrington (1969). Though criticized at the time, these books helped lay the foundation for evaluating the societal effects of federal poverty programs.

By 1975 some government entities were beginning to organize existing data and collect additional data for use in performance measures. Examples of measurement in state government included staff–client ratios in schools and health institutions, maintenance costs per mile of roadway, and cost per accident investigated in transportation agencies (The Urban Institute 1975, 1981). In the 1980s criticism began to focus on employees who administered

---

[5]Barnard started his career in the statistics department of AT&T and eventually became the president of New Jersey Bell. His public service included serving as a representative of the YMCA at the Just and Durable Peace Conference (1942) chaired by John Foster Dulles, heading the New Jersey Emergency Relief Administration (1931), and serving as the president of the Rockefeller Foundation in 1948 (Scott 1992; Wolf 1974).

these programs and on a perceived lack of service. Congress wanted a better way to control funds and maintain accountability (Chelimsky and Shadish 1997); hence more quantitative tools of measurement began to be used. Initial steps to incorporate the collection of data for evaluation began to be part of the program process instead of an after-the-fact activity often undertaken by an outside party rather than by organization employees. Still the use of performance measurement was relatively minimal. It was not really until the ideas of TQM, the reinventing government movement of the 1990s, and the National Performance Review (1993) put pressure on governments not only to measure productivity but also to measure quality and responsiveness to citizens and customers that performance measurement became a major tool for accountability. This created a profound redefinition of clients and citizens from passive recipients to customers demanding service and holding government accountable for that service.

Evaluation is now a legal requirement for many programs (Workforce Investment Act, No Child Left Behind Act) and is entrenched in contemporary ideas of professional management and accountability. Government has mandated collection of data and measurement by many nonprofits that provide contractual services; in turn, philanthropic foundations usually require that meaningful measurement be incorporated into any grant to government or nonprofits. Beginning in 1995, the U.S. United Way adopted these innovations and encouraged local United Ways to measure health and social service outcomes and allocate funds accordingly.

Goldenberg (1983) has theorized that there are three faces to evaluation. The first face of evaluation is *learning about a program's operation* and effects through operation and management controls. Under the second face, evaluation is *used as a control over the behavior* of those responsible for program implementation. Oversight (Goldenberg discussed congressional oversight) holds program administrators accountable to implemented standards. The objective of any audit, for example, is to ensure and enforce compliance. Measurement of outcomes is to ensure that a program is doing what it is purported to do. As evaluation becomes part of a program's administration, the third face of evaluation appears. Program administrators and evaluators take a more active role *using the information to improve the success of programs* rather than simply reporting results after the fact in an adversarial approach. Executives and managers use these results to influence decisions and funding of external policy makers. This third face expects the evaluating agency "to delay, detect, or channel the interventions of outsiders" (Goldenberg 1983, 515). It also moves evaluation and performance measurement from a tool of accountability of those with responsibilities of oversight to a means by which public organizations exert political influence by reporting their successes and lobbying for funding.

The power of personal computing devices, the increasing convergence of communication and information technologies, and the ever-expanding role of these technologies in the workplace make it possible to collect data from many sources, interrelate and store the information for extended periods, and retrieve it conveniently and in many formats. These capabilities give organizations greater power and flexibility to undertake a range of performance measurements—particularly those in which many performance data are by-products of organizational processes and systems rather than information that is gathered only for performance measurement. This same technology has made it possible to develop and use a variety of measures, including output, quality, outcome, productivity, and customer service measures. In discussing the types of performance measurement in more detail, we will also examine their utility to promoting accountability of public service organizations. Definitions of performance measures are listed in Table 6–1.

TABLE 6–1   What to Measure?

	General Definition	*Street Sweeping*	*Welfare: Job Training*
Output (or Process)	Volume of units produced.	Miles swept.	Numbers of people trained.
Outcome (or Result)	Quality/effectiveness of production: degree to which it creates desired outcomes.	Cleanliness rating of streets.	Numbers of people placed in jobs, working, and off welfare after six months, one year, and beyond. Impact on their lives.
Program Outcome	Effectiveness of specific program in achieving desired outcomes.	Cleanliness rating of streets as a result of sweeping.	Numbers of people placed in jobs, working, and off welfare after six months, one year, and beyond. Impact on their lives.
Policy Outcome	Effectiveness of broader policies in achieving fundamental goal.	Measure indicating how much litter citizens leave on streets.	Percentage of potential workforce unemployed, on welfare, and in poverty; percentage of welfare population on welfare more than one year, five years, etc.
Program Efficiency	Cost per unit of output.	Costs per mile of streets swept.	Cost per job trainee; placement; retained job, etc.
Policy Efficiency	Cost to achieve fundamental goals.	Cost for a given level of street cleanliness.	Cost to achieve desired decrease in unemployment, poverty rate, welfare caseload, etc.
Program Effectiveness	Degree to which program yields desired outcomes.	Level of citizen satisfaction with cleanliness of streets.	Numbers of people placed in jobs, working, and off welfare after six months, one year, and beyond. Impact on their lives.
Policy Effectiveness	Degree to which fundamental goals and citizen needs are met.	Do citizens want to use their money this way (for example, would they rather spend it on paving streets)?	Effects on larger society, such as poverty rate, welfare caseload, crime rate.

SOURCE: D. Osborne and T. Gaebler, *Reinventing Government*, Copyright © 1992 by David Osborne and Ted Gaebler. Reprinted by permission of Addison-Wesley Publishing Company. Inc. Osborne copyright Perseus Books, Cambridge MA with permission.

Measuring Outputs

We begin the discussion of the types of measuring with an explanation of output measures and their value. Outputs are usually used to measure ongoing programs and projects as opposed to the implementation of a program (Shadish, Cook, and Leviton 1991). Although the term *output measure* is relatively new, public organizations have always been good at reporting outputs. In a sense, these are the basics of performance evaluation of any organization. Annual reports of nonprofit social service agencies list outputs, as do the reports of state agencies to the legislature and federal agencies to Congress. Output measures are simple numbers of activities. The number of clients seen is a typical example, as is the number of dollars spent to serve clients. The presumption is that this information lets management control the internal workings of the public service organization (Overman and Loraine 1994). When reported on a regular basis, such measures (and more sophisticated measures) bring order to what appears as chaos, letting organizations compare their output performance against themselves over time and against other organizations engaged in the same activities.

These types of output measures can be of limited value if they simply record the past without regard to underlying reasons for the increase, decrease, or even stability of the numbers from one year to the next. Another limitation of output measures is that they may have little to do with policy outcomes or with the effort of staff. For example, a count of the number of clients seen says little about the number of clients' problems resolved or the effort involved in resolving problems for different clients. Research also shows that output measures may be better as a source of change than as a means of control (Overman and Loraine 1994). In 1954 Peter Drucker suggested that management by objectives (MBO) could be a change-promoting device. Objectives or goals are set by and for individual employees, units, or the organization as a whole. MBO treats these objectives as a type of output and then assesses achievement in reaching the stated set of objectives within a given reporting period (Locke and Latham 1984). Its benefit is that carefully chosen objectives can be aggregated from the individual level to the organizational level, each level supporting the next. An unintended consequence or downside to the use of MBO is that many managers of departmental units tend to favor modest objectives they are likely to achieve, avoiding risky and difficult objectives. This leads to less innovation over time.

Measuring Quality

When it comes to an organization's performance, measuring quality is a coin with two faces. The obverse face is determining what "quality" is—a quest that is often obvious but just as often intangible, subjective, and challenging to define in concrete terms. The reverse face is establishing mechanisms for monitoring and ensuring that the organization's outputs faithfully maintain those quality characteristics—a process that organizations variously dub "quality control," "quality review," "quality assurance," or variants of those terms.

Looking first at the definitional face, ask yourself how you would define quality for a social services program, a law or regulatory enforcement agency, an art museum, or something personal such as being served in a cafeteria or at the front counter of a local office. Then consider how you might quantify the characteristics you identify so that someone could monitor the organization's quality on a continuing basis for each of these situations. As philosopher Robert Pirsig observes, grappling with the fundamental attributes of quality can be an elusive task:

> Quality . . . you know what it is yet you don't know what it is. But that's self-contradictory.
> But some things *are* better than others; that is, they have more quality. But when you try to

say what the quality is, apart from the things that have it, all goes *poof!* There's nothing to talk about. But if you can't say what Quality is, how do you know what quality is, or that it even exists? If no one knows what it is, then for all practical purposes it doesn't exist at all. But for all practical purposes it really *does* exist. . . . Why else would people pay fortunes for some things and throw others in the trash pile? Obviously some things are better than others . . . but what's the "betterness"? . . . So round and round you go, spinning mental wheels and nowhere finding any place to get traction. What the hell is Quality? What *is* it? (Pirsig 1974, 163–64)

Quality takes on different meanings depending on the context and point of view involved. Garvin (1984) describes five perspectives, each with a different basis for considering quality for organizational outputs:

- *Transcendent:* innate excellence, the concept about which Pirsig ponders.

- *Product-based:* the object or service incorporates a desired attribute or ingredient (such as ease of access).

- *User-based:* satisfying a user's wants or needs.

- *Producer-based:* conforming to specifications—a concept program designers, auditors, purchase agents, and managers might use.

- *Value-based:* "affordable excellence"—the best output for a given investment.

Keeping multiple perspectives such as these in mind can be helpful in discussing quality with others, developing policies and programs, and establishing organizational performance measures.

The concept of output quality has evolved over time for organizations of all types. In the society of our Constitution framers living in a preindustrial age, *quality* pertained to finely crafted items "prized for their ability to satisfy, their durability, their utility—their perfection" (Nichols 1993, 39). But, writes historian Daniel Boorstin, an emerging industrial America, with its plainspoken emphasis on economy and practical function, fostered a new sense of what quality outputs ought to be:

> Americans had come to a new definition of what they meant by "quality." *Function* had come to displace *perfection*. . . . That first American system aimed to make products just good enough for their purpose. The aesthetic-that-was-not-functional, the ornament that was merely traditional, had no place in the American scheme. For Americans, a high-quality machine was not one that was polished and ornamented, but one that worked.
> . . . The late-twentieth-century American system went still further in outraging the Old World craftsman's ideal. For while the nineteenth-century system aimed to manufacture products that were *just good enough* for their purpose, the twentieth century actually aimed to manufacture products that were *no better than* they needed to be. . . . The name for this remarkable and little-celebrated American achievement was "Statistical Quality Control."
> . . . Obviously, . . . there was a negative as well as a positive side to quality control. Since "quality" was a colloquial synonym for "excellence," then to make the "control" of quality an objective of factory planning had some disturbing implications. For quality "control" actually aimed, as engineering historians have noted, to ensure that any product was not one iota "better" than it needed to be. (Boorstin 1973, 193–98)

Boorstin's chronicle introduces the second face of organizational quality: measuring it. *Quality control/quality assurance* (QC/QA), as it is often labeled, concerns measuring specific work processes or products to improve the output. It is a formal process, now often mandated by accrediting bodies, legislative requirements, and funders. But as Boorstin mentions, statistical quality control (SQC) began in the 1920s with the work of Walter A. Shewhart at Bell Laboratories. Shewhart developed a technique of tracking manufacturing defect rates, production volumes, and other assembly line–oriented factors using control charts on which the daily counts of, say, defective widgets, were recorded. A process would be considered under control if the defect count stayed within a certain range. A count outside the anticipated range—that is, "out of control"—was to be investigated and fixed so that the range returned to normal. Improvement would be reflected in the control charts by a narrowing of the range (less variance) or by a shift in the range to a more optimal level (consistently lower defect rate or higher production rate). Shewhart's work inspired W. Edwards Deming, who successfully repackaged the concept as part of total quality management—initially for postwar Japanese firms and later back in the United States (Aguayo 1990). What began in industry moved to private sector office settings and then into the public sector as well.

Organizations frequently use sampling techniques to measure output quality, subjecting sensitive work products to the most intensive levels of quality review. In hospitals, quality assurance began as simply ensuring accuracy of medical records, largely for proper billing and insurance purposes. Now teams and individual employees are involved in reporting the diagnosing of medication errors and improving the process of providing medication to patients; in addition, hospital employees collect data to determine the best treatments for different types of illnesses, developing "evidence-based medicine." Construction-intensive organizations, such as departments of transportation, use QC/QA to ensure the quality of building materials provided by contractors. In Goldenberg's terms, quality control/quality assurance has moved from the second face of evaluation, oversight, to an internal tool of management to improve the organization, the third face of evaluation.

QC/QA and other tools discussed thus far measure quality from an inside-the-organization perspective; output quality can also be measured from an external customer perspective. *Customer service measurement* looks at quality and other aspects of effectiveness as judged from the side of client or customer. Organizations across the spectrum now routinely survey citizens and customers to assess satisfaction. Whereas QC/QA and SQC evaluate based on some quantifiable measure of quality of a product, another way to measure quality is based on perceptions, usually of services. One theorized measurement of quality is the difference between an individual's *expectation* and the *perceptions* of performance or provision of the service (Parasuraman, Zeithaml, and Berry 1985; Zeithaml, Parasuraman, and Berry 1985). This definition recognizes that people have increasingly high expectations. We judge the speed of response of the ambulance service or the length of time waiting in the motor vehicle department based on our expectations of what is appropriate. True, we occasionally have no or low expectations and are pleasantly surprised; but more often we have high expectations, making this form of measurement rigorous as well as informative. Certainly high performance expectations can be threatening for many organizations; but proponents argue that concentration on reducing the difference between expectations and the perceived perception—the gap—can lead to greater efficiencies and greater satisfaction among employees as well. As the title of Kelly's (2002) article states, "If you only knew how well we are performing, you'd be highly satisfied with the quality of our service." But customers or citizens rarely see behind-the-scenes activities that lead to service (Overman and Loraine 1994), and they are interested in results rather than an organization's efforts.

Berman proposes that the "quality paradigm" is the "single greatest influence on productivity improvement in recent years" because "it drives new developments in productivity improvement" (1998, 266–67). As a tool of accountability, quality measures help complete the democratic cycle of accountability because the organization builds in quality rather than addressing individual citizen complaints voiced through elected officials. However, when the results are less than positive, these types of measures give political officials and other oversight bodies a means to assess and criticize performance, violating Deming's wish to drive out fear in the workplace (Walton 1986) and, to an extent, damping risk taking within some public organizations. These measures, too, add to programs' complexity, administration, and costs. These downside aspects noted, quality measurement is an essential element of organizational accountability and has substantial value as a tool for improving programs.

Measuring Productivity

In contrast to quality's amorphous characteristics, productivity has more precise and potentially quantifiable definitions. Productivity measures connote a rationality espoused by Frederick Taylor and the scientific management movement and support traditional organizational culture and structure. The Bureau of Labor Statistics within the U.S. Department of Labor defines *productivity* as a "measure of economic efficiency that shows how effectively economic inputs are converted into output. Productivity is measured by comparing the amount of goods and services produced with the inputs that were used in production." Often productivity is the term used for a specific resource (labor productivity, capital productivity, land use productivity) whereas the synonym *efficiency* is the term applied when general productivity (that is, aggregated input resources) is the focus and when inputs and outputs are monetized, usually to monitor cost savings as part of *cost–benefit analysis*.

Productivity measures typically use the formula [Outputs ÷ Inputs = Productivity ratio]. Because productivity is often framed in terms of labor, the productivity formula in such cases becomes [Outputs ÷ Work hours] or often [Outputs ÷ Cost of labor]. This distinction can be important, as can the process level or organizational level at which productivity is measured.

To use an example, an organization provides over-the-phone assistance through a bank of 20 call-receiving workstations staffed with two eight-hour shifts each day. Typically the operation has handled 10 incoming calls per workstation each hour, or 1,600 calls per shift; and during frequent high-volume periods, many callers would be on hold instead of receiving immediate assistance. Now, new technology automates assistance around the clock for what have been the most routine incoming calls—about half of the overall volume of calls—so phone assistance employees no longer receive them and the system can respond to them 24 hours a day. The remaining human-assisted calls are more challenging and usually take longer; consequently, employee productivity at the workstations has fallen by at least half, even though the volume of callers that the organization assists in a day has more than doubled. In other words, although productivity for *individual employees* drops, the overall operation experiences a dramatic productivity gain. Both productivity rates—at the individual level and at the organization level—are correct, but it is vital for observers to understand at what point the count is measured (the "point of count").

News magazines, websites, and other news outlets are apt to carry productivity measures in a graphic format, talking about the ratios as percentages while illustrating them with simple charts and graphs. Examples are everywhere: annual spending per pupil for different school districts, maintenance costs per mile of roadway, bushels harvested per acre of farmland, costs per accident investigated, charitable donation percentage absorbed by overhead costs, staff-to-client ratios. Measuring work output or productivity advances the theory of performance measurement by recognizing the degree to which inputs affect events. The emphasis is still on the measurement of efficiency—that is, cost savings—in that no one wants inefficient use of scarce resources. The scientific management movement, espoused by Frederick Taylor and others, embraces productivity measures that connote a rationality supportive of traditional organizational culture and structure. Productivity measures can be at the organizational level, the team level, or at the individual level; especially good productivity measures are those that "nest"—apply to different levels of the organization and its mission. Such measures are often used to create pay for performance, which may have a positive or negative effect on morale (see Chapter 8 for a discussion); they can also pressure officials in organizations to concentrate on short-term efficiencies at the expense of longer-term productivity.

Measuring Outcomes

Measuring outputs and productivity supports organizational efficiency but rarely measures effectiveness. *Effectiveness* measurement—more often called *outcome measurement*—assesses the degree to which programs and practices meet policy intents based on evidence of their outcomes. Outcomes are the end states that clients, constituents, and program officials aim to achieve. For example, an outcome of a medical service is, we hope, a patient's full recovery (based on the output of an office visit, hospital stay, medication, or therapy regimen). Because outcomes may take time to achieve and often take place away from the workplace (program implementation) setting, reliable outcome or effectiveness measurement can be challenging, especially for public organizations.

Efficiency and effectiveness sometimes reinforce one another (as when training helps employees complete tasks more quickly and accurately) and sometimes compete with one another (as when a push for speedy completion shortchanges accurate and complete handling). Consequently a precarious balance can exist between efficiency and effectiveness based on political decisions of government, a board, or an outside accrediting system (Pfeffer and Salancik 2005). On balance, government tends to lean toward concern for effectiveness over efficiency. Probably for nonprofits, effectiveness is also the stronger driver; but efficiency becomes almost as important because of the combination of scarce resources and fundraising competition.

An example of the use of outcome measurement is the mandated performance measurement system of the job training program funded under the Workforce Investment Act. Among the measures are wages earned and job retention of those who have completed training. Success is measured by a statistical process using regression to take into account differences in trainees' backgrounds. The training programs meeting standards receive a bonus, and those doing poorly risk losing the contract to provide service.

Oregon and Washington have used outcome measurement to measure the well-being of citizens of the state as a whole. These states have established statewide outcomes (goals) translated into measures at the department level. In the late 1980s the governor of Oregon established the Oregon Progress Board, comprised of public and private leaders, to create ambitious goals and *benchmarks* (standards by which to gauge success) for the state (Osborne and Gaebler 1992, 145; National Performance Review 1993). The legislature approved the board's recommended 160 benchmarks to measure three general categories of goals: exceptional individuals;

outstanding quality of life; and a diverse, robust economy. These broad goals and benchmarks were then tied to specific objectives for agencies.

States such as Oregon and Washington continue to work on this process by attempting to integrate goals with the budget process. This is known as *performance budgeting*. In a performance budget, the amount an agency receives depends not on line items but on the costs of producing and meeting the outcomes. The federal government joined this movement with the passage of the Government Performance and Results Act (GPRA) in 1993. The purpose is similar: to link funding of agencies to the priority of goals and success in meeting them. Performance budgeting has proven difficult to fully implement at the state and federal levels, and in most cases a performance budget runs parallel with a line item budget.

For public organizations, measuring outcomes that the community or society desires, such as those established by Oregon and Washington, must be balanced with the immediate need to measure specific programs such as the Workforce Investment Act and create accountability of program administrators (Campbell 2002). Outcomes, by their nature, are long-term goals when compared to the relatively shorter-term goals of productivity and efficiency. Organizations measuring community or societal outcomes may be viewed with skepticism: They deserve neither credit nor blame for phenomena they do not control.

An example of this is the ongoing debate about the meaning of measurement of schools (No Child Left Behind Act) and training programs. Those organizations involved in education and training programs measure student performance based on test scores, which are ostensibly an outcome measure of learning progress. This is a relatively easy measure to create because test scores can be standardized in ways that permit comparisons and accommodate controls for differences in students' backgrounds. Funding can be provided to schools successful at meeting the *short-term* goal of "learning progress." Yet society's real desire is to measure students' ability to participate in work and society—a *long-term* goal—not to measure test-taking ability or even learning progress itself. To measure the long-term goal we first might replace test scores with some sort of achievement measure, such as the percentage employed or in college within a year after completion of high school. Though such a measure is appealing, it is only a proximate measure of the outcome that society desires: a return on the investment society receives from funding education. Measurement of this outcome requires a longitudinal study. Though difficult, it is certainly methodologically possible to measure the return society receives (by tracking employment wage data, interviewing former students 5 and 10 years after school, comparing the use of welfare supplement programs by those who graduated and those who did not, or measuring income based on taxes paid). Unfortunately the further out in time the measurement takes place, the less reliably it relates to accountability of specific programs: The measurement becomes "muddy" or "confounded" because so many other factors have opportunities to contribute to whatever effect is being measured.

And that, in a nutshell, is the dilemma. Consequently, public organizations continue their struggle to identify and measure clear outcomes for their programs and, as legislation such as the Government Performance and Results Act (1993) mandates, link a specific level of investment to these outcomes.

Balanced Scorecards

Is it reasonable for an organization to identify a crucial specific measure—perhaps budgetary, perhaps mission-based—that lets its leaders and oversight bodies monitor how well that organization operates? No, according to Kaplan and Norton (1992, 1996; Kaplan 2001);

relying on a single measure is myopic and dangerous. Whatever preeminent measure emerges, it provides only one perspective about the organization's health. At the other extreme, using scores or hundreds of measures is equally unrealistic; they form an unorchestrated cacophony of indicators that does not clearly track the organization's overall performance. And they create information overload.

A *balanced scorecard* approach to organizational performance measurement uses just a handful of key indicators, grouping them into four perspectives: financial, customer or constituent, internal business, and learning and growth. Each perspective includes a small group of up to four performance measures appropriate for the organization—but rarely more than a dozen measures overall—that serve, as Kaplan and Norton (1992) explain, much like a pilot's cockpit instrumentation. Over time, measuring from four perspectives informs and strengthens a strategic management system by tracking necessary feedback about the organization in a way that does not put the organization's emphasis on a single dimension. Nanus and Dobbs (1999) reduce the types of measures to three: (1) social goods or production measures, (2) organization capital or measures of increase in services or clients, and (3) social energy or measures of developing commitment by volunteers and employees.

Suchman offers another approach: a typology that includes evaluating effort, performance, adequacy, efficiency, and process (1967, 60–66). *Effort* measures the direct activities and outputs of agency staff; *performance* measures the extent to which the results are those intended in the legislation or authorization; *adequacy* measures the degree to which the size and scope of the program are appropriate to the size of the problem; and *efficiency* focuses on the existence of less costly ways to achieve similar or better results. Each of these types of measures articulates a dimension of control. Ideally the combination of measures meets specific needs of program administrators, outside funders, oversight entities, and policy makers.

Whether using the balanced scorecard, the Bennis and Nanus measures, or the Suchman typology, good combinations of measures link to measures pertinent for lower levels of the organization; conversely, low-level performance measures "roll up" into higher-level measures to form a performance measurement hierarchy. A well-designed hierarchy of nested performance targets and measures enables managers and oversight officials to monitor how an aspect of performance at one level of the organization contributes to (or depends on) performance at another level of the organization (Nichols 1997). The combined qualities of comprehensiveness, simplicity, depth, and balance make the balanced scorecard approach a robust, practical performance measurement approach for public organizations.

Measurement Problems

But no system of organizational performance measurement is perfect. The question for our purpose is this: Does a set of measures contribute to organizational accountability? The balanced scorecard or similar approaches have the potential to operate vertically as well as horizontally to drive organizational performance. At the same time any measurement approach, whether of outputs, quality, productivity, or some combination, can be sabotaged if taken over by a PR campaign or employee morale booster campaign:

> Despite the best intentions of those at the top, lofty statements about becoming "best in class," "the number one supplier," or an "empowered organization" don't translate easily into operational terms that provide useful guides to action at the local level. For people to act on the words in vision and strategy statements, those statements must be expressed as an integrated set of objectives and measures. (Kaplan and Norton 1996, 75–76)

Performance measures exist to manage performance in areas that are key to the mission of the organization and create value. What an organization measures and rewards is what an organization gets, which can be ideal when measures and rewards are deftly targeted. But performance measurement has its dark side as well. Measurement pressure can be so much so that the act of measurement can lead to ignoring activities not measured and, at its worst, outright falsification of results and illegal activity (Miller 2005), illustrating what Downs has dubbed the "law of counter control": "The greater the effort to control, the greater the efforts to evade or counteract such control (1967, 147)." Even before the popularity of performance measurement as a means of accountability, Merton (1957) identified the problem of *goal displacement:* concentrating on the means rather than the ends or the true mission of the organization. Using the language of performance measurement, people tend to concentrate on what is monitored and rewarded rather than what is needed to meet an organization's mission.

Using organizational performance measurement as an accountability and control tool creates a range of technical problems, among which are insufficiencies in the techniques of performance measurement, lack of staff capacities and expertise in measurement, too little attention to performance measurement, the expense of the process, reporting time constraints, and lack of accessibility of data (Urban Institute 1975, 169–71; Finz 1980, 142–46; Shadish, Cook, and Leviton, 1991). Other drawbacks include the need for evaluation staff to manage the quality, interpretation, and statistical analysis of the data; otherwise the resulting measurements will follow the maxim "Garbage in, garbage out (or GIGO)."

A common concern is that even when data are correctly collected and analyzed, they will not be used in the organization's decision making (Urban Institute 1975, 169–70). This is at least in part what has occurred with the use (or the lack of use of) performance budgeting. Advocates of performance budgeting are enthusiastic about its ability to be used for accountability and budgeting. Legislators, however, still want to have a line item budget simultaneously with the performance budget, even though a performance budget provides a stronger relationship between program results and monies necessary to obtain results. The lack of use of performance evaluation, of course, surfaces less frequently when evaluation is mandated and when rewards are in place for meeting standards.

Performance measurement also may suffer from problems of accuracy and validity or from ambiguous and conflicting standards. The *validity* of a measure refers to the degree to which it measures what it purports to measure. Does it focus on the outcome (problems resolved and customers satisfied) rather than the output activity (forms processed)? Is it sufficient to determine performance in meeting the target (accuracy, timeliness, cost, satisfaction)? Validity is compromised whenever there is uncertainty or conflict over the definition of an organization's program outputs and outcomes. The level of serious disagreement determines the feasibility of using program measures as the basis for organizational control and accountability. For a performance measure to be useful and well-regarded, to be used to create accountability, it must exhibit other characteristics, as well:

- *Reliability:* Do the measures used provide similar results over and over, year after year, from office to office? Are the results credible? Are the data consistently reported by all necessary sources (such as different offices)?

- *Availability:* In what form is the measurement information available (estimates, samples, populations—in computer form or handwritten records)? Can the data be disaggregated as needed? In what units of measurement (percentages, current or constant dollars, time work units)? Are the data self-reported or independently reported?

- *Frequency:* Can the measurement data be captured at useful intervals (monthly, quarterly, annually)? How long after the interval before the data can be available?

- *Simplicity:* Is the measure easy to understand and calculate? Is it easy to relate to other measures? (Nichols 1997, 415)

The usefulness and accuracy of measurements may be compromised by intentional and unintentional *distortions* common to organizational communications of all kinds, such as filtering that results from messages passing through a chain of command, intentional alteration of emphasis and content to further the interests of senders, and misinterpretations from information overload or excessive jargon (see Chapter 5).

Downs (1967) identifies distortion as a general organizational problem, but it applies directly to performance measurement. Downs suggests several antidistortion devices. One is redundancy: using several sources of information, with different interests, as a check on accuracy. Alternatively, officials can discount known biases in reports, though this tactic may backfire if reporters change or biases are misunderstood. Upper-echelon officials may also cut through the normal channels of communication, bypassing possible sources of distortion. Frequent bypassing can lead to a breakdown of the regular communications and reporting channels; however, information technology is increasingly giving all levels of an organization fuller, faster, and more conveniently packaged access to potential performance data that the organization captures. Finally, requirements for report preparation themselves may limit distortion. Reporting formats that specify exactly what data are required and how calculations are to be done reduce distortion in the selection of information. Reporting formats that require quantitative data about activities or conditions also limit imaginative reporting.

Standards are ways by which organizations determine the results of outputs and outcomes. Standards can be based on historical data and set incrementally higher, set in comparison with other organizations, or set statistically. Support for measurement may run into difficulty when standards for determining appropriate levels become controversial. This occurs when arbitrary standards are set. There must be some basis to establishing an outcome of a 5 percent increase in productivity or a 5 percent reduction in costs! Standards or goals also must be set that are sufficiently challenging and realistic. Given this context, a great deal of power resides in those who design and manage performance measurement systems (Campbell 2002).

When vital information that is difficult and costly to collect is not used for program development, the control effort is delegitimized in the eyes of staff and becomes a meaningless exercise in information collection and paperwork generation. The cost of data collection and analysis is too great to relegate the whole process to the status of a symbolic gesture toward political accountability; consequently, cumbersome collection systems ultimately tend to fail because weak input priority, consistency, and quality undermine their potential utility. Occasional monitoring system collapses notwithstanding, accountability and control systems within organizations tend to increase over time as top-level officials and oversight bodies sense accountability problems; this is true even in periods when an organization's size and influence decline (Downs 1967).

These criticisms seem to question the value of performance management as an accountability system. Though far from perfect, the tool has been widely and effectively adopted. Alternatives (anecdotal reports and spot visits, for example) tend not to be acceptable in the long term. Widespread use of performance management coincides with the ability of leadership throughout organizations to use performance data as an ongoing mechanism of improvement. Pressure for greater accountability has helped foster these skills, and evolving workplace information technologies have served as a significant enabler. One useful trend, for example, has been to develop logic models that graphically show (through flow diagrams and other visual schematics) relationships among external factors and programmatic inputs, processes, and outcomes (Millar, Simeone, and Carnevale 2001). For leaders and analysts, logic models encompass much more of the complexity of the programs they oversee, ensuring that important aspects that are not quantifiable are still visible to policy makers.

Characteristics of evaluation that make accountability valuable also make it controversial. This illustrates again the pervasive ambiguity of accountability: Should it serve the information needs of internal systems adjustment or the requirements of political and legal accountability? To what extent can it contribute to both objectives? How—and what level of ongoing resource investment is necessary? The answers to such questions vary across organizations, missions, and eras; but the public's constantly rising expectations and the increasing sophistication of enabling technologies point toward greater accountability for government, nonprofit, and for-profit organizations.

In sum, the use of performance measurement and its results have practical, political, and ethical implications. Even when measurement is not mandated, program managers or advocates fear that evaluations are likely to result in the loss of autonomy, funds, or program authority (Campbell 2002). Deming is often cited for his assertion that 85 percent of all workplace problems are management- and systems-related, while only 15 percent are personnel-related (Walton 1986). Deming wanted measurement tools used to empower employees, support teamwork, and improve processes, but not to have tools used against employees and programs—that is, as Chapter 8 describes, to enable in a "Theory Y" fashion rather than to oppress in a "Theory X" fashion (McGregor 1957).

Factors associated with higher levels of evaluation utilization (through internal performance measurement and reviews by outside parties) include:

1. The direct relevance of the findings to policy makers or managers.
2. The direct communication of results to policy makers or managers, unfiltered by interested intermediaries.
3. The clarity of findings and the awareness by users of the implications of those findings for policy decisions.
4. The credibility of the findings, or the degree to which they agree with other information.
5. The existence of a strong political advocate for the findings (Shadish, Cook, and Leviton 1991; Leviton and Hughes 1981; Patton 1986).

None of these techniques is foolproof, but keeping them in mind helps organizations establish pragmatic performance standards, measures, and tracking systems.

Employee Involvement in Accountability Systems

Along with appropriate performance measurement, organizations can foster good accountability through aspects of organizational structure. Accountability involves giving workers and managers a level of authority commensurate with their responsibilities within the organization.

Consequently employees can be more effective and accountable if the structure is in place to allow them to solve problems, make decisions, and implement solutions within their designated areas of responsibility. Structure—often built on empowered teams, quality management concepts and techniques, and social structures such as labor–management committees, quality circles, and project management groups—puts employees in positions to make decisions. Employee involvement accountability systems turn accountability on its head by putting responsibility for performance in the hands of employees rather than leadership. This requires a change in the culture of many large organizations and, especially, top leadership support of employee involvement.

In general, *employee involvement* refers to organizational programs in which employees structured into teams take an active role in analyzing work processes, establishing standards of work, and monitoring results. In some cases work processes and decisions about implementation of programs may fall under review by a participatory body such as a labor–management committee or an appointed committee in nonunionized organizations. The human relations approach to organization theory (discussed in Chapter 8) generally promotes participation as a way to increase motivation and commitment to the organization, eschewing political reasons for fostering participation, as a means of real power sharing (Strauss 1963). Some organizations are acting on the premise that decision sharing between union and management is a positive way to solve problems (Ball 1996). Quality management approaches, such as TQM, make use of the fact that employees are in a better position to make certain decisions and solve certain problems than are their supervisors and managers (Walton 1986). Teams trained in problem-solving techniques review problems, collect data, implement solutions, and monitor the solutions to ensure that they work. As necessity and insight dictate, they adopt new solutions as part of continuous improvement of the organization's work processes.

Participation and teamwork are the cornerstones of employee involvement. Managers choose team members directly involved with the problem or process (such as handling many phone calls). The organizational hierarchy remains in place for coordination of work. Employees generally continue working at their principal jobs while involved in problem-solving teams for a designated period each week. Teams usually disband once a resolution is in place, but monitoring may become part of their jobs to ensure that improvements continue. Such employee involvement programs create a cultural commitment to group responsibility and shared decision making (Ouchi 1981; Walton 1986) and, of course, accountability. According to most quality management advocates, contemporary personnel policies, such as pay for performance, and temporary public relations gimmicks to rally increases in productivity are to be avoided because they create competition and thereby decrease team responsibility and accountability.

Participation also may be built into programs by enacting legislation or by a reviewing body. The Workforce Investment Act discussed earlier (which funds job training programs) requires involvement of contracting agencies working with state labor department representatives to monitor and modify performance measures applicable to their states. This is to ensure buy-in to the measures. Health care institutions are involved in reviewing and maintaining their own accrediting standards, just as schools of public affairs and administration review and modify their academic standards through the National Association of Schools of Public Affairs and Administration (NASPAA).

Participatory involvement seems to address Downs's "law of counter control." If accountability and control can be linked to a sense of commitment and motivation through participation or self-direction, some accountability problems can be eliminated. In practice, however, resistance will always occur because accountability to external entities is one reason for measurement. The motives and dynamics created by employee involvement are both sociological and political. Employee involvement can be interpreted as a form of co-optation—sometimes benign, sometimes manipulative. A number of unions rebel at employee involvement in what traditionally have been management responsibilities, whereas other unions support this role redefinition as fitting the union's mission of empowering employees. A major key to success is negotiation between labor and management representatives about the extent of workers' involvement and types of decisions (Lipskey and Brock 2002; Ball 1996; U.S.Secretary of Labor 1996). When the sides develop a shared sense of trust and purpose, practices can become institutionalized in ways that boost both employee involvement and accountability.

Employee Supervision and Monitoring

Supervising employees is a fundamental management task in all organizations. It involves monitoring behavior, processes, and activities to ensure compliance, usually at the individual level. It is obvious that supervising tasks and monitoring performance are markedly different means of creating accountability from that of developing employee involvement in decision making. Employee monitoring raises ethical and legal questions about the degree of trust managers should have in an organization's employees. For example, limited monitoring might increase creativity, support teamwork, and encourage self-leadership (see also Chapter 9). Substantial monitoring, on the other hand, is associated with a lack of trust and might be associated with a more formal hierarchical structure, a more traditional organizational culture, and a more mature stage in the organization's life cycle. Obviously some systems of monitoring are necessary whatever the culture, leadership, and structure of the organization.

Etzioni (1965) uses the term *control* to explain the process of supervising and monitoring. Organization control is the "means used by an organization to elicit the performance it needs and to check whether the quantities and qualities of such performance are in accord with organizational specifications" (Etzioni 1965, 650). Downs (1967) views control as an ongoing cycle of monitoring and correcting organizational activity ranging from issuing an order to collecting information about the performance of subordinates to evaluating the adequacy of performances and issuing corrective orders.

The theoretical question for organization theory is not whether to supervise but how much—and how much self-responsibility individuals have for their actions. Next we discuss a few approaches to a theory of employee monitoring and employee performance evaluation.

Types of Employee Monitoring

Monitoring employees involves the same concepts and some of the same techniques as monitoring the organization at different levels. Monitoring might focus on productivity, quality, behavior, or compliance with rules. Monitoring methods can range from continuous to random and can be hidden or visible to employees. Methods can be as simple as maintaining basic time and attendance records and as fundamental as reviewing production quantity rates or ensuring security. Monitoring can be as invasive as tracking e-mail and listening to phone conversations; requiring periodic lie detector tests or drug testing; employing sophisticated identification systems such as retinal scans and fingerprinting; or video surveillance. Few public organizations use most of these methods, but every organization uses some of them. (See Reading 6–1.)

READING 6–1   Punching Around-the-Clock Time Clocks

Employee surveillance by computers and video cameras is nothing new. The American Management Association reports that two-thirds of major American corporations now record their employees' phone conversations, review e-mail messages and computer files, or video-tape work performances. . . .

Less known, however, is the growing use of devices that generate an electronic trail of where employees go, what routes they take, and how fast they move about as they do their jobs.

"The potential for ubiquitous monitoring is growing rapidly, and there has never been a discussion about what this means in terms of stress and repetitive strain injuries and the quality of living," said Charley Richardson, director of labor extension at the University of Massachusetts in Lowell.

"It's not just that we're being monitored," he added. "It's that the information that's gathered through monitoring is fed back through the system and used to more tightly control us."

Truckers, who are meeting this week with officials of the Federal Motor Carrier Safety Administration and others in Washington, are the most vociferous in their hostility to location monitoring. But they are not the only ones being electronically tracked. Nurses, cooks, security guards, miners, casino change makers, couriers, public works employees, and others are increasingly being asked to wear badges, or carry gear, that records where they go.

"It's very easy to track who is going where, who is on every floor, who is talking to whom," said Christina Terranova, a nurse and legal representative to the New York State Nurses Association, who has deep reservations about the use of electronic tracking in hospitals. "We have nurses who say, 'Oh, it's great,'—and I want to shake them."

The nurses who think electronic tracking is great, though, argue that it helps them quickly find colleagues in mazelike hospitals and eliminates the tedium of keeping paper logs. Hospital tracking systems usually involve badges that emit infrared signals, which are picked up by sensors embedded in room and hall ceilings. The sensors can transmit the locations of hundreds, even thousands, of nurses, orderlies, doctors, housekeepers, and even patients as they go from place to place.

The people show up as color-coded icons, moving about on schematic floor plans that can be called up instantly on a computer screen, or stored and retrieved for future analysis if, say, a costly piece of equipment turns up missing, if a patient complains that his calls are going unanswered, or if nurses complain that certain departments or shifts are dangerously understaffed.

Some hospitals have used electronic monitoring to calculate the average time nurses spend on certain procedures and even punish those who linger too long at one task, Ms. Terranova said. "God forbid a patient was frightened and maybe you wanted to sit with them for five minutes," she said. . . .

Numerous municipalities have already put location-monitoring devices to work keeping track of where buses, snowplows, and other vehicles are. Once in place, though, the systems can also prove useful in improving civil service accountability. Denver announced earlier this year that it might soon begin tracking its 14,000 city workers, after an embarrassing local television exposé showed some of them playing cards, sleeping, and eating leisurely breakfasts during business hours. . . .

SOURCE: Abridged from Mary Williams Walsh, "Punching Around-the-Clock." The New York Times, September 27, 2000. Copyright © 2000 The New York Times Co. Reprinted with permission.

A number of reasons contribute to the need for employee monitoring. In practical terms, employers use various monitoring techniques because some laws encourage and others mandate the use of monitoring in certain circumstances. Our post-9/11 world has furthered this trend. Signing in and out of work relates to labor law issues of pay, and criminal record checks relate to legal requirements for hiring certain personnel. Another legal reason for monitoring is to maintain the confidentiality of those an organization services. Although few public service organizations are involved in trade secrets, they handle a host of information about their clients, members, and citizens protected by various privacy laws. Privacy laws have developed to ensure the confidentiality of data, rather than for the protection of employees, creating a need for monitoring employees to prevent loss or theft of this confidential information. Monitoring also occurs because employers have a good deal of discretion. Monitoring is primarily considered a management right in a unionized setting; in a nonunionized setting, the employment at will doctrine allows employers great flexibility in proscribing employee behavior and for setting up monitoring systems. Employees who do not conform may be fired at any time for any reason.

The cartoon by Ben Wasserman pokes fun at employee monitoring, but certainly there is a need for some monitoring. The concerns present during the Reagan era have expanded since 9/11. So when should monitoring occur to achieve accountability of employees? Privacy has always been a crucial right, so Martin and Freeman (2003) propose that those who monitor ask to what extent, if any, monitoring improves productivity and creativity. To what degree does monitoring lesson liability and increase security? They also ask whether it is paternalistic: What is the degree of social control? Monitoring will affect the organizational

culture, so these questions must be considered. In sum, do the effects of monitoring improve accountability, outweighing the possible loss in motivation and productivity? Computer monitoring, for instance, may minimize the sending and receiving of personal e-mail, down-loading pornography, and personal web surfing. Though this type of monitoring may be paternalistic, it can increase productivity, reduce costs from unrelated use of the Internet, and have other positive spillover. It also may limit productivity by heightening worker tension, boredom, and anxiety as employees feel less free to express ideas through e-mail messages and search for information on the Internet.

Opponents argue that most screening and monitoring is an invasion of privacy, going well beyond what is necessary to achieve control. In fact, privacy is a "hot button" organizational, ethical, and social issue. Although the U.S. Constitution does not cite privacy as an explicit right, the Fourth Amendment prohibits subjecting citizens to "unreasonable search and seizure," a phrase often interpreted to encompass personal privacy. But according to sociologist Amitai Etzioni (1999), privacy itself has limits; for Etzioni a person's right to individual privacy must be secondary to the common good. For example, a person's medical records should not be available to employers so that they can choose who might stay healthier versus who might need subsidized leave and medical treatment; however, organizations and institutions are entitled to medical and law enforcement information that might prevent coworkers or the public from being exposed to serious health hazards (such as a virulent communicable disease) or safety risks (such as sex offenders who might be placed in contact with potential prey).

Martin and Freeman also ask whether monitoring effectively leads to greater organizational security. On the one hand, thumbprints or swipe cards for entrance into a building or office help control who enters. Such measures may have a side benefit of mitigating workplace and domestic violence by preventing others from entering. On the other hand, if such measures lack a clear security purpose, they are likely to be ignored as employees allow fellow employees and visitors into the building.

Do such methods create too much social control? Again, that depends on the purpose; but they do appear to impede trusting relationships between an organization and its employees. In terms of behaviorism, individuals act based on reinforcements of behaviors, either positive or negative. Reinforcements are to create accountability and are not meant to impede trust. Employees conform because they will be rewarded for producing under surveillance or they will be disciplined. Monitoring methods can also cause *anticipatory conformity* (prudence). Employees conform in anticipation of the possible negative consequences, not actual consequences (Wood, A.M 1998 citing Zuboff 1988). It doesn't matter whether the drug test is random or scheduled; employees may choose to conform not wanting to risk the potential loss of a job. Some monitoring methods may also have the effect of implicitly condoning a minimal standard of performance (Katz and Kahn 1978). For example, professionals may see logging in or entering hours on the computer as irksome tasks rather than simple methods for security and keeping attendance.

Monitoring is one of many tools for supervision. Direct observation, performance evaluation, and employee socialization are also valuable in organizational settings. We explore these methods of accountability in the next few sections.

Direct Observation and Performance Evaluation

A primary method of ensuring accountability is daily interaction with employees. At the leadership level this is frequently called "management by wandering around" or MBWA.

The executive stops to meet with employees throughout the organization as a means of understanding what employees are doing and getting feedback about employee concerns. This is really more of a benefit for the executive; it helps establish a sense of trust and support for the organization through the visible presence of the leader. At lower levels, ongoing interaction through open-door policies, observation of work, and reports of employees help the manager keep the organization focused and functional. In the central office, direct observation is relatively simple and can include simply stopping by an employee's cubicle to get an update on work. But in the modern virtual organization, direct observation may be irregular and rare with greater reliance placed on employees' formally submitted reports. To the extent that these procedures or policies foster micromanagement (overly close and detailed supervision) they may create discontent (Filley, House, and Kerr 1976, 385–86), much as oppressive electronic monitoring may do. Although control and accountability are achieved, such policies and methods may become "dissatisfiers" (Herzberg, Mausner, and Snyderman 1959). Close supervision also goes counter to the purpose of many of the alternative forms of structure (participative, matrix, and adhocracies) discussed throughout this book. (See Chapters 4, 8, and 9.)

A more formal method is the performance appraisal or evaluation. Performance appraisals provide opportunities for supervisors and managers to give direct, personal feedback to employees. Appraisals are often used to guide employee development and training. Performance appraisals are used despite the fact that they are equally disliked by managers and employees, are considered a waste of time, are stressful to administer, and are subject to measurement errors. As a control mechanism, as documentation of poor performance, they are not particularly useful because evaluations are rarely conducted in a timely fashion related to the problem, and supervisors are uncomfortable giving poor evaluation ratings. Nevertheless, performance appraisal has a positive reason for existence even though it is imperfect and often misunderstood. By pointing to both positive and negative sides, the manager can make a clear and significant statement to establish benchmarks for merited rewards as well as for specific improvements in an employee's knowledge, skills, and abilities. Performance appraisals developed to measure objectives, MBO, are most successful in creating accountability. Objectives must be (1) clear and realistic, (2) measurable, and (3) sufficiently challenging rather than a paper exercise (Lawler 2000).

So in a sense, performance appraisals are a part of the scientific management movement that states that work can be measured and evaluated (Murphy and Cleveland 1995, 324–48). Actually developing a fair and objective performance appraisal is fraught with difficulties. Employees often see performance appraisals as subjective and biased, and these perceived (and real) inequities are difficult to eliminate. According to *equity theory,* individuals judge how much effort they will put into a task by comparing their effort, treatment, and rewards to those of others (Lawler 2000). Based on this calculation, individuals may increase, decrease, or maintain their level of productivity. Whether real or not, perceived unfairness of performance appraisals may increase problems of morale and motivation (see also Chapter 8) because the appraisal is seen as an attempt to monitor and control rather than as a vehicle for evaluating, rewarding, and helping employees improve their skills and knowledge. Tying pay to evaluations perceived as unfair further compounds problems of motivation and control.

To be useful, performance evaluations should also evaluate teamwork. It is a rare employee who works alone. Performance evaluations often fail to link what an individual does with the success of the organization. The relative importance of different activities to the success of the organization's mission can be hard to measure. For example, how does a supervisor evaluate what an administrative assistant does to meet the organization's mission and strategic objectives? The individual's work is vital, but it is one link in a long chain of actions by employees to meet the goals, as discussed in the "balanced scorecard" section earlier in this chapter. Some appraisals, such as results-oriented approaches (like management by objectives), do a better job of creating accountability than others. The "cost" trade-off, however, is that they are likely to be time-consuming, depend on frequent updating, and require creativity to apply effectively to many nonprofessional and technical jobs. When done thoughtfully, the price is modest compared with benefits to the employees, the organization, and the public they serve.

Organizational Commitment and Socialization

Employees monitor their own behavior, as well. The principle here is that the organization or some other agent in society succeeds in inculcating conformance with the goals and values of the organization. The goals of the individual and the larger entity become one and the same through organizational and professional commitment. Describing the ideal-type bureaucracy, Weber (1947) notes the importance of socialization to professional norms of impartiality, competence, and a career commitment to the organization. Similarly, Gulick argues that if everyone shares an idea, this circumstance alone often serves as a primary motivation for cooperative effort—this Gulick refers to as "leading through an idea" (1937, 37–38). Burns and Stalker's (1994) model of the "organic" form of organization (described in Chapter 4) also relies largely on an individual's commitment to the organization—as a resource contributing well beyond a narrow job description or technical profession—to create a community of interest.

This commitment occurs through *socialization*, the process of learning about how things are done in an organization or profession; this is another way of trying to ensure that employees hold the appropriate values and goals. Socialization occurs through planned activities such as orientation sessions and training, through the longer process of observation and imitation, and through professional school indoctrination and socialization (discussed under professional responsibility).

On-the-job socialization in an organization orients employees, regardless of their professional training and backgrounds, to the organization's norms and values. Informing employees about rules, policies, missions, and objectives can be done through communication tools such as handbooks, orientation sessions, retreats, and briefings. Much about the organization's sense of its real mission, importance, and character is instilled—both consciously and unconsciously—through informal gatherings around the coffeepot or through staff meetings. On these occasions employees learn the folklore of the organization, which often springs from points of crisis and stories of departed characters that become more mythical each year. Myths and symbols are important means for expressing and teaching organizational norms and important bases of commitment (Weick 1995; Pondy et al. 1983; Schein 2004; Ott 1989). Organizational mythology interprets and expresses the meanings of events and actions from the speaker's viewpoint. Myths help create, perpetuate, and evolve the organization's culture.

This process of formal and informal socialization helps create organizational commitment and a stable organizational culture. One Indiana state executive claimed that his agency had a Department of Oral History. The people in this "department" could remember why a policy was instituted, the debate surrounding it, and the reasons the eventual policy prevailed.

These oral historians provided a collective institutional memory that served as guidance for the organization. Then again, by circulating information about failed attempts, these informal historians stymied the Indiana executive when he wanted to make changes. The Department of Oral History sometimes erroneously claimed a policy reason for doing things when the policy had been rescinded or never even existed as a formal policy. So indoctrinated were they with the previous policy or way of doing things that they failed to adapt to the new one. So socialization has two sides: It can increase accountability to law or rule, and at the same time it can stymie traditional hierarchical accountability and change.

This theory of socialization is limited as an explanation for creating accountability because it does not elucidate why employees stay and work for the organization once socialized. One normative explanation of organizational commitment is a desire to serve the public interest. Etzioni (1965) theorizes that employees identify with the organization and share beliefs in the organization's goals whether it is a governmental, voluntary, religious, or ideological–political organization. The greater the *identitative* power of the organization, the greater the likelihood that an individual's loyalty and compliance will be strong enough to reduce the need for overt forms of control.

Further, Etzioni (1965) notes, identitative power varies with environmental conditions, such as the strength of public support for an issue (environmentalism or equal employment), the number of organizations competing for a member's loyalty, economic conditions affecting the funds available for such organizations, and the possibility of getting a job elsewhere. Herbert Kaufman (1967), writing the classic study of government organizational culture, *The Forest Ranger*, described the Forestry Service's ability to create conformance and accountability through the use of consistent rules, regimens, uniforms, hiring practices (hiring those with similar professional backgrounds), and reporting systems. These all shaped the forest rangers' ability to *identify* with the Forestry Service no matter whether stationed in Alaska or New York or handling the conflicting responsibilities of managing the land for commercial uses and preserving the land for environmental purposes.

Ideological commitment is a similar explanation and basis for accountability. We often think of this as applying to politically appointed employees in government, and indeed it does. But if we expand the term to mean commitment to the mission of the organization, it takes on broader implications. Employees may decide to work with a department or agency because they believe in its objectives. The missions of some organizations are more likely to elicit such commitments than others. The Central Intelligence Agency, law enforcement agencies, the military branches, and environmental groups probably have higher levels of commitment than, say, the Internal Revenue Service or the U.S. Postal Service because the former are clearly visible, sometimes controversial, and exciting, while the latter have much that is routine in the provision of services. The value of ideological commitment lies in the willingness of employees to exert energy and imagination for the organization or program goals. These can be some of the most dedicated and accountable employees. Yet if policies or managers change, those self-controlling commitments may lead to disenchantment from employees or obstruction of new policies or programs. This is certainly the fear of newly elected government officials, who see civil servants as the enemy.

Commitment may also be in the form of personal loyalty to a leader or mentor, or ideological commitment to the organization and its mission. Personal loyalty to a leader can be based, as Downs notes (1967, 156), on nepotism or long-standing trust and friendship. Charismatic leaders gain loyalty because of their ability to sway those around them.

The strength of these relations lies in the confidence that the mentor or leader can have in the cooperation and loyalty of the staff. Reliance on such personal relationships also has drawbacks. If the mentor leaves or becomes alienated and no longer adheres to policy, followers may well also defect, thereby compounding a loss. A series of strong personal loyalties can also disrupt other organizational command functions, especially if followers begin to develop a distorted view of their own authority, as distinct from their leader's authority.

Consequently there are downside aspects to socialization and organizational commitment. Socialization within an organization can lead to extreme commitment and fanatical behavior—attitudes that, like an aggressive cancer within the body, may ultimately destroy the organization itself (Schein 1968). Consider the fiascos of Enron, WorldCom, and Adelphia in the private sector; the City of Philadelphia in the 2000s; and, of course, the malignant nature of Watergate conspirators ("plumbers") in the Nixon era and Oliver North's misplaced allegiance in the Reagan era. When people think alike and reinforce one another's biases too strongly, they may make decisions that are unwise and contrary to the public interest, leading to behavior beyond permissible boundaries, and ultimately working to defeat the goals of the very organization they revere (Harvey 1988).

RESPONSIVENESS

If accountability emphasizes demonstrated adherence to rules and laws, responsiveness emphasizes meeting the needs of those being served, an equally important aspect of the mission of the organization. Simply following the letter of the law is not enough. Responsiveness is another side of accountability, and it has many definitions.

Responsiveness can be considered a form of professionalism. Professionals see being responsive to citizen, client, member, and customer needs as part of their professional duties. When extreme conformity to the rule or regulation occurs (perhaps through extreme socialization), the organization itself becomes dysfunctional (Merton 1957; Schein 1968). Slavish conformity and literalism are abdications of responsibility because responsible professionals are thinking professionals. According to Kearney and Sinha (1988), responsiveness goes hand-in-hand with a more professionalized, educated workforce. Of course Weber saw the ideal bureaucracy as composed of trained professionals, although he did not discuss responsiveness per se. Today fewer and fewer town managers and law enforcement officers have only a high school education, coming instead from a variety of educational backgrounds and professions. Public administration itself has been invaded by the professions, becoming more professional and aware of the need to be more responsive every decade. Critics of this perspective contend just the reverse—that increasing professionalism actually makes the bureaucracy less responsive and professionals more self-serving. Professionals, because of their education and socialization, have blinders to citizen perspectives: "I know better because I am more knowledgeable than the citizen about these things."

A second type of responsiveness is outreach to the public, in terms of both specific clienteles and the public as a whole (Cope 1997). Assistance-oriented responsiveness is most evident in social service organizations, whether public or nonprofit. Street social workers go to where the need is rather than waiting for those who are mentally ill or homeless to come to them for assistance. Other organizations exhibit this type of responsiveness as well. Community college systems are more apt to respond to employer needs for new training programs than state universities with their larger bureaucracies. The IRS holds tax preparation clinics in response to taxpayer needs. As discussed in Chapter 4, competition can promote responsiveness; yet by and large we restrict it in the public sector.

Part of this second type of responsiveness is quick action. When regulations are in place, a public organization is obligated to honor and administer those laws, as well as implement their programs. That is responsiveness. State labor departments have rapid response teams that respond to employer layoff notices by providing information and services about unemployment insurance, training programs, and job placement prior to the actual layoff. A hospital emergency department's triage of patients, determining the priority of patients, also fits with this notion of quick response. This conception requires organizations to act not only in a timely but sometimes an immediate fashion—a principle underscored by sluggish and inadequate public sector responses to Hurricane Katrina and other recent natural disasters. But (1) determining what it means to be responsive in a given situation and then (2) acting based on that determination can be difficult when decision makers face conflicting values, priorities, and solution alternatives or when essential information is scarce.

A third type of responsiveness is individualized service or customer service. The emphasis on this type of responsiveness arises with a changing organizational culture emphasizing quality improvement and structures utilizing employee participation and employee involvement. Many motor vehicle departments have improved service immensely, while others have not. Ironically, many that have improved service have moved to less personal contact, moving many functions to the Internet. Features of the reinventing government movement, such as contracting out services, may lead to this same kind of contradiction. In an effort to improve services and efficiency to the public as a whole—that is, to be responsive—government and elected officials may be less sensitive to an individual complaint or concern because the service is now provided through a contract.

At this point the balance between emphasizing by-the-book accountability, on the one hand, and over-the-counter responsiveness to an organization's clientele, on the other hand, seems to favor responsiveness, though expectations are high for both. This is appropriate. This delicate balance between accountability and responsiveness underlies the emphasis on *customer service* and *performance measurement* over the last two decades. The more impressive is an organization's responsiveness, the higher is its perceived performance; hospitals and even states routinely publicize "report cards" on their ability to respond. This balance favoring responsiveness rests on trust in an organization's employees to work autonomously. Trust is the integrative mechanism associated with taking risks for the organization and the creation of a culture of high performance (Ortman and Schlesinger 2003; Gould-Williams 2003).

Terry (2003) defines a fourth type of responsiveness: preservation of the institution, with the administrator as conservator. This is a less obvious definition when compared with others; nevertheless it can be crucial. Should the U.S. Department of Education exist? How about the Department of Housing and Urban Development (HUD)? The Interstate Commerce Commission (ICC)? The Civil Aeronautics Board (CAB)? Each of these federal agencies has been attacked at some point over the last decades. The Departments of Education and HUD mounted quick and effective defenses using argument, logic, and strong external support; today they remain intact and functioning much as they were originally designed. The CAB and ICC met a different fate; they withered as the industries they oversaw became increasingly deregulated. In the case of the ICC, it resisted shifting from case-based to rule-based policy making, and its multiheaded leadership (a board and a commission) could not argue its value successfully. Ultimately some functions of these departments were moved to other agencies; some were abandoned; and the two regulatory agencies were disbanded. Similar dynamics take place at state and local levels of government.

Nonprofit organizations are more exposed to deconstruction and mission shift. In a dramatic example, the March of Dimes "conserved" itself from an organization for the cure and prevention of polio to one for the cure and prevention of birth defects. The Girls Club was unable to "conserve" itself when its name was taken over by what is now known as the Boys and Girls Club, and it became a much smaller advocacy organization, Girls, Inc. These dramatic organizational disruptions can be bad or good, but top-level officials must argue their organizations' case. For them, personal responsibility as well as organizational responsiveness come into play.

RESPONSIBILITY

Whereas responsiveness largely pertains to the organization's relationship with those it serves, *responsibility* pertains to the individual within the organization and operates from two levels: individual administrative responsibility and professional responsibility. In public organizations both levels exist within the context of *democratic responsibility,* which is delegated to the individual through the formal policies and mechanisms of the organization, based on the laws and charters under which it operates. *Individual responsibility* is based upon one's own decision making ability and values; *professional responsibility* is based on the standards and ethical principles of the individual's profession.

By the nature of our democratic society, democratic responsibility is dispersed just as leadership is (Gardner 1990, 78–79). It does not fall simply on the shoulders of one executive. Leaders have a responsibility to encourage active involvement of constituents (citizens), but so do other employees. Democracy requires this. Responding to citizen and client concerns, ensuring participation and due process, and taking initiative for work to be completed are aspects of democratic responsibility. Further, each public employee has a responsibility to maintain the public trust, keeping the highest standards of action.

Responsibility incorporates both historical meaning and Weber's meaning of *neutral competence*: Public employees are hired and perform their work based on their technical knowledge and skills rather than their political contacts and ideologies. Today laws ensure this neutral competence by prohibiting certain forms of political activity by government and nonprofit employees in favor of nonpartisan service to the public as a whole. Although neutral competence is a highly relevant doctrine, particularly in administrative contexts such as quasi-judicial hearings and other forms of legal proceedings, it is difficult to reconcile with the goal of responsiveness in areas where employees are called on to exercise discretion. Consequently the neutral competence aspect of responsibility needs to be supplemented by individual and professional responsibility.

Individual Responsibility

Perhaps among the most important responsibilities of public employees are developing creative ways in which the organization can be effective within shifting budgetary constraints and political constraints. These constraints extend beyond short-term pressures associated with business cycles, economic downturns, or changes in products desired by the customer.

As one constraint is diminished or resolved, another invariably overtakes it. This is a typical situation among research and higher education institutions that depend on grant money from research funders and philanthropic foundations. Managers and employees in organizations funded this way must continually seek one contract or grant to replace another that may be winding down. Public employees everywhere need to be creative, innovative, and engaged in their responsibilities. Innovative managers and workers are critical for delivering services, improving the programs they work in, and helping reshape them as needs and opportunities emerge—all within an operating environment that sets their personal and organizational expertise and values within a larger political and budgetary framework.

Individual responsibility may take on another form: at times questioning and disagreeing with the organization's prevailing mindset about emerging issues and about practices taken for granted. Although whistleblowers (those who report violations of policy and illegal acts) are often viewed with suspicion, they are needed as a mechanism of accountability. That is why we try to protect whistleblowers who report wrongdoing when working through channels has been ineffective and the issue is significant. The need to disagree or call attention to problems does not have to be related to illegality. "Yes people" generally are not helpful to the organization or, by extension, to the public. Consequently one of the most difficult individual responsibilities is to disagree with leadership or even colleagues, based on one's competencies and general knowledge. Public employees have a responsibility to *communicate* and *act* when others do not communicate.

Though we, at first blush, think of disagreeing as creating conflict, and conflict as a problem in the workplace, it is probably more difficult to disagree than agree. That is, it is easier to go along with a group than to express a different opinion. Janis (1971/2005) coined the term *groupthink* to describe this situation. Groupthink occurs when people collectively agree about a critical decision when, individually and privately, they would disagree. They feel pressured to conform. Similarly, Harvey (1988) calls this "going to Abilene." But Harvey differs in his interpretation of why people do not speak up. The real problem, he states, is not peer group pressure, but one's own concern about being left out or being isolated from the group for disagreeing. Harvey does not deny that whistleblowers commonly risk being ostracized and losing their jobs when they report wrongdoing. Reports of whistleblowing that make the press do, indeed, demonstrate that it takes an incredible toll on the responsible professional. Rather, he suggests that people inflate the risk of disagreeing, imagining the worst-case scenario, when it is more likely that speaking up can change the course of events.

For organization theorists, the problem is to promote the right balance of individual commitment to the organization and to the group with a sense of individual questioning and responsibility. What mechanisms are available that will promote responsibility and discretion but not have individuals run rough-shod over the necessary rules? Harvey suggests that organizations need to be designed to allow people to make mistakes and to allow people to apologize. This involves technical and cultural accommodations that reward intelligent risk taking and, when appropriate, revere "noble failures." Others suggest a culture that values honesty and disagreement, an organizational structure that supports teamwork rather than competition, and leadership that promotes open communication rather than secrecy (Larson and LaFasto 1989; Walton 1986; Lawler 2000; Burns and Stalker 1994). This leads to a contradiction. At the same time that we want structural forms of organizations that use teamwork, the actual formation of those teams has the potential to reduce individual responsibility— hence the search for reasonableness and balance.

Professional Responsibility

Professional responsibility complements individual responsibility and is based on the socialization of an individual to his or her profession. It may include responsibility to professional codes of ethics. (See also Chapter 9, Executive Morality and Responsibility.) Professional responsibility develops through professional school socialization, internships, formal and informal networks, and ongoing continuing education and development. Professional school socialization provides technical information about state-of-the-art standards and values of the profession. For good or for ill, this socialization leads to a particular way of thinking about problems. Understanding and internalizing the values of the profession are important. The topic of ethics is routinely incorporated into the curricula of nursing, engineering, public administration, and other programs pertinent to public service–oriented professions. Coursework helps inculcate professional values, as does subtle training through exposure to successful role models at conferences, seminars, and informal discussions with professors and peers.

The selection process used by schools is a way to ensure that likeminded people fit the values of the profession. In general, Etzioni (1965) notes a relationship between selection and socialization; the more selective an organization can afford to be (the Air Force, medical schools), the more screening for technical competence and for values can be completed before entry, and the less emphasis need be placed on socialization in school. At least in the past, a relatively high proportion of West Point graduates came from families of West Point graduates (Janowitz 1960). Other elite institutions are subject to similar criticism for recruiting "legacies" (the children of alumni), affirming the importance of sustaining existing values over recruiting for diverse values.

Nurses, engineers, and many other professionals must meet testing and state licensing requirements to begin their careers with full standing. Once they begin practicing, they pursue continuing education, keep in touch with colleagues and evolving practices through professional societies, and conduct their work—no matter where they work—within the framework of their profession's formal code of ethics and, sometimes, state established review boards. In many ways their value set is more strongly aligned with their profession than with the organizations in which they practice. Because they are members of a state recognized profession, their organizations usually show them a special level of deference and substantial autonomy in decision making.

Upholding these ethics codes is a professional responsibility. Health care practitioners are among the most likely to employ their codes of ethics when resolving problems. Hospitals routinely set up ethics committees at the request of physicians, nurses, taxpayers, and family members. These committees often include community members and sometimes professional ethicists. The committees sometimes struggle with the ethical principles and standards themselves, though more often they weigh family and patient wishes to make determinations about care. Often applying one value to a situation (such as revering life) means paying less heed to another value (like diminishing pain and suffering). The decision, if one is needed, is made in the end by the person calling the meeting.

According to Kearney and Sinha (1988), *professionalization* is a matter of degree. Not everyone in the workforce is a member of a clearly identified and delineated profession with an explicit code of ethics. That does not mean they are not professionals; rather, it means the guideposts for professional responsibility are less clear—or at least less likely to be delineated clearly through a formal code of ethics. Even when leaders in nonprofit and government organizations come from professional and technical backgrounds, such as health and science, the ethics codes and expectations in their original professions may be insufficient to address the range of administrative responsibilities they acquire in managerial and leadership roles. After all, public sector executives must frame their responsibilities in terms of the community at large rather than a particular profession (Schein 1996). A librarian, psychologist, or engineer's code does not guide how to make administrative decisions about scarce resources and layoffs.

Nevertheless public administrators interested in doing so can tap broad-based codes of ethics framed by and for professionals in the public sector. Federal employees operate under a "Code of Ethics for Government Service," adopted in 1958 and written in the language of the day. For municipal managers, the International City/County Management Association (ICMA) has had a code of ethics since 1924. For anyone in public service, the American Society for Public Administration (ASPA) maintains a code of ethics built around five principles:

- Serve the public interest.
- Respect the Constitution and the law.
- Demonstrate personal integrity.
- Promote ethical organizations.
- Strive for professional excellence.

Of course codes of ethics are not panaceas that ensure professional responsibility in and of themselves. Rather, they help make internalized values explicit both for the professionals who operate using those values and for people the professionals serve and who hold them accountable.

Not all public sector workers know about the codes of ethics around them. Many codes, including these, are voluntary rather than mandatory because no review board examines allegations that a public employee has violated standard such-and-such of the code, and no sanctions are associated with violations of the code itself. Critics argue that codes of conduct are not useful unless they are enforceable. Supporters counter that broad codes such as these are impractical to mandate, monitor, and enforce; instead it is more desirable to rely on the employees' sense of responsibility combined with institutional accountability mechanisms such as ombudspeople, inspectors general, and oversight bodies.

Codes of ethics aside, workers with a sense of professionalism tend to exhibit *social responsibility*. This can involve cooperation with others in the profession to improve the well-being of clients, members, citizens, and the public as a whole. Information technology professionals recognize the need to cooperate to prevent threats to software and databases. Educators, health and social workers, law enforcement officials, and clergy have legal and social responsibilities to be activists in preventing child abuse and reporting it when it occurs. Social responsibility with its emphasis on responsiveness must be balanced with legal requirements and accountability. FEMA workers were put in the untenable position of having to defend legal requirements for privacy with the desperate need of family and friends to find loved ones after Hurricane Katrina (discussed in Box 6–2).

BOX 6–2 Social Responsibility or Legal Responsibility?

Efforts to locate 500 children still classified as missing after Hurricane Katrina are stalled because the Federal Emergency Management Agency, citing privacy laws, has refused to share its evacuee database with the National Center for Missing and Exploited Children, according to investigators tracking the cases.

Not until the White House and Justice Department intervened earlier this month did Department of Homeland Security officials agree to a compromise that grants FBI agents limited access to information that may provide clues to many of the unresolved cases.

In recent days, FEMA has released data that helped close 15 cases. Yesterday, after inquiries from *The Washington Post*, the agency sent the FBI a computer disk with the names of 570,000 evacuees.

But as the four-month anniversary of the worst natural disaster in U.S. history approaches, congressional leaders, law enforcement authorities, and family advocates say FEMA's slow response has meant that many families that could have been reunited this holiday season instead remain apart.

"We are deeply disappointed by the low priority FEMA assigned to the cases of missing children," Senators Susan Collins (R-Maine) and Joseph I. Lieberman (D-Connecticut) wrote yesterday to FEMA's acting director, R. David Paulison. "And while FEMA may not have sole responsibility to investigate cases of missing children, it should do what is in its power to assist other agencies in completing the investigations."

Officials believe it is likely that many of the 500 children are safe, perhaps even in the care of a family member. But a case is not closed until the relative who reported the child missing learns the youngster's whereabouts and is assured the child is unharmed.

- Under U.S. privacy laws, FEMA is prohibited from releasing information such as names and Social Security numbers to anyone.

"The information that people provide us when they are in the midst of, or recovering from, a life-altering event includes Social Security number, income levels, very personal information," said FEMA spokeswoman Nicol Andrews. "We take our charge to protect that information very seriously."

Cornelius J. Armstead, 25, said he has spent the past four months wondering and worrying about what happened to his 2-year-old son, who was with his mother a mile away when New Orleans flooded.

"The storm came. We all evacuated. I don't know which way they went," he said, recounting his frantic attempt to get to the housing project where his son and the child's mother lived. "I tried to get to them, but the water rose so high."

After calling the Red Cross, several shelters, and acquaintances, Armstead said, he dialed the missing children hotline, 800-THE-LOST. "I call it every day," he said.

When Katrina struck the Gulf Coast on August 29, the Justice Department and Louisiana officials asked the National Center for Missing and Exploited Children to handle missing-person reports.

The good—but certainly not surprising—news is that workers in public sector organizations tend to be motivated to do their best *because* they are part of public service and believe in its value. As Goodsell (2004, 105) sums it up, "Bureaucrats are mainly influenced by who they are. And who they are leads not to shirking and sabotaging but to conscientious, dedicated goal-seeking"—characteristics fundamental to shouldering professional responsibility.

SELF-REGULATING ORGANIZATIONS

As we just discussed, responsible behavior is a means by which individuals regulate what they do. Organizations also exhibit responsible behavior, adjusting their structure, actions, and outputs to accommodate external and internal changes while remaining effective in fulfilling their missions. The tendency for organizational self-preservation and self-regulation—or *cybernetic control,* as it is sometimes labeled—invites an analogy between organizations and self-regulating organisms (Scott, Mitchell, and Birnbaum 1981). Cybernetic theory and political accountability theories, although not incompatible, emphasize different values and attend to different phenomena. The cybernetic model, with its roots in systems theory, concerns self-controlling mechanisms that evaluate information about the state of the environment and adjust the system's activities to achieve equilibrium.

As organizations receive *inputs* from the environment, the inputs may spark adjustments through mechanisms of control, communication, and feedback (Scott, Mitchell, and Birnbaum 1981). Organizations and other complex systems maintain themselves at a point of equilibrium between activities and resources that is conducive to survival. The point of equilibrium almost always must change over time. For example, most public organizations survive and continue to be effective even when their sizes, funding levels, or scope of programs change somewhat from year to year. (See Chapter 10 for a discussion of consequences when an organization becomes out of sync with its environment.)

The role of information—*feedback*—in this theory is crucial. Information evaluated as showing an acceptable system state—positive feedback—dictates a continuation of current policies. Information evaluated to show a threat to system survival—negative feedback—indicates a need for change in policies. A further refinement of the feedback notion is *feed forward*. Here information known or theorized to be an index of the future state of the organization helps managers prepare for, rather than react to, changes (Filley, House, and Kerr 1976, 441–47). In a cybernetic system, mechanisms comparable to an organizational thermostat automatically monitor feedback and feed forward that trigger routines for taking corrective action. This feedback-and-action loop keeps the system self-maintaining.

Though cybernetic control differs from accountability, responsiveness, and responsibility, it points to the resilience of organizations. If times are austere, managers may cut back without a significant leadership intervention because the information is available to make that adjustment. The value of cybernetic theory is that it makes us think about how remarkable our organizations are at adjusting to new situations.

As control systems become increasingly sophisticated, managing organizations draws on an evolving combination of cybernetic and traditional forms of control. Some procedures stress chain of command, whereas others emphasize more accurate and comprehensive information systems. Both are valuable, which means that technology systems and individual responsibility make a strong combination, though the concoction is by no means problem-free.

Organizations, particularly in this era of performance pressure and concern about outside threats, sometimes overly rely on technological solutions and fixes, even in circumstances where they recognize that "[c]ontrol is a function of knowledge, and in uncertain environments knowledge often does not exist" (Landau and Stout 1979, 148). Technology is no substitute for knowledge, creativity, or good management. Program managers who overly rely on control systems may focus too much on reestablishing controls and restoring previous levels of outputs, without considering alternative program ideas or, even more important, without encouraging the political and professional debates and negotiations that constitute public management.

Perhaps the most serious consequence of overreliance on control systems is that management may become defined as a narrow, technical process of control rather than as the experimental process it really is. Micromanagement and other types of intensive control do not fit with today's notions of teamwork, democratically run organizations, and participative decision making. When developing control systems, what may be important is recognizing that government and nonprofit organizations work for the public. Consequently their systems of control, whether cybernetic or politically chosen, should create transparency.

CONCLUSION: TOWARD TRANSPARENCY

Transparency, or at least the word, is becoming the term of choice to describe the traditional notions of political accountability, responsiveness, and responsibility. To reiterate, *transparency* means that public services are both accountable and responsive—that is, answerable to the public and open to public scrutiny. Transparency connotes a respect for individual democratic rights and individual autonomy to make decisions. (See Reading 6–2.) Thus, for Stirton and Lodge (2001), transparency includes the ability of the citizen to exert influence or control on public services. Such transparency helps prevent abuse of authority and corruption and provides citizens, clients, members, and patients with informed choices. In this sense the idea of transparency goes beyond the individual and separate values of accountability, responsibility, and responsiveness.

READING 6–2   Homeland Secrecy

The government keeps too many secrets. It classifies information that would do no harm if published; this impedes information sharing within the government and erodes public confidence. Now the Department of Homeland Security is adding a new twist: aggressive secrecy concerning information that isn't even classified.

In recent months the department has been requiring new employees and contractors to sign nondisclosure agreements regarding "sensitive but unclassified" information they learn at work. Signers must acknowledge that they "could be subject to administrative, disciplinary, civil, or criminal action" for violations and that the government may "conduct inspections, at any time or place, for the purpose of ensuring compliance." In other words, as a condition of their employment, DHS workers have to accept a gag agreement and permit potentially intrusive searches as well.

Labor unions have understandably complained, and a DHS official says the agreements are being reviewed. This official explains that the agreements merely duplicate regulations that already protect certain categories of information; they don't actually do much at all, he says, and may therefore not be necessary. It's true they're not necessary, but antisecrecy activist Steven Aftergood disputes the contention that they would have little effect. He says they could chill whistleblowing and more basic discussion between government employees and the outside world. Mr. Aftergood notes that the military doesn't require its employees to sign such documents. DHS shouldn't either.

The department is also keeping secret Transportation Security Administration rules, known as "security directives," that guide who can get on an airplane. Not all criteria for airport screening should be public; they could give terrorists a road map for sneaking through. But there's no need for the entirety of all such directives to be secret. For basic legal authorities—the rules that define Americans' interactions with government—to be kept under wraps presents a challenge to the U.S. tradition of transparency in law. The department needs to remember that the homeland whose security it is protecting is one in which democratic debate is supposed to be open and freewheeling.

The notion of transparency is as much a product of scandals as it is a product of the information age. Watchdog organizations such as Transparency International promote transparency as part of public service reform, noting, "A principal tool in the fight against corruption is access to information" (2006). With the many new electronic technologies, organizations can provide—and citizens and clients can obtain—a wealth of information about an organization.

Mechanisms Fostering Transparency

Stirton and Lodge (2001) posit four mechanisms to create greater transparency: information, choice, representation, and voice. Voice and representation relate to the process of creating a service, and information and choice relate to the implementation and provision of the service. They theorize that through these mechanisms the public character of services can be maintained even when government itself does not directly provide the service.

Voice and representation allow constituents to be involved with policy creation and implementation, creating front-end transparency. When the public has some form of *representation* in an organization, this can include many groups and prevent the dominance of one group. (Of course we know from political science "capture theory" that groups often do dominate particular agencies.) Traditionally elected representatives provide the public a means of voice and representation in the management of all government organizations.

Voice involves mechanisms that allow the individual to have input. This occurs in nonprofit organizations when appointed board members are chosen to represent various interest groups. Community action agencies with funding from HUD, Human Services, and other state and federal agencies usually appoint a board member who is receiving those services to act as a voice. Transportation agencies, for example, now have advisory boards composed of advocates of bicycling and alternative modes of transportation; environmental groups; business groups; and abutters (those who may be directly affected by the project) to provide voice to the creation of major transportation projects. Transportation agencies, to continue the example, routinely hold public hearings to obtain public input when building public infrastructure. These committee and hearing mechanisms allow participation and help deter organizations from being unresponsive. Customer and citizen surveys are another mechanism to provide input. Above and beyond the traditional elected board or council (nonprofits and town councils), many organizations create additional formal committees (planning committees, comprehensive planning, fundraising committees) to help solve problems and supplement the work of the primary body.

Choice, the ability of the individual to choose services, and *information,* the adequate dissemination of information about choices, create transparency of implementation. The most controversial example is school choice, allowing parents to choose the schools their children attend. The idea is to create competition and increase accountability of schools for the progress of their students. Published results of tests in each school are an avenue for information about the schools. Performance measures can do much the same for other types of organizations. An example from the nonprofit sector are reports comparing money raised to the amount and percentage of an organization's funds going directly for services versus fundraising administrative costs. Reporting this information can help donors choose their charities.

In general, mechanisms that foster transparency tend to affect not only the way organizations *operate* but also how they are *structured.* When designed well, built-in transparency mechanisms are neither add-on processes nor barnaclelike structures that append to the edge of the organization. Rather, they become integral to the organization itself, vital for keeping it on track today and preparing for the future.

Accountability, Transparency, and Control

Accountability to officials, responsiveness to clients, and responsibility to duty all combine with transparency to make public organizations understandable and subservient to the public itself. They are means of control—but not control in the sense of arbitrary domination. These principles let the public, oversight bodies, and managers within their organizations assess what the organization is doing and how well. From such assessments people make informed decisions about whether society is being served, to what degree, and to what extent to support the organization's continuation.

Tools to support these principles—measuring outputs, quality, productivity, outcomes; advisory boards; sunshine laws and the like—are "enablers" in two ways. First, they provide the means for turning concepts and principles into practice. They make "the rubber meet the road." Applied well, such tools bring to life an important facet of organization theory. Second, measurement tools, means of public input, and accountability "departments" empower everyone involved because their knowledge about public organizations is no longer merely anecdotal and no longer largely guesswork. Officials gain the opportunity to see and fix what is wrong and to understand what can be made even better, serving a vital purpose in maintaining healthy public organizations.

FOR FURTHER READING

Anthony Downs's *Inside Bureaucracy* (Boston: Little, Brown, 1967; reissued Waveland Press: Prospect Heights, IL, 1994) considers the use of conventional quantitative and qualitative monitoring systems for control and such things as spies in bureaus in his political economy view of organizations. Martin Landau and Russell Stout outline the dilemmas of public managers who must establish clear standards for control with programs that are less than clear in their article "To Manage Is Not to Control: Or the Folly of Type II Errors," *Public Administration Review* 39, 1979: 148–56.

For a book that covers both government and nonprofit accountability, read Kevin Kearns's *Managing for Accountability: Preserving the Public Trust in Public and Nonprofit Organizations* (San Francisco: Jossey-Bass, 1996). John Burke provides insights about the theory of responsibility and its types in *Bureaucratic Responsibility* (Baltimore: Johns Hopkins University Press, 1986).

For complementary excerpts from the classics readings to go with this chapter, see most editions of Jay Shafritz and J. Steven Ott's (and coauthors) *Classics of Organizational Theory* (Belmont, CA: Thomson Wadsworth): Jeffrey Pfeffer and Gerald Salancik, "External Control of Organizations: A Resource Dependence Perspective" (6th edition); Al Gore, "Creating a Government That Works Better and Costs Less: Report of the National Performance Review"; Frederick Taylor, "The Principles of Scientific Management"; and Irving Janis, "Groupthink: The Desperate Drive for Consensus at Any Cost."

For complementary nonprofit case studies to go with this chapter, see Robert Goliembiewski and Jerry Stevenson's *Cases and Applications in Non-Profit Management* (Belmont, CA: Thomson Wadsworth, 1998): "Taking Risks for a Good Cause" and "After All, Nobody Got Hurt!"

REFERENCES

Aguayo, Rafael. 1990. *Dr. Deming: The American who taught the Japanese about quality.* New York: Fireside.

Bacchiega, Alberto, and Carlo Borzaga. 2003. The economics of the third sector. In *The study of the nonprofit enterprise*, 27–48. Ed. Helmut Anheier and Avner Ben-Ner. New York: Lower Academic/Plenum Publishers.

Ball, Carolyn. 1996. Is labor–management cooperation possible in the public sector without a change in law? *Journal of Collective Negotiations in the Public Sector* 25: 23–30.

Berman, Evan. 1998. *Productivity in public and nonprofit organizations: strategies and techniques.* Thousand Oaks, CA: Sage Publications.

Boorstin, Daniel J. 1973. *The Americans: The democratic experience.* New York: Random House.

Bozeman, Barry. 2000. *Bureaucracy and red tape.* Upper Saddle River, NJ: Prentice Hall.

Brandt, John. 1989. How organization counts: Incentives and inspiration. *Journal of Policy Analysis and Management* 8: 489–93.

Brody, Evelyn. 2002. Accountability and the public trust. In *The state of nonprofit America*, 471–98. Ed. Lester Salamon. Washington, DC: The Brookings Institution.

Brown, Laura K., and Elizabeth Troutt. 2004. A cooperative approach to accountability: Manitoba's family violence prevention program. *International Journal of Public Administration* 27: 309–30.

Brownlaw, Louis, Charles Merriam and Luther Gulick. President's Committee on Administrative Management in the Government of the United States (also known as the Brownlaw Committee). Jan 8, 1937.

Burke, John. 1986. *Bureaucratic Responsibility.* Baltimore: Johns Hopkins University Press.

Burns, Tom, and Gerald Stalker. 1994. *The management of innovation.* Rev. ed. Oxford: Oxford University Press.

Campbell, David. 2002. Outcomes assessment and the paradox of nonprofit accountability. *Nonprofit Management & Leadership* 12: 243–59.

Chelimsky, Eleanor, and William R. Shadish, eds. 1997. *Evaluation for the 21st century: A handbook.* Thousand Oaks, CA: Sage Publications.

Cope, Glen. 1997. Bureaucratic reform and issues of political responsiveness. *Journal of Public Administration Research and Theory* 7: 461–71.

Daniels, Mark R., and Clifford J. Wirth. 1983. Paradigms of evaluation research: The development of an important policymaking component. *American Review of Public Administration* 17: 33–45.

Downs, Anthony. 1967. *Inside bureaucracy.* Boston: Little, Brown. (Reissued Prospect Heights, IL: Waveland Press, 1994.)

Drucker, Peter F. 1954. *The practice of management.* New York: Harper.

Etzioni, Amitai. 1965. Organizational control structure. In *Handbook of Organizations.* Ed. James March. Chicago: Rand McNally.

———. 1999. *The limits of privacy.* New York: Basic Books.

Filley, Alan, Robert House, and Steven Kerr. 1976. *Managerial process and organizational behavior.* 2nd ed. Glenview, IL: Scott, Foresman.

Finz, Samuel. 1980. Productivity measurement systems and their implementation. In *Productivity improvement handbook for state and local government.* Ed. George Washins. New York: John Wiley & Sons.

Frederickson, H. George. 2003. *The public administration theory primer.* Boulder, CO: Westview Press.

Gardner, John W. 1990. *On leadership.* New York: The Free Press.

Garvey, Gerald. 1993. *Facing the bureaucracy: Living and dying in a public agency.* San Francisco: Jossey-Bass.

Garvin, David A. 1984. What does "product quality" really mean? *Sloan Management Review* (Fall): 25–43.

Goldenberg, Edie. 1983. The three faces of evaluation. *Journal of Policy Analysis and Management* 2: 515–25.

Goodsell, Charles T. 2004. *The case for bureaucracy: A public administration polemic.* Washington, DC: CQ Press.

Gould-Williams, Julian. 2003. The importance of HR practices and workplace trust in achieving superior performance: A study of public sector organizations. *International Journal of Human Resource Management* 14: 28–54.

Gulick, Luther. 1937. "Notes on the theory of organization." In *Papers on the science of administration.* Ed. Luther Gulick and Lyndall Urwick. (Reprint, Clifton, NJ: Augustus Kelley, 1973.)

Hansmann, Henry. 2003. The role of the nonprofit enterprises. In *The study of the nonprofit enterprise*, 115–22. Ed. Helmut Anheier and Avner Ben-Ner. New York: Kluwer Academic/Penum Publishers.

Harrington, Michael. 1969. *The other America.* New York: MacMillan.

Harvey, Jerry B. 1988. *The Abilene paradox and other meditations on management.* Lexington, MA: Lexington Books.

Herzberg, Frederick, Bernard Mausner, and Barbara Bloch Snyderman. 1959. *The motivation to work.* New York: Wiley.

Herzlinger, Regina. 1996. Can public trust in nonprofits and governments be restored? *Harvard Business Review* 74: 97–107.

Holland, Thomas. 2002. Board accountability. *Nonprofit Management & Leadership* 12: 409–28.

Janis, Irving. 1971. Groupthink: The desperate drive for consensus at any cost. In *Classics of organizational theory,* 185–92. Ed. Jay Shafritz, J. Steven Ott, and Yong Suk Jang. 6th ed. Belmont, CA: Thomson Wadsworth, 2005.

Janowitz, Morris. 1960. *The professional soldier.* New York: Free Press.

Kaplan, Robert S. 2001. Strategic performance measurement and management in nonprofit organizations. *Nonprofit Management & Leadership* 11: 354–71.

Kaplan, Robert S., and David P. Norton. 1992. The balanced scorecard: Measures that drive performance. *Harvard Business Review* (January–February): 71–79.

_____. 1996. Using the balanced scorecard as a strategic management system. *Harvard Business Review* (January–February): 75–85.

Katz, Daniel, and Robert Kahn. 1978. *The social psychology of organizations.* 2nd ed. New York: John Wiley & Sons.

Katzman, Robert. 1980. *Regulatory bureaucracy: The Federal Trade Commission and antitrust policy.* Cambridge, MA: MIT Press.

Kaufman, Herbert. 1967. *The forest ranger.* Baltimore: Johns Hopkins Press.

Kearney, Richard, and Chandan Sinha. 1988. Professionalism and bureaucratic responsiveness: Conflict or compatibility. *Public Administration Review* 48: 571–79.

Kearns, Kevin. 1996. *Managing for accountability: Preserving the public trust in public and nonprofit organizations.* San Francisco: Jossey-Bass.

Kelly, Janet M. 2002. If you only knew how well we are performing, you'd be highly satisfied with the quality of our service. *National Civic Review* 91: 283–92.

Kettl, Donald. 2002. Managing indirect government. In *The tools of government: A guide to the new governance*, 490–510. Ed. Lester Salamon. Oxford: Oxford University Press.

Kingma, Bruce R. 2003. Public good theories of the nonprofit sector. In *The study of the nonprofit enterprise*, 53–66. Ed. Helmut Anheier and Avner Ben-Ner. New York: Kluwer Academic/Penum Publishers.

Klausner, Michael, and Jonathan Small. 2005. Failing to govern? The disconnect between theory and practice. *Stanford Social Innovation Review,* Spring. [Accessed July 2005.] Accessible from Stanford University at www.ssireview.com.

Landau, Martin, and Russell Stout Jr. 1979. To manage is not to control: Or the folly of Type II errors." *Public Administration Review* 39: 148–56.

Larson, Carl, and Frank LaFasto. 1989. *Teamwork : What must go right, what can go wrong.* Beverly Hills, CA: Sage Publications.

Lawler, Edward E. III. 2000. *Rewarding excellence: Pay strategies for the new economy.* San Francisco: Jossey-Bass.

Leviton, Laura, and Edward Hughes. 1981. Research on the utilization of evaluations. *Evaluation Review* 5: 525–48.

Lipskey, David, and Jonathan Brock, eds. 2002. *Going public: The role of labor–management relations in delivering quality government services.* Champaign, IL: Industrial Relations Research Association.

Lipsky, Michael. 1980. *Street-level bureaucracy: Dilemmas of the individual in public services.* New York: Russell Sage Foundation.

Locke, Edwin A., and Gary P. Latham. 1984. *Goal setting: A motivational technique that works!* Englewood Cliffs, NJ: Prentice-Hall.

Martin, Kirsten and R. Edward Freeman. 2003. "Some problems with employee monitoring." *Journal of Business Ethics* 43: 353–361.

McGregor, Douglas.1957. The human side of enterprise. *Management Review,* November. Reprinted in *Classics of organization theory*, 179–84. 6th ed. Ed. Jay Shafritz, Steven Ott, and Yong Suk Jang. Belmont, CA: Thomson-Wadsworth, 2005.

Merton, Robert. 1957. Bureaucratic structure and personality. In *Social theory and social structure.* Rev. ed. New York: Free Press.

Millar, A., R. S. Simeone, and J. T. Carnevale. 2001. Logic models: A systems tool for performance management. *Evaluation and Program Planning* 24: 73–81.

Miller, Hugh. 2005. Performance, results, and outcomes: A problem. *PA Times.* June, p. 7+.

Moynihan, Daniel P. 1965. *The Negro family: The case for national action.* New York: Random House.

Murphy, Kevin, and Jeanette Cleveland. 1995. *Understanding performance appraisal.* Thousand Oaks, CA: Sage.

Nanus, Burt, and Stephen Dobbs. 1999. *Leaders who make a difference: essential strategies for meeting the nonprofit challenge.* San Francisco: Jossey-Bass.

National Performance Review (U.S.). 1993. *Creating a government that works better & costs less: The report of the National Performance Review.* Vice President Al Gore. New York: Plume/Penguin.

Nichols, Kenneth L. 1993. *Why public organizations adopt total quality management: Factors influencing decisions to invest in TQM.* Doctoral dissertation. George Mason University.

———. 1997. The crucial edges of reinvention: A primer on scoping and measuring for organizational change. *Public Administration Quarterly* 20, Winter: 405–18.

Noll, Roger. 1971. *Reforming regulation: An evaluation of the Ash Council Proposal.* Washington, DC: The Brookings Institution.

O'Regan, Katherine. 2005. Does the structure and composition of the board matter? The case of non-profit organizations. *Journal of Law, Economics, and Organization* 21: 205–27.

Ortman, Andreas, and Mark Schlesinger. 2003. Trust, repute, and the role of the nonprofit enterprises. In *The study of the nonprofit enterprise,* 77–114. Ed. Helmut Anheier and Avner Ben-Ner. New York: Kluwer Academic/Plenum Publishers .

Osborne, David, and Ted Gaebler. 1992. *Reinventing government: How the entrepreneurial spirit is transforming the public sector.* Reading, MA: Addison-Wesley.

Ott, J. Steven. 1989. *The organizational culture perspective.* Chicago: Dorsey Press.

Ouchi, William. 1981. *Theory Z.* Reading, MA: Addison-Wesley.

Overman, Sam E., and Donna T. Loraine. 1994. Information for control: Another management proverb. *Public Administration Review* 54: 193–96.

Page, Benjamin I., and Robert Y. Shapiro. 1983. Effects of public opinion on policy. *American Political Science Review* 77: 175–90.

Parasuraman, A., Valarie A. Zeithaml, and Leonard L. Berry. 1985. A conceptual model of service quality and its implications for future research. *The Journal of Marketing* 49: 41–50.

Patton, Michael. 1986. *Utilization focused evaluation.* 2nd ed. Beverly Hills, CA: Sage Publications.

Pfeffer, Jeffrey, and Gerald Salancik. 2005. External control of organizations: A resource dependence perspective. In *Classics of organizational theory,* 521–32. 6th ed. Ed. Jay Shafritz, J. Steven Ott, and Yong Suk Jang. Belmont, CA: Thomson Wadsworth.

Pirsig, Robert M. 1974. *Zen and the art of motorcycle maintenance: An inquiry into values.* New York: Bantam Books.

Pondy, Lewis, Peter Frost, Gareth Morgan, and Thomas Dandridge, eds. 1983. *Organizational symbolism.* Greenwich, CT: JAI Press.

Robey, Daniel. 1994. *Designing organizations.* 4th ed. Burr Ridge, IL: Richard D. Irwin.

Rohr, J. A. 1986. *To run a Constitution: The legitimacy of the administrative state.* Lawrence: University of Kansas Press.

Salamon, Lester. 1999a. *America's nonprofit sector: A primer.* 2nd ed. New York: Foundation Center.

———. 1999b. The nonprofit sector at a crossroads: The case of America? *Voluntas: International Journal of Voluntary and Nonprofit Organizations* 10: 5–23.

Schein, Edgar. 1968. Organizational socialization and the profession of management. *Industrial Management Review* 9: 1–16.

———. 1996. Three cultures of management. *Sloan Management Review* 38: 9–21.

———. 2004. *Organizational culture and leadership.* San Francisco: Jossey-Bass.

Scott, William G. 1992. *Chester I. Barnard and the guardians of the managerial state.* Lawrence: University of Kansas Press.

Scott, William, Terence Mitchell, and Philip Birnbaum. 1981. *Organization theory: A structural and behavioral analysis.* 4th ed. Homewood, IL: Richard D. Irwin.

Shadish, Jr. William R., Thomas Cook, and Laura Leviton. 1991. *Foundations of program evaluation theories of practice.* Newbury Park, CA: Sage Publications.

Stirton, Lindsay, and Martin Lodge. 2001. Transparency mechanisms: Building publicness into public services. *Journal of Law and Society* 28: 471–89.

Strauss, George. 1963. Some notes on power equalization. In *The social science of organizations.* Ed. Harold Leavitt. Englewood Cliffs, NJ: Prentice-Hall.

Suchman, Edward. 1967. *Evaluative research: Principles and practice in public service and social action programs.* New York: Sage Publications.

Taylor, Frederick. 1947. *Principles of scientific management.* New York: W. W. Norton. (Originally published in 1911.)

Terry, Larry. 2003. *Leadership of public bureaucracies.* 2nd ed. Armonk, New York: M. E. Sharpe.

The Urban Institute. 1975. *The status of productivity measurement in state government: An initial examination.* Washington, DC: The Urban Institute, State and Local Government Research Program.

———. 1981. *Developing client outcome monitoring systems.* Washington, DC: The Urban Institute.

Transparency International. 2006. Transparency International: About us. Available from Transparency International at www.transparency.org/about_us.

U.S. Secretary of Labor. 1996. *Working together for public service.* Report of U.S. Secretary of Labor's Task Force on Excellence in State and Local Government through Labor Management Cooperation, May.

Walton, Mary. 1986. *The Deming management method.* New York: Praeger.

Weber, Max. 1947. *The theory of social and economic organization.* Ed. and trans. A. M. Henderson and Talcott Parsons. New York: Free Press.

Weick, Karl E. 1995. *Sensemaking in organizations.* Thousand Oaks, CA: Sage Publications.

Weisbrod, Burton. 1975. Toward a theory of the voluntary nonprofit sector in a three-sector economy. In *The nonprofit organization: Essential readings.* Ed. D. L.Gies, J. S. Ott, and J. M. Shafritz. Pacific Grove, CA: Brooks/Cole, 1990.

Wolf, William B. 1974. *The basic Barnard: An introduction to Chester I. Barnard and his theories of organization and management.* Ithaca: New York State School of Industrial and Labor Relations, Cornell University.

Wood, A. M. 1998. Omniscient organizations and bodily observations: Electronic surveillance in the workplace. *International Journal of Sociology and Social Policy* 18: 136–74.

Zeithaml, Valarie A., A. Parasuraman, and Leonard L. Berry. 1985. Problems and strategies in services marketing. *The Journal of Marketing* 49: 33–46.

Zuboff, Shoshanna. 1988. *In the age of the smart machine: The future of work and power.* New York: Basic Books.

Chapter 7

Decision Making

By Ed Colley

Decision making is among the most complex and overtly political activities in organizations, whether those organizations are in the private, nonprofit, or government sector. Although elected officials and the courts formally make most basic policy decisions, unelected public service administrators in nonprofit and government organizations make crucial decisions about program implementation, staffing, and budgets—administrative decisions that have significant and lasting effects on public policy. Even apparently minor decisions about the day-to-day operating details of a program can have important consequences for how effective a program is and whom it reaches. The classic statement in public administration about the separation of politics and administration has become a debate concerning the proper domain of decision making in public organizations.

The methods or procedures that public organizations employ for decision making also have important political consequences. The decision method affects (and is affected by) who participates, how agendas are established, which alternatives are considered, how they are compared and analyzed, and which values dominate in the final selection. In no small way the *procedures* of administrative decision making affect the *substance* of choice. Therefore the method of decision making, like the domain, has important political consequences. Which method is best? On what grounds? For what problems or in what situations? Because of its importance,

> For many public executives, perhaps most, the exhilaration of choice is the primary reward for service and the chief ingredient in "morale." (Cleveland 1980, 183)

Organization theory is primarily concerned with the *methods* of decision making rather than the *domain*. For some time the organization theory field has focused on two decision-making methods and their variations: rational and incremental. The first is the classic model of *rational choice* among well-researched options. This is the implicit bureaucratic model of decision making in an expert hierarchy, and it has also been the classic model for economic and business decision making. The model has long been criticized as unrealistic; but it has more recently become linked to policy analysis, and as analysis has become more important, the rational method has gained new support and interest.

The *incremental–bargaining* method is the basic model of politics: conflict resolution through negotiation. Controversy surrounds this method, too. Many would agree that the method accurately describes decision making, but not as many support or condone choices made on this basis.

A third method has emerged in organization theory and administrative practice. Strategic planning, the Delphi process, and related techniques are termed here *aggregative* methods of decision making; organizations often introduce these complex and formal methods through the assistance of consultants and apply them in policy making and program development with staff or external governing boards. Consensus and equitable participation are hallmarks of such methods. An understanding of the political and technical implications of these methods is critical to successful use.

The fourth method, called by March and Olsen (1979a) the *garbage can* or non–decision-making (a somewhat misleading label) model, is an attempt to devise a descriptive model of choice that rejects even the limited rationality of incrementalism and focuses on the expressive character of decision making in organizations. Somewhat postmodern in its underlying approach, this model observes how discussions drift from their designated agendas to encompass a variety of personal and social issues as well as, or even instead of, the problems before the group. Some decisions emerge only by default and can almost be described as unintended. Perhaps most important, the decision-making process is viewed as uncovering and articulating goals in the process of discussing alternatives rather than evaluating the best way to achieve those goals. The process poses a serious challenge to conventional views of how nonprofit and government decisions are reached.

THE DECISION-MAKING PROCESS: SEARCH, ANALYSIS, AND CHOICE

This chapter considers these families of methods (that is, models) by focusing on three elements of decision making—the search for alternatives, the analysis of alternatives, and the choice criteria by which an alternative is finally selected and pursued—and placing these elements in a broader context that includes social and political influences, organizational culture, decision-making triggers, and action stemming from a choice. Thus the signal act of choice is only one element in the complex decision-making process, where the search for alternatives and the techniques for examining those alternatives are critical. Taken together the elements provide a general definition: *Decision making is a process that involves framing an issue or problem, identifying alternative courses of action, analyzing plausible alternatives based on subjective and objective criteria, and selecting among those alternatives (or deciding not to decide).*

Triggers

Organizations (more accurately, the people in them) make decisions at all levels for an endless variety of reasons. Most decisions are routine, and the conventions for when and how to make them are well established. However, for large issues and issues beyond the organizational routine, the organization typically must first recognize a need for affirmation or change as a precursor to working through a decision-making process. In other words, some pressure for change must *trigger* the search and decision process. For operational and policy issues, many things can serve as a trigger, but they tend to fall into categories. The first is an existing or anticipated performance crisis that could pertain to the organization, to one of its programs, or to a policy issue relevant to the organization (such as the prospect of a nonprofit organization's falling well short of a critical fundraising goal or the failure of an existing policy-based program to achieve key goals). The second category is criticism from outside the organization about real or perceived weaknesses and threats (such as a string of Mars probe failures at the National Aeronautics and Space Administration). The third category is a threat to the viability of an existing organization, organizational component, program or handling of a program, or current management approach (for example, any military facility listed for review by a Base Realignment and Closure Commission). For public organizations pressure to improve or else suffer some form of pruning can come from oversight organizations such as review boards and legislative subcommittees for federal agencies such pressure may come from the General Accountability Office (GAO). The fourth category is organizational leadership and vision. Whatever the impetus—internal, external, or both—something triggers the organization to embark on a nonroutine decision-making process, and that process begins with a search (Nichols 1993).

Search

Search embodies two phases. The first of these is to get smart about the issue or problem. If the focus is problem solving, the search involves separating symptoms from causes—sometimes called *root causes,* the term used in quality management settings. If the focus is a broader policy area, the search ranges across an array of factors that may include historical background, contextual influences, stakeholders and role of each group, and so on.

The second search phase is concerned with the organization's techniques for generating alternatives to improve current operations: The four families of decision-making methods differ radically in their search procedures. Brainstorming to identify innovations is a frequent feature of the aggregative method, whereas, by design, few truly novel alternatives emerge in the incremental method. Alternatives also originate from outside the organization. For all decision approaches, lures toward potential alternatives may include the widespread popularity of a possible solution (sometimes called the "bandwagon effect"), the promise a potential alternative seems to offer as a panacea (reorganizing or applying new technology), endorsements from consultants or key stakeholders (such as an oversight body), and personal interest or familiarity on the part of top leaders (for example, a new leader bringing ideas that worked from a prior organization) (Nichols 1993).

Analysis

The *analysis* element also clearly differentiates the methods. The rational method is typically quantitative and uses an array of analytic techniques, often from economics and engineering. Incrementalism also uses a sophisticated calculus; but this tends to be a political calculus, often based on determining how the benefits from each alternative are distributed among contending interests.

Choice

Finally, the *choice* element differentiates the methods. The rationalist method attempts to select the alternative that provides the optimal return for the resources expended, whereas the aggregative method places much weight on the preferences of key stakeholders. Table 7–1 compares differences among the methods in terms of search, analysis, and choice.

Contextual Definition

One other critical element in any decision-making process is how the issue is defined—an element that may lie largely beyond the influence of the administrator, especially if the process deals with sensitive policy issues. *Definition* influences search, analysis, and choice.

TABLE 7–1   Elements of the Decision Process

Decision Family	Search	Analysis	Choice
Rational	Preselected	Quantitative	Optimize gains
Incremental	Linked to status quo	Resource distribution	Group agreement
Aggregative	Brainstorming	Participation of experts	Group ranking
Garbage Can	Personal agendas	Sequential comparison	Choice is an artifact

How the problem gets defined often limits later processes, such as by disallowing search in certain areas of possible alternatives because of values, political beliefs, or the tactics of the administrators' political bosses. Likewise, definition influences evaluation of the problem, analysis of the allowed alternatives, and the basis for choosing among alternatives. Many times the definition is determined by the setting of the organization in the public sector.

THE SETTING OF DECISION MAKING IN PUBLIC ORGANIZATIONS

Several aspects of the settings for decisions in public agencies influence decisions. First, the domain or level of decision determines the degree to which administrators can act autonomously (at least under some constitutional arrangements) in making decisions—a consideration more true for government than for nonprofit organizations. Second, a number of theorists argue that the public setting limits the search for alternatives and thus narrows the options for choice. Third, the decision-making process in the organization is affected by the organization's communication, information-processing, and control systems. Finally, the public organization's political setting, its external relations, and the strength of its supporters and detractors influence the decisions made and perhaps the methods used as well because, in part, methods are linked to the substance of solutions.

Not surprisingly, questions about the proper domain of administrative decision making have been the subject of lengthy and intense debate in public administration. Kraemer and Perry (1983), in one of many portrayals of the various domains of organizational choice, suggest three levels of problems for organizations: operational, programming–management, and development or planning decisions. The appropriate type of analysis for problems at the day-to-day operational level is said to be the quantitative techniques such as operations research. These are choices where efficiency is the foremost concern and administrative autonomy in analysis and choice is most clearly appropriate. Kraemer and Perry further argue that decisions about program design are more appropriately made with a mix of qualitative and quantitative methods such as simulations of the specific social or economic system under analysis. Planning or development choices that involve organizational goals are seen as susceptible to qualitative analysis, such as the Delphi process.

Organization theory has not been particularly concerned with the link between the level of decision and the method of choice used to make it because the primary concern of the field as a whole has been with for-profit organizations, where such differences are usually matters of internal policy. A public organization perspective, however, must be concerned about this link because of the political and legal constraints on administrative authority over policy making.

Another characteristic of decision making in public organizations that has frequently been commented upon, especially by theorists writing from an economic perspective, is that the search for alternatives in public organizations is typically extremely limited; genuinely new options and innovations from which to choose are rare. A reason for this phenomenon, which is attributed to organizational factors in public organizations, is their reliance on standard operating procedures, scenarios, or what March and Simon (1993) term *performance programs*. What this term means is that the ways in which officials come up with alternatives are specified or programmed in advance. Most routine or programmed decisions are fully codified with respect to both the identification of options and the method and criteria for choice. This high degree of programming makes the public organization stable, consistent, and predictable, as required of an agent of law; but it also makes the organization rigid and reduces the possibility for innovation. The incrementalists are especially concerned with this constraint on decision making and discuss it at some length.

Decision making in any organization is also influenced by control and communication processes. As noted earlier, the communication system is the backbone of most types of organizational control because compliance with past program and policy choices is monitored through communication. Communication is critical to the integration of the specialized structures in the organization. It is also important in decision making because, regardless of the type of decision method used, some kind of information about the needs and opportunities of the organization, its resources, internal conflicts, and concentrations of influence is used as a basis for choice. If some information is suppressed or highlighted, and this is common (as described in Chapter 5), this distortion may be reflected in the decision. The timeliness of information, the extent to which the control system notices and can report departures from programs, the credibility and legitimacy of the information in the control system for professionals, and the degree to which we understand how to use the information in the control system to reform or improve the organization's programs all influence decision making. Each method of decision making has a different sensitivity to the weaknesses of communication and control systems, as discussed later in this chapter.

The political setting of decision making has a direct bearing on the specific choice made, and each model describes a different approach to incorporating political preferences—whether of officials or external actors—into the choice. For some policy analysts these questions are not broached, at least overtly, and issues are examined on the basis of economic factors. In other models of decision making, political factors are openly considered and choice involves a form of political calculus. The aggregative methods attempt to shun politics and eliminate it as an element in choice. The following discussions address assumptions about the role of the political setting in each model even though some models purport to ignore political issues.

The setting encompasses other characteristics, as well:

- Attitudes of stakeholders (including whether the concern involves an "our idea" versus "their idea" dynamic or an up-the-chain or down-the-chain recommendation).

- Whether officials within the organization use a goal-driven approach, a holistic approach, or neither.

- Whether the decision largely involves policy or administration and whether it is routine, involves some risk, or involves considerable uncertainty.

- Whether the decision is proactive or reactive.

- Whether the decision to be made involves a problem/transactional/defensive issue or a vision and transformation.

- Whether the decision is outcome oriented or process oriented.

- Whether the organization relies on centralized or decentralized decision making and individual or group decision makers: Is the prospective decision based on authority, majority, consensus, or unanimity? If it is a group decision, how is that group constructed (board, commission, ad hoc team)?

The purpose of this chapter, then, is to describe and contrast methods of decision making and to question the techniques and assumptions of each. After considering commonly raised criticisms of each method, the chapter contrasts decision methods in terms of search, analysis, and choice; the chapter then sets forth a contingency theory linking the methods to different conditions of choice.

THE RATIONAL–POLICY ANALYSIS METHOD

The rational method of decision making was long considered the ideal choice process in both the public and the private sectors. With an emphasis on analyzing a broad range of alternatives and a goal of optimizing efficiency and return on investment, the rational method was the ideal model for decision making. The emphasis on efficiency in achieving policy or goals set by external policy makers was well suited to the public sector role—at least in principle.

With the advent of research on administrative behavior, however, the rational method was criticized more and more for what were considered its unrealistic idealized assumptions, and it was overshadowed by the more empirically descriptive models, such as incrementalism and satisficing. The rational method has taken on new importance, however, in the context of policy and systems analysis. Modified forms of the classic rational model are now practiced as policy analysis, though they are used selectively due to their costliness and elaborateness. (See Table 10–1 in Chapter 10 for systems analysis techniques used in rational–analytic decision models.)

The rational–policy analysis method is *rational* in only one of two senses of the term. What we call *rational choice* is rational in that it attempts to select the most efficient means or instrument to realize a given purpose or goal; hence it is sometimes called *instrumental rationality*. It is concerned with identifying the alternative that produces the most of a desired effect or the greatest level of return. Efficiency is the only value that is promoted. In contrast, *substantive rationality* is concerned with many kinds of values and with the goodness of the goal or purpose itself. These questions are posed by substantive rationality: "Is it desirable?" "Should we want it if we are rational?" What is substantively rational is generally debated by political philosophers, and in more immediate terms by the legislative bodies, courts, and other policy makers in government. In general, administrative organizations may be more occupied with instrumental than substantive rationality, more with means than ends. Even so, the distinction between policy making and choosing the most efficient means or programs for the policy is not easily maintained in practice.

Instrumental rationality as a decision-making process is generally characterized by four steps (March and Simon 1993). First the goal or end of the policy is considered a given for the situation under consideration; that is, it is assumed that goals are set by external policy makers. It is also usually specified that all feasible alternatives or means to accomplish the goal are givens. Thus *in principle* search—the process that determines which alternatives will be considered—is not in the hands of administrators. This is one of the model's assumptions that is commonly found difficult and unrealistic. In fact, administrators usually determine the pool of alternatives to be analyzed, and political and technical considerations typically enter into the selection.

In the second step the alternative programs or procedures are thoroughly analyzed to identify all the consequences, desirable and undesirable, intended and unintended, associated with each alternative. These consequences may be known with certainty or may involve an element of uncertainty or risk. The analysis of these alternatives usually involves forecasting from experience.

The third step, a critical one, is to rank these alternatives according to a consistent ordering of preference for the set of consequences associated with each. Because each alternative has a different set of consequences, ranking the consequences becomes a step toward ranking the alternatives. For example, some alternatives under consideration may have economic and environmental consequences, others educational consequences. The importance of these consequences to the decision makers must be ranked before they can make an instrumentally rational choice.

In the fourth step the alternative with the greatest amount of the most valued consequences is chosen. The requirements of optimal efficiency have been met. The choice criterion is to optimize benefits or to select the alternative with the highest value. The simplicity of the final step is possible only because of the complexity of the preceding steps.

Instrumental rationality was long used as the normative standard against which to judge decisions in administration and elsewhere, despite the fact that by far the majority of decisions did not follow this method. Renewed interest in designing methods to improve instrumental rationality has sprung up with the advent of policy analysis and systems analysis in administration. Policy analysis is also concerned with examining the consequences of proposed alternative policies, programs, and operating procedures; it uses various economic and mathematical methods of analysis.

The rational decision method can be applied at any level of decision making. It is typically viewed as advisory to the policy-making process when goals and policies are at stake. The method is of direct and immediate administrative use for identifying efficient programs and operating procedures, however. Even though this distinction between decisions about means and ends is maintained in principle, it is not so clearly maintained in practice. This raises questions, of course, about the uses of the method.

Criticisms of the Rational–Policy Analysis Method

Questions have been raised about this decision-making method in terms of both its general feasibility and its use by public administrators. James March and Herbert Simon (1993) look at decision making as the core administrative activity and identify three unrealistic assumptions in the rational model. First, it is not clear how or by whom the alternatives to be analyzed and ranked are identified. Clearly not all possible alternatives are examined; imagination is limited, and selective perception is common. What sample of options is identified and studied, and on what basis are they selected? The model does not specify this or assumes that the alternatives are selected by policy makers. In essence, the research process, which is critical in determining the findings, is left unspecified. This may open the door to arbitrary or nonanalytic selection. The objectivity of the search process and its fidelity to the principle of efficiency are called into question if political considerations determine which possible programs will be analyzed.

The second of March and Simon's criticisms is that the rational method assumes the consequences of each alternative can be known, even if not with certainty. That is, the method assumes that the degree of risk or uncertainty will be known. This is a questionable assumption at best, as illustrated by such errors of planning and forecasting as the swine flu epidemic that never was and insufficient planning for the avian flu that poses a global threat, the aborted Iranian hostage rescue effort, the overestimation of the rate of increase in demand for electricity from nuclear power, and the underestimation of costs for programs such as Medicare. Not only do we overestimate or underestimate consequences, we also miss whole categories known as *unanticipated consequences*. This is not a criticism of the often considerable talents of forecasters and planners, but rather a counter to the grandiose claims made for the rational method and its comprehensiveness.

Finally, March and Simon criticize the classic rational method for its assumption that the decision maker, whether an individual or a group, has a consistent preference ordering for the consequences of the alternatives. The difficulty here is that few real options for new programs, for example, have only one *kind* of consequence; usually many consequences, desirable and undesirable, accompany a program. Fulfilling the requirements of the rational method involves not only comparing a set of alternatives on the basis of one type of consequence (environmental effects for example), but also comparing all the various consequences of the alternatives. For example, is the better choice Alternative A, which has some good but unlikely health consequences and some desirable environmental consequences, or is it Alternative B, which has a better chance of producing good health consequences but worse environmental and economic consequences? The problem is to establish a *consistent* ordering of preferences across the different alternatives being compared: This is an immense task even for a single individual, and the problem of finding such an ordering for a group is even greater. Economist Kenneth Arrow has shown that there is no unambiguous procedure for measuring and combining the preferences of two or more individuals to provide a ranking of total social preference (Stokey and Zeckhauser 1978, 276).

BOX 7–1 The Results of Absolute Efficiency

Are "efficiency" and "rational decision making" appropriate goals in and of themselves? Writers often test concepts and ideas by carrying them to their ultimate conclusion. Science fiction author Frank Herbert examines these two concepts in his series of books about Jorj X. McKie, Saboteur Extraordinary, and arrives at one possible outcome of such development. In his version, absolute efficiency and rationality are so dangerous that they must be stopped at any cost.

McKie began reflecting on his role in the affairs of sentiency. Once, long centuries past, consentients with a psychological compulsion to "do good" had captured the government. Unaware of the writhing complexities, the mingled guilts and self-punishments, beneath their compulsion, they had eliminated virtually all delays and red tape from government. The great machine with its blundering power over sentient life had slipped into high gear, had moved faster and faster. Laws had been conceived and passed in the same hour. Appropriations had flashed into being and were spent in a fortnight. New bureaus for the most improbable purposes had leaped into existence and proliferated like some insane fungus.

Government had become a great destructive wheel without a governor, whirling with such frantic speed that it spread chaos wherever it touched.

In desperation, a handful of sentients had conceived the Sabotage Corps to slow that wheel. There had been bloodshed and other degrees of violence, but the wheel had been slowed. In time, the Corps had become a Bureau, and the Bureau was whatever it was today—an organization headed into its own corridors of entropy, a group of sentients who preferred subtle diversion to violence . . . but were prepared for violence when the need arose.

The problem of finding a consistent preference ordering for the various consequences of different alternatives has been an important theoretical stumbling block for policy analysis. The way analysts have coped with this difficulty is to transform all types of consequences into one: money. Cost–benefit analysis is a key form of policy analysis. It is based on comparing the monetary value to society of all costs and all benefits of each alternative: then only one kind of consequence—financial—must be compared to find the optimal solution. The alternative that maximizes net benefit to society is the "best" and thus the one that is selected.

The rationale for this practice is found in two decision criteria. The Pareto criterion, named after the Italian economist and sociologist, states that a change should be made if at least one person benefits by it and no one is any worse off. This, of course, is a rare occurrence. More commonly applied is the Kaldor–Hicks criterion, named after two British economists, which argues that if a policy change makes the "gainers" so much better off that they can compensate the "losers" and still come out ahead, the policy should be undertaken. There is no requirement that this compensation actually take place, so in practice this criterion simply recommends maximizing net benefits—that is, benefits minus costs. This apparently undemocratic economic principle is justified on the grounds that, in the long run, the various program advantages will even out among the groups (Stokey and Zeckhauser 1978). Economist Lester Thurow, writing in 1980, promoted the role government plays in the redistribution of wealth. Recent analysis does in some cases look carefully at the specific distribution of a program's benefits to ensure that it will have the intended effect, though doing so does not address the problem of equity in distributing compensation.

Commonly noted drawbacks to the cost–benefit method point up further weaknesses in the rational–policy analysis method. The first is considerable disagreement over ways in which intangible benefits and costs are assigned monetary worth. This debate raises questions about race, gender, and other human political issues about which there is intense disagreement. In the area of public health and safety, how should life or the absence of disability be valued monetarily? Clearly different people expend different amounts of money and effort to preserve health; while some jog and eat broiled fish, others enjoy steaks and cigarettes. A widely used measure of the value of health is the amount of productivity lost to the economy by illnesses of various kinds. Income losses for workers of different types, for example, are taken as an estimate of lost productivity. The problem with such an estimate is that it places the highest value on preserving the health of young white males at the expense of women, minorities, and older people. Although correction factors are now used with such data, their use illustrates biases that can enter into efforts to monetize intangible factors.

Another drawback of cost–benefit analysis as the cornerstone of a decision-making method is that it substitutes judgment based on economic factors or technical efficiency for professional judgment. Cohen (1980) argues that the use of cost–benefit analysis in the area of weapons systems makes it impossible to consider the value of flexible or multiple uses and strategies of some systems. The analysis asks instead what the most cost-efficient means is to fulfill a particular policy or mission. Cohen argues that this question places economists and engineers in the position of assessing the capacity of various weapons systems to fulfill some narrowly defined functions without considering the political or psychological factors associated with war or the need for flexibility. For example, a nuclear-powered ship costs much more than a conventionally powered one; therefore, if both can perform the same mission it is rational to select the conventional ship. However, the psychological deterrence capacity of a nuclear-powered fleet may be greater than that of a conventionally powered one, and a nuclear ship may respond better in unanticipated conditions, so a military judgment would favor nuclear power. Thus Cohen shows that military judgments are overshadowed by the technical requirements of the choice process. In general there is concern that using the cost–benefit technique as the principal method of choice will result in far too much emphasis on the measurable quantitative aspects of the alternatives under analysis and too little attention to professional judgments and intangibles.

Advocates counter these criticisms, noting that some analysis is better than none and certainly better than politically motivated efforts to obscure differences among policies. Even flawed analyses improve our choices by forcing us to examine our assumptions and their consequences. For example, problems in monetizing intangibles often merely reflect current social practices that should be scrutinized and changed. In sum, even problematic analyses can lead to greater awareness of inequities in prevailing social and political practices, especially when augmented by forms of trade-off analysis that do not rely exclusively on monetized benefits and costs (Hammond, Keeney, and Raiffa 1998).

Finally, the issue of the political impact of the cost–benefit method has been the subject of some debate. In general, advocates of the method argue that it is objective and apolitical in any partisan sense, and that in the realm of policy making, its role is advisory rather than determinative. Thus they do not overstep the distinction between policy making and administration. Critics of the method argue that because it reflects a change in who makes decisions and how, changes in the political system are inevitable. Further, Gawthrop argues, "There are no neutral tools of administration, . . . and if, as some have contended, the analytical approach knows no politics, it will learn in short order if it is to survive" (1971, 75).

Illustrations of the political uses of some analyses include the finding by Merewitz and Sosnick (1971, 118) that program agencies, beneficiaries, and Democrats tend to favor low discount rates, a component of cost–benefit analysis that makes projects appear more efficient, whereas budget agencies, taxpayers, and Republicans tend to favor higher rates. Agencies may also place different discount rates on the same project, showing the degree to which the analysis is subject to differences of opinion. In debate over a major political policy like health care, the same data are used by the president, Congressional Republicans and Democrats, the Congressional Budget Office, and various interest groups to produce literally dozens of different results showing the impact of any particular set of programs, procedures, charges, and taxes. Thus both the possibility and the desirability of a wholly objective and apolitical stance for the rational–policy analysis decision process are questionable. Perhaps political questions require political solution processes. The incremental model is the most clearly political method.

THE INCREMENTAL MODEL AND RELATED METHODS

The 1950s brought behaviorism to the study of decision making and a concern for descriptive accuracy not met by the prescriptively oriented rational model in its original form. Decision making became an important focus of organization theory, perhaps because it was a relatively easily studied behavior. Decision theorists of that era developed several models that attempted to be empirically accurate—in particular the incremental and satisficing methods.

In general the incremental model portrays decision making as a bargaining process among interested participants, each of whom attempts to achieve some improvement in resources such as budgets, personnel, program authority, or autonomy. The "best" alternative is the one on which participants can agree. For the solution to be acceptable, each party must be better off by some increment of benefit. The classic description of the method was provided by Lindblom (1959).

Incrementalism is characterized by compromise—decisions that change programs or policies in small steps—and thus never departs far from the status quo. This is explained by the fact that incremental decision making is a bargaining process in which persuasion, debate, and negotiation, not analysis as the rationalist uses the term, are key features. Proposals and counterproposals are exchanged until a mutually acceptable solution is found. The immediate vicinity of the status quo is a good source of such solutions because only renegotiation of any new or changed resources and needs is required rather than comprehensive renegotiation of all resources. Such a renegotiation would be lengthy and conflict ridden. The incremental process strives to minimize conflict and allow the gradual testing of new ideas.

The incremental solution generally focuses on tangible programs and projects rather than on more abstract goals and policy statements. It is, Lindblom (1959) notes, much easier to compromise over concrete project components, such as the features of an educational grant or a highway project, than it is to bargain over ideology, principles, and goals. Program components can be apportioned among participants as part of the bargain, but goals and abstract policy statements are not so easily parceled out. Compromises about program size and resource share can be resolved without reopening the much more basic but intense issues of whether the goals are appropriate and the program should exist in the first place. In consequence, decisions made by the incremental method tend to be crisis oriented, internally fragmented, and even contradictory, and they are characterized as a series of changes in program activities rather than a specific statement of policy or organizational outcome.

Even as the incremental method is well suited to describing the activities of political decision-making groups such as legislatures, it also describes budget and policy decision making in public organizations, where multiple levels and divisions are involved in program development. In the case of administrative decision making, persuasion and bargaining occur among officials linked to professional, organizational, and constituency interests.

In summarizing the incremental over the rationalist method, Lindblom (1959) characterizes the incremental method as follows. First, clear value preferences are rare despite what the rationalist model claims. Generally decision makers can attach preferences only to specific proposals that may reflect abstract goals and values only indirectly. This is why incremental decision makers bargain over programs. A second characteristic deriving from this is that means (policies and programs) are not distinguishable from ends (goals and values). Third, the test of a "good policy" is that the actors agree on it, even though they may not be able to agree on its underlying values. Fourth, the analysis of alternatives is limited in both number and depth by considering only a few alternatives that depart marginally from the status quo. This means that some important new policy directions will be ignored and some legitimate values will not be heard; but Lindblom argues that the range of interests represented among the decision makers in the whole cycle is so broad that a nearly comprehensive range of realistically possible issues and options is, in fact, considered. Thus what appears as a fragmented process is really the working out of a decentralized pluralistic system that automatically coordinates itself as actors compete for support. The pluralistic assumptions of the method are a major justification for it; the method reflects the political system. Last, decisions reflect a series of successive approximations to multiple desired ends or values. This is necessarily

BOX 7–2 Comments on Rule Making: They Measure Pressure, Seldom Change Minds

There is more ado to interpret interpretations than to interpret the things and more books upon books than upon all other subjects; we do nothing but comment upon one another.
—Michel de Montaigne

The people in the Office of Adolescent Pregnancy Programs, with 80,000 written comments sitting in front of them, know what the 16th-century French philosopher was talking about.

When the Health and Human Services Department moved this spring to require doctors to notify a teenager's parents before dispensing contraceptive devices, the agency, thanks to a 1946 law, had to publish its proposal in the Federal Register and solicit public reaction. As a result, four staffers have been opening, sorting, analyzing, and summarizing comments for nearly six months.

Except in emergencies and special cases, the federal government must announce its intentions and invite response every time it tries to make or change a rule. This often means a time-consuming, exasperating, and predictable ritual for everyone involved—regulators, lobbyists, and citizens alike, according to those familiar with the procedure. Yet a recent effort to short-circuit the process has met with a strongly negative response by some of the same people who find it most exasperating.

Why does this procedural issue matter so much to so many people? According to lobbyists, government officials, and experts in administrative law, there are a variety of reasons, both theoretical and practical.

Philosophically, "it's important for the legitimacy of government to say, 'We will listen to anybody about this issue,'" said a former Carter administration regulatory expert. "I think it is fundamental that people have a chance to participate in decisions, however marginal that participation may be."

That's the theory. In practice, according to one lawyer–lobbyist who often drafts comments for a variety of regulatory agencies, "comments rarely change minds."

Groups . . . who use a comment period as a political referendum usually give regulatory officials few facts to consider but effectively convey the volatility of an issue. "This sort of thing is far more influential in terms of indicating the strength of the opinions held than giving us a particular view of the state of the world and answering the substantive questions we've asked," said Richard Wilson, an FERC official who has analyzed many of these comments.

Mike Roudemeyer, a staffer at the Federal Trade Commission, agrees. As a procedural device, he said, the comment period works to the benefit of lobbyists who object to something an agency proposes to do.

"Using comments as a referendum, a vote, that's not really very effective," Roudemeyer added. Yet when a friend suggested that he write HHS's Office of Adolescent Pregnancy Programs protesting the proposed rule on parental consent, he was tempted.

"I saw it as a political rule," Roudemeyer said, "and in that situation you should bring political pressure to bear."

SOURCE: Felicity Barringer, *Washington Post*, October 6, 1982, A23. Copyright © 1982, The Washington Post. Reprinted with permission.

a political rather than an empirically analytical process because we do not have the theoretical understanding of how to achieve policy success. Thus the incremental method of successive approximations avoids costly or lasting mistakes and moves gradually toward the multiple goals of a complex pluralistic society.

Innovation and Incrementalism

The search processes associated with the incremental method are constrained for several reasons. Lindblom (1959) argues that the bargaining process favors limited change. But other theorists see bureaucratic organization itself as responsible for limited search that favors options close to the status quo. The search for new programs and approaches requires planning, research, and professional development, all of which are costly and take personnel away from their ongoing work. Incremental changes are easier to correct if found to be wrong. The tendency of administrators to spend time on immediately pressing projects and to react to crises rather than to plan is commonly observed. The high degree of organizational and program specialization in most public organizations, especially the older, more entrenched ones, also works against the pursuit of novel programs (Downs 1967).

Another interesting and well-developed thesis about the causes of narrow search is that new decision options are limited by the organization's standard operating procedures. March and Simon (1993) characterize standard operating procedures as a series of organizational performance programs composed of an elaborate and more or less rigid set of prescribed routine activities. These programs are the product of program development and reflect operating improvements added over years to make program mechanisms operate smoothly, reliably, and efficiently. When a problem is encountered, an organization with highly codified procedures will be able to deal with the situation in an efficient, programmed manner, choosing the routine that dovetails with other established routines. Although this process is efficient, it limits the development of innovative alternatives to deal with problems. Graham Allison (1971) illustrates the drawbacks of highly codified performance routines in his study of the United States' response to Soviet missiles in Cuba: The routine procedures for classifying and acting on certain military situations virtually blinded military advisers to other alternatives.

James Q. Wilson, although agreeing that the use of standard operating procedures does limit choice processes, argues that the limitations come from the political environment and not from within the organization. First, the constraints that limit choices, which are said to be the result of the "bureaucracy's love of red tape," do not come from the bureaucracy at all. Most of the rules producing this complexity would not be generated by the bureaucracy if it had a choice, "and many are as cordially disliked by the bureaucrats as by their clients." These rules are imposed on the agencies by external actors, chiefly legislators. The rules are not bureaucratic but political ones. Legislators—whatever they may claim—value "fairness" over effectiveness (Wilson 1989, 121–22).

Second, the government organizations develop standard operating procedures to reduce the chance that an important contextual goal or constraint is not violated. The organization cannot serve a single, primary goal such as "making a profit." In addition to its primary goal, any government organization

> must serve a large number of contextual goals—that is, descriptions of desired states of affairs
> other than the one the agency was brought into being to create. For example, a police department
> not only must try to prevent crime and catch criminals, it must protect the rights of the accused,

safeguard the confidentiality of its records, and provide necessary health services to arrestees. These other goals define the context within which the primary goals can be sought. (129)

Whatever the cause of the development of standard operating procedures, once established these routines are not easily altered. Because they represent great sunk costs with respect to training, personnel, and specialized facilities and equipment, the most rational (efficient) response to a novel situation is to redefine the situation to fit the routine, or to modify in some small way an existing routine, or to combine existing programs. Only if protests or damaging failures result will new routines and new alternatives be created, usually at considerable cost. Other conditions associated with gaining extended search are new funds especially allocated for it (Montjoy and O'Toole 1979) and such things as allowing a long time for decision making, bringing many diverse people into the decision process, increasing the number of highly skilled people in the process, and isolating decision makers from other (especially short-term) responsibilities (Downs 1967, 185).

In sum, for the incrementalist, two lines of reasoning explain why final decisions and even the options for choice do not depart much from the status quo in public organizations. First, the bargaining process requires the distribution of limited resources to a coalition large enough to gain adoption of the alternative. Generally the easiest way to ensure such support is to distribute new resources on the basis of past resource distributions, rather than confronting fundamental questions of value. The latter course of action could result in conflict and deadlock. Second, the search process is limited by the standardized operating procedures that make the public organization consistent and efficient.

Satisficing

An alternative formulation that resembles the incremental method in several ways is the satisficing method of organizational decision making offered by March and Simon (1993). Compared with the rational method, both search and the process of analyzing alternatives are simplified, but these steps are somewhat more rational than the process in the incremental model. Satisficing takes the perspective of a single decision maker or a unified group and attempts to optimize, rather than maximize, the return or results from the choice among possible alternatives. The first step in this process, after agreeing on a goal, is for the decision maker to choose the desired level of response to be sought as the available alternatives are screened. The desired level is seldom, if ever, the best possible response, but instead is a choice aimed at what would appear to be a reasonable improvement given what is known about the current situation. It is an educated guess based on imperfect knowledge, and if a group is involved, it may be a choice based on agreement as to which step is to be taken without agreeing on the ultimate end of the policy. The agreement on a goal for "improvement," however, means that the decision maker is attempting to reach beyond the first alternative that shows any improvement in the situation to a predetermined level of improvement. This adds one level of rationality in the form of forethought about desired goals related to this decision.

Once the level of improvement is agreed upon, the first alternative encountered that meets or exceeds the decision maker's expectations or demands will be chosen. If, after search, such alternatives are not found, the decision maker's expectations and the minimum standard will decline. Thus the standard is flexible over time as experience with the environment informs the decision maker's expectations.

In contrast to the incremental model in which various alternatives are examined simultaneously, *satisficing* examines alternatives sequentially, being content with the first one to meet the minimum standard. Search is likewise sequential and is limited to the vicinity of the status quo for the reasons identified earlier. March and Simon contrast their method with the rationalist one as "the difference between searching a haystack to find the sharpest needle in it and searching a haystack to find a needle sharp enough to sew with" (1993, 162).

The differences between Lindblom's incremental model and the satisficing model are interesting. Satisficing assumes a preestablished standard rather than a group negotiation process. In this way satisficing is closer to the rational model. Also, the sequence in which alternatives are discovered is much more important in the satisficing model, so the search process, current environmental events, and professional interests are likely to have more of an impact with satisficing than with incrementalism. Both models reveal the dynamics of organizational decision making, however, and they may be related. Satisficing appears to describe how individual decision makers act, whereas the incremental model more often describes group or interactive decision making in larger, perhaps more political, settings.

Mixed Scanning

Mixed scanning is another variation on the incremental model, one that attempts to rectify some of that model's limitations. Etzioni (1967) describes *mixed scanning* as a dual method of search and decision making that does not fully accept either the rationalist model, which is expensive and slow, or the incrementalist model, which is biased toward status quo groups and issues. Rather, a cursory "big picture" review of all alternatives precedes zooming in for a detailed analysis of the most promising options. In this way innovations have a chance to be noticed, but a full-scale search need not be done each time. Government budgeting exemplifies this model: The entire budget receives initial consideration, including the budget's base (usually most of the overall budget); then the base is set aside so the increments (changed areas) are closely reviewed.

The decisions are also of mixed types. For example, a series of incremental decisions may follow a more fundamental choice of values. To focus on either type to the exclusion of the other is unwise and unrealistic.

Thus the mixed scanning method is offered as both a description and a prescription. It is descriptive in that fundamental change is more common than can be accounted for by the incremental method; it is prescriptive in its criticism of incrementalism and in its emphasis on the importance of fundamental, value-ordering decisions. For these reasons "mixed scanning seems to have an intuitive appeal to a fair number of scholars and action-oriented students of decision making" (Etzioni 1986, 13).

Criticisms

The incremental model is subject to criticisms on both technical and political bases. Technical criticisms include the fact that without systematic planning and analysis, decisions assume a short-term perspective, neglect basic social innovations, and lead to policy drift (Etzioni 1967). Available research and past experience may not be effectively incorporated into new choices. Conflict may become a major problem, sapping the energy of the decision process and leading to stalemate and costly delays in action. Innovation, as noted earlier, is not a common result of incrementalism, and this may retard program development as promising new alternatives are rejected or, more likely, never even considered.

Criticisms of the political consequences of the method include the charge by both Gawthrop (1971) and Etzioni (1967) that it disenfranchises significant portions of the population.

Etzioni further notes that the method is set to reflect only well-organized powerful interests that have influence with legislative and administrative decision makers; only those who have the skill and resources to play the game can participate. The pluralism claimed for the model is seen as providing only limited access to decision making. Further, Gawthrop argues that the process is dominated by intense regional interests to the detriment of less well-organized national interests. Finally, both Gawthrop and Etzioni note that the model is pro inertia and serves, in fact, as a justification for responsiveness only to influential interests. Intangible values, such as equity, are also generally ignored because they cannot be adapted to piece-meal distribution. In sum, incrementalism rests on a pluralistic model of American politics but cannot fully live up to the demands of that political model. At least partly in response to these criticisms, an attempt to eradicate influence from decision making is seen in the aggregative method.

PARTICIPATIVE METHODS OF DECISION MAKING

Over the years a third method of group (that is, participative) decision making has emerged in public and private sector organizations. The techniques included under this method are prescriptive—we are urged to use them to solve problems—and are designed to embrace multiple viewpoints. Examples of the method include strategic planning, scenario development and analysis, and consultant-assisted processes such as the Delphi technique and the nominal group technique (NGT).

In general, with these techniques group members are coached on how to generate a wide range of alternatives. One alternative is finally selected through some type of voting or consensus process. The final choice is said to be an accurate composite (or aggregation) of individual preferences rather than a negotiated synthesis of preferences such as what emerges in the incremental method. The aggregative methods seek to avoid the political conflict and stalemate that may arise under incrementalism. Advocates assert that the aggregative methods allow groups (1) to generate a broader, more diverse, and more innovative set of alternatives than either the rationalist or incrementalist methods; (2) to avoid the stifling influence of status and claims of expertise by some participants; and (3) to avoid the constraints of overly routinized standard operating procedures. Brainstorming is encouraged, and premature criticism of new ideas is avoided. The hallmark of these techniques is that they attempt to maintain a healthy, well-balanced level of group interaction without the excessive conformity or conflict found in some public organizations and elected bodies.

Groups using these techniques include staff, external expert advisory councils, and elected boards and councils. Often the techniques are used for planning, identifying and setting priorities among problems and projects, identifying future needs and resources, and goal setting. Implementation tactics and timetables may also be included in their process.

The *Delphi* technique is typically used as a planning or forecasting method in which experts in a field are assembled and are asked to individually generate a list of future states regarding some problem in the field. For example, the International City and County Management Association (ICMA) might want to know what the top priorities of city managers will be in the year 2010. These lists are collated and fed back to the group for discussion and another round of list making, ranking, and feedback. This process may be repeated several times to narrow the alternatives under consideration and reach consensus about priorities or future probabilities.

Even as the Delphi process intentionally affords much less interaction than the incremental method, the *nominal group technique* (NGT) allows less interaction than either the Delphi or incremental method and illustrates the procedures and assumptions of the increasingly popular aggregative method of decision making. The name of the technique, nominal group, tells us its orientation. The participants form a group in name only. Interaction of any kind, but especially political exchange, is kept to a minimum. Expressing individual ideas and preferences free from the influence of others is the technique's chief characteristic. In their description of the NGT, Delbecq, Van de Ven, and Gustavson note, for example, that it is important to "reduce status barriers among members, encourage free communication, and decrease the tendency for high-status individuals to be unduly verbal" (1975, 42). Each phase in the NGT shows its emphasis on minimizing interaction that could confound the natural inclinations of the participants.

The first stage in the process is establishing a clear question or problem for the group to work on. This is the consultant's job. The question should be clear, direct, and specific enough so that results will readily translate into action. Coke and Moore illustrate a good and a poor question:

> *Poor question*: "What are the goals to be achieved and the projects and programs to be undertaken in the city's community developments?" *Good question*: "What obstacles do you anticipate to carrying out the city's housing rehabilitation programs?" (n.d., 3)

The decision process itself begins with the "silent generation of ideas in writing" (Delbecq, Van de Ven, and Gustavson 1975, 44) in which each participant in a group of five to nine people works alone on a list of goals, projects, or whatever is needed. The purpose of this individual exercise is to maximize the variety of views expressed at the outset without inhibition from group criticism. The next step is to have each participant read aloud his or her list until all lists have been recorded. This simple step is important because it demonstrates to participants the breadth of possible solutions and the degree of consensus that already exists. It also prevents the group from prematurely settling on one definition of the problem (Delbecq, Van de Ven, and Gustavson 1975, 49).

Discussion of the items is not permitted until all the lists have been recorded so as not to inhibit ideas. After recording is completed, however, as the third step in the process, each item is given a limited discussion to clarify its meaning and logic. Lobbying for an item or arguments are seriously discouraged, however, and group leaders are urged to intervene nondirectively and move the discussion along to the next item if conflict occurs. The intention here is to prevent a high-status member from dominating the group "even though other members still disagree with his or her logic" (Delbecq, Van de Ven, and Gustavson 1975, 52).

The final steps in the process are concerned with voting to select the goal or program or to rank order the items generated. First, to reduce the number of items to be ranked, each participant is asked to select his or her highest priorities from the overall list, generally five of them, which are then combined into a joint list for the group. From this list the group then votes or uses some other ranking technique to identify the most favored items. Various voting procedures are used. For example, each participant may use a five-point numerical scale to rank items (5 being high and 1 being low). The item with the highest ranking is given top priority and so on. Having each participant use the more traditional system of voting for only one item is believed to underrepresent minority views and open the door to the kind of conflict and influence peddling that the technique is designed to avoid.

The objective of the technique is to foster the expression of individual judgment. Consensus based on the true preferences of group members can be fostered by having a preliminary round of rank ordering followed by discussion aimed at clarifying pros and cons of each item. Computer-assisted ranking procedures can also be used to identify the group's choice. With these techniques the participants vote their preferences on a comparison of each pair of items, which yields an overall rank ordering (Ostrowski, White, and Cole 1984).

Strategic Planning

A still more elaborate participative decision-making approach is *strategic planning*, a process organizations use to determine critical long-term goals and short-term actions that further the organization's mission. Strategic planning is distinct from other forms of organization-based planning in that it focuses on mission-critical goals, it involves an extended planning horizon of typically 5 or 10 years, and it tries to anticipate the organization's external environment over that time frame.

Increasingly an organization's strategic planning cycle meshes with its budget planning cycle. This is particularly true for federal organizations—largely thanks to the Government Performance and Results Act (GPRA) of 1993—and for agencies in states that have adopted outcome-based budget requirements. GPRA requires every federal department, agency, and bureau to

- Develop and maintain a strategic plan that articulates "a comprehensive mission statement" and sets out "general goals and objectives, including outcome-related goals and objectives, for the major functions," along with external factors than could affect agency performance.
- Develop an annual performance plan tied to the strategic plan, setting out anticipated results at a given level of investment for each program and measures by which to assess the target level of performance,
- Use the annual performance plan as the outline for its proposed budget.
- Provide an annual program performance report, highlighting actual investment and results for each program and explaining variances from the original performance plan (GPRA 1993).

In effect GPRA gives strategic planning formal status as a decision-making support tool for federal officials and congressional committees.

As Figure 7–1 depicts (and to some degree as GPRA prescribes), strategic planning involves several elements:

- Analyzing the organization's mission and its stakeholder groups.
- Articulating or reaffirming the organization's guiding values and vision for operating in the future.
- Establishing goals to achieve the mission.
- Identifying strategies to enable the goals.
- Defining measures by which to determine the organization's effectiveness in achieving its strategies, goals, and mission.
- Developing specific actions that bring the plan into being.
- Undertaking and monitoring those actions.
- Evaluating actions along with key aspects of the internal and external environment.
- Using the gained knowledge to revisit the organization's mission and its stakeholders.

FIGURE 7–1 Strategic Planning Cycle

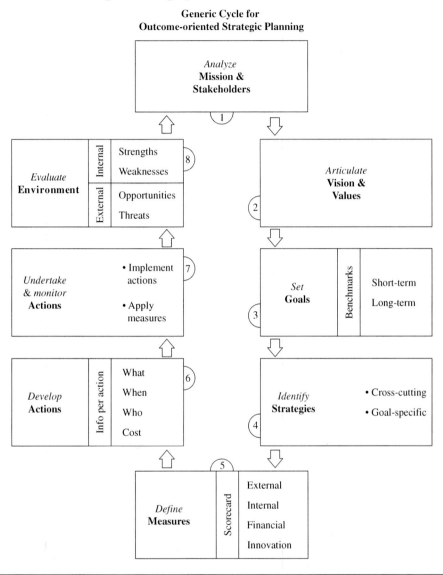

Generic Cycle for
Outcome-oriented Strategic Planning

Organizations adapt strategic planning to their own needs and culture, so the actual process varies greatly from one organization to another and even within the same organization over time. Organizations might add or skip steps and sequence them differently. At times several steps may be under way simultaneously. Officials in different components and levels of the organization may become involved at different stages in the process; for example, a variant known as Hosien planning has top executive levels setting overall direction and goals, then "bouncing" the plan down to officials at lower levels to fill in how those goals will be accomplished (that is, to describe the actions).

Analyze Mission and Stakeholders

Most organizations today have a brief mission statement articulating, in an easy-to-read sentence or two, what the organization is and why it exists. Often mission statements are more than a paragraph long. The first sentence or so constitutes the core mission, and the additional material provides context and goals. For government organizations the *mission statement* is drawn from the legislation that establishes the organization itself, though in more commonplace language; for nonprofit organizations the mission is based on what those who established the organization have set out in its charter documents. Creating a mission statement is a way of affirming to people inside and outside the organization what the fundamental purpose of that organization is. Though it usually need not change much over time (except to become shorter and clearer), the mission statement should be reviewed each planning cycle to be sure that it clearly and accurately reflects the essential purpose of the organization. Box 7–3 provides examples.

Organizations need a realistic understanding of their *stakeholders*—that is, groups likely to affect or be affected by the organization. Stakeholders can be classified into categories such as employees and vendors, clientele and the public at large, oversight entities, and competition and critics; each stakeholder group can be subdivided in ways appropriate to the organization.

Oversight entities vary depending on the organization and include, for example, parent agencies; governing boards; municipal councils; legislative subcommittees; accrediting bodies; and, for federal organizations, inspectors general (IG) and the Office of Management and Budget (OMB) within the executive branch and the General Accountability Office (GAO) within the legislative branch. Taken broadly, the category of oversight stakeholders may also encompass groups wary or critical of the organization and its objectives, such as interest groups holding countervailing perspectives on policy areas in which the organization is involved (for example, environmental groups and economic development groups as outside stakeholders for a state environmental regulation agency). Competition exists among government organizations as well as nonprofit organizations. Competition might come from other organizations providing similar services, from organizations seeking funding from a given source (such as appropriations and grants), and from a general phenomenon sometimes called "continuously rising expectations": not remaining satisfied with things as they are.

The most detailed stakeholder analysis is typically of the organization's clientele—individuals and groups the organization's mission is to serve, considering both who they are today and how they may change in the future. A regulatory agency, for example, may classify its clientele by business or household size (measured by any of a number of elements), type of regulation oversight required, compliance history, and other factors. Box 7–4 provides a classification example based on defensive and offensive client attitudes. A realistic understanding of clients, the public, and other stakeholders is essential not only for strategic planning but, more generally, for other types of informed organizational decision making.

Articulate Vision and Values

In strategic planning a *vision* is the organization's concept of the impact it aspires to achieve and how it hopes to operate at a given time in the future. (That given time is known as a *planning horizon*. Most organizations use 5- and sometimes 10-year planning horizons for strategic planning; however, organizations dealing with long-term infrastructure development may apply far longer planning horizons as they project needs many decades into the future.) For example, expressed in operational terms, the mission of Big Brothers Big Sisters is simply

BOX 7–3 Mission Statements from Government and Nonprofit Organizations

These mission statements come from a range of public organizations. Longer statements have been truncated or abridged.

American Association of University Women (AAUW)   *Nonprofit*
Promoting education and equity for women and girls.

American Association of School Administrators (AASA)   *Nonprofit*
. . . to support and develop effective school system leaders who are dedicated to the highest-quality public education for all children.

Big Brothers Big Sisters   *Nonprofit*
To help children reach their potential through professionally supported, one-to-one relationships with measurable impact.

International Committee of the Red Cross (ICRC)   *Nonprofit*
. . . to protect lives and dignities of victims of war and internal violence and to provide them with assistance.

Public Housing Authority, Fort Wayne, Indiana   *Local*
. . . to provide good quality, affordable housing and superior services to eligible members of the Fort Wayne community and to maintain an atmosphere that encourages self-sufficiency.

Florida Department of Highway Safety and Motor Vehicles   *State*
. . . making highways safe through service, education, and enforcement.

Florida Department of Juvenile Justice (DJJ)   *State*
. . . to protect the public by reducing juvenile crime and delinquency in Florida.

General Accountability Office (GAO)   *Federal*
. . . to support the Congress in meeting its constitutional responsibilities and to help improve the performance and ensure the accountability of the federal government for the benefit of the American people.

Office of Management and Budget (OMB)   *Federal*
. . . to assist the president in overseeing the preparation of the federal budget and to supervise its administration in executive branch agencies.

Internal Revenue Service (IRS)   *Federal*
[To] provide America's taxpayers top-quality service by helping them understand and meet their tax responsibilities and by applying the tax law with integrity and fairness to all.

World Trade Organization (WTO)   *Transnational*
The World Trade Organization (WTO) is the only global international organization dealing with the rules of trade between nations. At its heart are the WTO agreements, negotiated and signed by the bulk of the world's trading nations and ratified in their parliaments. The goal is to help producers of goods and services, exporters, and importers conduct their business. [Abridged]

BOX 7–4 Defensive and Offensive Clients of Organizations

Public organizations deal with segments of the public. Sometimes that relationship is involuntary on the part of the public (such as in dealing with tax and regulatory agencies); at other times members of the public deal with an organization voluntarily (for example, to obtain services for which they are eligible).

| *Stakeholder: Client/Public* | | | *Organization* |
Attitude	Character	Behavior	Response
Defensive	Newbie	Client is new to this program and may have little understanding of how to proceed.	Explain process and client responsibilities; guide client through process.
	Good faith	Client is generally familiar with this program and trying to comply but lacks confidence and is unsure of potentially relevant technical aspects.	Make guidance available and assist where requested; alert client to likely problems and opportunities.
Offensive	Aggressive	Client exploits questionable opportunities and loopholes in program.	Monitor/review client activity to ensure compliance with program parameters.
	Abusive	Client willfully evades the law or rules underlying the program.	Identify and prosecute willful evasion.

to "Provide a mentor for every child who wants or needs one." The mission has a larger social impact aspect: ". . . successful mentoring relationships for all children who need and want them, contributing to better schools, brighter futures, and stronger communities for all."

Organizations have the same values as the larger society they are part of. As with people, however, different organizations emphasize different values within the societal set of values. The Alexandria, Virginia, Fire Department, for example, declares that it values service delivery, people, integrity, leadership, community involvement, teamwork, employees, and communication.

Set Goals

Goals are high-level statements expressing aspects of how the organization pursues its mission. Sometimes goals are explicit within a mission statement: The "tripartite" mission of the University of Maine, for example, is expressed in terms of "learning, discovery [research], and service." Other times goals are derivable from the mission. Some goals are specific, shorter-term objectives, whereas others are longer-term and sustaining.

Identify Strategies

Strategies are basic approaches enabling the organization to address its goals. A given strategy may apply to a single goal (be goal-specific) or may contribute to several goals (be cross-cutting). For example, a nonprofit organization's strategy to increase membership may contribute to its goal of greater fiscal solvency and also to its goal of having a stronger voice in the policy arena.

Define Measures

During the planning process is the time to establish performance targets and mechanisms that track the extent to which the organization is achieving its mission, goals, and strategies. Performance measures need to be observable, reliable, and preferably quantifiable. "Capture mechanisms" are processes within the organization that secure performance data. Larger organizations often use "nested" performance measures so that lower-level performance measures relevant to the frontline aspects of the organization roll up into program-level measures and ultimately into a handful of mission-level or strategic performance measures (Nichols 1997). Good measures take into account multiple aspects of performance and accountability; consequently they do not focus only on efficiency or effectiveness, for example. This concept of multidimensional performance measures, discussed in Chapter 6, is sometimes known as a balanced scorecard; the scorecard incorporates measures that look at internal, external, financial, and innovation aspects of the organization's performance (Kaplan and Norton 1992).

Develop Actions

A strategic plan documents two levels of organizational decision making: At one level it is a policy blueprint articulating the organization's basic heading and priorities—a navigational guide. At a second level it is an operational blueprint for implementing strategies that support the organization's mission and goals. This second level is an implementation plan of specific actions that make the strategies and goals actually happen. What steps does it take—perhaps over several years—to put a given strategy in place to pursue a strategic goal? That step is called an *action*. Each action (such as setting up a new outreach program) involves (1) a thumbnail description of *what* is involved, (2) *who* in the organization has primary and cooperating responsibility for implementing the action, (3) the deadline *when* that action is to be completed or become operational, and (4) in rough terms the anticipated *cost* necessary to bring about the action.

Undertake and Monitor Actions

Unimplemented decisions remain only ideas, so an effective strategic planning process engages many parts or levels of the organization. This phase involves disseminating the planning information, orienting and training to bring the entire organization on board, undertaking actions the plan prescribes, tracking implementation progress, and beginning to monitor performance measurements at operational and strategic levels (Carr, Littman, and Condon 1995).

Evaluate Environment

This phase of a strategic planning cycle might as easily be listed as the first step. Looking outside as well as inside the walls of the organization is crucial for intelligent planning; fortunately useful evaluative decision support tools abound. Three of those tools are environmental scanning, trend monitoring, and SWOT analysis.

Environmental scanning is a practical look at what seems to be taking place outside the organization now and by a defined point in the future:

> Since plans are based on forecasts and forecasts are based on assumptions about the future, scanning the horizon is always prudent to identify new developments that can challenge past assumptions or provide new perspective to future threats or opportunities. Environmental scanning systems provide early warning about important changes and detect "weak signals" that indicate plans should be amended. (Gordon and Glenn 1994, 1)

Scans are easy-to-assimilate reports on "what's out there" that may be relevant to the organization and its own plans for the future. News media, trade publications, university research, reports about emerging technologies, growing environmental and social issues, and other materials—including selected interviews with experts in fields of interest to the organization—all contribute to the scan, which may be broadly based and general or may be targeted to a particular issue (perhaps specialized skills in the workforce).

Incipient trends identified through environmental scanning can be monitored to assess their potential impact as opportunities and threats for the organization. (Trends are discussed further in Chapter 10.) The information can then be used in an evaluation of the strengths, weaknesses, opportunities, and threats facing the organization. This is called a *SWOT* analysis. Strengths and weaknesses are internal assessments of the organization itself: What does the organization do especially well? Where does it chronically fall short? Being frankly realistic is important but hard for an organization to do, just as it is tough for us as individuals. Opportunities and threats are external to the organization. Recognizing upcoming threats well in advance may help organizations mitigate them or even approach them as opportunities.

Such evaluations set the stage for the strategic planning cycle to repeat. Given the state of the organization, its mission and vision, and the environment as it may unfold, is the mission still appropriate? The goals and strategies? The actions and measures? These are key organizational decisions, but they are informed decisions when organizations apply strategic planning as a basic decision support system.

Alternative Scenarios

Another decision support tool is *scenario development;* in fact, scenarios are at the heart of a related family of aggregative tools used to aid decision making. *Scenarios* are brief descriptions of conceivable future settings drawn from projected trends and events. "Because the past often is an inaccurate predictor of the future, it is misleading to simply project past events with straight-line trends and create a plan around the projection" (Carr, Littman, and Condon 1995, 116). Although they cannot predict the future, scenarios help decision makers envision what might be possible, probable, and even preferred—and how the organization might operate in the environments described.

By constructing alternative scenarios (for example, a straight-line forecast, a rosy outlook, a pessimistic scenario, and an offbeat or "wild card" alternative view), decision makers can examine the practicality of proposed policies and practices. Ringland observes that "scenario planning is a set of processes for improving the quality of . . . educated guesses and also for deciding what the implications are, and when to gamble" (1998, 11). Consequently, for public organizations the object of scenario analysis is to make decisions that are *robust* (that is, effective) under a range of possible future environments.

Scenarios can accompany the strategic planning process, and a few organizations cast their strategic plans as scenariolike narratives (Shaw, Brown, and Bromiley 1998). Scenarios can also be developed as an outcome of the Delphi process. But most frequently they are a component of the strategic planning process or they stand as decision support tools in their own right. They tend to be aggregative in that many parties contribute to scenario development and analysis. And they can be as simple or elaborate as the organization is ready to address.

Questions and Criticisms

Research on the uses and results of the group process approaches for organizational decision making poses questions to be considered when the processes are used. First, to what extent will the process be considered legitimate in an organization and by its clientele? The incremental bargaining process is so ingrained in political life that a decision that eliminates negotiation and avoids the real, known distribution of influence may not be accepted. If the legitimacy of the process is questioned, the results may never be implemented.

A second question concerns the assumption that a group process gives the truest reading of group preference. Every step in the process is designed to eliminate the influence or persuasiveness of high-status or politically skillful leaders. The assumption that politics always acts to distort rather than articulate genuine preferences or interests should not go unquestioned: It rests on the broader unspoken judgment that politics serves only to manipulate unwary participants into acting against their real interests. This narrow view of politics rejects the possibility that politics can be a vehicle for articulating broad social interests and principles and can provide an alternative to the strictly economic allocation system. Persuasion, as the first art of politics, can clarify as well as obscure interests. And bargaining, as the incrementalists show, is an effective way of resolving conflicts over goals and resources.

Yet group process advocates' desire to rid group decision making of seemingly useless conflict and delay is understandable, and the techniques described are effective for that purpose. Group members, as well as the external constituencies who depend on the group, become frustrated when stalemate and delay result from obstructive behavior. The incrementalists may consider these behaviors part of the process of partisan negotiation, but from the social–psychological perspective (refer to Chapter 3) of group process, they appear pathological and fruitless. At times stalemate also appears politically purposeless, though of course it represents the blockage of unacceptable action by one group against another.

In some situations participative decision-making processes fail to measure up to their potential because of confusion about what is involved in a consensus-based decision process, which falls between majority vote (where more than half of those expressing a viewpoint must favor the decision) and veto (where one person can stop the decision). *Consensus* involves general—but not necessarily total—agreement for a proposed decision. Not everyone needs to agree fully or enthusiastically. Individuals may express varying degrees of support:

- Enthusiastic support for the proposed decision.
- Full support for the proposed decision.
- Acceptance of the proposed decision, though with concerns.
- Serious objection(s) to the proposed decision.

Consensus for a decision generally means that no more than one or two individuals express serious objections (which the group first attempts to work out) and that most individuals support the decision.

OTHER DECISION MODELS AND TOOLS

Not all organizational decision-making approaches fit comfortably under the headings of participative, incremental, and rational–comprehensive. Rounding out the discussion are garbage can metaphors, ethical reasoning, and an array of decision support techniques and tools.

The Garbage Can and the "Nondecision" Models

March and Olsen's garbage can model of decision making (1979a) is an attempt to accurately describe decision making in organizations. It goes beyond the incremental model in identifying the limits in rationality; and it suggests, finally, that the incremental and satisficing models posit a level of clarity of intentions, understanding of problems, and predictability in the relationship between individual and organizational actions that is unrealistic for most organizations. In actuality, they argue, decision making is an unreliable, ambiguous process for selecting courses of action. However, it serves as a forum for individual and group expression of conflict, values, myths, friendships, and power. In important ways decision making in organizations is more expressive of social and personal needs than it is strictly instrumental.

The garbage-can model rejects standard models of rational decision making. Instead, the garbage can model views the decision process as

> a choice opportunity as a garbage can into which various problems and solutions are dumpted [*sic*] by participants. The mix of garbage in a single can depends partly on the labels attached to the alternative cans; but it also depends on what garbage is being produced at the moment, on the mix of cans available, and on the speed with which garbage is collected and removed from the scene. (Cohen, March and Olsen 1979, 26)

In nonmetaphorical terms, garbage-can decision making is a mix-and-match process built around four factors: apparent problems, potential solutions (that may or may not apply to the problems), choice opportunities, and participants. Problems drop into the garbage can, participants fish around for possible solutions, and sometimes the opportunity comes along to apply an available solution to a problem. Mid-sized problems receive the most attention, minor problems may be overlooked, and major problems may overload this type of decision process. The garbage-can decision approach can serve as an expressive activity that provides an opportunity for fulfilling roles or earlier commitments, defining virtue and truth, interpreting events and goals, distributing glory and blame, reaffirming or rejecting friendships and status relations, expressing or discovering self-interest or group interest, socializing new members, and enjoying the pleasures of a group choice (March and Olsen 1979b, 11–12).

From the standpoint of this model, the rational and incremental models err in assuming too much certainty and knowledge in decision making. In reality, most decision-making situations are plagued with ambiguities of many sorts. Objectives are ambiguous; no clear set of preferences represents the organization's intentions; causality is obscure; technology is difficult to define and environments are not easily understood; past events are interpreted differently by participants; and the attention and participation of key actors are uncertain because other activities and other decisions compete for their time (March and Olsen 1979b, 12).

The consequences of these factors are that decision making is not seen as a single-minded method for goal attainment in which the optimal means to the end is selected. Instead decisions reflect shifts in the goals, beliefs, and attention of participants. Goals are defined—to the extent that they are ever clearly specified—only in the process of considering particular proposals and debating whether to accept or reject them. This pattern is shown in some of the case studies in the March and Olsen volume (Olsen 1979; Rommetveit 1979) and, with some adjustment in theory, by Anderson (1983) in his analysis of the Cuban missile crisis.

Anderson found no evidence that a set of alternatives was considered and an optimal one selected in that case (as the rational or even the incremental model would have us believe). Rather, he found that the decision was made through a series of binary (yes–no) choices on specific proposals. The goals that were eventually said to be served by U.S. actions in the crisis were not mentioned in early sessions and were "discovered," Anderson suggests, during deliberations (1983, 211). For very difficult problems, the decision makers did not necessarily select choices they thought would solve the problems, but ones that had reasonably predictable consequences and were not expected to produce either dangerous or successful results—what Anderson, after March and Simon (1993), terms a *bland alternative*. All these characteristics of decision making support aspects of the garbage can model, though evidence of the expressive uses of the decision-making process was not studied in this case.

A variation on the garbage can model is the artifactual or nondecision model, which focuses on the unconscious and unintentional aspects of decision making. What we think of as decisions, Olsen suggests (1979; see also Bachrach and Baratz 1962), are often just a socially acceptable reconstruction of what has occurred. Calling something a decision does not necessarily mean that there has been an act of deliberative choice. This view of decision making illustrates a phenomenological perspective on organizations in which what we ordinarily think of as reality is largely a social construction. Decisions here are interesting fictions.

Questions and Criticisms

The garbage can model has been less widely discussed and studied (for an exception see Kingdon 1995) than incremental and rational–comprehensive models; correspondingly, its application in public organizations has received patchy attention even though it is inherent in organizational decision making. The garbage can model is meant to be descriptive, but the circumstances in which it would tend to be more accurately descriptive than the incremental model have not yet been well explored. Olsen suggests that the nondecision model will be most accurate under conditions of change—that is, when organizational goals and opportunities are most ambiguous (1979, 83–85); but the case studies that accompany his essay do not necessarily support his generalization. The model is also said to apply under conditions of organized anarchy, but the limits of that state are not clear.

Much is yet to be done with the model to explore its policy implications. It is an interesting model, however, that reflects the field's emerging concerns with socially constructed realities and the ways in which organizations integrate and socialize their members.

Ethical Decision Making

It is difficult to imagine any approach for making good decisions that does not encompass a solid ethical foundation. As Chapter 2 discusses, ethical behavior and decision making in organizations—particularly in public organizations—have taken a place as topics of ongoing concern in the public mind, just as they should. Adams and Balfour warn that inattention to ethics in decisions within government organizations can, on a large scale, result in what they term "administrative evil":

> Administrative evil may be masked in many different ways, but the common characteristic is that people can engage in acts of evil without being aware that they are in fact doing anything at all wrong. Indeed, ordinary people may simply be acting appropriately in their organizational role—in essence, doing just what those around them would agree they should be doing—and at the same time be participating in what a critical and reasonable observer, usually well after the fact, would call evil. (1998, p. xx)

This danger exists for nonprofit organizations, as well, though the risks are not as great because the scope and authority of nonprofit organizations are not as great. Ethically reasoned

---

BOX 7–5 Framework of Analysis for Ethical Dilemmas

First it is necessary to make sure that the problem faced is an ethical dilemma. To verify this fact, there must be a positive response to these questions:

- Are important values in conflict in this case?
- Can those values be identified, or must additional effort be made to discover them?
- Is it necessary to analyze, calculate, or reason about which of the competing values must be served?

The recognition of the ethical dilemma *and* its analysis require sensitivity to, and ability to understand the factors influencing, *at least* the five following areas:

1. **The law:** What can relevant laws tell me about what I am expected to do in this case? (The term *law* includes established rules and regulation interpreting the substance *and* process of more general statutes.)
    a. What does the statute say—both the specific language and the context?
    b. What does the statute *not* say, and is there any hint as to why that was left unsaid?
    c. Is it possible to go beyond the specific words of the law and understand the intent of those establishing the law?
    d. What do I do if the law is wrong or does not apply to my case?

2. **The philosophical and cultural setting:** Can I learn important factors about this situation by examining the basic philosophical and cultural elements that create ethical perceptions and determine what responses are acceptable?
    a. What can an understanding of the culture tell me about the way significant others perceive the issues I face and what their expectations are?
    b. Do the tenets of political philosophy on which our expectations are founded help to clarify the values that are important to the dilemma at hand, and can they help me frame the proper questions to ask?
    c. What are the basic American political values, and how can I guarantee that I stay true to them in my decisions and actions?
    d. Do the principal actors in the case at hand interpret the political values in the same way? If not, what are the differences in interpretation?

decisions do not happen automatically, especially when the decisions involve tension between underlying ethical values (fairness and compassion, honesty and loyalty) or what might be called the conflict of right versus right.

Ethical decision making is based on principled reasoning about the issues in a situation, the facts in dispute and not in dispute, the stakeholders and their varying interests, the ethical values (integrity, excellence) and principles (maximizing benefit while minimizing harm) that come into play, and a sense, based on these considerations, of "doing the right thing." Box 7–5 offers a framework for ethical decision making relevant for nonprofit and government settings.

Ethical standards based on shared values are a common substrate across a society, so subsets such as business ethics, medical ethics, and professional ethics are essentially

---

    e. How have society's values relative to this issue changed over the immediate past, and will change continue to occur?

    f. Must I take into account other factors, such as religious or political beliefs, to understand the values at play in the issue?

3. **Professions and professionalism:** Does my professional training or my broader sense of professionalism help me to understand what I should do?

    a. By remembering the characteristics of a "profession," can I better picture how I should approach and resolve this dilemma?

    b. Is this a problem regularly faced, in some similar form, by members of my profession? If so, how is it regularly resolved?

    c. What professional values can serve as a guide to action?

    d. Is the conflict between my role as a professional and my role as a bureau member?

    e. Am I hiding behind my profession to avoid decisions and actions?

4. **Organizational dynamics:** Is the organization in which I work, or my relationship with that organization, a part of the problem?

    a. What external forces related to the organization might be influencing the questions and alternatives that I face?

    b. Does the structure (size, type of hierarchy, centralization or decentralization, and so on) of the organization cause all or part of the problem or affect my ability to resolve it?

    c. Do the functions (procedures, outputs, and the like) carried out by the bureau cause or help solve the ethical dilemma?

    d. Does the organizational culture (values, rituals, and so forth) influence the type of ethical dilemma I face and the possible alternatives available to resolve it?

5. **Personal aspects:** What do I need to know about myself to deal adequately with this ethical dilemma?

    a. What about my personal background (family, religious and political beliefs, education, and so on) influences my perception and attitudes toward the ethical dilemma I face?

    b. How do my personality characteristics affect my ability to deal with complex ethical problems and the people with whom I must interact?

    c. At what level of maturity and sophistication do I deal with ethical dilemmas? Do I understand the maturity level of the others with whom I must deal in this situation?

SOURCE: *Ethics for Public Managers* by Harold Gortner. Copyright © 1991. Reproduced by permission of Greenwood Publishing Group, Inc., Westport, CT.

interpretations of those commonly held standards in the context of complex and technical situations. Our society expects individuals and organizations in the public sector to pay special heed to two ethical standards: One is to serve the public trust; the other is to avoid impropriety and the appearance of impropriety (Josephson 2005). Ultimately decision making in public sector organizations must fulfill an extended mantra of "Three Es": being ethical, effective, and efficient.

Decision Support Techniques and Tools

Many tools and techniques are available to help managers in organizations make good decisions. But whether we call them tools or techniques, processes or systems, they support decision making rather than substitute for it. Consequently decision makers must beware the fallacy of substituting data for judgment. Imagine this example:

> All field offices in an organization are subject to the same standards for performance measurement, and the organization's leaders scrutinize online performance measurement charts before each meeting. Field Office X tops the comparative performance measurement statistics in virtually every category; Field Office Y displays unevenness across key performance measures; and Field Office Z's performance trends, which had been good, have suddenly deteriorated.
>
> Does this mean that Field Office X is a great organizational component and should be acknowledged for it, that Field Office Y is so-so, and that Field Office Z should be penalized for its showing? After all, that is what the decision support tools seem to suggest. Maybe, but the measurement tool alone is insufficient for a judgment call. It may turn out that Field Office X is performing its mediocre usual, that Field Office Y has just brought on board several new employees who are still climbing the learning curve, and that Field Office Z, normally the best performing of the three offices, was just devastated by a natural disaster.

In short, decision support mechanisms signal areas to examine more closely, but they may not be sufficient in themselves. The bigger the organization, the more extensive and sophisticated these systems tend to be and the more distant and diffused are their sources. Thus the larger the organization, the more tempting and potentially damaging it is for decision makers to fall prey to the judgment substitution fallacy.

With this caution in mind, decision support tools are invaluable and ubiquitous in today's organizations, no matter what the organization's sector or size. Decision support tools and techniques vary according the decision maker's need. Here are some examples:

- Policy analysis uses white papers that examine in detail a possible course of action, options papers that present and weigh alternative policy choices, "even swap" and other trade-off evaluation methods, impact analyses, and performance measures of many kinds—economic, environmental, and so forth (Smith 2005; Hammond, Keeney, and Raiffa 1998).

- Budget development applies techniques that include benefit–cost and return-on-investment (ROI) analyses, life cycle cost analysis, and fundraising and debt capacity evaluations.

- Quality management approaches like total quality management (TQM) and Six Sigma rely on statistical process techniques such as process control charts that show variation in production and defect rates, Pareto analysis tools such as histograms to rank the frequency or significance of measured performance characteristics, and root–cause analysis techniques (such as the Ishikawa fishbone diagram) that document and array likely contributing causes for an observed problem (Brassard and Ritter 1994).

- Business process reengineering (BPR) and program design draw from structured design and analysis methods that build on flowcharting concepts, value analysis, quality function deployment (QFD), and an array of other techniques (Hammer and Stanton 1995; Hauser and Clausing 1988).

- Organizational development (OD) makes use of nominal group technique (NGT), affinity diagrams that help structure ideas or pieces of information, and decision assistance disciplines such as negotiation and conflict resolution.

The arsenal of techniques is versatile in that a technique favored for one area is certain to be adaptable for other applications. Moreover, the increasingly pervasive presence of digital information and communication technologies expands the availability, reliability, and convenience of tools and information for decision making throughout all levels of today's organizations.

These tools and the four models of decision making—rational, incremental, aggregative, and garbage can—will next be compared to assess their relative advantages and limitations, especially for decision making in public organizations.

SUMMARY AND CONTRAST OF THE METHODS

The four methods show interesting differences with respect to the elements of the decision making process discussed in the introduction: search, analysis, and choice. This section considers these differences after introducing assumptions about culture—especially those parts of culture related to participation, accountability, and organizational setting—behind each method. Finally, the last section of this chapter discusses the importance of these differences for a contingency theory of administrative decision making.

Culture

The everyday operations of an organization are affected by its culture. As described by Gareth Morgan, "organization is now seen to reside in the ideas, values, norms, rituals, and beliefs that sustain organizations as socially constructed realities" (1986, 14). Organizations are minisocieties that have their own ways of looking at the world and therefore of perceiving problems and establishing ways to resolve them:

> Thus one organization may see itself as a tight-knit team or family that believes in working together. Another may be permeated by the idea that "we're the best in the industry and intend to stay that way." Yet another may be highly fragmented, divided into groups that think about the world in very different ways, or that have different aspirations as to what their organization should be. Such patterns of belief or shared meaning, fragmented or integrated, and supported by various operating norms and rituals, can exert a decisive influence on the overall ability of the organization to deal with the challenges that it faces. (Morgan 1986, 121)

The culture of the organization therefore affects the way individuals operate, how the decision process is carried out, which of the various methods discussed in this chapter are acceptable, and what the probable outcomes or choices will be when resolving problems and opportunities. The composition of the membership, and the values and beliefs held by those individuals, will influence the choice of rational or incremental decision processes—or some method that falls between these extremes.

Search

The search process refers to staff activities, at all levels of the organization, to identify ways of improving the organization's policies, programs, and operations. Search is an ongoing process in that we are always looking for ways to improve management and program administration. But as Downs notes, recognizing a "performance gap" and deciding to change a basic program component meet a great deal of resistance because they disrupt the elaborate standard operating procedures that surround managerial and administrative activities. The need for some fundamental change may be recognized only with difficulty after a turnover in personnel or when a change in technology or in the power of the organization forces a reappraisal of the organization's performance (Downs 1967, 192–93). Inertia and the costliness of change battle against the desire by officials to make a revision so that they can do a better job, to fend off forced change from external actors, or to improve their own positions in the organization. Thus even though search is ongoing, decision making is not.

In general we would expect that the search process would be most exhaustive, systematic, and detailed under the rationalist method. The agenda of options would include policies, programs, or operational solutions that are new in the field, that have worked well elsewhere, or that seem, based on reason and experience, to offer some promise of success. These methods are most likely to be used where administrative staff with training in quantitative and economic analysis methods are the key participants and have major responsibilities for identifying the projects to be subjected to analysis.

In many discussions of the theory behind the rationalist–policy analysis method, little or no attention is paid to the search process. The identification of the alternatives to be analyzed is assumed to be part of the task of making policy and therefore done by political actors outside the government organization. This limitation on the administrative analysts' role is an attempt to keep them from setting the agenda and thus essentially determining the outcome of political decisions.

In practice, however, the specific alternatives are typically selected by the analysts so that the distinction between politics and administration is not maintained in the strict sense. Advocates of a clear demarcation between politics and administration find much to criticize, therefore, in the rationalist–policy analysis method (Goldwin 1980). Some view the method as a threat to the other branches of government by the bureaucracy.

In contrast, the incremental method's search process is characterized as limited, unsystematic, and perhaps too much controlled by outside political actors. Search in this method is generally not comprehensive, and innovative alternatives are usually not sought. Further, with incrementalism, because the emphasis is on minimizing conflict and fostering negotiation, the precise goals of a program and the differences among programs and policies may be obscured.

The breadth of the search and the number of options included depend on the diversity of interests represented by the participants. The greater the number, interest, and expertise of participants, the greater the number and variety of alternatives that will be considered (Downs 1967, 185). Incremental search processes will be used, in general, when participation is not limited to experts of one or another kind, but rather depends as much on the political as the technical capabilities of the staff.

Search in the aggregative method is less developed as a process or procedure than in the other methods. The focus of the process is as much on participation as it is on any particular kind of result. The breadth of the search and the depth of knowledge about a particular alternative depend on the expertise of the individual participants. Because the presentation of options occurs spontaneously in the group setting, detailed background research into the feasibility or consequences of an alternative, such as that found in policy analysis, is not possible. Nor are the political consequences of the alternatives always well known at this early juncture, as they would be in the incremental method where the distribution of benefits is an important attribute.

The aggregative method does, however, do much to encourage innovation in the design of alternatives. By training participants in the art of brainstorming—where the expression of untested ideas is encouraged—and by permitting only clarifications—not criticisms or debates about the merits of a proposal—the method fosters new ideas. What is lost in the method's capacity to critically assess alternatives is perhaps gained in its capacity to generate new ideas for programs or operations.

The search for new alternatives in the garbage can model is not systematic, but it may admit more creativity and a broader set of alternatives than the incremental view of search. Search is not separate from the actual process of discussing and choosing. Rejecting an existing alternative or discovering or articulating a goal may open the way to considering an option previously thought to be outside the realm of possibility or not imagined at all. Also, however, discovery of a new option may lead to articulating a new goal, so the process works both ways with this model. Search is clearly ongoing in the choice process and is not a separate prior activity.

Analysis

Analysis is concerned with examining alternatives in light of particular attributes such as feasibility, cost, and who the beneficiaries of the alternative will be. An alternative's feasibility is both a political and technical matter, and the techniques used to search for and evaluate alternatives are determined by the value placed on qualitative and quantitative data. In addition to simple efficiency and effectiveness, administrators must be concerned with the passage and funding of programs and with gaining support for (and from) the administrative actors who will must implement the plan. Questions of program technology and how to achieve the desired change in society, the economy, or foreign affairs are increasingly seen as issues for social science because they require considerable scholarly expertise.

Each method attacks the problem of analysis in a different fashion. The rational method uses policy analysis techniques to examine alternatives and identify the most cost-efficient ones. Policy analysis encompasses a variety of analytic techniques including cost–benefit analysis, some of the operations research models that project the cost and output of projects, and evaluation studies of the effectiveness and efficiency of programs. An enormous consulting industry has grown up around the use of these analyses at all levels of government as the rational–policy analysis method becomes more prominent.

The culture surrounding the decision process must accept the value of the scientific method, however. The analytical requirements of the rationalist method impose heavy costs because of the time, professional expertise, and organizational support needed; major decisions requiring substantial research can consume months or even years, lots of money, and huge amounts of human resources. Decisions regarding relatively small operational changes also consume the time of extremely well-trained experts. In some cases the expense of the analyses may limit the number of alternatives that can be compared. The expectation, however, is that the quality of the decision and the money saved by selecting the most efficient alternative will make up for these costs. This assumption is rarely tested.

Gawthrop (1971) notes that the rational–policy analysis approach is associated with centralized organizational structures in which decision-making authority is reserved for the upper executive levels. Centralization is required here to provide a clearinghouse for coordinating the large amounts of information used in decision making. The coordination and information-processing functions needed for the rational–policy analysis method add to the cost as well. The incremental method, by contrast, requires a decentralized structure, which permits the local autonomy needed to conduct negotiations.

In contrast, the analysis process of the incremental method is much less systematic and much less likely to be quantified. The basis on which an alternative is examined is the way it dispenses benefits, including intangible symbolic resources, to participants in the decision. This kind of analysis requires a combination of political and technical expertise. Judging the support potential for a proposal from other actors, professionals, appointees, and the external constituents of the organization is an important aspect of analysis under the incremental method.

The aggregative method depends on the individual judgments of participants, so systematic prior research or analysis of alternatives is not generally done. Participants may, of course, be experts and thus could use any research they wish in deciding whether to recommend an alternative; but because debate is not permitted, other participants would not be influenced. In general the method does not encourage in-depth analysis, political or technological, and for that reason might best be used to generate ideas rather than decide among them.

The view of analysis offered by the garbage can model is notably different from that described in the other models. Analysis is not separate from the decision process; rather, it is one of the things that happens in the course of discussion and debate. In the obviously fragmented environment (probably with many cultures interacting) where the garbage can model is useful, the reasons for rejecting or accepting alternatives (the bases for analyzing the "goodness" of an alternative) are especially complex because of the expressive, personal, and social nature of the decision process. Objections can be raised to a proposal to solidify a friendship or to play out a ritual, as well as to articulate a political or technical difficulty. Another distinctive characteristic of analysis in the garbage can model (at least according to Anderson [1983]) is that comparisons are not generally made directly between competing alternatives, but sequentially, as in the satisficing model. In consequence, an alternative that is rejected early may not be considered again later when goals have changed and other interests or social needs are uncovered, even though these objectives might be well served by a rejected option. Thus the order in which alternatives are considered is critical to the kind of analysis that occurs.

Choice

The choice criterion of a decision-making method is the basis on which one alternative is selected over another. The criterion reflects the organizational and political values assumed in the method and what they consider to be the best basis for making decisions for society. Economic, professional, and personal standards are also reflected in the methods.

The formal criterion of the rational–policy analysis method is the Kaldor–Hicks criterion, which, as noted earlier, recommends adopting projects for which total social benefits exceed total social costs. With this criterion we choose, by definition, the program that is most efficient. Such a choice seems appropriate for administrative decision making because the primary value in a bureaucratic organization is efficiency. Efficiency may be less appropriate as a criterion for decisions about society in general, however, where there are competing values such as equity and justice.

The rationalist method portrays the public administrator as an analyst without any discretion who works within the guidelines of goals established by external policy makers.

In principle then, the official is not really a decision maker under the rationalist method, but performs analyses for, and is accountable to, the legislative, judicial, and elected officials who do make policy. The reality is more complex. Often policy statements are vague and analysts have considerable autonomy in interpreting them. Furthermore, the control policy analysts have over search and analysis gives them considerable latitude in defining the options policy makers really have. Thus policy analysts can act as decision makers; but unlike colleagues operating under the incremental method, no compromises among competing claims can be negotiated (at least not openly) because nonanalytic issues are not overtly recognized.

The criterion that operates in the incremental method is selection of the policy or programs that can claim the support of a group of participants. This group must be large enough to fulfill the system's voting requirements, which may require in some cases less than a strict majority and in others total consensus. These requirements may be formal or informal. What the criterion reflects, however, is that the best alternative is the one that can gain the support needed for adoption. The criterion is a pragmatic one that puts the highest value on pluralism, the belief that trade-offs among diverse values are inevitable (Dahl 1991). Thus programs and policies arrived at by the incremental method are characterized by satisfying many specific interests simultaneously, with a plan reached by bargaining among participants in a stable, slowly changing system.

BOX 7–6 Public versus Private Management

In the government no one has the power to decide that this is the policy he wants to develop, these are the people who are going to develop it, this is how it's going to be decided, and these are the folks who are going to administer it. No one, not even the president, has that kind of power.

Take . . . the framing of a U.S. economic policy toward Japan. If the president said to me, you develop one, Mike, the moment that [it] becomes known there are innumerable interest groups that begin to play a role. The House Ways and Means Committee, the Senate Foreign Relations Committee, the oversight committees, and then the interest groups, businesses, the unions, the State Department, Commerce Department, OMB, Council of Economic Advisers, and not only the top people, but all their people, not to speak of the president's staff and the entire press.

So it's assigned to me, but I can't limit who gets in on the act. Everyone gets a piece of the action. I'm constantly amazed when I have the lead responsibility to find two people talking to each other and negotiating something—when I haven't assigned them any responsibility. They're not in the loop. But everybody wants to be in the loop.

Therefore, to control the development of a policy, to shape out of that cacophony of divergent interests and dissonant voices an approach that eventually leads to a consensus and can be administered in a coherent fashion is an entirely different task in the government than it is for the chief executive of a company. There you can control the process and tell group executive A, you're not involved, stay out of it. And he will, and he must. In government that's simply unworkable. So you have to learn to become one of a large number of players in a floating crap game, rather than a leader of a well-organized casino that you're in charge of. I should emphasize that this is not a complaint—that the diversity of interests seeking to affect policy is the nature and essence of a democratic government.

SOURCE: W. Michael Blumenthal, "Candid Reflections of a Businessman in Washington," *Fortune*, January 29, 1979. Reprinted with permission.

The aggregative methods select an alternative based on the number of supporters as well, but their criteria differ from those of the incrementalists. There is no mechanism for compromise or coalition building. The grounds for preference may or may not be scrutinized under NGT. Even when the group is composed of experts, the method is still not investigatory.

The choice criterion in the aggregative method seems to be based on a rather naive belief that majority rule will produce the best solution for all, and a fear that bargaining will lead to political manipulation. Because advocates of the method see themselves as rejecting political decision-making methods, they do not discuss, and may even be unaware of, the political values that underlie their procedures.

The final choice in the garbage can model is not necessarily an optimal one, as Anderson noted. Nor will it necessarily be the one expected by the participants or based on the goals established at the outset of the process (Rommetveit 1979). The basis on which the final choice will be made apparently varies in this model, and in some ways what we call decisions are only arbitrarily identified as such. Olsen, for example, in describing non–decision making, characterizes decisions as post hoc interpretations (1979, 83). According to Olsen, our ability to theorize and interpret events is greater than our capacity to actually make "goal oriented decisions" (1979, 83). The meetings, debates, and discussions that constitute the garbage can process continue until the agenda of instrumental and expressive items has been dealt with.

Haphazard Decisions versus Real Nondecisions

In an unfortunate way, the garbage can model is sometimes mislabeled by referring to it as a nondecision model: The garbage can model describes a comparatively haphazard process that results in conscious or unconscious decisions. However, decision-making processes do not inevitably lead to decisions—at least, not to affirming decisions. The outcome in some instances will be to defer or abandon making a formal decision. In such circumstances there tends to be a default decision to maintain the current situation (that is, the status quo). Sometimes decision makers obscure nondecisions by calling for further study or citing mitigating circumstances; at other times issues are openly stalled, shelved, or tabled.

Moreover, the decision process itself can be interrupted at any point, terminated, or shifted from one approach to another based on evolving circumstances, players, and priorities. On occasion decision makers may use multiple approaches in serial or in parallel. President Franklin Roosevelt, for example, would put different groups—unknown to one another—to work on the same policy problem; subsequently he would bring them together to discuss where and why their conclusions and recommendations might differ. In Box 7–7 presidential historian Arthur Schlesinger portrays part of FDR's decision-making style.

Action

The process of decision making does not end with a decision or even a nondecision. Decision making remains an abstract exercise until action is taken to implement the decision. In the case of status quo, the action is to maintain what is already in effect. In the case of decisions pertaining to policy or circumscribed with "in principle" or "in concept," promulgating the decision within appropriate circles sets the stage for future decision making.

BOX 7–7 Franklin Roosevelt: Strategies of Choice

Roosevelt . . . evidently felt that both the dignity of his office and the coherence of his administration required that the key decisions be made by him, and not by others before him. He took great pride, for example, in a calculation of Rudolph Forster's that he made at least 35 decisions for each one made by Calvin Coolidge. Given this conception of the presidency, he deliberately organized— or disorganized—his system of command to ensure that important decisions were passed on to the top. His favorite technique was to keep grants of authority incomplete, jurisdictions uncertain, charters overlapping. The result of this competitive theory of administration was often confusion and exasperation on the operating level; but no other method could so reliably ensure that in a large bureaucracy filled with ambitious men eager for power the decisions, and the power to make them, would remain with the president. This was in part on Roosevelt's side an instinct for self-preservation; in part, too, the temperamental expression of a restless, curious, and untidy personality.

SOURCE: Excerpt from *The Coming of the New Deal* by Arthur M. Schlesinger, Jr. Copyright © 1958, renewed 1986 by Arthur M. Schlesinger, Jr. Reprinted with permission from Houghton Mifflin Company. All rights reserved.

The differences among the methods on all four elements of the decision-making process are important for determining the particular strengths and weaknesses of each method. On the basis of these differences, we can explore the possibility of a contingency theory.

THE POSSIBILITY OF A CONTINGENCY THEORY

A contingency theory of decision making would specify the conditions under which each method would be most effective. These conditions might at least include the type of decision to be made; the costs involved; the degree of disagreement over known options; the supportiveness or homogeneity of the organization's constituency; the level of ambiguity and change in the system; and the availability of data.

The type of decision to be made appears to be a promising basis for a contingency theory. An earlier section of this chapter discussed three levels of decisions: (1) decisions about the broad policies or plans for the organization, (2) decisions about the programs and projects to undertake in pursuit of those goals, and (3) decisions about the operations of the programs and the organization's management system. Linking the methods of decision making to these decision levels could establish the beginnings of a contingency theory, albeit one in need of refining and testing.

Officials at the upper levels of organizations typically spend more of their time engaged in nonroutine, policy-oriented issues and far less time on fairly routine administrative decisions. The reverse is true at the lower levels of most organizations, with a mix of policy and administration decisions at middle levels within organizations. The cover of this book illustrates how the policy–administration ratio varies from one organizational level to another. Figure 7–2 illustrates a related conceptualization of the relationship between types of decisions and the organizational levels at which they are made; it distinguishes among decisions involving *uncertainty*, usually made by upper-level officials; risk, typically the domain of

FIGURE 7–2   Organization Levels and Types of Decisions

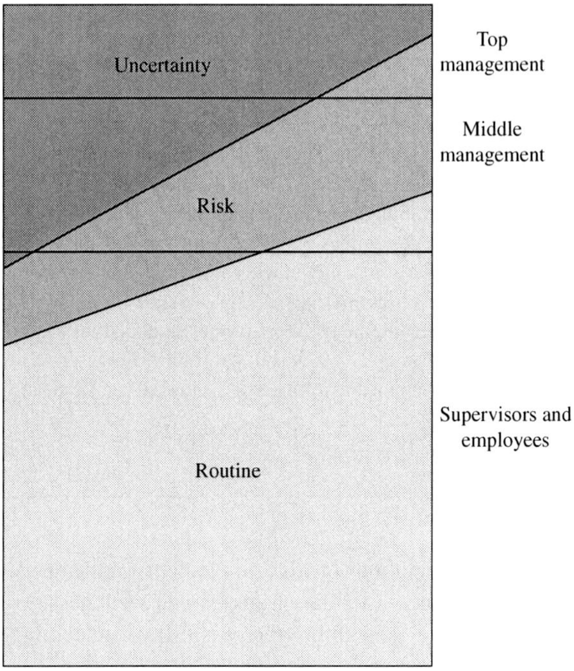

SOURCE: Harold F. Gortner, *Administration in the Public Sector*, 2nd ed. (New York: Krieger, 1986), 197.

midlevel administrators; and *routine* activity, largely the responsibility of lower-level offi-cials and line employees:

> Risk refers to those decisions where there is an element of prior experience that may be turned to, or where there is some knowledge of the probabilities of success when a particular alterna-tive is taken. Uncertainty refers to those decisions where there is no prior knowledge or expe-rience that may be turned to in making the decision and where there is no prior knowledge of the probabilities of success when a particular alternative is chosen. (Gortner 1986)

Routine decisions tend to be administrative; risk-related decisions tend to involve policy considerations; and uncertainty-related decisions tend to focus on policy concerns.

The rational method appears to be most appropriate at the level of operating decisions, such as determining the most efficient way to staff a program or design a bridge; these are the most common and immediate questions for public organizations. The operations research and quantitative analyses that are at the heart of the rationalist method are designed especially for these types of questions. The principal concern of the rational method is efficiency, and that is precisely what is desired at the level of operating decisions. On the other hand, questions of goals and values other than efficiency do not seem appropriate for this method.

The incremental method, alternatively, is not particularly well suited to making operations-level decisions because, by comparison with the rational method, it uses relatively little quanti-tative analysis. The advantage of the incremental method is not that it identifies the most efficient solution, but that it mediates conflict among officials who hold different values and must find an acceptable compromise. In doing so, the method produces program packages rather than policies. Thus it is appropriate for creating compromise programs that will be widely accepted, but not for deciding basic values about which there is generally no compromise.

The aggregative method may best be reserved for creating an initial rank ordered list of goals or programs to be subjected to further analysis and final selection under one of the other methods. Without a more developed capacity for technical analysis and without the legitimizing effect of political negotiations and compromise, the use of the method to make final choices is questionable. In practice we may find that the aggregative technique is also used as a last resort (attempting to change perceptions) when negotiations result in stalemate.

According to Olsen (1979, 85), the garbage can model is more likely, though not necessarily more desirable, where participants, goals, and issues are highly uncertain. This ambiguity is a characteristic of goal setting and planning decisions rather than operational decisions. At the planning and program levels, the political decisions at stake require the type of open expressive debate over the clarification of basic values that the garbage can model describes.

A difficulty in developing a contingency theory is that the advantages and limitations of each method are matters of political importance and therefore subject to disagreement. Devising a contingency theory of decision making is not simply a technical matter of collecting research findings, but involves political choices about who will control what kinds of decisions. The appropriate use of each method may therefore remain a matter for political debate.

CONCLUSION: GOOD DECISION MAKING EMERGES FROM PREPARED ADMINISTRATORS

So although the organizational decision-making process can be examined through a limited number of models, each with its own variants, the basic process itself can be expressed in a simple formula:

Decision making = Search + Analysis + Choice

Even an expanded version of the formula is pretty straightforward:

Decision making = Culture + Trigger(s) + Search (Probe + Alternatives generation) + Analysis + Choice + Action + Evaluation

The richness in organizational decision making comes from the substantial range of possibilities that each of these formula elements represents. It matters little whether the decision makers are based in a federal building, a town office, a nonprofit agency, a field site, or a conference taking place through cyberspace.

The prescribed decision-making process in organizations has undergone a good deal of change in the last half century—from the classic rational model to incrementalism and satisficing to the reincarnation of rationalism as policy analysis, and now to the group process method and expressive model. These changes are probably due to more than shifts in theory and new research findings. Rather, they reflect new popular and political views of what constitutes a legitimate role for the public administrators in policy making and what constitutes a legitimate process of choice. There appears to be a cyclical pattern in these changes in method as well—from the earlier view of organizational decision making as a matter of deferring to hierarchical authority and expertise to the acknowledgment of an overtly political role for administrative decision makers to the recent efforts to erase politics from the process, replacing it with analytic expertise and a leveling of power differences.

The reasons for the recent shift to analytic and purportedly apolitical methods of decision making in public organizations are not easily identified. One possibility may be that suspicion of the pluralist bargaining method generally grows from disillusionment with interest group liberalism and pork barrel politics in an era of budgetary constraints. The move from acknowledging a political method to the interest in the more technically deliberate methods may also be part of the larger recent interest in high technology and futurist thinking. Attempts in the past two decades to adopt more quantitative and analytic criteria of policy effectiveness may also be related to changes in decision processes.

These shifts in decision-making methods, in theory and practice, illustrate that an organization's most fundamental processes are not static; they respond to a variety of internal and external political and technological changes. The search for a single best decision-making process in government and nonprofit organizations may therefore be based on an unrealistic assumption about the stability of public organizations.

FOR FURTHER READING

A good overview of organizational decision making is Bernard Bass's *Organizational Decisionmaking* (Homewood, IL: Richard D. Irwin, 1983). The rational model of choice is clearly presented by Edith Stokey and Richard Zeckhauser in *A Primer for Policy Analysis* (New York: W. W. Norton, 1978). Charles Lindblom, in "The Science of Muddling Through," *Public Administration Review* 19, 1959: 79–88, sets out the incremental–pluralist model. Louis Gawthrop analyzes the political and structural implications of the rational and incremental–pluralist models in *Administrative Politics and Social Change* (New York: St. Martin's Press, 1971). Structured group choice models are introduced by Andre Delbecq, Andrew Van de Ven, and David Gustavson in *Group Techniques for Program Planning: A Guide to Nominal Group and Delphi Processes* (Glenview, IL: Scott, Foresman, 1975). The unpredictability of the choice process and its resemblance to a "garbage can" is described by James March and Johan Olsen in "Organization Choice under Ambiguity" in their *Ambiguity and Choice in Organizations*, 2nd ed. (Bergen, Norway: Universitetsforlaget, 1979). In their later work, *Rediscovering Institutions: The Organizational Basis of Politics* (New York: Free Press, 1989), March and Olsen discuss the relationship between choices and values. James G. March and Roger Weissinger-Baylon discuss the "garbage can" model further in *Ambiguity and Command: Organizational Perspectives on Military Decisionmaking* (Marshfield, MA: Pitman, 1986). Kenneth Kraemer and James Perry propose a means for linking the method of decision making and the level or type of decision to be made in "Implementation of Management Science in the Public Sector" in *Public Management: Public and Private Perspectives*, edited by James Perry and Kenneth Kraemer (Palo Alto, CA: Mayfield, 1983). Gareth Morgan discusses various metaphors for organizations and decision making in his *Images of Organization* (Beverly Hills, CA: Sage Publications, 1986).

For complementary excerpts from classics readings, see most editions of Jay Shafritz and J. Steven Ott's (and coauthors) *Classics of Organizational Theory* (Belmont, CA: Thomson Wadsworth). The volume includes "Understanding the Role of Power in Decision Making"

(1981) by Jeffrey Pfeffer and "Groupthink: The Desperate Drive for Consensus at Any Cost" (1971) by Irving L. Janis.

For a complementary nonprofit case study to go with this chapter, see Robert Goliembiewski and Jerry Stevenson's *Cases and Applications in Non-Profit Management* (Belmont, CA: Thomson Wadsworth, 1998): Case 30, "Putting the Pieces Together."

REVIEW QUESTIONS

1. What are the values, goals, and assumptions behind each of the four families of decision methods described in this chapter?
2. How would results be likely to differ if each of the methods was used in dealing with the same problem?
3. Would the structure or design of a nonprofit or government organization influence what decision methods the organization would be likely to favor? Would the structure influence which models would or would not be successful, if used? What is the reasoning behind your responses?
4. Why are many tools and techniques described as "decision support" methods?
5. Can the ethical framework for decision making be used with other decision models, or must it stand alone?

REFERENCES

Adams, Guy B., and Danny L. Balfour. 1998. *Unmasking administrative evil.* Thousand Oaks, CA: Sage.

Allison, Graham. 1971. *Essence of decision: Explaining the Cuban missile crisis.* Boston: Little, Brown.

Anderson, Paul. 1983. Decisionmaking by objection and the Cuban missile crisis. *Administrative Science Quarterly* 28: 201–22.

Bachrach, Peter, and Morton S. Baratz. 1962. Two faces of power. *The American Political Science Review* 56, no. 4 (December): 947–52.

Brassard, Michael, and Diane Ritter. 1994. *The memory jogger II: A pocket guide of tools for continuous improvement and effective planning.* Salem, NH: GOAL/QPC.

Carr, David K., Ian D. Littman, and John K. Condon. 1995. *Improvement-driven government: Public service for the 21st century.* Washington: Coopers & Lybrand.

Cleveland, Harlan. 1980. The future executive. In *Professional public executives.* Ed. Chester Newland. Washington, DC: American Society for Public Administration.

Cohen, Eliot. 1980. Systems paralysis. *The American Spectator* (November): 22–27.

Cohen, Michael, James March, and Johan Olsen. 1979. People, problems, solutions, and the ambiguity of relevance. In *Ambiguity and choice in organizations.* 2nd ed. Ed. James March and Johan Olsen. Bergen, Norway: Universitetsforlaget.

Coke, James, and Carl Moore. n.d. *Guide for leaders using nominal group technique.* Washington, DC: Academy for Contemporary Problems.

Dahl, Robert. 1991. *Modern political analysis.* 5th ed. Englewood Cliffs, NJ: Prentice-Hall.

Delbecq, Andre, Andrew Van de Ven, and David Gustavson. 1975. *Group techniques for program planning: A guide to nominal group and Delphi processes.* Glenview, IL: Scott, Foresman.

Downs, Anthony. 1967. *Inside bureaucracy.* Boston: Little, Brown. (Reissued Prospect Heights, IL: Waveland Press, 1994.)

284   Chapter 7   *Decision Making*

Etzioni, Amatai. 1967. Mixed scanning: A "third" approach to decision making. *Public Administration Review* 27 (December): 385–92.

_____. 1986. Mixed scanning revisited. *Public Administration Review* (January/February): 8–14.

Gawthrop, Louis. 1971. *Administrative politics and social change*. New York: St. Martin's Press.

Goldwin, Robert, ed. 1980. *Bureaucrats, policy analysis, statesmen: Who leads?* Washington, DC: American Enterprise Institute.

Gordon, Theodore J., and Jerome C. Glenn. 1994. Environmental scanning. *Futures research methodology*. Ed. Jerome C. Glenn. Washington, DC: American Council for the United Nations University, Millennium Project. [CD-ROM]

Gortner, Harold F. 1896. Administration in the public sector. New York: Krieger.

_____. 1991. Ethics for public managers. New York: Greenwood.

Government Performance and Results Act (GPRA). 1993. *U.S. Statutes at Large 107*, 1993: 285.

Hammer, Michael, and Steven A. Stanton. 1995. *The reengineering revolution: A handbook*. New York: Harper Business.

Hammond, John S., Ralph L. Keeney, and Howard Raiffa. 1998. Even swaps: A rational method for making trade-offs. *Harvard Business Review* 76 (March–April): 137–49.

Hauser, John R., and Don Clausing. 1988. The house of quality. *Harvard Business Review* 66 (May–June): 63–73.

Josephson, Michael S. 2005. *Preserving the public trust: Five principles of public service ethics*. Bloomington, IN: Unlimited Publishing.

Kaplan, Robert S., and David P. Norton. 1992. The balanced scorecard—Measures that drive performance. *Harvard Business Review* (January–February): 71–79.

Kingdon, John W. 1995. *Agendas, alternatives, and public policies*. 2nd ed. New York: Longman.

Kraemer, Kenneth, and James Perry. 1983. Implementation of management science in the public sector. In *Public management: Public and private perspectives*. Ed. James Perry and Kenneth Kraemer. Palo Alto, CA: Mayfield.

Lindblom, Charles. 1959. The science of muddling through. *Public Administration Review* 19: 79–88.

March, James, and Johan Olsen, eds. 1979a. *Ambiguity and choice in organizations*. Bergen, Norway: Universitetsforlaget.

March, James, and Johan Olsen. 1979b. Organizational choice under ambiguity. In *Ambiguity and choice in organizations*. 2nd ed. Ed. James March and Johan Olsen. Bergen, Norway: Universitetsforlaget.

March, James, and Herbert Simon. 1993. *Organizations*. 2nd ed. Cambridge, MA: Blackwell.

Merewitz, Leonard, and Stephen Sosnick. 1971. *The budget's new clothes*. Chicago: Markham.

Montjoy, Robert, and Lawrence O'Toole. 1979. Toward a theory of policy implementation: An organizational perspective. *Public Administration Review* 39: 465–76.

Morgan, Gareth. 1986. *Images of organization*. Beverly Hills, CA: Sage Publications.

Murensky, Catherine L. 2000. *The relationships between emotional intelligence, personality, critical thinking ability and organizational leadership performance at upper levels of management*. PhD dissertation, George Mason University.

Nichols, Kenneth L. 1993. *Why public organizations adopt total quality management: Factors influencing decisions to invest in TQM*. DPA dissertation, George Mason University.

_____. 1997. The crucial edges of reinvention: A primer on scoping and measuring for organizational change. *Public Administration Quarterly* 20 (Winter): 405–18.

Olsen, Johan. 1979. Choice in an organized anarchy. In *Ambiguity and choice in organizations*. 2nd ed. Ed. James March and Johan Olsen. Bergen, Norway: Universitetsforlaget.

Ostrowski, John, Louise White, and John Cole. 1984. Local government capacity building. *Administration and Society* 16: 3–26.

Ringland, Gill. 1998. *Scenario planning: Managing for the future*. Chichester, West Sussex, England: John Wiley & Sons.

Rommetveit, Kare. 1979. Decisionmaking under changing norms. In *Ambiguity and choice in organizations*. 2nd ed. Ed. James March and Johan Olsen. Bergen, Norway: Universitetsforlaget.

Shaw, Gordon, Robert Brown, and Philip Bromiley. 1998. Strategic stories: How 3M is rewriting business planning. *Harvard Business Review* 76 (May–June): 41–50.

Smith, Catherine F. 2005. *Writing public policy: A practical guide to communicating in the policy-making process*. New York: Oxford University Press.

Stokey, Edith, and Richard Zeckhauser. 1978. *A primer for policy analysis*. New York: W. W. Norton.

Thurow, Lester C. 1980. *The zero-sum society: Distribution and the possibilities for economic change*. New York: Penguin.

Wilson, James Q. 1989. *Bureaucracy: What government agencies do and why they do it*. New York: Basic Books.

Chapter 8

Motivation and Organizational Culture

By Ed Colley

Definitions of organizations discuss "positions" and "competencies" in a mechanistic way; however, organizations are ultimately human systems. Human beings fill those positions; human behavior is central to the functioning and effectiveness of competencies; and human motivation is the most basic psychological process in behavior. Motivation is of special consequence in public and nonprofit organizations because of the external limitations placed on managerial actions by the political environment and the general lack of resources available to hire and compensate people in a way competitive with the private sector.

The term *motivation* comes from the Latin "to move." Psychologically human motivation pertains to internal conditions or states; it is intangible. Motivation, then, is a hypothetical construct; it is based on what we infer about internal needs and the activity or behavior consequent to them. A well-stated definition is given by Bernard Berelson and Gary Steiner: "A motive is an inner state that energizes, activates, or moves (hence 'motivation'), and that directs or channels behavior toward goals" (1967, 240).

These goals, incentives, or rewards toward which motivation and activity are directed are desired by the individual for need satisfaction. Needs are internal; incentives or goals are more external or environmentally based. For example, hunger is a need, and food is the goal. An organization with a healthy culture (one that provides goals, rewards, or incentives appropriate for members' need satisfaction) will be more successful in motivating workers.

A good administrator does not work alone. No manager can singlehandedly maintain a high level of efficient and effective functioning. To achieve organizational goals, the energies and actions of others must be brought forth and directed. Because administrators usually must delegate to others to get things done, understanding the motivation processes and needs of these individuals increases both organizational and managerial effectiveness.

The patterns of individual behavior that organizations need for effective functioning have been identified by Daniel Katz and Robert Kahn (1982). First, organizations require that sufficient personnel join and stay in the system. Second, the dependable performance of assigned roles is necessary. A third and more subtle set of organization requirements is for actions to be carried out that are not specified by role prescriptions but are needed to meet unanticipated changes and contingencies. Spontaneous innovation, cooperation with other members, and behaviors that protect and create a favorable external climate for the organization are activities of this type. Each of these organization requirements depends on somewhat different motivational patterns.

Motivation theory is characterized by a diversity of models and theoretical frameworks. Because motivation is a multifaceted concept, this diversity provides researcher, practitioner, and student with a variety of insights and perspectives to choose from or combine. There are many possible ways of grouping the numerous motivation theories, ideas, and models. In this chapter we organize them by four major types: content models, cognitive process theories, behaviorist theories, and a relatively new theory based on an economic and rational self-interest perspective. In addition to describing the conceptual frameworks of various theories, we include elements allied to application—satisfaction and performance—where appropriate. The influence of the public sector on motivation theory is discussed.

Content models of motivation focus on identifying the substantive nature of individual needs; in other words, they attempt to determine what motivates individuals. Cognitive process theories attempt to explain how and why people are motivated. Motivation is presented here as a complex process in which cognition—especially perception and expectation—is important. The interaction of these psychological variables with other factors related to the situation or environment distinguishes process models. By contrast, internal psychological variables are excluded from the behaviorist perspective; only external factors count, mainly behavior and its response to environmental stimuli.

After examining these three approaches we consider their application to public sector organizations. This fourth perspective is discussed by Anthony Downs, whose model of motivation relates directly to bureau settings and opportunity structures. Downs's emphasis on self-interest and personal goals is carried further by a group of recent theorists who combine public choice theory with free market economics, rationalism, and self-interest to develop a principal–agent model of public employees. This perspective, developed beyond the ideas of Downs, adds to our understanding of individual motivation in bureaus by developing the idea that public policy and public interest goals are influenced by those working within the bureaucracies of the government and nonprofit organizations. However, the subject will be approached as allowing us to consider an additional facet of public organization life—not as the answer to how public servants operate. This additional insight lets us consider the traditional motivation theories and their application in the new management models currently in vogue within public organizations.

But before we look at these four models, think a bit about the impact of organizational mission and culture on motivation. Perhaps the best way to do this is to briefly discuss organizational cultures and how they can be categorized—because the categorizations become important in helping us understand what is going on when someone is motivated to do (or not to do) anything.

ORGANIZATION TYPES AND CULTURES

Structure and process are important, but ultimately the most important factor in getting the job done is gaining and maintaining the commitment of the people involved in carrying out the task(s). Motivation is the primary factor in determining why people participate in an organization, determining the extent to which they will allow others to direct and control their behavior, and influencing whether they strive to accomplish personal or organizational goals or both.

Motivation comes from several sources and is influenced by several factors related to the organizations within which people are operating. Perhaps the most important of these factors is the culture of the organization. Organization culture was defined at the beginning of Chapter 5; but let us here briefly note again that it is made up of the beliefs and behaviors of a group—in this case the particular organization. We can most easily understand varying cultures through motivation theory by recognizing that organizations can be grouped according to basic characteristics that help create commonality in the values and beliefs encompassed by the groups. These groupings are knows as *typologies*.

Some general typologies help us address the raison d'être for organizations and categorize some goals and values that influence their culture. Borrowing from several authors, let us separate the organizations we are studying into basic categories. Although there are six basic categories in Box 8–1, in our discussion throughout this book we are interested primarily in the first four.

The types of organizations presented here focus on two important issues: *why* people join organizations and *who* are the beneficiaries of the organizations. People join *normative organizations* because they believe in "the cause"—the theology, philosophy, or worldview

---

BOX 8–1 Types of Organizations

- *Normative:* Religious/political/environmental/social programs (such as Planned Parenthood).
- *Service:* Welfare/health/training for disabled or displaced.
- *Mutual benefit:* Social clubs/cooperatives/unions/professional associations.
- *Commonweal:* Serving the public at large.
- *Utilitarian:* Business/private sector/profit-oriented.
- *Coercive:* Mandatory asylum/prison/required service organizations.

In each case the type of organization notes the *primary* factor that influences the beliefs, perceptions, and behavior of the members of the organization. Obviously there are some elements of at least the first five types in each of the other four organizations; however, one is consistently, but not always, predominant. Coercive organizations may be special cases not as closely related to the others.

---

that is espoused, developed, and maintained by each organization. If a person believes and wishes to participate, for whatever reason, there is usually no other organizational choice available. To the extent that the person is committed and choices are limited, identification with the organization and its cause is a primary benefit gained from, or reason for, participation; and this focuses the individual's attention and loyalty. In dealing with outsiders there is often at least a secondary mission of bringing people into "the cause."

Service organizations exist to help or serve either specific groups or groups of people with common problems and needs. In this case the primary beneficiaries are client groups. A primary reason that people join such organizations is because they want to help those in need of the services—whatever those needs may be. Obviously people in these organizations are interested in the pay and other benefits (which we will talk about later in this chapter), but the sense of "doing good" is one motivator of agency members.

Mutual benefit organizations (also called *voluntary associations*) exist for the benefit of the members. Membership is maintained because of the gratification received by those who belong, and usually the benefits from membership cannot be gained or appreciated without common effort by groups. Thus an organizational structure develops to guarantee that the benefits continue and are shared appropriately. Sharing of information related to a profession, communication about and protecting common interests, the lower cost (or availability) of goods and services that cannot be delivered individually, and the satisfaction that comes from socializing with like-minded people are the benefits usually gained in such organizations. In a way mutual benefit organizations have some similarity to utilitarian ones; but the calculation of benefits is based primarily on nonquantifiable factors.

Commonweal organizations are established for the benefit of the public at large. When other types of organizations cannot guarantee particular protections or benefits, or distribute them properly and fairly, then it is essential to establish an order to accomplish these goals. This is considered the primary job of government, for instance, in a democratic society. Whereas other types of organizations appear to address specific parts of society, commonweal organizations work for all. Individuals join this type of organization for many of the reasons they participate in utilitarian organizations; but an element of public service and commitment to democratic goals influences the decisions and actions of many "civil servants."

Utilitarian organizations (business concerns) exist for the primary reason of making money. That profit is shared by the owners, and individuals work in the organization for remuneration. Both owners and employees calculate return or benefits for the cost (or type and amount of effort) in deciding whether to participate.

Finally, there are (we hope) a limited number of *coercive organizations* in society. Individuals are forced to participate in these organizations for a variety of reasons—because individuals cannot or do not control their own behavior, because they may have illnesses that require separation from the general society, or because they are required to carry out public service in either the military or civilian sectors of society. Actually both society and the individual involved may benefit from this type of organization. But those forced to participate do so under duress, and in a democratic society there is a sense of unease about use of coercive organizations and the amount of power over individual lives that should be given to such organizations. It is especially important to note that those running the organization are generally representatives of a commonweal organization or are allowed to function under the sanction and supervision of the government.

Each type of organization has a unique culture. As we look at the various motivation models or theories in the rest of this chapter, it will be useful to remember the types of organizations just described. It is especially helpful to think about how attempts to motivate people might have to vary to take these typological factors into account. In addition, cultures of organizations differ within each type. Within organizational types a unique culture is developed in each particular organization. Inevitably the values, beliefs, and mores that guide individuals and groups, and that make up particular cultures, develop from a variety of backgrounds; these cultures are principal factors in determining the success or failure of attempts at motivating organization members.

CONTENT THEORIES

It is natural to think about motivation in content terms: What motivates us as humans? Not surprisingly, the development of motivation theory began with the substantive aspects of motivation. Ancient Greek philosophers believed that humans are hedonistic—that they seek pleasure and try to avoid pain, deprivation, and loss. These basic assumptions endured in the much later social and economic theories of John Locke, Jeremy Bentham, John Stuart Mill, and Adam Smith. Still later the idea that motivation was based on instinct was introduced, and Freud and others proposed that unconscious desires motivate behavior. The modern study of work motivation is widely agreed to have begun with need or content theories.

Maslow's Hierarchy of Needs

It has become customary to introduce the discussion of work motivation theory with Abraham Maslow's hierarchy of needs. As a clinical psychologist, Maslow relied heavily on his patients' case histories; he did not use workers in an organizational context to derive his needs model. His theory was not developed specifically as a model of work motivation;

FIGURE 8–1   Maslow's Hierarchy of Needs

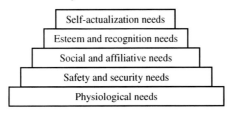

rather, it grew out of a more general interest in the interplay of heredity and learning in motivation. Despite this, the development of work motivation theory has been influenced greatly by Maslow's ideas (1987).

According to Maslow, individuals are motivated to satisfy unfulfilled needs. He postulates that individual needs form a hierarchy; that is, an individual does not consider higher-level needs as important or motivating unless lower-level needs have been more or less satisfied. The five need levels in Maslow's model are physiological, safety and security, social and affiliative, esteem and recognition, and self-actualization (see Figure 8–1). The foundation or first level of the need system is hereditary; but as a person moves up the hierarchy, maturation and learning become determining influences.

Physiological Needs

Our needs for such things as food, water, and shelter are inborn. Although these needs are not learned, acculturation and learning shape the manner in which they are expressed.

Safety and Security Needs

We acquire these needs or responses through experiences—being left alone, being hurt, being shaken by frightening or unpredictable events. Maslow included psychological and emotional as well as physical security needs. The order and structure of organizations, for example, may satisfy security needs of a psychological and emotional nature. Union contracts, work agreements, seniority, retirement plans, letting employees know what is expected of them, and giving them feedback on how they are doing are other ways for organizations to satisfy security needs.

Social and Affiliative Needs

We next acquire social needs as we realize that other people are important. In fact, whether we will be fulfilled or frustrated in satisfying our other needs depends on the actions and attitudes of other people toward us. Needs for love, belonging, and intimacy mark a crucial stage of human development. As the Hawthorne studies indicate (Roethlisberger 1941; Roethlisberger and Dickson 1939), individual needs for belonging—combined with group dynamics—have a far-reaching impact on satisfaction, productivity, and control in organizations. In part, informal groups and communication networks in organizations grow out of and satisfy social and affiliative needs.

Esteem and Recognition Needs

These needs are often referred to as "ego needs." They have to do with a desire to gain status and recognition in the eyes of others and to have a positive self-image. This level, Maslow points out, includes both self-esteem and esteem from others. Award ceremonies, articles in agency newsletters that feature individual accomplishments, praise from a superior or peers, and the respect of other professionals are sources of such rewards in bureaus.

Self-Actualization Needs

This is the fifth and highest need level in the hierarchy. Self-actualization involves an individual's need or desire to do what she or he is fitted for. Here the self-concept or perception of self is transformed into reality through action. Particular activities are performed for the stimulation and satisfaction of doing them; performing a given role or activity is self-rewarding. In other words, the individual finds his or her development and performance intrinsically satisfying.

A measure of the influence of a theory or idea is whether it stimulates further conceptual development, research, and application. By this measure Maslow's needs hierarchy is an important contribution.

Although the needs hierarchy is a very general theory of motivation, practitioners and theorists alike see its organizational significance: In the work setting, personal needs can be translated into work motivation. The theory has both the organizational potential for satisfying individual needs and the reciprocal potential of meeting individual needs as a basis for work motivation and the achievement of organizational goals. The concept of self-actualization raised especially interesting possibilities for linking personal needs and organizational tasks and goals.[1] And because of the simplicity of Maslow's theory and its descriptive treatment of needs, managers and organization scholars can link the needs in the model to relatively specific organizational incentives.

Herzberg's Two-Factor Theory

Frederick Herzberg's two-factor theory of motivation extended Maslow's work considerably. His theory was based on an initial study of about 200 professional employees (engineers and accountants) in Pennsylvania firms. Hundreds of additional interviews were later conducted that included a wide variety of occupational levels, types of organizations, and cultural milieus. Respondents were asked to

> Think of a time when you felt exceptionally good or exceptionally bad about your job, either your present job or any other job you have had. This can be either the "long range" or "short range" kind of situations, as I have just described it. Tell me what happened. (Herzberg, Mausner, and Snyderman 1993, 141)

Respondents fairly consistently associated bad feelings with factors related to the job context: poor working conditions, bad interpersonal relations, poor supervision, unclear company policy and administration, low salary and wages. Good feelings stemmed from a

---

[1]The idea of self-actualization, or at least the number of people who can (and do) achieve it, has been misinterpreted over time. Maslow believed that only a small percentage of individuals ever achieve self-actualization consistently or over any length of time. If he is correct, that limits the use of self-actualization as a general motivational tool. It must also be remembered that in this case, above all, the mode of motivation is *internal!*

TABLE 8–1 Herzberg's Two-Factor Theory

Hygiene Factors	*Motivators*
Job context:	*Job content:*
▪ Policies and administration	▪ Achievement
▪ Supervision	▪ Recognition
▪ Working conditions	▪ Challenging work
▪ Interpersonal relations	▪ Responsibility
▪ Money, status, security	▪ Growth and development

different set of factors that arose out of the content, not the context, of their work: opportunity for growth, advancement, responsibility, the work itself, recognition, and achievement. Factors intrinsic to the work yielded satisfaction; Herzberg called these *motivator factors.* The extrinsic conditions, which he termed *hygiene factors,* were linked to job dissatisfaction (see Table 8–1).

If we examine these factors it becomes apparent that *job dissatisfaction and the factors that cause it are different from, rather than opposites of, those causing satisfaction.* Herzberg concluded that satisfaction and dissatisfaction are separate concepts and not opposite ends of the same continuum.

The presence of motivators, analogous to Maslow's higher-order needs, increases worker satisfaction and performance. The absence of motivators does not lead to an equal sense of dissatisfaction. The (negative) presence of hygiene factors, analogous to Maslow's lower-level needs, creates dissatisfaction; but the absence of hygiene factors, or a positive presence, does not lead to satisfaction. Correcting hygiene factors, or trying to make them positive elements in the work experience, can reduce symptoms of dissatisfaction such as absenteeism and higher turnover; but by themselves positive hygiene factors do not motivate workers to greater productivity. Where dissatisfaction has been prevented, people work at minimally acceptable levels to avoid job or pay loss; but motivators are needed to boost satisfaction and motivate performance.

Some later studies confirm Herzberg's two-factor theory (Herzberg 1974; Bockman 1971; Grigaliunas and Herzberg 1971); others dispute it (Vroom 1995; Schwab, Devitt, and Cummings 1971). Nevertheless Herzberg's contributions are substantial. His studies increase the applicability of Maslow's needs hierarchy to work motivation and provide more specific descriptions of need content. The hygiene–motivator model has drawn attention to the importance of job content factors in motivation. Because these ideas gained popularity with managers, they have been applied in the workplace; for example, job enrichment, work group design, team management, and organization development rely on motivating individuals through opportunities for challenging work, recognition, respectability, and growth.

Alderfer's ERG Theory

A later content theory of work motivation was developed by Clayton Alderfer, who like Herzberg based his findings on research conducted in organizational settings (1972). Alderfer reformulates Maslow's five needs into three categories: *existence, relatedness,* and *growth*

FIGURE 8–2   Relationship among Alderfer's ERG Needs, Maslow's Hierarchy of Needs, and Herzberg's Two Factors

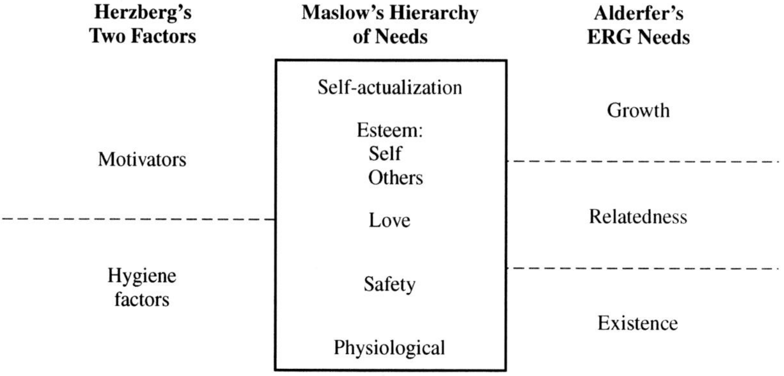

Herzberg's Two Factors	Maslow's Hierarchy of Needs	Alderfer's ERG Needs
	Self-actualization	Growth
Motivators	Esteem: Self Others	
	Love	Relatedness
Hygiene factors	Safety	
	Physiological	Existence

SOURCE: From Fred Luthans, *Organizational Behavior*, 4/e, p. 204. Copyright © 1985 McGraw-Hill Companies, Inc. Reprinted with permission.

(see Figure 8–2). The ERG theory's name is, of course, derived from these three terms. Existence needs equate to Maslow's physiological needs and in some aspects to his security needs; relatedness needs have to do with the desire for social acceptance and status in a group; and growth needs center on self-esteem and self-actualization. Alderfer's findings, however, do not point to a hierarchical ordering of needs and suggest a more complex relationship between need strength and need satisfaction. Depending on an individual's personal experiences or acculturation, for example, growth needs might take precedence over unfulfilled existence needs. Other research substantiates this conclusion, except that concern for higher-level needs tends to be precluded when lower-level needs are severely threatened (Lawler and Suttle 1972). If these needs are satisfied, higher-level needs assume importance to the individual. However, once growth or self-actualization needs kick in or become important, there is no specific experience of satiation: The self-actualizing individual tends to adjust goals higher, or to establish new and different goals, as previous ones are met.

Alderfer's theory fits well into the models already developed by both Maslow and Herzberg. To maximize the explanatory strength of these three theories it is best to look at their commonalities and how they fit into a relatively united whole. Even then interesting questions must be asked and answered to weave a complete fabric using content theories.

McClelland's Social Motives

David McClelland is a major critic of Maslow's work—particularly the adequacy of Maslow's conceptualization of self-actualization. Because many needs are socially acquired rather than biologically determined, they vary from culture to culture and from individual to individual. Therefore, McClelland reasons, perceptions of actualizing one's self and reaching one's potential differ among individuals and societies. McClelland's work illuminates both the content of self-actualizing needs and the possible effects of these need patterns on productivity, cohesion, and conflict, as well as leader–follower relationships in organizations.

The psychological research of McClelland and his followers is based on projective techniques. People who participated in their studies were shown a series of simple but ambiguous pictures; they were then asked to write a short story about each picture. Psychologists scored and analyzed stories based on three important themes or needs: affiliation, achievement, and power.

Affiliation Needs

People with high affiliation needs desire social interaction. High-affiliation individuals want to be liked by others, and in return they tend to be helpful and supportive. They can contribute greatly to organizations and groups through their efforts to promote positive interpersonal relations. Conflict can be diffused through their attempts to reduce tension.

After reviewing research addressing the need to belong, Baumeister and Leary (1995) found that

> it seems fair to conclude that human beings are fundamentally and pervasively motivated by a need to belong, that is, by a strong desire to form and maintain enduring interpersonal attachments. . . . (There are) multiple links between the need to belong and cognitive processes, emotional patterns, behavioral responses, and health and well-being. The desire for interpersonal attachment may well be one of the most far-reaching and integrative constructs currently available to understand human nature. (522)

Affiliation needs are, of course, an important reason for joining informal groups within an organization. These needs can influence both group cohesiveness and the extent to which informal group norms control a member's behavior (Cartwright 1968)—which in turn can enhance collaborative task efforts. Whether these needs are functional or dysfunctional for productivity and attaining organizational goals depends, however, on the congruence between the informal group norms and goals and those of the larger organization (Likert 1987).

Achievement Needs

Individuals whose behavior is consistently oriented toward successful performance according to some standard of competence or excellence are motivated by high achievement needs. People with high achievement needs (1) like to take personal responsibility for solving problems; (2) tend to set reasonably difficult goals, preferring to take moderate risks but not gambling on long shots; and (3) want concrete feedback on their performance (McClelland 1976).

Organizations and managers who set unreasonably high standards or goals are not motivating high-achievement members effectively because the high-achievement individual's satisfaction is strongest when the goal is attainable. Nor do goals that are set too low motivate the high-achievement worker.

Not surprisingly, high performance is likely to be related to high achievement needs. But a shift has taken place in achievement motivation research: Its focus has moved from the high-achievement individual to the organizational climate and opportunity structure that encourage and reward high achievement. Over three decades ago McClelland and David Winter (1971) pointed out that this phenomenon is contingent on organizational variables; the less bureaucratic the organization, for example, the more favorable the organizational context for high-achievement behavior.

Opinion is divided on the significance of achievement motivation for managerial effectiveness. McClelland believes that "it is fairly clear that a high need to achieve does not equip a man to deal effectively with managing human relationships" (1970, 30). Why? Because affiliation and power motivation are oriented toward others; however, achievement motivation "is a one man game which need never involve other people." McClelland concludes by noting,

"Stimulating achievement motivation in others requires a different motive and a different set of skills than wanting achievement satisfaction for oneself" (1970, 29–30). In a reiteration of this point, some new management methods, such as total quality management and some kinds of team management, actively discourage any special rewards based on individual achievement (Kohn 1993), looking instead at the total production system as the main basis for high achievement and quality (Carr and Littman 1993).

Other research findings reveal that leadership style and effectiveness vary with the degree of achievement need—high, moderate, or low. Unlike McClelland's image of the high-achievement individual as a loner who is not interpersonally effective, these findings suggest that *high-achievement managers* are optimistic about subordinates, use participative methods, and show concern for both people and production. (See the discussion of McGregor's "Theory X and Theory Y" leadership model later in this chapter.) Moderate achievers are more concerned with prestige symbols, and managers with low achievement motivation are mainly interested in safety and security. Each tends to try to motivate his or her subordinates as she or he is motivated (Zemke 1979; Blake and Mouton 1985).

Power Needs

Greater concern for having influence over, or a strong impact on, others characterizes people with a high need for power (Veroff 1957; McClelland 1970). But people are motivated by different visions or types of power. "There are," according to McClelland, "two faces of power. One is turned toward seeking to win out over active adversaries. Life is seen as a 'zero-sum game' in which 'if I win, you lose' or 'I lose, if you win' " (1970, 36). He calls this "personalized power." The other face of the power," he explains, "is more socialized" (1970, 36). Socialized power "expresses itself in thoughts of exercising power for the benefit of others and by feelings of greater ambivalence about holding power" (1970, 36).

There are differences in the ways personalized and socialized power are exercised and in their motivating effects on followers. Acting on a need for personalized power, the leader seeks to overwhelm others, to compel their submission through dominance. This behavior may evoke followers' obedience, but their passivity, or conversely their desire to resist, may be the price. McClelland notes another shortcoming of personal dominance: Whereas personal power may be effective in small groups, the process of influencing large organizations and groups requires more socialized forms of motivation.

Leaders who are motivated by socialized power needs are not inclined to force others to submit. These leaders are concerned with group goals—which entails not only their identification of those goals but also their promotion of the group's involvement in defining them. Socialized power engenders confidence in followers; they feel better able to accomplish whatever goals they share. Thus followers feel more rather than less powerful.

In our society we hold such a strongly negative view of power that as observers we are inclined to convert the positive face of power into a negative. That is, we believe that if a leader succeeds in an attempt to influence, that leader must have done so through dominance or manipulation. And "the more effective the leader, the more personal power tends to be attributed to him regardless of how he has achieved his effects" (McClelland 1970, 42). McClelland recognizes, however, that there is a realistic basis for this frequent misperception:

> In real life the actual leader balances on a knife edge between expressing personal dominance and exercising the more socialized type of leadership. He may show first one face of power, then the other. The reason for this lies in the simple fact that even if he is a socialized leader,

he must take initiative in helping the group he leads to form its goals. How much initiative he should take, how persuasive he should attempt to be, and at what point his clear enthusiasm for certain goals becomes personal authoritarian insistence that those goals are the right ones whatever the members of the group may think, are all questions calculated to frustrate the well-intentioned leader. (1970, 42)

Certain values in American culture may support acquiring strong personal power needs (for example, individualism and competitiveness), whereas others promote learning socialized power. Americans' fear of the abuse of power has led to a system of government that fragments authority. The process of exercising power requires some degree of taking into account and accommodating the goals of others—and often others' involvement in selecting and formulating those goals. This is especially germane, albeit problematic, in large-scale public bureaus where regulations and procedures abound, personal discretion and responsibility are curtailed, and public accountability is an enduring expectation. For those working in nonprofit organizations a similar problem exists. First, it is necessary to operate in a fragmented and regulated environment where public scrutiny is always present. In addition, any large project ultimately ends up requiring the involvement of numerous groups—often from various segments of society (government, private, and nonprofit)—and requires coalescing and coordinating these multiple organizations (and perspectives) in the furtherance of one specific goal that has to be relatively concrete in its visualization.

Katz and Kahn's Motivational Patterns

Daniel Katz and Robert Kahn (1982) approach motivation in organizations by looking at both individual and organizational factors. They discern different motivation patterns that combine psychologically based individual desires or values with organizational reward and control systems. Katz and Kahn identify four types of organizational incentive systems that tap into different motivation patterns and are good (or bad) for the organization in different ways (see Table 8–2). These motivational patterns are legal compliance, instrumental satisfaction, self-expression, and internalized values.

Legal Compliance

In legal compliance, motivation rests on the individual's internalized acceptance of the organization's authority and rules as legitimate. The completeness and clarity of role prescriptions and organizational controls are external elements related to sustaining this motivational and behavioral pattern (legal compliance). At best, however, this incentive system is limited by its inability to motivate members beyond routine compliance with role requirements. In a sense, this system places a floor on performance levels, but it also establishes a ceiling because an "emphasis on legalities of organizational control tends in practice to mean that the minimal acceptable standard for quantity and quality of performance becomes the maximal standard" (Katz and Kahn 1982, 408).

Instrumental Rewards

Motivation may also be linked to behavior by instrumental rewards. Katz and Kahn identify four types: general system, individual, approval from leaders, and approval from peers.

General system rewards come through membership and usually increase with seniority (retirement systems, sick leave, cost-of-living increases). These rewards reduce turnover and

---

TABLE 8–2   Motivational Patterns, Rewards Systems, and Organizational Behavior Outcomes

Incentive/Motivational Pattern	*Type of Behavior Produced*
Legal compliance: Internalized acceptance of authority or legitimacy of organization rules and/or external force can be used to compel compliance.	Minimally acceptable quantity of work can reduce absenteeism.
Instrumental satisfaction: General systems reward.	Minimal quantity and quality of role performance. Reduction in turnover and absenteeism.
Individual rewards.	Possible increase in productivity. Possible reduction in turnover and absenteeism.
Approval of leaders.	Possible decrease in turnover and absenteeism. Possible increases in productivity (or possible decreases).
Approval of peers.	Possible decrease in turnover and absenteeism. Possible increases in productivity (or possible decreases).
Self-expression: Self-concept, identification and intrinsic satisfaction with the work or job itself.	High productivity. Decreases in absenteeism.
Internalization of organization goals: Value expression, self-identification with goals of organization.	Increased productivity. Spontaneous and innovative behavior. Reduced turnover and absenteeism.

SOURCE: Based on Daniel Katz and Robert L. Kahn, *The Social Psychology of Organizations* (New York: John Wiley & Sons, 1982), 398–425.

---

are therefore most effective for retaining the organization's members. On an individual basis they will not lead to higher-quality or more work than is necessary to stay in the system. However, system rewards may account for differences in productivity between organizations because organizations that give better rewards than competing ones may be able to set a higher level of performance (Katz and Kahn 1982, 413).

Individual rewards, such as pay increases and promotion, are given on the basis of individual merit or performance. These rewards help attract people to an organization and hold them in it; they can also be effective in motivating members to meet or exceed standard performance, reducing turnover, and perhaps lowering absenteeism.[2] Where an individual's contribution(s) to a group product can be clearly differentiated, individual rewards are feasible; but where this differentiation is unclear or where teamwork receives greater emphasis, system rewards both are more advisable and foster higher identification with the organization.

---

[2]Even individual rewards and praise are questioned as productive methods to increase motivation by many motivation scholars and consultants. See the reading by Kohn in the section of this chapter discussing behaviorist theory.

Approval from leaders, with the concomitant gratification of praise from a powerful or respected person, is the third type of reward. Social *approval from one's immediate work group* is the remaining instrumental reward. Support or approval from either leaders or peers in the organization may reduce turnover. If these social relationships are unrelated to the tasks to be performed, however, they do not increase productivity or work quality. Chapter 9 discusses influence, power, and authority further.

Self-Expression

Because motivation based on self-expression is internalized, performance of the role activities carries its own rewards. Self-determination and self-expression are ego-satisfying motivations; the individual is motivated to establish a positive self-concept. If successful, this motivation pattern can result in high productivity and work quality as well as personal satisfaction. Central to self-expression is intrinsic job satisfaction or identification with the work, and this is aroused and maximized when the job itself provides sufficient variety, complexity, challenge, and exercise of skill to engage the worker's abilities. Hence the ongoing interest in job enrichment (Katz and Kahn 1982).

Internalization of Organizational Goals

The fourth type of motivation extends self-expression to the internalization of organizational goals. Here individuals regard these organizational values or goals (which are also their personal values) as appropriate to their own self-concepts. "People so motivated are usually described as having a sense of mission, direction, or commitment. In most organizations there is a small core of such committed members who have internalized the values of the system" (Katz and Kahn 1982, 362).

Partial internalization of organizational goals is more common than complete internalization. Identification with general organizational values that are not unique to the specific organization is one form of partial internalization. For example, a professional such as a lawyer may internalize the values of his or her occupational specialty—but not necessarily the values of the organization or firm in which she or he exercises it. Members often embrace the values and goals of a subsystem or unit rather than those of the larger organization. Both types of partial internalization are functional for the larger organization only to the extent that individual and group goals are congruent with organizational objectives.

Three additional conditions foster organization internalization: participating in decisions, contributing in a significant way to organization performance, and sharing in rewards for group accomplishment. Many organizations fail to provide these conditions, but the new participative management systems attempt to recognize and use these potential forces for employee commitment. When all is said and done, it is undoubtedly true that "the internalization of organization goals is at once the most effective motive pattern and the most difficult to invoke within the limits of conventional organizational practice and policy" (Katz and Kahn 1982, 425).

Content Theories Summarized

Content theory is based on individual needs, but its development has been marked by greater inclusion of situational variables and their applicability to work organizations. The content approach has branched out considerably from Maslow's hierarchy of needs, and it has become the theoretical basis for many new organization and management models that are currently in vogue.

The movement of content theory is toward a larger conceptual scope and greater usefulness for managers. A major contribution of the content approach is that its explicit treatment of needs bridges the gap between individual needs and organizationally based incentives. Efforts to discover the links between individual satisfaction and productivity and even organizational effectiveness also add to the development of work motivation theory and its organizational application.

Effectively linking incentives to motivation requires an understanding of worker needs and goals. Moreover, the organization must have access to appropriate resources, and managers need to have sufficient discretion or authority to make appropriate changes in reward systems—conditions that are more likely to be unmet in public and nonprofit than private organizations. In fact, public managers may come to grief even if performance improves and the costs of rewards to employees are highly effective in organizational savings and productivity.

BOX 8–2 It's Praise, Not a Raise, That's the Big Motivator

Ever since civilization removed the threat of death or starvation for people who did not work hard, managers have been arguing fiercely over how to motivate them. More pay? Sweet words? Company picnics?

A . . . survey by Robert Half International, a giant staffing services firm, suggests that money has lost its impact. Companies are in danger of losing good workers, the survey said, if they do not learn to nourish egos with warm adjectives and admiring nouns.

The poll of 150 executives from the nation's 1,000 largest companies found the single most common reason why employees left was lack of recognition and praise. Thirty-four percent gave that as the reason for losing workers, compared with 29 percent who cited low compensation, 13 percent who blamed limited authority, and 8 percent who mentioned personality conflicts.

The Half survey adds weight to the work of scholars who have been arguing lately that the carrot-and-stick ideas ruling corporate personnel departments do little to encourage more and better work. Researchers such as Edward Deci at the University of Rochester and Mark Lepper at Stanford University say that material rewards not only do not motivate well, but poison natural motivators such as curiosity and self-esteem.

"Companies that believe money is an employee's sole motivation for working are destined to lose some of their best people," said Half, the firm's founder. "Praising accomplishments provides psychological rewards that are critical to satisfaction in any professional setting."

Lynn Taylor, a vice president at Half, said managers often think they are praising workers more often than they actually do, and are far more likely to make negative than positive comments.

Grunting "nice job" in the elevator is not a sufficient solution, she said. "They should do it in public, in front of other people as much as possible," Taylor said. "They should do it frequently, but not to the point where it is insincere."

If they don't, she said, people will leave, damaging the reputation of the firm and making it more difficult to find replacements.

A 1991 poll showed that even among salespeople, allegedly fixated on cash, increased compensation was the least commonly cited reason for changing jobs.

SOURCE: From "It's Praise, Not a Raise, That's the Big Motivator" by Jay Matthews from *The Washington Post*, September 8, 1994. Copyright © 1994 The Washington Post. Reprinted with permission.

Public sector organizations cannot compete with private firms in tangible rewards such as salaries, bonuses, advancement, and promotion. Moreover, in government bureaus tangible rewards are dispensed on a system basis—that is, for being a member or employee and having seniority—rather than for an individual's above-average work performance. When merit systems are tried there is an abysmal record of finding ways to adequately measure "merit" and of funding systems adequately, so the end result is often frustration and cynicism. Promotion opportunities are often limited both by freezes on hiring and advancement and by time-in-grade rules and policies.

Because tangible rewards in public sector organizations are in short supply and management control over them is limited, it is common practice to substitute intrinsic and recognition rewards such as honor boards, office- or employee-of-the-month awards, and the like. Other opportunities for intrinsic and self-actualizing rewards are more promising. For example, members of agencies like the American Red Cross, the Chamber of Commerce, the American Cancer Society, or the Environmental Protection Agency can see themselves as part of movements helping achieve the public good within their particular spheres of operation. Internalized goals of community service can be rewarding to bureau members, especially at the local level where community needs and results are more proximate and visible. In the nonprofit area there is a strong sense of commitment to organizational goals by many employees, especially if they chose to work in the organization because of its mission.

We can point to content theory's normative significance as well. Implicit in this perspective is the belief that organizations do not have to be hateful, punitive places to be productive. A worker's motivation cannot be reduced to money as the sole motivator coupled with an inherent dislike of work. Potentially and empirically, the substance of worker motivation encompasses a far greater range of needs and incentives that are more socially and organizationally constructive. Content theory adds a scientific basis to the belief that work organizations can be invested with humanistic values.

COGNITIVE PROCESS THEORIES OF WORK MOTIVATION

Cognitive process models and operant conditioning (discussed in a following section of this chapter) also play an important role in motivation theory and research. They represent a shift away from the need-based emphasis of content theory toward a focus on either information processing and cognition or situation and job environment factors (Mitchell 1982).

Cognitive process models concentrate on identifying the factors, especially cognitive variables, that comprise the motivation process and on determining how and why these factors result in motivation. Their complexity results not merely from the inclusion of a number of variables, but rather from a concern with process—the relationships and interactions among variables. This idea of *process* in formulating models represents a significant advance in work motivation theory.

Expectancy Models

Two streams of thought form the foundation of expectancy models: (1) the utility or rational choice theories of classical economics, and (2) the cognitive theories of psychology. Expectancy theories include both internal/personality variables and external/situational factors. Human beings act and choose in ways that fit their personalities and needs, while at the same

FIGURE 8–3   VIE Model of Motivation

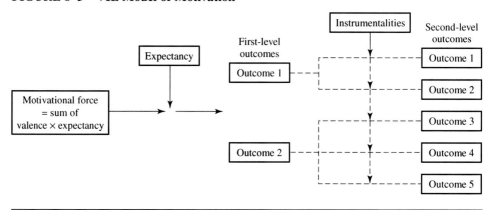

SOURCE: Adapted from Fred Luthans, *Organizational Behavior*, 3rd ed. (New York: McGraw-Hill, 1981), 187. Based on Victor H. Vroom, *Work and Motivation* (New York: John Wiley & Sons, 1964).

time taking account of the opportunities and constraints in the situation. Expectancy theory encompasses both the emotional (feeling) and cognitive (perceiving, evaluating, learning, and so on) aspects of choice and action. (See the decision-making models presented in Chapter 7.) People are emotional; they seek to satisfy their needs. And they are rational; they choose among alternative actions based on what they foresee as producing a satisfactory payoff.

Vroom's VIE Model

An early expectancy model of work motivation was developed by Victor Vroom (1995). The concepts in his VIE theory are valence, instrumentality, and expectancy (see Figure 8–3). *Valence* is the strength of a person's preference for a particular outcome. *Instrumentality* relates "first-level outcomes" to "second-level outcomes." The latter is the desired goal or payoff. For example, if a junior budget analyst perceives that outstanding performance is required if she is to be promoted to a higher grade in her agency, she will be motivated to achieve an outstanding rather than an average or above-average performance. Outstanding performance is the choice among first-level outcomes that leads to the desired second-level outcome—promotion to a higher grade. If the same woman's goal were job security and she perceived that an average performance was sufficient to ensure this outcome, her choice of first-level outcomes might be an average performance to achieve the preferred utility or second-level outcome of job security.

The concept of *expectancy* relates effort to first-level outcomes. Our budget analyst's motivation and effort would be affected by her beliefs about her ability to achieve her first-level outcome. Motivation would be determined, in part, by whether she believed the probability was high or low that she could achieve her first-level outcome of an outstanding or an average performance. In summary, motivational force is the product of the combined variables of valence, instrumentality, and expectancy.

Porter–Lawler Model

A more elaborate model of work motivation is the Porter–Lawler model (Porter and Lawler 1968), including the refinements added by Lawler (1994). The model's major variables are effort, performance, reward, and satisfaction (see Figure 8–4).

FIGURE 8–4   Porter–Lawler Motivation Model

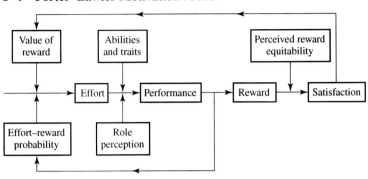

SOURCE: From Lyman W. Porter and Edward E. Lawler, III, *Managerial Attitudes and Performance*, p. 165. Copyright © 1968 Richard D. Irwin. Reprinted with permission.

The level of energy an individual puts into a given activity is termed *effort*. The amount of effort exerted depends largely on a combination of two factors: the value the individual places on the reward, and the perceived effort–reward probability. Effort is greater when a reward is highly valued by a worker who perceives that the probability is high that his or her effort will lead to the desired reward.

Effort is also affected by the expectancies added in Lawler's refinement: expectancy or probability that effort will produce the intended performance (E → P expectancy); and the likelihood that performance will result in a particular desired outcome (P → O expectancy). (See Figure 8–5.) According to Lawler, the external situation is the strongest determinant of E → P expectancies. Performance can be affected by such things as time availability, the level of cooperation necessary from others, and required procedures that may or may not be obstacles to performance. Internal factors such as self-esteem, role perception, and past experiences have an impact as well.

It is important to distinguish between effort and performance: Performance is the objective result of effort. There can be discrepancies between the amount of effort expended and

FIGURE 8–5   Lawler's Expectancies Refinement

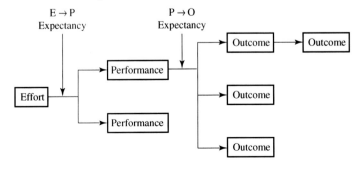

SOURCE: From *Motivation in Work Organizations* by E. E. Lawler, III. Copyright © 1973 by Wadsworth Publishing Company. Reprinted by permission of the author.

the effectiveness of performance; workers may expend colossal effort and still give ineffective performance. Their abilities and skills may be deficient; their role perceptions may be inaccurate; their efforts may be misdirected—or they may have little control over the outcomes of their efforts.

The link between performance and rewards is a central element in this theory. Rewards—and thus motivation and satisfaction—are contingent on performance. Common government practices such as automatic step increases in pay and across-the-board raises for everyone in designated job categories weaken this link because the rewards are not contingent on individual performance.

Porter and Lawler divide rewards into two types: extrinsic and intrinsic. *Extrinsic* rewards are external in that they come from the environment and not directly from the behavior or performance; money, for example, is an extrinsic reward. *Intrinsic* rewards are closely tied to internal feelings and are an outgrowth of a given performance or behavior. A sense of craftsmanship or professionalism, performing up to one's capacity, and completing a challenging assignment can be intrinsically rewarding.[3]

There are numerous constraints on monetary incentives in public sector organizations. Government organizations face statutory prohibitions, civil service restrictions, and uniformity requirements, while legislators are reluctant to surrender control of wage increases to supervisors and managers. All public and nonprofit organizations face an eternal problem of limited funds and public opposition to "highly paid bureaucrats," high overhead for administration, and the necessity of convincing donors or taxpayers that their money is being used wisely and efficiently. Monetary incentives of various types are relatively rare in government. Moreover, the most commonly used type, a performance-based wage increase, is weakly linked to performance due to the inadequacies of the appraisal systems and a history of inadequate funding for raises after the initial interest in the program wanes among the public and legislators (Greiner et al. 1981).

Promotion, another important extrinsic reward, is also comparatively limited. In a survey of 4,900 federal employees conducted by the U.S. Merit Systems Board, 62 percent said that they thought it unlikely that they would be promoted or get a better position if they worked harder in their present positions. Responses varied among agencies from 96 percent regarding promotion unlikely in the Office of Personnel Management to 55 percent in the Department of Health and Human Services to 29 percent in the General Services Administration (U.S. Merit Systems Board 1984, 18).

Nonmonetary rewards, such as pins, citations, plaques, feature stories in employee publications, or a visit with an agency head may pose fewer implementation problems, but no systematic studies show their effectiveness. In fact, Alfie Kohn (1993) argues symbolic rewards have a negative effect in most cases. Many professionals and others in government agencies are motivated by the work itself or by broader public service values, but systematic studies of how this affects performance are needed here. Job enrichment is a technique associated with intrinsic rewards and satisfaction. Although public sector use of job enrichment lags behind that in the private sector, the number of public efforts has expanded considerably in recent years with nonprofit organizations and local government accounting for most of the growth. Obstacles to broader use are personnel rules and job category systems, management and employee resistance, and union contracts and demands.

---

[3]Two points need to be emphasized here as the discussion of rewards continues. First, note how these models appear to support the findings of Herzberg presented earlier in the chapter. Second, many critics of rewards (such as Kohn 1993) argue that extrinsic rewards really do not motivate—that only intrinsic rewards motivate.

The work of Porter and Lawler greatly advances our thinking about satisfaction and reward–satisfaction relationships. They bring to our attention the fact that satisfaction is a cognitive state. Actual rewards only partly determine satisfaction; achieving satisfaction also depends on what rewards an individual believes are equitable for a given level of performance. Equitable reward and satisfaction levels are determined by the individual's perception of the degree to which actual rewards correspond to the perceived or expected equitable reward level. High satisfaction occurs when a reward received is perceived as nonmanipulative and equitable, and low satisfaction results from rewards that are inadequate or inappropriate based on the individual's perception of an equitable reward level.

Most previous thinking about work motivation, especially the human relations approach, assumed that satisfaction is an attitude that both precedes and causes performance. A major and revolutionary element of Porter and Lawler's theory is its proposition that performance causes satisfaction—mediated, of course, by rewards; or in any case, that satisfaction is more dependent on performance than performance on satisfaction.

In its complexity, the Porter–Lawler model gives us a more accurate motivation model than the comparatively simplistic content theories. The model can lead theorist and manager alike to useful insights. It depicts workers as active participants in the motivation process; they make decisions about their behavior on the basis of their expectancies about outcomes, and they choose behaviors that they perceive they can perform. The model also encourages attention to the differences in motives among individuals.

The model's complexity, while adding to its theoretical strength, has proven a drawback to its practical application—a problem acknowledged by Lawler:

> If we try to predict a person's behavior using our model, and if we gather complete data on all his perceptions of existing relationships, we might still predict behavior incorrectly because our model would be too complex to allow for valid predictions. (1994, 60)

Equity Theory

Developed during the same period as expectancy models, equity theory is also cognitively based. Its explanation of how motivation occurs derives from cognitive dissonance and exchange theories. Equity theory takes two forms. The first, discussed at some length by March and Simon (1993) and Downs (1994) and called *equilibrium theory,* entails the measurement of the cost of membership and participation against the benefits returned to the individual. A positive cost–benefit analysis (not a term used by the original authors but descriptive of the analytic process that goes on) leads a person to remain in the organization and may be a positive motivation for productivity and positive participation. A negative cost–benefit analysis, or disequilibrium, may have a damaging effect on participation and may ultimately lead to withdrawal from the organization.

Stacy Adams, the originator of the second and very similar model, *equity theory,* explains the basic point of his model in this way: "Inequity exists for Person whenever he perceives that the ratio of his outcomes to inputs and the ratio of Other's outcomes to inputs are unequal" (1975, 141).

Equity occurs when the ratios of outcomes to inputs are perceived as equal:

$$\frac{\text{Person's outcomes}}{\text{Person's inputs}} = \frac{\text{Other's outcomes}}{\text{Other's inputs}}$$

Adams's terms, *person* and *other,* refer to any individual who perceives himself or herself as being in an exchange relationship with some other individual or group, and to other individuals or groups with whom the individual feels that equity comparisons are relevant. If individuals perceive their ratio of outcomes to inputs as unequal to those of another relevant person, they are motivated to restore equality. The strength of the motivation to restore balance is proportional to the extent of the perceived inequity.

Efforts to restore equity, Adams points out, can take many forms. Individuals may change their outputs, increasing or decreasing the quantity or quality of their work; or they might try to change their outcomes. Asking for a raise in pay or making one's contribution more visible might change outcomes without increasing input. Some research suggests that piece-rate workers who perceive inequity try to improve their reward outcomes with little increase in input by turning out high-volume but low-quality products (Filley, House, and Kerr 1976, 205–6; Goodman and Friedman 1971). Other approaches may be used, such as attempting to change others' inputs or outcomes. A more drastic response is that of leaving an organization, work project, or group for a situation perceived as more equitable (Telly, French, and Scott 1971).

Attribution or Locus of Control Theory

Attribution theory is concerned with cause–effect perceptions and behavior. Human behavior is shaped by the perceptions or attributions of causality that an individual ascribes to relevant forces in his or her environment (Kelley 1972). These forces or attributes may be internal, such as personal skill and effort; or individuals may assign causality to external forces, such as organizational policies and rules or supervisor attitudes.

Individuals perceive that their outcomes in a work situation are either internally or externally controlled. Those who perceive internal control feel they can influence their outcomes through their own skill and efforts. Those who believe their outcomes are externally controlled do not feel they can control or influence them. These locus of control perceptions (and *perceived*, not *actual*, causes or determinants matter) affect behavior and performance.

Workers are more motivated to perform tasks well in environments where the payoff is certain and outcomes appear to be determined by their skill and performance; in this type of environment they are more likely to perceive an internal locus of control. Workers are less motivated to high performance in situations where the outcomes or payoffs are more random. Which environment is a better description of public organizations? Is external attribution among public employees fostered by factors such as broad and sometimes contradictory goals, accountability to outside and often conflicting actors, and reliance on system over individual rewards? In all likelihood the answer is yes, but further research is needed to determine both public–private differences and variations among different public contexts.

Attribution and locus of control theory can affect both worker satisfaction and management style. Individuals perceiving an internal locus of control tend to be more satisfied in their jobs than those perceiving an external control situation. And those working in what they see as internal and external control situations respond differently to leadership styles. Using a locus of control measure to assess the degree to which an individual sees the environment as responding to his or her behavior, researchers found that internals were more satisfied with a participative leadership style (Mitchell, Smyser, and Weed 1975). Under some conditions, however, the nature of the task may override the relationships between participation and follower responses. If tasks are highly ambiguous or stressful, participative leadership is positively correlated with satisfaction—regardless of followers' external and internal predispositions (House and Mitchell 1974).

Terrence Mitchell and his associates investigated how attribution affects management behavior, specifically leader responses to poor performance by followers (Mitchell and Wood 1979; Green and Mitchell 1979). Just as workers attribute internal or external locus of control situations, so do managers and supervisors attribute internal and external causes for poor performance. If they perceive that a subordinate's poor performance is due to internal factors—insufficient ability, effort, or attentiveness—their response tends to be punitive. But if they perceive the locus of control as external to the follower, they are more likely to respond sympathetically.

Something like an attribution process may operate on a macro level as well. The success or failure of a public or nonprofit agency may be attributed to internal or external causes. For example, the perception that a government bureau or a public sector service agency is ineffectual may be accompanied by a public attitude that the organization is lazy, administratively top-heavy, encumbered by red tape, or the like. If internal factors are blamed, the agency will be charged with incompetence. If external factors (conflicting goals, inadequate material and public support, unrealistic time constraints) are recognized as a major hurdle for agency success—and there is support for the organization's goals—there is a much better chance that the problems will be acknowledged and corrected.

Summary of Cognitive Process Theories

The assumption basic to all process theory is that internal cognitive states and situational variables interact in the motivational process. The individual is an active factor, selecting behaviors based on his or her needs and on expectations about what kind of behavior will lead to a desired reward. This perspective has greatly expanded our understanding of human motivation and its complexities. Process theories provide a good conceptual grasp of how elements of internal states and behavior are related. They also offer a wide range of diagnostic and operational alternatives that can be applied to motivation, but they are difficult for managers to apply on a daily basis.

Part of the difficulty is that process theories are far more abstract than content models, making it tricky to identify specific appropriate incentives. Further, process models deal not only with differences in individual needs but also with differences among individuals' perceptions of important elements of the situation, such as rewards, opportunity, equity, and control over outcomes. Linking the effect of specific rewards to an individual's work motivation (or satisfaction or performance) is complex when the effect of actual rewards is mediated by a number of subtle and internal processes of perception and expectancy. It is impractical and time-consuming for managers to attempt such an assessment of employees and organizational incentives.

For all public agencies, governmental and nonprofit, the application of process models is difficult in other ways as well. Over two decades ago Chester Newland identified several problems that still remain when working with something like the politically popular merit pay system. "Unless performance can be appraised well, it is impossible to relate pay to it," he points out (1984, 39). In addition, he notes that using pay to motivate performance is probably not an effective technique unless relatively large pay increases are available. Newland also cautions, in a statement prescient of later developments in total quality management and other participative methods, that individual rewards such as merit pay that focus on individually competitive behaviors "may frustrate modular and team management approaches" (39).

These two problems—rewards (their adequacy and appropriateness) and performance (its definition and appraisal)—are crucial to forging the principal link in process models: High performance results in desired and equitable rewards. The utility of rewards in bureaus is limited by constraints already discussed. Defining performance targets or goals and appraising performance are equally challenging. The link between effort and performance is stronger when performance standards or goals are clear and relatively specific.

Measures of administrative efficiency and the achievement of performance targets remain an important part of programs in both government and the nonprofit sector. Such measures may work for total organizations; however, the use of such tools for individuals is given mixed reviews (Deming 2000; Kohn 1993). In spite of debate by scholars, the use of techniques such as employee appraisal processes, work standards, and merit pay seems to be increasing in government. In such cases there is a danger that workload rather than efficiency or effectiveness criteria may be used because of the difficulty in setting specific organization goals and breaking these down into objective specific performance measures for individuals (Greiner et al. 1981). Compared to the more specific and tangible goals of firms, government agencies pursue goals that are diffuse and conflicting, and their performance criteria are less readily defined; nonprofit organizations often have difficulty in measuring the true impact of their services on clients, much less the larger community. The link between effort and performance, and thus the expectation that given performances will produce specific rewards, is weakened by the lack of goal clarity as well as by conflicting demands. Therefore the cognitive process models assume situational specificity, flexibility, and control over rewards that is somewhat unrealistic when applied to public sector managers.

The next approach, behaviorism and operant conditioning, offers an alternative, universalistic perspective that directly links individual behavior and organizational incentives or rewards. In our case we are interested in incentives and rewards in organizations.

BEHAVIORIST THEORY AND WORK MOTIVATION

Motivation theory explains behavior through a broad range of internal psychological processes such as needs, expectancies, and perceptions, but such unobservable inner states are irrelevant to behavioral researchers. What an individual's motivation is—indeed whether or not an individual is motivated—is irrelevant; from the behaviorist's perspective, only observable behavior and its consequences are important.

In a strict sense, then, behaviorist theories are not theories of motivation but instead are theories about ways to manipulate individuals. However, operant conditioning and expectancy theories (that depend on extrinsic rewards) are related in certain important aspects, despite differences in their underlying assumptions (*noncognitive* versus *cognitive*): "Both approaches argue that (1) rewards should be closely tied to behavior, (2) reward administration should be frequent and consistent, and (3) people are motivated by outcomes (expected or past)" (Mitchell 1982, 86). Thus although their theoretical bases differ, there are parallels in the actual applications of either approach, and both entail similar practices and policies by an organization.

Behaviorist theory concentrates primarily on two factors: behavior and its consequences. Its central thesis is that behavior is caused by its contingent consequences, the essential point being that the consequence must be contingent on the occurrence of a particular behavior.

In other words, behaviorist theory is concerned with how an action may be controlled by a stimulus that comes after it; when positive reinforcement follows a behavior, that behavior is likely to be repeated. Because behavior operates on the environment to produce a consequence, the term *operant conditioning* is used. It refers to the process through which behavior is learned and reinforced (Skinner 1976).

In operant conditioning, behavior is determined by four types of consequences: positive reinforcement, negative reinforcement, extinction, and punishment. *Reinforcers* are functionally defined by their observable effects. A reinforcer is anything that strengthens and increases a given behavior. Note how this way of defining *reinforcer* differs from the concept of reward in cognitive theories, where a reward is that which is *perceived* to be desirable: One definition relies on the external and observable, the other on the internal and subjective. The distinction is important to an understanding of the unique perspective of behaviorist and operant conditioning theory.

Positive reinforcers are satisfying or good consequences; negative reinforcers are unsatisfying or noxious ones. Individuals repeat a pattern of behavior that elicits a satisfying consequence (positive reinforcer) or one that precludes an unsatisfying or noxious one (negative reinforcer). Thus both positive and negative reinforcement strengthen and increase—that is, reinforce—a given behavior.

The effects of extinction and punishment on behavior are the opposite of reinforcers; they weaken or decrease a given behavior. The technique of extinction involves providing nonreinforcement; that is, nothing must happen as a consequence of behavior. If a manager recognizes and praises those who speak up and offer ideas in meetings, for example, participation is likely to increase. Participative behavior has been reinforced. But if a manager ignores such behavior, in time followers will no longer initiate participative behavior. Human beings rarely persist in behavior that is not rewarded or, in operant conditioning terms, reinforced. If both extinction and punishment weaken a given behavior, which technique should be used? If an undesirable behavior is relatively new, extinction may be sufficiently effective in eliminating it. But if the undesirable behavior is long-standing or very serious, punishment may be indicated, despite its drawbacks.

Punishment, like negative reinforcement, involves aversive stimuli or consequences. But its effect—moving to stop an unwanted behavior—is the opposite of negative reinforcement, which, as mentioned earlier, is used to strengthen a given behavior. Punishment, although widely used in organizational settings, has various defects and undesirable side effects. Most notable is that punishment suppresses undesirable behavior but often fails to eliminate it; when the aversive agent is removed or discontinued, the behavior recurs. Another problem with punishment is that its overall effects are hard to predict and are often dysfunctional to the organization. For example, only the particular behavior at which the punishment is directed is likely to be eliminated. Hence an employee made resentful by punishment may retaliate by engaging in other actions that are even less desirable but harder to detect. A punitive organizational climate can result in discipline problems, low morale, and absenteeism.

At best punishment is limited to eliminating undesirable behavior. Its greatest drawback is that it can show an individual what *not* to do, but not *what* to do (Hersey and Blanchard 2001). Punishment can be appropriate and necessary under some conditions. For an effective system of conditioning to operate, however, the manager needs to then identify the desired behavior and use positive reinforcement when it occurs to increase and strengthen it in the future.

READING 8–1   Punished by Rewards: The Trouble with Gold Stars, Incentive Plans, A's, Praise, and Other Bribes

Clearly punishments are harsher and more overt; there is no getting around the intent to control in "Do this or else here's what will happen to you." But rewards simply "control through seduction rather than force." In the final analysis, they are not one bit less controlling since, like punishments, they are "typically used to induce or pressure people to do things they would not freely do"—or rather, things that the controller believes they would not freely do. This is why one of the most important (and unsettling) things we can recognize is that the real choice for us is not between rewards and punishments but between either version of behavioral manipulation, on the one hand, and an approach that does not rely on control, on the other. . . .

If our goal is quality, or a lasting commitment to a value or behavior, no artificial incentive can match the power of intrinsic motivation. Think about someone you know who is truly superlative at his job. Now ask yourself whether he has a bumper sticker on his car that says I OWE, I OWE, IT'S OFF TO WORK I GO or THANK GOD IT'S FRIDAY or WORK SUCKS, BUT I NEED THE BUCKS. (One could scarcely imagine more vivid signs of an economic system in crisis.) Clearly this is not the sort of sentiment we associate with people who do excellent work. Such people may be glad to be paid, and even more glad to be well paid, but they do not see themselves as working primarily in order to collect a paycheck. They love what they do. Sometimes they even keep doing it on their own time.

This doesn't mean that our interest in a task fully accounts for how well we do it—or even completely explains why performance drops in the presence of rewards. But intrinsic motivation remains a powerful predictor of how good a job someone will do in the workplace or how successfully he or she will learn in school. As one group of researchers summed up the available evidence, "Intrinsically motivated people function in performance settings in much the same way as those high in achievement motivation do: They pursue optimal challenges, display greater innovativeness, and tend to perform better under challenging conditions." (Koestner et al., 1987, 389)

SOURCE: Alfie Kohn, *Punished by Rewards: The Trouble with Gold Stars, Incentive Plans, A's, Praise, and Other Bribes* (New York: Houghton Mifflin, 1993), 26, 68–69.

Summary of Behaviorist Motivation Theory

Operant conditioning is used continually in organizations, in most cases without organizational leaders or members having any formal knowledge of behaviorist theory. Surprisingly, the results are sometimes favorable. Unfortunately, however, inappropriate behavior is also often unintentionally reinforced (Kohn 1993).

Reinforcing dysfunctional behavior in public bureaus has ramifications beyond the individual and even beyond the organization. Government budget and appropriations practices are an example. Ordinarily public bureaus may not "save" or put aside surplus funds past the budget period for which they were authorized and appropriated. Such funds are to be returned to the government's general treasury. At the same time it is common wisdom among government administrators that they must avoid turning back funds because legislators will conclude that the bureau can get by on smaller future appropriations; therefore, as the end of a budget cycle approaches, unused funds are spent. Hasty expenditures on equipment, services, and travel are not desirable agency responses to legislators who oversee government agencies. Yet by spending leftover funds, agency officials avoid (negative reinforcement) lower appropriations in the future. We can only hope that last-minute expenditures have been planned and prioritized throughout the year so that undesirable results are minimized. Whatever the truth of the matter, these potentially negative practices are reinforced through the actions of outside overseers.

The behavioral approach offers a clear perspective on the problem of motivating workers to perform in ways that are useful to the organization and restraining them from behavior that is not organizationally desirable. However, the operant conditioning approach has strong detractors (see the reading by Alfie Kohn) who argue against the basic assumption that behavior can be controlled through external stimuli. When behavior modification is used intentionally, it should be remembered that the technique is best suited to simple behaviors. Moreover, such use requires that the desired behavior be specifically defined and that the organization can provide clear and proximate rewards for individual performance. Given the ambiguity of public goals and the relative lack of flexibility and control of rewards, this method's systematic use in any kind of public agency has serious limitations.

MOTIVATION AS EXPLANATION AND TOOL IN PUBLIC SECTOR ORGANIZATIONS

Human motivation and behavior are complex phenomena. They arise from interactions of both individual and situational variables. In addition, public sector settings introduce distinctive constraints, values, and opportunities for motivation. Government and nonprofit organizations differ from one another; and both differ, sometimes dramatically, from firms in the private sector. In this final section of the chapter let us consider three major uses of motivation theory as it applies to public sector agencies. Obviously these three approaches to understanding and using motivation theory only begin to address the myriad ways in which this information proves useful, but they let us work through some examples of how motivation theory is important to understanding life and action in public organizations. The three subjects to be addressed are what motivates people to join and participate in public organizations; how motivation theory affects the everyday life of public organizations; and how motivation theory lies at the base of the leadership theories and models presented in the next chapter.

The Decision to Join and Participate

Motivation and behavior are influenced by the *public* nature of an organization, and public organizations and policy are affected by the motivation and behavior of public employees and officials. Organization theories are needed that specifically address these types of organizations and behavior. The central questions are these: Why do people join public sector organizations? What directs their behavior (decisions and actions) as they participate in the mission and procedures of the public agency? These questions can be answered, at least in large part, by combining the ideas just developed with a "typology of bureau official motivation" developed by Anthony Downs (1994, 79–111). Although the bureaucratic context (remember that as organizations get larger they tend to be more bureaucratic) is an integral part of Downs's model, as is the interplay between individual motivation and policy preferences, it seems reasonable to apply the model to both governmental and nonprofit organizations. Of course different parts of the model apply with varying levels of congruency depending on the particular organization being considered.

Remember that organizations exist for many reasons; it may be necessary to go back to the beginning of this chapter and review the typology of organizations presented there. Nonprofit organizations usually fit into the first three categories (normative, service, and mutual benefit) whereas government organizations make up most of the commonweal category. However, there is spillover between these two types of organizations, and they face many of the same problems in promoting extraordinary performance. We will discuss these similarities and differences in the next section, which addresses how motivation theories are used in the public sector. But first let us examine why people join and participate in public sector organizations.

People in public organizations tend to be somewhat different from those in the private sector. People who choose public employment are apt to have a greater interest in serving the public interest—of doing something that helps society at large. Ultimately, though, public employees, like all individuals, vary in their personalities. And these characteristics change throughout each individual's career as external factors change and each person goes through the various stages of life and career (Schott 1986, 1987; Gale 1969; Crain 2000).

Downs (1994) describes at least five such different sets of characteristics. Downs's theory of five personality types of officials is in reality a set of practical observations about motivations in public organizations. He begins with two assumptions about human nature: (1) people are rational—their behavior is directed toward goals; and (2) they are motivated at least in part by *self-interest;* as a result they pursue goals that are in their own interest. But the prevalence of self-interest in the theory does not mean that officials do not take the interests of others into account; they have multiple goals, some of which are altruistic—that is, for the benefit of interests other than their own.[4] And some goals are mixed in that they may be part self-interest and part altruism.

Downs says that all bureau officials have multiple goals that derive from a set of general motives:

1. Power.
2. Money.
3. Income.
4. Prestige.
5. Convenience.
6. Security.
7. Pride in work proficiency.

---

[4]Downs's emphasis on self-interest is quite different—shall we say less intense—than what is found in current public choice theory and "self-interest models" used by economic interpretations of administrative behavior. Downs argues that self-interest is *one of many* motivators—and most prominent among some people—but that many other motivators are present, and sometimes prominent, within each individual.

8. Personal loyalty (either to one's own work group, the organization as a whole, or to a larger entity such as the government, the nation, or "the cause").

9. Desire to serve the public interest.

10. Commitment to a specific program of action.

These goals or motives do not represent an individual's overall goal structure; but they determine an official's behavior as it relates to his or her position in the public agency.

The first six motives are based on self-interest. Downs classifies the rest as mixed. One's desire to serve the public interest is altruistic; one's commitment to a specific program or policy is ambiguous—it may be altruistic, self-interested, or both.

Not all officials are motivated in the same degree by all motives; rather, each individual gives greater weight to some combination of motives. Downs concentrates on five combinations, and from these groupings he constructs a typology of officials based on their motivation structure; these officials are "ideal types."[5] Oversimplification is unavoidable here, as Downs acknowledges, because no reasonable number of ideal types can "encompass the bewildering variety of personalities and characters in the world" (1994, 88).

The five types of officials are climbers, conservers, zealots, advocates, and statesmen. The first two types—climbers and conservers—are motivated primarily by self-interest; the remaining three types—zealots, advocates, and statesmen—are mixed-motive officials. Each of these three types envisions organizational goals in terms of their perception of the public interest or the cause; and conversely, each type equates the public interest or the cause with their view of organizational goals. Their motives combine self-interest and altruistic loyalty to larger values, but the three types differ in the breadth of the larger values to which they are devoted.

In Downs's theory, as in content models, behavior is viewed as deriving from needs and goals that shape motives. Organization and position characteristics shape behavior, and the individual's beliefs about the probability of attaining his or her goal are also considered determinants of motivation. Motivation and behavior are also contingent on environmental variables and expectancies.

Climbers

The climber seeks to maximize his or her own power, income, and prestige by promotion, aggrandizement, and jumping between agencies. Promotion provides the greatest personal gain and is preferred. Aggrandizement entails increasing the power, income, and prestige associated with an individual's existing position by adding new functions or control over people or by achieving more than previous occupants of the position. Climbers will often consider moving to another organization either to get to the next career step or because long-term opportunities seem better. When climbers move into leadership positions there may be a tendency to use subordinates or to treat employees and others interacting with the agency as pawns. And because climbers are on the move—upward in the organization or hopping to another one—their leadership may be aimed at producing short-term results at the expense of long-term performance and the morale of others. Climbers tend to congregate in fast-growing agencies just as they tend to move from contracting or slowly growing organizations.

---

[5]Remember from Chapter 3 that an *ideal type* is a description of the characteristics that most perfectly meet the criteria of the group or subgroup. Thus an ideal type is an abstraction by which a set of characteristics is sharpened or clearly differentiated, and against which one may measure the level of achievement of those characteristics.

Climbers are receptive to organizational change because it can produce new opportunities for either promotion or aggrandizement. Because attachment to settled procedures and alliances is considered a hallmark of bureaucratic behavior, the climber's acceptance of risk can be useful to public sector managers who understand and channel it.

Conservers

These employees are motivated to maximize their security and convenience. Conservers resist change so they can avoid any risk to their existing power, income, and prestige, and because they do not have a strong desire for more of these. Change might harm them, and they do not strongly favor its potential rewards. Thus only changes that head off threats to their security or make their lives easier because less effort will be required of them are welcomed by conservers.

Conservers need only maintain acceptable performance levels and refrain from actions that invite failure and risk. In government, the safety of following bureau rules, together with various personnel practices (reliance on seniority, discharge only for proven cause, extensive procedural and appeals mechanisms), is usually sufficient to maintain security. For workers in all public sector agencies, accountability and neutrality norms reinforce and give added legitimacy to the conserver's by-the-book approach.

Individuals may be conservers because of personality factors, but occasionally conserver behavior is created by expectancies. In the latter group are competent people whose upward progress is barred by age, seniority, or other unchangeable traits. "In every bureau, there is an inherent pressure upon the vast majority to become conservers in the long run" (Downs 1994, 99). As a person becomes older and the expectations for substantial advancement grow slimmer, the tendency to become a conserver increases. Older and slower-growing organizations have more conservers, as do agencies that have developed a culture emphasizing formal rules and control (for example, welfare organizations where the emphasis has moved from "helping people get out of poverty" to "minimizing cheating").

The proportion of conservers is higher at the middle levels of an agency hierarchy than at the lowest and highest levels, and the proportion of conservers in any organization tends to increase over time. The "closing of the hierarchy" as one moves through a career limits the chances for advancement. When people remain in an organization for a long time it becomes harder—for a variety of reasons—to move elsewhere. And as individuals move up through the hierarchy they are increasingly required by the duties inherent in their positions to make decisions and take the chance of making a mistake (see Chapter 7). Climbers, if they are successful, at some point have a lot to lose! The climber often focuses on the fact that rewards are externally controlled rather than being an internal phenomenon. Because both the internal and external opportunity structures support and reinforce conserver rather than climber behavior, climbers "learn" to become conservers.

Conservers solve this dilemma by sticking to the rules; rules reduce the risks in decision making, and conservers are risk avoiders. Rule following lends stability to any organization's activity. It also ensures the accountability expected of officials because their positions are public, not private. But unduly rigid adherence to rules can impair agency responsiveness and hamper efficiency with red tape. If extreme, rule following can even be dysfunctional to the accomplishment of the agency's larger objectives and societal functions. Motivation must aim at maintaining a will to serve while recognizing the importance of security for these individuals.

Zealots

Zealots, like advocates and statesmen, are motivated less by self-interest than by higher-level needs. Although the concepts and models developed by Maslow and Herzberg are applicable in some measure, only Katz and Kahn's highest incentive structure directly touches on the distinctive motivation needs of these officials. The zealot perceives organizational goals and the public interest very narrowly by focusing on a "sacred" or special policy.

Because of the tremendous amounts of energy they help to generate and focus in the pursuit of their sacred policies, zealots can be a significant force in overcoming bureaucratic inertia, creating efficiency, and bringing about change. "Every bureau needs to encourage some zealots," Downs says, "and bureaus operating in rapidly changing environments need to nurture a great many" (1994, 110).

On the other hand, innovators and catalysts for change—especially zealots—generate conflict and resentment. In their willingness to vigorously attack the status quo on behalf of their "cause," or to protect it from either internal or external threats, zealots often draw attention to deficiencies in their organizations, emphasize their own remedies for overcoming the "problems," and make powerful enemies for themselves and their cause outside the organization. Because the end is so important to them, zealots often do not take into account the organizational and personal costs—material and political—of their suggestions or demands. They are most likely to engender resentment and resistance in conserver-dominated bureaus. And, paradoxically, conservers are more effective change agents than are zealots in agencies dominated by climbers and advocates because zealots tend to support only their own narrow interpretation of policy, "starving" any other developments.

Zealots usually make poor general administrators. They are unlikely to be found in top-level agency positions, although they can be found on high-level staffs. Only when a policy with which a zealot has become identified becomes suddenly and critically significant is this type of official likely to be elevated to a leading position. To a surprising degree, then, the external political environment conditions and shapes the rewards and reinforcements for zealot behavior. If it is possible to focus the efforts of zealots on organizational goals and in organizational processes, their internal motivators will keep them productive and useful.

Advocates

An advocate is motivated to promote whatever is in the best interest of the particular office he or she holds. Downs is not referring to self-interest here, but to advocates' loyalty to the organizations in which they work (1994, 102). Certain patterns—five are identified—characterize advocate behavior.

First, advocates do not focus on only one part of their organizational domain, but rather on the overall conditions and performance that are within their purview. Consequently they promote everything that is under their jurisdiction.

Second, advocates play the political game well in their external dealings, but they are impartial leaders and arbiters internally. The resources and prestige their organization or group receives depends on their success at external advocacy. In their external struggles advocates create conflict by competing and threatening the domains of others; but the other side of this conflict is that internal group unity and morale rise—members feel loyal to the advocate who champions their interests.

A third pattern is that advocates will persist in advocacy only if they believe the policies for which they have responsibility are significant and that there is a high probability they can influence those policies. If these conditions are not met, they will not continue acting as advocates over long periods, nor will they maintain the considerable expenditure of time and energy that advocacy requires.

Fourth, advocates rather than climbers are the most aggressive and persistent sources of "bureaucratic imperialism" (Holden 1966). They support innovation and expansion by their organization—and to obtain more resources, they magnify the problems facing their bureaus. Their practice of calling attention to unfavorable conditions and deficiencies is often disturbing to their superiors and to political leaders who prefer to give the public the impression that everything is under control. Compared to climbers and conservers, whose concern is limited to their own careers, advocates see their careers and the success of the bureau as intertwined. Thus advocates develop a broad, long-term perspective toward policy proposals and decisions related to the agency.

Finally, information flow becomes specialized as a result of advocates concentrating on a particular spectrum of activities and responsibilities. Specialized and differentiated information flow reinforces an official's sense of the relative importance of the position he or she occupies and its functions. Further, an advocate is a part of and is familiar with the processes by which alternatives are deliberated and evaluated in his or her own organization. On the other hand, she or he sees only the finished reports and recommendations from other organizations or parts of the bureau and knows little about the quality of the underlying choice process. As a result, nearly every official has greater faith in the reliability of his or her own part of the bureaucracy. Motivation to advocacy behavior, Downs concludes, is supported in this way:

> Special role expectations that encourage advocacy are attached to certain kinds of bureau positions. Because officials at all levels recognize the vital advantages of having advocates in charge of specialized bureaus, the role of bureau head (or department head, or division head, and the like) tends to be conceived as an advocacy role by most other persons who interact with that role, including the generalists at the top of the pyramid (such as the president). This expectation creates a further incentive for whoever performs each such role to behave like an advocate. (Downs 1994, 105)

In the case of bureau members and followers, this role expectation is especially strong because advocates' external effectiveness determines their resources and prestige.

Many factors in public organizational life cause officials to behave as advocates. Rewards, both external and internal, often accrue to advocates through their position and performance. A sense of achievement often comes with the territory. Their position in the bureau creates opportunities for influence and power. As liaison, their communication role (between their organization and the external environment) gives them visibility and recognition as well as information-based power. Others seek to affiliate with advocates. Advocacy and advancement are linked: The proportion of advocates increases at higher agency levels (Downs 1994, 109).

Statesmen

Loyalty to a very broad conception of the public interest motivates statesmen. Attentiveness to society and the nation as a whole receives philosophical support from everyone. Government political rhetoric is filled with exhortations to public administrators to serve the interests of the entire population; administrators, in turn, vow their loyalty to the citizenry. For nonprofit organizations, even though they are serving a particular sector of society, a primary goal is to carry out the agency's stated function in an effort to improve the overall quality of life for society. In reality, however, consistent statesmanlike behavior is rare due to the formidable obstacles in the politically charged environment, along with the structures and procedures that exist within governmental and nonprofit organizations. The pressures to become an advocate, which have already been described, also operate to stifle the more diffuse altruism of the statesman.

Officials whose behavior is statesmanlike in spite of the constraints they face and who forgo attending to the well-being of their own agencies usually earn the hostility of others in their organizations. These coworkers know that if all bureaus but theirs are being vigorously promoted, the stature (and resource allocation) for their organization may suffer. It is little wonder that statesmen are rarely promoted to the top ranks of their organizations.

Although rare, statesmanlike behavior does occur. If society's survival or that of the overall social or governmental structure is threatened, even officials with other motivation structures are inclined to act like statesmen. However, in less critical cases such behavior from officials is usually short in duration and specific in issue.

The nature of the bureaucracy is such a powerful inhibitor on statesmanlike behavior that under some conditions this fact of bureau life must be offset by specially structuring some positions. Sometimes, in an attempt to get more statesmanship into administrative decision making and policy implementation, advisory bodies are brought together to examine particular issues. The individuals in such bodies are often individuals recognized for their expertise and lack of an ax to grind. This is also the role played by advisers to the president on various areas requiring considerable knowledge of the relevant field (such as the president's science adviser) and time to analyze without specific daily tasks to pull attention away from the subject at hand.

Motivation and Organizational Commitment

Once we understand what motivates people to join and participate, it is possible to use that information in applying motivation theories as part of everyday life in the bureaucracy. Managers and supervisors must use the models of motivation to develop systems within the organization that reinforce productive behavior by creating an environment that helps individuals meet their own goals while also achieving the mission of the organization. The keys to success are maintaining

- Clear organizational goals (often complicated by the fact that the goals are set outside the organization).

- A focus on serving clients while remembering both individual needs and the public interest.

- A reward system that builds on employees' internal motivation and encourages commitment and effort toward achieving those goals.

Such a mission for managers and supervisors is no small task. To achieve effort and commitment in public organizations there must be a focus on the higher rewards, or satisfaction levels, of Maslow (1987), Herzberg (1974), and Katz and Kahn (1982). Security is assumed in most government organizations—although privatization, contracting out, and cutbacks in budget and staff through the last couple of decades have had a negative effect on these lower-level motivators. The workers in government increasingly understand the kinds of careers available in the public sector, as well as the probability and fairness of the rewards upon successfully carrying out their duties (review Figure 8–4 earlier in this chapter). Individuals working in nonprofit organizations are seldom doing so to get rich: They usually feel some commitment to the cause of the agency. Money, while important, is only one of many foci for most highly motivated workers outside the private sector (and probably in the private sector too). Interesting work, self-expression, internalization of goals, growth and development, responsibility, and a sense of achievement are the characteristics that can be affected by organizational leadership, structure, and process. These factors are increasingly the focus of motivation in most organizations, but they are about the only area of flexibility for public managers and leaders. If these theories are brought together, it is possible to develop at least a rudimentary model of motivation in the public sector.

At the same time the personnel and reward systems available to public sector organizations are quite different from those in the private sector. Politician and citizen attitudes toward the various public sector missions and procedures are unlike those held in reference to private organizations. Private organizations are assumed to work efficiently or they do not continue to exist, and people do not have to accept their products or services if the capitalist system is accomplishing its goal of competition. On the other hand, public sector organizations work in "glass houses" where interest groups, and often citizens in general, watch the functions and outputs/ends of those who are "spending their tax money" or "using their donations given for a specific cause" (and with the expectation of a specific outcome). And finally, because of these differences, the public response—laudatory, grateful, critical, or damning—has a strong effect on the morale and motivation of those working in the public sector. These differences do not mean that there must be a different theory of public motivation, but they require changes in the interpretation and application of the models.

In the United States the civil service operates within the general parameters of a merit system to cover most operational, non–policy-making positions at all levels of government. It is interesting to note that the perception of what is important in a merit system has changed over the last few decades, with decreased emphasis on political protection for workers. However, two cornerstone values of public personnel management that are perceived as important parts of the merit system are technical competence and equal pay for equal work. These two values have an interesting effect on the motivation systems used in government.

Technical or work-related competence was established as the criteria for selection, promotion, and related personnel choices; thus the merit system created a need to define what duties were entailed and what qualifications were required for a given position. Although clarity of job description helps limit manipulation of individuals in positions, it can, at the same time, lead to overspecialization and a narrow definition of duties. Job enrichment, or the use of an employee's "total capacity," can be difficult because government managers often find that their discretion in either shifting employees or adjusting the range of tasks to match individual abilities is hampered.

Equal pay for equal work is accomplished through position classification, which organizes all positions into groups or classes based on their duties, responsibilities, and required qualifications. Again the initial goal of equality in pay has had some unintended and detrimental effects on motivation. Salaries are attached to job classifications, not to individuals. Those who perform at an outstanding level and those who do enough to survive may make approximately the same salary. Implementing this aspect of the merit system has created job classification systems that are both highly complex and too simple. For example, all the myriad jobs in the federal bureaucracy are reduced to 16 or so categories. Because the salary and step increases are set for each category, there is little or no flexibility in pay.

The accountability norm further complicates the merit system. For example, the evaluation system encourages supervisors to give individuals middling evaluations because very high evaluations entail extensive justification and proof, whereas very low evaluations trigger even more extensive documentation and proof required because of grievance and appeal procedures. Thus the introduction of "merit pay" (based on performance on the job) or other attempts to differentiate between levels of performance at the same classification level often create as many, or more, problems than they resolve. In many cases merit pay systems have also failed because of the inability or unwillingness of legislators to fund the programs adequately. So the most widely accepted types of external motivation—money and promotion—cannot be used extensively by civil service managers. Internal motivators, which most students of motivation theory argue are more appropriate, must be depended on; but similar limits are placed on personnel and program management processes by the rules of accountability in public organizations.

Although nonprofit organizations may not face the same problem of rigid personnel systems, managers still must administer any such system constantly remembering that they have limited resources and that they also "live in glass houses." If a nonprofit uses federal funds, this fact immediately places certain limitations on how employees are treated. Likewise many community donors are sensitive to issues of equity, efficiency, and effectiveness; so the options for external or material motivation in nonprofit organizations are much more limited than those in the private sector. With volunteer workers in addition to wage-earning employees, nonprofit organizations must consider factors related to maintaining job satisfaction and loyalty to the organization and its leaders. Research points to the importance of relationships with supervisors and coworkers, seeing results from the work being done, and a sense that psychological contracts (the sensed or unwritten commitments from both sides beyond anything formally presented) are being met in return for workers' efforts.

A common approach to the issue of extrinsic rewards in public agencies is to use system rewards that are based on membership or seniority in the organization. System rewards—such as retirement plans, vacation policies, or personal leave time—are cheaper (at least in the short term) than monetary incentives, have lower visibility in the budget process, and thus have greater appeal to officials facing a taxpaying or dues-paying public. Such considerations allow flexibility in the work situation, and they are often increased based on seniority. But system rewards are not directly related to individual performance and therefore may serve primarily as a bottom line in motivating workers.[6]

Environmental factors and external climate strongly affect public organizations' motivation and reward systems. Decades of blaming bureaucracy have led to unfavorable attitudes about public employment and public agencies (both governmental and nonprofit). Failures such as the Federal Emergency Management Agency's initial debacle in handling Hurricane Katrina and the New Orleans/Gulf Coast catastrophe only underline and strengthen the general attitude toward public employees. To the extent that the general public holds unfavorable attitudes about public employment and public bureaucracies, it becomes increasingly

---

[6]If system rewards are based on seniority, they are ultimately rewards based more on longevity or staying with the organization than they are about excellent performance.

important to try to develop and maintain motivation-relevant employee perceptions such as self-worth and personal significance.

Bureaucrat bashing remains a favorite political sport, and combined with the downsizing of governments (caused by everything from tax limitations at the state level to budget deficits and philosophical restrictions at the federal level), there has been a general demoralization of government employees. The Clinton administration's attempt to improve the effectiveness and efficiency of government agencies had as one of its primary goals reducing the number of employees by dramatic amounts. This "disinvestment," as it is referred to by Lane and Wolf, has become a threat to what they call "governance capacity":

> The effects of continuing budgetary restrictions, antibureaucratic rhetoric, reorganizations, reductions in force, and various administrative retrenchments have adversely affected the quality of work life and sent the message that a public agency is the wrong place to invest personal energy and identity. As a result, organizational and program capacity is being lost daily as workers invest less of themselves in their work, make fewer commitments, and seek ways out of the system. (1990, 3)

The Bush administration came into office committed to privatizing programs and reducing the role of government within the total economy. Many of those aims were dramatically changed with the attack on the World Trade Center and the military actions in Afghanistan and Iraq that soon followed. Privatization of programs continued, however, and the emphasis on expanding the role of faith-based nonprofits led to continuing unsettlement in government and new challenges in the nonprofit area. Motivation theory and its application must be especially perceptive and sagacious in such an environment. New ways of using established models must be sought.

READING 8–2   Some Things Never Change!

In 1983 the message about working in the federal government was very negative. The impact of such a barrage of "antibureaucrat" (the term often used by denigrators of federal employment) propaganda is noted here.

The federal civil service system marks its centennial today unhappy, unhealthy, under siege. The assault comes from all quarters.

Even Madison Avenue has gotten into the act with advertisements for Federal Express that portray the employees of its competitor, the U.S. Postal Service, as surly, lazy, unresponsive. "The worst part of it was they were funny," said George Gould, legislative director of the National Association of Letter Carriers, whose protests helped push the hardest-hitting ads off the air.

Images have consequences. Since 1977, the lot of the federal worker has declined on a number of fronts.

- Government salaries, which by law are supposed to be kept at par with comparable private sector wages, are lagging a record 13.9 percent.
- The cost of government employee health premiums has gone up an average of 55 percent in the past two years while the benefits have been reduced an average of 12 to 16 percent.

- The jewel of the federal employees' compensation package, the retirement system, has been whittled back four of the past five years and now faces the most sweeping attack in its 62-year history.

- Since passage of the Civil Service Reform Act of 1978, designed to make the bureaucracy more responsive to political leadership, top-level careerists have enjoyed far less job security against policy or political purges.

From the viewpoint of some careerists, the loss of job protections, combined with the arrival of a batch of ideologically zealous political appointees who consider the government the enemy, has been a disaster. "It has gotten to the point where many of the nation's most capable public administrators are forced into being yes-men," said Bernard Rosen, a former executive director of the U.S. Civil Service Commission. "I've never seen it so bad." All of this has taken a predictable toll on morale.

"We are the new underclass of society," said G. Jerry Shaw, president of the Senior Executives Association, which represents high-ranking career bureaucrats. "People make jokes about us that they've stopped making about ethnic groups and minorities."

James Beggs, director of the National Aeronautics and Space Administration, said, "Anytime you are constantly told that you are a bunch of leeches on society, morale is bound to suffer." He worries, as do most top federal executives, that the image, pay, and morale problems are leading to a "brain drain" from government.

SOURCE: From "Federal Workers: Unloved and Under Siege" by Paul Taylor from *The Washington Post,* January 16, 1983. Copyright © 1983 The Washington Post. Reprinted with permission.

Of course things are little different in 2005, and policy makers are still trying to figure out what the problem is.

Worried that too many young Americans are turned off by the idea of working in government, Congress has provided $600,000 for a research project to develop strategies to raise interest among college students in federal service.

The "Call to Service Recruitment Initiative" will be run by the Office of Personnel Management and the Partnership for Public Service, according to the fiscal 2006 spending bill that covers OPM operations.

"The war for talent is a real one," Max Stier, president of the partnership, said. "The public sector is losing that war, and the consequences are going to become more severe."

The project will use surveys and other research efforts to test and evaluate various methods of reaching out to college students and to understand what messages or outreach activities might sway top-notch graduates to seriously consider a federal job.

Or as Stier put it, "Can we move the needle on students' interest in government as an employer of first choice?"

He noted that "the military has spent millions upon millions of dollars on understanding what talent they need to succeed, but virtually no research has been done on the civil service side of the house."

OPM and the partnership, a nonprofit group, launched the Call to Serve campaign in 2002 in an effort to educate young Americans about federal careers. The campaign has enlisted the help of 565 colleges and 62 federal agencies. . . .

Part of the project will focus on hard-to-fill occupations in the government. . . . For example, Stanford will look at how best to recruit engineering students; Ohio State will see what should be done to improve foreign language skills in the government; and New Mexico will examine new ways of attracting Hispanics to federal service, Stier said.

The partnership and OPM will produce reports that will hopefully help federal agencies improve their recruitment of college students and other young Americans.

Rep. Jerry Lewis (R-Calif.), chairman of the House Appropriations Committee, and Rep. Joe Knollenberg (R-Mich.), who chairs an appropriations subcommittee that oversees OPM, were key backers of the research project, Stier said.

A 2004 survey sponsored by the Council for Excellence in Government found that only 23 percent of young Americans were extremely likely or very likely to pursue a government career. By contrast, 35 percent said they were interested in working for a "community service organization."

Previous research by the partnership and Paul C. Light, a New York University professor, found that many Americans view federal careers as unappealing or believe that the government needs to be reformed, making it difficult for agencies to attract and keep talented employees.

SOURCE: Stephen Barr, "Congress Funds Project to Entice College Grads to Government Service," *Washington Post,* December 9, 2005, B2.

On the positive side, research indicates that public servants are attracted to public and nonprofit organizations for somewhat different reasons than those attracting individuals to private ones. Those who enter the public sector place less value on material reward than those who choose the profit sector (Rawls, Ulrich, and Nelson 1975; Gortner 1970). A desire to perform public service is cited by those entering public, but not private, careers (Gortner 1970). Some evidence points to greater security motivations among public respondents, but in other instances differences are less clear-cut (Gortner 1970; Rawls, Ulrich, and Nelson 1975).

Studies do point to somewhat different public and private patterns of commitment. The concept of commitment has several dimensions: desire to remain a member of the organization, willingness to perform at high levels, and acceptance of organizational goals and values. Private firms have considerable advantages and success in engendering commitment among their managers, whereas certain work setting and environmental characteristics of government and nonprofit organizations adversely affect motivation. An interesting question, for which there is no immediate answer, is to what extent the desire of public and nonprofit employees to function in public service offsets the commitment-limiting characteristics of those same organizations.

A comparative study of government and business managers found that an individual's perception of having contributed to organizational success has the greatest impact on his or her commitment (Buchanan 1974). Highly committed managers also feel a sense of challenge in their jobs, experience cohesion in their work groups, and perceive that the organization expects commitment. The substantive goals of most government agencies are diffuse, and agency effectiveness is hard to measure. As a result, the observable links between what a public manager does and the organization's success are harder to discern. Nonprofit organizations usually have a clearer sense of mission, so it is possible to emphasize the challenge and a sense of accomplishment when success occurs. This greatly increases the ability to use internal motivators in these organizations.

Another important factor is the stability of the organization's commitment to its goals. Nonprofit organizations generally continue to work toward specific goals (or ends) even if the means by which that goal is sought may change. Government organizations, on the other hand, confront circumstances—periodic ones like elections, as well as unpredictable shifts in public and political opinion—that lead to goal instability. Even when the publicly stated goal remains the same, the interpretation of what that goal means and the appropriate way to achieve it regularly change—especially if there are changes in party leadership or guiding philosophies among elected officials.

READING 8–3 Motivating Public Workers: Lessons from Nonprofit Management

At present, nonprofit management as an academic discipline is generally consigned to the role of a specialization within traditional public administration degree programs. The implication of this is that public management is a more mature and developed field, and especially well positioned to inform nonprofit management. However, close scrutiny of both chronic government problems and common nonprofit solutions leads one to see that nonprofits can actually teach the public sector some important lessons.

An illustrative example of this is in the area of employee motivation, a major challenge in government. Harvard University Professor Robert D. Behn characterizes a common public sector dilemma with the following lament: "How can you motivate anyone in the public sector? Everyone is protected by civil service rules. We can't fire anyone. We can't reward anyone. How can they expect us to get anything done?"

In part this is what social scientists call a "principal–agent" problem. Motivation requires knowledge of performance: A manager motivates employees either by rewarding excellent work or penalizing that which is substandard. Yet worker performance is difficult to monitor, creating incentives to shirk responsibilities. And uncontrolled performance means uncontrolled morale, leading to exit by the cream of the workforce.

The Importance of Nonfinancial Benefits

But motivation goes beyond simple control of the workforce. It also involves inspiration to achieve public purpose with vigor. Understanding this involves attention to the personal benefit calculation of public sector employees. Given the relatively low salaries in many government jobs, a significant portion of the compensation is certainly nonfinancial, as many authors in public management have noted. The core issue can be explained as follows. An employee in any sector earns compensation in wages, fringe benefits, and nonpecuniary compensation (such as job satisfaction, public-spiritedness, experience, career enhancement, and a host of other possible intangible benefits). If a potential employee chooses to work for government in spite of higher-paying alternatives in the private sector, it must logically be that nonmoney benefits are higher in government work for this employee. The lesson here is that under constrained financial resources—where wages are effectively fixed at a low level—the handle on worker motivation can be found in these nonfinancial benefits.

Nonprofit administrators deal with the most extreme form of this problem. Volunteer workforces are prevalent in the third sector, representing the case in which *all* compensation is nonfinancial. Thus an understanding of volunteer compensation is equivalent to understanding the power of nonpecuniary benefits in isolation. As such, nonprofit research is well placed to assist public management on this subject. What motivates someone to volunteer? In reviewing the literature, Boston College sociologist David Horton Smith has identified six basic categories of variables that lead to participation in nonprofit activities: demographic characteristics, geographic region, personality, the inherent propensity to participate in voluntary associations, attitudes toward the group of interest, and the interpersonal links involved in giving and volunteering. Obviously most of the benefits in these categories cannot be manipulated by managers. However, the nonprofit management literature has isolated several main nonmoney benefits that are major motivators to volunteers and that nonprofit managers *can* influence to one extent or another. These benefits include the perceived social meaningfulness of an activity; the skills-enhancing ability of a volunteer opportunity; the role of an opportunity as a substitute for market work; and a positive organizational culture.

Motivating forces for volunteers track fairly closely with those found among satisfied government employees: a sense of public service, skills acquisition, and a workplace environment that features more security and less stress than in the private sector (to name just three that researchers commonly find). As such, public HR managers might look to the nonprofit sector for designing retention, recruitment, and work quality appeals that exploit nonmoney benefits.

The marketing of volunteer benefits is evident and easy to find in practice throughout the nonprofit sector. To take one random example, Britain's Royal Horticultural Society advertises that the reasons people volunteer are as varied as the volunteers themselves. They paraphrase some of the most popular reasons thus:

- To meet people who enjoy gardening as much as I do.
- To get out in the fresh air in beautiful surroundings.
- To broaden my horticultural knowledge/horizons.
- To give something back.
- To create something for future generations to enjoy.
- To do more than my own garden/lack of garden permits.
- To learn from experts.

The principal nonpecuniary benefits discussed here are abundantly evident in this pitch to potential volunteers.

Benefits Need to be Codified

Nonprofits that are most successful in maintaining high-quality volunteer forces are those that give these types of benefits more than lip service. They design their programs in ways that deliver them to high-quality volunteers in a cost-effective manner. The lesson from this for public managers is that if nonmoney benefits to government workers are indeed an important currency of employment, managers need to codify and trade on them.

Beyond simple advertising for purposes of recruitment, some benefits might even be sufficiently within the control of managers to distribute on the basis of merit. For example, productive civil servants who are particularly interested in skills acquisition might be rewarded with internships in other departments or agencies. Similarly, good workers who prefer the public sector lifestyle to the rigidity and long hours in the private sector might receive merit bonuses in the form of, say, flextime or telecommuting privileges.

So what can we conclude from this?

- Clearly challenges in motivating public sector employees are not precisely the same as those in recruiting and retaining volunteers. In summary, however, we can see that the special circumstances of many nonprofits puts them in a unique position to inform public HR managers and that their experience makes the case for identifying nonpecuniary motivations for government employment.

- By understanding and (where possible) manipulating the relative value of different non-money benefits, managers can enhance the public sector workplace without necessarily increasing pay or tangible fringes.

- Marketing the most important intangible benefits of employment will aid in recruiting, retention, and employee motivation.

SOURCE: From Arthur C. Brooks, Associate Professor of Public Administration at the Maxwell School of Citizenship and Public Affairs, Syracuse University. Reproduced by permission of the Public Management and Policy Association.

Money is important! The importance of money does seem to fit into Maslow's hierarchy, with laborers emphasizing it more than white-collar workers. Employees in governmental and nonprofit organizations are aware of the differential in external rewards between their world and that of the private sector. And internally, within a particular organization, individuals compare salaries and pay raises as a major measure of their superiors' appreciation of individual effort and effectiveness. Nonetheless, studies over the years—in fact ever since the original research by Herzberg (1974; 1993)—suggest that job content and job challenge go a long way toward satisfying the needs of public employees.

Several factors may give public agencies some natural advantages in the formation of high commitment levels. The more distinctive and exciting the mission of an agency, the more likely members are to develop high commitment. Workers in the Red Cross have a strong commitment to their humanitarian efforts, and this is strongly reinforced at times like the dual hurricane strike along the Gulf Coast during the summer of 2005. In the Agency for International Development, managers and staff describe their agency's mission as humanitarian and important to foreign policy (Mahler 1985). The more lengthy and even stressful or hazardous the socialization, the higher the commitment level is likely to be (Van Maanen 1975a, 1975b; Kaufman 1967; Mahler 1985). A preestablished recruitment or entry pattern, reinforced by a distinctive image and mission (for example, the U.S. Marine Corps), makes self-selection effective as a means of creating organizational identification and commitment. So money is an important, but not necessarily a sufficient, motivator.

Motivation and Leadership

Finally, the third aspect of motivation in public sector organizations is related to leadership models and styles. The important point to make here is that the leadership style used by executives, managers, and supervisors (as well as the informal leaders in organizations) is determined by what motivates a leader (this is a case of "projection" from one's self to others) which in turn colors that leader's perception of the motivations influencing the people working under him or her. Leadership does not occur in a vacuum! *The perception of what motivates subordinates determines how a leader carries out his or her task.* This assertion can best be clarified and supported by looking at one of the early models of leadership, developed by Douglas McGregor, that interweaves the leader's perception of worker motivation and leadership style. He refers to his model as "Theory X" and "Theory Y" (McGregor 1956, 23–30; 1960). This model is presented here at the end of this chapter about motivation and culture because, either deliberately or by chance, the leadership models and theories developed over the last 60 years start from this most basic conception of the interaction of motivation and leadership. Because the model focuses on formal leadership in organizations, we use the term *management* instead of the more general term *leadership*.

After considerable study and reflection McGregor became convinced that the traditional organization with its centralized decision making, superior–subordinate pyramid, and external control of work is based on a set of assumptions about human nature and human motivation. These assumptions, which he calls *Theory X*, include the following:

1. Work is inherently distasteful to most people.
2. Most people are not ambitious, have little desire for responsibility, and prefer to be directed.
3. Most people have little capacity for creativity in solving organizational problems.
4. Motivation occurs only at the physiological and security levels.

This certainly sounds much like the charges made against public sector employees by many critics among both the general public and politicians. Because of the acceptance of these characteristics, a specific style of management is required:

1. Managers are responsible for organizing the elements of productive enterprise—money, materials, equipment, people—in the interest of achieving organizational ends.
2. Management is a process of directing people's efforts, motivating them, controlling their actions, modifying their behavior to fit the needs of the organization.
3. Without this active intervention by managers, people would be passive—even resistant—to organizational needs. They must therefore be persuaded, rewarded, punished, controlled—their activities must be directed.

Under these assumptions it is obvious that an authoritarian, control-oriented style of management (leadership) is bound to develop. McGregor argues that this type of management is likely to fail because it attempts to motivate employees in the wrong way. Management in this case depends on control, reward, and punishment, and ends up actually being a form of human manipulation (external) rather than motivation (internal). The major reason that this style of leadership fails is because *Theory X assumptions about human nature are generally inaccurate.*

The key to better management is a more accurate understanding of human nature and of what motivates a person at work. The proper perception of the worker, which McGregor calls *Theory Y,* assumes the following:

1. Work is as natural as play if the conditions are favorable.
2. Self-control is often indispensable in achieving organizational goals.
3. The capacity for creativity in solving organizational problems is widely distributed in the population.
4. Motivation occurs at the affiliation, esteem, and self-actualization levels, as well as the physiological and security levels.
5. People can be self-directed and creative at work if properly motivated.

With this view of workers, a new picture of management and leadership emerges. Managers are still responsible for organizing the elements of productive enterprise, just as is enunciated in the description of management style under Theory X; but the other steps in the process are dramatically different under Theory Y. According to McGregor,

1. Motivation, potential for development, capacity for assuming responsibility, and readiness to direct behavior toward organization goals are present in all people and employees. *Managers do not put these talents there.* It is a responsibility of managers to make it possible for people to recognize and develop these human characteristics for themselves.
2. The essential task of managers is to arrange organizational conditions and methods of operation so that people can achieve their own goals best by directing their own efforts toward organizational objectives. This is a process primarily of creating opportunities, releasing potential, removing obstacles, encouraging growth, and providing guidance.

Creating opportunities for employees and releasing their potential are at the opposite end of the spectrum from what many managers see as their traditional role—especially in the public sector, where there has been an emphasis on control over the years. It is also important to understand that organizational culture and how a person motivates or is motivated are inextricably intertwined. *A change in leadership style such as is suggested here inevitably changes the culture of the organization.* A better understanding of organizational culture, and of motivation and what it does (or how it can be used when it is an internal force in the individual), is central to success in public sector organizations.

Obviously McGregor's Theory Y deals with only one dimension of leadership, whereas the problem of leadership must be addressed from a systems approach and in a situational milieu. However, it helps to make the point that motivation—what people believe it is and how it affects people in organizations—is central to organizational life. This point will become even clearer as we move to the discussion of leadership styles in the next chapter.

CONCLUSION

If one theme emerges clearly from a review of the various work motivation theories and models, and how they are or can be used in the public sector, it is that research and application must include situational variables as well as individual factors. Some situations elicit organizationally effective behavior; others do not. These situations are often related to organizational culture, although external factors are also involved. Reward systems, nonmaterial employee support, and situational constraints in particular should be examined.

Governmental organizations appear to rely, for example, on security and system rewards. These types of rewards can elicit adequate role performance and reduce turnover. However, they do not promote high performance levels or activity that goes beyond role requirements. To heighten morale and dedication, a focus on organizational goals—and on higher-level, intrinsic motivational factors—must be developed in any motivation model for civil servants. Studies show that government employees have a sense of altruism, or desire to work for the public good, that influences their choice to work in the public sector.

Nonprofit organizations utilize as a motivator the commitment that many people bring to the organization and its cause. For volunteers this is especially important; but regular employees bring much of that same attitude, and any motivation plan must begin there. However, we must never forget that for employees who depend on material benefits for their livelihood, security must be found before other kinds of motivators can claim their true importance. In addition, participatory models of leadership (discussed in the next chapter) are essential to turning loose the creative, growth-oriented motivators that exist in most people.

Specialization of tasks, rigid job descriptions, detailed rules and regulations, required routines, and promotion based on seniority hinder motivation and minimize the recognition of individuality. Greater productivity is promoted when the content of work challenges through importance and complexity, allows for independent judgment, and offers opportunities for advancement. Rewards, when possible, must create a sense of equity and recognition of performance even though external actors and forces often make such goals difficult to achieve. Creating such a sense of equity and recognition requires that special attention be given to the characteristics of the individuals as well as the work.

Situational variables have strong and sometimes perverse influences on motivation. Government employees are subject to much disapproval—often falsely placed by a public and critics who perceive them as apathetic and rule bound. Yet their reward systems and environmental contexts elicit and reinforce conserver behavior. Equally frustrating and contradictory are society's expectations that public employees will operate in the public interest but simultaneously with political neutrality. The effort to balance these two close but distinct roles can create situations where decisions are hard to make and actions are difficult to take because the public servant realizes that whatever action is taken, there will be vociferous complaints from the losers in the process.

The nonprofit world may not be as volatile as that of the government worker, especially in the area of changing goals or interpretations thereof. However, there are often attempts by major donors, or by interested groups in the particular field of the agency, to reinterpret the goals of the organization and to pressure organization members to move in directions that do not fit into employee perceptions of what the agency exists for and is attempting to accomplish. Maintaining a high level of worker motivation and a clear sense of organizational mission is more difficult that one would surmise from the outside.

There is, however, room for optimism. The steady historical trend in American government has been toward a more professional and qualified public service. And despite popular perceptions or misperceptions, public employees as a group compare favorably to private ones in both motivation and productivity (Goodsell 1994). Likewise, American society has always emphasized voluntarism and the role of nonprofit organizations in meeting many needs of various sectors of society, and along with the increase in the importance of nonprofits has developed recognition of the importance of these people in serving the public interest. Productivity and efficiency throughout the public sector will always require that motivation, control, responsiveness, and accountability remain competing concerns (Frederickson 1997). Continuing study and application of organization culture and motivation theory as part of the total process of "making the public sector work" are central to success in maintaining all aspects of public life and the public good.

FOR FURTHER READING

Motivation is an area in organization theory that is characterized by the presence of separate and distinctive theories and models rather than synthesis. The writers who have had a major impact on the field include Abraham Maslow, who in *Motivation and Personality* (New York: Harper and Row, 1987) presents the basic argument for his hierarchy of needs model; David McClelland, *The Achieving Society* (New York: Irvington Publishers, 1976), in which he begins to develop his theory of individual maturity and the social attributes of motivation; and Frederick Herzberg, *Work and the Nature of Man* (London: Crosby Lockwood Staples, 1974), in which he develops his concepts of motivator and hygienic factors. A good example of the addition of cognition and the expectation of reward as parts of the motivation process is found in Lyman Porter and Edward Lawler III's *Managerial Attitudes and Performance* (Homewood, IL: Richard D. Irwin, 1968). An example of an attempt to combine and apply these various theories is found in Paul Hersey and Kenneth Blanchard's *Management of Organizational Behavior: Utilizing Human Resources*, 7th ed. (Upper Saddle River, NJ: Prentice-Hall, 2001). An interesting rebuttal of the behavioral approach to motivation is given by Alfie Kohn in *Punished by Rewards: The Trouble with Gold Stars, Incentive Plans, A's, Praise, and Other Bribes* (New York: Houghton Mifflin, 1993). One book explicitly examines the relationship between motivation and the bureaucratic environment: Anthony Downs's *Inside Bureaucracy* (Prospect Heights, IL: Waveland Press, 1994). New literature about the impact of privatizing and downsizing/rightsizing on morale and motivation appears regularly, and readers are encouraged to watch the appropriate journals and websites for information about this subject.

For classic readings, see most editions of Jay Shafritz and J. Steven Ott's (and coauthors) *Classics of Organizational Theory* (Belmont, CA: Thomson Wadsworth). Those that are especially relevant to this chapter include the excerpts from Taylor, "The Principles of Scientific Management"; Roethlisberger, "The Hawthorne Experiments"; Maslow, "A Theory of Human Motivation"; McGregor, "The Human Side of Enterprise"; Schein, "Defining Organizational Culture"; Cook and Yanow, "Culture and Organizational Learning"; Peters and Waterman, "In Search of Excellence"; and Acker, "Gendering Organizational Theory."

REVIEW QUESTIONS

1. What differences exist between the content theories, cognitive process theories, and behaviorist theories of motivation?
2. How can these different theories be combined to build a more complex and sophisticated theory of motivation in individuals?

3. Explain what part of, and how, the various theories presented in this chapter are operant when considering each of the five types of individuals that Downs says exist in organizations.
4. The authors of this book argue that motivation theories have to be interpreted and applied differently within the public sector than they are in the private sector (and that the same argument is true in the nonprofit sector). Prepare arguments both supporting and criticizing the authors' stance.
5. Consider the interactions between the motivation theories presented in this chapter and the communication and decision processes of organizations. How do they interact?
6. What impact can organizational structure and design have on motivation?

REFERENCES

Adams, J. Stacy. 1975. Inequity in social exchange. In *Motivation and work behavior,* 138–54. Ed. Richard M. Steers and Lyman W. Porter. New York: McGraw-Hill.

Alderfer, Clayton P. 1972. *Existence, relatedness, and growth: Human needs in organizational settings.* New York: Free Press.

Baumeister, Roy F., and Mark R. Leary. 1995. The need to belong: Desire for interpersonal attachments as a fundamental human motivation. *Psychological Bulletin* 117, no. 3: 497–529.

Berelson, Bernard, and Gary A. Steiner. 1967. *Human behavior: An inventory of scientific findings.* New York: Harcourt Brace Jovanovich.

Blake, Robert R., and Jane S. Mouton. 1985. *The managerial grid III.* Houston: Gulf Publishing.

Bockman, V. M. 1971. The Herzberg controversy. *Personnel Psychology* 24, no. 2 (Summer): 155–89.

Buchanan, Bruce II. 1974. Government managers, business executives, and organizational commitment. *Public Administration Review* 34, no. 4: 339–47.

Carr, David K., and Ian D. Littman. 1993. *Excellence in government: Total quality management in the 1990s.* 2nd ed. Arlington, VA: Coopers & Lybrand.

Cartwright, Dorwin. 1968. The nature of group cohesiveness. In *Group dynamics: Research and theory,* 91–109. Ed. Dorwin Cartwright and Alvin Zander. New York: Harper & Row.

Crain, William C. 2000. *Theories of development: Concepts and applications.* 4th ed. Upper Saddle River, NJ: Prentice-Hall.

Deming, W. Edwards. 2000. *Out of the crisis: Quality, productivity, and competitive position.* Cambridge: MIT Press.

Downs, Anthony. 1994. *Inside bureaucracy.* Prospect Heights, IL: Waveland Press. (Originally published by Little, Brown. Boston: 1967.)

Filley, Alan C., Robert J. House, and Steven Kerr. 1976. *Managerial process and organizational behavior.* 2nd ed. Glenview, IL: Scott, Foresman.

Frederickson, George F. 1997. *The spirit of public administration.* San Francisco: Jossey-Bass.

Gale, Raymond F. 1969. *Developmental behavior: A humanistic approach.* New York: Macmillan.

Goodman, Paul S., and Abraham Friedman. 1971. An examination of Adams's theory of inequity. *Administrative Science Quarterly* 16, no. 3: 271–88.

Goodsell, Charles. 1994. *The case for bureaucracy: A public administration polemic.* 3rd ed. Chatham, NJ: Chatham House Publishers.

Gortner, Harold F. 1970. *Student attitudes toward government employment.* PhD dissertation, Indiana University.

Green, Stephen G., and Terence R. Mitchell. 1979. Attributional processes of leaders in leader–member interactions. *Organizational Behavior and Human Performance* 23: 429–58.

Greiner, John M., Harry P. Hatry, Margo P. Koss, Annie P. Millar, and Jane P. Woodward. 1981. *Productivity and motivation: A review of state and local government initiatives.* Washington, DC: The Urban Institute Press.

Grigaliunas, Benedict S., and Frederick Herzberg. 1971. Relevancy in the test of motivation–hygiene theory. *Journal of Applied Psychology* 55, no. 1 (February): 73–79.

Hersey, Paul, and Kenneth H. Blanchard. 2001. *Management of organizational behavior: Leading human resources.* 7th ed. Upper Saddle River, NJ: Prentice-Hall.

Herzberg, Frederick. 1974. *Work and the nature of man.* London: Crosby Lockwood Staples.

Herzberg, Frederick, Bernard Mausner, and Barbara B. Snyderman. 1993. *The motivation to work.* New Brunswick, NJ: Transaction Publishers.

Holden, Matthew Jr. 1966. Imperialism in bureaucracy. *The American Political Science Review* 60: 943–51.

House, Robert J., and Terence R. Mitchell. 1974. Path–goal theory of leadership. *Journal of Contemporary Business* 3, no. 4: 81–97.

Katz, Daniel, and Robert L. Kahn. 1982. *The social psychology of organizations.* 3rd ed. New York: John Wiley & Sons.

Kaufman, Herbert. 1967. *The forest ranger: A study in administrative behavior.* Baltimore: Johns Hopkins Press. (Reissued by Resources for the Future. Washington, DC: 1993.)

Kelley, Harold H. 1972. Attribution in social interaction. In *Attribution: Perceiving causes of behavior,* 1–26. Ed. Edward E. Jones, David E. Kanouse, Harold H. Kelley, Richard E. Nisbett, Stuart Valins, and Bernard Weiner. Morristown, NJ: General Learning Press.

Koestner, Richard, Miron Zuckerman, and Julia Koestner. 1987. Praise, involvement, and intrinsic motivation. *Journal of Personality and Social Psychology* 53: 383–90.

Kohn, Alfie. 1993. *Punished by rewards: The trouble with gold stars, incentive plans, A's, praise, and other bribes.* New York: Houghton Mifflin.

Lane, Larry M., and James E. Wolf. 1990. *The human resource crisis in the public sector: Rebuilding the capacity to govern.* New York: Quorum Books.

Lawler, Edward E. III. 1994. *Motivation in work organizations.* San Francisco: Jossey-Bass.

Lawler, Edward E. III, and J. Lloyd Suttle. 1972. A causal correlational test of the need hierarchy concept. *Organizational Behavior and Human Performance* 7: 265–87.

Likert, Rensis. 1987. *New patterns of management.* New York: Garland.

Mahler, Julianne. 1985. *Patterns of commitment in public agencies.* Paper delivered at national convention of the American Society for Public Administration, Indianapolis, IN.

March, James, and Herbert A. Simon. 1993. *Organizations.* 2nd ed. Cambridge, MA: Blackwell.

Maslow, Abraham. 1987. *Motivation and personality.* 3rd ed. Rev. Robert Frager et al. New York: Harper and Row.

McClelland, David C. 1970. The two faces of power. *Journal of International Affairs* 24, no. 1: 29–47.
_____. 1976. *The achieving society.* New York: Irvington Publishers.

McClelland, David C., and David G. Winter. 1971. *Motivating economic achievement.* New York: Free Press.

McGregor, Douglas. 1956. The human side of enterprise. In *Adventures in thought and action: Proceedings of the fifth anniversary convocation of the School of Industrial Management,* 23–30. Massachusetts Institute of Technology.
_____. 1960. *The human side of enterprise.* New York: McGraw-Hill.

Mitchell, Terence R. 1982. Motivation: New directions for theory. *Academy of Management Review* 7, no. 1: 80–88.

Mitchell, Terence, Charles M. Smyser, and Stan E. Weed. 1975. Locus of control: Supervision and work satisfaction. *Academy of Management Journal* 18, no. 3: 623–31.

Mitchell, Terence, and Robert E. Wood. 1979. An empirical test of an attributional model of leaders' responses to poor performance. In *Academy of Management Proceedings,* 94–98. Ed. Richard C. Huseman.

Newland, Chester. 1984. Crucial issues for public personnel. *Public Personnel Management* 13, no. 1: 15–46.

Porter, Lyman W., and Edward E. Lawler III. 1968. *Managerial attitudes and performance.* Homewood, IL: Richard D. Irwin.

Rainey, Hal G. 1979. Perceptions of incentives in business and government: Implications for civil service reform. *Public Administration Review* 39: 440–48.

Rawls, James R., Robert A. Ulrich, and Oscar Tivis Nelson Jr. 1975. A comparison of managers entering or reentering the profit and nonprofit sectors. *Academy of Management Journal* 18: 616–22.

Rhinehart, J. B., R. P. Barrell, A. S. DeWolfe, J. E. Griffin, and F. E. Spaner. 1969. Comparative study of need satisfaction in governmental and business hierarchies. *Journal of Applied Psychology* 53 (June): 230–35.

Roethlisberger, Fritz J. 1941. *Management and morale.* Cambridge, MA: Harvard University Press.

Roethlisberger, Fritz J., and W. Dickson. 1939. *Management and the worker.* Cambridge, MA: Harvard University Press.

Schott, Richard L. 1986. The psychological development of adults. *Public Administration Review* 46: 657–67.

_____. 1987. Psychological development of adults: Further reflections and a rejoinder. *Public Administration Review* 47: 345–46.

Schwab, Donald P., H. William Devitt, and Larry L. Cummings. 1971. A test of the adequacy of the two-factor theory as a predictor of self-report performance effects. *Personnel Psychology* 24 (Summer): 293–303.

Skinner, B. F. 1976. *About behavior.* New York: Vintage.

Telly, Charles S., Wendell L. French, and William G. Scott. 1971. The relationship of inequity to turnover among hourly workers. *Administrative Science Quarterly* 16, no. 2: 164–72.

U.S. Merit Systems Board Office of Merit Systems Review and Studies. 1984. *Report on the significant actions of the Office of Personnel Management during 1983.* December.

Van Maanen, John. 1975a. Breaking in: Socialization to work. In *Handbook of work, organization, and society*, 67–130. Ed. Robert Dubin. Chicago: Rand McNally.

_____. 1975b. Police socialization: A longitudinal examination of job attitudes in an urban police department. *Administrative Science Quarterly* 20: 207–28.

Veroff, Joseph. 1957. Development and validation of a projective measure of power motivation. *Journal of Abnormal and Social Psychology* 54, no. 1: 1–8.

Vroom, Victor H. 1995. *Work and motivation.* San Francisco: Jossey-Bass.

Zemke, R. 1979. What are high-achieving managers really like? *Training: The Magazine of Human Resource Development* (February): 35–36.

Chapter 9

Leadership

In our society, leadership is more than ordinarily dispersed. Leaders are scattered around at every level and in all segments of our national life. Excessive dependence on central definition and rule making produces standardized solutions to be applied uniformly throughout the system. But the world "out there," the world to be coped with isn't standardized. It is diverse, localized, and surprising. (Gardner 1981, 11)

What Gardner is suggesting is that leadership does not arise at the executive level of the non-profit CEO or the town manager or the top nonpolitical position in state government; rather, leaders are at all levels. Leadership includes expecting the unexpected because change is constant, and even in the best possible days exceptions occur. Gardner developed this position during his many years of service in the federal government beginning in the 1960s Great Society programs of Lyndon Johnson and as the head of influential nonprofits: the Carnegie Corporation, the Urban Coalition, Common Cause, and completing his career as president of the Independent Sector. He saw potential in youth and in the ability to turn around difficult problems from poverty to lack of education. Many scholars reiterate his views of what a leader should be.

In this chapter we examine the various views of leadership by Gardner and others. Are leaders born or are leadership skills learned? Do some people have specific traits that make them leaders while others do not have these traits or personalities? Although numerous scholars and practitioners have studied leadership extensively, fundamental disagreements remain about what it is. In spite of such disagreements, there is unanimity about the need for leadership and great consternation about its absence. Perhaps the most damaging charge that can be made against a president is that he fails to lead the country. At the same time, of course, a standard accusation against public employees is that they are usurping responsibilities of politicians if they are innovative and energetic. The same might said for an ambitious assistant director or town manager. What seems clear is that we all believe that "leadership counts." That is how Behn (1989) began his important article contrasting leadership with analysis and organization. But what is leadership exactly?

DEFINITIONS: THE NATURE OF LEADERSHIP

Analyzing leadership yields an amazing number of definitions. James MacGregor Burns, in his study of leadership, found 130 definitions of the word (1978, 2). Here we define what leadership is at the executive, managerial, and supervisory levels of organizations (and for the most part exclude discussion of political leaders).We also discuss what it means to be an informal leader and to be able to lead one's self. Leadership takes place throughout the organization by people who are professionals, support staff, and technicians. Third, we examine five broad sets of theories in relationship to the four levels of leadership. Each theory—trait, transactional, transformational, attitudinal, and situational—attempts to explain how successful leadership occurs. We look at these theories in relationship to leadership of all types of government and nonprofit organizations.

Defining Leadership

As soon as leadership was recognized by thinkers as a special and important phenomenon, attempts were made to define what it was and to explain why some individuals became leaders while others did not. Plato, for instance, in *The Republic*, described how carefully chosen young men should be trained so that they will have the appropriate personalities and skills to serve as leaders of the city–state. Although it was the personal aspects of leadership that first attracted scholars' attention, they soon came to recognize the insufficiency of personality or trait theories, at which point the broader aspects of leadership theory began to receive attention. We now have a wide-ranging set of theories that attempts to explain what leadership is. When these various theories are combined in a comprehensive model, they help us understand leadership far better than we have in the past.

We can best approach the subject by noting the two elements where there is agreement and then expanding our ideas to include four additional concepts—symbolic leadership, the uniqueness of leadership, the achievement of the leadership role, and its power—that are necessary for this discussion.

The Two Common Elements—Group Phenomenon and Influence Process

Two elements are common to most definitions of leadership. First, leadership is a group phenomenon; two or more people must be involved. Second, leadership involves an influence process: The leader intentionally influences his or her followers. This influence may take many forms (discussed later in this chapter), but whatever its source it has the same goal—rallying people together and motivating them to achieve some common goal(s). Thus one physical condition (a group) and one process (influence) are necessary for leadership to occur.

Of course we immediately enter a debate as soon as causality and direction are considered in the influence process. Influence can flow from the leader to the group or flow from the group (employees) to the leader. In the former, employees grant the leadership role to whoever wears the mantle. Almost all organizations have a strong formal leadership component—an individual who is at the top of the organization chart. In the latter case, informal leadership, employees possess the ability to lead and to influence the leader. They do so because they are called on by others, they possess the requisite leadership characteristics, or they rise to the occasion. We discuss this situation in more depth in a later section about informal and self-leadership.

We focus now, however, on crucial but common interpersonal aspects of top leadership because it is here that major variations occur in its study and practice. Several concepts must be spelled out—the leader's symbolic role, the uniqueness of the role, the leader's achievement, and the leader's power—in more detail so we can discuss leadership in a truly meaningful context.

The Leader as Symbol

The leader personifies the organization's common purpose—not only to all who work in it, but also to the outside. What he or she does and says helps establish the culture of the organization (Weick 1995; Bennis and Nanus 1985; Schein 2004). The leader gives meaning to and manages the meaning of work, making sense of incoherent or chaotic situations. For nonprofits, the leader's actions affect the understanding of the volunteers as well (Ciulla 2004; Jaskyte 2004).

The Uniqueness of Leadership Roles

The leader's contribution, at the highest level, is expected to be indispensable and of considerable consequence to employees and the public. The group gains from accepting the individual as leader; the leader, in return, receives a variety of opportunities and benefits that make the position challenging and worthwhile.

After acceptance as leader by other group members, the leader acquires a set of expectations and interactions that make behavior by and toward her or him unique and differentiated. Leaders act differently than followers, and followers act differently toward a leader than they do toward their peers. For example, leaders may vary (obviously within limits) from what is considered acceptable group behavior as long as that behavior appears to pay off for the group by helping them to gain needed resources or achieve desired goals. Along with the differentiated role comes a change in expectations about contributions to the group.

The Achievement of Leadership Positions

The problem with the concept of leadership just presented is that it applies primarily to leadership in organizations after someone has become leader. However, an even more fundamental question is how the position of leadership is achieved in the first place. There are two answers. On the formal side a leader is appointed by the town, the board, or the legislature; but to the extent that a leader gains acceptance beyond this formal position, it must be gained from or granted by the group. On the informal side, the "leader without position" gains that status because it is granted by others. Stodgill (Bass 1990) argues that an individual is usually given leadership status because his or her behaviors arouse expectations in group members that lead them to believe that he or she, rather than some other member, will serve them more usefully. However, it would be inaccurate to believe that leaders always gain their position through willing conferral by followers; the formal appointment process takes precedence, and many leaders move from one organization to another. Boards, council members, governors, and presidents appoint without ever having seen the appointed leaders in action. Finally, achievement of a leadership position depends on the motivation of the individual to public service as discussed in Chapter 8. Research suggests that there are differences in motivation of those choosing public service careers (public service commitment, religious values, idealism) versus careers with for-profit organizations (Rose-Ackerman 1996; Perry and Wise 1990).

Power, Influence, and Authority

The conceptualization of leadership must also include an understanding of power, influence, and authority. *Power* occurs when leader A influences (or has the potential to influence) follower B's actions. *Influence* is the effect a leader has on attitudes, perceptions or behavior of others (Yukl 1998, 176). At a minimum, leaders attract followers to the group's goals through their words and deeds; further, leaders can gain even more loyalty to a cause through their charismatic qualities. The dual attachment to cause and person operates synergistically, thus creating combined ties that are greater than the sum of the two types of loyalty and commitment operating separately. Both Colin Powell, chairman of the Joint Chiefs of Staff and secretary of state (during the Clinton and George W. Bush administrations), and Daniel S. Goldin, longest-serving administrator of NASA, used charisma as well as their formal positions to gain strong commitments to their programs; hence their personal impacts on national politics and policies were tremendous.

Certainly when we use the word *power* we think of terrible dictators. James MacGregor Burns points out "that power as sheer domination [was] pervasive in [the] century of Hitler and Stalin" (1978, 52) as it probably is in every century. Such a statement, although true in the grossest sense of the term, causes us to lose any sense of sophistication in using the concept of power. Burns would not classify Hitler nor Stalin as true leaders. What he asserts is

BOX 9–1 The Bases of Social Power

1. *Reward power:* Based on the belief that person one has the ability to give person two pleasurable compensation for the second's obedience and loyalty.

2. *Coercive power:* Based on the perception that person one has the ability to inflict psychological or physical pain if person two is not obedient and loyal.

3. *Legitimate power:* Based on the acceptance of the idea that person one has a legal right to prescribe behavior for person two in a particular situation when that behavioral prescription is done in the proper manner.

4. *Referent power:* Based on one's psychological identification with a particular individual, group of individuals, or a particular goal or ideal that is embodied in the individual or group.

5. *Expert power:* Embodied in a recognized skill or knowledge.

SOURCE: Adapted from John R. P. French and Bertram Raven, "The Bases of Social Power," in *Studies in Social Power*, ed. Dorwin Cartwright (Ann Arbor, MI: Institute for Social Research, 1959), 150–67.

that having power is part of leadership, but power alone is not leadership. As we discuss later, without morals there is no leadership.

Power in a broader context is more than just domination. It occurs in a social exchange as a leader seeks to influence others (formally known as exchange theory). A leader has power because of his or her formal position (whether executive, manager, or supervisor) and because of his or her personal power—that is, charisma, expertise, or friendship. French and Raven (1959) expand these two types of power, positional and personal, to five types of power—reward, coercive, legitimate, referent, and expert power (see Box 9–1). Referent and expert power fit under the category of personal power, whereas the remaining types are more closely aligned with positional power. Only coercive power is specifically based on physical or punitive force; but legitimate power sometimes includes the implied threat of such force. Legitimate power is *authority* based on one's right by virtue of a leadership position. No position in an organization gives one absolute authority over all aspects of employee work life. Rather, a formal position has a sphere of competence that places specific limits on the authority. A leader, however, may have influence far beyond the authority that comes with his or her position.

The words *power* and *influence* are often used interchangeably because power is the outcome of influence. Influence is gained through the skillful playing of politics, and power is the reward received by the most skillful players. The nonprofit executive leader has at least as many and probably more stakeholders to influence than does the average nonelected government executive. He or she must seek to influence staff, the board of directors, clients and customers, volunteers, donors, policy advocates–lobbyists, other nonprofits, the business community, other civic organizations, the media, government agencies, and the community at large (Nanus and Dobbs 1999, 170–71). The success of any leader depends on his or her ability to use the variety of available influences in a way that gains support, compliance, and the achievement of goals (Yukl 1998, Chapter 8). In the political sphere many leaders (and for

BOX 9–2 Different Forms of Influence

1. *Legitimate request:* A target person complies with an agent's request because the person recognizes the agent's right to make such a request.

2. *Pressure and coercion:* A person is induced to alter his or her behavior by an agent's implicit or explicit demands.

3. *Exchange:* A person is induced to comply by the agent's explicit or implicit promises of benefits and rewards.

4. *Rational persuasion:* The person is convinced by the agent that the suggested behavior is the best way for the person to satisfy his or her needs or to attain his or her objectives.

5. *Rational faith:* A form of influence in which an agent's suggestion is sufficient to evoke compliance by the person without any explanation being necessary.

6. *Inspirational appeal:* The person is persuaded by the agent that there is a necessary link between the requested behavior and some value that is important enough to justify the behavior.

7. *Indoctrination:* The person is induced to act through internalization of strong values that are relevant to the desired behavior.

8. *Information distortion:* The target person is influenced, without being aware of it, by the agent limiting, falsifying, or interpreting information in a way that is conducive to compliance.

9. *Ingratiation:* The agent uses praise, flattery, and friendly behavior to obtain desired target attitudes and behavior.

10. *Personal identification:* The target person imitates the agent's attitudes and behavior because she or he admires or worships the agent.

11. *Consultation:* The agent allows the target person to participate in and have substantial influence over the making of a decision, thereby gaining the target person's identification with the final choice.

SOURCE: Gary A. Yukl, *Leadership in Organizations,* Copyright © 1994, p. 69–72. Adapted by permission of Pearson Education. Inc., Upper Saddle River, NJ.

that matter many employees) have several advantages: longevity, expertise, and information to influence policy (Rourke 1984; Jones 1984; Lindblom 1993). Influence can be obtained through coercive or noncoercive techniques. In Box 9–2 Gary Yukl (1998) identifies several possible forms of influence.

Four Levels of Leadership

Given our understanding of the group and influence process, we may create some order out of the numerous leadership theories by examining the material under the three most common levels of leadership: executive, managerial, and supervisory. We add a fourth level: informal or self-leadership. Informal leadership can occur in any organization and by any employee— from the receptionist to the technician to the professional. Quite frankly, much executive leadership literature is less theoretical than anecdotes relying on popular biographies of business executives and presidents. The management and supervision literature is based more on theoretical organizational literature with a major emphasis on identifying the functions of managers and supervisors. We supplement this with theories from political science, public policy, and public administration and some of the newer, though sparse, nonprofit literature.

By separating the discussion into levels and types of leadership, we are not arguing that the theories presented in each section apply only at that level of the organizational hierarchy. Indeed they cross levels; but the way they are interpreted and applied changes dramatically as we move from consideration of the executive to the manager, to the supervisor, and finally to self-leadership. As we look at the following material, remember that it can be useful to individuals at other leadership levels and that it must be interpreted to fit those different leaders, their roles, and their functions in the organization. We begin with a summary of the differences in leadership and then the application of theory to the different levels.

Levels of Leadership and Their Differences

Leadership occurs outside as well as inside the formal organization structure. Executives are expected to maintain a broad, general view of the organization and its place within the larger political and community environment. They must listen to public opinion and client, member, and citizen concerns. As the top officials, executives establish or interpret the agency's overall goals and attempt to create a general atmosphere or environment that will increase the probability of those goals being achieved (Urwick 1953). Finally, they must report to political officials and board members and satisfy their priorities.

Managers must interpret goals and policies in an ever more concrete manner into structures, procedures, and ultimately tasks. They may also be responsible for their section or department's budget. Supervisors implement the programs and supervise employees directly. They often are working supervisors providing hands-on service to citizens, clients, and members. Supervisors are directly responsible for the achievement of the organization's objectives and goals. They usually work with the most employees and handle day-to-day employee problems with responsibilities for hiring and training. Managers operate in the middle ground, being pulled in both directions by superiors and subordinates as they translate broad goals and policies into concrete actions. They are the coordinators and supervisors of supervisors.

Formal position in the hierarchy proves nothing about a person's leadership abilities; someone may hold any of the three positions in the organization without doing much in the way of leadership. Many nonsupervisory employees rise to the occasion and show leadership skills by dealing with crises, mentoring and motivating fellow employees, filling in for supervisors and managers, and implementing new ideas to complete work. It helps at all levels to use leadership skills; but the types of skills needed and the way they are applied of necessity differs.

SETTING THE GOALS: EXECUTIVE LEADERSHIP

Leadership at the executive level is a complicated series of actions. According to Phillip Selznick (1984) leaders must fulfill four functions integral to leadership:

1. Define the institutional mission and role (create and set goals).
2. Embody the purpose (build policy into an organization's social structure).

3. Defend the institution's integrity (maintain values and institutional identity).
4. Create order in internal conflict (reconcile the struggle among competing interests) (1984, 56–64).

In other words, these functions are not Gulick's functions (1937) in the sense of PODSCORB—planning, organizing, directing, staffing, coordinating, reporting, and budgeting—although these must be done. Gulick's functions are technical skills, some of which may certainly be necessary. Executive leadership is distinguished from managerial leadership when leaders carry out their jobs in a way that allows organizations to meet their missions. Leaders set the overarching goals. Burt Nanus (1992) refers to this approach as "visionary leadership" and argues that

> There is no more powerful engine driving an organization toward excellence and long-range success than an attractive, worthwhile, and achievable vision of the future, widely shared. (1992, 3)

But it is not enough to have a vision. The ability to achieve the vision is at the crux. It must be realistic; otherwise employees will not be willing to support the goals. Leaders must be able to communicate that vision as well (Bennis and Nanus 1985, 110–46; Nanus and Dobbs 1999, 75–96). By doing so, leaders begin to embody the purpose of the organization—Selznick's second function of leadership.

Leaders must also communicate this vision outwardly to volunteers and external groups, not just to employees. Leaders must consider this question: "What is the potential for mobilizing support for this program or mission?" Political feasibility shapes all aspects of establishing a vision. Internal and external support affects what can be done. Leaders need to solicit input and be flexible to infuse their vision into the mission of the organization:

> If leaders are rigid, inflexible, and unimaginative in adjusting their preferred styles to the political challenges they face, they have very seriously limited their chances of implementing their policy options. Hence, the final—and most crucial—ingredient in effective policy implementation involves the personal component of leadership. (Nakamura and Smallwood 1980, 167)

Such flexibility, though, cannot be at the expense of the loss of the integrity of the organization: Selznick's third function of leadership is to maintain the identity and integrity of the organization. At times the executive will need to take a crucial stand affecting this identity—which brings us to clarifying executive decision making. We discussed decision making in general terms in Chapter 7 but not specifically as it relates to executive leadership.

Decision Making

By creating and communicating a vision, a leader begins to embody the purpose of the organization. Certainly the most critical aspect of an executive's job is decision making—both daily and in times of crisis. The study and theories of decision making take us to the leader–hero, a president or executive who saved the day, even when there is a qualifier or disclaimer that the hero could not have done it without others. This "Great Man" theory of leadership assumes top-down authority and that a leader can and does motivate. These leaders have special traits and personalities that make them great.

But this is a simplistic view. Though this "Great Man" theory is appealing, particularly when we examine the success or failure of leaders involved in historic events such as our great wars or more recently 9/11 or Hurricane Katrina (in 2005), it narrows the theory of leadership to a study of crisis decision making and to elected officials and away from the daily activities of executives. Often the executive is a leader because of events imposed on him or her, and the leader rises to the occasion. For example, this is the case when an anonymous assistant director takes over temporarily after a sudden retirement, resignation, or death, succeeds beyond measure, and is promoted.

An executive is not necessarily different because of traits or personality (discussed in the manager section) but because of the sheer variety of decisions that must be made—the day-to-day decisions, the planning decisions, and the crisis decisions. Executive leadership is much more intimately involved in making decisions that involve more uncertainty and risk than those of managers, supervisors, or employees (Gortner 1986, 197). (See Chapter 7, Figure 7.2.) A leader must decide what goal to support, what process is correct to achieve the goal, what resources are available, what the political feasibility is, and what contingencies to consider. In almost every case there is at least one other perspective—often with equally ardent supporters.

Decision making is risky because there are many sources of disagreement (Sahr 2005) even in relatively innocuous decisions. There are differences in facts, the interpretation of consequences, ideology, and professional viewpoints as well as differences based on self-interest. Conservatives and liberals see problems and solutions differently. Anyone may obtain different and correct facts to support points of views; some facts may be readily available whereas others are known to select people. The executive may be missing information as well. Figures of wealth and poverty after Hurricanes Katrina and Rita (both in 2005) may be opposites of the same coin and both equally correct. However, data may not show the psychological impact on survivors. These figures may be difficult to determine. Policy decisions related to economic development, housing, and mental health after a hurricane may be based on an executive's ideology (conservative, liberal, Democratic, Republican), his or her profession, and self-interest. The executive who is trained as a social worker may arrive at a different decision than that of an accountant or engineer. Staff may bring different perspectives as well because of their professional training (see Chapter 6's discussion of professionalism). Risk increases in determining the consequences of, say, any particular policy to address the aftermath of hurricanes, whether it is an economic development policy, a housing policy, or related environmental policies.

Decisions in a time of crisis are the ones we remember most. For Peter Drucker, the decisions before the crisis are the critical ones. Drucker (1990, 9) states that the most important task of an organization's leader is to anticipate crisis, "perhaps not to avert it, but to anticipate it." To wait until the crisis hits is an abdication of responsibility. The executive has to make the organization capable of anticipating the storm, weathering it, and in fact being ahead of it.

To make risky decisions, the executive looks inward and outward to the board or political officials, to staff, and to the community when making decisions. Aside from the ongoing sources of disagreement, decisions are risky because of the many external factors (economy, technology, politics) outside the leader's control; yet he or she must seek to control or take them into account when making decisions. As noted by Harlan Cleveland,

> The executive's work often consists of meeting a series of unforeseeable obstacles on the road to an objective that can be clearly specified only when he is close to reaching it. He tries

to imagine the unforeseen by posing contingencies and asking how his organization system would adjust if they arose. Nevertheless, the planned-for contingency never happens; something else happens instead. (1972, 78)

Executives as Implementers of Policy

Cleveland's quote leads us to a related topic of decision making: the implementation and consequences of a specific decision, program, or policy. The amount of risk that leaders take depends on the degree of policy implementation responsibilities they have. The degree of responsibility depends on an executive's position in relation to the political actors, whether they are the board of a nonprofit, a government contracting agency, or political officials[1] (see Reading 9–1). Nakamura and Smallwood (1980) have described how government executives accomplish policy implementation by identifying five kinds of implementation roles: classical technocrats, instructed delegates, bargainers, discretionary experimenters, and bureaucratic entrepreneurs (see Box 9–3). We expand this to include the varying roles that nonprofit leaders play in implementing programs in their organizations.

READING 9–1   Managing in the Public Sector

Public managers who have been with their chief for more than one term—perhaps for years—have developed their own views of the chief's management ability and style. Typically, however, given the limited tenure of both chiefs and managers, the public manager finds himself or herself working for a new chief—often an inexperienced one.

From the point of view of the public manager, two types of newly elected chiefs are typically encountered: the generals and the policy makers.

The "generals" know that the job has to do with running government, and that management is involved somehow with getting programs going and making things work. But this chief does not really understand the process of implementation. The general sees management as a rather simple military exercise where the general tells the subordinates and the subordinates tell the troops until something finally gets done. This chief sees the problem as one of being demanding and tough; of giving enough orders that everyone gets the message and performs. These qualities may be admirable, but they are hardly sufficient to make government work.

While the general's style may work in the military (and it sometimes fails there), it certainly does not work well in the civilian part of the public sector. In the military the commander controls all or most of the resources needed to complete the task at hand. But in the public sector the chief rarely if ever has such unilateral control. In addition, the resources public managers do control are usually circumscribed by civil service rules, union agreements, and revenue levels. Furthermore, chief elected officials have no brig for the discipline of unruly or disloyal subordinates.

The general does not realize that, in government, implementation is very tough. It is one thing to decide that prison overcrowding must end but quite another to make it happen.

---

[1]Traditional management behavior literature tends to look inward, with the emphasis on improving the internal structure and functioning of the organization. Policy/implementation literature stresses the importance of understanding the factors that influence a leader's ability to carry out the functions described by Selznick and Nanus.

Nothing is more disheartening to a public manager than to deliver a particularly tough program or project in one year, only to have the chief resentful because it was not done in six months. Or worse still to have the chief announce at the outset that something will take six months when it cannot possibly be done in less than a year. Educating the "generals" about the realities of public management is an especially frustrating task for managers.

The second type of novice chief is the policy maker. For the policy maker, implementation and management are simply not considered an important part of the chief's responsibility. This chief does not really understand that he or she runs a complex organization, with money, people, and facilities which must be made to perform effectively. Policy makers typically come from legislative backgrounds—they see the job of chief as doing what they did before, only in a bigger way. The policy maker holds this view for a number of reasons: because it is more comfortable, because management may seem boring, because the chief does not really believe that anything can be done in the public sector anyway, or because the chief simply knows no better.

SOURCE: Gordon Chase and Elizabeth C. Reveal, *How to Manage in the Public Sector* (Reading, MA: Addison-Wesley, 1983): 27–28.

BOX 9–3 Five Kinds of Policy Implementers

Classical technocrats: Implementers have some technical discretion, but their power to make any overall policy decisions is strictly limited (applies primarily to government leaders).

Instructed delegates: Implementers have more power to determine the means that will be employed to achieve the policy makers' goals, with policy makers delineating clear goals that implementers agree on and delegating discretionary administrative authority (applies to government leaders and to nonprofit leaders with grants or contracts).

Bargainers: Implementers' power position vis-à-vis policy makers increases dramatically because they can exercise considerable clout through threats of noncompliance and nonimplementation (applies primarily to government leaders, but nonprofit leaders advocate for policies in legislatures).

Discretionary experimenters: Implementers experience a dramatic delegation of power away from policy makers and toward themselves. Nonprofit boards often rubber-stamp policy proposals and give broad discretion to leaders to implement policy (applies to nonprofits and government leaders).

Bureaucratic entrepreneurs: Power is shifted to implementers because they generate and control information, have continuity so they can outlast policy makers, and have and use entrepreneurial and political skills that allow them to dominate policy formulation. They formulate their own policy and convince policy makers (the board in a nonprofit; applies more to nonprofits than to government organization leaders).

SOURCE: Adapted from Robert Nakamura and Frank Smallwood, *The Politics of Policy Implementation* (New York: St. Martin's Press, 1980), 112–33.

Some executives act mainly according to the wishes of political actors, rarely making any suggestions or changes. They are the instructed delegates. After critical incidents, federal executives sometimes revert to even more limited decision-making power, acting as classical technocrats as Congress directs, investigates, and provides increased oversight. As for nonprofit leaders, federal, state, and even local policies have created a situation in which nonprofit executives negotiate with government entities over policy formulation and implementation of programs (Marwell 2004; Berman 1995), giving some nonprofit executives greater flexibility than their public counterparts have. They act strategically devising implementation plans (Nanus and Dobbs 1999, 111).

Especially since the Peters and Waterman book *In Search of Excellence* (1982) and the reinventing government movement, we have seen the growth of studies of entrepreneurial government executives (Doig and Hargrove 1987, Part II) and nonprofit executives (see Young 2001; Nanus and Dobbs 1999). Entrepreneurs are innovators who welcome the new rather than resisting it (Osborne and Gaebler 1992; Badelt 2003, 141; Drucker 1990, 14, 66–69). Entrepreneurship is about change and involves a good deal of risk taking. In government this has led to contracting out more and more services to nonprofits. Entrepreneurial nonprofit executives sometimes even create new nonprofits in response to grants or community demands. Nonprofit boards routinely defer to the executive, leaving nonprofit executives with more flexibility to be entrepreneurs (Rojas 2000) than many of their public counterparts. The recognition of an organization in decline might also trigger a new strategy by an entrepreneurial executive.

The executive's ability to innovate is often highly constrained. Leadership is inexorably entwined with the culture and structure of the organization. Executives (and upper-level managers) are often restricted from fulfilling their leadership responsibilities by the plethora of statutes, rules, regulations, court orders, prescribed procedures, and labor contracts set before their tenure. When we discuss federal and state agencies, there are countless examples of excessive verbiage restricting leadership. These rules ensure that executives do the job according to legal requirements, but they leave little room for innovative executives to do the right thing. Compounding the legal restrictions are the structures, traditions, and culture in place in the agencies. Many decisions are *programmed decisions* and actions (Kaufman 1981, 91; Rourke 1984). Work flows along because employees know how to do their work whatever the leadership. Executives may set the tone for the organization; but employees who have become accustomed to a certain method of operation are not likely to fall in line quickly with new ideas, and some may be unable to keep up with such changes.

Once a decision is made, any leader who makes progress or accomplishes a goal is aware that two personnel issues will result from his or her actions. First, some people will not appreciate what has been accomplished (although the leader hopes that many will). Second, the actions will generate controversy and perhaps even hatred. Certainly not everyone will love an intellectually active leader. This leads us to Selznick's fourth executive function: creating order in internal conflict (see also Drucker 1990, 126–27). This of course does not mean full agreement must take place; that would be groupthink. To quote Burns,

> No matter how strong [the] longing for unanimity, almost all leaders. . . must settle for far less than universal affection. They must be willing to *make enemies*—to deny themselves the affection of their adversaries. They must accept conflict. They must be willing and able to be unloved.[2] It is hard to pick one's friends, harder to pick one's enemies. (1978, 34)

---

[2]We must approach this idea from a position of moderation, remembering this caveat: The willingness to be unloved cannot be used as an excuse for riding roughshod over everyone else in the organization; the inevitability of making enemies does not justify practices that ensure doing so.

Again, decision making is risky. The question is not the inevitability of conflict but the function of leadership in encouraging, expressing, shaping, and eventually curbing it. Leaders who avoid conflict avoid one of Selznick's four executive functions.

If the handling of crises is what we remember most in our leaders, it is nevertheless the many other decisions that make the job. Some decision making is imposed (Kaufman 1981, 124) but can still create a series of risks. Selznick's third function is to defend the integrity of the organization. Defending its integrity involves the cycles of work such as budgeting, fundraising, hiring (such as for temporary summer programs), and labor negotiations. Not understanding or ignoring the budget can be a fatal error for executives. These imposed cyclical decisions can affect the mission of the organization and require attention despite and in addition to other pressing problems.

To summarize, executive leadership is inspiring or troublesome to those who keep the daily operations humming. Robert McMurray (1958) opined that management (that is, leadership) includes those who are stubbornly destructive and people who do not believe in delegation. McMurray lamented that (at least in business) it is not possible to delegate much beyond the top echelon. What most leaders are comfortable with is the Weberian model of a top-down hierarchical organization in which decision making is centralized in the leadership. This occurs even when leaders spout the human relations approach of concern for the interrelatedness of leaders and employees. Yet we do hear and know of many leaders who have embraced alternatives from project management to participative management. What we have been discussing is what writers have called *leadership style.* Leaders have different personalities, traits, and skills and use these traits and skills in different ways for the success of the organization.

Leadership Style

Studies of leadership style are more descriptive than prescriptive. McGregor (1960) in the seminal work *The Human Side of Enterprise* identified two approaches as Theory X and Theory Y (see Chapter 8). Theory X and Y are not so much theories as compilations and descriptions of what actually happens. By unconsciously or consciously choosing one of these approaches, leaders help establish the culture of an organization in both words and actions. Executive decisions supporting pay for performance, employee monitoring, or disciplinary step systems; hierarchical structures; and detailed policy and procedures all fall under Theory X, whereas executive decisions supporting flexible hiring policies, pay by grade and rank, flexible benefit plans, and earned time (rather than vacation/sick time); nonhierarchical structures; employee participation programs and teamwork; and slim policy and procedure manuals fit Theory Y.

Although Nakamura and Smallwood (1980) argue that particular leaders tend to operate in one of five modes, probably successful leaders adopt different styles of leadership over the years, depending on the prevailing values and assumptions of their political leaders, boards, and clientele; the interest groups that are watching their actions; and the public. These changes may occur gradually as the public's perception of the role of government and nonprofits shifts, or they may occur rapidly when a new executive takes over or a crisis intervenes.

Transactional versus Transformational Leadership

Can we develop a full-blown theory based on observation of leadership style? James MacGregor Burns (1978), later followed by Tichy and Ulrich (1984), contrasts two forms of leadership: *transactional* leadership and *transformational* leadership. Transactional leadership

TABLE 9–1   Transformational Leaders

Personality Characteristics	Behaviors	Effects on Followers
Charismatic	Acts as role model.	Trust.
Desire to influence	Shows competence.	Heightened goals.
Self-confident	Articulates goals and vision.	Identification with organization.
Moral values	Communicates high expectations;	Transforms follower ideas to support change.
	Acts on need for change.	

SOURCE: Adapted from Peter Northouse, *Leadership Theory and Practice,* 3rd ed. (Thousand Oaks, CA: Sage, 2004), 172.

theory is based on exchange theory. The transactional leader exchanges rewards for action or compliance. Through the control, monitoring, and encouragement of transactions, the leader uses a variety of resources—pay, monitoring, threats, information, and other factors of importance to ensure employee performance. Transactional leadership fits with conceptions from behaviorism (Kohn 1999) and traditional top-down management.

Transformational leadership theory is less straightforward in its theoretical underpinnings than transactional leadership theory. It is based upon the idea that a leader influences followers and employees (see Table 9–1). Through this process the transformational leader helps individuals and groups to recognize and achieve their higher and more humane aspirations, thereby moving human understanding and enterprise to a new moral and ethical level (Riggio, Bass, and Orr 2004; Bennis and Nanus 1985; Gardner 1990; Bass 1990; Burns 1978). The transformational leader helps individuals elevate themselves instead of simply looking to the leader for guidance and wisdom. Transformational leadership is closely tied to the idea of organizational change. The transformational leader recognizes the need for change, creates a vision of what the organization will be, and directs the change. To do this the leader becomes a role model for others and may change the culture of the organization. Followers learn to trust the leader and work to their highest performance to help institute the change.

Whether the transformational leader is charismatic is a question of theory and definition. Weber (1947) recognized the role of the charismatic leader as the basis of organization, although he thought a rational–legal basis for organization was preferable. Burns calls leaders who inspire others heroic (1978, 244). Bennis and Nanus (1985, 224) propose that charisma is the result of effective leadership rather than the precursor. Others have suggested that charisma is a necessary but not sufficient condition for transformational leadership (see Bass 1990, 54). Northouse claims that charisma is the influence creating the transformation. He defines charismatic leaders as having certain personal characteristics—dominance, a strong desire to influence others, self-confidence, and a sense of moral values—and having specific behaviors such as acting as a role model, showing competence, and articulating goals (2004, 171–74).

For transformational leaders the time and point of action are intensely individual and personal. The transformational leader is a change agent inspiring the effort of employees:

> The essence of leadership. . . is the recognition of real need, the uncovering and exploiting of contradictions among values and between values and practice, the realigning of values, the reorganization of institutions where necessary, and the governance of change. (Burns 1978, 43)

Transformational leadership as a theory may be relatively new, but its concepts have been widely adopted. Articulating the ideas of transformational leadership, James Q. Wilson wrote,

> [E]xecutives that not only maintain their organizations but transform them do more than merely acquire constituency support; they project a compelling vision of the tasks, culture, and importance of their agencies. The greatest executives infuse their organizations with value and convince others that this value is not merely useful to the bureau but essential to the polity. (1989, 217)

Studies of transformational leadership indicate that it is correlated with effectiveness and satisfaction with leadership (Northouse 2004, 184–85). However, because the theory is not conceptually clear, any study is subject to criticism. Further, it does not fit with many situations. Obviously not all organizations need to be changed. The transformational theory also has an undemocratic aspect to it. On the other hand, it places much more emphasis on followers and employee needs, values, and morals.

Executive Morality and Responsibility

This description of transformational leaders could include those who use their charisma for negative effects. Hitler inspired and transformed, but he did not elevate the goals of followers, nor did he use a code of ethics. He failed to recognize his moral responsibility (Barnard 1936). (See Reading 9–2.) For Burns and others, the transformational leader grapples with the contradictions using ethics to create the transformation. Burns (1978) notes that Max Weber contrasts two types of ethics in his writing: the "ethic of responsibility" and the "ethic of ultimate ends." The leader's behavior is measured according to adherence to "good" ends or "high" purposes. The ethic of responsibility, on the other hand, measures a set of actions by the leader including

- Acquiring the capacity to use a calculating, prudential, rationalistic approach.
- Making choices on the basis of many values, attitudes, and interests.
- Seeing the relationship of one goal to another.
- Understanding the implications of choice for the means of attaining it (the cost for the benefit).
- Recognizing the direct and indirect effects of different goals for different people and interests.

The leader using the ethic of responsibility carries out all of these calculations in a context of specificity and immediacy, and with an eye toward actual consequences rather than lofty intent (Burns 1978, 45). As Burns notes,

> For . . . leadership, the dichotomy is not between Weber's two ethics but between the leader's commitment to a number of overriding, general welfare–oriented values on the one hand and his encouragement of, and entanglement in, a host of lesser values and "responsibilities" on the other. (1978, 46)

Above all, the leader accepts and copes with ambiguity at the same time that she or he is attempting to develop and maintain the overall goals of the organization. Ethical decisions take on special importance for government and nonprofit executives because the decisions made affect people's lives, are made in the name of the public, and use public resources (Gortner 1991, 7, citing Harmon and Mayer 1986). The real importance of the leader

READING 9–2   Executive Responsibility

Executive positions (a) imply a complex morality, and (b) require a high capacity of responsibility, (c) under conditions of activity, necessitating (d) commensurate general and specific technical abilities as a moral factor. . . . (I)n addition there is required (e) the faculty of *creating* morals for others. . . .

(a) Every executive possesses, independently of the position he occupies, personal moral codes. When the individual is placed in an executive position there are immediately incumbent upon him, officially at least, several *additional* codes that are codes of his organization.

(b) The capacity of responsibility is that of being firmly governed by moral codes—against inconsistent immediate impulses, desires, or interests, and in the direction of desires or interests that are consonant with such codes. Our common word for one aspect of this capacity is "dependability," by which we mean that, knowing a man's codes—that is, being aware of his "character"—we can reasonably foresee what he is likely to do or not to do, usually under a variety of circumstances.

(c) Generally the conditions of executive work are those of great activity. . . . It is clear that the higher the position the more exposed the incumbent to action imposed from numerous directions, calling for the activity of decision.

(d) The capacity of responsibility is in executive ranks rather a constant, and the tendency of activity to increase with scope of position is often controllable. The increase in complexity of moral conditions, however, is not controllable by the person affected, so that despite control of activities the burden increases from conflicts of morals as the scope of the executive position broadens. . . .

The moral complications of the executive functions, then, can only be endured by those possessing a commensurate ability. While, on one hand, the requisite ability without an adequate complex of moralities or without a high sense of responsibility leads to the hopeless confusion of inconsistent expediencies so often described as "incompetence," on the other hand, the requisite morality and sense of responsibility without commensurate abilities leads to fatal indecision or emotional and impulsive decisions, with personal breakdown and ultimate destruction of the sense of responsibility. The important distinctions of rank lie in the fact that the higher the grade the more complex the moralities involved, and the more necessary higher abilities to discharge the responsibilities, that is, to resolve the moral conflicts implicit in the positions. . . .

(e) The distinguishing mark of the executive responsibility is that it requires not merely conformance to a complex code of morals but also the creation of moral codes for others. The most generally recognized aspect of this function is called securing, creating, inspiring of "morale" in an organization. This is the process of inculcating points of view, fundamental attitudes, loyalties, to the organization of cooperative system, and to the system of objective authority, that will result in subordinating individual interest and the minor dictates of personal codes to the good of the cooperative whole.

But there is another aspect of moral creativeness that is little understood, except in the field of jurisprudence. This is the inventing of a moral basis for the solution of moral conflicts—variously called "handling the exceptional case," "the appellate function," "the judicial function." This function is exercised in the cases that seem "right" from one point of view, "wrong" from another. . . . Probably most of [these cases] are solved by substitute action, [but even in these cases] the codes governing individual relationships to organized effort are of wide variation, so that either action or failure to act in these cases does violence to individual moralities, though the alternatives will affect different persons in different ways.

[Executives are also responsible for] morally justifying a change or redefinition or new particularizing of purpose so that the sense of conformance to moral codes is secured. One final effect is the elaboration and refinement of morals—of codes of conduct. . . . That it can degenerate into mere subtlety to avoid rather than to discharge obligations is apparent in all executive experience. The invention of the constructions and fictions necessary to secure the preservation of morale is a severe test of both responsibility and ability, for to be sound they must be "just" in the view of the executive, that is, really consonant with the morality of the whole; as well as acceptable, that is, really consonant with the morality of the part, of the individual.

SOURCE: Chester I. Barnard, *The Functions of the Executive* (Cambridge, MA: Harvard University Press 1968): 271–81 p. (Introduction by Kenneth R. Andrews). Reprinted with permission from the publisher. Copyright © 1938, 1968 by the President and Fellows of Harvard College. Copyright © renewed 1966 by Grace F. Noera Barnard.

---

is to create and manage a culture (Schein 2004). This culture is one in which the leader models ethical behavior so that such behavior becomes a given for employees. When leaders fail to act ethically, it affects not only their own organizations but also the trust the community has in similar organizations.

Ciulla (2004) identifies an additional ethic related to nonprofits but equally applicable to government social service agencies: the ethic of charity.[3] Public service agencies provide a service or benefit to individuals or groups, and their leaders have an obligation to this principle that should guide decision making both in times of crisis and daily.

To make these moral decisions, leaders need to use intellect guided by ethics with action. Hurricane Katrina presented a situation in which many government and nonprofit leaders had to use intellect and translate it into immediate action. It takes only a few examples of fence-sitting, intellectually oriented leaders who allow the opportunity to pass while collecting the last bit of information for a decision to recognize that action is necessary for the transformational leader. On the other hand, there are just as many stories about the "bull in the china closet" who charges off without having done enough thinking and creates havoc for others. What is needed is an analytical leader who deals with both analytical and normative ideas and brings them both to bear on the environment through timely action (Burns 1978).

Research indicates that effective leaders use a combination of transactional and transformational behaviors (see Yukl's summary 1998, 325–28). Transformational leadership fits with themes of the 1990s and 2000s for organizational structures and cultures that recognize the value of the individual's contributions to the organization. But research also shows that it is unclear how to achieve this. For instance, how does one attain a vision for an organization? How does one gain the trust of employees? Transactional leadership, although a more simplistic theory and perhaps at odds with some of our beliefs, fits with many daily actions we

---

[3]Although the term *charity organization* is rarely used as a general description of nonprofits any more and has become obscured with the application of business principles, it is a major factor in the difference between nonprofits and business.

see from our leaders and with related motivational theories discussed in Chapter 8. As we leave the discussion of executive leadership and move to discuss middle management and team leadership, it is apparent that leaders can set the style of management, but they cannot accomplish the tasks of leadership alone.

LEADERSHIP IN THE MIDDLE: THE MANAGERS

Managers are in the middle in several ways. Managers must fulfill contradictory roles: Subordinates expect them to represent their interests upward to higher officials, whereas higher officials expect them to present organizational goals downward to employees and to see that those objectives are achieved. Although managers may have provided a service in the past, they are now the ones responsible for program management. They set the time lines and are the coordinators between and among departments. Whereas those below them handle specific tasks or functions and those above them consider broad policy and goals, managers must turn those policies and objectives into outputs by developing and coordinating structures and functions. The epitome of the manager in the middle is the city manager (sometimes called an administrator).

James Svara (2003) has addressed this push–pull situation of the city manager in his discussion of mayoral leadership. The city manager provides professional leadership to the staff and at the same time supports elected officials in accomplishing their goals. According to Svara, "the city manager rather than being a bureaucratic force whose resistance must be overcome is obligated to use his/her leadership in the service of elected officials and the citizens of the community." Svara characterizes mayors in city manager forms of government as being facilitative leaders, and he states that managers "can and frequently do use the same style in their own behavior." The manager who uses the facilitative approach is committed to helping other officials accomplish their goals, promotes open communication among officials, and approaches conflict by stressing collaboration in which the interests of the leader and others are mutually satisfied. This characterization describes the incredible difficulty of being the manager—the one in the middle.

In addition to the difficulty of the job, middle management is the focus of much public dissatisfaction with bureaucratic inefficiency. Because it is hard to put a value on what is done by managers, they are often charged with inefficiency and ineffectiveness and are cut first by organizations. For instance, the National Performance Review claimed that reducing the "over-control and micromanagement in government" would create the possibility to

> pare down the structures that go with them: the oversized headquarters, multiple layers of supervisors and auditors, and offices specializing in the arcane rules of budgeting, personnel, procurement, and finance. We cannot entirely do without headquarters, supervisors, auditors, or specialists, but *these structures have grown twice as large as they should be.* (1993, 5–6; emphasis added)

Managers are difficult to describe and theorize about (although that has not stopped anyone from trying) because just as the position and practice of management fall in the middle, so does the study of it. Managers interact with both leaders and subordinates and must serve as a link between them (Likert 1987, 1967). Because they have a connection with both ends of the continuum, theories of leadership that are identified principally with the two ends—executives and supervisors—tend to apply to managers as well.

In his thought-provoking books, *Why Leaders Can't Lead* (Bennis 1989b) and *On Becoming a Leader* (Bennis 1989a), Bennis has stated that "leaders do the right things" and

BOX 9–4 Distinctions between Managers and Leaders

- The manager administers; the leader innovates.
- The manager is a copy; the leader is an original.
- The manager maintains; the leader develops.
- The manager focuses on systems and structure; the leader focuses on people.
- The manager relies on control; the leader inspires trust.
- The manager has a short-range view; the leader has a long-range perspective.
- The manager asks how and when; the leader asks what and why.
- The manager has his eye always on the bottom line; the leader has his eye on the horizon.
- The manager imitates; the leader originates.
- The manager accepts the status quo; the leader challenges it.
- The manager is the classic good soldier; the leader is his own person.
- The manager does things right; the leader does the right thing.

SOURCE: Warren Bennis, *On Becoming a Leader* (Reading, MA: Addison-Wesley, 1989), 45.

"managers do things right" (see Box 9–4). Although this seems critical of managers, in fact there are a host of important tasks managers must do if leaders and organizations are to succeed. This is no better stated than by Levin (1993) in his scenario on why management matters. He poses a situation in which an AIDS vaccine has been developed, and now administering an immunization program is a matter of management. Political officials make *point decisions;* the less glamorous job of management is handling what Levin calls *line decisions.* Three skills are necessary: assembling, coordinating, and bargaining.

> The line decision involves a complicated line of many decisions about many elements. It involves a good deal of bargaining among many actors. A great deal of effort goes into controlling and coordinating these various actors and various elements of the program. (442)

In other words, ideas are not self-executing; they need to be implemented. Managers have to be concerned with correct and effective implementation (Levin 1993, 444). Behn (1998), supporting this viewpoint, believes that line decisions take leadership, albeit a different type, because many line decisions are reviewed by the judiciary. They must be executed carefully to meet democratic principles. These decisions may also come under the scrutiny of numerous others—citizens, clients, and customers. We can safely say that what managers do fits closely with Gulick's (1937, 12) PODSCORB: planning, organizing, directing, staffing, coordinating, reporting, and budgeting.

Behn (1998) further adds (specifically relating to government agencies but applying to many nonprofit service organizations) that at times managers must lead because of executive failures, legislative failures, and judicial failures. Elected officials (and executives) direct activities for specific priorities, but they may ignore others where the manager must step in. The legislature sometimes provides ambiguous or conflicting legislation that the manager must interpret (such as promoting public use of the parks and at the same time preserving the parks). Because of the litigiousness of our society, the manager (and executive) may have to carry out court remedies conflicting with larger public policy issues. For example, corrections officials must ensure the incarceration of the convicted while administering a court-remedied early release program because of overcrowding.

Manager Effectiveness

Traits

Scholars throughout the twentieth century and now the twenty-first century have had an ongoing interest in the particular traits, skills, needs, and values exhibited by leaders. Conceptually these categories are not always clear and overlap. *Traits* refer to a manager's personality, personal qualities, and attitudes but can also include needs, motives, and even values that are usually considered relatively stable throughout a person's life. *Skills* often refer to a manager's ability to perform aspects of the job, such as budgeting or handling interpersonal problems in the workplace, and so are learned. In practice traits and skills might be a combination of learned and inherited abilities.

Originally researchers were interested in discovering what traits were present among leaders but did not exist among followers, or which existed to a greater degree among leaders. That is, they were interested in the personality of the leader. More recent research has focused on the application of *trait theory* to the practical aspects of recruiting and selecting supervisors and managers and to predicting managerial success.

The most thorough review of trait theory (and leadership theory in general) appears in *Bass & Stogdill's Handbook of Leadership* (Bass 1990, Chapters 4 and 5). Stogdill conducted a comprehensive survey of leadership articles published between 1904 and 1947 to assess the personal factors (such as traits, age, scholarship, and knowledge) associated with leadership. He then surveyed another 163 articles that appeared between 1948 and 1970. From the first study Stogdill concluded that the average leader exceeded followers in intelligence, initiative, and a number of other traits. He was able to classify the most common traits as falling under "capacity, achievement, responsibility, participation, and status" (see Box 9–5). But Stogdill's

---

BOX 9–5 Stogdill's Leadership Traits

1. *Capacity:* Intelligence, alertness, verbal facility, originality, judgment.
2. *Achievement:* Scholarship, knowledge, athletic accomplishments.
3. *Responsibility:* Dependability, initiative, persistence, aggressiveness, self-confidence, desire to excel.
4. *Participation:* Activity, sociability, cooperation, adaptability, humor.
5. *Status:* Socioeconomic position, popularity.
6. *Situation:* Mental level, status, skills, needs and interests of followers, objectives to be achieved, and so on.

SOURCE: Bernard M. Bass, ed., *Bass & Stogdill's Handbook of Leadership,* 3rd ed. (New York: Free Press, 1990), 76.

most important contribution was his conclusion that "qualities, characteristics, and skills required in a leader are determined, to a large degree, by the demands of the situation" (75). This research area has become known as *situational leadership* theory (discussed in more depth later in the chapter).

After the publication of Stogdill's initial research in 1948, scholars began to analyze leaders in a situational context. Stogdill's second survey of leadership literature through 1970 supported the earlier summary but introduced a more general explanation:

> The leader is characterized by a strong drive for responsibility and task completion, vigor and persistence in pursuit of goals, venturesomeness and originality in problem solving, drive to exercise initiative in social situations, self-confidence and sense of personal identity, willingness to accept consequences of decision and action, readiness to absorb interpersonal stress, willingness to tolerate frustration and delay, ability to influence other people's behavior, and capacity to structure social interaction systems to the purpose at hand. (Bass 1990, 87)

No longer do scholars believe that leaders are born; nor do they believe that a specific set of traits is essential to leader success. Instead there is agreement that the traits just noted, and perhaps some others, greatly increase the probability of success as a leader, although they do not guarantee success. Similarly psychologists believe five personality traits, known as the *big 5*, relate to performance, but not specifically to leadership: "extraversion, emotional stability, agreeableness, conscientiousness, and openness to experience" (Barrick, Mount, and Judge 2001). This line of research suggests that it is possible for two leaders facing the same situation to have different traits, or for a leader to be successful in one situation and not in another. The context changes the traits necessary to solve problems and lead. In addition, certainly the intelligence and experience of a leader, as well as his or her skills, are important to the success of followers and the organization.[4]

Closely related to this trait research are some other approaches to the study of leadership that focus on the motivation and values held by managers and executives. Numerous individuals have zeroed in on managerial motivation. For example, David McClelland's research indicated that three needs—for achievement, power, and affiliation—were central to the effectiveness of managers (McClelland 1975; see also Winter 1973). In established bureaucracies the dominant motive of most successful organizational managers is the need for power; but the need for achievement has to be present as well.[5] Along with a drive for power appears to go the self-confidence and assertiveness that are necessary to lead and control a large and complex group. The successful leader also has a moderate need for affiliation, in some cases only to be able to fulfill the social and public relations activities that are inherent in managerial and executive positions—but more importantly because affiliation is essential to the leader's establishing effective interpersonal relationships with subordinates, peers, and superiors. After all, commitment and loyalty tend to be reciprocal feelings. Obviously a balance of the three drives is necessary, with the levels being determined by the situation facing the organization and the leader.

---

[4]Some research indicates that stress moderates the relationship between intelligence and decision-making ability. Under high stress intelligent leaders can and do make terrible decisions. Greater experience can moderate this stress and lead to better decisions (Yukl 1994, 308).

[5]Among entrepreneurial executives the need for achievement appeared to be dominant; therefore achievement would probably be the motivating factor for someone successfully directing a new and struggling organization.

Values

Underlying these traits and needs may be the values that a manager holds. Numerous attempts have been made to identify and categorize the values held by managers deemed successful (Gordon 1975, 1976). Values might include fairness, justice, courtesy, cooperation, upholding democratic principles, and knowing right from wrong. These values may be what creates the motivation, or helps create the motivation, in managers and others. The manager serves as a role model for other employees based on his or her values.

Gordon reported six major values:

1. *Support:* Being treated with understanding, kindness, and consideration; receiving encouragement from other people.

2. *Conformity:* Following regulations; doing what is accepted, proper, or socially correct.

3. *Recognition:* Attracting favorable attention; being admired, looked up to, or considered important.

4. *Independence:* Being free to make one's own decisions or do things in one's own way; experiencing freedom of action.

5. *Benevolence:* Being generous and other-directed; sharing with and helping those who are less fortunate.

6. *Leadership:* Having authority over people; being in a position of influence or power. (Gordon 1975, 22–25)

Our concern is not so much that managers hold certain values but that when they take action, they support the values of the democratic process and a civil society. Ultimately what may be necessary (for any level of leadership) is upholding the agreed values of society and the Constitution: justice, liberty, equality of opportunity, the dignity of the individual, and the sanctity of private religious beliefs (Gardner 1990, 75, 77). These values guide our management thinking, yet they often conflict or at least compete for attention (see Table 9–2). Values don't easily lend themselves to a rational model of thinking or decision making.

TABLE 9–2   Competing Values

1a	Ultimately there is but one truth.	1b	There are two sides to every story.
2a	Nothing is so meaningful as a job well done.	2b	Greatest meaning derives from loving relationships.
3a	Custom deters progress.	3b	Wisdom favors tradition.
4a	The only constant is change.	4b	Order follows regulation.
5a	Establish the rule and allow no variation.	5b	Be tolerant, for each rule has its exception.
6a	Never do less than your individual best.	6b	Seek understanding, for it brings cooperation.
7a	Be wise as a serpent and gentle as a dove.	7b	Act aggressively or the moment will be lost.
8a	Dream well, for thy dreams shall be prophets.	8b	Do well the little things that lie nearest.

SOURCE: Robert Quinn, *Beyond Rational Management* (San Francisco: Jossey-Bass, 1991), 30. Copyright © 1991 by Jossey-Bass. Reprinted with permission.

When traits, needs, motivation, and values are combined with the specific skills needed for a particular managerial position, we have the components considered important to successful management. Putting these together are the managers in the middle. Such symbolic documents as codes of ethics and mission statements attempt to promote the organization's values; but it is the manager who actually does this through his or her actions, acting as a role model for others.

Managerial Tasks and the Fulfillment of Multiple Roles

The number and variety of tasks performed by the manager are actually larger than our imagination allows us to perceive and comprehend. Successful managers describe the reasons for their successes by aphorisms such as "flying by the seat of my pants," "using my sixth sense," and "following my gut reactions." Behn (1988) calls this "management by groping along." This is not because they don't know what to do. Good managers have a vision of what needs to be done; they do not necessarily know the steps to get there. They grope along through a series of small successes and mistakes to turn the vision into a success.[6] This is just one way to describe the tasks that managers fulfill.

Henry Mintzberg (1973; for a discussion see Yukl 1998, 23–25), using his own research and research of others, gleaned a set of 10 distinguishing characteristics and roles to describe what managers do in a variety of organizations. In a hierarchical organization, these might form the backbone of the job description. The relative importance of the roles is determined by situational factors including position in the hierarchy, technology used by employees, the culture of the organization, type of organizational unit, and threats to the organizational unit's survival (for local government, see Morgan et al. 1996). These roles, of course, can and do overlap with other leadership levels. We briefly describe these roles and note their applicability to other leadership levels.

1. *Figurehead role:* Managers hold formal positions within the organization, and these positions create an obligation to participate in organizational duties, rituals, and ceremonies. These vary from signing certain documents and greeting visitors to holding retirement lunches. These actions help set the culture. (This description applies to the executive role as well.)

2. *Leader role:* Managers must hire, train, direct, praise, motivate, integrate, and even dismiss employees. Managers create conditions that allow work to be done efficiently and effectively.

3. *Liaison role:* Communication and coordination between the various units inside and outside the organization are accomplished by establishing contacts via the cell phone, Web, and networks of relationships. Who is relevant to a manager depends on an individual's position. By making contacts, doing favors, and keeping an ear to the grapevine, each manager attempts to sway influential others, who in turn can affect the success of the manager's operations.

4. *Monitor role:* Managers monitor information from a variety of sources. Some is passed on to subordinates or to outsiders (other managers in the organization or relevant individuals or groups in the environment). But most of the information is analyzed in a constant search for problems and opportunities so that both external

---

[6]He actually was discussing the very highest level, politically appointed positions, but used the word *manager*. Managers may also fail if they do not grope (654). See also Chapter 2 for discussion of "muddling through."

events and internal processes can be better understood. In this way managers can correct situations causing difficulty, encourage success, and prepare for future events.

5. *Disseminator role:* Managers have access to information often not available to subordinates. It is the manager's function to assimilate and properly interpret the information and pass it to those who need it.

6. *Spokesperson role:* Managers serve as transmitters of information about their units to their superiors, other managers, and external parties. The manager must act as lobbyist, public relations officer, and negotiator because she has the best knowledge about her unit and its environment. (This applies primarily to executives.)

7. *Entrepreneur role:* The entrepreneur role may seem at first blush an inappropriate one for a government or nonprofit manager; but on further consideration it becomes obvious that this role is essential in all sectors of society (Lewis 1980). As noted by Matthew Holden (1966), there is a high degree of "bureaucratic imperialism" in public agencies. Therefore chief executives and managers must at least be on the lookout for bureaucratic marauders who may attack by snatching bits of authority and resources from their units or who may try to grab the entire operation and place it in a disadvantageous situation. By the same token, managers watch for opportunities to strengthen or expand their operations, hopefully in ways that make sense or lead to better service for the public. Managers also act as initiators and designers of changes that are aimed at improving the situations of their units. Such changes might include the purchase of new equipment, the reorganization of formal structure, or the development of a new and needed program. Mintzberg describes the entrepreneur as a juggler. "At any one point in time he has a number of balls in the air. Periodically, one comes down, receives a short burst of energy, and goes up again. Meanwhile, new balls wait on the sidelines and, at intervals, old balls are discarded and new ones added" (1973, 81).

8. *Disturbance handler role:* Sudden internal crises, client complaints, program changes, staff conflicts, computer problems, or the loss of key staff take up much of a manager's time. (This also applies to supervisors and to executives for external crises.)

9. *Resource allocator role:* Managers use their control over money, material, and personnel. It is rare for a manager in a hierarchical organization to have complete control over the budget and staffing and more common in other structural forms of organizations. (This applies primarily to executives.)

10. *Negotiator role:* When a manager acts in this role, he or she is probably involved because of several of the other roles such as the spokesperson and resource allocator.

Each of these roles exists for most managers. The combination of roles important at any one time and how much emphasis to place on each varies with the managerial position. As discussed earlier, we increasingly see managers and executives as entrepreneurs.

GROUP LEADERSHIP: SUPERVISORS AND TEAM LEADERS

At the productive heart, the staff that is getting the work done is led by supervisors and team leaders. Supervisors have three major foci in all their activities: production, maintenance of morale, and maintenance of group cohesiveness. Their jobs directly relate to day-to-day human resource concerns of employee turnover, absenteeism, job satisfaction, and organizational commitment.

Supervisors and team leaders make sure that the particular tasks and goals of their groups are completed properly. They need a combination of conceptual, technical, and human relations skills (Katz 1955; Mann 1965). Or do they? Conceptual skills relate to the supervisor or team leader's analytic abilities; interpersonal skills to knowledge and ability to understand feelings, attitudes, and human behavior; and technical skills to the knowledge and techniques of conducting a specialized activity.

One unanswered question in the literature is how much technical skill the supervisor or team leader must have to manage the group. Departments of Transportation (DOTs) are composed largely of engineers. Engineers have little time in their professional training to learn management skills. They may have a course in project management, and that might be the extent of their management training. Yet they are most often the team leaders and project managers for projects costing millions of dollars. Some DOTs are experimenting with having nonengineers serve as project team leaders, but most still promote engineers into these positions. Is this a better idea? In the following section we try to tease out any answers regarding supervisory and team leader effectiveness from the theoretical literature.

Supervisor/Team Leader Effectiveness

What makes this job different from the other levels is that the supervisor or team leader usually works directly with his or her staff. Theoretical work on the effectiveness of supervisors begins with the Ohio State University studies of the 1950s conducted by Stogdill and his colleagues (Hersey and Blanchard 1993). Military and civilian personnel were provided 150 items on which to judge the leadership behavior of their supervisors. The analysis defined two dimensions of effective supervisory behavior and attitude: consideration and initiation of structure.

Consideration is the extent to which a leader exhibits concern for the welfare of the other members of the group. Considerate supervisors express appreciation for good work, stress the importance of job satisfaction, maintain and strengthen self-esteem of subordinates by treating them as equals, make special efforts for subordinates to feel at ease, are easy to approach, put subordinates' suggestions into operation, and obtain approval of subordinates on important matters before going ahead. *Initiation of structure* refers to the extent to which a leader initiates work, organizes it, defines how it is to be done, establishes standards, and sets deadlines. Initiation of structure also includes the amount of structuring of the leaders' and subordinates' roles (Bass 1990 , 358–59).

Many studies of the relationship between consideration and initiating structure have been conducted (see Yukl 1998, Chapter 3). Not surprisingly, these studies have shown that supervisors high in consideration experience fewer grievances and lower turnover among their subordinates than supervisors who emphasize the structuring of behavior (Fleishman and Harris 1962; Skinner 1969). Sometimes structuring is necessary and where a substantial amount of structuring is required, a high level of consideration alleviates much dissatisfaction. But many studies have shown inconsistent relationships between consideration and performance and structuring and satisfaction. The most consistent relationship is found between consideration and employee satisfaction. Certainly no one wants an inconsiderate supervisor. Job satisfaction, however, does not always lead to increased performance or productivity; employees may simply be satisfied but not productive (Herzberg, Mausner, and Snyderman 1993; Lawler 2000).

An alternative way of understanding supervisory effectiveness is known as the *managerial grid* (Blake and Mouton 1985).[7] The grid is based on two dimensions of behavior—"concern for people" and "concern for production"—that are similar to consideration and initiating structure. No two people operate the same way. Nor does one supervisor act the same way from one situation to another. Some of us will be better on one dimension than on another. According to the managerial grid, the goal is balancing the need for production while emphasizing a concern for people. Blake and Mouton (1985) assert that

> The [team management] theory of managing presumes a necessary *connection* between organizational needs for production and the needs of people for full and rewarding work experiences. The leader's desire is to contribute to corporate success by involving others so that they too may contribute. Such a "can-do" spirit is contagious, inspires a "win" attitude in others, and promotes enthusiasm, voluntarism, spontaneity, and openness. Contribution with caring in the sense of a genuine desire to help others reach their highest potential is basic to creativity, commitment, and cohesion. (82)

Achieving such a relationship with subordinates creates the feeling of a common stake in the outcome of their endeavors and allows for a much higher chance of success in achieving the organization's goals and its continued existence over the long run. The managerial grid is often used in training programs, as are other similar assessments (such as Myers–Briggs). Blake and Mouton's work on the managerial grid suggests that by understanding ourselves, we can be better supervisors.

Both the Ohio State studies and the managerial grid are *attitudinal* theories of leadership. They describe and guide rather than predict. Attitudinal theories, like trait theories, contain a gap in explanation: Attitudes do not necessarily correlate with effectiveness. Some unidentified action needs to take place between attitudes and effectiveness. To find a comprehensive theory, we need to return to situational theories.

Specific research on effective teams (both executive and project management teams involved in creative projects, problem solving, and defined work) suggests that supervisors and team leaders are transformational leaders (Larson and LaFasto 1989).[8] The most effective teams, according to Larson and LaFasto, have

- A clear and elevating goal.
- A results-driven structure.
- Competent team members.
- A unified commitment.
- A collaborative climate.
- Standards of excellence.
- External support and recognition.

Working well together, creating the collaborative climate means that the team (including the leader) has to feel a sense of trust, honesty, and a willingness to share. As Larson and LaFasto point out, once a person lies, trust in that person may collapse to zero (86–87).

---

[7]The grid deals with management at all levels of the organization, but it focuses on the functions that we have identified as primarily supervisory.

[8]Larson and LaFasto use the phrase *principled leadership,* a synonym for *transformational leadership.*

Situational Theories of Group Leadership

Situational theories recognize that a leadership style needs to be chosen in relationship to the work. The needed skills, behaviors, and traits depend on the context that includes the leader's peers, subordinates' ability, the task at hand, and the external environment—politics, customers/ citizens, and the community. These situational variables require different behaviors. For example, a director of the American Lung Association who moves to the American Cancer Society may find that success in one agency does not translate to another because of the different situational variables.[9]

One of the better known situational theories of leadership is the contingency model proposed by Fiedler (1964, 1967). *Contingency* models or theories explicitly recognize that certain variables moderate the ability of leaders to be effective. Contingency theories examine these variables to determine when a leader is more likely to have success. Leader effectiveness is depends on the match between, say, the team leader's style or traits and the situation. To test the theory, Fiedler had leaders rate themselves on a trait he identified as the *least preferred coworker* (past or present) to create an LPC score to predict effectiveness. (Individuals who are critical of their least preferred coworker receive low LPC scores, and those who are tolerant receive high ones.) Although the interpretation of LPC scores has changed several times over the years, the situational moderating variable involved has remained constant. The variable around which the LPC scores and leader effectiveness revolves is the extent to which the situation gives a leader influence over subordinate performance. This level of influence is measured according to three criteria:

1. *Leader–member relations:* If leaders enjoy the loyalty and support of subordinates, enthusiastic compliance with their wishes and orders usually follows. The opposite can be expected if attitudes and feelings toward the leader are reversed.

2. *Position power:* If a leader has substantial power built into a position, he or she can use it to reward and punish compliance or noncompliance with wishes or orders. A leader who does not have such power must rely on other sources of influence to gain compliance.

3. *Task structure* If tasks are highly structured, standard operating procedures exist, finished products or services are clearly defined, and the quality of work done by subordinates is clear, control and guidance are easier. If task structure, procedures, and end products are not so clear, the leader has less control and gives less guidance, and workers can find more ways to circumvent the leader's wishes and orders.

Fiedler goes on to suggest that when situational control is either very high or very low, based on these three criteria, a team leader with a low LPC score will be more effective, whereas in situations with intermediate levels of situational control, team leaders with high LPC scores will be more successful. Fiedler operationalized in his theory what long had been recognized but had not been dealt with in a formal way: Proper leader behavior must be based on an evaluation of the situation in which it occurs.

---

[9]See Behn's (1988) discussion of the failure of the Massachusetts Director of the Employment and Training to apply his successful "groping along" to a similar position in Kansas.

Hersey and Blanchard (1993) have applied the situational construct to develop the tridimensional leader effectiveness model. This model fills the gap of the Ohio State studies that left unresolved how to translate attitudes into effectiveness. Hersey and Blanchard begin with a combination of two dimensions: task behavior and relationship behavior (similar in meaning to the structure and consideration concepts of the Ohio State studies). They add the third dimension—the environment or the situation. Effectiveness is the right combination of the two constructs for the situation.

This theory suggests that for leaders to be effective they must consider a variety of situational variables such as the maturity or readiness level of followers. This situational variable is particularly relevant to any discussion of leadership of today's workforce composed of knowledge workers. These high achievers, as McClelland (1961) identified them (and elaborated upon by Hersey and Blanchard), have the capacity to set high but attainable goals (achievement), concern for personal achievement (motivation), a willingness to take responsibility, and the education and experience to do the job. The combination of relationship and task-oriented behaviors of the supervisor should change as subordinates' maturity or readiness increases (see Figure 9–1). Task-oriented behaviors steadily decrease as subordinates achieve higher levels of maturity. On the other hand, relationship-oriented behavior increases as subordinates advance from immaturity to a moderate level of maturity. Then, as subordinates move on to a higher level of maturity, the amount of considerate, supportive, consultative behavior is reduced as the leader delegates responsibility and increases the independence of employees. Mature employees, because of their initiative, self-confidence, and commitment, do not need as much supportive behavior from their superiors.

For Hersey and Blanchard, when the style of the leader is appropriate for the given situation, it is defined as effective (1993, 130). For example, in a crisis a leader might choose high task and low relationship as the best combination; but once the crisis is over, he or she might return to another combination (132). This appears to indicate that effectiveness is an either–or perspective, but Hersey and Blanchard characterize effectiveness as a continuum. As Hersey and Blanchard state,

> consistent leadership is not using the same leadership style all the time, but using the style appropriate for followers' level of readiness in such a way that followers understand why they are getting a certain behavior, a certain style from the leader. (1993, 134)

Perhaps the model that uses the most comprehensive set of intervening variables is the multiple linkage model of leader effectiveness developed by Gary Yukl (1998, 276–283). Yukl looks at an extensive set of situational variables that affect individual and group performance as well as the ability of the supervisor—traits, power, behavior—to influence the intervening variables determining that performance. As a first step in the model, Yukl presents the intervening variables that influence performance and effectiveness. These include

1. *Subordinate effort:* The extent to which subordinates make an effort to attain a high level of performance and show a high degree of personal responsibility and commitment toward achieving the work unit's goals and objectives.

2. *Subordinate role clarity:* The extent to which subordinates understand their job duties and responsibilities and know what is expected of them and have the skills to do the job.

3. *Subordinate task skills:* The extent to which subordinates have the experience, training, and skills necessary to perform all aspects of their jobs effectively.

FIGURE 9–1 Situational Leadership®

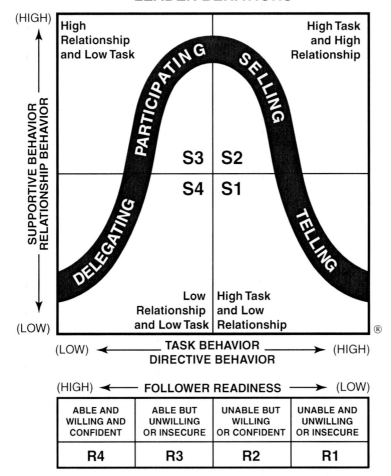

LEADER BEHAVIORS

4. *Resources and support services:* The extent to which subordinates can obtain the materials, equipment, supplies, and support services to do their jobs.

5. *Task–role organization:* The extent to which the work unit is effectively organized to ensure efficient utilization of personnel, equipment, and facilities and the avoidance of delays, duplication of effort, and wasted effort.

6. *Group cohesiveness and teamwork:* The extent to which subordinates get along with each other, share information and ideas, and are friendly, helpful, considerate, and cooperative (1994, 295–96, 154).

The performance of individual subordinates depends on the first four variables; the performance of the group as a whole is related to the next two. All six intervening variables interact to determine the levels of individual and group commitment, morale, and productivity; and the intervening variables are themselves influenced by a set of situational variables that Yukl classifies in three categories (1998, 278).

The first category of situational influences directly affects one or more of the six factors just spelled out, thus indirectly influencing individual and/or group performance. Examples of this type of variable are the recruitment and selection system, training, the formal reward system, the budgetary and resource allocation system, and the size of the work group. The second type of situational influence is the job itself. Technology, for example, may change and increase or decrease the skill needed by workers, the attractiveness of the job, or the amount of time required to give subordinates feedback if they are doing something either well or poorly. If the nature of the job requires few supplies, equipment, and support services, then such intervening variables will not be important. So too the level of cooperation is affected by the nature of the work.

Finally, the third type of situational influence in Yukl's model deals with organizational constraints on leader actions to alter directly the intervening variables (1998, 279–280). Kerr and Jermier (1978) more descriptively call these "substitutes for leadership." Structural

BOX 9–6 Yukl's Categories of Managerial Practices

Making Decisions

Planning and organizing: Determining long-term objectives and strategies; allocating resources according to priorities; determining how to use personnel and resources to accomplish a task efficiently; and determining how to improve coordination, productivity, and the effectiveness of the organizational unit.

Problem solving: Identifying work-related problems, analyzing problems in a timely but systematic manner to identify causes and find solutions, and acting decisively to implement solutions to resolve important problems or crises.

Consulting: Checking with people before making changes that affect them, encouraging suggestions for improvement, inviting participation in decision making, and incorporating the ideas and suggestions of others in decisions.

Delegating: Allowing subordinates to have substantial responsibility and discretion in carrying out work activities, handling problems, and making important decisions.

Influencing People

Motivating and inspiring: Using influence techniques that appeal to emotion or logic to generate enthusiasm for the work, commitment to task objectives, and compliance with requests for cooperation, assistance, support, or resources; and setting an example of appropriate behavior.

Recognizing: Providing praise and recognition for effective performance, significant achievements, and special contributions; and expressing appreciation for someone's contributions and special efforts.

Rewarding: Providing or recommending tangible rewards such as a pay increase or promotion for effective performance, significant achievements, and demonstrated competence.

arrangements, budgetary systems, procurement systems, ability to control rewards and punishments, discretion over work assignments, procedures, and union contracts all may constrain or act as substitutes for leadership. The effect of this situational influence depends on the leader's position, power, and organizational policies and the leader's behavior.

These organizational constraints can lead to employees who are apathetic, confused about their work, and fail to work as a team. Because this model is both prescriptive and explanatory, Yukl prescribes a whole host of behaviors to address many of these organizational constraints. In Box 9–6 we have grouped these behaviors under four primary processes of managing that are appropriate for use in different situations (43, 69). The relative importance of these behaviors depends on the level of leadership—executive, manager, team leader. The leader who fails to correct is ineffective and may even increase deficiencies (1994, 301–302).

Here we see what may be the most complex formal model of situational leadership behavior that has been developed to date. It uses the same approach as the other theories mentioned, but it increases the complexity, sophistication, and delicacy of the calculations that must occur. In each case the (executive, supervisor, manager, or team) leader is expected to evaluate the situation; the set of circumstances related to the internal and external forces

Building Relationships

Networking: Socializing informally; developing contacts with people who are a source of information and support; and maintaining contacts through periodic interaction, including visits, telephone calls, correspondence, and attendance at meetings and social events.

Managing conflict and team building: Facilitating the constructive resolution of conflict; and encouraging cooperation, teamwork, and identification with the work unit.

Developing and mentoring: Providing coaching and helpful career advice; and doing things to facilitate a person's skill acquisition, professional development, and career advancement.

Supporting: Acting friendly and considerate, being patient and helpful, showing sympathy and support when someone is upset or anxious, listening to complaints and problems, and looking out for someone's interests.

Giving and Seeking Information

Monitoring: Gathering information about work activities and external conditions affecting the work, checking on the progress and quality of the work, evaluating the performance of individuals and the organizational unit, and analyzing trends and forecasting external events.

Clarifying roles and objectives: Assigning tasks; providing direction in how to do the work; and communicating a clear understanding of job responsibilities, task objectives, deadlines, and performance expectations.

Informing: Disseminating relevant information about decisions, plans, and activities to people who need it to do their work; providing written materials and documents; and answering requests for technical information.

SOURCE: Adapted from Gary A. Yukl. *Leadership in Organizations,* 4th ed. (Englewood Cliffs, N. J.: Prentice-Hall, Inc., 1998), 60.

YUKL, GARY A., LEADERSHIP IN ORGANIZATIONS, 4TH Edition, Copyright © 1998. Adapted by permission of Pearson Education, Inc., Upper Saddle River, NJ acting in or on the organization and the existing characteristics of the organization; and the strengths and weaknesses associated with the organization's employees, resources, processes, and objectives. Once this is completed, the leader decides what behavior or leadership (style) is appropriate at this time. He or she must look at both the short- and long-term effects of the style and balance its costs and benefits. (Obviously each style has a variety of specific component behaviors attached to it.) In the meantime, the leader must have a built-in barometer to constantly measure reactions to the current style and predict when it is time to reinvestigate the situation or change the style of leadership in use.

At the upper levels the evaluation of the situation will lead to a general style that will probably be relatively stable. Recall that trait and attitudinal theory suggest traits, values, and hence behaviors are relatively stable. Yet dramatic change may be required in case of a crisis. When Hurricane Katrina occurred, FEMA Director Brown used the same leadership style he had used in other recent hurricane situations. He did not assert direct leadership once his New Orleans FEMA contact informed him of the dire situation. He failed to change his style appropriate for his followers' level of readiness (Hersey and Blanchard 1993, 134). His style may have been appropriate for the planning functions of FEMA (removed when FEMA merged into Homeland Security) or smaller emergencies.

We can interpret this situation using the multiple linkage model.[10] The situational variables, the resources of FEMA, and the job itself, responding to emergencies, had not changed since the previous emergency response. What did change was the magnitude of the external event (the environment), transforming the job into one that required massive internal and external coordination. The other differences were the failure of Director Brown to influence intervening variables, to modify his own traits and behaviors to the needs of the emergency as well as his failure to coordinate FEMA's responsibilities with outside organizations (state, local, and nonprofit).

READING 9–3   Catastrophes and Leadership

For 16 critical hours, Federal Emergency Management Agency officials, including former director Michael D. Brown, dismissed urgent eyewitness accounts by FEMA's only staffer in New Orleans that Hurricane Katrina had broken the city's levee system the morning of August 29 and was causing catastrophic flooding, the staffer told the Senate yesterday.

Marty Bahamonde, sent to New Orleans by Brown, said he alerted Brown's assistant shortly after 11 a.m. that Monday with the "worst possible news" for the city: The Category 4 hurricane had carved a 20-foot breach in the 17th Avenue Canal levee.

Five FEMA aides were e-mailed Bahamonde's report of "water flow 'bad'" from the broken levees designed to hold back Lake Pontchartrain. Bahamonde said he called Brown personally after 7 p.m. to warn that 80 percent of New Orleans was underwater and that he had photographed a 200-foot-wide breach.

"FEMA headquarters knew at 11 o'clock. Mike Brown knew at 7 o'clock. Most of FEMA's operational staff knew by 9 o'clock that evening. I don't know where that information went," said Bahamonde, a 12-year FEMA staffer who has worked full-time since 2002 as a public affairs official.

---

[10]No set of variables can be complete. A true analysis of the handling of Hurricane Katrina would take much more space than a paragraph.

Testifying to a bipartisan Senate panel investigating the response to the hurricane, Bahamonde said his accounts were discarded by officials in Baton Rouge and Washington headquarters amid conflicting information.

His disclosures add significantly to public knowledge of how much information Brown and FEMA officials had about the damage Katrina caused, and how soon they were aware of it. The federal government has been widely criticized for its slow, uncoordinated response to the hurricane, which left 1,053 people dead in Louisiana, most of them in New Orleans.

President Bush, Homeland Security Secretary Michael Chertoff, Defense Secretary Donald H. Rumsfeld, and Richard B. Myers, then chairman of the Joint Chiefs of Staff, have all said they were told that the city's flood walls did not fail until August 30. They said they assumed that the worst was over during a daylong window when operations could have been launched to rush aid to the Louisiana Superdome or rescue more than 50,000 residents and tourists before streets and homes were flooded.

"This disconnect . . . is beyond disturbing. It's shocking," said Senator Joseph I. Lieberman (Connecticut), the senior Democrat on the Senate Homeland Security and Governmental Affairs Committee, which is leading the investigation.

Bahamonde said he found it "amazing" that New Orleans officials continued to let thousands gather at the Superdome, even though they knew that the area around it was going to flood. Ten people later died at the Superdome.

"Urgent reports did not appear to prompt an urgent response," said panel chairperson Susan M. Collins (R-Maine). She asked "why the city continued to send people to the Superdome, when it appears they should have evacuated the Superdome?"

As recently as this week, Chertoff told a House Katrina investigation, "The report—last report I got on Monday [August 29] was that the levees—there had not been a significant breach in the levees. It appeared that the worst was over."

In contrast, Bahamonde, who was dressed in a dark suit and spoke somberly to senators for nearly three hours, said, "I believed at the time and still do today, that I was confirming the worst-case scenario that everyone had always talked about regarding New Orleans."

In a series of increasingly dire, angry e-mails and phone calls, Bahamonde updated Brown, aides, and top spokespeople for FEMA beginning August 28 from the New Orleans emergency operations center and then from the Superdome across the street.

"Issues developing at the Superdome. The medical staff at the dome says they will run out of oxygen in about two hours and are looking for alternative oxygen," Bahamonde wrote to FEMA Region VI spokesman David Passey on August 28.

That night 25,000 people were inside, including 400 people with special medical needs and 45 who required hospitalization. The center was short of toilet paper, water, and food, the last of which was adequate through Tuesday only because a Coast Guard helicopter crew found and broke into five abandoned FEMA trailer trucks at Bahamonde's direction, Bahamonde said yesterday.

About 7 p.m. August 29, Bahamonde said, he called Brown and warned him of "massive flooding," that 20,000 people were short of food and water at the Superdome and that thousands of people were standing on roofs or balconies seeking rescue.

Brown replied only, "Thank you. I'm going to call the White House," Bahamonde said.

It is unclear what Brown told his superiors or the president's aides. He has testified to receiving "conflicting information" about 10 a.m. Monday that the levees had broken and at noon or 1 p.m. that "the levees had only been topped. So we knew something was going on between 10 and noon on Monday."

Bahamonde contradicted accounts by Brown that FEMA had positioned 12 staffers in the Superdome before the storm, that Bahamonde's reports Monday were "routine," and that FEMA medical personnel were on hand before Tuesday.

At 11:20 a.m. August 31, Bahamonde e-mailed Brown, "Sir, I know that you know the situation is past critical . . . thousands gathering in the streets with no food or water . . . estimates are many will die within hours."

At 2:27 p.m., however, Brown press secretary Sharon Worthy wrote colleagues to schedule an interview for Brown on MSNBC's *Scarborough Country* and to give him more time to eat dinner because Baton Rouge restaurants were getting busy: "He needs much more than 20 or 30 minutes."

Bahamonde e-mailed a friend to "just tell [Worthy] that I just ate an MRE . . . along with 30,000 other close friends so I understand her concern."

SOURCE: Spencer S. Hsu, "Aide Says FEMA Ignored Warnings; Testimony Covers Communication as Levees Breached," *Washington Post,* final edition, October 21, 2005, A01.

Copyright *The Washington Post Company* October 21, 2005.

This situational approach to leadership is the generally accepted explanation of leadership effectiveness. It recognizes the interaction of leadership with the innumerable cross pressures that exist. Its strength is also its weakness. As a prescriptive model of leadership, it is difficult to follow. It involves keeping in mind many factors at the same time. However, this may simply reflect reality. A leader has to take into account individual, organizational, and political demands to achieve efficiency and effectiveness.

INFORMAL AND SELF-LEADERSHIP

We began this chapter with a quote from Gardner that we can find leaders everywhere. The fourth level of leadership is informal or self-leadership. Formal leaders do not work alone to ensure that the mission of an organization is met. This involves making sure that employees can do their jobs and establishing the trust of employees. Employees and volunteers of FEMA, the Red Cross, the Salvation Army and many other organizations helped make a very bad situation better after Hurricane Katrina.

Many of us have valued the help of a mentor; but the idea of developing the leadership abilities of others is actually a relatively new idea in the leadership and organizational literature. McGregor took up this idea in his discussion of Theory X and Theory Y. Describing Theory Y, McGregor suggested,

> The essential task of management is to arrange organizational conditions and methods of operations so that people can achieve their own goals best by directing their own efforts toward organizational objectives. (McGregor 1957, 183)[11]

---

[11]Shafritz, Ott, and Yong (2005) excerpt an article version of McGregor's ideas about Theory X and Y that became the basis of McGregor's important study, *The Human Side of Enterprise.*

McGregor also was one of the first to support the idea of participative/consultative management and greater decentralization. What he described is what today's theorists are advocating: self-leadership. A leader's role is one of developing the leadership abilities of employees (Manz and Sims 1990; Bennis 1989b, 1989a).

Perhaps a weakness in earlier theories and particularly our reliance on Weber's ideal-type bureaucracy is that they say little about supporting employees: the administrative assistants, the plumbers, the help desk employees, the police officers, and similar kinds of nonsalaried personnel. Can Weber's ideal type be extended to include those people? Although U.S. labor laws have changed relatively little since the 1940s, we increasingly identify jobs as professions ranging from the professional administrative assistant to the professional police officer, nurse, or plumber—suggesting that we can indeed incorporate them into the idea of career professionals who have competencies to be leaders.

The trend in organizational development is to treat leadership as a series of competencies that can be developed (for examples see Joint Commission on the Accreditation of Health Care Organizations n.d.; Coast Guard 2004). The theory has roots in the work of McClelland and his colleagues (McClelland and Steele 1973). Competencies are a combination of knowledge, skills, traits, and underlying motives. The theory behind competency development is that we can indeed learn leadership skills that will translate into effective behavior. We learn through a variety of means: traditional education, skill demonstration, mentors, and colleagues and supervisors. Organizations from the state of Maine to the Coast Guard have identified and developed training programs in competencies necessary to succeed in different levels of leadership. The Coast Guard, for example, defines leadership competencies as measurable patterns of behavior essential to leading: understanding your own abilities, working with others, and applying these competencies to job performance. Developing competencies is part of a lifelong learning process.

Bowman (2004) sees the professional, whether working for a public, nonprofit, or private organization, as needing three competencies. He or she is a technical professional with expertise in human resources, information technology, and performance management. Second, the professional is an ethical decision maker with the tools to make decisions based on morals and values. And third, the professional can assess situations in terms of tasks, people, and the organizational needs.

Two particularly important competencies are social intelligence (the ability to recognize what is expected and respond accordingly) and emotional intelligence (an awareness of one's emotions leading to self-management). Emotionally intelligent people can manage their emotions and create a positive work environment (Murensky 2000). Leaders have the trait of being intelligent—probably more intelligent than the average person—but as McClelland points out, that is not enough to be a true leader. Leaders need to be something more: They need emotional intelligence.

WOMEN AND LEADERSHIP

Even today some people are sufficiently ignorant to ask whether women have the competencies to be leaders. Certainly we have many examples of women leaders, and studies show that male and female leaders differ little in effectiveness (Northouse 2004, 270–71). Women leaders have similar traits to men, but they tend to be less autocratic and more democratic in style—although the tendency is not as predominant in more male-oriented organizations (Northouse 2004, 270). Thus this question is more of a rhetorical question than a factual one. But why is it even asked rhetorically? It is because we know that there are far fewer women leaders in the highest positions than men leaders. Just as leadership is a function of the situation, the possibility of women in high leadership positions seems to be situational. The context, the predominance of male or female positions, the type of structure, and the associated culture affect the ability of women to enter leadership positions. Organizations are *gendered* (Guy 1992, 2, 220–21; Acker 1992). When the professions are predominantly male (such as in engineering-related organizations), the structure is hierarchical, and the culture is more rule oriented, the organization is more apt to be dominated by male leaders. Organizations that have more participatory decision making, have a more diverse array of professions, and are less hierarchical are more apt to have women leaders. The fact that fewer women hold leadership positions as the level of command in the hierarchy rises is known as the *glass ceiling*. That is, there are structural impediments to women obtaining leadership positions. What occurs, then, has disparate impact on women's abilities to move ahead in organizations. The gendered office perspective suggests that women may be precluded from leadership unintentionally (and sometimes intentionally). Rooting out the causes of discrimination will assist women who seek leadership positions.

Carol Gilligan (1993), a psychologist and author of *A Different Voice*, offers a different perspective about women and decision making and hence leadership. She proposes that women perceive, hear, see, speak, and interpret events differently. They have "a different voice," a voice that is not better or worse than a man's voice. But their perceptions are different. Women perceive and interpret in terms of relations rather than in terms of self. This perspective of a different voice fits nicely with recent interpretations that diversity in the workplace (ethnic, religious, gender, race, color) is a benefit. Individuals from various groups and professions add different opinions and different ways to solve problems and thus can increase organizational effectiveness.

CONCLUSION

After looking at much literature about leadership and applying it to government and nonprofit organizations, we see that recent theorists believe that leaders can be developed and are not born; leadership can be defined as set of competencies. Although different aspects of the leadership role are emphasized more at some levels and sectors, there is overlap. To a degree, fulfilling a leadership role in a nonprofit or government organization today depends on two powerful influences of the external environment: rapidly changing technology and the global economy. Leadership in this rapidly changing environment is not so different in large and small organizations. Informal leadership occurs often because informal leaders have some characteristics that are ascribed to leaders. They have learned the competencies to fulfill some leadership functions.

Choosing among policies and programs assumes ethical decision making for the well-being of immediate clients, constituents, customers, and citizens at large. The job of the nonprofit or government leader is often considered doubly difficult due to the political environment that must be added to any choice. And of course in many cases the choices and action taken lack time for calculation. Being a successful executive, manager, supervisor or team leader, or even informal leader is not an easy task; it is simply a task that must be done to carry out the mandate of serving the public and helping to maintain the democratic system. If a leader is able to overcome the difficulties, carry out the tasks, and make the significant value choices that are inherent in the position, then she or he embodies the leader role and can look forward to success and a feeling of deeply satisfying accomplishment. When the internal situation changes (policy, technology, organization size, or group dynamics) or the external situation changes (political environment, economic situation, or a crisis), the process of analysis, understanding, choice, and action must begin anew. The reward for successful leaders is the challenge.

FOR FURTHER READING

The major compendium of leadership theory over the years, which is useful as a place to start, is Bernard M. Bass's *Bass & Stogdill's Handbook of Leadership*, 3rd ed. (New York: Free Press, 1990). Two other works are suggested here because they trace the development and use of multiple-variable models to analyze the organizational environment and the development of leadership. They are Paul Hersey and Kenneth H. Blanchard's *Management of Organizational Behavior*, 6th. ed. (Englewood Cliffs, NJ: Prentice-Hall, 1993) and Gary A. Yukl's *Leadership in Organizations*, 4th. ed. (Englewood Cliffs, NJ: Prentice-Hall, 1998). Perhaps the best classic work on leadership, and one that is worth rereading occasionally, is Chester Barnard's *The Functions of an Executive* (Cambridge, MA: Harvard University Press, 1936/1968). A major work that tries to address political leadership by combining psychological, social, and cultural perspectives is James MacGregor Burns's *Leadership* (New York: Harper & Row, 1978). James Q. Wilson's *Bureaucracy: What Government Agencies Do and Why They Do It*, 2nd ed. (New York: Basic Books, 2000) does a masterful job of presenting the problems faced by individuals at each level of leadership in various sections of his book's discussion of operators, managers, and executives. When examining the managerial level of leadership, the place to start, because of its examination of the multiple roles of the manager, is Henry Mintzberg's *The Nature of Managerial Work* (New York: Harper & Row, 1973). Martin Levin shows the detail of a manager's job in his 1993 hypothetical scenario "The Day after an AIDS Vaccine Is Discovered: Management Matters" in *Journal of Public Policy Analysis and Management* 12: 438–55.

For those interested in understanding teamwork and supervision, an excellent source is Carl Larson and Frank LaFasto's *Teamwork* (Newbury Park, CA: Sage, 1989).

Those interested in leadership from a cross sector perspective should read John Gardner's *On Leadership* (New York: The Free Press, 1990). To learn more about John W. Gardner, visit "John Gardner: Uncommon American" at http://www.pbs.org/johngardner/. Norma Riccucci's *Unsung Heroes: Federal Execucrats Making a Difference* (Washington, DC: Georgetown University Press, 1995) and Burt Nanus and Stephen Dobbs's *Leaders Who Make a Difference* (San Francisco: Jossey-Bass, 1999) do an excellent job of describing the real-life experiences of public and nonprofit sector leaders. For an interesting insight into the portrayal of nonprofit leaders, see Mordecai Lee's 2004 article "What Does Hollywood Think Nonprofit CEOs Do All Day? Screen Depictions of NGO Management" in *Public Organization Review* 4: 157–76.

For complementary excerpts from the classics, see most editions of Jay Shafritz and J. Steven Ott's (and coauthors) *Classics of Organizational Theory* (Belmont, CA: Thomson Wadsworth); Max Weber, "Bureaucracy"; Luther Gulick, "Notes on a Theory of Organization";

Tom Peters and Robert Waterman Jr., "In Search of Excellence: Simultaneous Loose–Tight Properties"; and Peter Senge, "The Fifth Discipline: A Shift of Mind."

For a complementary nonprofit case study, see Robert Goliembiewski and Jerry Stevenson's *Cases and Applications in Non-Profit Management* (Belmont, CA: Thomson Wadsworth, 1998): Case 2, "Friends, Volunteers, and Adversaries: Sorting Out the Players."

REVIEW QUESTIONS

1. Scholars agree that leadership is a critical element that pulls together all other aspects of organizational life. Do you agree? Is the leader as important in determining success in a private organization compared to a nonprofit or government organization? In what ways?
2. What are the major differences in the tasks or functions of individuals operating at the three leadership levels of an organization? How do they differ from those of the informal leader?
3. Explain how the situation helps determine an individual's style of leadership. Does situational theory work at all levels of the organization? Is the leader's style determined by the situation, or can the leader control the situation?
4. Bennis distinguishes between managers and leaders. What values and assumptions might underlie the statements made by the author in Box 9–4? How are those values and assumptions correct or incorrect? Do they apply equally to government and nonprofit leaders?
5. When you look at the distinction made by Bennis between managers and leaders, how do theories or models in this and previous chapters help to clarify the meaning of the statements?

REFERENCES

Acker, Joan. 2005. Gendering organizational theory. In *Classics of Organizational Theory*. Ed. J. Shafritz, J. S. Ott, and Y. S. Jang. Belmont, CA: Thomson.

Badelt, Christoph. 2003. Entrepreneurship in nonprofit: Its role in theory and in the real-world nonprofit sector. In *The nonprofit enterprise*. Ed. Avner Ben-Ner and Helmut K. Anheier. New York: Springer.

Barnard, Chester. 1936. *The functions of an executive*. Cambridge, MA: Harvard University Press. (Reprinted in 1968.)

Barrick, Murray R., Michael K. Mount, and Timothy A. Judge. 2001. Personality and performance at the beginning of the new millennium: What do we know and where do we go next? *International Journal of Selection & Assessment* 9: 9–30.

Bass, Bernard M. 1990. *Bass & Stogdill's handbook of leadership: Theory, research, and managerial applications*. 3rd ed. New York: Free Press.

Behn, Robert. 1988. Management by groping along. *Journal of Policy Analysis and Management* 7: 643–63.

_____. 1989. Leadership counts. *Journal of Public Policy Analysis and Management* 8: 494–500.

_____. 1998. What right do public managers have to lead? *Public Administration Review* 58: 209–24.

Bennis, Warren G. 1989a. *On becoming a leader*. Reading, MA: Addison-Wesley.

_____. 1989b. *Why leaders can't lead: The unconscious conspiracy continues*. San Francisco: Jossey-Bass.

Bennis, Warren, and Burt Nanus. 1985. *Leaders: The strategies for taking charge*. New York: Harper & Row.

Berman, Evan. 1995. Public–private leadership and the role of nonprofit organizations in local government: The case of social services. *Policy Studies Review* 14: 235–46.

Blake, Robert R., and Jane S. Mouton. 1985. *The managerial grid III*. Houston: Gulf Publishing.

Bowman, James. 2004. *Professional edge: Competencies in public service*. Armonk, NY: ME Sharpe.

Burns, James MacGregor. 1978. *Leadership*. New York: Harper & Row.

Ciulla, Joanne. 2004. The ethical challenges of nonprofit leaders. In *Improving leadership in nonprofit organizations*. Ed. Ronald Riggio and Bernard M. Bass. San Francisco: Jossey-Bass.

Cleveland, Harlan. 1972. *The future executive*. New York: Harper & Row.

Coast Guard (U.S.). 2004. *Coast Guard leadership development program*. February [accessed November 2005]. Available from http://www.uscg.mil/leadership/leadci/encl1.htm.

Doig, Jameson W., and Erwin Hargrove, eds. 1987. *Leadership and innovation: A biographical perspective on entrepreneurs in government*. Baltimore: Johns Hopkins University Press.

Drucker, Peter. 1990. *Managing the nonprofit organization: Practices and principles*. New York: HarperCollins.

Fiedler, Fred E. 1964. A contingency model of leadership effectiveness. In *Advances in experimental social psychology*. Ed. Leonard Berkowitz. New York: Academic Press.

———. 1967. *A theory of leadership effectiveness*. New York: McGraw-Hill.

Fleishman, Edwin A., and Edwin F. Harris. 1962. Patterns of leadership behavior related to employee grievances and turnover. *Personnel Psychology* 15: 43–56.

French, John R. P., and Bertram Raven. 1959. The bases of social power. In *Studies in social power*, 150–67. Ed. Dorwin Cartwright. Ann Arbor, MI: Institute for Social Research.

Gardner, John W. 1981. *Leadership: A sampler of the wisdom of John W. Gardner*. Minneapolis: Hubert H. Humphrey Institute of Public Administration, University of Minnesota.

———. 1990. *On leadership*. New York: The Free Press.

Gilligan, Carol. 1993. *In a different voice: Psychological theory and women's development*. Cambridge, MA: Harvard University Press.

Gordon, Leonard V. 1975. *The measurement of interpersonal values*. Chicago: Science Research Associates.

———. 1976. *Survey of interpersonal values: Revised manual*. Chicago: Science Research Associates.

Gortner, Harold F. 1986. *Administration in the Public Sector*, 2nd ed. New York: Krieger:

———. 1991. *Ethics for public managers*. New York: Greenwood Press.

Gulick, Luther. 1937. Notes on the theory of organization. In *Papers on the science of administration*. Ed. Luther Gulick and Lyndall Urwick. New York: Institute of Public Administration.

Guy, Mary. 1992. Summing up what we know. In *Women and men of the states: Public administrators at the state level*. Ed. Mary Guy. Armonk, NY: M.E. Sharpe.

Harmon, Michael, and Richard T. Mayer. 1986. *Organizational theory for public administration*. Boston: Little, Brown.

Hersey, Paul, and Kenneth Blanchard. 1993. *Management of organizational behavior: Utilizing human resources*. 6th ed. Englewood Cliffs, NJ: Prentice-Hall.

Herzberg, Frederick, Bernard Mausner, and Barbara Snyderman. 1993. *The motivation to work*. 2nd ed. New Brunswick, NJ: Transaction. (Original edition 1959.)

Holden, Matthew Jr. 1966. "Imperialism" in bureaucracy. *The American Political Science Review* 60: 943–51.

Jaskyte, Kristina. 2004. Transformational leadership, organizational culture, and innovativeness in nonprofit organizations. *Nonprofit Management & Leadership* 15: 153–68.

Joint Commission on the Accreditation of Health Care Organizations. n.d. *Overview of the 2007 Hospital Leadership Chapter revisions in progress*. [Accessed November 2005.] Available from http://www.jcaho.org/.

Jones, Charles O. 1984. *An introduction to the study of public policy.* 3rd ed. Monterey, CA: Brooks/Cole.

Katz, Robert L. 1955. Skills of an effective administrator. *Harvard Business Review* 33: 33–42.

Kaufman, Herbert. 1981. *The administrative behavior of federal bureau chiefs.* Washington, DC: Brookings Institution.

Kerr, Steven, and John M. Jermier. 1978. Substitutes for leadership: Their meaning and measurement. *Organizational Behavior and Human Performance* 22: 376–403.

Kohn, Alfie. 1999. *Punished by rewards: The trouble with gold stars, incentive plans, A's, praise, and other bribes.* 2nd ed. Boston: Houghton Mifflin.

Larson, Carl, and Frank LaFasto. 1989. *Teamwork.* Newbury Park, CA: Sage.

Lawler, Edward E. III. 2000. *Rewarding excellence: Pay strategies for the new economy.* San Francisco: Jossey-Bass.

Lee, Mordecai. 2004. What does hollywood think nonprofit CEOs do all day? Screen depictions of NGO management. *Public Organization Review* 4: 157–76.

Levin, Martin. 1993. The day after an AIDS vaccine is discovered: Management matters. *Journal of Public Policy Analysis and Management* 12: 438–55.

Lewis, Eugene. 1980. *Public entrepreneurship: Toward a theory of bureaucratic political power.* Bloomington: Indiana University Press.

Likert, Rensis. 1967. *The human organization: Its management and value.* New York: McGraw-Hill.

———. 1987. *New patterns of management.* New York: Garland. (Reprint of original published by McGraw-Hill, 1961.)

Lindblom, Charles E. 1993. *The policy-making process.* 3rd ed. Englewood Cliffs, NJ: Prentice-Hall.

Mann, Floyd C. 1965. Toward an understanding of the leadership role in formal organization. In *Leadership and productivity: Some facts of industrial life.* Ed. Robert Dubin et al. San Francisco: Chandler.

Manz, Charles C., and Henry Sims Jr. 1990. *Superleadership: Leading others to lead themselves.* New York: Berkeley Books.

Marwell, Nicole P. 2004. Privatizing the welfare state: Nonprofit community-based organizations as political actors. *American Sociological Review* 69: 265–91.

McClelland, David C. 1961. *The achieving society.* Princeton, NJ: Van Nostrand Reinhold.

———. 1975. *Power: The inner experience.* New York: Irvington.

McClelland, David, and Robert Steele. 1973. *Human motivation: A book of readings.* Morristown, NJ: General Learning Press.

McGregor, Douglas. 1957. The human side of enterprise. In *Classics of organizational theory.* Ed. Jay Shafritz, J. Steven Ott, and Yong Suk Jang. Belmont, CA: Thomson, 2005.

———. 1960. *The human side of enterprise.* New York: McGraw-Hill (25th anniversary ed., 1985).

McMurray, Robert. 1958. The case for benevolent autocracy. *Harvard Business Review* 36: 82–90.

Mintzberg, Henry. 1973. *The nature of managerial work.* New York: Harper & Row.

Morgan, Douglas, Ron Banch, Charles Cameron, and Robert Deis. 1996. What middle managers do in local government: Stewardship of the public trust and the limits of reinventing government. *Public Administration Review* 56: 359–66.

Murensky, Catherine. 2000. *The relationships between emotional intelligence, personality, critical thinking ability, and organizational leadership performance at upper levels of management.* PhD dissertation. Fairfax, VA: George Mason University Psychology Department.

Nakamura, Robert T., and Frank Smallwood. 1980. *The politics of policy implementation.* New York: St. Martin's Press.

Nanus, Burt. 1992. *Visionary leadership: Creating a compelling sense of direction for your organization.* San Francisco: Jossey-Bass.

Nanus, Burt, and Stephen Dobbs. 1999. *Leaders who make a difference: Essential strategies for meeting the nonprofit challenge.* San Francisco: Jossey-Bass.

National Performance Review (U.S.). 1993. *Creating a government that works better & costs less: The report of the National Performance Review.* Vice President Al Gore. New York: Plume/Penguin.

Northouse, Peter Guy. 2004. *Leadership: Theory and practice.* 3rd ed. Thousand Oaks, CA: Sage.

Osborne, David, and Ted Gaebler. 1992. *Reinventing government: How the entrepreneurial spirit is transforming the public sector.* Reading, MA: Addison-Wesley.

Perry, James L., and Lois Recascino Wise. 1990. The motivational bases of public service. *Public Administration Review* 50: 367–73.

Peters, Thomas, and Robert Waterman. 1982. *In Search of Excellence.* New York: Warner.

Quinn, Robert E. 1991. *Beyond rational management.* San Francisco: Jossey-Bass.

Riccucci, Norma. 1995. *Unsung Heroes: Federal execucrats making a difference.* Washington, DC: Georgetown University Press.

Riggio, Ronald, Bernard M. Bass, and Sarah Smith Orr. 2004. Transformational leadership in nonprofit organizations. In *Improving leadership in nonprofit organizations.* Ed. Ronald Riggio and Bernard M. Bass. San Francisco: Jossey-Bass.

Rojas, Ronald R. 2000. A review of models for measuring organizational effectiveness among for-profit and nonprofit managers. *Nonprofit Management & Leadership* 11: 97–104.

Rose-Ackerman, Susan. 1996. Altruism, nonprofits, and economic theory. *Journal of Economic Literature* 34: 701–28.

Rourke, Francis E. 1984. *Bureaucracy, politics, and public policy.* 3rd ed. Boston: Little, Brown.

Sahr, Robert. 2005. *Sources of uncertainty and disagreement about public policy.* Unpublished paper. Corvallis: Oregon State University.

Schein, Edgar H. 2004. *Organizational culture and leadership.* 3rd ed. San Francisco: Jossey-Bass.

Selznick, Phillip. 1984. *Leadership in administration: A sociological interpretation.* Berkeley: University of California Press. (Originally published by Harper & Row, 1957.)

Shafritz, Jay , J. Steven Ott, and Suk Jang Yong. 1995. *Classics of Organizational Theory.* Belmont, CA: Thomson Wadsworth.

Skinner, Elizabeth W. 1969. Relationships between leadership behavior patterns and organizational–situational variables. *Personnel Psychology* 22: 489–94.

Svara, James. 2003. Effective mayoral leadership in council–manager cities: Reassessing the facilitative model. *National Civic Review* 92: 157–72.

Tichy, Noel, and David Ulrich. 1984. SMR forum: The leadership challenge—a call for the transformational leader. *Sloan Management Review* 26: 59–68.

Urwick, Lyndall F. 1953. *Leadership and morale.* Columbus: Ohio State University, College of Commerce and Administration.

Weber, Max. 1947. *The theory of social and economic organization.* Trans. and ed. A. M. Henderson and Talcott Parsons. New York: Oxford University.

Weick, Karl E. 1995. *Sensemaking in organizations.* Thousand Oaks, CA: Sage.

Wilson, James Q. 1989. *Bureaucracy: What government agencies do and why they do it.* New York: Basic Books.

Winter, David G. 1973. *The power motive.* New York: Free Press.

Young, Dennis. 2001. Nonprofit entrepreneurship. In *Understanding nonprofit organizations: governance, leadership, and management,* 218–22. Ed. J.Steven Ott. Boulder, CO: Westview.

Yukl, Gary. 1998. *Leadership in organizations.* 4th ed. Englewood Cliffs, NJ: Prentice-Hall.

Chapter 10

Change and Stability

By Ed Colley

Change—change in organizations, change in public organizations. In a sense organizational change is what this book on public organization theory is about: first because organizations are imperfect—always have been, always will be—and second because organizations exist in a changing environment. Chapter 1 introduced organization theory as it applies to government and nonprofit organizations; Chapter 2 examined their increasingly blended nature; and Chapter 3 laid out pivotal controversies that tug at the shape and purpose of those organizations. Chapter 4 looked at organizational structure as it continues to evolve; Chapter 5 considered classic and emerging communication issues public organizations share; and Chapter 6 chronicled the shift from control to accountability. Chapter 7 examined organizational decision making; Chapter 8 probed organizational culture and behavior; and Chapter 9 studied leadership as it applies to public organizations. Each of these subjects is both the object of change and the lever for organizational change.

At its root this book is about organizational change because organizations do not just happen. People create them, use them, complain about them, alter them, and discard them. This means we are the masters of organizations: Our public organizations are not simply artifacts of the environment whose deficiencies we must endure. Consequently knowledge about organization theory—about the way organizations work—helps give us means, motives, and opportunities for making our government and nonprofit organizations better than they used to be and better than they are today.

Two closely allied elements are paramount when we pursue change in public organizations. The first element is to be faithful to the public interest. Government and nonprofit organizations (that is, *public* organizations) may have targeted primary clienteles, but public organizations pursue their designated roles as a way to further the common good. For example, a regulatory agency that begins to pander to those being regulated has become a malignant organization. The second element is to operate within the ethical parameters of society. Pursuing the public interest through unethical practices undermines the organization's value to society, harming society rather than aiding it. Violating either precept also damages the organization itself.

This chapter examines aspects of planned and unplanned change in public organizations. It looks at forces driving change, mechanisms for channeling change in public organizations, and resistance to organizational change. To set the stage, the chapter considers the vital role of stability in enabling effective change.

YIN AND YANG: STABILITY AND CHANGE

A *counterintuitive observation* is one that seems the opposite of what a reasonable person would expect, at least initially. For this discussion of organizational change, a counterintuitive assertion might be that guided organizational change—even big change—requires a stable base if it is to be effective. Although beneficial change can happen when everything is in flux, change is most readily managed from a solid anchor point or foundation. This section looks at the significance of turbulence in the organization's environment, how change affects different levels of society, and how change materializes in different patterns.

Turbulence in an Organization's Environment

An organization's environment has a tremendous impact on its need to change and its ability to change in a healthy, managed fashion. Moreover, environments vary in their dynamics over time.

Levels of Turbulence

Chapter 4 mentions a classic analysis by Emery and Trist (1965) in which they define four levels of environmental turbulence. They define Level I as a steady state, exemplified by slow change and scant competition. Level II, moderate turbulence, is characterized by rapid change and significant competition. Level III, extreme turbulence, involves swift, radical change and fierce competition. And Level IV, chaos, is a state in which civilization is suspended and no rules apply. Organizations can exist in Levels I through III. Highly adaptive organizations can do well in Levels II and III. But because organizations and societies depend on rules, a Level IV environment makes their effective operation impossible.

Fortunately chaotic environments (by this definition) are rare in the modern world. Bosnia and Afghanistan under siege are recent examples. When a Level IV situation occurs, one option is to hunker down until the turbulence subsides—the sit-and-wait strategy. A more proactive strategy involves working with others to forge new rules that overlay the turbulence and provide a new foundation from which to operate. Public sector organizations are unavoidably in the vanguard when this is necessary.

Chaos Theory

Chaos is a term that comes up frequently in change literature and actually has a somewhat different meaning than Level IV of Emery and Trist. The underlying concept is that everything in the environment is interconnected—basically through the environment itself, which is made up of vastly complex systems. Therefore even a minor, seemingly random action in one part of the environment may have enormous effects in an apparently unrelated part of the environment. This is sometimes referred to as a "tipping point" (Gladwell 2002). The classic illustration is known as the "butterfly effect": The fluttering of a butterfly's wing in one part of the world may disturb air currents in a way that results in a cataclysmic weather event in another part of the world (Lorenz 1993). In other words, "chaos occurs when a small change in the starting conditions of a process produces a big change in the outcome of the process," suggesting that complex systems—especially those in which feedback has the potential to alter the systems' development—have built-in chaos (Gribbin 2004, 255). And organizations are complex systems.

This fundamental complexity and interconnectedness embody concepts such as attractors and simplicity. In chaos theory an *attractor* is a point at which many systems settle down if left alone. For example, some organizations mature into routines that remain consistent over time, barring outside influences. *Simplicity* is the concept that all activity in a system can ultimately be described by a few simple rules that explain the systems, its components, and their interactions. In practice, discovering simplicity is tougher than it seems; nevertheless, pioneering rule articulation efforts in organization theory help make sense of how hierarchical organizations work. (Consider Max Weber's description of the principles—or simple rules—underlying an "ideal hierarchy," discussed in Chapter 4.)

Levels of Society

Society too can be looked at in levels, with change affecting each level differently. The most superficial level is that of fads and fashion. Change is easy and relatively rapid at this level of society, but the impact of such change is negligible. Clothing, entertainment, slang, and diet choices fall into this category; changes are measured in months or a few years. The middle level of society is the institutional level involving business practices, education approaches, government operations, and the like. Deeper change happens at this level; but it takes place more slowly, with more resistance and with a more lasting impact. Policies and politics play a significant role at this level of societal change, where changes are measured over years or decades. Our transportation, energy, and communication industries exemplify this level (and pace) of societal change.

The most fundamental level of society encompasses its cultural values and mores. This level is the slowest to change—and the toughest. The time frame for this type of change ranges from decades to generations to centuries. Issues involve cultural values such as understanding the health hazards of smoking, expanding our sense of social equity, and appreciating the value of protecting the natural environment. At this level public institutions— both government and nonprofit—often follow but sometimes lead. Consider, for example, where the U.S. civil rights movement would have been without the persistent efforts of organizations such as the National Association for the Advancement of Colored People (NAACP).

Change as a Vector

Whether within an organization or in its environment, change is by no means a constant phenomenon. Change has properties similar to what, in mathematics and physics, is termed a *vector*. A vector combines direction, in that something is moving from one status to another, and velocity, in that something is taking place with a given velocity or intensity. Huber, Sutcliffe, Miller, and Glick (1995) have identified characteristics that might cause or constrain change, including the environment, the organization's strategy, the organization's performance, the organization's structure, and manager characteristics. When analyzing organizations and their environments, trends embody the same pair of properties: direction and intensity. Trends, however, are more complex than vectors because trends come in many patterns. (See Figure 10–1). Staying alert for potentially relevant trends is a way of monitoring, mapping, and anticipating meaningful change. Trends in communication and information technologies, for example, continue to alter how organizations operate.

The scope of change can vary in two basic ways. One is the intensity of its impact, from negligible to huge; another is the breadth of its impact, from affecting only a handful of people to affecting an entire country or beyond. Figure 10–2 illustrates how breadth and intensity interrelate: A small change that affects many parties may have greater overall significance than a large change affecting only a few. When officials in organizations evaluate the potential significance of a change they can control (such as rolling out a new program), these two dimensions are important. A third dimension—likelihood (that is, probability)— becomes nearly as crucial when potential change is not within our control (such as for public organizations involved in disaster relief). The series of major hurricanes that devastated the U.S. Gulf Coast in 2005, for example, would beforehand have been considered a low-probability but high-impact succession of events.

Events can also signal or trigger change. The terrorist strikes of September 11, 2001, on New York City's World Trade Center and on the Pentagon in Washington, D.C., comprised an event that changed the mood of the nation. The 9/11 attack prompted organizational

FIGURE 10–1   Basic Trend Configurations

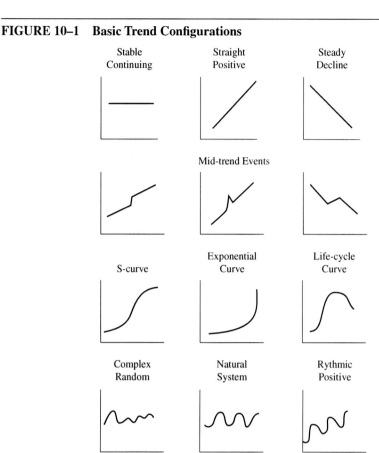

responses from all levels of society. When events that are typically stand-alone occurrences turn out to occur repeatedly, they may mark emerging trends. The Government Performance and Results Act (GPRA) of 1993 offers a variation on this example: At the federal level it tied together strategic planning and performance-based budgeting (see Chapter 7), drawing from experiments in a few states and municipalities and giving impetus to other states and localities to adopt similar outcome-based budgeting practices.

Periodicity is another factor in change cycles or trends. Seasonal cycles affect organizations just as they affect local weather patterns. Most organizations see peak (very busy) periods at certain times of the year and valleys (less busy periods) at other times, and these peaks and valleys can be forecast with reasonable accuracy. Cycles relevant for organizations can range from glacial to micro scale. Economic cycles are important for government and nonprofit organizations alike (Alexander, Nank, and Stivers 2001). So, for many public organizations, are political cycles—and public sector organizations often must staff and budget based on program cycles and fiscal cycles. Many organizations, especially those that cannot control

FIGURE 10–2   Impact Dimensions of Change

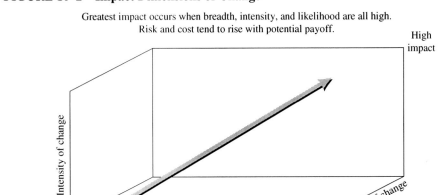

Greatest impact occurs when breadth, intensity, and likelihood are all high.
Risk and cost tend to rise with potential payoff.

incoming workload, anticipate varying staffing needs on different days of the week or even hours of the day. For example, organizations dealing with unscheduled visits or calls from the public may staff more heavily on Mondays or at the beginning of the day and at lunchtime to accommodate workload peaks. Periodicity, then, is repetition of essentially the same routine; consequently such cycles can be factored into trend analyses to help distinguish normal variation from longer-term change.

Life cycle change is inherently an important aspect of periodicity for organizations. Organizations have life cycles that evolve through stages comparable to living beings. As economist Anthony Downs observes, organizations, like humans, are especially vulnerable when they are young. In adolescence they tend to grow rapidly, slowing as they reach maturity. As organizations age, they grow more conservative and less flexible in adapting to change. Eventually they may outlive their usefulness and succumb, or their components may be absorbed into newer organizations. But Downs (1967) and Kaufman (1976) point out that government organizations face less competition than most other kinds of organizations and so may experience longevity beyond their utility. Life cycle considerations come into play whenever organizations develop products and services or new operating technologies because they too are subject to life cycles.

But perhaps the most profound change vector is a *paradigm shift*. Sometimes called a "Kuhnian paradigm" after philosopher and historian Thomas S. Kuhn (1970), a paradigm shift takes place when a new way of thinking overtakes a society or discipline. This indeed is profound change. For organizations, whether public or private, an apparent current paradigm shift among developed nations is that organizations must operate with the same kind of social conscience and social responsibility that we expect of individuals. For most of the industrial age organizations were expected only to operate within the law; free market dynamics neither expected nor demanded that they embody a strong social conscience. That was for people. The focus was on private sector organizations, and the key to success was becoming the prime competitor. When examined more closely, however, not all organizations fit or followed this model. Government organizations, especially in democracies such as the United States, existed to serve the people's business. Charities helped the poor. Nonprofit organizations worked for women's suffrage, workers' rights, and environmental causes. Some business leaders and their firms undertook philanthropy with a percentage of their profits. Thus the properties of organizational conscience were discernible in spite of commonly held perceptions to the contrary. As the twenty-first century unfolds, perceptions are shifting—and so are expectations. Irrespective of their primary missions, organizations (like people) are increasingly expected to behave not only within the law but also as exemplary citizens, acting in a manner that is ethically upstanding, socially conscious, politically correct, environmentally benign, contributing to the community, and respectful of everyone's background. The paradigm shift (if in fact it is one) will be complete when such behavior is taken for granted rather than viewed as quixotic.

Stability through Adaptation

By their nature paradigm shifts are extremely rare events. Indeed we enjoy a relatively stable environment—one in which organizations can cooperate and compete with one another under only moderate turbulence. Relative stability provides extensive opportunity for an organization to maintain stability or change in a managed, advantageous fashion. When the environment has some level of turbulence, an organization must change (adapt to the changing environment) so it can continue to be effective in fulfilling its mission. Box 10–1 illustrates how an organization in a changing environment can lag in keeping abreast of environmental change, can stay in tune, or can overanticipate, often with unhappy consequences. This is why "stability" itself is a relative concept and a common reason that static (highly conservative, risk-averse) organizations tend to become less effective over time.

Drivers of Change

What pressures within the environment and within organizations override stability and induce change? What drives change? "Everything" is the short answer, but that answer is not useful. Different aspects of our environment propel change, so a first step is to recognize and define those aspects. As strategic planners and trend analysts monitor the environment for potential impacts, they sometimes apply a standard set of categories (realms) known as *"STEEP analysis,"* which is an acronym for "society, technology, environment, economics, and politics" (Glenn 1999). The World Future Society, a Washington-based nonprofit organization, employs a similar set of categories in its publications (see Box 10–2). Events and trends in any realm—especially those that span realms—can drive organizations to change, but the specific categories are less important than the wide angle such categories provide for comprehensive monitoring.

Public sector organizations face myriad environmental phenomena that are driving change. *Globalism* (also referred to as "globalization") is a trend that can catch organizations unprepared. Foreign affairs columnist Thomas Friedman (2005) uses the expression "the world is flat" to portray a fundamental change in contemporary life: worldwide interconnectedness at all levels. Whether the topic is wildlife habitats and conservation easements, health care programs that involve importing medical expertise or reimporting pharmaceuticals, Internet-based research, regulatory enforcement agreements, or managing contracts for outsourced services, society has entered the era of routine transnational activity—activity that touches governments, giant institutions, individuals, and organizations of every size and function. Ultimately globalism affects every organization in tangible ways, putting slow-to-adapt organizations at odds with their evolving environment (Møller 2000; Dichter 2001). Friedman coins a complementing term ("glocalize") as he admonishes, "The more you have a culture that naturally *glocalizes*—that is, the more your culture easily absorbs foreign ideas and best practices and melds those with its own traditions—the greater advantage you will have in a flat world" (2005, 325). Viewed through a glocalizing lens, the term *diversity* broadens to reflect the way healthy organizations act as well as the way they staff themselves and serve their publics.

Technology advances represent a second phenomenon driving changes in organizations and their environments. Swiftly converging information and communication technologies have been remaking how organizations operate—a trend that may accelerate through the next decade. No organization is immune from these technologies. The concept of "open source" is gathering momentum, moving from its software development origins into the realm of social technology, where collaboration among organizations is becoming easier and its practice more valued. Ever more robust information technology is enabling a movement toward an "intellectual commons" that extends beyond current Internet resources, which are already nurtured through thousands of information-rich public sector websites. This budding movement's huge knowledge-building potential has roots in libraries and educational and research institutions, but it may become a knowledge superhighway in a fashion akin to the World Wide Web on the Internet as a contemporary information superhighway. Both the commons and the Web facilitate e-government services.

Biotechnology trends in pharmacology, genomics, nanotech, and other frontiers are beginning to exert change pressure, as well—pressure that organizations are likely to experience based on the effects of biotech innovations (such as a healthier and longer-living workforce, new issues in public policy and ethics, and new threats and opportunities for dealing with the natural environment) even more than from direct use of these technologies. And together globalism and technology drive issues of security. Physical security, data security, economic and environmental security, and the recently articulated domain of homeland security (for example, see Kettl 2004) pose new levels of challenge (and, for some, opportunity) for all organizations—but especially for government and nonprofit organizations because they must be sensitive to both the need for openness and public convenience, on the one hand, and, on the other hand, client privacy, worker safety, and mission effectiveness.

A third change driver in the environment is the diverse nature of the public that nonprofit and government organizations serve. "The public" is more accurately "the publics"—a dynamic mosaic of humanity with diverse and evolving needs and with ever-rising expectations. This creates mostly good pressure. Government organizations have come to realize that the public, in addition to being citizens and constituents, consists of customers who deserve to be treated with courtesy, dignity, and respect as well as with efficiency. Standards of service, effectiveness, and promptness that customers expect of private sector organizations have appropriately become standards the public expects from nonprofit and government organizations. This—coupled with expectations of transparency, pursuit of the public interest, and responsive performance—can challenge public organization workers who do not realize that service standards are continually rising and may not appreciate that they serve many publics (younger people, older workers, recent arrivals unused to dealing with government, and so on).

Rising expectations combined with interest in creative careers and lifestyles put pressure on organizations to provide more creativity as well as productivity. This means shaping

BOX 10–1 Organizational Dynamics in Changing Environments

An organization must stay in tune with its environment if it is to remain healthy. Private sector organizations failing to stay synchronized soon lose to competitors and go out of business. But notwithstanding Herbert Kaufman's reasonable question, "Are government organizations immortal?" (1976), public organizations can find themselves out of sync with changing times and shifting environments, putting those organizations in danger of collapse. This is particularly the situation for government organizations, which typically face milder competition than many nonprofit organizations.

We think of organizational change as difficult but necessary, which it is. On one hand, lack of change is invariably dangerous over time. On another hand, too much change is equally possible in theory, and it occasionally happens in the real world of the public sector. One of the motives behind the schema illustrated here is, in fact, to acknowledge the salience of overdevelopment as well as to acknowledge that collapse or catastrophe is not necessarily the end of an organization—or at least its parts. Moreover, every large organization will enjoy several of theses states over time, just as mortals do.

The set of change assumptions under the schematic is crucial to understanding conditions that account for growth, decline, and why an organization occupies a particular state. (This is perhaps akin to explaining why electrons undergo phase shifts and jump from one level to another.) These assumptions illustrate questions the model does and does not address:

1. The focal organizations are large, complex, mature bureaucracies.
2. Status shifts substantially depend on type and texture of the environment.
3. Different parts of the same organization may occupy different states.
4. Perceived status and status shifts are functions of interaction with other organizations and with the broader environment.

The arrows on the graph on the facing page indicate directions in which the organization's state may shift. The associated plus (+) or minus (−) by each state indicates whether the state tends to be a healthy or unhealthy condition for the organization itself and for its future—not whether the state is necessarily good or bad for directly affected constituents or for the public as a whole. In rare cases an organization experiencing catastrophic collapse may *nova*—that is, reemerge in a dynamically balanced or developing state.

SOURCE: Adapted from material prepared by Brack Brown (2005), professor emeritus of public and international affairs, George Mason University.

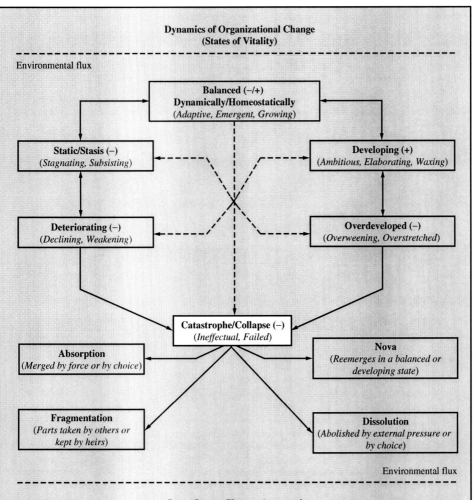

Dynamics of Organizational Change
(States of Vitality)

Environmental flux

Balanced (−/+)
Dynamically/Homeostatically
(*Adaptive, Emergent, Growing*)

Static/Stasis (−)
(*Stagnating, Subsisting*)

Developing (+)
(*Ambitious, Elaborating, Waxing*)

Deteriorating (−)
(*Declining, Weakening*)

Overdeveloped (−)
(*Overweening, Overstretched*)

Catastrophe/Collapse (−)
(*Ineffectual, Failed*)

Absorption
(*Merged by force or by choice*)

Nova
(*Reemerges in a balanced or
developing state*)

Fragmentation
(*Parts taken by others or
kept by heirs*)

Dissolution
(*Abolished by external pressure or
by choice*)

Environmental flux

Some Status Change Assumptions

1. The focal organizations are large, complex mature bureaucracies.
2. Status shifts substantially depend on type and texture of the environment.
3. Different parts of the same organization may occupy different states.
4. Perceived status and status shifts are functions of interaction with other organizations.
5. Status changes are a sum of interactions between parts, other organizations, and the environment.

By Dr. Brack Brown
Prof. Emeritus
George Mason University
December 2005

BOX 10–2 Trend Categories from the World Future Society

About World Trends and Forecasts

The trends and forecasts in this section [of the magazine *The Futurist*] are divided into the six categories commonly used in business planning:

Demography covers specific population groups, family composition, public health issues, and the like.

Economics includes finance, business, work and careers, and management.

Environment includes resources, ecosystems, species, and habitats.

Government includes world affairs, politics, laws, and public policy.

Society covers lifestyles, values, religion, leisure, culture, and education.

Technology includes innovations, scientific discoveries, and their impacts.

In many cases a single trend could be discussed in several different sectors. By categorizing a trend in one sector, however, the editors intend to focus attention on a specific aspect of the trend.

SOURCE: World Future Society, *The Futurist* (bimonthly).

organizations and communities to support fulfilling, higher-wage jobs, according to Richard Florida in his *Rise of the Creative Class* (2002, 40):

> Creative people come in many different forms. Some are mercurial and intuitive in their work habits, others methodical. Some prefer to channel their energies into radical big ideas; others are tinkerers and improvers. Some like to move from job to job, whereas others like the security of a large organization. Some are best working in groups; others like nothing better than to be left alone. Moreover, many people don't fall at the extremes—and their work and lifestyle preferences may change as they mature.
>
> What all of these people have in common is a strong desire for organizations and environments that let them be creative—that value their input, challenge them, have mechanisms for mobilizing resources around ideas, and are receptive to small changes as well as the occasional big idea. Companies and places that can provide this kind of environment, regardless of size, will have an edge in attracting, managing, and motivating creative talent. The same companies and places will also tend to enjoy flow of innovation, reaping competitive advantage in the short run and evolutionary advantage in the long run.

Given the focus on fostering creative organizations, creative communities, and a creative economy, "the public" as a driver of change operates at multiple levels. For public organizations, particularly, the public is a fundamental driver.

From a broader and longer-term perspective, futurist Jim Dator (1997) identifies five fundamental drivers to which he refers as "tsunamis of change":

- *The demographic tsunami*: Global population growth and mobility are inducing inexorable change in the way we live. The world now has 6 billion people and, of necessity, is becoming increasingly urban. "While the global population is growing, some parts of the world are experiencing population stability, and others population decline."

Population throughout the poorest regions of the world is growing the fastest, whereas developed nations are growing the most slowly—with huge ramifications. The U.S. population is aging (that is, the ratio of older Americans is increasing)—also with huge ramifications.

- *The environmental tsunami:* Evidence for global environmental change is compelling on many fronts, including "future global climate change; scarcities in food, water, and energy; pollution; sea level rise; and new and renewed diseases." To doubt or ignore the evidence is "playing a massive, global game of Russian roulette." Dator cites the Australian government's Commission on the Future: "If we act as if it matters and it doesn't matter, then it doesn't matter. But if we act as if it doesn't matter and it matters, then it matters."

- *The economic tsunami:* "Since communism is so clearly dead, many people falsely assume that capitalism won. But this is not the case. Communism merely died first. Both systems are unsustainable." The era of a global economy is "beyond the effective control of any nation" to operate by practices that "are sustainable, fair, and future-oriented," which is a legacy we owe one another and generations to come.

- *The governance tsunami:* Globalism is not a future condition. It has arrived. We have already become next-door neighbors to everyone on earth, creating unavoidable challenges to address issues multilaterally. "But the nation–state is already nearly dead," and the lead contender for running the planet is a troubling "vision of the future as a global economy controlled by a handful of 'competing' multinational corporations." Self-governing communities, global governance, and a measure of direct "electronic" democracy offer other possibilities—and risks.

- *The technological tsunami:* Marshall McLuhan has said, "We shape our tools, and thereafter our tools shape us." Technology continues to give us new powers and new risks. Dator sees technology as having the potential to be hugely beneficial despite the challenges of using it as a positive force. But as we modify ourselves through science and technology, our sense of humanness is itself likely to change.

Dator puts a dramatic spin on forces shaping the environment and everything in it, organizations included. Others emphasize drivers with potentially more positive consequences. Whatever observers track and forecast, those forces don't stay on separate tracks. To the contrary, they are "major forces racing toward us, which will crash together, along with our wit and will, to create the future" (Dator 1997). Anticipating and understanding them helps us shape what happens.

PLANNED AND UNPLANNED CHANGE

Organizational change is a phenomenon we can strongly influence, if not completely control. This section looks at the growing body of literature about aspects of planned and unplanned change as well as organizational responses to it. Unplanned change (that is, change driven by forces beyond control of the organization) involves external and many internal factors and takes up much of the time of top management in any organization. Of special interest to nonprofit and government managers is the political context or environment in which their organizations operate; however, numerous other factors are important, including social, demographic, economic, environmental, and technological influences.

Theories about Change

Every school of organization theory has its own set of assumptions about the meaning of change and its objectives or ends. The objectives, in turn, lead to assumptions about the process involved—when, how, and why change occurs. Although the literature about change in organizations takes numerous forms and discusses widely divergent issues, five themes are generally consistent:

1. *Adaptability:* Organizations need to be capable of adapting to external change in the political, social, economic, and technological environments. In fact, we increasingly expect organizations to anticipate likely change in the external environment that might demand (or enable) organizational change. This often means questioning existing policies and processes rather than relying on the if-it-ain't-broke-don't-fix-it approach valued in less competitive, less turbulent environments. To adapt successfully, organizations must be able to create new knowledge, processes, and technology.

2. *Decision quality:* A general call for greater rationality in decision making exists in organizations. Improved decision making can take many forms, however, and what is meant by *rationality* varies depending on the type of organization being discussed and, for public organizations, both the political and managerial philosophy of the critic. For contemporary organizations, decision quality also addresses issues of who decides, how, how quickly, and with what accountability.

3. *Outcome impact:* The goal of improving management or changing an organization's structure or process has, for nearly half a century, been to improve "efficiency" and "effectiveness"; since the 1990s the vocabulary has expanded to feature organizational "performance" and "outcomes." The public sector does not and cannot rely on profit as a defining organizational imperative; yet it lacks unequivocal, clear definitions of these and similar terms. Even so—or perhaps because of the importance of having a goal that reflects the complexity of advancing the general welfare—much of the debate about what should be done occurs around these four concepts.

4. *Worker/member empowerment:* The goal of change efforts carried out by many social scientists is to reduce "organizational pathology." *Pathology* here refers to "deviation from propriety or from an assumed normal state." Having established what they believe is proper or normal behavior in groups, social scientists attempt to correct deviations from that behavior, improve human development and human relations within the organizations and beyond, increase members' motivation and commitment, reduce alienation, and increase freedom (autonomy or self-determination) among organization members.

5. *Constructive conflict:* To at least a limited extent, the goals just listed are also involved in attempting to reduce conflict or redirect it in constructive ways. This applies to conflict both within and between organizations. Some conflict can be eliminated, but much of it is not only inevitable but also useful when directed toward appropriate channels and controlled in ways that keep it from diverting the individuals involved from the organization's goals.

Organization theories prominent over the years each address some of these goals. However, particular theories leave out important elements or stress selected factors. By contrast, change theories are more likely to deal with all five goals.

Rationalist and incremental theories, for example, attend to a few of the five goals, but neither tackles them all. Rationalist theory focuses on greater rationality and improved efficiency and effectiveness; but it fails to recognize the importance of being able to adapt to external change, reduce organizational pathology, or reduce and redirect conflict. Adapting to external change and reducing conflict are major points stressed in the incrementalist model of decision making. Change theories tend to argue that all five factors warrant *proper*, not necessarily *equal* (depending on the situation), emphasis for an organization to achieve its objectives efficiently and effectively. Other areas of organization study (motivation, accountability and control, communication, leadership, and so on) are marked by the same partial attention to all five goals. Organizational change literature attempts—with differing levels of success—to develop a more universal theory.

PLANNED CHANGE

Accountability and responsibility influence any discussion about change within public sector organizations. Change is an inherent and ubiquitous fact of life for any organization. If this were not so, we could simply program the activities of organizations and not worry about most of the problems discussed throughout this book. Things are evolving, however, both inside and outside the organization; this is just as true for the public organization as it is for the private corporation. Great efforts are being made to increase the area of planned change for organizations, which is the goal of theorists as they systematically study organizations. The first step is description, but the end products involve anticipating events and prescribing ways to handle them—or better still, finding ways to handle opportunities or avoid problems.

Planned organizational change is undertaken using many labels and is by no means new. For example, scientific management, which Frederick Taylor ushered in at the beginning of the twentieth century, was ripe with organizational efficiency experts. The pursuit of planned change appears to be growing, especially as organizations develop greater capacity for collecting, storing, and using information.

Not all growth is good. A worry expressed by critics of developing mega-organizations (both national and international) is that these organizations are so large and powerful that they can impose control on parts of the environment beyond their immediate boundaries but affecting their functions and interests. The danger, of course, is that hegemonic organizations may arrange conditions that are best for them but damaging to society as a whole. Similar damaging behavior can take place within organizations, where one part of the organization creates an advantage for itself at the expense of another organizational component; such intraorganizational behavior is known as *suboptimizing*.

Regarding organizations in general, well-planned change is fostered through understanding the organization itself, understanding the environment in which it functions, reasonably anticipating future possibilities, anticipating resistance to change efforts, and taking reasonable risks to implement change plans. Planned change typically occurs in three major areas of organization life: behavior and values, structure, and process and technology. Each of these is considered briefly here.

Planned Change in Behavior and Values

A major aspect of planned change is influencing *organization behavior,* the fundamental elements of which include individuals in groups, groups combined into organizations, the actions of individuals and groups in organizational settings, and by inference the values that are the basis for action by both individuals and groups. This area of study and change is known as *organization development*—or "OD" (pronounced "oh-dee")—when undertaken by itself, such as to improve morale, worker cohesiveness, or ethics sensitivity. (Planned changes in organizational behavior also take place in larger-scale change activities such as quality management and reengineering.) According to OD practitioners, organization development is *applied* organization theory and behavior. OD draws from sociology, psychology, cybernetics, political science, and related fields. Thus OD, in its broadest sense, can be considered applied research in the subarea of social sciences relating to organizational phenomena (Argyris and Schon 1978).

The field has developed from two important techniques that draw on additional tools to better understand the structures, processes, culture, values, and behavior within organizations—and, when beneficial, to fabricate ways to change them. Introduced in 1946 as a method for understanding and influencing small-group behavior, the first of the two techniques is *laboratory training groups* (or T-groups). The approach temporarily brings together strangers from within the organization and uses facilitated discussion to help participants more fully understand one another's feelings and perspectives. Because T-groups have a potential to involve emotional intensity, they have been largely superseded. OD projects in complex organizations typically work with teams who work together or regularly interact, which fosters a more focused impact and better retention over time. The second technique for capturing and modifying values and behavior is *survey research and feedback* involving members of an organization. Through this technique participants can find out what people believe and feel about their organization, its objectives, and its members' values and behavior.

From these two basic techniques—laboratory training and survey research and feedback—a multitude of programs have evolved to intervene in ongoing organizations (thus the name OD interventions) and thereby alter the structure, processes, behavior, and values of individuals and groups.

Over the years OD activities have had an important impact on public sector organizations; but other approaches for planned organizational change have eclipsed OD efforts—and have themselves been overtaken. The quality management movement, led by total quality management or TQM (Deming cited by Walton 1986; Crosby 1984; Juran and Gryna 1988), is a holistic approach to organizational change that incorporates elements of organizational development. (See the related discussion in Chapter 3.) Systems concepts have proven at least as durable. Reinventing government, showcased on the local and state levels by Osborne and Gaebler (1992) and at the federal level by the Clinton administration's National Performance Review (1993), emerged in the 1990s. They endure, as do the concepts of intrapreneurialism (employee willingness to turn an idea into a profit-making product within and for a company and be rewarded—see Pinchot and Pinchot 1993); the learning organization (Senge 1994); customer-oriented public and private organizations (Peters 1994; Whiteley 1991); and value engineering, core business systems, and business process reengineering (Hammer and Stanton 1995). Acquiring fresh attention are the concepts of creative workers and creative organizations (Florida 2002; de Bono 1985), and surviving well are the concepts of distributed organizations and virtual organizations. The world of organizational change comes in many flavors, of which some focus on behavior and values while others embrace this category more lightly. As we go along, we'll feature some of these flavors of planned organizational change.

Just as complexity plays a major role in diagnosing and undertaking organizational change, there is an increasing emphasis on culture and values as core factors in determining the success of organizations over time. The ultimate goal of those who work to create what

BOX 10–3 Stages in Developing Learning Capacities

Stage One: New Cognitive, Linguistic Capacities

People see new things and can speak a new language. This allows them to see more clearly their own and others' assumptions and actions and the consequences of both. Typically they find it hard to translate these new cognitive and linguistic competencies into fundamentally new actions. They may begin to behave differently; but the basic rules, assumptions, and values are the same.

Stage Two: New Action Rules

As old assumptions "loosen" in response to the cognitive insights of Stage One, people begin to experiment with action rules based on new assumptions so they can see what they yield. They may need to rely on the new language to produce new actions, and they will find it difficult to access or string together new rules when under stress.

Stage Three: New Values and Operating Assumptions

People can string together rules that reflect new action values and operating assumptions. They can enact these rules under stress and ambiguity, continuing to aid their own and others' learning. By this stage, people will have adapted the rules into their own particular models, speaking in their own voices.

SOURCE: Peter Senge, *The Fifth Discipline: The Art and Practice of the Learning Organization* (New York: Currency/Doubleday. 1990), 377.

are often now called "learning organizations" is to create a culture that guarantees common understanding of the organization's goals and then allows open questioning of assumptions, actions, and the consequences of both. Distinct stages of growth occur along the way to becoming a learning organization (see Box 10–3).

If an organization achieves the third level of development, then Senge says that it and the people in it become able to understand the world and how the organization can create its future instead of "just surviving" in its world. Through analysis, adaptation, and "generative learning" (learning that enhances the ability to create), the organization can become an active partner in defining and developing its role in the larger world (Senge 1990, 14).

There is a danger of overselling what can be done in a public organization, however. Even public sector organizations that accomplish their goals of organizational change may not satisfactorily accomplish their public service missions. That can be a disappointing problem. A second potential problem is the fine line between attempting to motivate workers by helping them modify their values and behavior and manipulating workers through skillful external controls and through maneuvering rewards and values to get subordinates to do what others want them to do. Thus both leaders and members of the organization are wise to distinguish between motivation and manipulation.

A third problem is that even successful change efforts may decay as time passes, the immediacy of the training and learning decreases, and new actors enter the organization. Although this can be ameliorated through long-term commitment and maintenance, doing so can be tough: The rate of decline may not be readily recognized, maintenance is never glamorous, priorities shift, and leaders (including elected and appointed officials) move on. Successive political leaders may pursue contrasting agendas. Moreover, turnover among appointed officials is often greater than that of politicians, making continuity problematic as organizations pursue long-term goals. Many political appointees naturally seek objectives that allow them to leave an imprint on the organization and its programs during their time in office. For them, success must be measurable before the next election or even sooner (perhaps when they expect to resign and move to another position in government, the nonprofit arena, or the private sector). Leadership in many nonprofit organizations can also be transient—especially for those close to the political process—but a nonprofit's volunteer staffing is the most likely area to exhibit high turnover rates. Consequently volunteer-dependent nonprofit organizations must often combat "change decay" by investing substantially in training and addressing learning curve challenges.

Fourth, planned organizational change in values and behavior is an area where accountability becomes paramount. The degree to which nonprofit organizations should be democratized is flexible; the degree to which government organizations should be democratized is debatable; and the degree to which both kinds of public sector organizations are involved in "blended sector" programs (that may, in fact, also include private sector organizations) is constantly increasing. (See the related discussion in Chapter 2.) But is a changed organizational culture likely to increase an organization's responsiveness to its leadership, to the public it serves, or to the organization's goals? Will members understand how the organization's goals fit into the surrounding social and political fabric? Public sector workers tend to have strong commitments to their agencies, their programs, and their clienteles; thus it is difficult to know how clearly they can see the big picture (politically, economically, or socially) in the same way that other parties might.

Although values and behavior play important roles in the overall change and development of public sector organizations, they are aspects of a larger mosaic wherein society, technology, and other factors influence the shape and operation of public organizations—including planned change that affects organizational structure.

Planned Change in Structure

Structure plays two roles in the process of planned change. First, much planned change occurs in the area of structure. When it appears that an organization must change, an obvious place to look is at its structure; in many cases doing so is appropriate because structure can influence the organization's ability to carry out all the other functions of management. In fact, newly appointed leaders in organizations routinely examine its structure, which is a way to have a visible impact on the organization.

Second, to cope with the demand for planned change, most organizations of any size have established planning offices. These offices look into the future and envision the programs, policies, and structures of the organization in ways that allow leaders to plan for changes that may be necessary. For example, the Internal Revenue Service (IRS) has long maintained an office that, as one of its primary functions, monitors and forecasts likely impacts of demographic, labor, and technology trends on the way the IRS may handle its work in the future. The IRS is by no means unique. United Way regional offices examine trends in donor giving and in nonprofit "help" agencies' operations to anticipate how United Way offices can best organize and operate to support local nonprofits. Hospitals across the

country continually assess their structures and interrelationships to contain costs and anticipate needed services. Many local governments have planning offices that specifically deal
with the physical development of the community; these offices offer models of their envi-
sioned community of the future. Both kinds of offices—those dealing with physical planning
and those involved in structural and procedural planning—are an accepted part of successfully functioning public sector organizations.

Within organizations there is much discussion of creating more fluid and responsive
structures and processes through flattening hierarchies, developing teams, creating quality
initiatives, focusing on clients as customers, and in general applying the new social science
technologies. Chapter 4 describes traditional and contemporary approaches to planned organizational design; the central point here is that every design approach carries with it political
benefits and drawbacks. Gawthrop (1983) points out four approaches to organizing for
change: organizing for control, organizing for bargaining, organizing for responsiveness,
and organizing for analysis. Different structures help to accomplish whatever major objective is paramount for the leader or legislature establishing or changing the organization. Each
of Gawthrop's approaches results in a different structure—yet they all exist to an extent in
every organization, though one will predominate.

An ongoing political focus toward organizational change is cost savings through workforce downsizing (cutting the size of the workforce) and reducing midlevel management—a
phenomenon defined differently by various participants in the debate. (See the definitions of
various terms and an assessment of their value in Box 10–4.) Both nonprofit and government organizations are under unrelenting pressure to "work lean." The major emphasis
seems to be on efficiency and the lowering of "bureaucratic" or "nonvalue-added" costs; certainly, downsizing can reduce cost outlays over the short term. However, lowering costs is
not equivalent to improving efficiency or effectiveness, both of which require a retooling of
the work process (Hammer and Stanton 1995). In fact, neither effectiveness nor efficiency is
explicitly among the four reasons Gawthrop gives for structural change. Reducing an organization's size, including its middle management positions, can make sense, but only as a
consequence of other organizational improvements and only in the larger context of all four
of Gawthrop's factors; otherwise an unintended consequence of the reductions may be
diminished organizational utility. Restoring the organization's effectiveness may ultimately
cost more than was saved. Those costs can extend beyond funding to mission effectiveness
and public confidence in the organization itself.

Organizing for Control

Organizing for control is central to the overall idea of organization existence. To guarantee that
an organization's objectives are being achieved—which is the responsibility of every public
sector manager—control mechanisms must exist. The typical hierarchical structure is central to
control; through its use, someone is always responsible when things go right or wrong. If change
creates problems that must be dealt with, there are people responsible for making whatever organizational adjustments are necessary. Whether they fail or succeed, they can *supposedly* be held
responsible and acknowledged for their effort in an appropriate manner. *Supposedly* is emphasized because, as discussed in Chapter 6, accountability systems in government and nonprofit
organizations have shortcomings, and those shortcomings can have unanticipated consequences.

An equally important aspect of control when we discuss organizational change is the
interface with other organizations. Most organizations have parts of their structure that are

BOX 10–4 A Lexicon of Valid Approaches, Pseudo-Approaches, and Nonapproaches to Restructuring Government

Centralize (a valid approach in some cases): To gather services, programs, or functions into and administer them through one decision-making structure. *The agency centralized the personnel functions of its line departments into a single new human resources department.*

Consolidate (valid in some cases): To unite or combine different agencies, programs, or services that do the same thing. *The town consolidated its police agency and the county sheriff's office.*

Decentralize (increasingly valid and desirable): To break up centralized or consolidated structures and move the decision making to local, line, or operating unit groups. *"It is not possible for a society to de-massify economic activity, communications, and many other crucial processes without being compelled to decentralize government decision making as well"* (Alvin and Heidi Toffler).

Delayer (valid but often used as a pseudo-approach): To remove one or more levels of management in a hierarchical organization. *The agency delayered its deputy director positions to enhance communication among directors and line managers.*

Devolve (valid in some cases): The transfer of power, a program, or a service from a central government to a local government. *The federal government devolved its welfare programs to the states, leaving it up to them to figure out how to run and pay for the programs.*

Downsize (a nonapproach): To make an agency smaller by reducing the number of its staff members, usually through layoffs, early retirement, or shedding services. Downsizing does not imply improvement or other changes. *The county executive ordered agencies to downsize their staffs by 10 percent.* According to Peter Drucker, dean of American management experts, "Downsizing has turned out to be something that surgeons for centuries have warned against: 'amputation before diagnosis.' The result is always a casualty."

Entrepreneurial government (valid): According to David Osborne and Ted Gaebler, who coined the term, this means public institutions that constantly use their resources in new ways to heighten their efficiency and effectiveness. We have no example sentence because entrepreneurial government covers just about everything positive about reinventing government. However, . . . the entrepreneurial approach can be risky.

Lean and mean (a nonapproach): Refers to an organization that has been repeatedly downsized to the point that it can barely meet its mission. This is the result of a macho, meat ax approach that leaves the survivors feeling not lean, but certainly mean. *Across-the-board budget cuts left the agency dangerously lean in some areas and still too fat in others.* In industry *lean production* (a valid approach) refers to a management system characterized by

especially sensitive to, and need to be protected from, change in the environment. James Thompson (2005) argues that the structure of a complex organization specifically takes this part of the system into account when he notes that "boundary spanning units" protect the technological core from environmental buffeting (as described in Chapter 4). The part of the organization that cannot operate efficiently under the pressure of change or constant surveillance flexible processes with fast cycle times and little waste, cross-trained and self-managed workers, vendor partnership, and continuous improvement.

Privatize (valid in some cases; sometimes a pseudo-approach and nonvalid): To move a public service or asset into the private sector. . . . *The city privatized waste water treatment by selling its treatment assets and powers to a group of private investors.*

Redesign or reengineer (valid when the situation calls for it): To completely reconfigure a process, changing nearly every component of it to gain a quantum leap in performance. . . . *By establishing new processes and using information technology, the city, county, and state governments reengineered customer contact processes in several agencies to consolidate them into a single-point-of-contact system.*

Reinvent (always valid): To fundamentally question the mission and methods of government with the intent of restructuring it to focus on outcomes desired by citizens. *By selling its public housing assets, issuing rental vouchers for the most needy, and providing tax credits and other assistance to private developers, the city reinvented the way it ensured low-cost housing for poor citizens.*

Rethink (always valid): Peter Drucker says rethinking goes beyond reinventing because the rethinking asks, "If we were not already doing this, would we now go into it?" He's referring to an agency's basic mission, not its operations. Rethinking leaves open the alternatives of completely eliminating agencies with outmoded missions or agencies that have not produced desirable results for reasons no one can determine. *"If no rational rethinking of government performance [occurs], it is predictable that the wrong things will then be cut—the things that perform and should be strengthened"* Peter Drucker, *The Atlantic Monthly*, February 1995.

Reorganize (a pseudo-approach and often a nonapproach): As it is most commonly practiced in government, this means to shift around the boxes in an organizational chart without changing anything else. *After severe criticism for ineffective handling of a crisis, the agency director published a reorganization plan that put work units involved in the crisis under the control of the deputy director in charge of crises, a newly created position.*

Rightsize (a pseudo-approach): To adjust the size of the workforce until there is a balance between the work to be done and the number of people available to do it. Usually synonymous with downsizing because it does not include process improvement. *The agency rightsized its workforce to meet capacity needs.*

Streamline (valid if you use our definition; a pseudo-approach if you don't): To change a process by minimizing non–value-added work steps and maximizing value-added steps. *The agency streamlined its procurement process by eliminating unnecessary sign-offs and paperwork and raising spending authority limits.*

SOURCE: David K. Carr, Ian D. Littman, and John K. Condon, *Improvement Driven Government: Public Service for the 21st Century* (Washington, DC: Coopers and Lybrand, 1995), 357–60.

from a fickle public or press (such as working undercover or managing confidential records) is protected by the structure in ways that allow its vital function to be carried out in a steady or "private" manner, thereby benefiting overall organization activity. In fact, Landau (1969) points out that critical controls, processes, and systems within an organization (akin to the safety systems in our vehicles) need to be redundant to keep the organization working well—as apparently inefficient as the duplication may seem at first. Steady operation requires the guarantee of resources necessary to that operation, whether the production of a material good, the delivery of a particular service, or the handling of a procedure. Government organizations advance this goal by ensuring the flow of necessary resources through long-term appropriations, charging fees, arrangements with influential constituents or consumers of the service or product, or a guarantee of resources to that part of the organization before other parts are considered; nonprofit organizations proceed in much the same fashion, substituting sustained donor funding for long-term appropriations. In other words, the organization attempts to cushion the vital part of its structure from the exigencies of a turbulent environment. (Private organizations may also use vertical or horizontal integration.)

Similarly, public and private organizations tend to protect themselves from constant observation and second-guessing by employing structures that remove much of the decision-making process from the public's view. This may be accomplished through the use of executive sessions, closed-door negotiations, adopting security classifications to inhibit the release of information, claims of "professional privilege," and other devices aimed at limiting public disclosure. Designated segments of organizations help clarify where such processes are possible and legal and aid all other parts of the organization in using these processes properly.

For public sector organizations, these devices may become the focus of controversy because they may shield precisely what outsiders want to observe or influence. Consequently a paramount test becomes what is in the public interest (which is not always clear) rather than what is convenient for an organization and its leaders. For government organizations more than for nonprofits, such legislative tools as sunshine laws, sunset laws, and time limits and other constraints on appropriations may draw these activities into the limelight and the political fray when challenged organizations argue that such attention limits the agencies' ability to function in a rational, efficient, and effective manner.

Whatever the control issue may be, emphasis on it tends to give special power to those with formal positions of authority in the hierarchy. This power is also supported by legal mandate as established by the legislative body and ratified by the chief executive. Therefore, outside control with its concomitant power is always present in government agencies to a greater extent than is common within nonprofit organizations or the private sector.

Organizing for Bargaining

Organizing for bargaining requires that people with the appropriate expertise in both the politically and technically relevant areas be available in the organization; that these people (whether lawyers, scientists, social scientists, or politicians) be placed in positions where they can carry out the required negotiations for the organization's decision makers (if they are not the decision makers themselves); and that they be protected (by their position descriptions or by knowledgeable and sympathetic superiors) from negative reactions to the wheeling and dealing (as long as it is within the bounds of propriety) inherent in such a role.

Organizing for Responsiveness

Organizing for responsiveness requires that an organization's structure allow appropriate external forces (clients, professionals, legislators, and so on) to be involved in the decision making related to the fulfillment of organizational objectives (O'Regan 2005). Thus the organization must create structures that allow outsiders to participate in establishing priorities and procedures and in evaluating the degree to which the organization accomplishes those objectives. The phrase *maximum feasible participation* was used during the 1960s in the Johnson administration's War on Poverty programs; today the expression *participatory democracy* is more common. The concept leads to new structures in government (and sometimes in "blended" nonprofit organizations operating on behalf of government), especially at the local level (Brown and Troutt 2004). These structures guarantee that citizens in areas affected by a program have input about how and where federal money is spent. Obviously this alters power relationships within public service organizations as well as relationships between the organizations and those they serve. Responsiveness creates this type of structural change—and it generates discomfort and insecurity among those not committed to the concept.

Two types of citizen boards exemplify responsiveness-spawned organizational structures: advisory boards and review boards. Their members are likely to be appointed rather than elected. Although both types of boards are most often found at the local government level, comparable boards appear at other government levels and as part of many nonprofit organizations. Arts commissions, public television stations, hospital groups, land use and public utility boards, and public universities are among the public service entities where representatives of the public are likely to have a direct voice through these boards. How active and influential that voice is varies among organizations and with the dynamics of the individuals involved.

A second example of structural organizational change to improve responsiveness is an ombudsperson office, which is designed to look into complaints from individuals about their treatment by the organization. Ombudsperson positions can be found around the globe in any type of organization, but they are most common in public sector organizations. The term comes from nineteenth-century Sweden; it surfaced in the U.S. Navy in the 1970s, after which many federal agencies began to adopt the practice, if not the label. The Internal Revenue Service, for example, staffs and operates its ombudsperson service under the title of "Office of the National Taxpayer Advocate" (26 USC 7811). Outside government, ombudsperson offices are most common among news media and health care organizations. Ombudspeople's activities and effectiveness vary across organizations, but typically they perform three functions. First, they (or their staffs in larger organizations) assist individuals who have tried unsuccessfully to have their concerns dealt with through the organization's normal channels; second, they identify systemic patterns of such failures and bring them to the attention of the organization's decision makers; third, they represent the public within the organization when key programmatic decisions are considered.

Responsiveness, structure, and technology combine to provide more possibilities. Telephone help centers have become commonplace in private sector organizations: Customers call in to inquire about products and services, to complain, or to secure technical assistance from knowledgeable workers or from computers with synthetic voices. Many public sector organizations have equivalent operations—suicide hotlines, disaster relief phone banks, do-not-call registers, tax assistance, and phone-in tax returns are just a few examples. Technology enables these services, but new and often complex organizational structures support them. (Occasionally organizations outsource their telephone operations.) Technology, expertise, and organizational structure likewise combine to propel the fast-growing phenomenon of Internet access to the organization and its services. Many organizations have no sophisticated telephone sites, but almost every organization has a presence on the World Wide Web, with vastly differing levels of service available through those sites. Because telephone centers and websites can be so helpful to the public, they raise equal access issues regarding members of the public unable to use these windows into public sector organizations. Addressing these issues often prompts further changes to an organization's structure. All institutions face a form of self-competition in constantly rising expectations on the part of their customers or constituents; consequently this cycle of continuous adaptation is unlikely to abate.

Organizing for Analysis

Finally, organizing for analysis puts those with technical and analytic skills in places of influence with respect to information and decision making—a situation economist John Kenneth Galbraith (1967) termed "technocracy." Formal authority may have little impact in such an organization. Individuals who are traditionally "staffers," with all the drawbacks inherent in such positions, may unexpectedly play major roles in deciding the priorities and processes that influence their organization's fate. Although the organization's structure need not reflect the analysts' elevated power, that structure may change over time to reflect the shifting status and roles of various actors. At least this is true for some organizations. But the structure of other organizations may change in quite a different fashion because technology increasingly enables people throughout the organizational hierarchy to tap skills and information formerly accessible only through a technical staff. The bottom line is that in one fashion or another, competent analysis must combine appropriate skills with access to information. The next section of this chapter includes a more detailed discussion of organizing for analysis.

Planned Change in Process and Technology

Technological change—especially its scope and speed—has moved from news to an accepted way of life. During the 1970s, 1980s, and 1990s Alvin Toffler (1970, 1980, 1995), John Naisbitt (1984, 1994), and Thomas J. Peters (1994) made a handsome living by writing about and defining the idea of the technological society—explaining what has happened in the last few decades and predicting what the future will be like as the new technologies take root and flourish in society. This subfield of nonfiction remains popular, with voices such as Ray Kurtzweiler, Harry Rheingold, and Tom Friedman; sleek publications such as *Wired Magazine;* and posh conferences such as *Pop!Tech* (www.poptech.org) adding to the mix. Although much of this discussion of change is educated guesswork (admittedly good in many cases), it points out how change is a constant in determining the way organizational objectives are set and met.

Systems Analysis

Perhaps the most cohesive set of skills regularly applied to the problems of procedural and technological changes comes from a set of quantitative and qualitative techniques referred to as *systems analysis.* These techniques have roots in the biological sciences, where it became obvious that a single organism or phenomenon could not be studied in a vacuum. In biology each organism is part of a much larger system (for example, the food chain); to understand individual parts we must also appreciate how seemingly disparate elements interact over wide geographic areas and long periods (Boulding 1956). Think of it as "nested complexity."

A systems approach, with its nested complexity and organic parallels, applies handily to the study of organizations. Systems analysts apply an array of techniques and examine multiple factors as part of understanding and changing organizational structures and processes (see Table 10–1). Although the systems approach does not replace experience and personal

TABLE 10–1 Systems Analysis Techniques

Technique	Description or Purpose	Complexity Level
Bayesian analysis	Analyzing conditional probabilities based on subjective probability estimates. Used to predict the probability of the occurrence of future events.	Moderate
Decision trees	Analyzing branching choice possibilities, focusing on the value of each outcome weighted for the probability of its occurrence. Used to assess alternative courses of action involving several branching decision points.	Moderate
Dynamic programming	Analyzing the occurrence of an event based on the occurrence of events immediately prior to the target event. Used to structure solution sets to complex problems.	High
Flowcharting	Simple graphic representation of the elements, processes, and linkages in a system. Used to model the "flow" or progression of activities within a system.	Low
Game theory	Analyzing the probability of outcomes in a competitive choice situation. Used to construct models of alternative outcome possibilities in a conflict situation.	Moderate
Inventory analysis	An analytical method of projecting demand for resources under conditions of uncertainty. Used to estimate the demand for resources in a system.	Moderate to high
Linear programming	A technique (may use graphs) used to select the optimal mix of resources in a project. Used to plan resource allocation in a project.	High
Markov process	A technique used to determine the probability of achieving alternative outcomes based on prior event probabilities. Used to model system performance probabilities.	Moderate
Program evaluation and review technique (PERT); critical path method (CPM)	Mapping time relationships for completing parts of a project. Used to plan the timing of a project and estimate ways of reducing total project time through the strategic allocation of resources.	Low
Payoff matrix	Evaluating alternative strategies under various conditions. Used to evaluate action alternatives when implementation circumstances are uncertain.	Low to moderate
Queuing theory	Analyzing waiting times for service in a system. Used to model resource demands on a system.	Moderate to high
Simulation	Quantitative analysis of the performance of interrelated variables in a system. Used to model system performance under varying conditions.	Moderate to high
Time series analysis	Employing linear regression to evaluate variable relationships over time. Used to model future system performance based on past system performance.	Moderate

SOURCE: Prepared by John Ostrowski (1997), professor of public administration, California State University–Long Beach.

insight, its quantitative and qualitative managerial techniques help reduce reliance on intuition by pointing out unexpected consequences, sharpening goals, clarifying processes, and generally disciplining managerial thinking. According to proponents of systems analysis in the public sector,

> The entire intellectual orientation is toward explicit conceptual models of phenomena relevant to [a given area of inquiry]. There are models that aid the detection of problems, models that aid decision making, and models that aid the institutionalization of the decisions or designs chosen in response to the problems recognized. Our logic is in the first place cybernetic and, as a consequence of our concern with models, structuralist. Additionally, we tend toward the normative/idealistic rather than the descriptive/realistic. We are concerned with how things are organized, but at least as much with how things might be organized. (White et al. 1980, 9)

Applying such approaches to public sector organizations can be difficult because the ultimate private sector objective of financial profit is rarely the appropriate yardstick. Although private sector firms have a more intense interest than public sector organizations in competition, businesses are usually less concerned with externally controlled conditions such as funding source (appropriations for most government organizations; donations for many nonprofits) and program direction (from the legislative body and parent agencies for government entities; from boards and members for nonprofits)—in other words, the political environment that surrounds public sector organizations. Put simply, private sector organizations are in greater control of their destiny. As White and his colleagues elaborate, "Public management is a political process in which the political demands, internal and external, are concerned with how the services are produced as well as with their characteristics as end products, and with who gets the services as well as with how much is produced" (1980, 4).

Teams

At the opposite end of planned change at the procedural level, the focus of attention becomes the individual job and the flow of work within an agency. The major developments in this area are job enrichment and moving from individually defined jobs to teams. To improve employees' satisfaction and quality of work, their jobs are being restructured so they are not so repetitive and fragmented; the tasks performed by an employee are enriched (Herzberg 1964). Where in the past a social worker may have been involved in only one major aspect of a client's case, she or he may now handle the entire case. It is hoped that this approach will allow the caseworker to use all his or her skills to make the work more interesting. At the same time it is hoped that the broadening of the caseworker's scope in the process will improve the quality of the counseling and aid the client receives because the caseworker can consider all aspects of the client's problems and the interrelationship of the pieces as decisions are made about the situation. An accountant may be given certain accounts to administer rather than having responsibility for only one step in the accounting process; or a park groundskeeper may be given a small park to maintain rather than being in charge of mowing or tree trimming.

In each case the important element is the attempt to remove the monotony from work and to allow workers who wish to do so the chance to use all their skills and develop new ones. And of course leaders plan all changes in techniques and procedures with the ultimate end of improving the organization's overall performance.

Likewise, the use of teams is meant to make workers more satisfied with their work while improving the quality of the product delivered by the organization. The idea has been around for some time and is at the center of the matrix organization structure presented in Chapter 4. Further impetus came from emphasizing quality circles and other participative aspects of quality management approaches such as total quality management. In addition to gaining pooled knowledge, teamwork can lead to greater commitment to the goals of the organization. Of course the success of this concept depends on how the idea is carried out. Michael Schrage argues that

> most companies simply assign people to teams and expect those selected to be ready, willing, and able to collaborate. The belief is that any group of people within the organization can be assembled into a team where the whole is greater than the sum of the parts. (1995, 222)

If top management knows its individuals well, that plan may work; however, there are numerous ways of setting up teams, and every situation calls for a unique procedure for creating working groups.

The concept of teams means more than putting a group of people together to work on a project. According to Katzenbach and Smith (2003, 45), a team is a small number of people with complementary skills who are committed to a common purpose, performance goals, and approach for which they hold themselves mutually accountable. That short definition includes several specific factors that often take a good deal of time and effort to achieve; to achieve these factors the authors present a set of questions (see Box 10–5) that must be answered affirmatively before the designation of "team" fits any group that is working together. As they answer these questions, special problems often arise for public administrators. These problems are related to the political environment within which the government or nonprofit organization operates.

The introduction of new techniques automatically means that procedures will change, and the opposite is usually—although not always—true. As computers played an increasing role in organizational activity, procedures changed accordingly. Now, with the permeation of microcomputers, even faster and greater changes are occurring in the structure and procedures of public agencies. Introducing teams changes the communication, decision making, and product delivery procedures in an organization.

Along with such changes come alterations in values and behavior. The roles of workers are changing, with less division of labor along strict substantive and procedural lines. Top managers can now prepare, send, and receive messages quickly and efficiently, cutting out the middle steps of dictating, typing, and mailing information. Of course this means that managers must get rid of their aversion to keyboards, which is based on an attitude of superiority toward secretaries and, at the same time, a fear of the technical knowledge required to do this supposedly demeaning work. Likewise, managers must also change their attitudes toward status in organizations because different individuals will step into and out of leadership roles during the development and delivery of program goals, whether they are concrete products, social services, or intellectual property. This kind of fluctuation can lead to role ambiguity, at least in the short term, and the necessity of playing different parts for relatively short periods in the larger organizational scenario.

Communication

Chapter 5 described the vital role communication plays in every organization. Technology has helped to create an environment that allows rapid change in roles and the building of teams with large pools of commonly shared information. In large part this is because ever

BOX 10–5 Questions Related to the Formation of Teams

Answering the following questions can establish the degree to which your group functions as a real team, as well as helping to pinpoint how you can strengthen your efforts to increase performance. The questions set tough standards, and answering them candidly may reveal a harder challenge than you may have expected. At the same time, facing the answers can accelerate your progress in achieving the full potential of your team.

1. **Small enough in number:**
   a. Can you convene easily and frequently?
   b. Can you communicate with all members easily and frequently?
   c. Are your discussions open and interactive for all members?
   d. Does each member understand the others' roles and skills?
   e. Do you need more people to achieve your ends?
   f. Are subteams possible or necessary?

2. **Adequate levels of complementary skills:**
   a. Are all three categories of skills either actually or potentially represented across the membership (functional/technical, problem solving/decision making, and interpersonal)?
   b. Does each member have the potential in all three categories to advance his or her skills to the level required by the team's purpose and goals?
   c. Are any skill areas that are critical to team performance missing or underrepresented?
   d. Are the members, individually and collectively, willing to spend the time to help themselves and others learn and develop skills?
   e. Can you introduce new or supplemental skills as needed?

3. **Truly meaningful purpose:**
   a. Does it constitute a broader, deeper aspiration than just near-term goals?
   b. Is it a *team* purpose as opposed to a broader organizational purpose or just one individual's purpose (perhaps the leader's)?
   c. Do all members understand and articulate the purpose in the same way? And can they do so without relying on ambiguous abstractions?
   d. Do members define the purpose vigorously in discussions with outsiders?
   e. Do members frequently refer to the purpose and explore its implications?
   f. Does the purpose contain themes that are particularly meaningful and memorable?
   g. Do members feel the purpose is important, if not exciting?

smaller, more powerful and portable, and less expensive communication technologies can make information that was once the private domain of top management available to individuals throughout the organization. Thus the sacredness of position becomes harder to protect because much of the deference to superiors has been based on the supposition that people at the upper levels of an organizational hierarchy have better information than their subordinates.

4. **Specific goal or goals:**

   a. Are they *team* goals versus broader organizational goals or just one individual's goals (such as the leader's)?

   b. Are they clear, simple, and measurable? If not measurable, can their achievement be determined?

   c. Are they realistic as well as ambitious? Do they allow small wins along the way?

   d. Do they call for a concrete set of team work products?

   e. Are their relative importance and priority clear to all members?

   f. Do all members agree with the goals, their relative importance, and the way in which their achievement will be measured?

   g. Do all members articulate the goals in the same way?

5. **Clear working approach:**

   a. Is the approach concrete, clear, and really understood and agreed to by everybody? Will it result in achievement of the objectives?

   b. Will the approach capitalize on and enhance the skills of all members? Is it consistent with other demands on the members?

   c. Does the approach require all members to contribute equivalent amounts of real work?

   d. Does the approach provide for open interaction, fact-based problem solving, and results-based evaluation?

   e. Do all members articulate the approach in the same way?

   f. Does the approach provide for modification and improvement over time?

   g. Are fresh input and perspectives systematically sought and added—for example, through information and analysis, new members, and senior sponsors?

6. **Sense of mutual accountability:**

   a. Are you individually and jointly accountable for the team's purpose, goals, approach, and work products?

   b. Can you and do you measure progress against specific goals?

   c. Do all members feel responsible for all measures?

   d. Are the members clear on what they are individually responsible for and what they are jointly responsible for?

   e. Is there a sense that "only the team can fail"?

SOURCE: Reprinted by permission of Harvard Business School Press. From *The Wisdom of Teams: Creating the High-Performance Organization* by Jon R. Katzenberg and Douglas K. Smith. Boston, MA, p. 62–64. Copyright © 2003 by the President and Fellows of Harvard College, all rights reserved.

Such may not be the case as successive waves of sophisticated information technology permeate the workplace and, in the process, liberate many organizational activities from being place-bound, hierarchy-bound, and specialist-bound. Deference to superiors may be based, to a much greater extent in the future, on proven performance in the job as perceived by subordinates who are relatively well informed about the organization's internal and external situation.

Authoritarian management styles may be much harder to camouflage and justify because information on which decisions are based will be much more readily available to all participants in the agency, and it will become increasingly normal for others than "bosses" to play the role of group leader based on expertise. Thus management style and motivational techniques will be influenced by the new technologies that are currently gaining widespread use. And we cannot even imagine some of the techniques that will exist in the near future.

A question government and nonprofit administrators must face is the impact these new technologies have on the ultimate objective of serving immediate clients and the citizenry at large. How, for instance, does the integration of computers in the workplace and in our daily lives affect law enforcement? First, the types of crimes that are occurring are changing rapidly; now crimes are committed not only "on the street" but also on "the information highway" created by the Internet. Therefore skills needed within the law enforcement profession are changing. Second, the ability of law enforcement agencies to deny individuals their civil rights is greatly enhanced by the sophisticated new equipment; at the same time, new definitions of privacy and civil rights must be developed for new and emerging technologies (Etzioni 1999). Therefore officials must be deeply committed to the basic tenets of democracy and aware of both the short- and long-term results of the use of new technologies on those basic values. The type of law enforcement agency and officer that must exist in the future is being dramatically changed by the technology developing around them. To quote an anonymous police chief about problems facing police executives,

> The most challenging aspect of a police administrator's job is leading an organization through necessary change, a half step behind the society we interact with. We cannot be pace setters for societal change yet must adjust to it rapidly in order not to lag too far behind. (Witham 1985, 124)

Another example of technology's impact on public administration is how changes in information and communication systems affect citizen participation. The impact of changing information technology on citizen participation may be dramatic. For instance, cable television and Internet streaming allow citizens to observe the debates of governmental bodies from Congress to the local library board; and some technologists argue that direct democracy could become commonplace by letting citizens vote on most issues that face the community. However, the kind of civic participation that would be required by such procedures is not now part of most citizens' values and behavior. Thus the results of such procedures may be quite skewed and even damaging to the community if ways are not found to guarantee the appropriate use of the technology (Kamarck and Nye 1999). Citizens' values will necessarily change; but how does that come about without manipulative strategies having long-term implications for individual rights and liberties? How does participative government operate intelligently given the time and attention constraints on most citizen participants? And how does this recast the role (and possibly the boundaries) of public organizations? What new responsibilities and interdependencies emerge for both government and nonprofit entities? The danger of manipulation does not suggest that workable procedures cannot be developed; it does argue that constructing solutions to such problems is extremely difficult and requires special creativity so that these technologies can be applied effectively to larger social and political questions. The question of how increased citizen participation might change public organizations' functioning is an issue that can be raised here—but not answered.

Shared Decision Making

Finally, in looking at changes in social technology and the impact on public administration, what if teams and other shared decision-making constructs in public organizations grow significantly in their influence on the decisions and processes of organizations? Will accountability be diluted (an issue from Chapter 6)? Will public administrators in nonprofit and government organizations remain servants of the people? What might guarantee that the tenets of public choice theory do not become true and that the members of the organization act in their own interest instead of the public interest? Such issues in public administration ethics have been debated regularly by earlier scholars including Dwight Waldo (1948) and Paul Appleby (1949, 1952), and later by Robert Greenleaf (2002), John Rohr (1989), Terry Cooper (1991), Harold Gortner (1991), Paul Light (2005b), and Michael Josephson (2005), to cite but a few voices. If the public choice advocates are correct that individuals ultimately always act in their own self-interest, the debate may be futile, and evolving social and technical procedures may make democracy more difficult to maintain. But if we accept that individuals respond to the general obligations of citizenship and that public servants understand and act in the public interest, then vetting and applying new organizational change techniques becomes as necessary as it is desirable. The unceasing search to "work smarter" in our public organizations ultimately helps maintain the democratic system even when threatened by shifting social and technical pressures. Organizational change, both proactive and reactive, underscores

> the need for deep commitments by our public officials to civic virtues, democratic values, and constitutional procedures. . . . (T)he traditions of republicanism, democracy, and constitutionalism ground the common values of the cadre of civil servants that we need today as they did the corps of expert administrators envisioned by Woodrow Wilson. (Garvey 1993, 220)

The Folly of "Mono-Change"

The preceding discussion necessarily takes a separate look at planned change in various spheres of the organization. In practice, change in one aspect of an organization precipitates change in other dimensions. The combination is both necessary and healthy. As reengineering authority Michael Hammer describes, major organizational change (in this case through business process reengineering) begins with—but is more than—"the fundamental rethinking and radical redesign of business processes to bring about dramatic improvements in performance" (Hammer and Stanton 1995, 3). When approached thoughtfully, it entails

> fundamental rethinking and radical redesign of an entire business system—business processes, job definitions, organizational structures, management and measurement systems, and values and beliefs—to achieve dramatic improvements in critical measures of performance (cost, quality, capital, service, speed). (Hammer 1994)

Hammer's observation applies to any serious change, whether planned or unplanned. The organization's mission and programs frame the need for particular work processes. Work processes in turn largely determine the organization's jobs, skills, staffing, and structure. These elements require tailored management and measurement approaches, and those approaches do much to shape the organization's values and beliefs. Values and beliefs underlie the organization's mission and enable its work processes. Together they define the organization; consequently changing one element triggers change—or the need for change—in each of the others.

Change and Conflict

Finally, one area where there is an attempt to control and make change positive within organizations is the area of conflict analysis and management. Although conflict management has been inherently a part of public management, its recognition as a specific field of analysis, theory, and practice has occurred primarily during the last decade. In 1925 Mary Parker Follett argued that

> As conflict—difference—is here in the world, as we cannot avoid it, we should, I think, use it. Instead of condemning it, we should set it to work for us. Why not? What does the mechanical engineer do with friction? Of course his chief job is to eliminate friction, but it is true that he also capitalizes friction. The transmission of power by belts depends on friction between the belt and the pulley. The friction between the driving wheel of the locomotive and the track is necessary to haul the train. All polishing is done by friction. The music of the violin we get by friction. We left the savage state when we discovered fire by friction. We talk of the friction of mind on mind as a good thing. So in (organizations), too, we have to know when to try to eliminate friction and when to try to capitalize it, when to see what work we can make it do. (Graham 1995, 67–8)

Over the decades a variety of public organizations have made special efforts to understand and guide conflict into positive, constructive, collaborative activities (Fisher and Ury 1991). Specific groups have been set up to deal with interpersonal conflicts within agencies, and managers are given training on handling intergroup and interorganizational problems. And especially in the area of regulation, officials search for ways to constructively resolve long-standing conflicts between groups in the community and between government agencies and interest groups of all kinds rather than just assuming that those conflicts are inevitable and eternal.

Critical to the study of conflicts in and between organizations is the definition of what we are examining. People assumed for a long time that conflicts occurred because of different beliefs or different desired results that were part of a zero-sum game: Only one side could win and the other must lose. The newer definition of conflict accepts differences in beliefs and desired ends. But it argues that by getting both sides to understand and lay on the table their beliefs and desires it is often possible to arrive at what Mary Parker Follett called an "integrative solution" (Graham 1995, 68–86) and today we would characterize as a super-solution or win–win outcome. In an integrative solution both sides find a place for their desires so that neither side has to sacrifice the most important factors. However, the analysis, understanding, and negotiation processes have usually changed the priority listing of the conflicting groups as part of the conflict management process. (See Box 10–6 for one public leader's approach to negotiation.)

Of course the political system is itself a structure established to allow the civilized and productive resolution of conflicts that cannot be settled at lower levels of the society. But the focus of conflict analysis goes beyond understanding conflicts and looks for ways to use conflict productively and to turn it into collaborative, joint problem solving that can be useful to all sides (Burton 1990). Likewise it is recognized that conflict and change are inextricably bound together—one seldom happens without the other. As L. David Brown (1983, v) notes,

> Change is often closely tied to conflict. Sometimes change breeds conflict; sometimes conflict breeds change. Effective conflict management is often critical to constructive change processes. Change is important if inequitable and unacceptable conditions exist for some party, but so too there is a need for order, consensus, and common goals *within and between organizations and between organizations and the public they serve* in an open society.

BOX 10–6 Attila the Hun on the Art of Negotiation

Negotiation is one way antagonists resolve conflicts. Attila the Hun offers advice on this skill and how to use it to "win" when negotiating—which may or may not always fit the needs of public administrators.

"The techniques of negotiation are not easily taught. It is for both Hun and chieftain to learn skills useful in negotiating. These are mastered only through understanding gained by experience. . . . Now I give to all assembled my counsel, in the hopes that it will serve to add to your wisdom and your expertise in the leader's vital art of negotiation:

- Always maintain the diplomatic initiative in all negotiations. Be on the offense always—never lose contact with your enemy. This will place him in a lesser position, and you will have the upper hand.
- Always negotiate at the lowest level possible. This will serve to resolve small things before they grow out of proportion and make negotiating impossible.
- Never trust negotiation to luck. Enter every session armed with knowledge of the enemy's strengths and weaknesses; knowing his secrets makes you strong and allows you to better deceive him as to your ultimate goals.
- Keep negotiations secret! They must be conducted in private. . . . Only the policies should become public knowledge. How they were negotiated should remain confidential, saving a loss of face.
- Time is your ally when you're negotiating. It calms temperaments and gives rise to less spirited perspectives. Never rush into negotiations.
- Never arbitrate. Arbitration allows a third party to determine your destiny. It is a resort of the weak.
- Never make negotiations difficult on immediate, lesser points at the cost of a greater outcome. Acquiescence on lesser issues softens the spirit of your adversary.
- In negotiation you must take well-studied risks. Try to foresee all possible outcomes to determine those that will yield favorable results.
- Be aware of the temperament in your foe's camp. Take advantage of troubles and turmoils that arise during negotiations.
- Never overestimate your own adroitness. You may simply be negotiating with a weak opponent. Though fortuitous, this will not always be the situation.
- Never intimidate.
- Honor all commitments you make during negotiations lest your enemy fail to trust your word in the future.
- Remember, agreement in principle does not dictate agreement in practice. It does, however, serve to save face at the moment.
- Be bold in facing the inevitable. Acquiesce when resistance would be pointless or when your victory can be gained only at too high a cost. Of this you may not approve, but it is your duty to do so for the good of all Huns.
- Be keenly aware of time. Present appealing alternatives that are appropriate to your opponent's situation at the moment of your negotiations. Otherwise he will dismiss your propositions.

Now you mighty chieftains must come to an understanding of a final simple fact. It is never wise to gain by battle what may be gained through bloodless negotiations. Reserve the potential loss of your warriors for great causes not attainable without waging battle."

Public organizations must play an important part in social and political conflicts. Unless individuals within such organizations understand the dynamics of the conflicts within which they are major actors and know how to turn negative feelings toward more constructive paths, they may easily exacerbate the problems they are mandated to fix. Ultimately such action, taken in ignorance, can harm the fabric of society. Often that destructiveness occurs because there is no understanding of the different cultures that may exist in the conflicting groups. Wallace Warfield addresses this problem by suggesting that, in many cases, a third party intervenor skilled in public policy conflict resolution may be needed to help the various sides work through the misunderstandings. Warfield notes, for example, that

> Low-power cultural groups, who have traditionally been kept away from the negotiating table, see the origins, processes, and outcomes of conflict through the lens of values that have historically shaped their relationships with the dominant culture. They bring different voices to the negotiating process that often do not fit the protocols of interest-based bargaining. At the same time, public organizations are complex entities that have cultures of a different kind. . . . When these forces are joined in conflict, the third-party intervenor must find a way to bridge the cultural gap. Frequently, this means playing an interpreter role for one side or both, in a way that provides a context for the actions and language of the opposing side. (1993, 190)

What is sought in conflict *management* is a "balance of conflict." Too little conflict leads to complacency and no desire for change or to the inability to face issues of friction, imbalance in distribution of costs and benefits, or other factors that may, when not noticed and dealt with early, become issues of bitter hostility and confrontation at a later date.

Internal organizational culture is dramatically affected by the types of conflicts that occur between individual members and between groups. All efforts at changing the values of the group, improving intraorganizational cooperation and collaboration, focusing attention and getting agreement on the goals of the organization, and attempting to improve overall efficiency and effectiveness will depend on developing an acceptance of conflict as a normal individual/organizational phenomenon and learning to deal with it constructively. Used constructively, conflict can be a powerful tool for clarification of individual, group, and organizational values, ideas, and actions and the development of greater understanding and collaboration between all the actors. When conflict is recognized as a normal factor in organizational life, it can be calculated into the set of variables that can be addressed on a regular basis. If conflict in organizations is not recognized and dealt with, it becomes one more external factor (discussed later in this chapter) that randomly influences organization functionality.

Ultimately change breeds resistance in any human situation, and that resistance must be handled for change to become effective. This requires understanding the motives for resistance, addressing them, and, when necessary, excising unjustified resistance that will not be quelled. Doing so requires effective leadership, compassion, perseverance, and toughness (Hammer and Stanton 1995). As Hallmark president Robert Stark once commented, "We are going on a journey. Along the way, we will carry the wounded and shoot the stragglers" (Hammer 1994). Executing planned organizational change is frequently necessary but rarely easy.

The Continuing Debate over Planned Organizational Change

So what is necessary or desirable change for public sector organizations? This chapter's discussion has focused on a general theory of organizational change and techniques used in accomplishing that change; however, this is a means-oriented or process-oriented discussion that different organizations in different circumstances can use to achieve different ends or results. Agreeing on what the results of change should be—or even whether to pursue change—must be its own discussion. There are alternative models for organizational behavior and values, structure, and process. Not everyone wants the organization to look or act the same; many models exist for public sector organizations (as Chapter 4 describes); and results differ even in applying a chosen model. After all, each model is based on a different set of assumptions about organizational objectives, the roles of government and nonprofit organizations in society, and the way people are expected to function in them.

We have discussed systems of participatory control in Chapter 6 and elsewhere in this book. Justification for participatory systems varies from implementing particular aspects of Marxist philosophy to practicing humanistic psychology; in addition, these systems vary according to the culture of the particular country or society—or organizational culture, as Chapter 8 illustrates. Therefore considering participatory management systems also involves considering culture and the objectives in using that system.

If the objective of a participatory system is to improve control, the type of participation encouraged may be quite different from that sought when the objective is to improve overall efficiency or effectiveness or ethical decision making. Still another type of participation may be encouraged if the objective is to increase identification with a particular organization. In each case the point at which participation is encouraged may also change. If improved control is the goal, participation may be encouraged only after organization objectives and plans have been completed, and the participation may occur only in specific areas of organizational activity. But if the goal of the participation is to increase identification with the organization, there may be an attempt to involve members (who could be defined as employees, engaged constituents, advisory groups, or members of a member-based nonprofit) as quickly as possible in defining organization goals and plans so that they will have a sense of ownership in those important organizational elements. Of course there is always the problem of deciding the degree to which the members and clients of a public agency should set their own goals or whether the goals should come from elected representatives of the people. It is even possible to question how much leeway organization members should have in establishing their own procedures; the answer appears to be determined primarily by the way in which we perceive human beings in general—that is, whether public interest will outweigh self-interest.

Each approach to participation results in a different structure. If identification with the organization is important and participation in the establishment of goals and procedures is encouraged, an agency creates strong communication circuits that work both up and down. These circuits will be apparent in the organization's structure, and offices that play an important role in the communication system will be given higher status and protected so they can function without feeling threatened by either internal or external forces unsympathetic to the organization's established philosophy. It is likely that such an organization will have a relatively flat hierarchy. On the other hand, if the primary goal of the organization is control, no matter how much participation is encouraged, the organization will undoubtedly have a taller hierarchy with more managerial layers. Similar differences can be found for almost any organizational goal and the type of structure and processes occurring because of that primary goal.

Another factor that influences the structure of public organizations, determines whether they should change, and decides how that change should take place is directly related to the type of service that organizations deliver and the structure required to carry out that service. Many organizations in the public sector were originally set up to deliver concrete products.

The early role of the government was primarily helping to tame the wilderness and aiding in the creation of our industrial might: Highways had to be built, harbors developed, and floods controlled. Much of government had an industrial look. The organizational structure and process emulated that of business.

Later government became more involved in delivering services to citizens and to other organizations in society, while early nonprofits formed around social services and member protection. All of the roles discussed here have always existed in government, although their relative importance changed dramatically at different points in our country's development. Service organizations have a different configuration than organizations of an industrial, product-oriented nature. In fact, many tensions in government relate to misunderstandings that occur when people try to judge the performance of a service organization by production organization standards. Many people have not yet recognized the difference between the two, including occasional political figures who try to apply standards of efficiency from industry to government and nonprofit programs such as subsidized housing, earned income credit, mail delivery in rural areas, or hospice care.

Another developing governmental role that has created much controversy is the function of regulation. In our interdependent world it has been determined by the legislature that certain business communities need to be regulated because of either inefficiency or failure in the normal market processes. Regulatory activities have a dynamic all their own, and it is impossible to judge the efficiency or effectiveness of such organizations by any industrial standard. Questions of due process, equity, and public interest are paramount in these activities instead of simple measures of the number of cases handled or pieces of paper pushed. Careful understanding of the goals for which these organizations were established, and the dynamic of the process over time, is critical in making judgments about change in objectives, organizational culture, structure, and process.

A new major role in government is that of information broker or information organizer. In this role a principal mission for some organizations (such as the Bureau of the Census, the Bureau of Labor Statistics, and the National Intelligence Agency at the federal level; or the Conference Board among nonprofits) is collecting, analyzing, using, and dispensing to appropriate others information generated and needed throughout major sectors of society. This information is needed simply to keep the government, and the social or business sectors of society, functioning effectively in our highly technological and interdependent world. If the organization does not directly furnish this service, it often regulates the part of society that is collating and delivering the information. This new type of organization requires a different set of knowledge and skills; the structures of authority, communication, and decision making, and the procedures followed in carrying out the mission, are quite different from those of the types of organizations previously noted. Because of the immense amount of expertise required and the phenomenal rates at which technology and external demands change, these organizations often assume the characteristics of the virtual organization discussed in Chapter 4. The nature of these organizations is often highly disquieting to politicians because it makes it hard for them to maintain political control over such dynamic activities. The governmental policy-making machinery is deliberately structured to operate slowly through a coalition-building process that requires special majorities to achieve temporary closure on any issue. Organizations at the forefront of technology may change structures, processes, and even objectives several times in the span of time that their legislative masters require to make policy. And while this is happening, these new technologies and the organizations using them are often capable of carrying out activities that could be quite injurious to the health of our democratic system. This situation places many public managers and executives in positions where they must make serious ethical and political decisions about appropriate behaviors, procedures, and objectives for their agencies.

Finally, we must not assume that change is necessarily good. No single model or structure of organization is "right" or should be always sought; no particular structure is guaranteed to be better than another. Instead we must decide what is appropriate for an organization, what change is necessary, and what the new structures and processes should be after careful consideration of the environment in which the agency is working and what its goals are. At that point decisions can be made about the necessity of change and what the goals are for that change. In many cases alternative models are not improvements. Any attempt to create change in an organization without carefully weighing all of these issues opens us to the charge of being in favor of change for change's sake or being enamored of the excitement of change rather than interested in accomplishing preordained goals. Such a charge, if true, is damning; if untrue, the charge is still damaging and must be immediately rebutted by a careful enunciation of the goals of the change. Not everyone may agree with the goals, but at least we can refute the charge of thoughtlessness. That is vital to success. It is also vital to know if insufficient thought has gone into the process so that the changes can be either halted or corrected before serious damage is done to the organization. The final decision about what structure is correct or better for public organizations can be made only by some combination of policy makers (politicians or board members), bureaucrats, clients, and other interested parties in the political/administrative process.

UNPLANNED CHANGE

Outside the organization, the political, economic, and social characteristics of our society are constantly changing. Other countries also play important roles in influencing activities in our government. For example, our perception of the military might of the Soviet Union and its interest in using that military strength to foment trouble around the world once had a dramatic impact on the amount of resources available for other activities within our government. The end of the Cold War, when it came, was expected to reap a "peace benefit" that might help other government programs. Such a surplus did not appear, and the political mood changed to one of cutbacks and reduction of the government's role in society; consequently international changes were offset, as far as government programs were concerned, by social value changes. The oil crisis of the 1970s and the "war on terror" at the beginning of this century each created an upheaval throughout our society that affected all types of public and private organization policies, structures, and procedures. The crises pointed out inevitable long-term problems and choices that would have to be made at some point in the future. Government, industry, the public, and international relations have not been the same since those times. We may question whether the Pony Express was efficient and effective (historical debunkers argue that the Pony Express was romanticized and not nearly as efficient as we are led to believe); but there is no doubt that the completion of railroad and telegraph systems across the United States rendered the Pony Express obsolete and that commercial package delivery firms and pervasive electronic communication are similarly challenging today's postal service. Good or bad management was not then—and is not now—the central issue.

Likewise the civil rights movement, which reached a peak of activity during the 1960s, changed how all organizations (public and private) conducted personnel activities as employees were hired, trained, and promoted. Affirmative action and equal employment opportunity programs were central to all personnel functions in public organizations. Now an effort is being made to reduce or stop affirmative action programs at the federal level and in some states; in 1996 the governor of Louisiana mandated an end to those programs, arguing that even Martin Luther King would support this action. Nonprofit and government managers inside individual organizations cannot control these forces but must react to them in the best possible way. No matter how effectively and responsibly an organization is managed, the next election may bring into office a political leader whose mandate includes eliminating or shifting programs important for a particular government agency or a nonprofit enterprise. Hence all public organizations must react to changing priorities among the general public, legislative bodies, the courts, and events and sentiments beyond our borders.

Perhaps the whole concept of workforce diversity is a good example of external changes that require response within organizations. The various changes in demography related to race and ethnicity, gender and gender preference, age and disability, and other factors that have occurred regularly in our society have led to bitter disputes and numerous laws. This is an area that was always changing more than was realized. The magnitude of change in organizations of the future was forcefully spelled out in *Workforce 2000: Work and Workers for the 21st Century* (William and Packer 1987). Now it is a problem and an opportunity that play a central role in much of our social and political consciousness. (See Box 10–7.) Affirmative action and equal employment laws have tried to address these changes; but the only way to really cope with current changes in the workforce is to specifically face the issue of diversity that exists, and will increase, in organizations as in society. Specific efforts must be made to accommodate changes that diversity brings. The values, goals, and processes related to workforce diversity must be established by political decision makers and public administrators—in collaboration with organization members and the larger society. Those who argue for "diversity programs" do so because they believe it is easier to handle such issues when the organization acts proactively rather than reactively (Golembiewski 1995). Public leaders in this case are attempting to plan for external forces over which they may have little control but which they know exist and are bound to affect the overall success of their organizations.

Inside the organization unplanned changes may not be of the same magnitude, but they are just as important when they occur. The loss of a critical employee during peak activity may cause temporary backlogs in the processing of cases, slow the decision-making process, delay experiments, and otherwise disrupt crucial activities. An equipment breakdown can have comparable effects. For example, perhaps the most common complaint currently heard in large offices is that work is delayed because "the (fill in the blank) system is down." Numerous activities of employees and managers also have unanticipated consequences; these unforeseen results of what are thought to be planned changes often create serious problems for everyone involved (Tenner 1997; Gillon 2000; Nichols 2005).

Change in the Political System: The Focus for Public Organizations

Unplanned change requires quick and appropriate reaction; thus organizations must maintain the flexibility to respond to it. Those that do can prosper; those that do not can expect hard times. Public organizations must be aware of all aspects of their environment, but their

BOX 10–7 Major Sources of Advantage and Disadvantage in Managing Diversity in the Public Sector

1. *Legal:* Failure to manage diversity will result in high costs of litigation as well as adverse judgments by the courts.

2. *Costs:* The costs of doing business will be higher with failure to manage diversity—communication will be more difficult, employee involvement will be reduced, relationships will be strained if not adversarial, and so on, as organizations become more diverse.

3. *Intergroup conflict:* This is a special case of costs with broad implications for the quality of working life, labor–management relationships, and the quality of unionization. Conflict will be greater where managing diversity is less successful.

4. *Attractiveness to potential and actual employees:* Failure in managing diversity will be a major disincentive for existing as well as potential employees; this is of special significance in the public sector, which has well-known disadvantages in recruitment and retention. This attractiveness holds not only for minorities, who will form large portions of the pool of employees, but also for others interested in a public workforce that "looks like America."

5. *Attractiveness to budgeting authorities:* Government agencies derive their life's blood from complex executive–legislative views of requests for appropriations. Poor performance in managing diversity may become a growing factor in adverse reviews.

6. *Attractiveness to clientele or customers:* Unsuccessful diversity efforts may have direct implications for how an agency serves its clients or customers. The latter will become increasingly diverse over time; their needs presumably will be more accessible to diverse workers and managers; and the comfort level for both service providers and clients or customers should increase.

7. *Attractiveness to managers and executives:* Not only are more managers tasking subordinates with diversity goals, but performance on those goals is taken into increasing account for promotions and salary judgments.

8. *Creativity and problem solving:* Many observers argue that organizations successful in managing diversity will bring broader perspectives, different experiences, and lessened attachment to past norms and practices, all of which can be expected to have a positive effect on creativity and problem solving.

9. *System flexibility:* Agencies with successful diversity efforts will be more accustomed to dealing comprehensively with a changing environment and hence more fluid and perhaps less standardized, as well as arguably more efficient and effective in responding to environmental turbulence.

10. *System legitimacy:* Success in managing diversity is associated with core values in our political and social philosophy, so that success also should have regime-enhancing tendencies.

11. *System image:* Successfully managing diversity provides another opportunity for government to exercise leadership as a model employer.

SOURCE: Robert T. Golembiewski, *Managing Diversity in Organizations* (Tuscaloosa: University of Alabama Press, 1995), 47.

attention is focused primarily on one area. All public agencies have one overwhelmingly important characteristic that colors all thought about change. Organizations are inextricably bound up with the political system and the variations in public opinion and policy that are a constant part of political life. The organization's original broad objectives are established in the whirlwind of political, public interest group, and legislative activity; even though administrative leaders form these relatively malleable objectives to the advantage of the organization, there is only so much flexibility in the available interpretation. Similarly the physical resources and political support for programs change as time goes by, sometimes dramatically but always inevitably; these changes are often totally unrelated to success or failure in meeting the organization's stated objectives. Public administrators must recognize this ubiquitous change in the environment and learn not only how to survive but also how to turn this environmental characteristic into a useful tool when it is appropriate to do so. The important task is to recognize the appropriateness of manipulating the environment: There are times when a program is no longer wanted or needed by the citizens that it supposedly serves. When this is the case, it is essential to arrange a decent and timely organizational death. In many instances, however, organizations are simply experiencing the normal swings of the public opinion pendulum, and popular and unpopular programs will trade places in the polls after an unspecified period. Such is the nature of the political world.

Members of public organizations must remember that (1) any particular period in the life of an organization is probably temporary; (2) each period creates opportunity for at least one of the types of change discussed in this chapter; and (3) all changes must be planned with the assumption that unless the change is occurring in a crisis situation, the basic objectives of the organization remain the same or change only slightly. This means that any proposed changes must fit into the organization's overall goals, and change is justified only if it improves the organization's ability to meet those goals.

Public administrators must have both a short- and long-term outlook as decisions about the necessity and feasibility of change are considered. It is essential to think how a particular change—in design, process, or values and behavior of members—will work in the present situation. It is also necessary to realize that the political environment may change tomorrow, or most certainly in a few years; and the anticipated change will have to either fit a new set of demands or be easily adjusted. Quick fixes often portend future difficulty that is exacerbated rather than alleviated by the instant solution that fails to calculate future costs.

The biggest problem in this area is that many decisions that affect a public sector organization are made outside of it, and thus organization leaders have no control over an initial externally made decision about change. If a governor decides to run for a national office and, as an element of campaign strategy, promises to decrease the number of that state's employees and services contracted through nonprofit agencies, public managers have no say over the initial decision: The governor will mandate such cuts. The problem for the manager is to find a way to turn this externally mandated change into a positive action within the agency. One possibility is using the governor's mandate as an impetus for carefully studying the organization's functions, structures, and processes to see where changes can increase the efficiency and effectiveness of the operation while adhering to the political leader's orders. Quality circles may be helpful—or reengineering or other change techniques this chapter has discussed. If such new procedures can be found, it is possible to use the external pressure to justify and promote changes ultimately valuable to the organization anyway. This is a variation on the saying that "necessity is the mother of invention."

Normally groups of clients and interested citizens support any new program as it starts (Downs 1967); public administrators must turn to these people as a new program gets under way. Many initial supporters will lose interest as time goes by, or they will disagree with how the program is run and therefore stop supporting it as ardently as they did originally. In our political system, almost every program or policy can expect to have a group of dissenters or opponents who will look for an opportunity to attack and destroy the current program or to exchange it for one they want.

The wise public administrator therefore builds bridges to new groups that may replace those lost or help balance the growing number of opponents (such as other nonprofit organizations offering the same service or other government agencies vying for a bigger slice of the municipal budget). In addition, the leader looks ahead for situations that surface opposition and situations that give the organization an opportunity to advance its cause; both inevitably occur. Then the leader has intelligence about opposition, compromises, or new proposals (including adjustments to goals or new objectives) that can be brought to bear on the situation. Thus what may appear to be a compromise or a retreat may in fact be a change for the organization that has been planned and waiting for just such a situation so that it can be presented when the time is ripe. Long-term changes, however, can be difficult to implement in the public sector because people tend to have relatively short attention spans, and elected leaders move in and out of office rapidly and at inopportune times. Therefore it may be necessary to find a way to divide long-term goals into a series of short-term, easily identifiable, and supportable projects or modules that will ultimately achieve the organization's long-term goals but will also allow those who must operate under shorter time constraints a sense of achievement as they observe what has been accomplished during their tenure. This approach matches in many details the argument presented by students of decision making: Major decisions may be accomplished through a series of incremental ones as long as there is some general agreement on objectives. Strategy and tactics become important in organizational change in the public sector just as they are important in any other decision-making situation.

CONCLUSION: WE HAVE THE RESPONSIBILITY AND ABILITY TO SHAPE PUBLIC ORGANIZATIONS THOUGHTFULLY

We shape our public organizations, and in turn they help shape society itself. So we can examine what organizational designs are possible, what designs are probable, and which among those are preferred. This is both an opportunity and a responsibility. Nonprofit organizations create their missions based on the needs of their members or a need in the public. Government organizations exist with certain mandates from political leaders; they try to carry out those mandates in particular ways. In the political world it is normal to expect opposition; after all, that is how and why an issue is handled in the political world. For any organization working for and with the public, there is no way to achieve unanimity on what objectives and procedures should be.

Moreover, as Denhardt and Denhardt (2003, 150) point out, "Public organizations are increasingly limited in what they can do on their own. Many other groups and organizations must be involved." This requires effective public organizations and their leaders to mobilize and sustain the attention of a wide range of stakeholders—something Harlan Cleveland (1985) refers to as leadership through "brokering" rather than through hierarchical authority, which he too sees as a declining organizational configuration given the complexity of real-world interconnections within and among contemporary organizations. The Denhardts build on an observation by Jeffrey Luke:

> "Governance in the United States is characterized by a dynamic interplay among government agencies, nonprofit service providers, business enterprises, multinational corporations, neighborhood groups, special interest and advocacy groups, labor unions, academia, the media, and many other formal and informal associations that attempt to influence the public agenda" (Luke 1998, 4). Moreover, the most substantial problems we face today cross organizational, jurisdictional, and sector boundaries. What happens in one place or what one organization does is likely to affect the problem only in a marginal way; all the other groups and organizations interested in the same issue are also affecting the issue. In other words, there is an underlying web of interdependence and interconnectedness that ties many different groups together. Without the involvement of all those interconnected groups and organizations, little can be done to effectively address complex public problems. Moreover, given the passionate commitment and highly focused interest of most of these parties, it's often difficult to exclude anyone. (Denhardt and Denhardt, 2003, 150)

The constant tension generated around public programs generates a stasis or balance in which the organization operates—but that stasis is never permanent. Once the balance shifts, the organization must adapt to meet the new situation. This is a never-ending cycle. Usually society is shifting slowly enough so that the adjustments can be made relatively easily, almost without being noticed, and without discomfort to organizational members, clients, and interested parties who are not directly affected. At other times changes are uncomfortable and even threatening to actors in the process. But the synthesis that results is developed from opposing views.

All of this can be painful because government organizations represent the institutionalization of power in society. This is true, as well, for nonprofit organizations even though they are self-organizing: Once they exist, they focus and reflect their supporters' power. Those who assert themselves in shaping public organizations and those who prevail in the political process get to decide the goals, structure, and procedures used by the organizations that carry out their policies. Public policies, the decisions that guide them, and actions to implement them all tend to be incremental in nature; so an examination of governmental bureaucracy offers a good picture of who in society has won and lost over the last few decades. Political dilemmas are generated through change and pressure to change; such pressures come from many sources, but a major source is within public sector organizations themselves. Who has the "right" to change how things are done? How will changes affect the balance of power within society? Can dramatic, internally generated change occur without affecting the balance of accountability and responsibility within public organizations, and will that change affect our democratic principles? There are no easy answers to such questions, yet answers are essential. None of these questions rules out change within government and nonprofit organizations; rather, they point out the care we must take in shaping the organizations that serve us, the ubiquitous presence and relevance of those organizations, and the inevitable impact that organizational change in the public sector can have.

FOR FURTHER READING

You have finished this textbook examining organization theory in the context of nonprofit and government institutions, but the issues traced here represent only the surface of an extensive, ongoing conversation involving many voices and topic threads. The reading suggestions in this section and the earlier chapters offer possibilities for pursuing threads and voices that capture your interest.

The choices are extensive. Shelves in the management and business sections of today's bookstores are ripe with prescriptive tomes on how to tinker with organizations; how to rebuild them completely; and how to make them greener, leaner, more profitable, more nimble, more virtuous, more virtual, more market-savvy, more customer-centered, and more results-oriented. This is a healthy trend, even though which of these books and which scholarly articles will endure as valued classics is problematic. Organizational change became a best seller in 1982 with Thomas Peters and Robert Waterman's *In Search of Excellence,* which shared space in popular culture with Alvin Toffler's *Future Shock* (1970) and *The Third Wave* (1980) and with John Naisbitt's *Megatrends* (1984). Planned change within public sector organizations—specifically government—achieved best-seller status in 1992 with David Osborne and Ted Gaebler's *Reinventing Government* and Michael Barzelay's less widely read *Breaking through Bureaucracy* (1992), and the federal government itself generated popular interest in 1993 with *Creating a Government That Works Better and Costs Less,* the report of the National Performance Review under the direction of Vice President Al Gore. Also in 1993 Michael Hammer and James Champy's *Reengineering the Corporation* popularized the value of large-scale process change for organizations; Hammer and Steven Stanton recast the concept in more concrete and helpful terms with the publication of *The Reengineering Revolution: A Handbook* in 1995.

Articles worth exploring include Samantha Durst and Charldean Newell's "The Who, Why, and How of Reinvention in Nonprofit Organizations" (2001); and Martin Landau's 1969 essay "Redundancy, Rationality, and the Possibility of Duplication and Overlap," published in *Public Administration Review.* Jay Shafritz, Steven Ott, and Yong Suk Jang's sixth edition of *Classics of Organization Theory* (2005) includes James Thompson's "Organizations in Action" (1967); Tom Burns and G. M. Stalker's "Mechanistic and Organic Systems" (1994); Richard M. Burton and Borge Obel's "Technology as a Contingency Factor" (1998); Daniel Katz and Robert Kahn's "Organizations and the System Concept" (1966); and Glen Carroll and Michael Hannan's "Demography of Corporations and Industries" (2000).

But the conversation about stability, change, and public organizations has a far broader base than these mainstream administrative treatises, well-considered though they are. The extended conversation embraces science, culture and values, world affairs, technology, administrative mechanics, history, conjecture about the future, and other topics that influence and are influenced by public organizations.

Thomas Kuhn's widely regarded *Structure of Scientific Revolutions* (1970), originally published in 1962, examines the history of science, and John Gribbin's *Deep Simplicity* (2004) describes how simple rules transform chaos into complexity; both books have conceptual implications for public organizations and institutions. With its substrate of cultural diversity and communication technologies, globalism's profound impact on public organizations is discernable in Francis Fukuyama's *State-building* (2004), J. Ørstrøm Møller's *The End of Internationalism* (2000), and Tom Friedman's *The World Is Flat* (2005). Howard Rheingold's *Smart Mobs* (2002) and Glenn Reynolds' *An Army of Davids* (2006) look at how communication technologies reshape power structures and redefine communities here and around the world.

The impact of information technologies on society and its institutions is awesome and often positive. But it also provokes thoughtful caution from observers such as Neil Postman and Amitai Etzioni. Postman's *Technopoly* (1993) and *Building a Bridge to the Eighteenth Century* (1999) consider the degree to which humans dominate technology or are dominated by it. In *The Communitarian Reader* (2004), Etzioni and others explore the needed balance between citizens' rights and responsibilities; in *The Limits of Privacy* (1999), Etzioni examines public organizations' mandate to ensure the public's welfare by increasingly employing policies and technologies that circumvent personal privacy. Information technologies alter the roles of public organizations and the processes through which they operate. Four perspectives on how technology can affect public organizations include Elaine Kamarck and Joseph Nye's *Democracy.com?* (1999), which is the most conceptual of the four; Katherine Barrett and Richard Greene's *Powering Up* (2001), the most nuts-and-bolts of this group; William Eggers' *Government 2.0* (2005); and G. David Garson's *Public Information Technology and E-governance* (2006).

What public organizations do and how they go about doing it are themselves complex threads with multiple viewpoints. Eugene Dvorin and Robert Simmons examine these issues in *From Amoral to Humane Bureaucracy* (1972), as do Janet Denhardt and Robert Denhardt in *The New Public Service: Serving, Not Steering* (2003). Similar questions are considered through the lens of postmodernism by David John Farmer in *The Language of Public Administration* (1995) and by Hugh Miller and Charles Fox in *Postmodernism, "Reality" and Public Administration* (1997). Gareth Morgan continues the postmodern theme in *Imaginization* (1997) and *Images of Organization* (2006), doing so in often-visual ways that are simultaneously conceptual and applied. Emphasis is on the "how" as well as the "what" question in Lester Salamon's *The Tools of Government* (2001), whereas Paul Light's *Four Pillars of High Performance* (2005) and Michael Beitler's *Strategic Organizational Change* (2006) pay more attention to the means by which organizations pursue their goals.

Jerome Glenn's *Futures Research Methodology* (1999) prescribes ways organizations can identify and evaluate possibilities about the future, including the likelihood and implications of those possibilities. John Petersen, in *Out of the Blue* (1999), presents and then uses similar forecasting tools. Tae-Chang Kim and Jim Dator, in *Co-creating a Public Philosophy for Future Generations* (1999), apply ethical values along with future-research tools, as they and others consider obligations that societies and institutions have toward unborn generations.

The threads are many, the conversation is there to join, and the relevance for public organizations and organization theory is immense. Enjoy. In fact, add your voice.

REVIEW QUESTIONS

1. Is organizational change basically good or bad? In what ways?
2. What kinds of phenomena precipitate organizational change? What phenomena tend to prevent or hinder organizational change?
3. In what way(s) does an organization's outside environment influence how it operates?
4. Does technology tend to drive organizational change, or does it enable organizational change? What is your basis for this assessment?
5. What is the role of stability in enabling effective organizational operations and effective change endeavors?
6. Why are many observers skeptical about downsizing and similar approaches to organizational change? What is your view?
7. How do organizational culture, political trends, and ethical considerations influence change? Give an example.

8. What is the toughest aspect of organizational change? How would you deal with it? How might you approach change differently if you were in a government organization?
9. In what ways do government organizations, nonprofit organizations, and private sector organizations approach change differently? Why? Regarding change, what do the different kinds of organizations share in common?

REFERENCES

Alexander, Jennifer, Reneé Nank, and Camilla Stivers. 2001. Implications of welfare reform: Do nonprofit survival strategies threaten a civil society? In *Understanding nonprofit organizations*, 276–82. Ed. J. Steven Ott. Boulder, CO: Westview Press.

Appleby, Paul H. 1949. *Policy and administration*. Montgomery: The University of Alabama Press.

_____. 1969. *Morality and administration in democratic government*. New York: Greenwood Press. (Originally published in 1952.)

Argyris, Chris, and J. Schon. 1978. *Organizational learning: A theory of action perspective*. Reading, MA: Addison-Wesley.

Barrett, Katherine, and Richard Greene. 2001. *Powering up: How public managers can take control of information technology*. Washington, DC: CQ Press.

Barzelay, Michael. 1992. *Breaking through bureaucracy: A new vision for managing in government*. Berkeley: University of California Press.

Beitler, Michael A. 2006. *Strategic organizational change: A practitioner's guide for managers and consultants*. 2nd ed. Greensboro, NC: Practitioner Press International.

Boulding, Kenneth E. 1956. General systems theory—The skeleton of science. *Management Science* 2: 197–208.

Brown, Brack. *Organizational dynamics in changing environments*. Unpublished material. Fairfax VA: George Mason University.

Brown, L. David. 1983. *Managing conflict at organizational interfaces*. Reading, MA: Addison-Wesley.

Brown, Laura K., and Elizabeth Troutt. 2004. A cooperative approach to accountability: Manitoba's family violence prevention program. *International Journal of Public Administration* 27: 309–30.

Burns, Tom, and G. M. Stalker. 1994. Mechanistic and organic systems. In *The management of innovation*, 119–25. Rev. ed. Oxford: Oxford University Press. Reprinted in *Classics of organization theory*, 198–202. 6th ed. Ed. Jay Shafritz, J. Steven Ott, and Yong Suk Jang. Belmont, CA: Thomson Wadsworth, 2005.

Burton, John. 1990. *Conflict: Resolution and prevention*. New York: St. Martin's.

Burton, Richard M., and Borge Obel. 1998. Technology as a contingency factor. In *Strategic organizational diagnosis and design: Developing theory for application*, 224–34. 2nd ed. Boston: Kluwer Academic. Reprinted in *Classics of Organizational Theory*, 239–47. 6th ed. Ed. Jay Shafritz, J. Steven Ott, and Yong Suk Jang. Belmont, CA: Thomson Wadsworth, 2005.

Carroll, Glenn R., and Michael T. Hannan. 2000. Demography of corporations and industries, 193–200. Princeton: Princeton University Press. Reprinted in *Classics of organization theory*, 533–44. 6th ed. Ed. Jay M. Shafritz, J. Steven Ott, and Yong Suk Jang. Belmont, CA: Thomson Wadsworth, 2005.

Cleveland, Harlan. 1985. *The knowledge executive: Leadership in an information society*. New York: Dutton.

Cooper, Terry L. 1991. *An ethic of citizenship for public administration*. Englewood Cliffs, NJ: Prentice-Hall.

Crosby, Philip B. 1984. *Quality without tears: The art of hassle-free management*. New York: Plume/New American Library.

Dator, James. 1997. *Will you surf the tsunamis of change?* Speech before the Pacific Islands Club. Honolulu: Hawaii Research Center for Futures Studies, May 9.

de Bono, Edward. 1985. *Six thinking hats*. Boston: Little Brown and Company.

Denhardt, Janet V., and Robert B. Denhardt. 2003. *The new public service: Serving, not steering*. Armonk, NY: M. E. Sharpe.

Dichter, Thomas. 2001. Globalization and its effects on NGOs: Efflorescence or a blurring of roles and relevance. In *Understanding nonprofit organizations*. Ed. J. Steven Ott. Boulder, CO: Westview Press.

Downs, Anthony. 1967. *Inside bureaucracy*. Boston: Little, Brown. (Reissued by Waveland Press. Prospect Heights, IL: 1994.)

Durst, Samantha L., and Charldean Newell. 2001. The who, why, and how of reinvention in nonprofit organizations. *Nonprofit Management and Leadership* 11: 443–57.

Dvorin, Eugene, and Robert Simmons. 1972. *From amoral to humane bureaucracy*. San Francisco: Canfield.

Eggers, William. 2005. *Government 2.0: Using technology to improve education, cut red tape, reduce gridlock, and enhance democracy*. Lanham, MD: Rowen and Littlefield.

Emery, E. F., and E. L. Trist. 1965. The causal texture of organizational environments. *Human Relations* 18: 21–32.

Etzioni, Amitai. 1999. *The limits of privacy*. New York: Basic Books.

_____. 2004. *The communitarian reader: Beyond the essentials*. Lanham, MD: Roman and Littlefield.

Farmer, David John. 1995. *The language of public administration: Bureaucracy, modernity, and post-modernity*. Tuscaloosa: University of Alabama Press.

Fisher, Roger, and William Ury. 1991. *Getting to yes*. New York: Penguin Books.

Florida, Richard. 2002. *The rise of the creative class . . . and how it's transforming work, leisure, community, & everyday life*. New York: Basic Books.

Friedman, Thomas L. 2005. *The world is flat: A brief history of the twenty-first century*. New York: Farrar, Straus and Giroux.

Fukuyama, Francis. 2004. *State-building: governance and world order in the 21st century*. Ithica, NY: Cornell U. Press.

Galbraith, John Kenneth. 1967. *The new industrial state*. New York: Signet.

Garson, G. David. 2006. *Public information technology and e-governance: Managing the virtual state*. Sudbury, MA: Jones and Bartlett.

Garvey, Gerald. 1993. *Facing the bureaucracy: Living and dying in a public agency*. San Francisco: Jossey-Bass.

Gawthrop, Lewis C. 1983. Organizing for change. *The Annals of the American Academy of Political and Social Science* 446: 119–34.

Gillon, Steven M. 2000. *"That's not what we meant to do": Reform and its unintended consequences in twentieth-century America*. New York: W.W. Norton & Company.

Gladwell, Malcolm. 2002. *The tipping point: How little things can make a big difference*. New York: Little, Brown.

Glenn, Jerome C., ed. 1999. *Futures research methodology*. The Millennium Project. Washington, DC: American Council for The United Nations University. [CD-ROM]

Golembiewski, Robert T. 1995. *Managing diversity in organizations*. Tuscaloosa: University of Alabama Press.

Gortner, Harold F. 1991. *Ethics for public managers*. New York: Greenwood Press/Praeger.

Graham, Pauline. 1995. *Mary Parker Follett—Prophet of management: A celebration of writing from the 1920s*. Boston: Harvard Business School Press.

Greenleaf, Robert K. 2002. *Servant leadership: A journey into the nature of legitimate power and greatness*. Mahwah, NJ: Paulist Press. (Originally published in 1977.)

Gribbin, John. 2004. *Deep simplicity: Bringing order to chaos and complexity*. New York: Random House.

Hammer, Michael. 1994. *Reengineering: The implementation experience.* Educational material. Boston: Center for Reengineering Leadership.

Hammer, Michael, and James Champy, 1993. *Reengineering the corporation: A manifesto for business revolution.* New York: HarperBusiness.

Hammer, Michael, and Steven A. Stanton. 1995. *The reengineering revolution: A handbook.* New York: HarperCollins.

Herzberg, Frederick. 1964. The motivation–hygiene concept and problems of manpower. *Personnel Administration* 27 (January–February): 3–7.

Huber, George, Kathleen Sutcliffe, C. Chet Miller, and William Glick. 1995. Understanding and predicting organizational change. In *Organizational change and redesign.* Ed. George Huber and William Glick. New York: Oxford University Press.

Josephson, Michael S. 2005. *Preserving the public trust: The five principles of public service ethics.* Bloomington, IN: Unlimited Publishing.

Juran, Joseph, and Frank M. Gryna Jr., eds. 1988. *Quality control handbook.* 4th ed. New York: McGraw-Hill.

Kamarck, Elaine Ciulla, and Joseph S. Nye Jr., eds. 1999. *Democracy.com?: Governance in a networked world.* Hollis, NH: Hollis.

Katz, Daniel, and Robert Kahn. 1966. Organizations and the system concept. Reprinted in *Classics of organization theory,* pp. 480-90. 6th ed. Ed. Jay M. Shafritz, J. Steven Ott, and Yong Suk Jang. Belmont, CA: Thomson Wadsworth, 2005.

Katzenbach, Jon R., and Douglas K. Smith. 2003. *The wisdom of teams: Creating the high-performance organization.* New York: Harper Business Essentials.

Kaufman, Herbert. 1976. *Are government organizations immortal?* Washington, DC: Brookings.

Kettl, Donald F. 2004. *System under stress: Homeland security and American politics.* Washington, DC: CQ Press.

Kim, Tae-Chang, and James A. Dator, eds. 1999. *Co-creating a public philosophy for future generations.* Westport, CT: Praeger.

Kuhn, Thomas S. 1970. *The structure of scientific revolutions.* 2nd ed. Chicago: The University of Chicago Press.

Landau, Martin. 1969. Redundancy, rationality, and the problem of duplication and overlay. *Public Administration Review* 29 (July/August): 346–58.

Light, Paul C. 2005a. *The four pillars of high performance: How robust organizations achieve extraordinary results.* New York: McGraw-Hill.

———. 2005b. Rebuilding public confidence in charitable organizations. *Public Service Brief* #1 (October).

Lorenz, Edward N. 1993. *The essence of chaos.* Seattle: University of Washington Press.

Luke, Jeffrey S. 1998. *Catalytic leadership: Strategies for an interconnected world.* Somerset, NJ: John Wiley & Sons.

Miller, Hugh T., and Charles J. Fox, eds. 1997. *Postmodernism, "reality" and public administration: A discourse.* Burke, VA: Chatelaine Press.

Møller, J. Ørstrom. 2000. *The end of internationalism: Or world governance?* Westport, CT: Praeger.

Morgan, Gareth. 1997. *Imaginization: New mindsets for seeing, organizing, and managing.* Thousand Oaks, CA: Sage.

———. 2006. *Images of organization.* Thousand Oaks, CA: Sage.

Naisbitt, John. 1984. *Megatrends: Ten new directions transforming our lives.* New York: Warner Books.

———. 1994. *Global paradox: The bigger the world economy, the more important its smallest players.* New York: W. Morrow.

National Performance Review (U.S.). 1993. *Creating a government that works better and costs less: The report of the National Performance Review.* Vice President Al Gore. New York: Plume/Penguin.

Nichols, Kenneth L. 2005. Technology transfer and diffusion. In *Encyclopedia for the life support systems*. Oxford: Baldwin House.

O'Regan, Katherine. 2005. Does the structure and composition of the board matter? The case of non-profit organizations. *Journal of Law, Economics and Organization* 21: 205–27.

Osborne, David, and Ted Gaebler. 1992. *Reinventing government: How the entrepreneurial spirit is transforming the public sector*. Reading, MA: Addison-Wesley.

Ostrowski, John. 1997. *Systems analysis techniques*. Unpublished material. Long Beach: California State University.

Ouchi, William. 1981. *Theory Z: How American business can meet the Japanese challenge*. Reading, MA: Addison-Wesley.

Peters, Thomas J. 1994. *The pursuit of wow! Every person's guide to topsy-turvy times*. New York: Vintage.

Peters, Thomas J., and Robert H. Waterman. 1982. *In search of excellence: Lessons from America's best-run companies*. New York: Harper and Row.

Petersen, John L. 1999. *Out of the Blue: How to Anticipate Big Future Surprises*. Lanham, MD: Madison Books.

Pinchot, Gifford, and Elizabeth Pinchot. 1993. *The end of bureaucracy & the rise of the intelligent organization*. San Francisco: Berrett-Koehler.

Postman, Neil. 1992. *Technopoly: The Surrender of culture to technology*. New York: Vintage.

———. 1999. *Building a bridge to the eighteenth century: How the past can improve our future*. New York: Alfred A. Knopf.

Reynolds, Glenn. 2006. *An army of Davids: How markets and technlolgy empower ordinary people to beat big media, big government and other goliaths*. Nashville: Nelson Current.

Rheingold, Howard. 2002. *Smart Mobs: The Next Social Revolution*. Cambridge, MA: Perseus.

Roberts, Wess. 1987. *Leadership secrets of Attila the Hun*. New York: Warner Books.

Rohr, John. 1989. *Ethics for bureaucrats: An essay on law and values*. 2nd ed. New York: Marcel Dekker.

Salamon, Lester M. 2002. *The tools of government: A guide to the new governance*. New York: Oxford University Press.

Schrage, Michael. 1995. *No more teams! Mastering the dynamics of creative collaboration*. New York: Currency/Doubleday.

Senge, Peter M. 1990. *The fifth discipline: The art and practice of the learning organization*. New York: Doubleday/Currency.

Shafritz, Jay M., J. Steven Ott, and Yong Suk Jang. 2005. *Classics of organization theory*. 6th ed. Belmont, CA: Thomson Wadsworth.

Tannenbaum, Arnold, et al. 1974. *Hierarchy in organizations*. San Francisco: Jossey-Bass.

Tenner, Edward. 1997. *Why things bite back: Technology and the revenge of unintended consequences*. New York: Knopf Publishing Group.

Thompson, James D. 2005. Organizations in action. Reprinted in *Classics of organizational theory*, 491–504. 6th ed. Ed. Jay Shafritz, J. Steven Ott, and Yong Suk Jang. Belmont, CA: Thomson Wadsworth. (Originally published in 1967. Reprinted in *Classics of organizational theory*, 3–24. 3rd ed. New York: McGraw-Hill, 2003.)

Toffler, Alvin. 1970. *Future shock*. New York: Random House.

———. 1980. *The third wave*. New York: Morrow.

———. 1995. *Creating a new civilization: Politics of the third wave*. Atlanta: Turner.

Waldo, Dwight. 1948. *The administrative state: A study of the political theory of American public administration*. New York: The Ronald Press. (Reissued by Holmes and Meier. New York: 1984.)

Walton, Mary. 1986. *The Deming management method*. New York: Perigee Books.

Warfield, William. 1993. Public policy conflict resolution. In *Conflict resolution theory and practice: Integration and application*, 176–93. Ed. J. Dennis, D. Sandole, and Hugo vander Merwe. New York: Manchester University Press.

White, Michael J., et al. 1980. *Managing public systems: Analytic techniques for public administration.* North Scituate, MA: Duxbury. (Paperback reprint by University Press of America. Lanham, MD: 1985.)

Whiteley, Richard C. 1991. *The customer driven company: Moving from talk to action.* Cambridge, MA: Perseus Books.

William, B. Johnston, and Arnold E. Packer. 1987. *Workforce 2000: Work and workers for the 21st century.* Indianapolis: Hudson Institute.

Witham, Donald C. 1985. *The American law enforcement chief executive: A management profile.* Washington, DC: Police Executive Research Forum.

Name Index

Subject Index